Praise for Dominick Dunne and
FATAL CHARMS

"Powerful and personal . . . Dunne is at his brisk, acerbic best." —*Chicago Tribune*

"Nick has an unsurpassed eye for detail and atmosphere. . . . I have always known him to be accurate. P.S. I am very glad he is my friend, not my enemy." —Elizabeth Taylor

"Insightful, sometimes frightening portraits . . . By all means snap up *Fatal Charms*." —*Boston Herald*

"The charm of Somerset Maugham and the bitchiness of Truman Capote." —*Tulsa Daily World*

"Great fun to read . . . Full of insight and quotable quotes . . . Dunne is one of our best chroniclers of the monied and famous. . . . A master at showing his subjects hoist on their own petards." —*Houston Post*

"A new perspective on the high-society human condition . . . [Dunne] knows how the rich are different from you and I and, more importantly, he understands how they work. And how to get them to talk." —*Milwaukee Journal*

Please turn the page for more reviews. . . .

Praise for Dominick Dunne and
THE MANSIONS OF LIMBO

"Like sitting in an exclusive restaurant, listening to a plummy voiced intimate of the rich and famous tell us all about their foibles and follies."
　　　　　　　　　　—*The Washington Post Book World*

"The closest thing Americans can get to an official chronicler of modern-day nobility."　　—*San Francisco Chronicle*

"Awesome . . . If you missed any of these [in *Vanity Fair*], or even if you didn't, buy this book now. Don't put it off. . . . This book is a key to America. It has a Renaissance intensity. It shows us the Wheel of Fortune, the Wages of Hubris. It points out the horrid and satisfying truth that the higher you climb, the more inexorably you fall."
　　　　　　　　　　—*New York Newsday*

"Captures the greed, egomania, and personal excesses that ripped away at America's social fabric during those long ten years."　　　　　　　　　—*Buffalo News*

"A card-carrying citizen of the glittery world about which he writes."　　　　　　—*The Philadelphia Inquirer*

"Highly entertaining and razor-sharp."　　　—Liz Smith

"Superlative."　　　　　　　—*Boston Sunday Herald*

FATAL CHARMS

AND OTHER TALES OF TODAY AND

THE MANSIONS OF LIMBO

BY DOMINICK DUNNE

Fiction

*Another City, Not My Own**
*An Inconvient Woman**
*People Like Us**
*A Season in Purgatory**
*The Two Mrs. Grenvilles**
The Winners

Nonfiction

*Fatal Charms**
*The Mansions of Limbo**

*Published by The Ballantine Publishing Group

DOMINICK DUNNE

FATAL CHARMS

AND OTHER TALES OF TODAY AND

THE MANSIONS OF LIMBO

BALLANTINE BOOKS • NEW YORK

A Ballantine Book
Published by The Ballantine Publishing Group

All rights reserved under International and Pan-American Copyright Conventions. Published in the United States by The Ballantine Publishing Group, a division of Random House, Inc., New York, and simultaneously in Canada by Random House of Canada Limited, Toronto. *Fatal Charms and Other Tales of Today* was originally published by Crown Publishers, Inc., in 1986. *The Mansions of Limbo* was originally published by Crown Publishers, Inc., in 1991. All of the essays originally appeared in *Vanity Fair*.

Ballantine and colophon are registered trademarks of Random House, Inc.

www.randomhouse.com/BB/

Library of Congress Catalog Card Number: 98-96665

ISBN: 0-345-43059-X

This edition published by arrangement with Crown Publishers, Inc.

Cover design by Min Choi
Cover photo © Gasper Tringale/*Vanity Fair*

Manufactured in the United States of America

First Ballantine Edition: March 1999
10 9 8 7 6 5 4 3

For E.G.D. with love

To Tina Brown
who held out her hand,
with thanks and love

Contents

. . . AND MORE

Introduction to This Edition

If I were ever to write my autobiography, I would devote a whole chapter to a Sunday night Tex-Mex dinner in the kitchen of journalist Marie Brenner's house in the Chelsea area of New York City. The year was 1983. Although I have been socially gregarious for my entire life—out every night, here, there, everywhere—I hadn't wanted to go to Marie's that night. I was leaving in two days for Los Angeles to attend the trial of the man who had murdered my daughter nine months earlier. I was not in a party state of mind, and there were many practicalities to be dealt with, as I was to be gone for several months. Further, feelings of dread for the upcoming trial weighed me down. I thought of backing out of Marie's invitation, but I didn't, and I've been glad ever since. As always, at her table the people were smart and the conversation was heady; I was briefly able to forget my troubles. Kindly, no one asked me about the murder or the upcoming trial. I was not yet at the stage where I could discuss it without becoming visibly upset. I sat next to a young Englishwoman, a friend of Marie's, who was visiting New York. She was the recent editor of the British magazine *The Tatler*. The impression I received was that she was in New York looking for work in the magazine world. We talked mostly about Hollywood, which fascinated her. I had once lived there and had a career in television and films that ended rather ignominiously a few years earlier. Hollywood is a topic on which I never run dry in the story department. I told her my Elizabeth Taylor stories, from when I had produced one of Elizabeth's movies, *Ash Wednesday*, and my Sharon Tate stories, from when she was the girlfriend of my barber, Jay Sebring, who was later murdered with Sharon that terrible night of the

Manson murders on Cielo Drive in Beverly Hills. The next day Marie called me. She told me that the young lady I had sat next to the night before wanted to have lunch with me. I said I couldn't possibly, that I had too much to do before leaving for California. Marie replied, "Do it," giving me an order, which I obeyed. She reminded me that her friend's name was Tina Brown. At that time Tina Brown was not a droppable name. Nor was Tina as glamorous as she has become, but what I had recognized about her the night before was that she was headed for the big time in a big way.

We met at La Goulue, a fancy restaurant on the Upper East Side of Manhattan favored by the European set. It's one of those restaurants where people call out, "Hi, darling," and blow kisses, but Tina got right down to business as soon as we'd ordered our Perriers and lemon. At that time, I had just become a writer. I was brand-new at it at age fifty-three, and I was not being sought after as a writer. My first novel, which was the sequel to a perfectly awful novel by Joyce Haber, the late gossip columnist for the *Los Angeles Times*, had just been mocked in the *New York Times* and quickly remaindered. Although my wounds of Hollywood failure had nearly healed, I was still unused to people paying attention to me. Tina told me I shouldn't be wasting all my Hollywood stories at dinner parties. She told me I should be writing for a magazine. She said it would take her years to train someone to have the kind of contacts I had. But I put the brakes on. No, no, I can't. I'm a late-life writer. I never put pen to paper until I was fifty years old. I said I wouldn't have a clue how to write for a magazine. Unfazed about my negativity, she said she could teach me. She told me she was about to become the editor of *Vanity Fair* magazine, although it was a deep secret that would not be announced as yet. Then she got to the touchy part, the part about the murder and the trial that was to start in a few days' time. She said, "We've all read about trials, but I've never read about a trial written by a participant in one. Keep a journal every day. Write it all down. Come and see me when you get back."

If I hadn't kept that journal, as Tina suggested, I would have gone mad. What I saw in the courtroom filled me with the kind of rage that only writing about it could quell. It infuriated me that the rights of the defendant on trial exceeded the rights of the victim, and I was determined to do something about it. The story of that trial, entitled "Justice," opens this book. That trial was in its day a mini-version of the O. J. Simpson murder trial fifteen years later—cameras, flashbulbs, a controversial judge, etc.—and the similarities of incident and character of John Sweeney, the man who murdered my daughter, and O. J. Simpson, who was acquitted of murdering his wife, Nicole, are utterly startling. The story of the O. J. Simpson murder trial ends this book.

A week before the issue came out on the stands, Tina took me out to lunch again, this time to the Rose Room at the Algonquin, where William Shawn, the fabled editor of *The New Yorker*, was having shredded wheat for lunch at a nearby table. I felt like I was in the swing of magazine life, and I liked the feeling. Tina said, "When this issue comes out next week, every magazine in New York is going to want you to write for them. But you're mine, and I want to sign you up." Or words to that effect. You never saw anybody leap so quickly at a job offer as I did. She saw something in me that I didn't know I possessed, and she helped me refind in myself the confidence that I thought I had lost forever. There began my long tenure with *Vanity Fair* magazine, from which all of the articles in this book are drawn. A wise man in publishing once whispered in my ear when I first started to write, "There is nothing the public enjoys reading about more than the rich and the powerful in a criminal situation." Bells rang in my head, and I knew I had found my subject matter. Trials became a mainstay of my contributions to the magazine. I made no pretense of doing balanced reporting about murder. I was appalled by defense attorneys who would do *anything* to win an acquittal for a guilty person. I said exactly what I thought. I was the first person to say on television after the acquittal of O. J. Simpson, "A guilty man has been acquitted." Of course, you make a lot of enemies when you take a stand. I got death threats, but nothing ever happened.

I have always had an insatiable curiosity about other people's lives, and *Vanity Fair*, first under Tina and then under Graydon Carter, who has been its brilliant editor since 1992, when Tina left to go to *The New Yorker*, gave me a forum where I could march right in and ask questions of some of the most famous people of my era. I am still filled with wonder at the places my assignments have taken me to over the years. Imagine being in a beach house in Honolulu with Imelda and

Ferdinand Marcos only days into their exile, after their fall from grace in Manila. Imagine riding all alone in a jeep across the desert with Queen Noor of Jordan a week or so before the start of the Gulf War. Imagine being at a Fifth Avenue lunch party with Claus von Bülow and his mistress Andrea Reynolds—butlers in white gloves, champagne and lobster salad—during Claus's trial for the attempted murder of his heiress wife, Sunny. Imagine sitting across the aisle from the Kennedy sisters and a Kennedy sister-in-law, all of whom I knew, during the Palm Beach rape trial of William Kennedy Smith. Imagine ringing the doorbell of Phyllis McGuire's mansion in Las Vegas and having the door opened by a guard with a machine gun in his hand. Imagine sitting next to the Goldman family on one side and the Simpson family on the other when the jury acquitted O. J. Simpson of double murder. All events of high drama, and I was there. I couldn't ask for a better life.

Dominick Dunne
New York, January 1999

FATAL CHARMS

A WORD ON A LATE START

Several years ago, when breaking up a house I had lived in for years in California, I came across a long-forgotten box of letters from World War II which I, as a young soldier of eighteen and nineteen, wrote to my mother, father, and sisters from several combat zones in the European theater of operations. In the same box were letters that my family had written to me in return that I must have carried around in my pack and saved. Reading what I wrote to my family, and what my family wrote back to me, after thirty-five years was an eerie experience: an almost day-by-day account of their life in Hartford, Connecticut, during wartime concurrent with mine as a teenage private in France, Belgium, and Germany in 1944 and 1945. More startling than our separate histories, however, was the revision of a resentment I had long nurtured about my late father. For years I believed he had considered me to be a disappointment as a son because my interests were always more artistic than athletic. To my astonishment his letters were filled not with the stern admonishments which were my memory of him but with pride that I was fighting for my country, admiration for my descriptions of the events of war, and some long-term advice that I should give some thought, after completing college, to a career in writing.

I didn't take his advice. My father died before I finished Williams College, and my life choices were my own to make. I had been bitten by the theater bug at Williams and decided on a career in television in New York during that early period of live drama that has subsequently become known as the Golden Age. Then came Hollywood where I spent twenty-four years in television and movies as both a producer and studio executive, and began a long fascination not only with the film industry but also with the social life of the industry, where so many of the business decisions had their genesis.

Within me lurked some sort of documentarian's need to record the extraordinary insider's life that became available to me. For nearly a decade I kept copious scrapbooks and photograph albums with the intensity of someone who knew that none of it was going to last, at least for the recorder of the events. In these books are pictures of my serene and beautiful wife and our children staring out from a variety of exotic settings, and invitations to and photographs of party after party after party. There is a photograph of Natalie Wood applying lipstick, using the blade of a dinner party knife as a mirror; there is Cecil Beaton using a spoon to eat the ice cream from an ice-cream cone; there is Warren Beatty playing the piano in black tie at a Vincente Minnelli party; there is Truman Capote in a deep dancing dip with Tuesday Weld; there is a married acting couple called Nancy Davis and Ronald Reagan who, even then, before politics, were gazing fondly at each other.

In 1978 I repaired to a small cabin in the Cascade Mountains of Oregon to lick the wounds of defeat in Hollywood. My once glamorous life in that community had gone awry, and the pain of a failed marriage that I was not able to let go of, and a failed career that had let go of me, had led me to self-destructive excesses. It was there in the cabin on the Metolius River near a community called Camp Sherman that I finally took up my father's wartime advice and began writing a novel. The process of writing was not unknown to me. In my previous career I always worked closely with writers and, long before I began to write, I often read the in-progress work of my writer friends and felt creative stirrings. An inner contentment that had long eluded me began to come back in Oregon, and I gave serious thought to remaining permanently in that sylvan glade.

Then two things happened. I received a surprising letter from Truman Capote, another dabbler in self-destructive excesses. A longtime acquaintance, although never a friend, he had several times been a guest at our house in Beverly Hills during the jubilant days of my marriage. His was a letter of encouragement and admiration that I had dropped out of my life in order to try to pull it together again. Perhaps he knew it was what he should have done himself. "But remember this," he wrote, "that is not where you belong, and when you get out of it what you went there to get, you have to come back to your own life." Shortly thereafter one of my brothers committed suicide, and I flew east from Oregon to attend his funeral. It was then that I realized it was time for me to begin another chapter.

I returned to Beverly Hills just long enough to sell every possession I once thought I could never live without—pictures, furniture, even all my books—and with two suitcases and a typewriter moved to a little apartment in Greenwich Village to start a new life and a new career. I finished the book I began in Oregon, and it was published with not only no stir but also with a lousy review in the *New York Times*. However, I was thrilled that at past fifty I was published at all and even reviewed in the *Times*, no matter how badly, and, undeterred, I set about writing a new novel that eventually became *The Two Mrs. Grenvilles*.

At five o'clock in the morning on October 31, 1982, I received a call in my New York apartment from a detective in Beverly Hills to tell me that my youngest child and only daughter, Dominique, had been brutally attacked by a former boyfriend of hers and taken to Cedars-Sinai Hospital in Los Angeles. My wife, Lenny, with whom I had remained friendly after the divorce, got on the telephone after the detective. Suffering now from multiple sclerosis and confined to a wheelchair, she filled me in on the terrible details. When I hung up, I knew from her that there was no hope for our daughter. My sons and I left for Los Angeles immediately and, for over a year, until after the trial of John Sweeney for the murder of my daughter, the lives of all of us simply stopped. . . .

Dominick Dunne
New York, 1987

JUSTICE: A FATHER'S ACCOUNT OF THE TRIAL OF HIS DAUGHTER'S KILLER

It was the beginning of a long hot summer. I flew to Los Angeles on July 5, 1983, for an indefinite stay. Throughout the flight from New York I engaged in diligent conversation with the stranger next to me, postponing as long as possible facing the feelings of dread within me. My two sons, Griffin and Alex, had preceded me out from New York. Alex, the younger one, met me at the airport, and we drove into Beverly Hills to the house where my former wife, Ellen Griffin Dunne, called Lenny, lives. Griffin was already there. It is not the house we lived in as a family. It is smaller and on one level. Lenny has multiple sclerosis and is confined to a wheelchair. We were gathering, a family again, for a murder trial.

The first time I saw Lenny she was getting off a train at the railroad station in Hartford, Connecticut. She was ravishing, and I knew that instant that I would marry her if she would have me. We had a large wedding at her family's ranch in Nogales, Arizona, in 1954, and after living briefly in New York, we moved to Beverly Hills, where I worked for twenty-five years in television and films. We had five children, two of whom died when they were only a few days old. Long divorced, we have, rightly or wrongly, never become unmarried. Often I have felt through the years that our lives might have been better if we had just stuck out the difficult years of our marriage, but I do not know if she would agree with that. We never venture into the realm of what might have been. I refer to her in conversation as my wife, never my ex-wife, and there is not a day in which she does not occupy my thoughts for some period of time. We communicate regularly and mail each other clippings we cut out of newspapers, and I no longer resent, as I once did, addressing her as Mrs. E. Griffin Dunne rather than as Mrs. Dominick Dunne.

When the telephone in my New York apartment woke me at five o'clock in the morning on October 31, 1982, I sensed as I reached for the receiver that disaster loomed. Det. Harold Johnston of the Los Angeles Homicide Bureau told me that my twenty-two-year-old daughter, Dominique, was near death at Cedars-Sinai Medical Center. I asked him if he had notified my wife. He said he was calling from her home. Lenny got on the phone and said, "I need you."

"What happened?" I asked, afraid to hear.

"Sweeney," she answered.

"I'll be on the first plane."

I called Griffin, then twenty-seven, who lives two blocks away from me in New York, and within minutes he was at my door. He called TWA and reserved a seat on the next flight. Then he went to an automatic teller machine and got me money. As I threw clothes into a suitcase, I hesitated over my black suit and tie, thinking they might be bad luck, but I packed them. Before I got into the taxi, I hugged Griffin and kissed him. He was to go then to the apartment of my second son, Alex, and break the news to him. Uniquely individual, Alex chose to live with no telephone on Pitt Street in a relatively inaccessible part of New York. Only Alex, of the four of us, had voiced his dislike of John Sweeney when Dominique introduced him into our lives.

She had brought him to New York several months earlier for the boys and me to meet. Dominique was a successful young television actress, who had just made her first major feature film, *Poltergeist*. Sweeney was the head chef at Ma Maison, a West Hollywood restaurant so concerned with its fashionable image that it had an unlisted telephone number to discourage the *hoi polloi* from entering its portals. We watched an episode of the television series "Fame" in which Dominique was the guest star, and then went out to dinner. At one moment when the four of us were alone, the boys teased Dominique about marriage, and she said, oh no, she was not getting married, and I knew she meant it. I was relieved, for although I could see Sweeney was excessively devoted to her, there was something off-putting about him. That night I phoned her mother and said, "He is much more in

love with her than she is with him," and Lenny said, "You're absolutely right."

The next morning Alex told me of an incident that had occurred in
P. J. Clarke's after I left them. While Sweeney was in the men's room, a
man at the bar recognized Dominique as the older sister in *Poltergeist*
and called out one of her lines from the film: "What's happening?"
Dominique screams that line when evil spirits start to take over her
home and cause frightening things to happen. A film clip of that scene
has been shown so often on television that the line was familiar to people all over the country. There was no flirtation; it was the case of a
slightly tipsy fan delighted to be in the presence of an actress he had
seen in a film. But when Sweeney returned to the table and saw the
man talking to Dominique, he became enraged. He picked up the man
and shook him. Alex said that Sweeney's reaction was out of all pro-
portion to the innocent scene going on. Alex said he was scary.

The following day I arrived a few minutes late at Lutèce, where I
was meeting Dominique and Sweeney for lunch. They had not yet arrived, so I sat at a table in the bar to wait for them. I finished one Perrier and ordered another, and was beginning to think there had been a
misunderstanding about either the time or the place when they entered the restaurant. It was a hot summer day, and Dominique looked
marvelous in a starched white organdy dress, very California-looking. I
was immediately aware that she had been crying, and that there was
tension between them.

The chef made a great fuss over Sweeney. There was kissing on
both cheeks, and they spoke together in French. At the chef's suggestion we ate the *spécialité* of the day, whatever it was, but the lunch was
not a success. I found Sweeney ill at ease, nervous, difficult to talk to.
It occurred to me that Dominique might have difficulty extricating
herself from such a person, but I did not pursue the thought.

On the Fourth of July the three of us dined at the River Café under
the Brooklyn Bridge. It was a lovely night, and we were at a window
table where we could watch the fireworks. Sweeney told me he intended to leave Ma Maison. He said he had backing from a consor-
tium of French and Japanese businessmen and was going to open his
own restaurant in Melrose Park, a highly desirable location in Los
Angeles. Never once did he speak affectionately of his employer,

Patrick Terrail, a member of the French restaurant family that owns the Tour d'Argent in Paris. In fact, I suspected there were bad feelings between them.

On that endless flight to Los Angeles I did not allow myself to consider the possibility of her death. She was making a pilot at Warner Bros. for an NBC miniseries called "V," and I remember thinking that they would have to shoot around her until she was on her feet again. Five weeks earlier she had broken up with John Sweeney, and he had moved out of the house they shared in West Hollywood. Her explanation to me at the time was, "He's not in love with me, Dad. He's obsessed with me. It's driving me crazy."

Two other daughters preceding Dominique died in infancy from a lung disease once common in cesarean births known as hyaline membrane disease. Dominique was all three daughters in one to us, triply loved. She adored her older brothers and was always totally at ease in a sophisticated world without being sophisticated herself. She was a collector of stray animals; in her menagerie were a cat with a lobotomy and a large dog with stunted legs. She went to Westlake School in Los Angeles, then to Taft School in Connecticut, then to Fountain Valley School in Colorado. After that she spent a year in Florence, where she learned to speak Italian. Twice she and I took trips in Italy together. Extravagantly emotional, she was heartbroken when Lenny gave up the family home on Walden Drive because her worsening condition made it unmanageable. I was not surprised when Dominique announced her intention to become an actress. Griffin, who is an actor and a producer, later said jokingly that one day she decided to become an actress and the next week she was on a back lot making a movie, and that from then on she never stopped. It was very nearly true. She loved being an actress and was passionate about her career.

By the time I arrived in Los Angeles at noon that Sunday, the report that Dominique had been strangled outside her home by her former boyfriend and was in a coma at Cedars-Sinai Medical Center was on all the news channels and stations. Mart Crowley, the author of *The Boys in the Band*, the film version of which I had produced, met me at the airport and filled me in with what little information he had got from Lenny. Lenny's house on Crescent Drive was full of people when we got there. (It would stay that way from early morning until late at night for the next seven or eight days, during which relay teams of friends manned the telephones, screened the calls, handled the coffee detail, accepted the endless deliveries of flowers, made all the arrangements for our day-to-day living.) All the television sets and radios were on for news bulletins. In the midst of this confusion sat Lenny in her wheelchair. She was very calm. "The news is not good," she said to me. And within minutes I heard the words "brain damage" being whispered around the house.

Lenny's mother, who had heard the news on the radio, was on her way from San Diego. Griffin and Alex's plane would be in in a few hours. My relatives in Hartford called, and, as the news spread, so did friends in New York and London. A doctor at the hospital telephoned for my permission to insert a bolt into Dominique's skull to relieve the pressure on her brain. Was it absolutely necessary? I asked. Yes, he replied. All right, I said. I asked him when we could go and see her. Not yet, he said.

The boys arrived, ashen-faced. When the time came to go to the hospital, we were full of dreadful apprehension. Some friends said to Lenny, "You mustn't go. It would be a terrible mistake to look at her this way. You must remember her as she was." They were, of course, thinking of Lenny's health; stress is the worst thing for multiple sclerosis victims. She replied, "The mistake would be if I didn't see her. That is what I would have to live with."

The four of us proceeded in silence through the maze of corridors leading to the intensive care unit on the fifth floor of Cedars-Sinai. One of us, I don't remember which, pushed Lenny's wheelchair, and the other two flanked her—a formation we would automatically fall into many times in the year that followed. Outside the double doors of the unit are printed instructions telling you to buzz and announce yourself. I did so: "The family of Dominique Dunne is here." We were told to wait, that someone would come out and get us.

Several people were standing there, among them the actor George Hamilton. We exchanged greetings. George said his brother was also in the ICU, and that he had been there the night before when Dominique was brought in. Another man introduced himself to us as Ken Johnson, the director of the pilot Dominique was working on. Waiting nearby was a young actor in the same film named David Packer, his eyes red from crying. Packer, we learned, had been in Dominique's house at the time of the attack and had called in the police, albeit too late. Later we also learned that Packer became so frightened by the struggle he heard outside on the lawn that he left a message on a friend's answering machine saying, "If I die tonight, it was by John Sweeney."

A nurse appeared and told us that after we had seen Dominique the doctors would want to talk with us. She said that no one but immediate family would be allowed in, and asked us to show identification. They were afraid the press would try to pass themselves off as members of the family. She warned us that it would be a shock to look at her, that we should be prepared.

I worried about Lenny and looked over at her. She closed her eyes, bowed her head, and took a deep breath. I watched her will strength into herself, through some inner spiritual force, in a moment so intensely private that I dared not, even later, question her about it. Of the four of us, she was the strongest when we entered the room.

At first I did not realize that the person on the bed was Dominique. There were tubes in her everywhere, and the life-support system caused her to breathe in and out with a grotesque jerking movement that seemed a parody of life. Her eyes were open, massively enlarged, staring sightlessly up at the ceiling. Her beautiful hair had been shaved off. A large bolt had been screwed into her skull to relieve the pressure on her brain. Her neck was purpled and swollen; vividly visible on it were the marks of the massive hands of the man who had strangled her. It was nearly impossible to look at her, but also impossible to look away.

Lenny wheeled her chair to the bed, took Dominique's hand in hers, and spoke to her in a voice of complete calm. "Hello, my darling, it's Mom. We're all here, Dominique. Dad and Griffin and Alex. We love you."

Her words released us, and the boys and I stepped forward and surrounded the bed, each touching a different part of Dominique. The nurses had said that she could not hear us, but we felt she could, and took turns talking to her. We prayed for her to live even though we knew that it would be best for her to die.

There was a small conference room in the ICU where we met periodically over the next four days to discuss her ebbing life. Dr. Edward
Brettholz told us that the brain scan was even, meaning that it showed
no life, but that it would be necessary to take three more scans so that,
in the trial ahead, the defense could not claim that Cedars-Sinai had
removed Dominique from the life-support system too soon. This was
the first mention of a trial. In the shocked state in which we were operating, we had not yet started to deal with the fact that a murder had
taken place.

On the fourth day Lenny said, quite unexpectedly, to the doctors,
"When Dominique dies, we would like her organs donated to the hospital." The boys and I knew that was exactly what Dominique would
have wanted, but it would not have occurred to us to say so at that moment. Lenny, ill herself with a disease for which there is no cure,
understood. Dr. Gray Elrod, with tears in his eyes, said two patients in
the hospital were waiting for kidney transplants. We then went in and
said good-bye to Dominique for the last time before they took her off
the support system. She was wheeled to surgery for the removal of her
kidneys, and transplant operations took place almost immediately. Her
heart was sent to a hospital in San Francisco. Then her body was
turned over to the coroner for an autopsy.

In the *Los Angeles Times* a day or so after the attack, Patrick Terrail,
the owner of Ma Maison, described his chef, John Sweeney, as a "very
dependable young man" and said he would obtain the best legal representation for him. He made no comment about Dominique, whom
he knew, as he knew us, and throughout the long ordeal that followed
he did not call on us or write a letter of condolence. Since it was too
early then to deal with the magnitude of my feelings for the killer of
my daughter, Patrick Terrail became the interim object of my growing rage.

Obtaining the best legal representation for Sweeney took an
economy turn when a public defender, Michael Adelson, was assigned to handle the case. We heard from Detective Johnston that
Adelson was highly acclaimed and doggedly tough. Assisting the public defender, however, was Joseph Shapiro, the legal counsel for Ma
Maison and a member of the prestigious law firm of Donovan,

Leisure, Newton & Irvine. Although Shapiro's role on the defense team was later played down, he was an ever-present but elusive figure from the night following the murder, when he visited Sweeney in the Beverly Hills jail, right up until the day of the verdict, when he exulted in the courtroom.

At the time of the murder Dominique was consistently identified in the press as the niece of my brother and sister-in-law, John Gregory Dunne and Joan Didion, rather than as the daughter of Lenny and me. At first I was too stunned by the killing for this to matter, but as the days passed, it bothered me. I spoke to Lenny about it one morning in her bedroom. She said, "Oh, what difference does it make?" with such despair in her voice that I felt ashamed to be concerned with such a trivial matter at such a crucial time.

In the room with us was my former mother-in-law, Beatriz Sandoval Griffin Goodwin, the widow of Lenny's father, Thomas Griffin, an Arizona cattle rancher, and of Lenny's stepfather, Ewart Goodwin, an insurance tycoon and rancher. She was a strong, uncompromising woman who has never not stated exactly what was on her mind in any given situation, a trait that has made her respected if not always endearing.

"Listen to what he's saying to you," she said emphatically. "It sounds as if Dominique was an orphan raised by her aunt and uncle." Lenny looked up with a changed expression. "*And*," added her mother, to underscore the point, "she had two brothers as well."

"You handle it," Lenny said to me. I called the publicist Rupert Allan, a family friend, and explained the situation to him. "It's hurtful to us. It's as if we had not only lost her but been denied parentage as well," I said. "It'll be taken care of," Rupert said, and it was.

On the morning of November 4, while the autopsy was going on, I went to visit the elderly monsignor at the Church of the Good Shepherd in Beverly Hills to make the arrangements for Dominique's funeral. In years past this church was jokingly referred to as Our Lady of the Cadillacs for the affluence of its parishioners. The housekeeper at the rectory told me the monsignor was in the church saying mass. I waited in the front pew until he finished. Then I went back into the vestry with him and explained my reason for coming. He had read of

the murder in the newspapers, and I thought I detected in him a slight
hesitation over having the funeral of a murder victim in the Good
Shepherd Church. I explained to him that we had once been members
of the parish, that Dominique had been christened here by him
twenty-two years earlier, and that he had come to our home afterward
to the reception. The memory was dim to him, so I persisted. I said
that Martin Manulis, the producer, who would be giving the eulogy at
the funeral, was Dominique's godfather, but that evoked no remembrance either. I then said that Maria Cooper was Dominique's godmother, and at that he looked up. He remembered Maria well, he said,
the beautiful daughter of Rocky and Gary Cooper. He told me he had
given Gary Cooper the last rites when he died, and had performed the
funeral mass. He said he had always hoped Maria would be a nun but
that, alas, she had married a Jewish fella (the pianist Byron Janis). By
now the church was a certainty. We discussed the music that I wanted
played, and settled on eleven o'clock, Saturday, November 6, for the
funeral.

On November 5 we discovered that the monsignor had also
booked a wedding at eleven on Saturday morning. The mistake came
to light when the groom-to-be read in one of Dominique's obituaries
that her funeral was to be at the same time and in the same place as his
wedding. He telephoned the church, and the church notified us.

Griffin, Alex, Martin Manulis, and I went to the rectory in the afternoon to try to straighten matters out. We waited endlessly, but the
monsignor did not appear. The boys became impatient and began
yelling up the stairs of the rectory. Finally a priest with a heavy Flemish
accent came down, but he did not seem anxious to get mixed up in an
error that was not of his making. When we pointed out to him that
pandemonium was likely to occur the following morning unless steps
were taken, he cooperated in figuring out a plan. As the wedding people refused to move their marriage up an hour, we agreed to have the
funeral an hour later. It was too late to inform the newspapers, so we
arranged for twelve ushers to be at the church at 10:30 to tell the people arriving for the funeral to come back an hour later.

"I cannot comprehend how such an error could have been made,"
I said to the priest.

"It's even worse than you realize, Mr. Dunne," he replied.

"What do you mean?"

"The groom in the wedding is a friend of the man who murdered your daughter."

That night on the news we watched John Sweeney being arraigned for Dominique's murder. He was accompanied by the defense team of Michael Adelson and Joseph Shapiro. As we watched, we all began to feel guilty for not having spoken out our true feelings about Sweeney when there was still time to save Dominique from him. In the days that followed, her friends began to tell us how terrified she was of him during the last weeks of her life. I found out for the first time that five weeks previously he had assaulted her and choked her, and that she had escaped from him and broken off her relationship with him. Fred Leopold, a family friend and the former mayor of Beverly Hills, told us during a condolence call that he had heard from a secretary in his law office that John Sweeney had severely beaten another woman a year or so earlier. We passed on this information to Det. Harold Johnston, who stayed close to our family during those days.

Later that night, the eve of the funeral, Dominique appeared on two television programs that had been previously scheduled. Also on television that night was a film I had produced, never before seen on television, and another film my brother had written, also being shown for the first time. We did not watch any of them.

The day of the funeral, November 6, was incredibly hot. Riding the few blocks from Lenny's house on Crescent Drive to the Good Shepherd Church at Santa Monica Boulevard and Bedford Drive, I noticed that the tinsel Christmas decorations were going up on the lampposts of Beverly Hills. As the limousine pulled up in front of the church, I was deeply touched to see Dr. Brettholz from Cedars-Sinai in the crowd arriving for the service. Lenny, her mother, Griffin, Alex, and I were in the first car. When the chauffeur opened the door for us to get out, a hot gust of wind blew multicolored wedding confetti into the car.

The boys helped their grandmother out, and then we got the wheelchair out of the trunk and moved Lenny from the car into the chair.

"There's the mother," we heard someone say, and a phalanx of photographers and television cameramen descended on us, coming within a foot of Lenny's face. Because there were so many steps in the front of the church, we decided to take the wheelchair around to the back, where there was a ramp entrance for handicapped people. The cameramen and photographers walked backward in front of us, shooting film. "No matter what they do, don't say anything," I said to the boys.

Lenny has extraordinary dignity. Dressed curiously for a funeral in a long lavender dress with pearls and a large straw hat, she made no attempt to turn away from the television cameramen. They seemed to respect her, and one by one they dropped away.

The church was filled to capacity, not with curiosity seekers attracted by the sensationalism of Dominique's death, but with people who knew her and loved her. During the service the boys read a poem by Yeats, and Martin Manulis, who had brought me to California twenty-six years earlier to work for him on "Playhouse 90," delivered the eulogy. "Every year of her life," he said, "we spent Christmas Eve together at a carol sing at our house. When she could barely talk, she stood between her brothers and sang what resembled 'O Little Town of Bethlehem' and spoke a single line from the Gospel of Saint Luke, taught to her by her doting parents: 'Because there is no room at the inn.' And standing there with those huge grave eyes, she was, in life, an infanta by Goya, only more beautiful."

A few nights after the funeral, Lenny and I sat in her bedroom, she in her bed, I on it, and watched Dominique in "Hill Street Blues." The episode had been dedicated to her on the air by the producers. We did not talk. We did not cry. We simply stared at the set. She looked so incredibly young. She played a battered child. What we would not know until the trial was that the marks on her neck were real, from John Sweeney's assault on her five weeks before he killed her.

On my first day back in New York after the funeral, I was mugged leaving the subway at twelve noon in Times Square. I thought I was the only person on the stairway I was ascending to the street, but suddenly I was grabbed from behind and pulled off balance. I heard the sound of a switchblade opening, and a hand—which was all I ever saw of my assailant—reached around and held the knife in front of my face. From out of my mouth came a sound of rage that I did not know I was capable of making. It was more animal than human, and I was later told it had been heard a block away. Within seconds people came running from every direction. In his panic my assailant superficially slashed my chin with the blade of his knife, but I had beaten him. I had both my wallet and my life, and I realized that, uncourageous as I am about physical combat, I would have fought before giving in. Whoever that nameless, faceless man was, to me he was John Sweeney.

If Dominique had been killed in an automobile accident, horrible as that would have been, at least it would have been over, and mourning could have begun. A murder is an ongoing event until the day of sentencing, and mourning has to be postponed. After several trips west for preliminary hearings, I returned to Los Angeles in July for the trial.

For a while I drove Dominique's electric blue, convertible Volkswagen. It had stood unused in the driveway of Lenny's house since the murder, a reminder of her that we neither wanted to look at nor could bear to get rid of. I felt strange in the car; too old by far to be driving it, I could always imagine her in it, young and pretty, driving too fast, her beautiful long hair streaming out behind her. In the glove compartment I found a pair of her sunglasses, the ones she called her Annie Hall glasses. I had bought them for her in Florence when I visited her in school there. I took them out of the glove compartment and put them in my briefcase. Throughout the trial, when the going got rough, I would hold them in my hand, or touch them in the inside pocket of my jacket next to my heart, as if I could derive strength from her through them.

Alex was living on Crescent Drive with Lenny. Griffin and his girlfriend, the actress Brooke Adams, had rented a house in Malibu. I was staying at my old friend Tom McDermott's house in Holmby Hills. On the Saturday afternoon before the Monday morning when the jury selection was to start, Lenny rounded us up at her house. She had received a call from a journalist friend of the family, who said he wanted to meet with us to deliver a message from Mike Adelson, the defense attorney representing John Sweeney. We all had curious feelings about the meeting. Why should the lawyer of our daughter's murderer be contacting us through a journalist rather than through the district attorney? At that point in the proceedings our relationship with the district attorney, Steven Barshop, was still very formal. We called him Mr.

Barshop, and he called us Mr. and Mrs. Dunne. We did not even have his home telephone number. We decided in advance that no matter what was said to us at the meeting we would listen to the message and make no comment.

The purpose of the journalist's visit was to offer us a plea bargain so that the case would not have to go to trial. He said that Sweeney was full of remorse and was willing to go to prison. Sweeney would plead guilty to a reduced charge of manslaughter and would serve seven and a half years, but he wanted the assault charge, based on his attack on Dominique five weeks before the murder, dropped. The journalist said that Adelson saw the case, not as a crime, but as a tragedy, of "a blue-collar kid who got mixed up in Beverly Hills society and couldn't handle it."

We had been down the plea-bargain road before. Five months earlier, in February, after the preliminary hearing on the assault charge, a plea bargain had been offered to us by Adelson through the district attorney. At that time we had accepted it, feeling that Lenny's health would be endangered by the trial. I had also seen at that hearing what a ruthless player Adelson was in the courtroom. Later, in May, Adelson had reneged on the plea bargain and opened up the whole matter of the trial, which we thought had been put to rest. Now, within two days of the beginning of jury selection, we were being offered, through a third party, another plea bargain, from which the district attorney had simply been excluded. I felt distrustful and manipulated. I despised the fact that we were supposed to be moved that Sweeney was remorseful and "willing" to serve seven and a half years.

Although the journalist was only a messenger in the situation, the meeting became strained as he presented Adelson's viewpoints. Doubts were put in our mind about the ability of Steven Barshop. There was even a suggestion that Dominique was a participant in the crime. Neighbors would be called, we were told, who would testify that fights were commonplace between Dominique and Sweeney. The journalist said that if the two snitches who had come forward were put on the stand, Adelson would "cut them off at the knees." At that time I didn't know what snitches were; they were fellow prisoners who betray confidences of the cell for lessened sentences. (One prisoner reported that Sweeney had confessed to him that he thought he had the

JUSTICE

police believing he had not intended to kill Dominique, and another said that Sweeney had told him that Dominique was a snob, too ambitious, who deserved what she got.)

The journalist talked a great deal about a lawyer called Paul Fitzgerald. In the months ahead I was never to meet Fitzgerald, but he was often presented in conversation as a sage of the court system, with the detractors as vocal as his admirers. A former public defender, Fitzgerald was occasionally appointed as a conflict lawyer by Judge Burton S. Katz, in whose courtroom the case was being tried. A rumor persisted after the trial that he wrote Judge Katz's astonishing reversal speech on the day of the sentencing. He was also a close friend of Michael Adelson's. On that Saturday afternoon, before the jury selection had begun, Paul Fitzgerald was identified as the source of the information, reiterated again and again by the journalist who visited us, that Mike Adelson was a wonderful man.

It had not been my personal experience to find Mike Adelson a wonderful man. Twice during the February preliminary hearing he had addressed me in the corridor outside the courtroom as Mr. Sweeney, as if mistaking me for the father of the killer rather than the father of the victim. A seasoned courtroom observer suggested to me that since I was a sympathetic figure in the courtroom, it had been Adelson's intention, by this obvious error, to incite me to make some kind of slur on him in public. During that same hearing, a young friend of Dominique's named Bryan Cook recounted a night on the town with his girlfriend, Denise Dennehy, and Dominique and Sweeney during which several bottles of champagne were consumed. Singling Dominique out from the quartet of celebrants, Adelson, in questioning Cook, asked several times, "When Miss Dunne got in from the bars, how drunk was she?" The obvious intent of this ugly repetition was to give the impression in the courtroom that my actress daughter was an out-on-the-town drunkard. No amount of laudatory comment, after those preliminary hearings, would ever convince me that Mike Adelson was a wonderful man. Mustached and extremely short, his head topped with a full toupee, Adelson made me think of an angry, miniature bulldog.

The journalist's mission, though instigated with good intentions, only engendered bad feelings.

At nine o'clock on Monday morning, July 11, we gathered in Steven Barshop's office in the Santa Monica Courthouse. Alternately tough-talking and professional, the district attorney is about forty. He achieved public recognition for his prosecution of the killers of Sarai Ribicoff, the journalist niece of Senator Abraham Ribicoff. We felt lucky that Barshop had been assigned to our case by Robert Phili-bosian, the district attorney of the Los Angeles County, but we felt that he did not want any personal involvement with us. Although never dis-courteous, he was brusque, and he made it very clear that he was run-ning the show and would not tolerate any interference.

Barshop was angered when we told him that a plea bargain had been offered to us by Adelson through a journalist. "You didn't accept it, did you?" he asked. We said we had not. "The matter is out of your hands," he said. "The state wishes to proceed with this trial."

That day he gave us his home phone number, and for the first time we called each other by our first names.

The cast of characters was gathering. Down the corridor from the dis-trict attorney's office, several hundred potential jurors were milling about, waiting to be called for examination. Observing the scene from benches along the wall was a group known as the courthouse groupies, old people from Santa Monica who come to the courthouse every day to watch the murder trials. They know all the judges, all the lawyers, all the cases, and all the gossip. An old man in a blue polka-dot shirt and a baseball hat with "Hawaii" on it announced to the group that he was waiting to see Sweeney.

"Who's Sweeney?" asked an old woman with jet black, tightly permed hair.

"The guy who killed the movie star," he answered.

"What movie star?"

"Dominique somebody."

"Never heard of her."

I asked a middle-aged woman in black slacks and a tan blouse who was carrying a small red suitcase and peering in the windows of the doors to Courtroom D where everyone was. She said they had broken for lunch. I asked what time they would be back, and she said at two o'clock. I thanked her. My son Alex told me the woman was Sweeney's mother, who had just arrived after a two-day bus trip from Hazelton, Pennsylvania. I had not thought of Sweeney in terms of family, although I knew he had divorced parents and was the oldest of six children, and that his mother had been a battered wife. It was a well-known fact among the people who knew John Sweeney that he had long since put distance between himself and his family. Alex said that he had been sitting next to Mrs. Sweeney in the courtroom earlier, not knowing who she was, when Joseph Shapiro came over to her, addressed her by name, and said that he disliked being the one to give her the message, but her son did not wish to see her. Alex said her eyes filled with tears. For the next seven weeks we sat across the aisle from her every day, and though we never spoke, we felt compassion for her and knew that she in turn felt compassion for us in the dreadful situation that interlocked our families.

The jury selection took two weeks. Each side could eliminate, by way of peremptory challenge, twenty-six people from the main jury before arriving at the twelve, and six from the alternate jury before arriving at the six. People who had had violent crimes in their families were automatically excused. Women activists and people of obvious intelligence who asked pertinent questions were eliminated by the defense. "What I'm looking for are twelve facists, and Adelson's looking for twelve bleeding-heart liberals or weirdos, and we'll arrive somewhere in between," said Steven Barshop to me at one point. Adelson had announced that his defense would be based mostly on psychiatric findings. A writer-photographer who was being questioned said he would not accept the testimony of psychiatrists and psychologists as fact. He further said he found defense attorneys manipulative, to which Adelson replied, "Suppose you don't like the way I comb my hair. Would that affect the way you listen to the testimony?" I found this an extraordinary image for a lawyer who wore a toupee to use, and then I realized that he must think that we thought that the quarter pound of hair taped to the top of his head was real. This would help me later to understand the total conviction with which he presented his client's version of the events surrounding the murder, which he knew to be untrue.

Presiding over the case was Judge Burton S. Katz. In his forties, Judge Katz gives the impression of a man greatly pleased with his good looks. He is expensively barbered, deeply tanned, and noticeably dressed in a manner associated more with Hollywood agents than with superior court judges. He has tinted aviator glasses, and on the first day he was wearing designer jeans, glossy white loafers, and no necktie beneath his judicial robes. Every seat in the courtroom was filled, and Judge Katz seemed to like playing to an audience. His explanations to the prospective jurors were concise and clear, and he made himself pleasing to them. He said funny things to make them laugh, but then was careful to warn them against levity.

The completed jury consisted of nine men and three women. The man who became the foreman ran a string of bowling alleys. One of the men was a postman, another a butcher. One worked for an airline and another for a computer company. One was a teacher. One had a juvenile delinquent son serving on a work team. Two of the men were black. One of the women was an Irish Catholic widow with six children, including a twenty-two-year-old daughter. Although we had hoped for more women, we were pleased with the makeup of the jury. On the instructions of the judge, not so much as a nod was ever exchanged between us, not even when we lunched in the same restaurant or met in the lavatory. However, I felt I grew to know them as the weeks passed, even though Steven Barshop often told me, "Don't ever anticipate a jury. They'll fool you every time."

Judge Katz's relationship with the jury bordered on the flirtatious, and they responded in kind. If the court was called for ten, Judge Katz invariably began around eleven, with elaborate and charming apologies to the jury. One Monday morning he told them he had had a great weekend in Ensenada, that he had had the top down on his car both ways, and that he wished they had been with him. The ladies laughed delightedly, and the men grinned back at him.

Our family was never favored with Judge Katz's charms, not even to the point of simple courtesies. For seven weeks he mispronounced Dominique's name, insistently calling her by my name, Dominick. People wandered in and out of the courtroom; lawyers from other cases chatted with the clerk or used the bailiff's telephone. The microphone on the witness stand fell off its moorings innumerable times and either went dead or emitted a loud electronic screech, and it was never fixed.

It is the fashion among the criminal fraternity to find God, and Sweeney, the killer, was no exception. He arrived daily in the courtroom clutching a Bible, dressed in black, looking like a sacristan. The Bible was a prop; Sweeney never read it, he just rested his folded hands on it. He also wept regularly. One day the court had to be recessed because he claimed the other prisoners had been harassing him before he entered, and he needed time to cry in private. I could not believe that jurors would buy such a performance. "You mark my words," said Steven Barshop, watching him. "Something weird is going to happen in this trial. I can feel it."

On July 20, Barshop called us to say that Adelson did not want Lenny at the trial because her presence in a wheelchair would create undue sympathy for her that would be prejudicial to Sweeney. She was to appear in court the following day so that the judge could hear what she had to say and decide if it was relevant to the trial.

We began to worry. It was becoming apparent that nearly everything Adelson requested was being granted. Adelson recognized Katz's enormous appetite for flattery and indulged it shamelessly. A camaraderie sprang up between the judge and the public defender, and the diminutive Adelson made himself a willing participant in a running series of "short" jokes indulged in by the judge at his expense to the delight of the jury. It was becoming equally apparent that the district attorney, Steven Barshop, was ill-favored by the judge.

Lenny did not take the stand the following day. She was preceded by Lillian Pierce, who had been a girlfriend of John Sweeney's before my daughter. Det. Harold Johnston had tracked her down after receiving a telephone tip from Lynne Brennan, a Beverly Hills publicist, who had once been her friend and knew her story. Lillian Pierce appeared by subpoena issued by the prosecution and was known in advance to be a reluctant witness. Later we heard that she had sat in a car outside the church at Dominique's funeral and cried, feeling too guilty to go inside. At Adelson's request, her testimony was given out of the presence of the jury in order to determine its admissibility as evidence.

An attractive and well-dressed woman in her thirties, Lillian Pierce was very nervous and kept glancing over at Sweeney, who did not look at her. She had, she admitted, been in contact the day before with

Joseph Shapiro, the Ma Maison lawyer. When the district attorney started to question her, her account of her relationship with John Sweeney was so shocking that it should have put to rest forever the defense stand that the strangulation death of Dominique Dunne at the hands of John Sweeney was an isolated incident. He was, it became perfectly apparent, a classic abuser of women, and his weapon was his hands.

Lillian Pierce said that on ten separate occasions during their two-year relationship he had beaten her. She had been hospitalized twice, once for six days, once for four. Sweeney had broken her nose, punctured her eardrum, collapsed her lung, thrown rocks at her when she tried to escape from him. She had seen him, she said, foam at the mouth when he lost control, and smash furniture and pictures. As she spoke, the courtroom was absolutely silent.

Adelson was incensed by the impact of Lillian Pierce's story, made more chilling by her quiet recital of all the acts of violence that she had survived. He became vicious with her. "Were you not drunk?" he asked her. "Were you not drugged?" His implication was that she had got what she deserved. He tried repeatedly to get her to veer from her story, but she remained steadfast.

"Let me remind you, Miss Pierce," he said testily at one point, shuffling through a sheaf of papers, "when you met with Mr. Joe Shapiro and me for lunch on November third, you said ..." I stopped following the sentence. My mind remained at the date November 3. On November 3, Dominique was still on the life-support system at Cedars-Sinai. She was not pronounced legally dead until November 4. So even while Dominique lay dying, efforts were being made to free her killer by men who knew very well that this was not his first display of violence. Adelson knew, and sent a journalist to our house with the lachrymose message that he saw Dominique's death not as a crime but as a tragedy. Patrick Terrail had told Detective Johnston that he had seen Sweeney act violently only once, when he "punched out" a telephone booth in the south of France. It is a fact of the legal system that all information gathered by the prosecution relevant to the case is available to the defense. The reverse is not true. If Detective Johnston had not learned about Lillian Pierce from a telephone tip, her existence would have been unknown to us. I felt hatred for Michael Adelson. His object was to win; nothing else mattered.

Steven Barshop cross-examined Lillian Pierce. "Let me ask you, Miss Pierce, do you come from a well-to-do family?" Adelson objected. "I am trying to establish a pattern," Barshop told the judge.

At that moment—one of the most extraordinary I have ever experienced—we saw an enraged John Sweeney, his prop Bible flying, jump up from his seat at the counsel table and take off for the rear door of the courtroom which leads to the judge's chambers and the holding-cell area. Velma Smith, the court clerk, gave a startled cry. Lillian Pierce, on the stand, did the same. We heard someone shout, "Get help!" Silent alarms were activated by Judge Katz and Velma Smith. The bailiff, Paul Turner, leapt to his feet in a pantherlike movement and made a lunge for Sweeney, grasping him around the chest from behind. Within seconds four armed guards rushed into the courtroom, nearly upsetting Lenny's wheelchair, and surrounded the melee. The bailiff and Sweeney crashed into a file cabinet. "Don't hurt him!" screamed Adelson. Sweeney was wrestled to the floor and then handcuffed to the arms of his chair, where Adelson whispered frantically to him to get hold of himself.

Sobbing, Sweeney apologized to the court and said he had not been trying to escape. Judge Katz accepted his apology. "We know what a strain you are under, Mr. Sweeney," he said. I was appalled at the lack of severity of the judge's admonishment. What we had witnessed had nothing to do with escape. It was an explosion of anger. It showed us how little it took to incite John Sweeney to active rage. Like most of the telling moments of the trial, however, it was not witnessed by the jury.

Mike Tipping, a reporter from the *Santa Monica Evening Outlook*, saw the episode and reported it in his paper. At the behest of Adelson, the court admonished Tipping for exaggerating the incident. The same day, a court gag order was issued to prevent anyone involved in the case from speaking to the press.

From then on, I felt, and continue to feel, that John Sweeney was sedated in the courtroom so that such an incident would never be repeated in front of the jury. He was asked under oath, not in the presence of the jury, if he was sedated, and he said he was not, except for some mild medicine for an upset stomach. The district attorney asked the court for either a blood test or a urine test to substantiate Sweeney's reply, but Judge Katz denied the request.

When Lenny took the stand the first time, the jury was again not present. Judge Katz had to decide on the admissibility of her testimony, but he wrote notes through most of it and scarcely looked in her direction. Lenny described an incident when Dominique came to her house at night after being beaten by Sweeney—the first of the three times he beat her. Dominique's terror was so abject, Lenny said, that she assumed a fetal position in the hallway. Sweeney had knocked her head on the floor and pulled out clumps of her hair. Adelson asked Lenny if she knew what the argument that precipitated the beating had been about. Lenny said she did not. He asked her if she knew that Dominique had had an abortion. She didn't. I didn't. The boys didn't. Her closest friend didn't. It remained throughout the trial an unsubstantiated charge that, to the defense, seemed to justify the beating. The look on Lenny's face was heartbreaking, as if she had been slapped in public. Judge Katz called her testimony hearsay and said he would make his decision as to its admissibility when the trial resumed on August 15 after a two-week hiatus.

During this period, our great friend Katie Manulis died of cancer. Our lives have been intricately involved with the Manuli, as we call them, for twenty-five years. Back at Martin's house after the funeral, I told Sammy Goldwyn that I had grave doubts about the judge. I cited his solicitousness toward Sweeney after his outburst in the courtroom, as well as his discourtesy with Lenny. Sammy said he was dining that evening with John Van de Kamp, the attorney general of the state of California, and he would get a rundown on the judge for me.

He reported back that Judge Katz went to law school at Loyola University and then served as a deputy district attorney for fourteen years. He had been unpopular in the district attorney's office, where he was considered a theatrical character. In 1970, he prosecuted members of the Charles Manson "family" for the murders of Shorty Shea and Gary Hinman. In 1978, he was appointed to the municipal court by Governor Jerry Brown, and in 1981 he was appointed to the superior court. He was considered highly ambitious and was said to like cases with high media visibility, like this one.

Judge Katz ruled that the prosecution could not use the testimony of Lillian Pierce to show the jury that John Sweeney had committed previous acts of violence against women. He said he would allow Miss Pierce to take the stand only in rebuttal if Adelson put expert witnesses, meaning psychiatrists, on the stand to testify that Sweeney was too mentally impaired by emotion to have formed the intent to kill. Once Judge Katz ruled that, Adelson threw out his psychiatric defense. Later in the trial, when the possibility of putting Lillian Pierce on the stand was raised again by Steven Barshop, Katz ruled that the "prejudicial effect outweighed the probative value." The jury would never know of Lillian Pierce's existence until after they had arrived at a verdict.

Judge Katz also ruled that Lenny's testimony about Dominique's coming to her in hysterics after Sweeney first beat her on August 27 could not be used by the prosecution during the main case. The judge once again agreed with Adelson that the prejudicial effect of the testimony outweighed its probative value; and he told Barshop not to mention the incident in his primary case. He said he would decide later in the trial whether her story could be used to rebut a mental-impairment defense for Sweeney.

Judge Katz agreed with Adelson that all statements made by Dominique to her agent, her fellow actors, and her friends regarding her fear of John Sweeney during the last five weeks of her life must be considered hearsay and ruled inadmissible as evidence.

It was not an auspicious opening to the trial. The loss of the Lillian Pierce testimony was a severe blow to Steven Barshop. Our hopes were buoyed by Barshop's opening argument in the case. He began with a description of the participants. Sweeney: twenty-seven, six foot one, 170 pounds. Dominique: twenty-two, five foot one, 112 pounds. He gave a rundown of the charges in the two incidents, the assault on Dominique on September 26 and the murder on the night of October 30. He described how Sweeney had walked out of Ma Maison restaurant at 8:30 that evening and proceeded on foot to the house, where he argued with Dominique and strangled her. He said that Dominique was brain-dead there at the scene of the strangulation, despite the fact that she was kept on the life-support system at Cedars-Sinai until November 4. He said that the coroner would testify that death by strangulation took between four and six minutes. Then he held up a watch with a second hand and said to the jury, "Ladies and gentlemen, I am going to show you how long it took for Dominique Dunne to die." For four minutes the courtroom sat in hushed silence. It was horrifying. I had never allowed myself to think how long she had struggled in his hands, thrashing for her life. A gunshot or a knife stab is over in an instant; a strangulation is an eternity. The only sound during the four minutes came from Michael Adelson and John Sweeney, who whispered together the whole time.

Our daily presence in the courtroom annoyed Adelson throughout the trial. Defense lawyers in general don't like jurors to see the victim's family. Friends of ours had advised us to leave town until the trial was over. The organization known as Parents of Murdered Children advised us to attend every session. "It's the last business of your daughter's life," a father of a young girl stabbed to death by a former boyfriend said to me on the telephone one night. We sat in the front row behind the bailiff's desk in full view of the jury: Lenny in the aisle in her wheelchair, Alex, Griffin and his girlfriend, and I. We were within six feet of John Sweeney. As the weeks crept by, the boys became more and more silent. It seemed to me as if their youth were being stripped away from them.

In the row behind us sat representatives from Parents of Murdered Children; some had been through their trials, others were awaiting theirs. Many of Dominique's friends came on a daily basis; so did friends of ours and friends of the boys. There were also representatives from Women Against Violence Against Women and from Victims for Victims, the group started by Theresa Saldana, an actress who was brutally stabbed a few years ago and survived.

"If any member of the Dunne family cries, cries out, rolls his eyes, exclaims in any way, he will be asked to leave the courtroom," we were told by the judge at the behest of Adelson.

"Your honor, Alex Dunne had tears in his eyes," Adelson called out one day. When Sweeney took the stand, Alex and Griffin changed their seats in order to be in his line of vision. Adelson tried to get them put out of the courtroom for this. We were intimidated but never searched. How easy it would have been to enter with a weapon and eradicate the killer if we had been of that mind. As the last week approached, Alex said one morning, "I can't go back anymore. I can't be there where Sweeney is."

Dominique's friends Bryan Cook and Denise Dennehy flew in from Lake Forest, Illinois, to testify about the time, five weeks before the murder, when Sweeney attempted to choke Dominique after their night on the town. She had escaped from her house that night by climbing through a bathroom window and driving her Volkswagen to the home of an artist friend named Norman Carby. (Lenny was in New York at the time.) Carby, appalled by the marks of attempted strangulation on her neck, had the presence of mind to take photographs. The pictures were the prosecution's prime exhibit of the seriousness of the assault. Adelson belittled the pictures. There was, he said, a third picture in the same series showing Dominique laughing. Carby explained that Dominique had a reading that morning for the role of a battered child on "Hill Street Blues." Carby said he told her that at least she wouldn't have to wear any makeup for it, and that had made her laugh.

One of the snitches appeared in the courtroom. He was the one who claimed Sweeney had said he thought he had the police believing that he had not intended to kill Dominique. He claimed further that Sweeney had asked him, "Have you ever been with a girl who thought she was better than you?" Snitches are known to be unreliable witnesses, whom jurors usually dislike and distrust. This man's dossier, forwarded by his prison, depicted a disturbed troublemaker. His arms were tattooed from his shoulders to his wrists. Steven Barshop decided to dispense with his revelations. He was not put on the stand.

On one of the color pictures of the autopsy there was a bruise on Dominique's shoulder, which gave rise to disagreement. No one was quite sure if it had been incurred when she fell to the ground after being strangled, or if it had been caused by the life-support system, or if it was a result of the autopsy. Adelson was determined that the jury not see the photograph with the bruise, and the arguments went on endlessly while the jury waited in an adjoining room. Judge Katz solved the matter: with a pair of scissors provided by Velma Smith, the court clerk, he simply cut off the picture below the neck so that only the actual strangulation marks were visible to the jury.

Dep. Frank DeMilio, one of the first to arrive at the scene of the crime, testified on the stand that Sweeney had said to him, "Man, I blew it. I killed her. I didn't think I choked her that hard, but I don't know, I just kept on choking her. I just lost my temper and blew it again."

I wondered then and wonder still what the word *again* meant. Did it refer to one of the other times he attacked Dominique? Or Lillian Pierce? Or is there something else in this mysterious man's mysterious past that has not yet come to light? Sweeney had no car and no driver's license, an oddity for a young man in a city totally dependent on wheels. And although he had worked as head chef in one of the most prestigious restaurants in the city, he was nearly totally without funds. Furthermore, an informant at Ma Maison told Detective Johnston of another former girlfriend, then somewhere in France, against whom Sweeney had committed at least one act of violence.

After Steven Barshop rested his case, Judge Katz delivered another devastating blow to the prosecution. He agreed with a request from Adelson that the jury be allowed to consider only charges of manslaughter and second-degree murder, thus acquitting Sweeney of first-degree murder. In asking Katz to bar a first-degree murder verdict, Adelson argued, "There is no premeditation or deliberation in this case," and Katz agreed. Barshop argued that the jury should decide whether there was sufficient premeditation or deliberation. He said Sweeney had enough time to consider his actions during the period—up to six minutes, according to the coroner's testimony—that it took him to choke Dominique. Katz emphasized that Sweeney had arrived at Dominique's house without a murder weapon, although he knew that Sweeney's hands had nearly killed Lillian Pierce and that his hands had nearly strangled Dominique five weeks before he killed her. He also cited the fact that Sweeney had made no attempt to escape.

Rarely do twelve people on a jury agree: most verdicts are compromises. If this jury had had the option of first-degree murder and were in dispute, they could have compromised at second-degree. With first-degree ruled out, if there was a dispute, their only compromise was manslaughter.

Det. Harold Johnston was in the courtroom that day. He believed this was a case of first-degree murder, just as we did. Means of escape and means of method have nothing to do with premeditation, he told us. An informant at Ma Maison had told us that just before Sweeney left the restaurant to go to Dominique's house on the night he murdered her, he had ordered two martinis from the bar and drunk them. He felt that Sweeney must have decided that if he couldn't have Dominique, he wasn't going to let anyone else have her either.

Harold Johnston had become a friend over the year, since the night that he rang the doorbell of Lenny's house on Crescent Drive at two in the morning to tell her that Dominique was near death in Cedars-Sinai. He had also questioned Sweeney on the night of the murder. He told me in the corridor outside the courtroom that day that the judge's ruling had made him lose faith in the system after twenty-six years on the force.

One day Adelson's wife and little boys came to the trial. As if to offset his unpleasant image in front of the jury, Adelson elaborately played father. "Now don't you talk," he admonished them, wagging his finger. Several times Judge Katz's mother and father also came to observe the proceedings. They were seated in special chairs set up inside the gate by the bailiff's desk and whispered incessantly. Invariably Katz showed off for their benefit. On one occasion, after both Barshop and Adelson had finished with the witness David Packer, the actor who was visiting Dominique at the time of the murder and who called the police, Judge Katz started an independent line of questioning, about eyeglasses, that had not been introduced by either the prosecution or the defense: Did David Packer wear them? Did he have them on the night he saw Sweeney standing over Dominique's body? The questions advanced nothing and muddied what had gone before.

———

A photographer from *People* magazine appeared in court one day, weighed down with equipment. I happened to know him. He said he had been sent to take pictures of our family for an article his magazine was doing on the trial. Neither Griffin nor Alex wished to be photographed, but the photographer stayed in the courtroom and took pictures of the session with Sweeney and the lawyers. At the lunch break, the judge signaled to the photographer to see him in his chambers. Later, out in the parking lot, I ran into the man. He told me he had thought the judge was going to ask him not to shoot during the session. Instead, the judge had said he wanted his eyes to show up in the pictures and had tried on several different pairs of glasses for the photographer's approval.

Adelson had never intended to have Sweeney take the stand. However, when he had to throw out his psychiatric defense to keep the jurors from knowing about Sweeney's previous acts of violence against Lillian Pierce, he had no choice but to put the accused on. Sweeney was abjectly courteous, addressing the lawyers and judge as sir. He spoke very quietly, and often had to be told to raise his voice so that the jurors could hear. Although he wept he never once became flustered, and there was no sign of the rage he exhibited on the day Lillian Pierce took the stand. He painted his relationship with Dominique as nearly idyllic. He gave the names of all her animals—the bunny, the kitten, the puppy. He refuted the testimony of Bryan Cook and Denise Dennehy and denied that he had attempted to choke Dominique after their night on the town five weeks before the murder. He said he'd only tried to restrain her from leaving the house. He admitted that they had separated after that, and that she had had the locks changed so that he could not get back in the house, but he insisted that she had promised to reconcile with him and that her refusal to do so was what brought on the final attack. He could not, he claimed, remember the events of the murder, which prompted Barshop to accuse him of having "selective memory." After the attack, Sweeney said, he had entered the house and attempted to commit suicide by swallowing two bottles of pills; however, no bottles were ever found, and if he had swallowed pills, they did not have any apparent effect on his system.

From the beginning we had been warned that the defense would slander Dominique. It is part of the defense premise that the victim is responsible for the crime. As Dr. Willard Gaylin says in his book *The Killing of Bonnie Garland*, Bonnie Garland's killer, Richard Herrin, murdered Bonnie all over again in the courtroom. It is always the murder victim who is placed on trial. John Sweeney, who claimed to love Dominique, and whose defense was that this was a crime of passion, slandered her in court as viciously and cruelly as he had strangled her. It was agonizing for us to listen to him, led on by Adelson, besmirch Dominique's name. His violent past remained sacrosanct and inviolate, but her name was allowed to be trampled upon and kicked, with unsubstantiated charges, by the man who killed her.

"Look at her friends!" I wanted to scream at the judge and the jury. "You have seen them both on the stand and in the courtroom: Bryan Cook, Denise Dennehy, Melinda Bittan, Kit McDonough, Erica Elliot, and the others who have been here every day—bright, clean-cut, successful young people. That is what Dominique Dunne was like. She wasn't at all the person whom John Sweeney is describing." But I sat silent.

When Dominique's friends closed up her house after the funeral, her best friend, Melinda Bittan, came across a letter Dominique had written to Sweeney, which he may or may not have received. The letter had been filed away and forgotten. In the final days of the trial, Melinda remembered it one day when a group of us were having lunch together. Steven Barshop introduced it in his rebuttal, and as the court reporter, Sally Yerger, read it to the jury, it was as if Dominique was speaking from beyond the grave.

"Selfishness works both ways," she wrote. *"You are just as selfish as I am. We have to be two individuals to work as a couple. I am not permitted to do enough things on my own. Why must you be a part of everything I do? Why do you want to come to my riding lessons and my acting classes? Why are you jealous of every scene partner I have?*

"Why must I recount word for word everything I spoke to Dr. Black about? Why must I talk about every audition when you know it is bad luck for me? Why do we have discussions at 3:00 A.M. all the time, instead of during the day?

"Why must you know the name of every person I come into contact with? You go crazy over my rehearsals. You insist on going to work with me when I have told you it makes me nervous. Your paranoia is overboard. . . . You do not love me. You are obsessed with me. The person you think you love is not me at all. It is someone you have made up in your head. I'm the person who makes you angry, who you fight with sometimes. I think we only fight when images of me fade away and you are faced with the real me. That's why arguments erupt out of nowhere.

"The whole thing has made me realize how scared I am of you, and I don't mean just physically. I'm afraid of the next time you are going to have another mood swing. . . . When we are good, we are great. But when we are bad, we are horrendous. The bad outweighs the good."

Throughout Steven Barshop's closing argument to the jury, when he asked them to find Sweeney guilty of murder in the second degree, the maximum verdict available to them, Judge Katz sat with a bottle of correction fluid, brushing out lines on something he was preparing. Later we learned it was his instructions to the jury. I thought, if he isn't listening, or is only half listening, what kind of subliminal signal is that sending to the jury? During Adelson's final argument, on the other hand, he gave his full attention.

"This will be the toughest day of the trial," said Steven Barshop on the morning of Adelson's final argument. "Today you will hear Adelson justify murder." We had grown very close to Steven Barshop during the weeks of the trial and admired his integrity and honesty. "You don't have to sit through it, you know," he said. But we did, and he knew we would.

I lost count of how many times Adelson described Sweeney to the jury as an "ordinarily reasonable person," as if this act of murder were an isolated instance in an otherwise serene life. Every time he said it he separated the three words—ordinarily reasonable person—and underscored them with a pointing gesture of his hand. We who had seen every moment of the trial knew of thirteen separate instances of violence, ten against Lillian Pierce and three against Dominique, but the jurors at this point were still not even aware of the existence of Lillian Pierce. Through an informant at Ma Maison, our family also knew of other acts of violence against women that had not been introduced into the case, but we sat in impassive silence as Adelson described the strangler as an ordinarily reasonable person.

He returned to his old theme: "This was not a crime," he told the jury. "This was a tragedy." It didn't matter that he knew it wasn't true. They didn't know it wasn't true, and he was concerned only with convincing them.

He talked about "that old-fashioned thing: romantic love." He made up dialogue and put it in the mouth of Dominique Dunne. "I, Dominique, reject you, Sweeney," he cried out. *"I lied to you, Sweeney!"*

We were sickened at his shamelessness. Leaving the courtroom during a break, I found myself next to him in the aisle. "You piece of shit," I said to him quietly so that only he could hear.

His eyes flashed in anger. "Your Honor!" he called out. "May I approach the bench?"

I continued out to the corridor, where I told Lenny what I had done.

"That was very stupid," she said. "Now you'll get kicked out of the courtroom."

"No one heard me say it except Adelson," I said. "When the judge calls me up, I'll lie and say I didn't say it. Everybody else is lying. Why shouldn't I? It's his word against mine."

Steven Barshop appeared.

"Is he going to kick me out?" I asked.

Barshop smiled. "He can't kick the father of the victim out of the court on the last day of the trial with all the press present," he said. Then he added, "But don't do it again."

Judge Katz drank soft drinks from Styrofoam cups as he read instructions to the jury explaining second-degree murder, voluntary manslaughter, and involuntary manslaughter. Later, after the sentencing, the jury foreman, Paul Spiegel, would say on television that the judge's instructions were incomprehensible. During the eight days that the jury was out, deadlocked, they asked the judge four times for clarification of the instructions, and four times the judge told them that the answers to their questions were in the instructions.

—————

I was now living in the Bel Air home of Martin Manulis, who had returned east after Katie's death to complete postproduction work on a new miniseries. The jury had been out for over a week, and we knew they could not understand the instructions. Lenny, Griffin, Alex, and I were terribly edgy, and one evening we all went our separate ways. I paced restlessly from room to room in the Manulis house. I hadn't looked at television that summer except occasionally to see the news, but I suddenly picked up the remote-control unit and flicked the set on. I froze at the voice I heard.

There, on television, was Dominique screaming, "What's happening?" I had not known that *Poltergeist* was scheduled on the cable channel, and the shock of seeing her was overwhelming. I felt as if she were sending me a message. "I don't know what's happening, my darling," I screamed back at the television set, and for the first time since the trial started, I sobbed. The next day the verdict came in.

The waiting was endless. Joseph Shapiro, the Ma Maison lawyer, regaled the reporters with an account of an African safari in the veldt where the native guides serving his party wore black tie. One of the courthouse groupies said that three buzzes to the clerk's desk meant that a verdict had been reached. Five minutes before the jury entered, we watched Judge Katz sentence a man who had robbed a flower shop in a nonviolent crime to five years in prison. Sweeney entered, clutching his Bible, and sat a few feet away from us. Mrs. Sweeney sat across the aisle with Joseph Shapiro. The room was packed. A pool television camera, reporters, and photographers filled the aisles.

The jury entered, and the foreman, Paul Spiegel, delivered two envelopes to the bailiff to give to the judge. Katz opened first one envelope and then the other, milking his moment before the television camera like a starlet at the Golden Globes. Then, revealing nothing, he handed the two envelopes to his clerk, Velma Smith, who read the verdicts aloud to the court. The strangulation death of Dominique Dunne was voluntary manslaughter, and the earlier choking attack a misdemeanor assault. There was a gasp of disbelief in the courtroom. The maximum sentence for the two charges is six and a half years, and with good time and work time, the convict is paroled automatically when he has served half his sentence, without having to go through a parole hearing. Since the time spent in jail between the arrest and the sentencing counted as time served, Sweeney would be free in two and a half years.

"I am ecstatic!" cried Adelson. He embraced Sweeney, who laid his head on Adelson's shoulder. Shapiro clutched Mrs. Sweeney's hand in a victorious salute, but Mrs. Sweeney, of the lot of them, had the grace not to exult publicly that her son had got away with murder. Then Adelson and Shapiro clasped hands, acting as if they had freed an innocent man from the gallows. Not content with his victory, Adelson wanted more. "Probation!" he cried. As we sat there like whipped dogs and watched the spectacle of justice at work, I felt a madness growing within me.

Judge Katz excused the jury, telling them that even though other people might agree or disagree with the verdict, they must not doubt their decision. "You were there. You saw the evidence. You heard the witnesses." He knew, of course, that they would be hearing from the press about Lillian Pierce in minutes.

He told them that justice had been served and thanked them on behalf of the attorneys and both families. I could not believe I had heard Judge Katz thank the jury on behalf of my family for reducing the murder of my daughter to manslaughter. Rage heated my blood. I felt loathing for him. The weeks of sitting impassively through the travesty that we had witnessed finally took their toll. "Not for our family, Judge Katz!" I shouted. Friends behind me put warning hands of caution on my shoulders, but reason had deserted me.

Katz looked at me, aghast, as if he were above criticism in his own courtroom.

"You will have your chance to speak at the time of the sentencing, Mr. Dunne," he said.

"It's too late then," I answered.

"I will have to ask the bailiff to remove you from the courtroom," he said.

"No," I answered. "I'm leaving the courtroom. It's all over here."

I took Lenny's wheelchair and pushed it up the aisle. The room was silent. At the double doors that opened onto the corridor, I turned back. My eyes locked with Judge Katz's, and I raised my hand and pointed at him. "You have withheld important evidence from this jury about this man's history of violence against women."

The jury foreman, when asked later by the press what finally broke the deadlock, replied on television, "A few jurors were just hot and tired and wanted to give up."

The trial was over. Sentencing was set for November 10.

There was an uproar in the media over the verdict, and KABC radio ran an on-the-hour editorial blasting it. Letters of outrage filled the newspapers as stories of John Sweeney's history of violence against women became public knowledge. The *Herald-Examiner* published a front-page article about the case: "Heat of Passion: Legitimate Defense or a Legal Loophole?" Judge Katz was severely criticized. In the weeks that followed, a local television station released the results of a poll of prosecutors and criminal defense lawyers in which he tied for fourth-worst judge in Los Angeles County.

Several days after the verdict I returned to the courthouse to retrieve from the district attorney the photographs and letters and videotapes of television shows that Lenny had lent him. The receptionist said I would find Steven Barshop in one of the courtrooms. As I passed Courtroom D, out of habit I looked in the window. At that instant Judge Katz happened to look up. I moved on and entered Courtroom C, where Barshop was busy with another lawyer. The doors of the courtroom opened behind me, and Judge Katz's bailiff, Paul Turner, who had wrestled Sweeney to the ground several months earlier, asked me to go out into the hall with him. "What are you doing here?" he asked me. He was stern and tough.

"What do you mean, what am I doing here?" I replied.

"Just what I said to you."

"I don't have the right to be here?"

"There's been a lot of bad blood in this trial," he said. I realized that he thought, or the judge thought, that I had come here to seek revenge. Then Steven Barshop came out into the corridor, and the bailiff turned and left us.

———

In the month between the verdict and the sentencing, we tried to pick up the pieces of our lives, but the aftermath of the trial continued. Joseph Shapiro appeared at the wrap party given by 20th Century-Fox for the film *Johnny Dangerously*, in which Griffin costars, and the producers asked him to leave the lot.

According to Proposition 8, the victim's bill of rights, the next of kin of murder victims have the right to take the stand at the sentencing and plead with the judge for the maximum sentence. We were told that Adelson intended to cross-examine us if we did this. We were also told that Adelson, in order to get Sweeney released on probation that day, intended to put on the stand psychiatrists and psychologists who would testify that Sweeney was nonviolent. And we were told that Adelson intended to show a videotape of Sweeney under hypnosis saying he could not remember the murder.

On the day of the sentencing, pickets protesting the verdict, the judge, and Ma Maison marched and sang on the courthouse steps in Santa Monica. Courtroom D was filled to capacity. Extra bailiffs stood in the aisles and among the standees at the rear of the room. A young man called Gavin DeBecker sat next to the bailiff's desk and made frequent trips back to the judge's chambers. DeBecker provides bodyguard service for political figures and public personalities.

Throughout the several hours of the proceedings John Sweeney remained hunched over, his face covered by his hands, so unobtrusive a figure that he seemed almost not to be there.

Two of Sweeney's sisters took the stand and asked for mercy for their brother. Mrs. Sweeney described her life as a battered and beaten wife. Griffin took the stand and presented Judge Katz with a petition that had been circulated by Dominique's friends; it contained a thousand signatures of people protesting the verdict and asking for the maximum sentence. Lenny spoke, and I spoke.

We were not cross-examined by Adelson. No psychiatrists or psychologists took the stand. No videotape of Sweeney saying he could not remember the murder was shown. But a whole new dynamic entered Courtroom D that day and dominated everything else: the outrage of Judge Burton S. Katz over the injustice of the verdict arrived at by the jury.

He mocked the argument that Sweeney had acted in the heat of
passion. "I will state on the record that I believe this is a murder. I believe that Sweeney is a murderer and not a manslaughterer. . . . This is
a killing with malice. This man held on to this young, vulnerable,
beautiful, warm human being that had everything to live for, with his
hands. He had to have known that as she was flailing to get oxygen,
that the process of death was displacing the process of life."

Judge Katz then addressed Sweeney: "You knew of your capacity
for uncontrolled violence. You knew you hurt Dominique badly with
your own hands and that you nearly choked her into unconsciousness
on September 26. You were in a rage because your fragile ego could
not accept the final rejection."

He said he was appalled by the jurors' decision over Sweeney's first
attack: "The jury came back—I don't understand it for the life of
me—with simple assault, thus taking away the sentencing parameters
that I might have on a felony assault."

He called the punishment for the crime "anemic and pathetically
inadequate." Having got the verdict we felt he had guided the jurors
into giving, he was now blasting them for giving it.

He went on and on. It was as if he had suddenly become a different
human being. However, all his eloquence changed nothing. The verdict remained the same: manslaughter. The sentence remained the
same: six and a half years, automatically out in two and a half.

Surrounded by four bailiffs, Sweeney rose, looking at no one, and
walked out of the courtroom for the last time. He was sent to the
minimum-security facility at Chino.

Gavin DeBecker pursued us down the hall. He said Judge Katz would
like to see us in his chambers. Lenny declined, but I was curious, as
was Griffin. DeBecker led us to Katz's chambers. "Burt," he said, tap-
ping on the door, "the Dunnes are here."

Judge Katz was utterly charming. He called us by our first names.
He talked at length about the injustice of the verdict and his own
shock over it, as if all this was something in which he had played no
part. He said his daughters had not spoken to him since the verdict
came in.

He gave each of us his Superior Court card and wrote on it his unlisted telephone number at home and his private number in chambers so that we could call him direct. What, I thought to myself, would I ever have to call him about?

Back in the crowded corridor again, I was talking with friends as Michael Adelson made his exit. He caught my eye, and I sensed what he was going to do. In the manner of John McEnroe leaping over the net in a moment of largesse to exchange pleasantries with the vanquished, this defender of my daughter's killer made his way across the corridor to speak to me. I waited until he was very near, and as he was about to extend his hand I turned away from him.

When Michael Adelson was asked in an NBC television interview if he thought Sweeney would pose a threat to society when released from prison in two and a half years, he pondered and replied, "I think he will be safe if he gets the therapy he needs. His rage needs to be worked upon." Judge Katz, when asked the same question by the same interviewer, answered, "I wouldn't be comfortable with him in society." Steven Barshop told a newspaper reporter, "He'll be out in time to cook someone a nice dinner and kill someone else." Paul Spiegel, the jury foreman, in a television interview, called the judge's criticism of the verdict a cheap shot. He said the judge was concerned over the criticism he himself had received since the trial and was trying to place the blame elsewhere. Spiegel said he felt that justice had not been served. He said the jury would certainly have found Sweeney guilty if they had heard all the evidence. "If it were up to me," he said, "Sweeney would have spent the rest of his life in jail."

Not one of us regrets having gone through the trial, or wishes that we had accepted the plea bargain, even though Sweeney would then have had to serve seven and a half years rather than two and a half. We chose to go to trial, and we did, and we saw into one another's souls in the process. We loved her, and we knew that she loved us back. Knowing that we did everything we could has been for us the beginning of the release from pain. We thought of revenge, the boys and I, but it was just a thought, no more than that, momentarily comforting. We believe in God and in ultimate justice, and the time came to let go of our obsession with the murder and proceed with life.

Alex decided to stay with his mother in California and finish his

college education. Griffin had to return to New York to start a new
film. Lenny became an active spokeswoman for Parents of Murdered
Children. I returned to the novel I was writing, which I had put aside
at the beginning of the trial.

It was my last day in Los Angeles. I had said my farewells to all, knowing I had experienced new dimensions of friendship and family love. I
was waiting for the car to drive me to the airport. Outside it was rain-
ing for the first time in months. Through the windows I could see the
gardeners of the house where I had been staying in Bel Air. They were
watering the lawn as usual, wearing yellow slickers in the insistent
downpour.

There was plenty of time. I told the driver to take me to Crescent
Drive first. I wanted to say good-bye to Lenny again. I knew what an
effort it had been for her to put herself through the ordeal of the trial.
She was in bed watching "Good Morning America." I sat in her
wheelchair next to her bed and held her hand. "I'm proud of you,
Len," I said to her. "I'm proud of you too," she said to me, but she
kept looking at David Hartman on television.

On the way out I took a yellow rose from the hall table.

"I want to make one more stop," I said to the driver.

We went out Whilshire Boulevard to Westwood. Past the Avco theater complex, the driver made a left turn into the Westwood Cemetery.

"I'll be just a few minutes," I said.

Dominique is buried near two of her mother's close friends, the actresses Norma Crane and Natalie Wood. On her marker, under her
name and dates, it says, "Loved by All." I knelt down and put the yellow rose on her grave.

"Good-bye, my darling daughter."

---

*John Sweeney, the murderer of my daughter, was released from prison af-
ter two and a half years. For a while, I hired the famous private detective
Anthony Pellicano to follow him and track his movements, but after
some time I decided that I didn't want to live in a state of revenge and
desisted. Fourteen years later, when I mentioned John Sweeney's name*

in an article I wrote about Anthony Pellicano at the O. J. Simpson trial, a man in Florida contacted me to say that his daughter was engaged to be married to a man named John Sweeney. He was a chef in a top restaurant in Seattle. It was the same John Sweeney. He had not told his fiancée that he had ever been in prison, nor had he told her that he had killed a girl. The marriage did not take place. He claimed to fellow workers that I was harassing him. He changed his name. The most fervent wish of my life is that I never encounter him.

THE WOMAN WHO KNEW
TOO LITTLE

She was a kept woman on the skids, an actress-model who neither acted nor modeled, living on the wrong side of town in an apartment from which she was about to be evicted for nonpayment of rent. Amid the half-packed bags and unwatered plants, remnants of a past life bespoke more affluent times: a luxurious white sofa, a Chinese porcelain dish on a teakwood stand.

He was a homosexual-schizophrenic-alcoholic on the fringes of show business, a collector of celebrities' telephone numbers, who basked for a while in the light of the scarlet woman's illicit fame. They were old friends who had met as patients in a mental hospital and who tolerated each other's transgressions and failures. After he moved in, he found he was buying the groceries and even making the monthly payments on a car she had totaled when she was drunk. She treated him like her slave boy, sending him out to get her bagels and cream cheese, to walk her dog, to find her a new place to live. She spent most of her time in bed, too paralyzed with fear at what was happening to her to function. Her money and glamour gone, she felt that her options for ever recovering her former status had been exhausted. In the end she drove him to the breaking point, and he did for her what she could not do for herself: he killed her.

He waited until she went to sleep. He took her son's baseball bat, adjusted the lights, turned on the water so that the neighbors wouldn't hear anything through the paper-thin walls, and bludgeoned her with the bat until she was dead. She was lying under $500 gray-bordered Pratesi sheets embroidered with her initials, V.M. Next to her bed, on a Formica table, were an empty bottle of Soave wine and a paperback by Carlos Castaneda.

He drove to the North Hollywood police station and confessed. "She wanted to die," he said, and then he gave her credentials, as if seeking approval for the quality of life he had just extinguished. "Don't you know who she is? Are you aware of her background? It was on the front page of every newspaper because Alfred Bloomingdale was on Ronald Reagan's kitchen cabinet. . . ."

Everybody knew the story. Vicki Morgan established herself in tabloid history as the $18,000-a-month mistress of Alfred Bloomingdale, the department-store heir and founder of the Diners Club, when she filed a $5-million palimony suit against the dying millionaire, claiming he had reneged on a promise to provide her with lifetime support and a home of her own. The suit, which sent shock waves through the social world, was instigated after Bloomingdale's wife, Betsy, cut off the corporate checks Vicki had long been receiving. Mrs. Bloomingdale, a leader in Los Angeles and international society and a close friend of Mrs. Ronald Reagan's, refused to be intimidated by her husband's mistress and held her ground throughout the scandal.

The names came pouring out of the killer, a reverential litany of fame and power. People who had never heard of Marvin Pancoast, for that was his name, were part of his confession to the murder of Vicki Morgan.

Pancoast, who didn't usually command much attention, had the detective riveted. In jail two days later, he told a reporter from the *Los Angeles Herald-Examiner* that he expected to be sentenced to the gas chamber. But that was before anyone had heard of the sex tapes. And before he had a lawyer.

Vicki Morgan's fourteen-year-old son attended her funeral at Forest Lawn Mortuary with his Mohawk-cut hair dyed green. The service was sparsely attended, but even as it was taking place, new headlines were in the making. A Beverly Hills attorney announced to the press that he had in his possession three videotape cassettes showing high ranking members of the Reagan administration in sexual frolics with Vicki and other women.

From Beverly Hills to Washington, in the months that followed, rumors flourished. Wasn't it just too convenient that this woman should end up dead? Broke and at the breaking point, did Vicki Morgan threaten to sell the sex tapes if she was not bought off? Surely, people speculated, Marvin Pancoast had been planted in her house three weeks before her death. Was Pancoast taking the rap for a crime he did not commit—for which he would be found insane, serve a short sentence, and be well remunerated? His clothes had not been blood-spattered after the murder. There were no fingerprints. And the drawers had been ransacked. Where were the tapes? Where was the tell-all memoir Vicki was supposed to be writing?

The murder trial of Marvin Pancoast got under way in June, eleven months after Vicki Morgan's death. When I arrived in Los Angeles, it had already been in the courtroom for three weeks, two weeks of jury selection and a week of prosecution testimony. But it appeared that there was a virtual news blackout on the story.

Although Pancoast had recanted his confession and his lawyers said they would prove that someone else killed Vicki Morgan because she was planning to use the sex tapes for purposes of blackmail, the story was rarely more prominently featured than on page 5 or 6 of the *Los Angeles Herald-Examiner*, with hardly a mention in the *L.A. Times* or newspapers around the country. Even the courtroom, in the city of Van Nuys, out in the San Fernando Valley, was never more than half-filled, often considerably less, and most of those people were court watchers. Was this because pressure had been brought to bear to downplay a story that might prove embarrassing to the Reagan administration? Or was it because the stars of the piece were dead and the leading players at the trial had been no more than bit players in the drama, hangers-on and acolytes of the discredited mistress of a disgraced multi-millionaire?

Rumors die hard, though. Shortly after I arrived in Los Angeles, a friend of mine, a movie star, said to me, "Oh, no, darling, Marvin's not guilty. We knew Marvin. He worked for my ex-husband. Nutty as a fruitcake, yes. A murderer, no. You check his mother's bank account after this whole thing is over, and you'll see she's been taken care of for life. They'll just put Marvin in the nuthouse for a few years. It's Marilyn all over again. Did you ever know that the C.I.A. went into Marilyn's house afterward and cleaned out everything? I bet they did that at Vicki's too. That's where the tapes went."

Even at his own trial Marvin Pancoast was not a dominant figure. He has an easily forgettable face, a West Hollywood mustache, and the kind of white skin that turns sunstroke scarlet after five minutes' exposure to the sun. He was always meticulously groomed. Every time he entered the courtroom, he waved to people he knew—his mother, his lawyer's wife, a friend with a ponytail, pierced ear, and turquoise rings on most of his fingers. At times he read *The Shining*, by Stephen King.

Pancoast met Vicki Morgan in 1979, when they were both patients at the Thalians Community Mental Health Center, in Los Angeles. Vicki was there, at Alfred Bloomingdale's expense, for depression following the collapse of her third marriage. Marvin, who had been in and out of such institutions for years, was also in for depression. At various times Marvin had been diagnosed as schizophrenic, manic-depressive, psychotic, and masochistic. They became friends.

He worked in subservient positions for such luminary Hollywood institutions as Rogers & Cowan, the publicists, where he was a gofer, and William Morris, the talent agency, where he operated the Xerox machine. He bragged of knowing famous people in the film business, and his telephone book contained numbers of many celebrated individuals he had never met.

For thirteen months he worked in the office of Hollywood and Broadway producer Allan Carr. "I remember him," said Carr. "He stole my Rolodex with all my celebrity phone numbers, and we couldn't get it back. Finally he sent us back the Rolodex frame, but all the cards were gone."

I remarked to Virginia Peninger, a court watcher seated next to me, that Marvin seemed heavily sedated.

"Oh, he is," she replied. "Ask his mother. She'll tell you. He gets agitated if he doesn't get his medication."

Pancoast had two lawyers defending him, Arthur Barens and Charles "Ted" Mathews, who had been hired by Pancoast's mother and his grandmother. Barens was the star of the courtroom. Trim, handsome, and fashionably dressed, with gold jewelry glistening at each wrist, he drives a Jaguar with initialed license plates and lives on one of the best streets in Beverly Hills. His business card reads: "Arthur Barens, Attorney at Law, A Professional Corporation." This is his third murder trial. Before, he had been mainly a personal-injury lawyer, known as a P.I. He had also worked for years in real estate with Pancoast's mother. A curious twist in his background is that Vicki Morgan, at Pancoast's suggestion, went to ask him to handle her pali-mony suit after she fired the well-known lawyer Marvin Mitchelson. He admits to having met with her three times, but says he turned her down because he felt that "she could not possibly win the suit."

Ted Mathews is heavy bellied and wears suspenders. He made no secret of his revulsion for his client's lifestyle and sexual practices, but he kept pressing home the point that those things should not be brought into consideration when the jury was deciding the guilt or in-nocence of Marvin Pancoast. Barens and Mathews made an odd cou-ple. In the corridor outside the courtroom, day after day, they tititllated a handful of press and television reporters with promises that people who had viewed the sex tapes would appear, that presidential coun-selor Ed Meese had been subpoenaed, and that Marvin Pancoast would take the stand.

"This whole case is full of people who want nothing more than to have their faces on the six o'clock news," said a disgusted witness as she made her way past the nightly sideshow.

"Have you ever represented Marvin before when he has been in trouble?" I asked Arthur Barens.

"Just fag stuff. Lewd conduct charges," he said.

Representing the prosecution was Deputy District Attorney Stanley Weisberg. Wry, wise, probably witty in circumstances other than these, he was without flash, glamour, or fancy rhetoric. He stuck to the facts. While Barens and Mathews could talk about a police cover-up, the sex tapes, blackmail, hypnosis, drugs, and unnamed higher-ups in the ad-ministration, Weisberg had nothing more to go on than Marvin Pan-coast's confession. As the days went by, Weisberg became the favorite of the court watchers.

Presiding over the court was forty-two-year-old Judge David Horo-witz. Fair and unbiased, he never allowed his courtroom to turn into a circus. When evidence of the existence of sex tapes was not forth-coming, he disallowed the defense claim that Vicki Morgan was using the tapes for purposes of blackmail, and sustained all objections of the prosecution when the defense asked hearsay questions about the tapes.

One of the most fascinating aspects of the case was the colossal ineptitude of the police work. No fingerprints were taken at the scene of the crime. An officer lamely explained that since Marvin Pancoast had confessed, the police didn't see any point in taking prints. Nor did they seal the house afterward; therefore, anyone possessing a key had access to it in the days following the murder—a strange state of affairs in a case in which missing tapes, both audio and video, played such a large part. The coroner testified that when he arrived at the murder scene at seven o'clock in the morning, he was not able to examine the murder weapon, the baseball bat, for blood, skin, or hair, because the police had sealed it in a plastic bag. It is an almost elementary fact of police work that evidence containing blood, or any body fluid, is never wrapped in plastic, only paper or cloth, because plastic creates a humidity chamber in which bacteria grow and destroy such evidence as blood and tissue. "If this is not an inept police investigation, then it's a deliberate cover-up," said Ted Mathews.

Far more revealing and potentially dangerous than any of Vicki's lurid testimony in the deposition for her palimony suit, in which she recounted in detail the sadomasochistic sexual practices of Alfred Bloomingdale, were her accounts of the personal conversations she had had with Bloomingdale. "Alfred continuously confided in me by telling me his private opinions about influential and important people with whom he was intimately involved, such as Ronald and Nancy Reagan, and he would relate specific instances involving them; and he told me about his involvement in secret and delicate matters such as campaign contributions for Mr. Reagan."

In the second week of the trial, Pancoast's lawyers called a writer named Gordon Basichis to the stand. Basichis had been working with Vicki Morgan on *Alfred's Mistress*, her revenge memoir about her affair with Bloomingdale. Basichis had been introduced to her by a film producer for whom Basichis was writing a screenplay, and with whom Vicki Morgan had had an affair during her affair with Alfred Bloomingdale. Basichis is married to a television executive, has an eighteen-month-old son, and had been working with Vicki for eight months preceding her death. He is dark and intense, and on the stand was sweaty and nervous.

The contract drawn up by Morgan's lawyer, Michael Dave, provided that Basichis was to deliver to her the first chapter of the book plus an outline of the remaining chapter by August 1, 1983. If she disapproved of the material, she had no obligation to proceed with Basichis or compensate him.

Almost immediately after meeting, Basichis and Morgan began a love affair. Eight months after the contract between them was signed, despite nearly daily contact, the initial chapter and outline were still not written. There is some argument as to how many hours of microcassette audiotape were recorded. Vicki's mother, Connie Laney, and Marvin Pancoast, who moved in with Vicki three weeks before her death, recalled that there were many hours of recorded conversations. The tapes were kept in a safe-deposit box to which both Vicki and Basichis had keys. After Vicki's death, when the tapes were ordered to be turned over to the estate, only six hours of tape were forthcoming. What happened to the other tapes, if there were others, has never come to light. Basichis says the six hours of tape he submitted were all that were recorded. What exactly he and Vicki did during the eight months of their collaboration remains a mystery.

One week before her death Vicki Morgan broke off her romantic relationship with Basichis and fired him as her collaborator. A fight occurred, and there were two versions of it. Basichis admitted to having pushed Morgan around. Vicki's mother said Vicki told her that Basichis had hit her and punched her in the face. There were black-and-blue marks on her face and body. In Marvin Pancoast's confession, he said about Basichis, whom he referred to as the writer, "He beat the shit out of her."

The police did not question Basichis until three months after the murder—and then only after prompted by a reporter—even though he was Vicki's known lover, her known collaborator, and thereby privy to the secrets of her life; even though it was a documented fact that she had fired him and that he had fought with her and struck her.

Basichis denied on the stand that he was responsible for the black-and-blue marks on Morgan's face and body. He denied feeding her Valium habit or buying her cocaine. He said that he and Vicki had made up on the night before her death and that he had spent the night with her. He said that on the following night, the night of the murder, he was home with his wife watching the All-Star Game on television, which his wife later corroborated on the stand.

"How often did you go to bed with her?" Barens asked him.

"I didn't keep count."

When a break was called, Basichis stood up and walked across the courtroom to where I was sitting. "Hello," he said, and called me by my first name. I was stunned. Later he told me he had submitted a manuscript of one of his early books to me in 1976, when I was a film producer.

"They're trying to pin this murder on me," Basichis said, talking rapidly into my ear. He kept jagging his finger into his shirt collar. "I didn't kill her. I swear to you. I was deeply in love with her. I would never harm her."

"Who do you think killed her?" I asked him.

"Marvin," he answered, and then added, "with help."

"Help from whom?"

He shrugged and did not reply. His dislike of Arthur Barens and Ted Mathews was matched only by their dislike of him. Barens and Mathews said on television and to the press that Basichis was a definite suspect, a drug taker, and a drug supplier to Vicki, and that he might possibly have made a deal with "someone" to turn over the missing audiotapes based on his eight months of conversations with Vicki. Basichis said that Barens's relationship with Vicki Morgan had involved more than just three office meetings.

That night Basichis called me at my hotel and asked if he could see me. He said he had things to tell me and offered to let me read *Alfred's Mistress*. I asked if we could talk on the telephone, and he said that the telephone might be tapped. He arrived more than an hour late, after his wife had called to say that he had lost his credit cards and money but that he would be there.

Basichis rarely completes a sentence. He begins, thinks of something else, switches to it. He talked nonstop for two hours. His nervous presence was compelling, a frightened man masquerading under a tough bluff, but when the tape of our meeting was transcribed, by a woman in Santa Monica who was so shocked by the profanity she left black spaces, page after page read like incoherent ramblings. He claimed there were no videotapes of Vicki Morgan cavorting with government officials. He said he would have known if there had been, because he and Vicki had spent so much time together. He said, "She had a sense of vanity that went so deep she wasn't going to spread herself out among a whole bunch of those guys in their white fleur-de-lis boxer shorts."

When he left my hotel room after midnight, I read *Alfred's Mistress*. It had, he told me, been turned down by his publisher because another writer, one of seven doing a book on the same subject, had told the publisher that Basichis was the murderer.

Basichis hadn't completed even the first chapter of *Alfred's Mistress* during the eight months of his collaboration with Vicki Morgan. He wrote the book sometime after her death in July 1983 and before Marvin Pancoast's trial for her murder in June 1984. When he showed it to me in June, it had already been rejected by ten publishers.

It is a curious book, told completely in the third person, as if the eight months of conversation, taping, and lovemaking between the author and the deceased has not taken place. Some of it is culled from the deposition that Vicki filed at the time of her palimony suit. Her meeting with Bloomingdale, their first assignation, his sado-masochistic tendencies, and the financial terms of their long affair were all things I had read about before. Some of the other facts in the book are inaccurate: a depiction of Mrs. Bloomingdale as foul-mouthed is totally off the mark. Most important, none of the big administration names that had long been whispered as having connections with Vicki are mentioned; there is nothing in the book that would embarrass the administration.

It is Vicki Morgan's life story. It tells of her three marriages (her first ex-husband went to jail for dealing drugs in order to make enough money to win her back from Bloomingdale). It tells of her love affairs with the convicted financier Bernie Cornfeld, the King of Morocco, and a Saudi Arabian princess, as well as of a romance with Cary Grant.

Most compelling is the picture of Bloomingdale, caught in the grip of living a double life, too involved with each to let go of the other. A scene where Bloomingdale tells Vicki that he has cancer as he is leaving for England with his wife to attend the festivities connected with the royal wedding of Prince Charles and Lady Diana, and a scene where Bloomingdale is carried to Vicki's house by a male nurse for their final lunch, for which Vicki spent $1,000 on flowers and appointments for what she called her "Betsy table," made crystal clear the complicated nature of their relationship.

"What about all this stuff she was supposed to have known concerning campaign contributions and personal things about people in the administration?" I asked Basichis.

He said her information was fragmented—pieces of a story, but not the whole story. Most of what she knew, he said, was more embarrassing than dangerous, gossip about the private and family lives of top figures.

The book tells her history, but it doesn't explain her. What did she have, this girl? What was her allure? Why did a king fly her to Rabat? Why did the princess charter a yacht to sail her to Honolulu? Why did a man who had everything risk it all on her? I once saw her at the Christmas party of a film-company business manager. "That's Alfred Bloomingdale's girlfriend," the daughter of one of Alfred Bloomingdale's friends told me. What I remember most about her were her eyes, taking in everything from the sidelines, meeting the looks of people who looked at her. Friendly-aloof. And pretty. But Hollywood parties are full of pretty girls who are somebody's girlfriend.

The moot point of the trial remained the celebrated sex tapes. There was not a person in the courtroom who had not heard that a certain member of the administration was supposed to be shown on them dallying with Vicki, with pink carnations in his pubic hair. But where were they? Do they exist? Did they ever exist? The main source of information about them was Marvin Pancoast, known to be pornography-mad. Could they have been a figment of his imagination? Vicki's close friend of fourteen years, Sally Talbert, said under oath that she had never heard Vicki mention the tapes. Even Gordon Basichis, everyone's enemy in this story, said Vicki never mentioned the tapes to him. The first public mention of the tapes was by Robert Steinberg, who was, for twenty-four hours, Marvin Pancoast's lawyer. Two days later, when asked for proof that the videotapes existed, Steinberg said that he had seen them, but that they had been stolen from his office. Later Steinberg was indicted for filing a false robbery report. When the defense called him to the stand during the Pancoast

trial, he took the Fifth Amendment nine times because the misdemeanor charges for the robbery report were still pending.

A secretary from William Morris who knew Pancoast when he
worked there said she had heard about the tapes a year and a half before Vicki died. This woman, who wished to remain anonymous, believes they did exist. She also believes that Pancoast definitely struck
the fatal blows. "Marvin's craving in life was to be famous. The people
Marvin had been in contact with all the time in the business have what
Marvin has an absolute blood-lust for: they are famous. It goes beyond
rich. I believe he's guilty. I have from the outset. Marvin's motive for
killing Vicki was convoluted but to his mind very logical. She represented one of his closest links to the spotlight because of Bloomingdale. This made her a star to Marvin. When she no longer had the
backing that made her a star, she began to lose value to him. That was
reason enough for him to kill her, that she wasn't famous anymore.

"The last time I visited Marvin in jail," she said, "he had on his lap
a file folder of all the newspaper front pages that he had been on, and
he was stroking that folder and showing me, 'Look, I'm on the front
pages.' If that folder had been a human being, it would have had the
most incredible orgasm of its life. I thought to myself, I have now seen
obscenity. I didn't go back to see him again. I couldn't."

On July 5, after only four and a half hours of deliberation, the ten-
woman, two-man jury returned a verdict of guilty of murder in the first
degree. They believed the confession on the night of the murder, and
the defense had not proved that the all-important tapes ever existed or
that a conspiracy had taken place. The defense's contention that Gordon Basichis had held Vicki Morgan's Doberman pinscher while an
unknown assailant delivered the fatal blows and then had hypnotized
Pancoast into thinking that he had killed Vicki—this drew muted guf-
faws in the courtroom—apparently held no weight with the jury either.

Arthur Barens reported that Marvin Pancoast was devastated by
the verdict. As he was led from the courtroom by bailiffs, Pancoast,
who had sat through the trial in medicated silence, snapped at a photographer taking his picture, "Fuck off, man. Leave me alone."

From his cell in Los Angeles County Jail, Pancoast told a psychiatrist that he believes that Betsy Bloomingdale and Ronald Reagan are

in a conspiracy against him and that he is being monitored by the F.B.I. and the C.I.A. through radios and television sets.

The same day that Pancoast was convicted, a full-page color picture of Betsy Bloomingdale cutting roses in the garden of her Holmby Hills Palladian villa appeared on the cover of *W.* The article, about her widowhood, was called "Betsy in Bloom." Van Nuys, where the trial took place, on the other side of town, was farther away from her than New York or London or Paris. She is the survivor of this story.

Vicki Morgan was the victim twice over. She was only thirty when she died, and only seventeen when, according to her, the fifty-four-year-old Bloomingdale picked her up in a Los Angeles restaurant by pressing an $8,000 check into her hand. Their liaison lasted twelve years, starting the day Vicki joined Bloomingdale and several other women for a bout of sadomasochistic play and ending with his death, when she said of his wife, who had interred him privately without any announcement to the press, "She buried him like a dog."

Vicki Morgan was a mistress who led a mistress's life. She shopped and spent while a limousine waited with a driver to carry her packages. She worked on her tan, took social drugs, took acting lessons, and went to the same hairdresser that the wives of Bloomingdale's friends went to. She drove expensive cars, but she never had a pink slip of ownership. She lived in expensive houses in fashionable areas, but she never had the deed to a house. She heard secrets that could have made her solvent for life, but, sadly for her, she couldn't remember most of what she heard.

For years I believed that other persons than Marvin Pancoast actually killed Vicki Morgan, while he was merely a bystander who took the rap for money. I always meant to visit him in prison, but he died there of AIDS before I could. I wrote a bestselling novel about this story called An Inconvenient Woman, *which was made into a highly rated television series. The book got me into a lot of trouble with prominent figures in Los Angeles society.*

CANDY'S DYNASTY

It is no secret that the movie rich live rich. What is less well known is that the television rich live even richer, because, except for a few film people like Ray Stark, Steven Spielberg, and George Lucas, the television rich *are* richer than the movie rich. And more flamboyant. While the movie rich have settled into the relatively conservative habits of "old money," the television rich, long considered second class in the rigid caste system of filmland society, are bringing back to Hollywood a way of life and a standard of living that have not been around since what are nostalgically referred to as "the great days," when big spender William Randolph Hearst built Marion Davies a castle in the sand at Santa Monica.

The name on every lip and in every column these days is Candy Spelling, wife of television supermogul Aaron Spelling, who is reputed to be the most successful, most powerful, and richest independent producer in Hollywood. In a community inured to tales of extravagant lifestyles, Candy Spelling is setting new parameters. Recently the Spellings paid $10,250,000—in cash—for the cream-colored stone mansion Bing Crosby owned when he was married to Dixie Lee. Then, after discussing plans for structural changes with some of the priciest architects on the West Coast, they decided to tear the 43,000-square-foot house down to the ground and start again from scratch. "What she ended up with is a $10,250,000 lot," commented one of the outraged neighbors. The new house will be even bigger and will include, when it is completed in two years, an indoor ice-skating rink, a bowling alley, and a zoo. Before a curtain is hung or a carpet is laid, Aaron Spelling will have spent close to $25 million on it.

Stories about Candy Spelling have reached mythic proportions. They say she wears $4 million worth of jewels to lunch, and that she carries her own jeweler's loupe when she attends auctions at Sotheby's. They say that one Christmas Eve a couple of years ago, studio teamsters drove all night with truckloads of snow in order to cover the lawns of her estate so that the Spelling children could have a white Christmas. That when she walks on the beach at her Malibu house, she has been known to send a nanny ahead to plant rare and beautiful shells in the sand so that her daughter can find them. That when she and her husband are in Las Vegas, where they vacation, in the Presidential Suite of the Desert Inn surrounded by bodyguards, they have slot machines brought up to their rooms. That she once summoned dress designer Carolina Herrera to fly her latest collection and three models from New York to Las Vegas for a private fashion show and then bought the entire collection, including bags and hats. That her five-year-old son wears a monogrammed smoking jacket. That the Lucite invitations to her New Year's Eve party were so heavy they each cost $1.47 in postage to mail locally. And on and on.

The source of this bounty, fifty-nine-year-old Aaron Spelling, grew up in poverty in a Texas ghetto, the son of a Russian immigrant tailor. He wore hand-me-down clothes, and was called Jewbaby by the local bullies. I first knew him in the mid-fifties, when we worked together on "Playhouse 90"; Aaron was a sometime actor and fledgling writer, I was the assistant to the producer. Shy and socially insecure, he seemed a highly unlikely candidate for success, power, and multimillionairedom. In the early sixties, we connected again at a film studio called Four Star, where he was already on his way as a television producer, creating such series as "Zane Grey Theater" and "Burke's Law."

In the 1983-1984 season Aaron Spelling's shows represented a record seven hours of network-television prime time, all on ABC. His company, Aaron Spelling Productions, of which Candy Spelling is secretary and treasurer, produced "Dynasty," "The Love Boat," "Hotel," and "Matt Houston," and under the Spelling-Goldberg banner he produced "Hart to Hart," "Fantasy Island," and "T. J. Hooker." The man has turned out thousands and thousands of hours of film, including more than ninety motion pictures for television. Every hour of every day his series are playing in syndication somewhere. Estimates of Aaron Spelling's income by industry observers exceed $20 million annually.

Candy married Aaron Spelling nearly sixteen years ago. Before that she had worked briefly as a hand model, by some reporters as a sales-girl at Saks, and as an interior decorator. Both of them had been mar-ried before. His first marriage, to actress Carolyn Jones, lasted eleven years. Candy was very young at the time of her first marriage, about which little is known.

My several encounters with Candy over the years have been brief but vivid. On one occasion I was producing a television film about Hollywood climbers for her husband's company, and we were shoot-ing on location in a Sunset Boulevard mansion a few blocks from the Spellings' house. It was late, and we had just one sequence left to shoot, an exterior scene showing extras arriving at a Hollywood party dressed in evening clothes and furs, when we discovered that by mis-take the wardrobe had been returned to the studio. I made an emer-gency call to Candy's house and told her the jam we were in, and she sent her driver over with enough fur coats from her fur vault to dress all the extras.

During the same period I ran into her at a Hollywood party and ad-mired an armload of diamond bracelets she was wearing. "This one's for 'The Rookies,' " she said, ticking them off playfully, "and this one's for 'The Mod Squad,' and this one's for 'Starsky and Hutch.' "

Another time she called to ask me about a beach house that be-longed to a film-star friend of mine. She had heard it was going to be up for sale, and she wanted to get inside and have a look.

"The thing about that house," I said, "is it's not very beachy. It's more like a Beverly Hills house at the beach."

"That's perfect!" said Candy without any hesitation, and I remem-ber thinking to myself at the time, These people are getting rich.

After not being in touch with them for years, I wondered if Candy would see me for an interview. I was informed that it was a very busy period for her. She was preparing for her first trip to Europe, which required extensive planning. Because her husband will not fly, they were going to travel to the East Coast in a private railroad car with a chef, a maid, a nanny for each child, guards, and her majordomo. For the ocean crossing, they had reserved a cluster of suites on the *QE2*. She was also involved in the spring fair at her children's school, and she was organizing a benefit dinner for her favorite charity, the fight against retinitis pigmentosa. Moreover, she runs several businesses in addition to being an officer of her husband's company. But she agreed to be interviewed.

The Spellings live in Holmby Hills, a small enclave of superaffluence north and south of Sunset Boulevard between Beverly Hills and Bel Air which contains some of the most extravagant dwellings in the United States. Their house, like most houses in the area, is protected from the prying eyes of tourists and curiosity seekers by a wall, gates, and electronic surveillance. Across the street from the entrance, an old lady sitting under a black umbrella sells guide maps to the movie stars' houses. Within walking distance are the homes of Burt Reynolds, Barbra Streisand, Gregory Peck, and Rod Stewart.

Outside the gates on a steel pole set into the asphalt is an intercom over which I announced my name and business to a guard inside. A closed-circuit television camera was trained on me; then the wrought-iron gates swung open. The driveway goes uphill to the courtyard. At the top of the hill was a black-and-white Los Angeles police car, which I later learned is a permanent fixture, pulled from one of Spelling's television series to discourage the uninvited. Spelling has given his neighbor, producer Ray Stark, a similar one for his courtyard. Beyond were two white Lincoln limousines, one for Aaron, one for Candy. An armed guard waved me up to the entrance of the mansion. He accompanied me to the front door and unlocked it, and I entered the lavish world of Candy Spelling.

It is a world of big houses, big cars, big jewels, big parties, and Big Plans. It is not merely rich, it is "Dynasty"-rich, and I felt I was stepping into a television set and becoming a character in an episode of that series. Either Blake and Krystle Carrington are based on Aaron and Candy Spelling, or Aaron and Candy Spelling are based on Blake and Krystle Carrington.

Candy's publicist received me, and Candy's secretary, seated behind an antique desk in the library, made polite conversation. The majordomo—the chief steward of a noble house, according to the Random House dictionary—passed busily through the room. The butler stood at attention by the door, appearing not to listen, waiting, one supposed, for orders. (In the course of the afternoon he periodically brought us fresh Tabs in fresh Baccarat glasses to replace Tabs in Baccarat glasses that we had barely touched.) We were all minor players in the episode, setting the scene for the arrival of the star.

"Hello," Candy said, ten minutes later, walking into the room, holding out her hand, moving like a woman who is coming from an important engagement and will soon be leaving to go to another. She is not the sort of rich woman who languishes in luxurious indolence. There are lists in her head of things to be done; a household to oversee, businesses to be run, menus to be planned for the chef of the chartered railroad car, blueprints of the new house to be checked, an art class to be taught at her children's school, a cocktail party at Chasen's for her husband's company.

She is thirty-seven years old, slender, sleek, manicured, exercised, massaged, well dressed, and very glamorous. She was nervous about being interviewed. She said she had been savaged by a national magazine last year and had cried for a week afterward. She laughed when I reminded her of our past encounters. Her speaking voice has the regionless sound of those models who have speaking lines in cosmetics commercials. It is probably a voice in transition. Her conversation is full of film references. For example, she says "lap dissolve" to denote the passage of time in a story she is telling: "Aaron promised his mother that as long as she was living he would never fly in another plane. Lap dissolve. She's no longer living, but he's now built it up in his mind he's going to die the next flight he takes."

Chain-smoking cigarette after cigarette, she told me her back story. She grew up in Beverly Hills affluence. "We lived right next door to Barbara Stanwyck," she said. "There were four in help in the house, and I was allowed to cross the street to play with my girlfriend only in the company of a maid."

As she spoke, she changed, almost imperceptibly, the position of a vase holding a spray of cymbidium blossoms. Telephones and doorbells rang, and she went right on talking as if she had heard nothing, knowing the messages would be taken. When Candy was eight, her father, who was in the furniture business, suffered severe financial reversals, and the family moved to an apartment in the area known as South of Wilshire. She took buses to school for the first time and learned to cook. She looks upon those years as the most important of her life, for they taught her, as she put it, "what the dollar meant, where it had to go, and what you had to do with it." She began to read the *Wall Street Journal* as a child.

She has a computerlike mind for the factors and figures concerning anything that interests her: television, orchids, architecture, furniture, travel. She can tell you the advantages of having the screen in her new projection room rise from the floor rather than lower from the ceiling. She can describe to you the difficulty of installing a Dolby sound system. She can explain precisely why she has had the floor plans and elevations of her new house made up at the scale of a half inch to a foot. She knows that the private railroad cars fueled with propane cannot travel farther east than Chicago, and she knows which cross-country train routes offer the best sightseeing with the fewest number of stops.

On her finger was one of the greatest jewels in the world, a pear-shaped, D-flawless, forty-carat diamond, purchased from the estate of the late Shah of Iran. She can explain, with the expertise of a gemologist, the color graduations of diamonds from D, the highest, through I.

"How do you know all this?" I asked.

"I can just look at a diamond and tell you exactly how many carats it has," she answered.

"But how?"

"I've been told I have a better eye than the late Harry Winston," she said.

She talks constantly about her husband and children. "We don't like to go out a lot, to social parties. We love our house, and we love being home together with our family, and it makes a lot of sense to have everything we love the most around us."

On the piano is a silver-framed color photograph of the two Spelling children, five-year-old Randy and eleven-year-old Tori, an aspiring actress, who has guest-starred in twelve episodes of her father's television series. In the photograph, the children are standing on the winding stairway in the front hall, wearing eighteenth-century French court costumes with powdered wigs, jewels, and shoes with buckles.

"What was the occasion?" I asked.

"Halloween," she replied, adjusting the position of the frame by a fraction. "Nolan designed those costumes."

Nolan is Nolan Miller, her personal couturier and the designer of the clothes worn by Joan Collins and Linda Evans on "Dynasty," as well as the clothes of five other Aaron Spelling series. Candy owns 50 percent of his business, Nolan Miller, Ltd. She also owns, with her partner, Marcia Lehr, a successful boutique in Beverly Hills specializing in party planning, antiques, and gifts, in which she is an active participant and buyer. Gifts for guest stars on all of Aaron's shows come from her boutique. Party favors at her own parties are so plentiful she provides bags that match the tablecloths to carry them home in.

"What exactly is your input in 'Dynasty'?"

"The books," she replied.

"The books?"

"I go over the books."

She knows if money is being wasted, and where. She understands cost and schedules and overtime and double time. Aaron comes home late in the day to spend time with the children. Often she returns to the studio with him at night to watch the dailies and rough cuts of his movies and series. Aaron is said to rely greatly on her opinions, both financial and creative. She has an eye for discovering talented young people. An insomniac, she does most of her work after midnight, when the house is quiet.

She claims to relax by straightening out, in meticulous color sequence, "from white to cream to bone to beige, from lemon to yellow, from pink to red," the blouses and slacks in her mirrored and marbled dressing room. She does the same in her husband's closets, where the socks are strictly separated, the brown in one drawer, the blue in another, the black in a third.

"Will all this furniture go in your new house?" I asked.

"Oh, no. Just the antiques."

"Who will be your decorator?"

"I will," she said.

The new house, country French in style, will make Blake and Krystle Carrington's place on "Dynasty" look like a guest house. It will be 360 feet long, or, as the majordomo explained, "longer than a football field." The house is fulfilling a lifetime dream, which includes the double staircase she has wished for since she first saw *Gone with the Wind*. She knows exactly what she wants; she has already arranged most of the furniture on outsize floor plans, and she is in the process of picking fabrics and colors and papers even though construction is just getting under way. "I'm going to need a thirty-eight-inch table here and an eight-foot sofa there," she said, pointing at the plans. She has sent her architect to France to study, not the great châteaux in the country, but the large new houses "in whatever the Bel Air or Beverly Hills of France is."

Even the Spellings's philanthrophy has elements of a scripted television drama, with a beginning, a middle, and an end. Watching the news with Aaron one night last year, Candy was moved to tears by the story of a black college student named Derrick Gordon, who was suffering from a hereditary heart disease that had already killed an older brother. He needed a heart transplant, and his family still needed to raise $100,000 more for the operation. The Spellings had their accountant issue a check for the entire amount, and their driver delivered it along with $500 worth of steaks to the Gordon family. When Aaron received an N.A.A.C.P. Humanitarian Award three months later, Derrick Gordon was among the honored guests on the dais.

Except for Saturday nights, when the Spellings show films to a small group of intimate friends, Candy's entertaining is almost exclusively business-oriented. She claims she has no social ambition, although the dining table in her new house has been designed to seat twenty-eight. Their appearances in public are mostly at wrap parties celebrating the completion of a film or series, testimonial dinners, charity benefits, industry galas, and the Golden Globe, Emmy, and Oscar awards. For these occasions Candy is ablaze with jewels from her famous collection. She has sets in all the colors.

Following in the tradition of the great film moguls of an earlier time, the Spellings have started a racing stable of thoroughbreds and are regulars at the track. Recently Candy's attention has also turned to art. The pictures in her present house are not top-drawer and will probably not make the move to the new house. Her husband's partner,

Douglas Cramer, a noted collector of contemporary American art, tried to influence her in the direction of his taste, but she is said to have been much more taken with the Impressionist collection of Mrs. William Goetz, the daughter of the legendary Louis B. Mayer and for forty years the leading *grande dame* and hostess of the film industry. "I said to Aaron," reported Candy, "let's cool it on the jewels for a while and get into art." A few days later they bought a Monet, their first major picture.

The Spellings have long settled comfortably into their enormous and beautifully furnished mansion. They entertained Prince Charles there during his last visit to Los Angeles. The house is a regular stop for the tour buses that take out-of-towners to see the movie stars' homes. By now, Aaron and Candy Spelling are considered members of the Old Guard in Hollywood society. Their daughter, Tori, has become a prominent television star, and their son, Randy, also appears on one of his father's series.

IMELDA IN EXILE

Directly under my balcony at the Kahala Hilton hotel, porpoises frolicked in a pool. Beyond them, past the palm trees blowing in the breeze, a Secret Service man was patrolling the beach with a bomb-sniffing dog. Out in the calm Pacific, flanked by two more Secret Service men in bathing attire, Secretary of State George Shultz was enjoying a 6:30 A.M. swim. Two other Secret Service men, in blue blazers and beige slacks, carried walkie-talkies and stared back at the balconies of the hotel.

After a few moments the secretary of state came out of the water, dried himself with a towel, and walked back to the hotel, encircled by his attendants, one of whom let his surveillance of the balconies flag long enough to observe the playful activities of the porpoises in the pool. In Honolulu on a two-night stopover, Mr. Shultz was on his way back to Washington from the summit meeting in Tokyo, via Manila, where he had called on the new president of the Philippines, Corazon Aquino. The previous day a reporter had asked him if he intended, while he was in Honolulu, to call on the former president of the Philippines, Ferdinand Marcos, and his wife, Imelda, who were in temporary residence less than two miles down the beach from the Kahala Hilton. "No!" the secretary of state had snapped.

Later Mr. Shultz went further and publicly rebuked Ferdinand Marcos for using his safe haven in Hawaii as a base from which to foment difficulties for President Aquino's government. "He is causing trouble," said Shultz, and Jaime Cardinal Sin, the archbishop of Manila, echoed the secretary of state's remarks. The cardinal said that Marcos was financing demonstrations against Mrs. Aquino, and in some cases paying people 100 or 150 pesos ($5 or $7.50) to dress up as priests and nuns in order to attract favorable press attention for him abroad. The Marcoses were definitely in Dutch.

For four days I had sat on my balcony over the porpoises, waiting for Imelda Marcos to respond to my request for an interview. Contact with the former first lady of the Philippines had been made for me, not through political or diplomatic connections, but through friends of hers in high society. For as everyone now knows, in addition to being the first lady for twenty-one years and the chatelaine of Malacañang Palace, Imelda Marcos had been a card-carrying member of the jet set, numbering among her friends Lord and Lady Glenconner, the British aristocrats, who are friends of the royal family; the Count and Countess of Romanones, members of the Spanish nobility; Princess Firyal of Jordan; the Agnelli and Niarchos families; and American multimillionaries like David Rockefeller and Malcolm Forbes. In recent years, however, those closest to her had been less socially exalted: Adnan Khashoggi, the Arabian billionaire, for whom she entertained extravagantly in her New York mansion; Cristina Ford, the Italian-born former wife of Henry Ford; George Hamilton, the suave and debonair Hollywood actor, and his mother, Anne; Van Cliburn, the acclaimed pianist; and Franco Rossellini, of the New York and Rome film world.

On my arrival in Honolulu, I had written her a personal note. For four days it had gone unheeded. I had seen Mrs. Marcos once during that time, but from a distance. The previous Sunday, Mother's Day, also happened to be the thirty-second wedding anniversary of the Marcoses, and a real estate broker in Honolulu who had been instrumental in finding a house for them to live in told me that the local pro-Marcos Filipino-American community was planning a celebration in their honor. I arrived at the Blaisdell auditorium at eleven A.M. to ensure getting a seat and stayed until the program ended, at five in the afternoon.

Of the 115,000 Filipinos in Hawaii, approximately 15,000 are pro-Marcos, and most of those are from Ferdinand Marcos's home province of Ilocos Norte. The crowd of cheering Filipinos in the auditorium that day was estimated at between four and five thousand, and the event was long and tedious. Children from the Hawaii Talent

Searchers Club sang Cyndi Lauper and Huey Lewis vocals to instrumental tracks recorded on cassettes. There was a demonstration of ballroom dancing by a gray-haired woman and a younger female partner. Following that was a magic act, and then, to the delight of the audience, a leading pop star called Anthony Castillo, who had arrived from Manila the day before to take part in the festivities, sang a medley of songs.

When Ferdinand and Imelda Marcos arrived, about an hour before the end of the celebration, the crowd waved V-for-victory signs to them and broke into song:

> *We love you, Mr. President,*
> *First Lady, and family.*
> *We thank God for you again,*
> *For what you are and what you'll be.*
> *Our country is more beautiful*
> *Because of you and what you did.*
> *We who are here will be with you.*

Despite all the cheering, the Marcoses appeared subdued. Mrs. Marcos, dressed in the same green dress, black patent-leather shoes, and matching pearl costume jewelry that she had worn for every public appearance since her arrival in Hawaii, blew desultory kisses at the crowd. Then she took the microphone like a nightclub artiste and began to sing. She knew how to work the stage, playing first to one side, then to the other, and even though her famous singing voice was woefully out of tune, she did not seem to care. Her eyes had a distant look. Next the president came forward and joined her in a Philippine love song. Taller than her husband, Mrs. Marcos easily upstaged him. There seemed to be no intimacy between them; they were together only in the sense of being side by side.

Before the speeches became political and the anniversary celebration turned into what sounded like the opening of a campaign to return Marcos to power, the speaker rose and told a long and rambling anecdote about longevity in marriage. He said that once when Henry Ford was asked to what he attributed the success of his long and happy marriage, he replied, "I have never changed models." The speaker added triumphantly that Mr. Marcos had never changed models either. The speaker was, it turned out, talking about the grandfather of the present, thrice-married Henry Ford. One of international society's favorite and most persistent rumors over the years has been about Mrs. Marcos's supposed romantic attachment to a member of the Ford clan, on whom she is said to have showered gifts of jewelry, but obviously the rumor was unknown to both the teller of the Ford anecdote and the audience that delighted in his story. In a country where poverty is endemic, the Marcoses' wealth—their real estate holdings, their jewels and paintings, their extravagant entertaining—has always been an extremely sensitive issue. Yet, for the most part, the people cheering for them that day were the poor of the Philippine community in Honolulu. The comparison of Imelda Marcos to Evita Perón is said to distress Mrs. Marcos, because Evita Perón started her rise as a prostitute, but the fact remains that Imelda Marcos inspires a similar adoration in some of her subjects.

When Mrs. Marcos moved to the microphone to speak, her listlessness evaporated. She spoke in her native language, sprinkled with occasional English words, like *security guards* and *television crews*. After a few moments she was crying, and many in the audience were crying too. She extended her arms above her head and, with tears streaming down her face, said in English, "When I hurt, I do not cry, but I cry when you overwhelm me." As theater, it was a magnificent moment.

Then Mr. Marcos made a speech in the dialect of his province, Ilocos Norte. "As your elected president," he began, and when that brought cheers he reiterated: *"As your elected president . . ."* But he had already been completely overshadowed by his wife.

On my fifth morning in Honolulu I received a call from Mrs. George Ariyoshi, the beautiful Japanese-American wife of the governor of Hawaii. Old friends of the Marcoses', the Ariyoshis had placed friendship before political considerations in going to Hickam Air Force Base in February to greet and place leis around the necks of Imelda and Ferdinand Marcos when they arrived from Guam after being forced to flee the Philippines. The gesture brought criticism down on Mr. Ariyoshi, and if he had not been a lame-duck governor it might have proved disastrous; the people of Hawaii did not want the Marcoses to settle there and did not let up in their demands for them to leave. Although the two couples ceased to see each other publicly, Mrs. Marcos and Mrs. Ariyoshi remained friends and talked every day on the telephone. I had been invited to lunch with Mrs. Ariyoshi the day I arrived, and I was hoping that she had been able to appeal to Mrs. Marcos on my behalf.

Mrs. Ariyoshi informed me that Mrs. Marcos would not see me. She assured me it had nothing to do with me personally; it was just that a policy had been made against interviews. She said that Mrs. Marcos was sorry I had made the trip from New York for nothing. If I called the Marcos house immediately, she said, Mrs. Marcos herself would explain why it was impossible. Mrs. Ariyoshi had done all that she could do.

When I called, Mrs. Marcos came immediately to the telephone. She was strong-voiced and definite. She had not, she reminded me correctly, ever promised me an interview. "The problem," she said, "is that it is premature for me to give interviews at this point in time. With all these cases pending against us all over the world, an interview might prejudice people against me. This is not the right time for me to give my side of the story. There is such an overwhelming force against us. As much as possible we would like to keep our silence for the time being."

"I'm sorry, First Lady," I replied. (I had been told to address her as either First Lady or Ma'am by someone better acquainted with protocol than I.)

"Our life is so disorganized," she added, and the finality in her voice sounded a bit less final.

"At least I can say when I go back that I saw you, First Lady," I said.

"But I don't go out. Where did you see me?" she asked.

"I went to the celebration of your thirty-second wedding anniversary at the Blaisdell auditorium on Sunday."

"You did?"

"Yes."

"Why?"

"I wanted to see you and the president."

"When were you there?"

"I was there for all five hours."

"But we didn't come until the end."

"I had no way of knowing that."

She hesitated for a moment, then asked, "Where are you staying?"

"At the Kahala Hilton."

"It's down the beach from where we are."

"I know."

She hesitated again. "I will meet you," she said. "What time is it?"

"It's twenty minutes past nine."

"At ten o'clock. There must be no pictures."

"Fine."

"No tape recorder."

"Fine."

"No questions. This is not an interview."

"Fine."

"And only," she concluded, "for ten minutes."

She gave me the address: 5577 Kalanianaole Highway. Of course, I already knew where she lived; everyone in Honolulu knew. I had driven by the house every day since I had been there, and once I had parked my car nearby and walked along the beach to the Marcoses' place. I was able to look through the shrubbery and stare at the house for fully five minutes before two guards, sitting on chairs and chatting together, noticed me. The security provided by the state had been taken away from the Marcoses three and a half weeks after they arrived in Hawaii; these guards were part of a volunteer security force made up of pro-Marcos members of the Filipino colony in Honolulu. They had walkie-talkies but no guns that I could see; however, when I realized that they had spotted me, I quickly turned and walked away.

A Hawaiian real estate agent claimed to me that the Marcoses owned two homes in the fashionable Makiki Heights section of Honolulu, one worth $1.5 million and the other worth $2 million. The houses are said to be in the names of two well-to-do Filipinos. The Marcoses cannot admit to owning the houses, for fear the present Philippine government will put a claim on them. Because of the Marcoses' political unpopularity, it had been hard to find anybody anywhere who would rent to them. For example, an approach had been made through an emissary for the Marcoses to rent one of the great houses on the fashionable Caribbean island of Mustique, but because Mustique is a favorite vacation retreat for members of the British royal family, it was thought that the Marcos presence might prove embarrassing. However, according to a prominent resident of the island, if the United States were to request that they be given haven, or if the Marcoses were to make a proper gesture, such as building a $65 million airstrip on nearby Saint Vincent, new consideration for their future welfare in Mustique might be taken into account.

They pay $8,000 a month for the house they finally did find, and since they have a severe cash-flow problem, brokers are on the lookout for a house at half that rent in case the Marcoses are forced to remain in Honolulu. Each Sunday after mass, which is said privately for them in the house, members of the pro-Marcos Filipino community in Honolulu arrive with food, flowers, and money for the couple and their entourage.

In the beginning of their stay, demonstrators collected in front of the house with signs saying, MARCOS, MURDERER, GO HOME or HONK IF YOU WANT THE MARCOSES TO LEAVE. To the distress of the neighbors, the honking went on all day and all night. Since the bombing attack on Libya and the nuclear fallout at Chernobyl, however, the press has turned its attention away from them, and the demonstrations have stopped, but the former first family remain in a sense incarcerated, behind the locked gates.

In a sane real estate market, the Marcos house would be described as an $80,000 or $90,000 single-family dwelling on valuable beachfront property. There are neighbors close by on both sides, with no walls or fences between the houses. Shrubbery and a high wooden fence with two gates that are kept locked at all times protect the house from the highway. I waved and yelled through the fence, and the gate was finally opened when I made it clear that Mrs. Marcos was expecting me. Five or six old cars littered the short driveway. Parking was difficult, and the guards were unhelpful. The entrance to the single-story, shingle-roofed, ranch-style house was visually marred by an electric blue tarpaulin strung up haphazardly between two trees to protect the guards from the sun. Beneath it stood a wooden table and a couple of chairs. On the table were a plate of

ripening mangoes and several empty Pepsi-Cola cans. One had a
sense of "there goes the neighborhood" about the place.

Entering the small front hallway, a visitor is immediately confronted
with the presidential seal, which fills an entire wall. Next to it on a pole
is the flag of the Philippines. The house consists of a living room, a
dining room, a kitchen, three bedrooms, a maid's room, three bathrooms, and a lanai, a sort of porch furnished like a living room which
is a feature of most Hawaiian houses. Next to the house is a separate
one-room guest house. There are, I learned, more than forty people
living here. Most of the original furniture has been removed and replaced by rented furniture. A plain, wooden table on the terrace was
covered with a white plastic tablecloth and surrounded by card-table
chairs with MGN RENTAL stenciled on the back. In the living room
were several television sets, a VCR, and both audio and video recording equipment. (A Honolulu rumor has it that the Marcoses ruined
their friendship with President and Mrs. Reagan by videotaping a private conversation they had with them and later giving the tape to the
television stations.) An upright piano and a synthesizer were pushed
against the wall of the lanai. On practically every table surface, there
were mismatched bouquets of tropical flowers, many wrapped in alu-
minum foil or tied with homemade bows, unwatered, dying or dead.
There were flies everywhere. All the books on the tables, with the single exception of David Stockman's *The Triumph of Politics,* were by
Ferdinand Marcos, including *The Ideology of the Philippines.*

About a dozen men in Hawaiian shirts were seated about the room.
In a gray suit, shirt, and tie, I felt overcitified. President Marcos, we
were told, had a toothache and was at the dentist, but the first lady
would be with us presently. For the first time it occurred to me that all
the people there had been summoned, as I had, to see her. I made conversation with a Filipino journalist from New York who had worked in
the consulate when Marcos was in power, and with Anthony Castillo,
the pop singer from Manila, who told me that one of the first things
Corazon Aquino had done was abolish all the cultural programs
started by Imelda Marcos. All the artists in the country, he said, stood
behind the Marcoses.

And then the first lady entered the room, the strong scent of heady
perfume preceding her. She moves in an extraordinarily graceful man-

ner; even in those simple rooms she was like a queen in a palace. All of
those seated jumped to their feet the moment her presence was felt. As
if a party line of "stay poor and lie low" were in force to counteract the
stories of excess that had dominated the media for months, Mrs. Marcos was again dressed as she had been dressed on every public appearance since she arrived in Hawaii: the green dress, black patent leather
shoes, and pearl earrings and ring which were obviously costume jewelry. Her black hair was majestically coiffed.

She gave instructions to a servant to offer coffee to everyone. She
greeted a university professor and discussed briefly a paper he was
preparing. She exchanged affectionate words with a group of Filipinos
who had come from California and New York to participate in the
wedding-anniversary celebration. People addressed her as either First
Lady or Ma'am. She pointed out to another visitor a huge color
photograph in an ornate gilt frame of the president and her with their
children and grandchildren which had been an anniversary gift. I
understood before she came to greet me that I was part of a morning
levee, one of a group being offered an audience and a few words of
greeting. She offered her hand. Her crimson fingernails had been carefully manicured with white moons and white tips. She is, at fifty-seven,
still a beautiful woman. We exchanged a few unmemorable words.
When I conveyed greetings from the people who had brought me into
contact with her, she indicated that I should take a seat on the lanai.
Then, on instructions from her that I was not aware of, the room
cleared and we were alone.

Imelda Marcos had been described to me by a friend who knew her
well as a woman who understood luxury better than anyone in the
world. Flies buzzed around us in great profusion, but she seemed not
to notice them. She never waved them away. I had the feeling that she
had simply ceased to pay any attention to the surroundings in which
she was living. There is a sense of tremendous sadness about her, but if
she is at times despondent, she manages to shake herself into positive
pursuits. Was this the same woman who had boogied the nights away
in the various private discotheques of her various private residences
with her jet-set friends, wearing a king's ransom in jewels on her wrists,
fingers, neck, and bosom?

Stories of Imelda Marcos's extravagance abound. "Please, for

God's sake, don't use my name," several of her former friends said to me. People in society are notoriously loath to have their names quoted in stories about events in which they have participated, although they don't mind filling you in on the details. Former houseguests at Malacañang Palace tell how the streets of Manila were cleared of people when Imelda took them about the city, and how the guest bathrooms in the palace were so well equipped down to the smallest luxury items that ladies even found packages of false eyelashes in their medicine cabinets. They tell how Imelda abolished mechanized street cleaning in Manila and dressed the homeless of the city in yellow-and-red uniforms and provided them with brooms and the title Metro Aide—instead of street cleaner—so that the streets would be immaculate around the clock.

On a balmy evening a little over a year ago, Malcolm Forbes gave a dinner cruise around Manhattan aboard his yacht, the *Highlander,* in honor of Mrs. Marcos. While the party was still in progress, a lady-in-waiting went around the ship and issued impromptu invitations to a select number of Mr. Forbes's guests to continue the party back at the first lady's New York town house on East Sixty-sixth Street. On arriving there, guests were taken up to the sixth-floor discotheque, where an enormous supper had been laid. The amount of food on display was said to be embarrassing—ten entrées to choose from, including lobster and steak. Since they had all just eaten Malcolm Forbes's sumptuous buffet, they had to pass up Mrs. Marcos's food, choosing instead to dance to the live orchestra that awaited them. As the festivities came to an end and guests started leaving, Mrs. Marcos proved again that there were inner circles within inner circles by asking a few people to stay behind so that she could show them the private floor of her mansion, where her bedroom and sitting room were. Two large, leather caskets, each about the size of half a desk, were brought out by maids. Each contained seven or eight drawers filled with jewelry, which were emptied onto the floor so that the remaining guests could try them on. That was said to be her favorite late-night entertainment, to forestall going to bed. A Madison Avenue jeweler who specializes in estate jewelry told me that Mrs. Marcos had a passion for canary diamonds until last year, when the color yellow became associated with the ascendancy of Corazon Aquino. The town house was furnished out of a Park Avenue triplex maisonette that had belonged to the late philanthropists Mr. and Mrs. Leslie R. Samuels. Mrs. Marcos had tried to buy the triplex for $9 million, but she was turned down by the co-op board of that building because her presence would have posed too great a security risk. Instead she bought the entire contents of the enormous apartment so that she could do up the Sixty-sixth Street town house in just a few days in order to be ready for a party she was giving for Adnan Khashoggi.

Although she was reverential about royalty, she had been known to upstage the crowned heads she revered. She once arrived at a party for the shy and retiring Queen of Thailand, for example, with her own television crew to film her being received by the queen. On another occasion, at a small private party at Claridge's in London attended by the former King Constantine of Greece, Mrs. Marcos arrived to the cheers of London's Filipino community, who mysteriously material- ized outside the hotel right on cue.

"The last two and a half months," Mrs. Marcos said, looking around the plain rooms filled with rented furniture, "have been so enriching. This is a good period for enlightenment. I have no bitterness in my heart."

Disinclined to be questioned, she was more than inclined to talk, and for the three and a half hours that the promised ten minutes eventually stretched into, she talked nonstop on a variety of topics, as if she had been starved for conversation. If I sometimes asked things that she did not wish to comment on, she kept talking as if she had not heard me. Thirty minutes into our visit, I asked if she minded if I wrote down something she had said so that I would be able to record her words accurately. She didn't respond yes or no, but she didn't ask me to stop writing either, and from that moment on her whole manner and delivery changed. I felt I was watching a well-rehearsed performance as she expounded at great length on the subject of love, couched in a series of mystical, Rajneesh-sounding philosophical phrases.

"Beauty is love made real," she said. "Beauty, love, and God are happiness and peace. Love has only one opposite. The opposite of love is not hate. The opposite of love is selfishness. A human being has three levels: his body, his mind, and his spirit. In the spiritual world, you find peace, and none of this matters." She gestured expansively with her hands and arms to indicate her surroundings. "I am completely devoid of basic human rights, but I am blessed. Everything we have here comes from people. All our valuables were impounded. We do not have a single dollar. What can you pick up in an hour's time when you are told to pack up and leave? Your whole lifetime is exposed to the world.

"Peace is a transcendent state. I was a soldier for beauty and love. I was completely selfless. They say about me that I was extravagant, but I gave. Your magazines and papers say that I bought art. It is true. I bought art, but I bought art to fill our museums so that people could enjoy beauty.

"I was born in a family that gave much of themselves in love. There were eleven children. I married a president. I was the first lady for twenty-one years. Very few have been as privileged as I have. If you are successful and have everything, destiny has a way of imposing money, power, and privilege on you.

"Across the sea is my country, and sometimes when I sit here, I think that I can see it. This house is very modest, but your real home is the home within. I am so glad that I have one good dress and one good pair of shoes. Now I don't have all that hassle about clothes and what to wear."

Long stretches of this material I had seen her deliver on tapes left behind in the Sixty-sixth Street house in New York. The irony was that on the tapes she had been expounding her philosophy in a champagne toast to the munitions entrepreneur Adnan Khashoggi.

Her face is unlined and looked to me unlifted. "People say I have spent a fortune on plastic surgery," she said, understanding my stare, "but I have not. The only time I thought of having it done was to cover this scar from the assassination attempt on my life." She held up her arm and showed me the ugly scar from a knife wound inflicted on her in 1972. "My husband said to me at the time, 'Don't have it covered. Wear it as your badge of courage.' Once Queen Elizabeth said to me, 'Imelda, how did you live through it?' "

Mrs. Marcos looked past me but continued talking. I assumed that I had lost her attention and that it was time to leave. She was, in fact, looking at her daughter Irene, who had come out onto the lanai and indicated by gesture that there was a telephone call for her. "This is my beautiful daughter," she said, her face filled with love as she looked at her. They exchanged a few words in Pilipino. "I'm so sorry," she said. "I must take this call. It's Margot Fonteyn." Dame Margot Fonteyn had helped Mrs. Marcos found the ballet company of Manila. For that, Mrs. Marcos had given her an award with a pension attached to it. She gave a similar award and pension to Van Cliburn.

Several times she evinced a mildly gallows-type humor. Speaking of the *tsunami*, a tidal wave from the Aleutian Islands that had threatened to devastate Honolulu a few days earlier, she told how a helicopter had hovered over the house while a man inside shouted orders on a bullhorn to them: "Pack your clothes and get out!" "But we just did that in Manila," she said she had told her family, and she laughed as she recalled the story.

Trapped in a Catch-22 situation, the Marcoses were broke. Their tangible assets, including the money and jewelry they entered Hawaii with, had been frozen by the U.S. government. Talking about the generous Filipinos in Honolulu who bring them food and clothing, she said, "They even bring me shoes." In the manner of an expert storyteller, she let a few seconds pass and then added, "Who knows, soon I may have three thousand pairs."

Again Mrs. Marcos looked beyond me to someone entering. "Oh, here comes the president," she said. Out onto the lanai walked Ferdinand Marcos, surrounded by aides. He no longer looked the way he had during his last days in office or when he got off the plane at Hickam Air Force Base outside Honolulu, as if he were going to die later in the day. His color was healthy; his step was sure. He was wearing a three-piece suit of beige gabardine with a white shirt, cuff links, and tie, but he was still a far cry from the dynamic world leader who had held total control over 50 million people for twenty-one years. Mrs. Marcos rose and walked toward him. When she introduced me to him I sensed he was displeased to find a journalist in his house with notebook in hand. Later, thinking back, it occurred to me that if I had stayed for only the ten minutes that the visit was supposed to be, I would have been long gone before the president returned from the dentist.

"How is your tooth, Ferdinand?" asked the first lady, like any wife concerned with her husband's welfare and, at the same time, distracting him.

"You know, Imelda," he replied, speaking English in a high-pitched, singsong fashion and pointing to a tooth in his open mouth, "it wasn't my tooth after all. There was a fish bone in my tooth. The dentist took out the fish bone, but he didn't take out the tooth." The president was delighted with his story, and all his aides laughed appreciatively. Mrs. Marcos joined in. They actually seemed for a moment like a Filipino Ma and Pa Kettle. Then the president excused himself, saying he had to return to work with his lawyers.

After he left, she spoke proudly of him. Sometimes she called him Marcos, sometimes "the president," sometimes just "my husband." "My husband wrote two or three dozen books," she said, "including *The Ideology of the Philippines*—the only world leader to write an ideology of his country. Your media," she said, in the scoffing tone she used every time she mentioned the U.S. press and television coverage of their downfall, "said that Marcos's medals from World War II were fake. But his medals were awarded to him by General Douglas MacArthur. Is General Douglas MacArthur a fake too? Your media says that my husband had no money when he became president, that he became rich in office by stealing from the Treasury. That is completely untrue. My husband was a flourishing lawyer in Manila for years before he became the president." She walked out of the lanai into the living room, disappeared down a short hallway, and returned almost immediately. "Let me show you the only thing I kept," she said, placing a large diamond ring in my hand. "This is my engagement ring from thirty-two years ago, eleven years before he became the president. You can see from this ring that my husband wasn't exactly poor then." She told me that the jewelry firm of Harry Winston had appraised the ring several years ago at $300,000.

After I handed the diamond ring back to her, she again left the lanai. This time she returned with another thing she had obviously kept, one of the world's most famous diamonds, called the Star of the South, which she said the president had given her for their twenty-fifth wedding anniversary. She said it was listed in the Harry Winston book, and it is. The kite-shaped, 14.37-carat, D-color diamond has belonged to the late Evalyn Walsh McLean, the owner of the ill-fated Hope diamond, as well as to the Duchess of Windsor's great friend Mrs. George F. Baker. The Winston book says that the jeweler sold it again in 1981— two years after the Marcos's twenty-fifth wedding anniversary.

It had been widely reported that the gangs of international social figures who had danced in her discotheques and been recipients of her bounty had, for business or social reasons, deserted her in her decline and disgrace. A host of one of the major, upcoming, international society balls said, "We were going to invite Imelda, but, you know, it's less easy now." Another onetime friend said, "I'd like to call her, but it's bad for business."

"Have you been disappointed by your friends?" I asked. She looked at me but did not answer. "Have you heard from them?"

She replied slowly, choosing her words. "Those who had our telephone number in Hawaii, yes. Those who had the time, yes. But this is when you find out who are your real friends, and this is when you cut out the fakes." Again she thought for a time and then added, "I have no bitterness in my heart."

"Do you suffer when you read what is said about you in the press?"

"I don't read anymore what they say about me. I only read straight news. I am not a masochist. I am a very positive human being. I have so much energy that I sleep only two hours a night. In the end we will be judged by history, not what they write about us now.

"I want to show you something," she said. She called inside to have a television-and-VCR set rolled out onto the lanai. Anthony Castillo, the pop singer, operated the machine for her. She wanted me to watch a tape that had arrived a few days before from the Philippines, showing pro-Marcos demonstrations in Manila, which, she said, had become daily occurrences in the city even though the Aquino government would not grant permits for such demonstrations. She obviously knew every frame of the hour-long tape and, snapping her fingers, gave frequent, excited instructions to Castillo. It was suddenly easy to see her as a woman used to giving orders and used to having them obeyed.

"Go forward. More. More! Stop here. Listen to what these people

are singing: 'You can imprison us, but you cannot imprison our spirits.' That's their song. There are a million people in that crowd. Go
forward. More. Go to the demonstration for Mrs. Aquino. Stop! Look
at *her* crowds. The people are just not there for her. Mrs. Aquino is
an out-and-out Communist. America doesn't want to believe this, but
it is true. The minister of labor is a Communist. Go forward. To
the nuns and the priests. Look at them. 'Marcos,' they are yelling.
Nuns. Look here, Mr. Dunne, do you see that woman? She is a famous film star. All those people there are artists and writers. All the
creative people are for Marcos. Go forward. Watch here. See that
child on the shoulders of his mother? The Communist Mrs. Aquino's
soldiers are going to shoot that child. Watch. Listen to what they're
saying about Cardinal Sin. They say, 'Cardinal Sin is the officer in
charge of hell!' "

When the tape ended, we sat for a few moments in silence. "Would
you like to see my house?" she asked. In the kitchen a half-dozen
women were preparing lunch, setting out big plates of mismatched
food, like a potluck dinner. "The people here bring us our food," she
said, exchanging greetings with the women. "Two people sleep on the
floor of this room," she said, opening the door of a tiny laundry room
with a washer and dryer. She then opened the door of the maid's room.
Lined up on the floor were canvas cots, and there were women asleep
on several of them. She walked in and stood in the small space between two of the cots. "Sixteen women sleep in here," she said. "In
shifts. The nurses and the women in the kitchen and the others." The
sleeping women slept through her talking.

We next walked through the garage. On a shelf were a pile of unopened legal-looking envelopes. "Look," she said, pointing to them
and then holding them up for ridicule. "Do you know what these are?
They're subpoenas. We're being sued by people all over the world.
Even my daughter is being sued. Even my baby grandchild! Someone
thinks valuables and Philippine currency were smuggled out in the
baby's clothes." She shook her head at the lunacy of it. I followed her
as she walked along a cement walkway between the garage and the
one-room guest house next to it. "Forty-two men sleep in this room,"
she said, indicating it with a toss of her head.

"There were forty-two, Ma'am," said the chief of the guards. "There are only fifteen here now."

Inside were rows of cots with clothes piled on the floor beside each one. Some men were eating, some were sitting on their cots, some were sleeping. It was hot, and the room smelled. It looked like an enlisted men's barracks badly in need of inspection. The men stared out as we stared in.

Mrs. Marcos moved on across the lawn, stopping to look for a moment at a neighbor next door. No greeting passed between them. We went in the side entrance of the house and were in the hallway to the three main bedrooms. One bedroom was his. One was hers. Six people slept in the third bedroom, including the Marcoses' eight-year-old adopted daughter, Aimee, the grandchild of Mrs. Marcos's late brother and sister-in-law. A vibrant personality in the beleaguered household, Aimee had the previous Sunday patiently fanned Ferdinand Marcos in the hot auditorium during the anniversary proceedings. Their daughter Irene and her husband and children have their own house elsewhere. When I asked where her daughter Imee, a former member of Parliament, and her son, Ferdinand junior, the former governor of the province of Ilocos Norte, who is known as Bongbong, were, she did not answer. I had heard rumors that they were in Mexico seeking a haven for the family. The hallway was full of suitcases, piled high one on top of the other, cheap blue plastic cases next to expensive Louis Vuitton cases—the old kind of Louis Vuitton cases, before they were mass-marketed. On one bag was a tag saying "Mink Coat."

"We won the election by a million and a half votes," she said, becoming impassioned again, "but the world media makes Mrs. Aquino look like Joan of Arc." Her loathing of Corazon Aquino was evident in every word. "Even the people in her own province voted for my husband. She was the underdog because of Karma. She has abolished the constitution. What she is is a dictator. They are beginning to discover just how far to the left she is."

She found a book about herself that she had been searching for. Page after page of it was filled with her cultural and political accomplishments. "I have been in more corridors of power than any woman in history," she said. "I have been received by every head of state, including two Russian heads of state. Only five months ago I was received by Gorbachev. I went to Tripoli and personally made a treaty with Qaddafi, the only treaty that he has ever honored."

She turned the pages of the book. "I had this building built in a hundred days," she said. "Our Cultural Center, which I commissioned, was built before the Kennedy Center and the Sydney Opera House. Reagan, when he was still the governor of California, came over to dedicate the center. I founded the University of Life. President Giscard d'Estaing came himself to see my University of Life so that he could build one in France. Today the literacy rate of the Philippines is 90 percent, and the literacy rate of the city of Manila is 100 percent!" A further litany of her accomplishments followed: "I planted . . . I founded . . . I built . . . I commissioned . . . I opened . . . I had composed . . . I began . . ."

She paused dramatically. "Do you read about any of that in your papers? No. Your magazines showed a picture of me, saying, 'Mrs. Marcos was blazing in diamonds and rubies.' " Her voice was filled with scorn. "What they don't understand was that the necklace was false. They are pop-in beads. I'll show you. I've got them here. Most of the jewelry I wear is imitation, made by the artisans and craftsmen of my country." I looked at her incredulously. Just then a maid passed through the front hall, where we were standing, and Mrs. Marcos spoke to her in Pilipino. When the maid returned, she was carrying six or seven necklaces, each in a stiff plastic case with snaps. "Look at these," said Mrs. Marcos. She handed me the cases of necklaces, and I put them on the seat of a chair and knelt down to look at them. I do not know if they were imitation or not. Certainly they were beautiful, and the workmanship was extraordinary. On one necklace, canary diamonds alternated with pink diamonds. She said that the settings had been dipped in gold so that they would not turn her neck black.

"I thought you weren't able to keep any of your jewelry," I said.

Mrs. Marcos replied that these necklaces were left behind in Malacañang Palace when they fled, and that Mrs. Aquino had no interest in them because they were imitation. Later they were stolen from the palace. A friend of hers in Manila recognized them, bought them for 20,000 pesos, or $1,000, and sent them to her in Honolulu.

At that moment, from behind a small louver window looking out from the hall onto the front porch, came the words, "I'm listening, Imelda," loud and clear. The window opened vertically, and Ferdinand Marcos, displeased, was framed in it. In an instant, Mrs. Marcos whipped off a shawl from her shoulders and threw it over the cases of necklaces, covering them. "My husband doesn't like me to show the jewelry," she whispered to me. There was urgency in her voice. The president came out the door, and I felt ridiculous as I stood up in front of the chair to block his view. In another instant Mrs. Marcos was at his side. She took his hand affectionately. "Do you know, Ferdinand," she said, "Mr. Dunne has written a best-selling novel that is going to be made into a film in Hollywood."

"Oh?" he said, smiling. "In Hollywood!"

In a wonderfully complex moment of stunning social pyrotechnics, Mrs. Marcos had diverted her husband's attention and also acknowledged for the first time that she knew things about me. We chatted pleasantly, and then the president excused himself, saying he had to get back to work on one of the many lawsuits pending against them.

"How much is this one for, Ferdinand?" she asked.

"Oh, twenty-four billion," he joked, and they both laughed.

It was time to leave. We shook hands good-bye. "For four hundred years we were a subject people," she said. "When Marcos became president, we had been independent for only twenty years. We were a mixture of races. We had to identify who we were. We helped our people to understand what it meant to be Filipino."

Imelda got mad at me after I wrote this piece, furious, in fact. She cut me dead one night at Mortimer's, the famed watering hole on the Upper East Side of New York, during the time she was being taken care of by the billionairess, Doris Duke. A couple of years ago, I received a call at my house in Connecticut from the actor George Hamilton, who was a great friend of Imelda's. He said Imelda was anxious to do her autobiography and she was interested in having me write it. No way. But it's interesting the way people change. A lot of them who were upset with me after I wrote about them in these articles now have me to dinner. Actually, of all the people I ever interviewed, Imelda was the most fascinating—so utterly charming, so manipulative, the drama queen of all drama queens. These past years back in her native land have been tough on her. She's been brought to her knees by life, but she keeps getting up and soldiering on. You have to admire that.

BEVERLY HILLS COUP

"It's *King Lear*, isn't it?" said the person on the telephone discussing the drama of the Silberstein sisters with me.

"King Lear?" I asked.

"You know. Goneril and Regan, that sort of thing, with the father manipulating it all."

"I see."

In truth, I had not thought until then of Goneril and Regan, but I had thought of another sister act, closer to Beverly Hills, where the Silberstein drama was unfolding: the Mayer sisters, octogenarian Edith Goetz and septuagenarian Irene Selznick, whose father, Louis B. Mayer, the legendary movie mogul, by favoring one in his will and ignoring the other, contributed to their well-known dislike of each other, a dislike refueled recently in Mrs. Selznick's memoir, *A Private View*.

In the case of the Silberstein sisters, Muriel Slatkin and Seema Boesky, their father, Ben L. Silberstein, a Detroit real estate magnate and hotel tycoon, left them equal shares—48 percent each—in the world-famous Beverly Hills Hotel, the current market value of which has been estimated at around $125 million. Alas, he left the remaining 4 percent to his sister in Detroit, and therein lies the story.

In the early 1950s, the tale goes, when the girls were teenagers, their father took them and their mother to the hotel for the first time. The opulent structure, which had been built in 1912 and long referred to affectionately as the Pink Palace, dazzled young Muriel, representing glamour and beauty to her in a way that Detroit never had. She is reputed to have said to her father, "Daddy, if you want me to be interested in your business, why don't you buy this hotel?" And Ben

Silberstein, who doted on Muriel, did just that, for the then outrageous price of $5.5 million. He bought it from Hernando Courtright, the colorful owner, a bona fide member of Los Angeles society, whose financial backers included such prominent figures of the film world as Loretta Young and Irene Dunne. The plan was for Courtright, who knew everyone, to stay on for five years as president and general manager.

The relationship between the cigar-chomping Ben Silberstein, who dressed in knit shirts and slacks, and the elegant Hernando Courtright, who sometimes wore serapes and sombreros, was strained from the start, and their distaste for each other turned to downright hatred when Silberstein, after divorcing his wife, fell in love with Courtright's wife, Rosalind, a nightclub chanteuse, and later married her. Courtright went on to buy the Beverly Wilshire Hotel, which he proceeded to turn into a first-class rival to the Beverly Hills Hotel.

Silberstein's marriage to Rosalind Courtright was short-lived. In anticipation of its collapse, he moved his official residence to Florida in order to avoid California's community-property laws, which would have allotted half of his earnings during the period of marriage to his wife. In Palm Beach, following his divorce from Rosalind, Silberstein met and eventually married a beautiful former show-girl-turned-socialite named Bonnie Edwards, whose numerous husbands have included playboy Tommy Manville, the asbestos heir and tabloid darling of the period. The marriage of Ben and Bonnie endured, and they resided most of each year in the Beverly Hills Hotel, where Bonnie Silberstein became much loved by the staff and the community.

Silberstein was always referred to as Mr. S. by the staff so that the guests would not realize he was the owner. To the surprise of all, he never accepted large groups or conventions, as the other big hotels did, and he was dedicated to preserving the country-club atmosphere that made the Beverly Hills such a famed gathering place for film stars, visiting royalty, and the power elite of Hollywood. But he never lost his abrasive manner.

One morning at breakfast in the coffee shop, General David Sarnoff, president and chairman of the board of RCA, said to Silberstein, "I spend so much time here, you should give me a discount."

"I'm thinking of charging more for people who stay here too long a time," replied Silberstein.

In the meantime, the Silberstein sisters, Muriel and Seema, both married Detroit boys. There had always been a degree of friction between the sisters, possibly even fostered by their father, who was said to favor Muriel, and their marriages brought this friction to the surface. Their father was delighted with Muriel's choice, Burton Slatkin, whose family ran a jewelry store, but not remotely pleased with Seema's choice, Ivan Boesky, whose family owned a couple of Brass Rail restaurants. Burt Slatkin quickly became the son Ben Silberstein never had, and went to work for his father-in-law at the Beverly Hills Hotel. As for Ivan Boesky, anyone who knows the family will tell you—and none more graphically than Muriel—that Ben Silberstein considered him a bum and a ne'er-do-well, destined to amount to nothing. "My father was always disappointed with my sister's choice of husband," Muriel told me when I first contacted her. She is an attractive woman in her early fifties, dark-haired, with a svelte figure, of whom a friend has said, "What's on Muriel's mind is on her tongue." "I was *not* my father's favorite, as people say, but my father approved of my husband and despised Ivan. I was always the peacemaker in the family, and I would say to my father, 'Don't make Seema miserable because you don't approve of her husband.' "

A public indication of the low esteem in which Ivan Boesky was held can be inferred from Sandra Lee Stuart's book *The Pink Palace,* a gossipy history of the hotel published in 1978, a year before Ben Silberstein's death. In the book Ivan Boesky is never mentioned by name, and his wife is dismissed in these nonprophetic words: "Silberstein's other daughter, Seema, now Mrs. Seema Boetsky of New York, is not involved in the hotel." The name Boesky is even misspelled.

In 1973 Burt Slatkin became the president and chief operating officer of the hotel, although he was still answerable to his father-in-law. The Slatkins had two sons, Tom and Edward, and it was the dynastic wish of Silberstein that these two grandsons, who received their education in hotel administration, would someday run the place. With the help of Silberstein, Muriel and Burt built, on Beverly Hills Hotel property which was deeded over to them, the kind of house that can best be described as a showplace—a Regency mansion with a copper mansard roof and a courtyard designed by the eminent Los Angeles

architect Caspar Ehmcke, and a perfectly puffed-pillowed interior designed by the prestigious William Chidester.

With a fortune, a mansion, and a hotel behind her, Muriel Slatkin
had more credentials than most to make it as a social figure in Beverly Hills. She was never asked to join the Amazing Blue Ribbon, the
ultimate distinction for women of social achievements in Los Angeles, but she had a double cabana at the Beverly Hills pool, where she
entertained important visitors for lunch, and she always occupied the
same table in the celebrity-filled Polo Lounge. Her parties at home,
famous for the extravagance of the food, were duly reported on in
the society pages of the *Los Angeles Times* and *Herald Examiner,* as
well as in the gossip columns of the *Hollywood Reporter* and *Daily
Variety.* She took tables at all the major charity events and gave cocktail parties for famous writers stopping at the hotel on their book
tours. She even had a brief film career, playing a San Francisco society matron in Allan Carr's movie *Can't Stop the Music.* When she became actively involved in the redecoration of the hotel, she was given
an office near her husband's, and she had pink-and-green bordered
business cards made up proclaiming her proprietor of the Beverly
Hills. The hotel became her principality, and every time she walked
in or out of it, everyone, from the doorman on, bowed to her and
treated her like a princess.

Like her father, she was not universally loved, although her supporters are passionate in her defense. A complaint often heard about
her is "She's the type who's your best friend one day and looks right
through you the next." However, like her or not, everyone in Beverly
Hills took cognizance of Muriel Slatkin.

While Muriel became a personality in Beverly Hills, Seema lived in
New York with her husband, whom she adored, and their four children in a large Park Avenue apartment provided by Ben Silberstein.
In contrast to Muriel, who sought out recognition, Seema worked
hard at remaining anonymous. A trim-figured, high-spirited woman
with dark hair and vibrant blue eyes, Seema bears a strong resemblance to her sister. While her relatives in Beverly Hills downplayed
her husband's business abilities, others, nearer to the mark by far, described Ivan Boesky as a late bloomer. With the emergence of arbi-
trage on Wall Street, the man whose in-laws had considered him a

bum unquestionably found his vocation. Arbitrageurs are, according to a December 1984 article about Boesky in the *Atlantic*, "professional gamblers who bet on the outcome of corporate transactions. They invest in securities that are the subject of an announced tender offer, a merger, or a liquidation, and then realize a profit in the spread between their purchase price and the selling price when the announced event is consummated."

In 1979 Ben Silberstein became ill, and his illness exacerbated the trouble between the sisters. Muriel went to the U.C.L.A. Medical Center every day to visit her father and complained to anyone who would listen that Seema should have spent more time there too; she felt that Seema was not carrying her share of the load. Silberstein left each daughter 48 percent of the Beverly Hills, and before he died, in an effort to provide a secure future for the hotel he loved, he advised Muriel to give half of her shares to her husband, Burt. Bonnie Silberstein, Ben's widow, who had grown closer to Seema than Muriel, received an apartment on Sutton Place in New York, an apartment in Palm Beach, and visiting privileges in the Beverly Hills Hotel, but, contrary to popular belief, no shares in it. The remaining 4 percent went to Ben Silberstein's sister, Gertrude Marks, of Detroit, and her two children.

Burt and Muriel Slatkin offered to buy the 4 percent from Gertrude Marks, but they balked at the price she asked. That was a fatal error. "Burt's tight," explained a close observer of the situation to me. "He lost the fucking hotel because he's tight. When you're in a takeover, you don't quibble about money. If the old lady wanted a hundred bucks, you gave her three, and if she wanted a million bucks, you gave her three million. That's what his brother-in-law did."

Ivan Boesky didn't balk at the price. Gertrude Marks died a year after her brother, and her son, Royal, a concert-pianist-turned-art dealer, then controlled the swing points. Whatever price Royal asked for them, Boesky, unbeknownst to the Slatkins, paid without question. With that 4 percent, plus Seema's 48, Ivan Boesky, in an intrafamily coup, became in 1980 the principal stockholder in the Beverly Hills Hotel. It was a sweet revenge for him.

Muriel Slatkin's explanation of why Royal Marks sold the swing points to Ivan Boesky rather than to Burt Slatkin was that there had been bad blood between her father and Royal Marks, and Burt had had to serve as intermediary between the two.

In the most recent *Forbes* magazine list of the four hundred richest people in the United States, Boesky's personal fortune was given as $150 million—more money than Ben Silberstein ever had. Boesky is said to have grossed about $50 million on the 1984 acquisition of Getty Oil by Texaco, and later that year he grossed about $65 million on the acquisition of Gulf Oil by the Standard Oil Company of California. The Boeskys now own a large estate in Westchester County, New York, as well as an apartment in Paris. Seema Boesky is often seen at sales of Impressionist paintings at Sotheby's, bidding and buying, and there are Renoirs on her walls.

After Boesky's takeover in 1981, the Slatkins waited for the other shoe to drop. Meanwhile, their marriage fell apart. Muriel continues to live in the Regency mansion, but Burt now lives elsewhere. Muriel has a boyfriend, a Chilean named Ricardo Pascal. Pascal is younger than Muriel, and the relationship has caused tension between Muriel and her two boys. When one of the sons, Tommy, got married last July, there was public controversy over whether or not he had invited his mother to the wedding ceremony. She made an appearance at the reception.

Burt Slatkin continued as president of the hotel and oversaw all building and refurbishing of the bungalows on the grounds. He also continued to handle routine management problems, such as that presented by the aging and ailing Norton Simon, the multimillionaire industrialist and art collector, who for a time lived in one of the bungalows. Simon took to appearing in the Polo Lounge for breakfast wearing pajamas, a bathrobe, and slippers, and no one on the staff had the nerve to challenge him. Finally Slatkin made a discreet appeal to Simon's wife, the former film star Jennifer Jones, suggesting that her husband's attire in the public rooms of the hotel might encourage other guests to follow suit.

Ivan Boesky held the controlling interest in the hotel for almost five years before he made his move. Opinions differ as to why, after waiting so long, he struck when he did—pulling the rug out from under his sister-in-law, Muriel Slatkin.

"She said something to Seema about Ivan that went too far, and Ivan retaliated," said one observer.

Another explanation was that she called him a moron once too often at the counter of the coffee shop.

Whatever, it happened. In July 1985, Ivan Boesky arrived in Beverly Hills and checked in at his regular suite, 135–36, which had been redecorated to his specifications and which was rented or lent to his friends when he was not there. He called a meeting of all employees, from executives to bellboys, even those on their day off, in the Crystal Room, the principal ballroom of the hotel. There he announced to the startled staff that from that moment on the president and chief executive officer of the hotel was no longer Burton Slatkin but Adalberto M. Stratta, president of Princess Hotels International when it was owned by D. K. Ludwig. Slatkin was give the title of chairman of the board, but the implication was clear to all: Boesky's man, Stratta, was now the man in charge.

Muriel Slatkin was stripped of all her perks. Her office in the hotel was taken away, and she was informed that she was no longer welcome in any capacity other than guest, with the same privileges as any other paying guest. Her double cabana at the pool was confiscated, although she could rent it by the day if she called and it had not already been booked. Her favorite table in the Polo Lounge was no longer hers to command. Her charges in the drugstore were no longer to be paid by the hotel. "She was so embarrassed she didn't dare walk through the lobby," said one of her friends. Muriel Slatkin without the Beverly Hills Hotel was like King Zog without Albania. Shamed by her treatment and inconsolable, she took to her bed and saw no one, except Ricardo Pascal and a few close friends, for six weeks.

Now a family showdown is brewing. Muriel, recovered, and Burt, from whom she is not divorced, have jointly hired the Washington, D.C., law firm of Edward Bennett Williams to protect their interests. And Ivan Boesky has poured a fortune into the hotel, amid rumors of a sale. Seema Boesky declined to be interviewed for this article and declined for her husband as well.

"Could you just tell me about the four percent, Mrs. Boesky, whether your husband . . ."

"Do your own research," replied Seema Boesky.

I called Muriel Slatkin in Beverly Hills to ask her if she would see me if I flew out. She was undecided. "I love my sister. I don't understand why she is doing this to me," she said. "She is humiliating me. She has taken away everything. I don't even get a ten percent discount anymore." Reflecting on their childhood, she said, "My sister was heavy and not as popular as me. I'm not going to become bitter about it. My sister is the culprit. She wants to annihilate me."

I flew to Beverly Hills and checked in at the Beverly Hills Hotel. Grant Tinker, chairman of NBC, was making a telephone call in the lobby. Alan Ladd, Jr., the president of MGM/UA, strolled through with Guy McElwaine, the chairman of Columbia Pictures, and Barry Diller, the chairman of Twentieth Century-Fox, rushed past on his way to a meeting. In my room I found a bouquet of flowers, a bottle of wine, a basket of fruit, and a personal note of welcome from Burton Slatkin, chairman of the board. The telephone operator called me by name on my first call. In spite of everything, the Beverly Hills Hotel was still the Beverly Hills Hotel.

"Can you have lunch today?" I asked Muriel Slatkin when the hotel operator put me through to her house.

"No, I'm having lunch at the Bistro Garden with my boyfriend," she replied.

"Tomorrow?"

"I have houseguests for the weekend."

"When?"

"Monday tea?"

"Fine."

"Three o'clock in the Polo Lounge," she said. Later she changed it to three o'clock at her house. Later still she canceled altogether. "Eddie Bennett Williams said under no condition can I talk to you," she said.

Since Seema wouldn't talk, and Muriel was now silenced, I turned to their cousin Royal Marks, who by selling his 4 percent had started the war. When I called him at his art gallery in New York and identified myself by name and magazine, he replied, "I'm not interested in a subscription."

In the long run, everyone lost in this story. The plans of Ben Silberstein for his daughters fell apart. Muriel Slatkin lost her foothold at the hotel. Ivan Boesky went to prison. Seema Boesky divorced him but had to pay him a considerable amount of money. The Sultan of Brunei bought the Beverly Hills Hotel, then closed it down for several years while doing it up in a garish manner. It reopened in 1995 to great fanfare, but it has never regained the prominence in the hearts of the citizens of Beverly Hills that it once had.

LAZARAMA

"I'm trying to find Janet de Cordova."

"She's seated in that corner between Tom Selleck and Johnny Carson. At the table next to Jimmy Stewart's."

"I feel like I'm going to be trampled to death by movie stars."

"Nobody but Swifty could get all these people under one roof. Nobody."

When Mrs. William Backhouse Astor, Jr., built her vast Fifth Avenue mansion in 1857, she had the ballroom designed to dance four hundred guests, and for her first ball she called on the social arbiter of that time, Ward McAllister, to draw up a list of New York's four hundred grandest people. There was much jockeying for McAllister's favor, as well as gnashing of teeth by those not invited, and from then on society itself became known as the Four Hundred.

In recent years, in Hollywood of all places, an unlikely successor to Ward McAllister has emerged in the person of Irving Paul Lazar, the diminutive septuagenarian agent, known far and wide as Swifty. The Academy Awards party he and his wife, Mary, have hosted for twenty-five years has become *the* place to be, and his guest list, as carefully honed as Ward McAllister's, varies each year as people gain or lose prominence. On Lazar's list, success has replaced McAllister's criterion of pedigree. "Are you going to Swifty's?" people in Hollywood ask weeks in advance. Immense pressure is brought to bear on both Lazars by people who have not been invited, but Swifty has not got to the top of the heap in Hollywood and remained there for almost four decades by being a softy. "NO!" is the answer people say he gives. Or, if the person calling, or being called about, interests him, the answer is

"Come after dinner." Sometimes he even qualifies that by adding, "Late!"

Although Spago, the trendy West Hollywood restaurant where the party has been given for the last two years, is smaller than Mrs. Astor's ballroom, nearly the same number of people crossed its threshold during the three waves of this year's nine-hour party. In the first wave were 190 members of the Hollywood establishment and a few billionaires. In the after-dinner crowd were people who had attended the ceremony but bypassed the Academy's Governor's Ball. In the third wave came those who had also gone to the ball. All evening Swifty moved through the rooms like a ringmaster, directing traffic, telling people to get back in their seats.

"I can't see anything," complained one man. "I mean, it's hard to say to Raquel Welch, 'Hey, Raquel, you're blocking the TV.' " "I'd like to be a fly on that table where Jessica Lange, Meryl Streep, Kathleen Turner, and Sally Field have their heads together," said his friend.

Audrey Hepburn, who had presented an Oscar, arrived late to a standing ovation.

"Audrey!" cried Elizabeth Taylor.

"Elizabeth!" cried Audrey Hepburn, leaning over a table to kiss her.

"Ouch! You stepped on my toe!" yelped Elizabeth Taylor to a passerby.

"Oh, God, William Hurt brought the whole *Spider Woman* crowd with him," said Mary Lazar.

"Where are Jack and Anjelica?"

"They had to go to that damn ball."

First Mary Lazar died. Then Irving died. The town lost its most colorful hosts. Vanity Fair *magazine has come closest to replacing the Lazars' famous Academy Awards party each year.*

THE MORTIMER'S BUNCH

Mortimer's, the restaurant on the corner of Lexington Avenue and Seventy-fifth Street, is the best show in New York. If you can get a table. But don't count on getting a table. Far less well known to the general public than fancy places like Le Cirque, the Four Seasons, or Lutèce, where the concentration is on *grande cuisine*, Mortimer's is all about ambience. On any given day you are likely to see, at lunch or dinner, alone or in combination, Jacqueline Onassis, Ahmet Ertegun, Brooke Astor, Bobby Short, Peter Duchin, Marietta Tree, Fran Lebowitz, Placido Domingo, William S. Paley, Valerian Rybar, Katherine Graham, Mark Hampton, Mariel Hemingway, Oscar de la Renta, Mike Wallace, Patricia Kennedy Lawford, Jean Kennedy Smith, Lord Snowdon, Yasmin Khan, Marsha Mason, C. Z. Guest, Greta Garbo, Jean Vanderbilt, Jeanne Vanderbilt, Gloria Vanderbilt. The A list goes on and on.

Gloria Vanderbilt says Mortimer's is like Rick's Café in *Casablanca*, with Glenn Bernbaum, the owner, in the Humphrey Bogart role. "The things that go on there!" she exclaims. "And, you know, he lives upstairs in that incredible place. There's nothing like it in New York."

"I think Glenn Bernbaum is one of the most charming hosts that I've ever encountered in any establishment," says the record mogul Ahmet Ertegun. "He's low-key. He's elegant. He's a gentleman. His place has become—along with Elaine's—the other meeting place."

Irving Lazar, the Hollywood literary agent and social martinet, says that "Glennbaum," as he calls him, has "a genius for seating."

One afternoon recently, arriving at Mortimer's to have a late lunch with Bernbaum, I found him in a grumpy mood. The computer service that prepares the payroll for his staff of sixty had made the checks out on the wrong bank, and the error had definitely put him out of sorts. He was wearing a tweed jacket, an ecru custom-made shirt, gray flannels, and, surprisingly, Top-Siders. His clothes are beautifully cut and tailored, the kind that last forever. His hair is trimmed short, in the Ivy League style, and he wears horn-rimmed glasses with brown tinted lenses. He is sixty-one years old.

"You missed a good lunch," he said, when he had finally calmed down. He was not referring to the food but to the cast list of the day, and he began reeling off the names of some of the people, at the same time pointing out by number the tables where he had seated them.

Bernbaum will deny to you that the restaurant is snobbish, but make no mistake about it: it is. "We don't take reservations," you are told when you phone to book a table, "except for parties of five or more." And when you arrive to take your chances, the eyes of the captain at the door can be as unwelcoming as if you had walked into the sacrosanct halls of the Knickerbocker Club or the Brook Club without being a member. Yet there always seem to be tables for the high-profile names of New York. "Well," conceded Bernbaum when I asked him about this, "we don't take reservations, but we do, of course, take care of our friends." Behind his glasses, his eyes retreated into thought about what he had said, and he qualified his remark. "On the other hand, if I see someone who's an attractive person, the kind we want in the restaurant, with inherent style, there's always a place for that kind of person." He thought again and added, "If liking people with style is being a snob, then I'm a snob, I suppose."

Michael Connolly, one of the two waiters called Michael who handle the celebrity section during lunch, paused with a tray on which was a tin of beluga caviar that Bernbaum was sending to the table where Mercedes Kellogg, the wife of Ambassador Francis Kellogg, was giving a birthday lunch for two to Hubert de Givenchy, the French couturier.

"Does this look all right?" asked Connolly.

"Hmmmm," replied Bernbaum, examining the tray. He changed the position of a lemon wedge.

"Should there be watercress on the tray?" asked Michael.

"Good God, no, and that spoon's all wrong. Get a bigger spoon."
Bernbaum added, "If you're going to do it, do it right." It is one of the
rules he lives by.

Bernbaum grew up in private splendor in Philadelphia. A World
War II army friend, Boy Scheftel, who knew him when he was a lieutenant in psychological warfare, describes the Bernbaum wealth as
"Philadelphia money and a lot of it." Before starting Mortimer's in
1976, Bernbaum had achieved success as executive vice president of
the Custom Shop Shirtmakers.

In Bernbaum's stylish apartment upstairs over the restaurant, there
is a drawing of his family's town house on Delancey Place in Philadelphia. The apartment is one open effect of a vast room in an exotic
country house. There are lacquered cabinets, paintings of Turkish sul-
tans, a French desk, and sofas covered with fur throws. Over the fireplace hangs a portrait of his late mother, with hands on hips, dark hair
cut in bangs, wearing black velvet and pearls, and looking almost exactly like Vita Sackville-West. There's a photograph in a silver frame of
his mother and her great friend, the opera star Lily Pons, and another
of the first lady, Nancy Reagan, in an affectionate pose with her adju-
tant, Jerry Zipkin. Over one of the sofas is an eighteenth-century
painting of a hound attacking a felled stag.

"It's a Baldassare de Caro," said Bernbaum, looking up at it. Then
he added, "Maybe," and smiled.

When Bernbaum opened Mortimer's ten years ago, he knew nothing about running a restaurant. Two friends, Bill Blass and Steve Kauf-
mann, brought him together with Michael Pearman, who had created
such famous New York establishments as Michael's Pub and the Running Footman. "He didn't know where to get coffee, or meat, or how
to hire staff," said Pearman, from Palm Beach, where he now lives.
Bernbaum concedes that Pearman got his backers to frequent Mortimer's (which was named after Mortimer Levitt, who owns the Custom Shop Shirtmakers), but adds, "I also knew a few people quite
well: Bill Blass, Kenny Lane, and Jerry Zipkin. They were immediate
boosters of the restaurant. Of course, we can't detract from the location. Everyone lives close by."

"There are two cardinal rules in the restaurant business," said Pearman. "Never take a drink in front of the staff, and never, ever, sit down

with a customer, no matter how well you know them. Glenn does both these things."

"Pearman wanted the restaurant to reflect his personality, and I wanted it to reflect mine," said Bernbaum.

The arrangement between the two did not work out, so Pearman withdrew and returned to Palm Beach. Sometime later he dined in the restaurant with a friend and complained that his chicken paillard was protruding over the edge of the plate. Meant constructively, the criticism was resented by Bernbaum, and he walked off without replying. Pearman has not visited the restaurant since.

Bernbaum is sensitive to any criticism of the food he serves. Jerry Zipkin and he temporarily fell out over Zipkin's criticism of the spinach. Zipkin claimed, according to Bernbaum, that the spinach was always creamed. Why couldn't the restaurant serve leaf spinach? Bernbaum replied tartly that creamed spinach had to be leaf spinach before it became creamed spinach, and if Zipkin wanted leaf spinach he should ask for it. Except for private parties, the fare at Mortimer's is simple—crab cake, twinburgers, chicken paillard, and fresh fish—and the prices are remarkably cheap for so tony an establishment.

There are other rifts. A current one is with Kenneth Jay Lane, the jewelry designer and man-about-town, whom many people credit with the enormous success of the restaurant. The art historian John Richardson says, "As Pratt's Club in London caters to the personal friends of the Duke of Devonshire, so Mortimer's in New York caters to the personal friends of Kenny Lane."

"Tell me about Glenn," I asked Kenny Lane when I ran across him at the Morgan Library looking at drawings from the Albertina.

"The social arbiter?" he replied, eyebrows raised, a note of irony in his voice. Bernbaum had been so described in a recent magazine interview. "I seem to have been dropped by Mr. Bernbaum. However, I'm delighted that the restaurant is doing so well that I can no longer get a reservation there."

Their rift was over seating. According to Bernbaum, Lane was displeased with the table he was shown to, and simply moved his party of four to a better one, which was reserved for someone else. Bernbaum was annoyed.

Bernbaum is a complicated man, paradoxically rude and kind, distant and warm, sad and funny. He is invariably well informed on the comings and goings of other people. "Mrs. Reagan is having lunch at Mrs. Buckley's today," he will tell you. Or "Oona Chaplin's apartment burned and she's moved to the Carlyle." Or "I hear Princess Margaret's smoking like a chimney, and after that lung operation."

Bernbaum has not been without his share of gossip and melodrama. While vacationing on the island of Crete in 1975, he was so impressed by a waiter called Stefanos that he asked him to move to New York and work at Mortimer's. It then developed that Stefanos had a wife and child, and Bernbaum agreed to move them to New York too. He made Stefanos a captain, and the young man's charm ingratiated him with the regulars of the establishment. But Stefanos gambled, and soon he was heavily in debt to the kind of people who break your legs if you can't pay. Bernbaum, in the meantime, had made out a new will, leaving Mortimer's to Stefanos, and he told Stefanos that he would be his heir. Impatient to pay off the underworld figures, who were after him, Stefanos sought to hurry along the inheritance process by contracting two hit men to do away with his benefactor. His plan was discovered, and the two hit men who arrived at the restaurant turned out to be F.B.I. agents. Stefanos was arrested on the spot, tried, and sent to the slammer.

The incident was reported in the press, and Taki Theodoracopulos wrote about it in graphic detail in the pages of the *Spectator*. Such is the level of sophistication at Mortimer's, however, that when Taki's book *Princes, Playboys, & High-Class Tarts*, which includes the piece on Bernbaum and the Greek waiter, appeared, Bernbaum gave the publication party at the restaurant, because it was Taki's favorite New York hangout.

Bernbaum is famous for the private parties he arranges at Mortimer's. Several years after opening the restaurant, he expanded into the building next door and turned the new space into a second dining room, suitable for private parties. Last year he expanded further by adding the Café Mortimer around the corner on Seventy-fifth Street; it serves sandwiches and pizza and also functions as a room for small parties.

"I gave the first party at Mortimer's," Kenny Lane told me. "One hundred of the A list in twelve different languages. Glenn provided the food, and I provided the people. The guests never left. They're still there."

I arrived one afternoon to find Bernbaum arranging white lilacs and pink roses in small glass vases for a private party that evening. He treats each party as if he were the host, and he proudly displays albums filled with color photographs of Cornelia Guest's coming-out party, Bill Blass and Oscar de la Renta's party for the publication of Diana Vreeland's book *D.V.*, opera patron Sybil Harrington's birthday party for Placido Domingo, and the 1984 red-white-and-blue, election-night party hosted by the Ahmet Erteguns, the Irving Lazars, and the Abraham Ribicoffs.

Joel Gerbino, one of the three maîtres d'hôtel, rushed into the restaurant and delivered six swatches of Liberty of London prints to his employer. The following night the American-born Lady Keith, known as Slim in the circles in which she travels, was giving a dinner for twenty in honor of her daughter, Kitty Hawks (from her marriage to the late Howard Hawks), her stepdaughter Brooke Hayward (from her marriage to the late producer Leland Hayward), and her stepdaughter Lady Camilla Mackeson (from her marriage to Lord Keith). Bernbaum wanted to make the evening special, and he fussed over which of the six fabrics would make the proper tablecloths for Lady Keith's party. Invariably he adds extra touches at his own expense if he feels they will make the evening exceptional. He rapidly figured on a piece of paper that each tablecloth would come to $250. "I hate to spend that much money and not get something I really like," he said. "I can't very well charge Slim Keith for print tablecloths from Liberty of London that she didn't order, but I'll be able to use the tablecloths again, and isn't it more important to get it done right?" He looked out the window and patted the back of his head.

"No one but a nut would agonize like this over a dinner for twenty."

By party time the next evening the Café Mortimer looked as if it were for a children's party, a rich children's party, which is what it was, even though the children were all grown up and divorced themselves. Helium balloons with silver lamé streamers hugged the ceiling. The centerpieces were large jars of candy, and *Wind in the Willows* bean-bag animals anchored the place cards on the candlelit tables, which

were covered with Liberty of London tablecloths rushed to completion for $250 apiece. "Dim the lights so we can see how it's going to
look," Bernbaum said to Michael Connolly. He crossed his arms and
stared up at the balloons. "Give me a scissors," he said. "These ribbons are too long."

"Taste this tofu that Gloria Vanderbilt sent over this morning," said
Bernbaum to his chef, Stephen Attoe, formerly of the Connaught Ho-
tel in London. Tofu dessert is the latest product carrying the illustrious
Vanderbilt name. "I must say I never saw ice cream delivered so beau-
tifully," he went on. "Her own car. Her own driver. Gloria's got style.
What do you think of it?"

Stephen Attoe sampled the three flavors and liked them all.

"Reinaldo Herrera gave a lunch at Le Cirque for Princess Margaret
yesterday," Bernbaum said to his chef. "It would have been here if the
poisson had been cooked properly the other night when Reinaldo
came in for dinner. It was underdone, he said." There was a slight rep-
rimand in his voice.

He likes royalty and apparently royalty likes Mortimer's. On one of
the Princess Margaret's visits to New York, she was entertained at the
River Café in a small party that included Jack and Drue Heinz, of the
pickle-and-ketchup Heinzes, and Bill Blass. A ripple of excitement ran
through the restaurant as the elegant party made its way to the table.
"There's Bill Blass," the celebrity watchers whispered, while Her Royal
Highness went virtually unrecognized. She was not pleased. The following night the princess was given a large party at Mortimer's by the
Venezuelan socialite and landowner Reinaldo Herrera and his dress-
designer wife, Carolina. Glenn Bernbaum, who had heard the story of
the River Café, instructed the piano player to play "There'll Always Be
an England," and "Rule Britannia," and he prompted the diners in the
main room to stand and applaud the queen's sister. As the princess was
leaving the party, she informed Bernbaum that he had given her her
most pleasant evening in New York.

Another night, the king and queen of Spain entertained in the
restaurant. Bernbaum was determined to keep their evening at Mortimer's private. "No one knew he was coming," said Bernbaum.

"Not even the staff. I put the family name on the reservation list."

"What is the family name?"

"It's slipped my mind for a minute, but I'll look it up for you."

He did. It was Bourbon.

"They had the window table in the second room. I seated the king at the head of the table with his back to the window. The security people had a fit. Because of the Basque separatists. How was I to know the Basque separatists were out to get him? Well, Pierre Cardin was also having a dinner in the restaurant the same night, for the same number of people, and I thought of swapping tables, but I left the king at the window table. I just moved his seat so the head of the table was against the brick wall. The next day the embassy in Washington called to say that this was the only place in New York where there weren't TV cameras. I even assigned the waiter who always waits on Garbo to the king's table."

One night, quite late, three men entered the restaurant, pulled guns, and told the remaining diners to lie on the floor while they emptied the cash register. "Thank God the Aga Kahn and Sally had just left," said Bernbaum.

It *is* Rick's Café, and he does have a genius for seating. Claus von Bülow, shortly before his second trial for the attempted murder of his wife, the utilities heiress Martha "Sunny" Crawford von Bülow, was lunching one day in Mortimer's with Grace, Countess of Dudley, and John Richardson. Directly behind von Bülow, Bernbaum seated Arthur Schlesinger and Lally Weymouth, the daughter of Katherine Graham, the owner of the *Washington Post*, even though Mrs. Weymouth had written a series of articles unfavorable to von Bülow at the time of his first trial.

Von Bülow maintained his high profile in New York between trials by lunching at Mortimer's several days a week, usually with his girlfriend, Andrea Reynolds. He always entered the restaurant like a film star. His detractors, and there are many, voiced disapproval at his presence there; his supporters, and there are many, greeted and joked with him.

Bernbaum performed a delicate balancing act whenever von Bülow's stepchildren, Alexander von Auersperg and his sister Ala von Auersperg Kneissl, who believe him guilty of having attempted to murder their mother, were in the restaurant at the same time as von Bülow. Bernbaum always seated them at a distance from each other so that no unfortunate incidents could occur.

The von Bülow presence at Mortimer's was not a subject that Bernbaum wanted to talk about, but it was unavoidable. He is too good a restaurateur to be unmindful of the theatrical effect von Bülow had on other customers.

"I never showed him off," said Bernbaum. He weighed his words carefully. "His stepchildren no longer come here," he said. "Claus has never been anything other than a gent. I don't think it's up to me to pass judgment on him. If anybody didn't act properly, that would be another story."

"Have you ever barred anyone from the restaurant?"

"Several people."

"Why?"

"Unpleasant. Ungentlemanly. Unladylike."

"Who?"

He smiled, shrugged, and didn't reply.

Michael Ludwig, the other waiter called Michael, came over and asked, "Do you want to give a reservation for Sunday lunch to Harrison Goldin?"

"Who's Harrison Goldin?" asked Bernbaum.

"The comptroller of the City of New York," replied Michael. Neither of them seemed impressed.

Bernbaum looked out the window for a moment, patted the back of his head, looked back at Michael, and replied, "Oh, give it to him."

After writing this article, I became part of the Mortimer's bunch myself. I went there three or four times a week every week for the next ten years. It had the feeling of a country club in the city, where all the members knew each other. Glenn was thrilled when I used it as a centerpiece in my New York society novel, People Like Us, *changing the name to Clarence's, although it was unmistakably Mortimer's. When the producers of the mini-series of that book went to the restaurant to look at it for a location, they were shocked and terribly disappointed at its simplicity and rejected it out of hand for the film. They wanted something grander looking. Glenn loved that. He died this year, all alone in his apartment over the restaurant, snobbish to the end. His will dictated that the restaurant be closed forever on the day of his death. The six hundred or so people he favored as regulars can't find a substitute for their favorite meeting place. They never will. Only Glenn Bernbaum would dare to put up the barriers he put up.*

THE WOMEN OF PALM BEACH

Palm Beach people talk about Palm Beach people constantly. It is a subject that never seems to exhaust itself, and any one of them, at any event where they are gathered, can give you an instant précis of any other one's life. "She's Mollie Netcher Bragno Bostwick Wilmot. She lives next to Rose Kennedy, and last year a tanker ran aground on her seawall and practically landed in her living room." . . . "The man in the receiving line, third from the end, is Paul Ilyinsky. He's on the town council. His father was a Russian grand duke who married Audrey Emery, Paul's mother, and his second cousin was the last czar of Russia." . . . "The lady with the long blond hair who never misses a dance is Sue Whitmore, the Listerine heiress. She was practically born at the old Royal Poinciana Hotel. She single-handedly runs the International Red Cross Ball every year, which is the only one of the big charity parties the chic people go to." . . . "There, with the deep tan and the mustache, is Douglas Fairbanks, Jr. I don't have to tell you who he is, except that his house, for some reason, is called the Vicarage." . . . "That elderly lady being helped across the dance floor by Charlie Van Rensselaer is Mary Sanford, Laddie Sanford's widow—you know, the polo player. They call her the Queen of Palm Beach. Don't say I called her elderly." . . . "The guy with the pale pink lipstick and the plucked eyebrows and the big diamond ring in the color photograph in the window of Kohn's on Worth Avenue is Arndt Krupp, the German munitions heir. Last year he gave a big party for the Queen of Thailand, but nobody's seen him this year." . . . "She's Lilly McKim Pulitzer Rousseau. Everybody loves Lilly. She's Ogden Phipps's stepdaughter, and she used to be married to Peter Pulitzer, years before all that awful Roxanne business, and they were the most beautiful couple in Palm Beach. Now she's married to Enrique Rousseau, one of the Cubans, and Enrique's ex-wife is now married to Charlie Amory, who used to be married to Chessy Patcevitch. I hope you can keep all this straight." . . . "That's Bill Ylvisaker. He's the polo group. Sundays everyone goes to Wellington for the polo." . . . "The tall man sitting next to Estée Lauder is Joe Sobotka. He's one of the better extra men down here. Sometimes you have to scrape the bottom of the barrel for good extra men for these parties." . . . "The beautiful redhead in the gold dress is Fern Tailer Gimble Denney, Tommy Tailer's daughter, Edith Baker's granddaughter, and the man she's talking to is Alfonso Fanjul. One of the Cubans. Sugar money. Rich, rich, rich." . . . "At the next table, in the T-shirt, carrying her gardening book, is C. Z. Guest, Mrs. Winston Guest, the famous gardener. She's become rather independent down here. And sitting next to her, in the black bathing suit with the long blond hair, is her daughter, Cornelia, who's always in the papers." . . . "There's Suzie Phipps, perfectly beautiful and sitting on twenty-six acres in the middle of Palm Beach. She, I suppose, is the real Palm Beach." . . . "That's Dorothy Spreckels Munn. She lives in an Addison Mizner–style house on what was the Munn compound with ten indoor servants. You can't get any higher than Dorothy Munn and the Phippses in Palm Beach."

"Everybody who ever writes about Palm Beach always gets it wrong," said a very grand lady to me during a lunch party on my first day there. She stared down at the silver platter of gnocchi that was being served to her, shook her head no to the maid, changed her mind, and took a minuscule portion. "They come down here, these writers, stay too short a time, don't get to the Bath and Tennis Club or the Everglades, never meet anyone, except all those old dragons who love publicity and aren't Palm Beach at all, and then they go back to wherever they're from and think they're authorities on Palm Beach and write the most awful things about us. Did you ever see that English television show they did? I mean, really. None of us even knew who those grotesques were they interviewed for that show. And it's always like that. Not one person was Real Palm Beach."

Just who is and who isn't "real Palm Beach" is a recurring theme in Palm Beach conversations. The grand lady, her morsel of gnocchi consumed, lit a cigarette and threw back her head as she exhaled, as if to stress how the journalistic portrayals of her winter resort annoyed her. She was tanned and slender and pretty, wore a print silk dress, pearls, and a straw hat, and would, when this lunch was over, play bridge until dinner. "The trouble is," she continued, "that everyone thinks Roxanne Pulitzer is Palm Beach." She pronounced the name Roxanne Pulitzer with an intonation that let you know in no uncertain terms exactly what she thought of that person, which wasn't much. "She's not Palm Beach, and never was, and none of us ever saw Roxanne and Peter, even before that horrible divorce. They were always with the Kimberlys, and that's a different group entirely. And as for Mr. Armand Hammer! Puhleeze!"

Mr. Armand Hammer, the chairman of the board of Occidental Petroleum, won the eternal enmity of most of the real Palm Beach for his high-handed treatment of them when he presided over a charity ball during the visit of Prince Charles and Princess Diana to the resort in November 1985. The real Palm Beach boycotted the affair.

The grand lady stared down at the dessert plate that had been placed in front of her by the maid, lifted off the spoon and fork, and transferred the finger bowl and doily from the plate to the table. "You see," she went on, "Palm Beach, I mean the real Palm Beach, is behind walls, and very private, and that's why none of you people who come down here to write about it ever get it right."

The lush and lovely Florida island, which faces the Atlantic Ocean on one side and Lake Worth on the other, is the winter counterpart of such northern summer resorts as Newport, Southampton, and Bar Harbor. It is only twelve miles long. Here rich people can enjoy being rich without fear of criticism, because almost no one lives in Palm Beach except other rich people enjoying being rich. During the sixties and seventies, some of the Old Guard, fearing that Palm Beach had seen better days, abandoned it and took or built houses in Acapulco or on smart Caribbean islands like Jamaica, but the unsightly poverty, "the racial thing," and the fear of uprisings brought them back to where their eyes need only look upon other people living exactly as they are living, in large and lovely pastel-colored villas with well-tended lawns and hedges and well-trained staffs to manage them. But even here, in this most rarefied existence of rank and privilege, there is heard a constant lament that things are not as good as they used to be.

It's possible to go to Palm Beach bearing all the right credentials, spend the season in a pretty house or the Colony Hotel or the Breakers, and never lay eyes on any of the people you've heard about, or read about, all your life, who are, as the saying goes, the real Palm Beach. But they're there, behind their walls, just as the grand lady said to me, and their social life, for those of them who like social life, is relentless. There are lunch parties and cocktail parties and dinner parties, and a great deal of stopping by friends' houses for drinks on the way to the parties or on the way home from the parties. And there are charity balls, although there is a hierarchy of charity balls, and this group attends only the three or four where the guest list is limited to "people we know." In between the parties, the same people see one another at the Bath and Tennis Club, called the B. and T. by its members, or the Everglades Club, for lunch, or dinner, or tennis, or croquet, or golf, or a swim. They are mostly dressed alike, the men in lemon or lime or raspberry linen trousers with blue blazers and loafers without socks, and the women in very understated beach or golf wear, except for the group that plays bridge every afternoon, who are slightly dressier.

Exclusivity is the name of the game in the real Palm Beach: being with your own kind and your own kind's houseguests, excluding, for the most part, all others. To be asked to join the two clubs that count; to be invited to the Coconuts on New Year's Eve, the most in of the in New Year's Eve parties, with its receiving line of twenty men; to be invited to buy tickets for the Planned Parenthood and the Community Foundation dinner dances and the Preservation Foundation Ball— these are all signs that you're accepted, or that you've made it. But unless your name appears on one of the two overlapping lists of under three hundred names with unlisted telephone numbers that are sent out each year, like mini-social registers, one in the form of a Christmas card by the enormously rich Fanjul family, the other by the socially prominent Realtor Anthony Boalt, you're not really the real Palm Beach. "People are dying to get on those lists," one lady told me in the snobbese characteristic of people who believe that inherited wealth is superior to earned wealth, "but, you know, there are some business people on them now. When Charlie Munn used to do the list every year, there were only social people on it."

In the swell houses on South Ocean Boulevard the living is indeed very swell and being shown through the cool and elegant rooms and the grounds on a sort of privately conducted tour by the owner is part of each visit. In one, a butler in a well-tailored white jacket and white gloves stood at the end of a chintz-upholstered drawing room, a presence but not a participant, waiting to replenish drinks and hors d'oeuvres while we talked. On the wall hung, as there hangs on the wall of almost every fashionable house here, a portrait of the lady of the house painted by Alejo Vidal-Quadras, the resident Boldini of Palm Beach.

"Need I tell you what people talk about in resorts?" asked my hostess of that day, reclining on a sofa beneath her Vidal-Quadras portrait. "'The gardener didn't come.' 'I hate my new maid.' 'Who did you sit next to at Chessy's last night?' I mean, it goes like that, day in, day out."

She has been coming to Palm Beach most of her life, as has her mother, who lives nearby. She sipped her Perrier water, declined an hors d'oeuvre with a shake of her head to the butler, and petted a King Charles spaniel that had jumped up on the sofa next to her. Like everyone else, she lamented that Palm Beach was not the way it used to be. "It's too bad about all those other people coming to Palm Beach," she said, lowering her voice, although she was in her own drawing room, "you know, the fifty percent, but we never have to see them. That is what's so wonderful about the clubs. You can't even bring them there as a guest. You'd get a little letter in the mail if you did, and then, if you did it again, bye-bye membership in the Bath and Tennis."

"Those other people," the 50 percent she was talking about, referred to what is most commonly called "the Jewish thing," about which no one likes to commit himself, although it is a constant in conversation. One man told me, "Palm Beach is the only unabashedly Wasp community left in the United States, but we're up-front about it." Other people consider Palm Beach a bastion of anti-Semitism. Because the Bath and Tennis and the Everglades clubs are restricted, the rich Jews of Palm Beach are ineligible for membership. As David Marcus of the *Miami Herald* wrote last year, in a series of articles on the private clubs which incensed many of the Old Guard, "No matter how wealthy, how prominent or how impeccable their credentials, Jews are not welcome at these exclusive social institutions." The feeling is that this sort of thing is better left unsaid.

What makes the matter a constant source of beneath-the-surface acrimony is the so-called guest rule, and members of both clubs are divided in their feelings about it. While it nowhere states in the rules that Jews, blacks, or other ethnic minorities cannot come as guests of members, the guest rule at the Everglades states that members may not bring anyone they "might reasonably believe would not be accepted as a member." Quite simply, this means that these clubs will not even permit a Jew to walk through the door as the guest of a member.

There are endless stories of acutely embarrassing situations that have occurred when people have brought Jewish friends to the clubs and the friends have been asked to leave the golf course, or the tennis courts, or the dining room. In one particularly irksome case, the head of the Palm Beach branch of an international company cannot bring the chairman of the board of the company to his clubs, even though the chairman of the board is a winter resident of Palm Beach.

The Everglades Club was built in 1917 on 160 acres of prime real estate by Addison Mizner, the architect who developed the Palm Beach style, a rococo olio of Moorish, Spanish, and Italianate elements. Originally conceived as a convalescent home for mentally disturbed servicemen by the multimillionaire Paris Singer, a lover of Isadora Duncan and one of the twenty-five children of Isaac Merritt Singer, the sewing-machine magnate, it was converted into a private social club two years later. An oil portrait of Paris Singer hangs inside the double doors, past the MEMBERS ONLY sign. Although it was Singer who restricted the membership of the club, Palm Beach legend has it that he himself was suspected of being Jewish. Herbert Bayard Swope, Jr., a radio and television commentator and a member of the croquet set, says, "On that rumor alone, Paris Singer wouldn't get into the club to see his own portrait today."

A mile down the road is the Bath and Tennis Club, facing the Atlantic. It was built in 1926 in the Mizner tradition.

In the 1950s the Jews founded their own club, the Palm Beach Country Club, where the initiation fee is reputed to be $50,000, higher than the initiation fee at either the Everglades or the Bath and Tennis, and the annual dues are $4,000. Eligibility for membership in this club is unique in that it has to do more with an applicant's recognized involvement with charitable contributions than with social standing, good schools, and the right connections. Members of the Palm Beach Country Club can bring Christians as guests, although there is only one Christian, Phil O'Connell, Sr., among the 325 members.

At the turn of the century, when the first great hotels like the Royal Poinciana and the Breakers were being built to lure the New York and Newport aristocracy to the new winter paradise, there developed nearby, on what is today condominium-lined Sunrise Avenue, a shantytown known as the Styx, inhabited by the blacks who were brought in to build the hotels. According to local lore, the unsightly community offended the eye of Henry Flagler, known as the founder of Palm Beach, and other town fathers. In a magnanimous-appearing gesture, they invited the entire population of the Styx over to West Palm Beach to a circus performance and barbecue, and during their absence burned the shantytown to the ground. The workers were relocated permanently in West Palm Beach.

"Money talks."

"Honey, money shrieks."

The two ladies were discussing the imminent arrival on the Palm Beach scene of two of the most successful young businessmen in America, Leslie Wexner and Donald Trump. Last season Wexner, the low-profile head of The Limited and some 2,500 specialty apparel shops, with a personal fortune of $1 billion, was the subject of much speculation when he purchased the magnificent estate of Charles and Jayne Wrightsman for $10 million as a companion piece to his recently purchased $6 million house on the Upper East Side of Manhattan. Then, in a spectacular, Candy Spelling gesture that shocked Palm Beach, he razed the famous house to the ground. He is now in the process of building himself a Versailles-type mansion. He is unmarried and thus far virtually unknown in Palm Beach.

In January, Donald Trump, of the real estate fortune, and his wife, Ivana, purchased for a mere $5 million the 118-room mansion called Mar-a-Lago, former house of the late Marjorie Merriweather Post, which had been on the market for $15 million. Mar-a-Lago was conceived by a Ziegfeld set designer in a mélange of architectural styles.

The Trumps have hired a Palm Beach decorator and claim they plan to spend several months of the year here. There is, however, a lurking suspicion among a lot of members of the Bath and Tennis Club, which is next door to Mar-a-Lago, that the Trumps have inside knowledge that gambling is returning to Palm Beach, and that they intend to turn Mar-a-Lago into a gambling casino.

"They'll never get into the clubs," says one faction about the Trumps. Another faction isn't so sure. "They'll let him a little bit in," they say. "Earl E. T. Smith is behind them." Earl E. T. Smith is a former ambassador to Cuba, a former mayor of Palm Beach, a onetime husband of a Vanderbilt, and his support is considered as good as you can get. And the Trumps—whom one woman referred to as "the new darlings of Palm Beach"—have made a smart social move to start off their life here: they have offered Mar-a-Lago to the Preservation Foundation of Palm Beach for its annual ball.

The *Palm Beach Daily News* is known affectionately as the Shiny Sheet because it is printed on a superior quality of glossy paper which guarantees that it can be handled without soiling the fingers or staining the white morning linen. A ninety-two-year-old institution, the Shiny Sheet is devoted exclusively to Palm Beach life, both social and everyday. MRS. VINCENT DRADDY SUES FOR DIVORCE was the headline of one recent front-page story, which recounted the details of the latest in Palm Beach's predilection for messy, no-holds-barred divorces. Another read: FOUNDATION DINNER-DANCE LIVES UP TO ITS BILLING. Another, HARD CASH GETS TRUMP A BARGAIN, referring to the purchase of Mar-a-Lago. There was a subhead: "Trump Pays Extra for Estate's Furniture."

While the real Palm Beach crowd tend for the most part to keep their pictures out of the Shiny Sheet and the other five publications covering Palm Beach life, except when they attend charity balls or committee meetings in preparation for the balls, the rest of the out-every-night population is not reluctant at all to pose as often as possible, and some have become bona fide social celebrities, like Mrs. Helen Tuchbreiter, who is a regular first-nighter at the Royal Poinciana Playhouse and the organizer over the past twenty years of twenty-eight charity balls which raised $10 million for assorted good works.

Helen Bernstein, who writes a regular column for the Shiny Sheet, is the wife of the man who built the New York Telephone building and the great-niece of Kate Wollman, who gave the skating rink in Central Park. A kind and witty lady, she is a perceptive observer of Palm Beach social life. "Here everything is sanitized," she said, sitting in the living room of her dramatic house overlooking Lake Worth. "They pick up the garbage five days a week. Everything that's negative, or not so great, is over the bridge in West Palm Beach."

One of her favorite themes is social climbing. About one of the most prominent ladies in the winter colony, she said, "She's so desperate about it. She doesn't take a moment's vacation from it."

"Do social climbers ever make it?" I asked her.

"To Dorothy Munn's house? No. But, on the other hand, they probably don't even know who Dorothy Munn is. No one makes it to the top of the ladder. The successful ones make it about three-quarters of the way. Some fall back from fatigue, but a true social climber doesn't have the sensitivity to know it's only three-quarters of the way. Let me tell you something about social climbing: it's good for the economy. The serious social climbers underwrite the charity balls. The doors are closing in Palm Beach. In a few years, it won't be easy to see anyone."

When the Shiny Sheet reported that Helmut Newton and I were coming to Palm Beach to do an article on the community for *Vanity Fair*, we had a few experiences of our own. The mother of a postdeb delivered a letter to Helmut at the Breakers, imploring him to moonlight from his *Vanity Fair* assignment to photograph her daughter's cocktail party.

The party, she wrote, "will bring together the town's top Young Socialites in a more natural, typical setting . . . including our friends, the Sargent Shrivers from Washington, D.C. Mrs. S. is Eunice Kennedy, as you know—and all five boys are here, using Mrs. Kennedy's house, of course. They attended [my daughter's] debut two years ago, and are always included amongst her parties. The young Charles Revson (Countess Ancky too), are coming. Please do come—you'll enjoy yourself immensely, as well as seeing our Mirós, Picasso & Chagall." On a separate page, she added, "We will render payment in American dollars, not F.F."

Another lady called me at the Colony Hotel. "It would be a shame if you don't talk to me," she said. "It would be like coming to Palm Beach without a dinner jacket. I'm sort of an interesting story. My husband invented the milk carton. He was on CBS news on Monday night as one of the great people who passed away this year.

"I was one of the hostesses of Palm Beach for many years. The last people I entertained were the Queen's cousins. I'm sort of an Elsa Maxwell. I have been the chairman of more balls than you can count in the last twenty years. I own the Duchess of Marlborough's house.

"Would you be kind enough to call me Celia *Lipton* Farris. That's the name I'm known under. I was a household name at fifteen in England. Right now I'm recording my new album in Miami."

Palm Beach goes to a lot of people's heads. Although plenty goes on alcoholically and sexually in the upper circles, the real Palm Beachers tend to forgive one another's transgressions. "I always have to do over my phone book each year because of all the divorces," a well-known hostess told me. "Usually you start to hear about the divorces in April, after the season." At one party I attended, the guests were regaled with hilarious accounts of how a friend of theirs, an outraged wife, had taped romantic telephone conversations between her husband and her former maid, whom he had set up in West Palm Beach. Another tale, told with sadness, concerned a lady whose life had recently nose-dived, after several divorces, into alcoholism, drug addiction, and unfortunate liaisons, culminating in a marriage everyone frowned on, followed by her almost immediate death. It is only when social figures go public in the newspapers with their transgressions that the others can be, and are, unforgiving.

"Gregg's not allowed in anyone's house" was a line casually said about Gregg Sherwood Dodge Moran. "Roxanne has been squeezed out" was another line I heard, about Roxanne Pulitzer, as if she were a Florida orange. For these two ladies, and many other, less publicized ones, the paths of Palm Beach have been rocky. Although Mrs. Dodge and Mrs. Pulitzer continue to live in the environs of the grand world they once were a part of, today they are like fallen angels, castoffs, in the social scheme of things. Their futures are in the hands of literary agents, paperback publishers, and TV producers if, but only if, they tell it like it was.

"Do you ever see Gregg Dodge?" I asked a lady who once worked on ball committees with her.

"Gregg and I don't have the same kind of friends," she replied.

"Do you ever see Gregg Dodge?" I asked another lady who once knew her well.

"I saw her at Razook's trying on a full-length mink coat, so she must have gotten an advance on that miniseries of hers." She thought for a moment and then added, "No one sees Gregg Dodge anymore."

I saw Gregg Dodge, and she still looks like Lana Turner, with whom she once acted in *The Merry Widow*. Gregg was a little girl from Wisconsin whose real name was Dora Fjelstad. She became a Miss America contestant and later the Chesterfield Girl, at twenty-seven married Horace Dodge, the automobile heir, had a son by him, became his widow after several months of separation, inherited $13.5 million, married her bodyguard, Danny Moran, who used to be a New York cop, lived in a mansion in Palm Beach, a Fifth Avenue apartment, an estate in Greenwich, Connecticut, a house in the South of France, a country house in Windsor, England, and a yacht, the *Delphine*, 355 feet, which had a crew of fifty-five. She went bankrupt, had all her possessions sold out from under her by court order to pay her creditors, went through more lawsuits than you could count, including one for libel against her onetime best friend, Mary Sanford, the Queen of Palm Beach. She was with Danny Moran in their bedroom when he shot and killed an intruder, and within hearing range when he shot and killed himself. She is currently living in reduced circumstances in Palm Beach with her son, John Dodge, thirty-two, and her small grandson.

She didn't want me to go to her house. She picked the nearby Epicurean Restaurant, where we met for late-afternoon tea for me and vodka martinis for her. "I don't usually wear all this jewelry in the daytime," she said, about her diamond rings and diamond-and-onyx earrings, "but I was being photographed by Helmut Newton." She is pretty, funny, wounded, down but not out. Although she was most recently Mrs. Danny Moran, she calls herself Mrs. Horace E. Dodge again. Her ocean-to-lake estate on South Ocean Boulevard has been sold. John DeLorean now lives in her apartment at 834 Fifth Avenue. Leona and Harry Helmsley now live in her Greenwich, Connecticut, estate. The other places and the yacht are gone too.

She is used to telling her story and tells it well, as if she were pitching it to a producer or an editor. "I buried my second husband and my mother in the same week," she said. "I went through $13.5 million. . . . I know Palm Beach. It's a social battlefield."

"Are you still a member of the clubs?" I asked.

"No," she replied. "No one asked me to resign. I couldn't afford the dues anymore. Now if I joined, I'd have to pay up past dues, which are fifteen or twenty thousand in each club."

"Do you ever hear from any of the people you used to know down here?"

"The women are the generals down here," she replied. "They run everything. The men just become black-tied, silent bystanders. Mary Sanford and I used to run this town socially. Nobody gave a party without checking with us first. Many people in Palm Beach think they're social, but they're just ticket buyers, meeting other ticket buyers. True society in Palm Beach is in the home."

"Do you ever hear from any of the people you used to know down here?" I repeated.

Her eyes filled with tears. We sat for a moment in silence. "I don't choose to see those people," she said. "I haven't wanted to see anyone. I've been recovering my energies."

"Where do you live?" I asked Roxanne Pulitzer.

"Do you know where the mall is?" she replied on the telephone from Inger's Workout in West Palm Beach, where she is now an aerobics instructor.

"No."

She gave me detailed instructions to a neighborhood across the bridge in West Palm Beach, far removed from where she and Peter Pulitzer used to live. "You'll see the house. There's a Porsche in the carport."

What you see first, after the Porsche in the carport, in Roxanne Pulitzer's pleasant house, are two junior-size bicycles belonging to her eight-year-old twin sons, Mac and Zac. And there is Roxanne herself, the scandalous lady of the messiest divorce case in the history of Palm Beach society. After all the stories of cocaine addiction, sexual promiscuity, and lesbianism, I expected her to be defensive, but she isn't. Roxanne, who was married to multimillionaire Herbert "Peter" Pulitzer for seven years, got a measly $50,000 in the divorce settlement.

"I read somewhere you lived in a dump," I said.

"I did right after the divorce, but it wasn't fair for the boys to come from Peter's house to my little place. I got some money when I posed for *Playboy*, so I decided that Mac and Zac and I were going to have a nice place for a year. I'll probably have to move out when the lease is up, unless something happens from the book I'm writing or the miniseries."

"How often do you see your sons?"

"I lost custody of the boys, so I only get to see them four days a month," she said. "And I wasn't even declared an unfit mother. It's a gyp."

"When you run into people from the clubs, do they speak to you?"

"They were cool to me at first, but after I did *Playboy* and was on the 'Phil Donahue Show,' some of them sided with me."

"Do you regret things?"

"The biggest mistake I made was during the trial, when I said to the kids, 'No matter what, we'll always be together,' and then I lost custody of them, and they resented it. But they're getting over that now. All my friends deserted me. People I asked to be character witnesses for me left town. Listen, I had a good time on coke for a while, up until the end, and then it turned and became bad. We stopped going to bed together, and slept at different times, and then everything fell apart.

"Jacquie Kimberly was my best friend. She and Jim and Peter and I were always together for years. Jacquie took me to Petite Marmite for lunch before the trial and said, 'The handwriting's on the wall, and I can't afford to be seen with you,' and I've never laid eyes on her again. She didn't even send me a note when I lost my kids. I can't forgive that."

There's no reason in most people's minds that the girl got rooked. It takes two to tango, but the real Palm Beach closed the circle around one of their own, and the outsider got left outside with no kids, no home, and no money.

"Would you go back over the bridge to that life again?"

"The rich life? You'd have to be stupid to go down that road again."

Dorothy Spreckels Munn's house on North County Road is one of a pair of side-by-side mansions built in the 1920s by her late husband, Charles Munn, who was always known as Mr. Palm Beach, and his brother, Gurnee Munn, in the Spanish-Moorish style, with large rooms, wide corridors, high ceilings, and majestic stairways. Mrs. Munn, in her widowhood, has made no concessions to changing fashion in interior decoration. Entering her house is like stepping back into the thirties. A maid opened the door and directed me to a stairway, where a butler preceded me across an immense tiled hallway to a tapestry-hung library, where Mrs. Munn, two male guests, and a companion sat in what seemed to be a tableau in a time warp.

People in Palm Beach tell the story of how one night Dorothy Munn walked into a restaurant where she was well known and a favored customer. The restaurant was filled to capacity, and there was no table for her. The maître d'hôtel was abject with apology, begged Mrs. Munn's forgiveness, and offered as an explanation that it was Thursday.

"Thursday?" queried Mrs. Munn.

"Cook's night out," he explained.

"Do you mean to say that all these people are cooks?" cried Mrs. Munn.

The acknowledged *grande dame* of Palm Beach, Mrs. Munn sat tall and straight-backed in a tall and straight-backed Spanish chair.

"You must have a drink," she said, looking from me to her butler.

"Perrier," I said.

"Everybody's drinking Perrier," she replied.

In recent years Mrs. Munn has absented herself from active participation in Palm Beach social life. "She doesn't go out twice a day anymore," one of her friends said to me. In Palm Beach parlance, this means she goes out either to lunch or to dinner, but never both on the same day. "You sometimes see her at people's houses, although mostly people go to her. She still loves to play cards."

"You must tell us everything about Claus von Bülow," she said to me.

"I don't think he did it," said her companion emphatically.

"Oh, I do," said one of the male guests.

"She was beautiful, Sunny," said Mrs. Munn.

Mrs. Munn is interested in writers and writing. As she has difficulty sleeping, she pays someone to read to her, sometimes until as late as four in the morning. She had recently gone through the manuscript of a biography based on the life of her mother, Alma Spreckels, of the sugar family, a dominant figure in San Francisco society in the early decades of the century.

"How was it?" I asked.

"The dates are all there, and all the chronological order of things— she crossed the Atlantic, she did this, she did that—but there's nothing of my mother, her personality, how she was. My mother was a friend of Loie Fuller, the dancer, who was a friend of Queen Marie of Romania, and my mother and Queen Marie became friends, and . . ."

Her guests sat and listened with rapt attention.

I felt that I had finally found the Real Palm Beach.

All sorts of new people with vast fortunes have moved into Palm Beach, and the Old Guard is, understandably, vexed. These new people don't care if they can't get into the Bath and Tennis Club or the Everglades. The houses they are building are the size of football fields with pavilions and loggias and marble halls, palaces that have all the amenities, and more, of the clubs. I go there for a week or so every winter. Social manipulation has always interested me. Palm Beach is one of the few places where it really exists.

AVA NOW

"Let's not talk about Mickey, or Artie, or Frank," she said, looking up from lighting a cigarette, exhaling smoke. She was talking about Rooney, and Shaw, and Sinatra, of course, the husbands of her three brief marriages, the last of which ended in 1957. Every interview she ever gave, she said, ended up being a discussion of the same old stories, true and untrue, that had been told oh so many times. "Let's not go into the stuff you always read about me."

"O.K.," I replied.

"Is that a tape recorder?"

"Yes."

"Oh, honey, uh-uh. I'm more scared of those things than I am of the camera."

"O.K."

"Don't write," she said later when she saw me taking notes. "Let's just talk."

Ava Gardner, the ravishing love goddess of the 1950s, still has the walk, the style, and the excitement of a movie queen. Her glorious face, untouched by cosmetic surgery, is remarkably unravaged by decades of tabloid-reported riotous living. A North Carolina accent occasionally seeps through the deep, lush MGM-trained voice, which is overlaid with a glossy international patina. She moved to London in 1968 after a long sojourn in Madrid, where she engaged in a lifestyle so flamboyant it caused her neighbors, the exiled Peróns of Argentina, to seek residence elsewhere. Time and England have brought tranquillity to her life.

It is no accident that she gravitated to this civilized nation's capital.

The respect for privacy, the quieter way of life, and even the weather appeal to her. She wanders the streets of London, usually unrecognized and unintruded upon, a rootless, beautiful, fiercely American expatriate. She is a lady in retirement, but most certainly not retired. At sixty-two she is soon to make her television debut as Agrippina, the evil mother of Nero (played by Anthony Andrews), in the forthcoming NBC miniseries "A.D." She enjoyed shooting on location in Tunisia, and the possibility of a new career in a new medium looms.

Her most successful films were those in which the parts she played—like the barefoot contessa in the film of that name and Lady Brett Ashley in her friend Ernest Hemingway's *The Sun Also Rises*— meshed with the famous wild persona she created off the screen, elevating her to an almost mythic, Hollywood-star status. Her last major role was in Tennessee Williams's *The Night of the Iguana*, under her favorite director, John Huston. Her appearances since then have been mostly cameo roles in undistinguished films, but there is no sense of the washed-up or has-been about her. She walked away from her career but retained her stardom. Her name still evokes tremendous curiosity among the generation who adored her.

We met during a photographic session at the Launceton Place studio of Lord Snowdon in London. Although a fashionable hairdresser and a makeup man had been engaged by Lord Snowdon, Ava Gardner arrived already made up and coiffed—she had done her face and hair herself. She claimed she was nervous about the sitting, but she seemed to enjoy the experience. In a magical star gesture, a throwback to her MGM days, she signed the photo release form as if she were bestowing an autograph at a premiere.

Later we walked from the studio, in Kensington, to her home, in Knightsbridge, through back streets and mewses and across parks. She knows London like a tour guide. Stepping off a curb, I looked left instead of right, in the American manner, and nearly got nipped by a passing taxi. "You better hold my hand," she said with a smile, and held it out to me. We stopped to visit her veterinarian on the way; some pills he had prescribed for her corgi were causing listlessness. "You'll like Keith," she said to me about the veterinarian. Waiting for Keith, who was in conference, she talked about homeopathic cures for pets with a woman who had two gray cats in a box. Midway through the conversation I saw the moment of recognition in the woman's eyes when she realized she was talking with Ava Gardner. But with true English tact she suppressed her delight.

Ava Gardner's apartment is in a cream-colored Victorian mansion that faces on a communal garden. "The king of Malaysia lives in that house when he's in London," she said, pointing out a neighboring building. For obvious reasons there is a made-up name on the outside bell of her house. She buzzed a signal upstairs—two shorts and a long, or two longs and a short.

"Señora?" came the voice through the speaker.

"Sí, Carmen," she replied, and we were buzzed in to the downstairs hall. Upstairs a door opened, and the corgi barked with a wild excitement—matched by his mistress's cries of greeting. She calls the corgi Morgan, after her American business manager.

Carmen, uniformed, who has been with her for years, stood at the front door and acknowledged an affectionate introduction. The apartment is extremely handsome, with large rooms and wide halls. Elaborately curtained windows open onto a long, shrub-planted balcony that fronts the house. Marble-topped consoles, gilt mirrors, lacquered cabinets, French and Regency chairs and Chinese screens fill the rooms in actressy splendor. The dining room is book-lined. A drink tray with ice and glasses had been set on a table in the drawing room, where a fire blazed invitingly. It is a very well run household.

There we were finally, settled in, strangers meeting. She smoked constantly, selecting each cigarette from a Georgian silver box and using a heavy cut-glass and ormolu table lighter in the shape of a pineapple. Lighting a cigarette is a two-handed operation, almost ritualistic, occupying her attention totally. It is another movie-star gesture in the grand tradition.

She avoids the social whirl and first nights of London life, preferring to pop in on her small coterie of friends when they are not entertaining. She attends the ballet, opera, and theater in preview performances, often with her neighbor and great friend, the English actor Charles Gray, who lives so close by that they talk to each other from their balconies. I asked about her celebrated friendships with

Robert Graves, Tennessee Williams, Noel Coward, Maria Callas, and, of course, Hemingway and Huston. She smiled in recollection. "Those weren't day-to-day friendships, not through thick and thin," she said, and then added, "but they were intense on the occasions we met."

She has a habit of speaking to her dog to convey messages to you or to avoid questions she considers invasions of privacy. I told her a gossipy story a mutual friend of ours had told me involving adultery and black satin lingerie and duplicity. She clearly didn't see the need for the story to have been told, either by our mutual friend to me or by me to her, and told her dog so: "That's not a nice story." It dawned on me that Ava Gardner, who was the subject of so much gossip for so many years, never gossiped herself. Once, when the name of someone who had not behaved well with her came up, a look crossed her face that told me she had a lot she could say about that person, but she said nothing.

It is the reason she will never write a book, although offers are constant. Several unauthorized biographies have been written about her, but she scoffed at them, saying they were written from gossip columns and reviews of her pictures. Despite her strong sense of forthrightness, she disapproves of the kind of sexually graphic autobiographies that certain actresses of her generation have written, telling all, naming names.

Late at night, walking again, we went into a crowded pub. The mass of young patrons did not part for the entrance of the bareheaded, mink-jacketed star with a corgi on a leash, and I searched her face for disappointment, but found none.

"She seeps into you in a haunting kind of way," her friend Roddy McDowall said about her, and it is true. She is by turns complicated and mysterious, direct and honest, witty and melancholy. "I haven't taken an overdose of sleeping pills and called my agent," she said, quoting a much repeated line of hers from times past. "I haven't been in jail, and I don't go running to a psychiatrist every two minutes. That's something of an accomplishment, isn't it?"

Oh, how I loved that great movie star on the occasion that I met her for this article. Ava Gardner may have come from a simple rural Southern background, but this was a lady, a great lady, with the added asset of mystery about her. We kept in touch. Ava died in London in 1990.

HIDE-AND-SEEK WITH DIANE KEATON

Diane Keaton, the most reclusive star since Garbo, does not sit in positions of relaxation. All during our interview she seemed poised for flight, one patent-leather-shod foot in constant motion as she goes reluctantly through this chore of stardom. A pile of curls bobs on her forehead when she speaks, and a single, purple, plastic hoop earring jiggles from her lobe. She is prettier than she photographs, and friendly, but wary. She pushes up, pulls down, then pushes up again the sleeves of her blouse, dying to be finished with the task at hand.

She lives in a glass aerie high above Central Park. Stepping off the elevator into the foyer outside her front door, one is immediately confronted with evidence of her unique style—a large, tracklit artwork, which, on closer inspection, turns out to be hundreds and hundreds of yellow plastic bananas, piled in a corner by the actress herself. The apartment is white on white on white, floor, ceiling, walls, kitchen tiles, furniture, even the thick diner cups and saucers—its starkness broken by several huge floor vases of flowers and by arrangements of art objects that have caught her eye, such as a plastic bust of Pope John Paul II that she found in a curio shop in Toronto, a trio of reindeer that she saw at a roadside stand while driving through Massachusetts, and a grouping of huge papier-mâché boulders that she got in a theatrical-prop shop. "I'm sort of a junk collector," she tells me. "What I really need is a warehouse. I like to change things around. For a while it's fun to look at them, and then I don't want to look at them anymore." For the moment, at least, her critically admired collages and photographs have been packed away in a back room, and she is disinclined to let me see them. There is a sense of fastidious neatness throughout—no clutter, no books or pictures littering the tabletops—and, of course, her Academy Award is nowhere in sight. Her home is like an art gallery, with changing shows.

The apartment has a 360-degree view of the city; it looks down twenty floors onto the park's sailing pond on one side, onto the copper green turrets of the majestic Dakota on another, across the West Side to the Hudson River on the third, and smack into the windows of the matching twin-tower apartment of Mary Tyler Moore on the fourth.

"Do you wave to each other?" I ask.

"Oh no. We've never met," she replies. "In fact, I've never even seen her."

Since the place is high up, safe, spacious, and very private, I am surprised when she says it is on her mind to move. She explains that the large living room, with its thirties bamboo-and-canvas furniture, and the dining area, with its huge table and chairs on casters, are pleasant but functionless rooms for her kind of life. "I never entertain," she says. She does, however, share the apartment with three large old cats, each with its own domain. She says she would like to own a loft or a building where she could have more room for work—a studio for her photography, space to edit her documentary films, and an office for her production company, where she could meet with writers to discuss projects. After nearly twenty years in New York, she tells me, she sometimes toys with the thought of returning to California to live. Then she breaks off saying, "Listen, it's cat-hair city here. You're going to hate me when you leave."

Keaton is much more at ease talking about other people, like Mel Gibson, the hot costar of her latest movie, *Mrs. Soffel*, than about herself. "It was not difficult for me to imagine what it was like to be hopelessly in love with Mel," she says. "It was wonderful for me to play opposite him. I didn't have any idea how much emotional range he had."

Mrs. Soffel is, according to her, "a big love story," based on a true event that took place in Pittsburgh in 1901. Keaton, who plays the wife of a prison warden, gives an extraordinary and disturbing performance as a fervently religious woman who falls madly, hopelessly in love with a condemned bank robber so handsome that women wait outside the prison to send gifts in to him by the guards. Without thought of consequence, she helps the outlaw and his brother to escape and then willingly forsakes husband, children, and reputation to accompany the pair on an ill-fated, three-day race with death. The part is shocking and fascinating and a risky one for a star. Who could care about a woman who does what Mrs. Soffel does? As Diane Keaton plays the part, you may not approve, but you do understand.

She loved the role. "The idea of playing someone who had never been touched emotionally or romantically in her whole life and then gives way to an urge so strong that she cannot help herself—all the terror and excitement of it was wonderful for me." The smoldering presence of Gibson combines with Keaton's enigmatic and elusive quality to create the kind of sexual sparks that are rarely seen on the screen.

During the long and arduous shooting in Canada in twenty-degree weather, the two stars admired each other's talent but did not socialize together in their free time. "I never got to know Mel very well," says Keaton. "I wanted to keep a distance from being friendly with him. If you start hanging out together you lose the kind of tension it takes to play a part like that."

With *Reds*, *Shoot the Moon*, *The Little Drummer Girl*, and *Mrs. Soffel*, Diane Keaton has put her Annie Hall image to rest forever. Gone is every vestige of the beloved character created by Woody Allen and based on her own skittish and jittery personality. At thirty-nine, she is a major star at the peak of her talent.

"She is the dream actress that every director should have," says Gillian Armstrong, the Australian director of *My Brilliant Career*, who made her American directorial debut with *Mrs. Soffel*. "In a practical sense she is absolutely professional. There's none of that sort of star business about being late or not turning up or staying out all night, or any of those things. She is absolutely dedicated and hardworking, and she gave me the same intensity in take after take."

Working back-to-back on *The Little Drummer Girl* and *Mrs. Soffel* meant being out of the country on distant locations for nearly a year. "I don't want to do that ever again," says Keaton. "I don't want to go away and work for months and months and move every two weeks to another hotel in another country and be away from people that I love. I don't want to do that. I felt like I'd left my life for quite some time. I felt alone."

After a series of heavily dramatic roles, she longs to play comedy again, but finding the right script has not been easy. "I was spoiled by Woody," she says. At the age of twenty-three, she was cast by Allen in the stage version of *Play It Again, Sam*, and she later acted the same role on the screen. She also appeared with him in *Sleeper*, *Love and Death*, and the brilliant *Annie Hall*, for which she received an Academy Award in 1978. Her relationship with Woody Allen, both professional and romantic, remains a pivotal part of her career and life. Long apart, they have managed to maintain their friendship even through other relationships, including Allen's long liaison with Mia Farrow.

"In the comedy zone there's nobody like Woody," she continues. "I just had great roles. I would love more than anything to do a comedy again. I'd love it. But for some reason, I don't know . . ." Her voice drifts off.

So far her own attempts at developing a comedy for herself have not been successful. The most promising was called *Modern Bride*, a romantic comedy about a thirty-six-year-old woman who is getting married for the first time just as her parents are getting divorced. She would have coproduced and starred, but after several attempts at a script, including one by Nora Ephron and Alice Arlen and another by John Sayles, the project fell into abeyance.

Another film idea, a comedy about friendship, would star Keaton with two close friends, the actress Kathryn Grody (wife of actor Mandy Patinkin) and Carol Kane, whom she met when the three of them were in the film *Harry and Walter Go to New York*. "I'm going to stick with trying to do something with these projects, but to be honest with you," says Keaton wistfully, "I think my skills as a producer, or a person who is able to get a movie together, and get it on, and actually realize it, are . . . uh . . . it's not my . . . uh . . . gift, or, I don't think I have those capabilities in putting people together to make it happen. Now, there's a long sentence."

When talking about herself, she sometimes borders on the inarticulate, expressing self-doubt, stopping, starting, changing direction, interrupting her thoughts, advancing in disorder.

"I'm not going to quit," she says. "I'm going to continue to try to be in a movie that's funny. I'd love to do something with Woody and Mia." She jumps up from the sofa and looks out the window.

"These serious movies are hard on me. I find acting not . . . uh . . . not . . . uh . . . oh, I don't know. It's hard. It's very hard, and it brings out things in me that I don't like, which is . . . uh . . . steady, constant worry. I just worry every day. Am I O.K.? Am I all right? Look . . . I don't want to say that it's not a privilege, and it's not something I don't want to do, because I do like doing it, really, but I'm glad I'm not doing it right now."

I went to see her again in Los Angeles, where, the press agent for *Mrs. Soffel* told me, she was producing a documentary.

"What kind of documentary?"

"You'll have to let Diane tell you that. It's a private thing she's doing."

"Can't you tell me what it's about?"

"Heaven."

"Heaven?"

"Heaven."

"What about heaven?"

"You better ask her when you get out there."

She was at a hotel in Santa Monica called the Shangri-La. The nonconformist movie crowd, who have always eschewed the splendors of the Beverly Hills, Beverly Wilshire, and Bel Air hotels in favor of the bohemian atmosphere of the Chateau Marmont, have of late picked up on the offbeat, seaside charm of Shangri-La. Built in the forties as an apartment hotel, it has been handsomely transformed into a hotel in the Art Moderne style and it has become Keaton's favorite stopping-off place. "Diane likes the funkier kind of places," says Kathryn Grody.

When I arrived at the Shangri-La, Keaton stuck her head around a corner and called out, "Hi!" indicating the direction of her suite with a head gesture. The sleek gray living room in forties streamline revival suited her. Her clothes have a distinctly rummage-sale/swap-meet look about them, but there is an eye for design in the layering which is as complicated and of a piece as one of her performances. That day she was a study in black and white: a mid-calf, houndstooth-check skirt over black leggings, white push-down socks that flopped onto black patent-leather "Thriller" shoes, a black blouse pushed up at the sleeves, a black-and-white hair rag tied in a bow atop her head in a style somewhere between Carmen Miranda and Cyndi Lauper, and one hoop earring. She is often able to walk unnoticed on the street. Neither needing nor wanting to be recognized, she is assimilated into the anonymity she craves without resorting to the movie-star disguise of oversize sunglasses and fur coat. It is perhaps her bizarre manner of dressing that protects her, drawing, as it does, the gaze of passersby to her clothes rather than her face.

"Look out here," she said, gesturing again with her head. Outside, a terrace ran the length of her penthouse suite. Across Ocean Avenue were giant palm trees on the palisades. Far below was the broad Santa Monica Beach, and beyond it the Pacific Ocean. The sky was blue and cloud-filled, the scene picture-postcard beautiful.

"Great, huh?" she asked, leaning on the rail, looking out at the sea, serene, content, enjoying the moment.

It was.

"I have this longing to be here again," she said quietly. "I'd like to have a place right here in Santa Monica. I like the whole area. I like the little mall where you walk around. I can walk to a store. I can walk to a restaurant. And, of course, there's the water. I guess everybody loves Santa Monica now, though, don't they? It's the place."

After a pause, she said, "Maybe I will come back. My family's out here." Her family, with whom she is deeply involved, consists of her mother, father, two sisters, brother, and grandmother, ninety-three-year-old Grammy Hall. Her family name is Hall, but she took her mother's maiden name of Keaton because there was already a Diane Hall in Actors' Equity.

"Let me put on some water for coffee," she said, going to the bathroom for water. Her coffee machine was brand-new and unfamiliar, and she continued to talk as she tried to make it work, and then apologized for the coffee. "It's not hot enough is it? It never really boils. Is it too strong? I don't have any cream or sugar."

"Hungry?" I asked.

"Yeah."

Not far from the Shangri-La, in the trendy Venice art colony, is the new restaurant of the moment, 72 Market Street, owned by actor-producer Tony Bill, Dudley Moore, and two partners, and backed by such celebrities as Liza Minnelli. It is the place where everyone wants to go and no one can get a table.

"Do you mind if I drop your name?" I asked before calling for a reservation.

"It won't help," she replied.

"Yes it will."

It did.

The restaurant is spacious and stunning and makes, the maître d' said, an architectural statement. We were ushered in in grand style and well seated although Keaton makes a point of wanting no special treatment. "She disavows all the trappings of fame," says writer Lynn Grossman, one of her close friends. She would never, ever, use her name to get into a crowded restaurant in New York. "She's not waiting for heads to turn at the Russian Tea Room," says Kathryn Grody. She stands in line at the movies and has been known to decline offers by theater managers to pass her in ahead of the crowd. Sometimes she seems almost too good to be true, for a movie star. A well-known New York playwright received a letter from her, rejecting his play, that he said was the nicest letter he had ever received, so nice that he wrote her back thanking her for it, saying that her letter was better than his play. She is so shy that at 1985's Toronto film festival's Tribute to Warren Beatty, her former great love, she remained hidden in the audience and refused to be acknowledged, not even standing to wave when Beatty himself introduced her from the stage. And it is a known fact that in the newspaper ads for *Reds*, of Keaton and Beatty embracing, it was her wish that only the back of her head be shown.

"Don't you enjoy being famous?" I asked.

"I think I like to deny it. It suits me to deny it. It's more comfortable for me to deny it, but I suppose that's another one of my problems. Look, I don't think it's such a big deal, I don't think I'm that big a thing. You know, uh, I'm a movie star. I get to play the leads in movies, or I have so far, maybe not so much, you know, after, uh, whatever. . . . But I don't feel I'm one of those prime . . . uh . . . people don't really . . . uh . . . I don't get a lot of . . . uh . . . I mean I can walk down the street, it's no big deal. For the most part, people don't stop me. They kind of treat me nice. You see, I'm not an idol or anything like that. They don't bother me. Sure, it's great to be . . . uh . . . I'm really lucky, obviously I'm really fortunate, and I'm grateful, but I think it's nice not to be too well known. I hope I can continue like that."

"You're pretty well known, Diane."

"Pretty well known, but not *recognizably* well known. It's not like being Woody Allen. '*That's* Woody Allen,' they say. Or Mary Tyler Moore. Now, *she's* famous. Or Jack Nicholson. He's the most comfortable person being a movie star I've ever seen. I've never seen anybody like him. I'm a big fan of his. He's got the right attitude about it, you know, being famous. He says, 'This is what I do, and having your picture taken, and being recognized, it's all part of it.' "

When she travels, she takes driving trips with her friends to places like the Grand Canyon or New Mexico, or to Memphis to see Graceland, Elvis Presley's home. She loves to drive. "She likes any odd, out-of-the-way, eccentric nook or cranny, like the diner most people wouldn't stop at," says Kathryn Grody, a frequent traveling companion. Lynn Grossman, who accompanied Diane to Graceland, says she enjoys "hanging out, eating fries at roadside stands, singing songs. She's a middle-class girl with the soul of an artist." They say they have never seen her be rude to a fan, "even under the most gross conditions."

In both *Shoot the Moon* and *Mrs. Soffel*, Keaton acts motherhood as well as it has ever been acted, but she has no children. Does she want them?

"Yeah, well, sure. . . . You know, I'm thirty-nine, and I don't know how much time, I mean, there's still time. Early on I made a career choice, and now, I hope it's not too late. Sure I do. Yes, I'd like to."

Her personal life remains her own, and intrusions are not welcome. Recently there have been items in gossip columns linking her romantically with a young director whom she was said to be taking home to meet her family. When I showed her the clippings, which she had not seen, she shrugged off the stories with a smile. "Oh, that Liz," she said in mock exasperation, meaning Liz Smith, in whose column one of the items had appeared.

These are areas she does not wish to share. Don't bring up Warren

Beatty, I had been told in advance by one of her closest friends. She doesn't want to talk about Warren. Nevertheless, questions about their famous romance, now ended, were churning in my mind, should the moment present itself. Did Warren take her away from Woody? Does Woody hate Warren? Is it true that Woody's movie *Zelig*, with its famous people commenting on the nonentity Zelig, was meant to be a send-up of Warren's movie *Reds*? Questions like that. But where to begin?

"Have you—uh . . . remained friends with Warren?" I asked, feeling my way.

She changed her position, breathed in deeply, and withdrew into her privacy. For an endless moment, we waited in silence as she moved the carpaccio around on her plate. "Let me say this," she answered finally. "The experience of making *Reds* is one that I will always treasure. I have the deepest respect for Warren, both as a director and as an actor. *Reds* is a film that I am very proud of."

"And that's it on Warren?" I asked, sensing a note of termination.

"Yeah," she answered, drawing out the word.

"Let's talk about heaven," I volunteered.

"Oh, sure, heaven," she said with evident enthusiasm for the subject of her new documentary, and our awkward moment vanished.

"I've seen films depicting heaven, and there were extraordinary visual images. The whole notion of heaven frightened the hell out of me, so I thought maybe it would be interesting to put together a little documentary where you just ask everybody, as many different kinds of people as possible, what they think about heaven and how they feel about it."

She found the people around Hollywood Boulevard, and on the streets, and at various associations and churches. "I think a lot of people are afraid to think about what it's like after death. They hope for something more, but a lot of people are afraid to think about it."

"Who talks to the people and asks the questions?"

"I do."

"As Diane Keaton?"

"Oh, no, just an off-camera voice, although some of the people did call me Diane. It's a talking-heads kind of movie. We shot a lot of film. It's going to be a huge editing job."

"How much will it cost?"

"Oh, gosh, a lot."

"Who's paying for it?"

"One of the cable stations."

"Would you call that one of the perks of fame?"

"Yeah," she answered. "That's the good part, being able to do things like this little documentary, and publishing my books on photography."

It was late. Back at the Shangri-la we said good-bye. She was going that evening to the new Los Angeles Museum of Contemporary Art for the viewing of a laser work donated by her friend Doug Wheeler. Watching her retreat into the lobby, I was struck by her walk and by her extraordinary style, which no one else could ever quite bring off the way she does. I liked her. I missed her already.

The next day, before returning to New York, I caught up with family at the hotel for lunch. When Beverly Hills people say "the hotel," they mean only the Beverly Hills Hotel. It is the hub of activity, where you buy the *New York Times*, get your shoes shined, have breakfast, lunch, or dinner, and run into a wide assortment of people. At the entrance to the Polo Lounge, talking to Pasquale, the maître d', I saw the back of a woman wearing a black-and-white houndstooth-check skirt over black leggings, white push-down socks falling onto "Thriller" shoes, and a black-and-white hair rag tied in a style somewhere between Carmen Miranda and Cyndi Lauper. It was Diane Keaton, who, her friends had assured me, never, ever went to places like the Beverly Hills Hotel. We said hello again.

Later, during lunch, heads turned in the Polo Lounge as Warren Beatty entered the room. He has the kind of star presence that even the most sophisticated people do not take in their stride.

"Hi," he said to me in passing. "I hear you had an interesting day yesterday." He continued on through the Polo Lounge to the glass door that opens out to the terrace. At the farthest end of the patio, he sat down at the table where Diane Keaton was waiting. They have, it appeared, remained friends.

Ms. Keaton has gone right on being a movie star. I went to a big Holly-wood party in her honor a couple of years ago, when she was nominated for an Academy Award for Marvin's Room. *A sign of the respect that she commands is that all the big movie names turned out to honor her. She had a great personal success in* The First Wives Club *with Goldie Hawn and Bette Midler. Watch her step into character roles. Watch her stay around for a long time.*

THE RED QUEEN

In 1972, in Cortina d'Ampezzo, a mountain resort in the Italian Dolomites, Elizabeth Taylor, Henry Fonda, and Helmut Berger starred in a film I produced called *Ash Wednesday*. Elizabeth was then in the waning period of the first of her two marriages to Richard Burton. Being with the Burtons, as they were always called, was like being in a state of almost surreal celebrity. Late, late one night, during an all-stops-out conversation, Elizabeth said to me, "You know, I can't remember when I wasn't famous." It was a statement made without the slightest braggadocio, simply as a fact of her celebrated life. Except for that other Elizabeth, the queen of England, who else, then or now, could make it?

In September of this year I went to the London home of Elizabeth's film-producer friend Norma Heyman, where Elizabeth was staying, to take her to the photo session for this article. The photographer Helmut Newton was there, along with the dozen or so necessary people who arrange her hair and make up her face and provide her clothes and carry her jewels. We waited four hours for her to get ready, drinking pots of coffee, passing the Sunday papers back and forth across the kitchen table. "Elizabeth is chronically late," Richard Burton once said about her. Her lateness is as much a part of her as her violet eyes. Bulletins from above were sent down from time to time. She had slept on her left side, and her left eye was puffed up. Were there cucumbers in the house? Were there tea bags? She had not liked all the Yves Saint Laurent dresses sent over from Paris. She had called in the Emanuels.

More than once Helmut Newton wondered if the already problematic light would last.

Finally, of course, she appeared, descending the stairway in great good humor, unperturbed by the chaos she caused, and all, as always, was instantly forgiven in the wake of her never diminishing splendor. Even if you know Elizabeth Taylor, it is not uncustomary to gasp a little when you see her. She is a sight that never ceases to fascinate. Now, in the forty-third year of her stardom, she is voluptuous and ravishing again. The recent image of obesity and alcoholism and Percodan addiction is behind her. Except for her recurring back problems, she radiates good health and a maturing beauty. "Sheran sends her love," she said to me about her childhood friend Sheran Cazalet Hornby, at whose country house she had spent the weekend. Unhurried, she examined herself in a hall mirror, the left side of her face, the right side of her face, moistened her lips, evened her lipstick with the little finger of her left hand, and adjusted a strand of her frosted black hair.

"There are lots of *paparazzi* in front of the house," I said to alert her.

"So what else is new?" she answered.

"You look great."

"Thank you, love."

Outside, the sky was suddenly bright for the first time that day.

"You see, the sun is better now," she said to Helmut Newton, as if she had done him a favor by being late.

"You're torturing me," he replied.

"No, I'm toying with you," she said.

Trained like royalty to understand and undertake the obligations of her calling, she moved forward to the reporters and news photographers waiting for her in front of the house. She stopped, smiled, waved, posed, and spoke to the ones she recognized.

"How is Rock Hudson?" asked an English reporter.

She shrugged and blinked slowly, as if her eyelids were suddenly weighty.

"Have you visited him?"

"Yes."

"Will he get better?" persisted the reporter.

"No," she replied. With her security man, her secretary, and her chauffeur in attendance, she moved on into her Rolls-Royce and raced across London for the picture session.

If she understands the duties of a star, she also expects the perks of a star, as she demonstrated at the end of the session.

"I want the red dress," she said to the woman who had arranged the sitting. As she spoke she adjusted her makeup in the mirror, moving her little finger back and forth over her lipstick.

"The Emanuel?"

"No," she said, "I already have that."

"The Yves Saint Laurent?"

"Yes."

"I don't really have the authority," the magazine's representative said.

"Ask," she said with the perfect certainty that the dress would be hers. (It was.)

Her permanent home these days is Los Angeles, where she grew up as a child star at MGM and where she returned in 1982 to reestablish her roots. Her house, which is hidden from view, set behind gates equipped with closed-circuit television to screen callers, once belonged to Nancy Sinatra, Sr. Taylor bought it for $2 million after separating from her sixth husband, United States Senator John Warner. From her terrace one looks out over the hills of Bel Air onto Los Angeles below. The house is both sprawling and simple, elegant and comfortable. A living room opens into a game room, which opens into a dining room. The first floor is monochromatically decorated in off-white; all the color comes from her art collection and a profusion of enormous orchid plants in full purple bloom.

On a lacquered table in the game room are silver-framed photographs of her: being greeted by the queen of England, talking with President Gerald Ford, laughing with Marshal Tito, being welcomed at the Iranian Embassy in Washington by her onetime suitor Ambassador Ardeshir Zahedi, posing festively at Ascot with Richard Burton and Noel Coward in gray top hats. There is an inscribed photograph from Princess Grace and Prince Rainier of Monaco, another from David Niven. Her two Oscars, for *Butterfield 8* and *Who's Afraid of*

Virginia Woolf?, are prominently displayed in the center of book-shelves crammed with other, lesser awards.

While I waited for her in the living room, Liz Thorburn, who runs her house, brought tea and placed a fresh pack of Salems, opened, with several cigarettes pushed forward for easy access, in front of the place on the sofa where Elizabeth would sit. Next to it she placed a lighter. A Cordon Bleu chef, the Scottish Miss Thorburn, young and attractive, formerly worked at Kensington Palace for Princess Margaret. "I've gone from a princess to a queen," she observed with a twinkle in her eye. In contrast to the glamorous chaos of the old life-style I associated with Elizabeth Taylor—trunks being packed and un-packed constantly—this was the well-run, very organized household of a woman settled in her own surroundings with her own things.

No one who knows Elizabeth Taylor ever calls her Liz. Used to homage, she did not remember to thank me, when she arrived, for a $100 bouquet of flowers in her favorite color, lavender, which I had sent her, and which was nowhere in sight. She was dressed in pink silk lounging pajamas and flat-heeled shoes instead of the spikes she habit-ually wears. It is always surprising to realize how small this majestic woman actually is. Her only jewelry was the thirty-three-carat Krupp diamond that Richard Burton gave her, which she wears day and night, dressed up or dressed down. Her face was deeply tanned, but her beautiful skin seemed to bear no ill effects from the California sun. Her figure nearly retained the slimness she had achieved last year, when she lost forty-five pounds in two months on a diet program of her own devising. "I read in the paper that someone had a fat picture of me on her refrigerator door to keep her from eating, and I said to myself, well, if it helps her, it ought to help me. You should see the aw-ful picture I have of myself on the icebox door. I don't crave booze at all," she added, "but I do crave sweet things."

Her reverence for Richard Burton, who died last year, is absolute, and private, and she was emphatic in stating that she did not wish to share her thoughts and feelings about him. Her stare is unflinching when she makes such a point. In an interview, even a friendly one, she is on her guard. "I've been burned so many times," she warned me. She said she had never read Kitty Kelley's book, *Elizabeth Taylor: The Last Star*. "I've been told I should sue, but it would mean reading the book, and I just can't stomach it." If there were long moments of silence, she did nothing to fill them in. At other times, on certain subjects, she said, "This is off the record," or motioned for the tape recorder to be turned off, with the expertise of someone who had been through the procedure a thousand times before. Several times she pulled out a handbag from behind some pillows and brushed on pink lipstick as a way of changing the subject. When I asked her about her short-term, highly publicized engagement last year to Frank Sinatra's crony Dennis Stein, she said into her mirror, "Let's just say I almost made a mistake," and then added, "but I didn't."

Settled among the the soft cushions of her deep sofa, she lit a cigarette. "My only vice," she explained, inhaling deeply. On the wall behind her were a Modigliani, a Renoir, a van Gogh, a Rouault, a Degas, and a Monet. Elsewhere in the room Utrillos, Vlamincks, and other treasures hung. Her late father, Francis Taylor, ran an art gallery in London and Beverly Hills when Elizabeth was a child, and her knowledge of art was formed early. There are other evidences of wealth. She owns two racehorses, and the racing colors she chose, cerise and chartreuse, are the colors she wore in *National Velvet*. In the driveway outside was her new car, an Aston Martin Lagonda, for which she had paid $153,000, on the spot, one day when she went shopping for a Rolls. "It's all money I've earned," she said. "I've never asked for alimony in my life."

Chief among her accomplishments over the last several years was her seven-week stay at the Betty Ford Center near Palm Springs. Her admiration for Betty Ford is boundless. "My God, what she's done for women alcoholics is just phenomenal! She's lifted the stigma." She went to the center through family intervention. She was at Saint John's Hospital in Santa Monica when her brother and his wife, her sons, and one of her daughters arrived to tell her that she could go to the Betty Ford Center by choice or she would eventually end up killing herself. She admits to being riddled with guilt and shame, but the decision to go was her own.

Like most people who have conquered an addiction, she talked openly and freely about it, without embarrassment, aware that the example she had set was a help to other people.

"I'd been taking sleeping pills every night for thirty-five years. I was hooked on Percodan. I had reached a point where I would take one or two Percodan mixed with booze before I could go out in the evening and face people. I think you know how horribly shy I really am. I thought it would help me, because that combination would make me kind of talkative. I felt I was being charming. I was probably boring as hell, but it gave me false courage.

"During the course of an evening, like every four hours, I'd take another two Percodan. And, of course, I had a hollow leg. I could drink anybody under the table and never get drunk. My capacity to consume was terrifying. I didn't even realize that I was an alcoholic until I'd been at the center for a couple of weeks. Just because I wouldn't get drunk doesn't mean it wasn't poison for me."

"How soon after you went to the Betty Ford Center did the press pick up that you were there?" I asked.

"I'd been there over a week, but I have an uncanny sense about the press. I had a feeling in my gut that it was going to leak out, so I talked to Betty Ford about it, and she agreed that I should announce it and get it in print, because otherwise the press would make up a story about me being in a straitjacket, or carried down, or God knows what. I was right. They were onto it, but I beat them by a few hours."

"What was your first encounter with the other people there like? You must have caused a sensation."

"They'd never had a celebrity before. They told me later, the counselors, they didn't know what to do with me, whether they should treat me like an ordinary patient or whether they should give me some sort of special isolated treatment. They decided to lump me in with everyone else, which of course was the only way to do it, and it's the way they treat celebrities now. It doesn't matter who you are. We get all kinds down there: street junkies, preachers, priests, doctors, psychiatrists, and society ladies—you name it."

"Was it hard for you to talk in front of those people?"

"In the beginning, yes. I felt like I was giving interviews. I talked about my childhood and my past in a very couched way, giving the version I would give to the press and keeping the true version to myself. And then I broke all those barriers down and told the truth. Like an onion, I was peeled down to the absolute core."

"Did you have a roommate?" I asked.

"Yes," she replied, then thought about it for a moment and added with a smile, "It was the first time in my life I'd ever shared a room with a woman."

Relaxed now, she sank deeper into the cushions and lit another cigarette. Her Pekingese, complete with lavender bow, passed through the room. Her Burmese cat walked across the top of the sofa, down her arm, and settled comfortably in her lap. "Don't you love the way cats come in and insinuate themselves on you?" she said. "Who do you think you are?" she said to the cat. For a while we sat without talking.

"There's a nice feeling in this house," I said.

"I love this house," she replied.

"What's that room up there?" I asked, pointing across the patio to a second-story aerie surrounded by treetops.

"That's my bedroom, and no one gets in there without an engraved invitation."

"Hmmm."

"I suppose you want to see it?"

"Sure."

"I'll show it to you, but don't write about it."

"Elizabeth," I said to her, "this is really the first extended period in your life when you are, uh, uh . . ."

"Single?" she asked, finishing the sentence for me.

"Yes."

"It is. I think maybe finally I'm growing up, and about time. Being alone doesn't frighten me. And it's not like I'm alone." Elsewhere in the house the sounds of visiting grandchildren could be heard, and she made a movement of her head in that direction and said with a smile, "Because I'm not."

Her attention shifted back to the cat staring up at her, and she continued talking in measured sentences as she returned the stare. "I'm dating several men, but I'm in no rush to get married. I've broken two engagements. I'm being very cautious. I'm sure I will remarry once more, but"—holding up her index finger and shaking it—"*only* once more, and, boy, it's going to be right. I'm taking no chances."

She has had seven marriages and six husbands, four of whom are dead: hotel heir Nicky Hilton, actor Michael Wilding, showman Mike

Todd, and superstar Richard Burton. Her other husbands were singer
Eddie Fisher and Senator John Warner of Virginia. She has four chil-
dren and five grandchildren. By Michael Wilding she had two sons:
Michael, an actor, who is married to Brooke Palance (daughter of
Jack), with two children by his previous marriage; and Christopher, an
artist, married to Aileen Getty, the daughter of Paul Getty, Jr., by
whom he has two children. Her daughter Liza, a sculptress, married to
Hap Tivey, was born shortly before her father, Mike Todd, died in a
plane crash. Her other daughter, German-born Maria, was adopted by
Elizabeth and Richard Burton; she is married to agent Steve Carson
and has one daughter.

An extremely handsome young child entered the room and interrupted our conversation.

"Elizabeth, can I go . . ."

"I'm busy now, love," she replied.

"But, Elizabeth," he insisted, "I want to . . ."

She gave him her full attention. "Can't you see I'm talking to Mr.
Dunne? Say hello to Mr. Dunne. This is Balthazar Getty," she said to me.

Balthazar strode purposefully across the room and held out his
hand. "How do you do?" he said in a manner to make a parent proud.

"Hello, Balthazar," I replied.

"Now outside, until I finish," she said, smiling. "Stay by the pool,
where I can see you."

"O.K., Elizabeth," said the child, opening and then pulling together the sliding doors to the patio. Balthazar, she explained, is the
nephew of her daughter-in-law Aileen Getty Wilding. He is the son of
Aileen's brother Paul Getty III, who gained international fame when
his ear was cut off by kidnappers in Italy, and who subsequently became physically incapacitated after he suffered a stroke. Aileen and
Christopher and their two babies were staying with Elizabeth until
their new house in Bel Air was ready.

For a moment it was almost possible to believe her claim that she is
semiretired from the film business, devoting herself to family life,
horse racing, and good works. But anyone who knows anything about
the film business knows that semiretired means simply until the next
good script comes along.

———

Elizabeth Taylor is the national chairman of AFAR, the American Foundation for AIDS Research. On October 2, 1985, Rock Hudson, her great friend and costar in *Giant*, died of AIDS. Two weeks earlier, on September 19, Elizabeth, dressed in black lace and emeralds, entered the main ballroom of the Bonaventure Hotel in downtown Los Angeles, and three thousand of her peers rose and cheered her with a wild ovation. By lending her name and considerable support to APLA, AIDS Project Los Angeles, for the benefit entitled "Commitment to Life," she had helped raise over a million dollars in a single evening, and the huge turnout of stars that night attracted international publicity for the plight of AIDS victims.

Amid the pandemonium, she remained socially graceful, finding the right thing to say to each person she greeted, from Whoopi Goldberg to Cyndi Lauper to Burt Reynolds to Shirley MacLaine to Gregory Peck, talking intimately and laughing as if a hundred flashbulbs were not exploding in her face and security men were not holding back the crush of people who wanted to get nearer to her. "I don't want to talk to her, I just want to *look* at her!" one beautifully dressed woman pleaded with a guard.

"I'm stunned," said a young, female studio executive sitting next to me at Elizabeth's table. "I've never seen anything like this. I've been with Barbra and Jane in public, but it's nothing like this."

After four decades of making headlines with her marriages, her divorces, her tragedies, and her near-fatal illnesses, she has passed from super-stardom into legend. "That comes with aging," she told me modestly. The public has seen her at the top, in the middle, and, supposedly, washed up. But Elizabeth Taylor will never be washed up. She is Ol' Man River. She just keeps on rollin' along.

Elizabeth Taylor is still rollin' along, against all odds. I lived out a chapter of my life with her when we made the ill-starred Ash Wednesday film in Cortina in 1973, and I've stayed in touch with her ever since, never ceasing to be amazed by this amazing woman. Her loyalty to her friends is extraordinary. Plagued by ill health, she remains an American presence, beloved by the public like the national treasure she is.

GLORIA'S EUPHORIA

At the window table in Mortimer's on New York's Upper East Side, Jerry Zipkin, Nancy Reagan's close friend, was celebrating his seventieth birthday with a group of social figures that included Nan Kempner, Chessy Rayner, Mica and Ahmet Ertegun, and Carolina and Reinaldo Herrera, all of whom were passing elaborately wrapped gifts to him. Mica Ertegun's present, which Zipkin opened and held up, was a nineteenth-century painting of a boar, with the name Zip on a small brass plate attached to the frame, and the joke was greeted with hoots and screams from the assembled company.

At a nearby table, faced away from the merriment, sat Gloria Vanderbilt, alone, waiting for her luncheon companion. And at the bar, all the people waiting for tables were staring at her, not at the riotous party behind her.

"She looks wonderful," said a lady in a feathered hat.

"Marvelous," her friend replied.

They spoke with that proprietary tone New Yorkers reserve for a cherished celebrity—a survivor as well, in this case, against all odds of being one—who continues to cast a magic spell.

"No one told me you were here!" she cried, greeting me at the door of her red library. "Have you been waiting long?" She was contrite. She always rises before six, and at that hour, shortly after nine, she had been about the business of her life for several hours.

Gloria Laura Madelaine Vanderbilt diCicco Stokowski Lumet Cooper is, like the queen of England and Elizabeth Taylor, a lifetime celebrity, famous from childhood. She was wearing brown cashmere, and she settled elegantly into the corner of a chintz sofa. The great-great-granddaughter of Commodore Cornelius Vanderbilt, who founded the family railroad and shipping fortune, lives in a penthouse on Gracie Square with her two teenage sons by her last husband, writer Wyatt Cooper, who died in 1978. Outside, beyond the terrace, tugboats lumbered by under the Triborough Bridge on the sun-dappled East River—that magical view you see so often in movies about rich people in Manhattan.

She speaks in a breathless, whispery, society-girl voice, and there is a trace of a stammer, under control and attractive. Her much photographed flour-white face, so prominent at theatrical and social parties in New York, was scrubbed and clear. Her hair, no longer black and severe, is now chestnut-colored, and it moved freely as she talked and gestured. She looked healthy and fresh and much younger than her well-documented age of sixty-one.

That evening a gossip column had announced that she might be on the verge of marrying again, and she giggled luxuriously over the item, her dimples deepening, her eyes sparkling, at the same time dismissing and enjoying it. She was, even in the morning, decidedly glamorous. She held a gold cigarette case with a sapphire clasp that she had bought at an auction. Inside, engraved, were the words "To Gertie from Noel" and the notes to the opening phrase of "Some Day I'll Find You."

"Isn't it divine?" she asked. She had bought it specially for her great friend Bill Blass, the dress designer, and had intended to leave it to him in her will, but Blass, a constant smoker, had recently lost his own cigarette case, which had been left to him by the late Billy Baldwin, the interior designer, so she had decided to give it to him when they met for lunch later that day, rather than leave it to him after she was dead.

Behind her on a red lacquered wall was a photograph of a painting of Vanderbilt ancestors, the original of which hangs at Biltmore, the massive French château in Asheville, North Carolina, built by her great-uncle George Vanderbilt. She said she had spotted the painting in the background of a scene in the film *Being There*, which was shot in that house, and had had it reproduced. Beneath the photograph was an etching depicting all the great Vanderbilt mansions, both town and country, erected in the early years of the century, when the Vanderbilt family was busily establishing itself as the grandest in the land.

Her large apartment on two floors has the feeling of a country house in the city. Her library and bedrooms are memorabilia-filled with heirlooms, oil portraits, and family photographs in silver frames everywhere. There is a sense of roots and permanence and of ancestors having lived in these rooms before her, but it is a performance created by Vanderbilt herself. The poor little rich girl of the thirties, who was the central figure in the most sensational child custody case in the history of the United States, never had a room of her own until she was fifteen years old. Left fatherless before she was two, on the death of the alcoholic Reginald Vanderbilt, she was shunted from hotel to hotel, from rented house to rented house, from continent to continent, by her beautiful, thoughtless, pleasure-bent, widowed young mother, Gloria Morgan Vanderbilt. When, finally, she secured a degree of permanence of location, in her aunt Gertrude Vanderbilt Whitney's vast country house, Wheatley Hills, in Old Westbury, Long Island, her assigned room, next to her aunt's, was the former room of her late uncle, the sportsman Harry Payne Whitney, which had been left intact since his death. Nothing was changed to accommodate a girl of ten, and for five years she lived with her uncle's horse prints and brown carpets, his curtains and chairs.

The dining room of Gloria Vanderbilt's apartment is dominated by a full-length portrait of her mother, painted in Paris when she was a child bride of the already dying Reginald Vanderbilt. Another painting of her mother occupies a wall of the guest room. There are photographs of her mother taken by Dorothy Wilding, the society photographer of an earlier time, and a drawing by Cecil Beaton of her mother with her equally beautiful twin sister, Thelma, Lady Furness, once the mistress of the Prince of Wales. There is, throughout the apartment, a sense of *hommage* to the woman the courts found unfit to be her mother.

She said, confidentially, about women like her mother, "You know, the kind of social strata they were in—they really in a sense were not meant to be mothers, because their instincts were not in that direction." She quotes her late husband Wyatt Cooper on her mother, when he first met her, in the final years of her life, living quietly with her twin sister in a small bungalow in Beverly Hills crammed with furniture that had once graced larger rooms: "This woman does not understand one thing that ever happened to her."

Five years ago Barbara Goldsmith wrote a highly successful book based on the *Matter of Vanderbilt*, as the custody case was legally called, entitled *Little Gloria . . . Happy at Last*. Alden Whitman, writing in the *Philadelphia Inquirer*, called it "a Proustian picture of the American upper class and the international society of which it was a part." It was a Book-of-the-Month Club main selection and for four months remained on the *New York Times* best-seller list. It was a well-known fact in New York at the time that the book greatly distressed Vanderbilt. She had refused to be interviewed by Goldsmith. "She called me, which fascinated me, and said 'I'm ready to interview you.' I said, 'From one professional writer to another, why should I give you material? Someday I'm going to write my own book.' " She claims never to have read Goldsmith's book, saying, "I have rarely read anything about myself." She implored her friends not to read it, declined an invitation to one of hostess Alice Mason's dinners when she found out Goldsmith would be present, and even stopped speaking to one of her friends, Maureen Stapleton, for playing the role of Dodo, her beloved nanny, in the four-hour television miniseries based on Goldsmith's book. The story, Vanderbilt felt, was hers to tell, and the time would come when she would be ready to tell it.

Now, five years later, she had told it, in a searing personal memoir entitled *Once Upon a Time*, subtitled, "A True Story." It is the account of the celebrated, lonely child who figured at the center of the custody trial rather than the story of the trial itself. In it she records the events of her extraordinary childhood, as she remembers them, in the language of the age she was at the time of the events—a series of long-suppressed memories finally come to life. "This is the way I have chosen to tell it," she said, "because this is the way I experienced it." It is an interesting twist that the book has been brought out by the same publishing house, Knopf, that issued Goldsmith's book, and that the same editor, Bob Gottlieb, has worked on both and managed to retain the good graces of both authors.

Even the genesis of writing the book has elements of the phantasmal quality of Vanderbilt's life. A discarded baby picture of Gloria Vanderbilt and a cousin, Emily Vanderbilt, taken in Central Park nearly sixty years ago, was saved by the maid of a relative and sent to Vanderbilt. And that picture inspired her book.

"Fate is so extraordinary," she said. "I looked at that picture of the baby in the carriage and I thought, 'I know this person. Me. I'm going to sit down and write about her.' And I did. I started writing just before the New Year, just after Christmas, and I couldn't stop writing. It was like being obsessed with it. And I wrote, and I wrote, and I wrote, and I finished it by April." Some days she wrote without stop for eight hours.

Throughout the book there is the sense of longing of the child for her mother. "Sometimes our hands touched," writes Vanderbilt. "But then she would go away, down the long corridors of hotels, down staircases, along avenues in her pale furs, snow-sprinkled, disappearing into the velvet caverns of waiting cars and borne away, away, away, away. . . . Would I ever see her again?"

Vanderbilt's Grandmother Morgan, her mother's mother, a curious, strong-willed woman who disapproved of her daughter's flagrant lifestyle, and Vanderbilt's nanny, Dodo, were the people most important to her in her early life. "No father anywhere reachable, and Mother who was always coming in and then going out—mostly going out," she writes. When her father died in Newport before her second birthday, her mother, who was only nineteen years old, was at the theater in New York City. That night the little girl was taken to the Breakers, her paternal grandmother Alice Gwynne Vanderbilt's Newport mansion.

Early on in life the susceptible child was manipulated to be frightened of her mother, principally by her nanny and her maternal grandmother, Laura Morgan, who feared that the young widow, who was in love with Prince Friedel Hohenlohe, nephew of Queen Marie of Romania, would take the child to live in Germany. The grandmother persuaded the immensely rich and powerful sculptress Gertrude Vanderbilt Whitney, sister of Reginald and founder of the Whitney Museum of American Art, to go to court and fight with her sister-in-law over Gloria's custody. "You must show your Aunt Gertrude how much you love her," Vanderbilt quotes her grandmother as telling her. "You must hug her more and kiss her a lot."

She described arriving at the courthouse, at the age of ten, in the backseat of her aunt's gray Rolls-Royce limousine as hundreds of spectators peered in the windows and jostled the car, and then her passage up the steps as photographers took her picture and a crowd surged around her.

"Was there any thrill to that?"

"What a question! Are you mad? It was terrifying," she answered. "They were screaming, 'You treat your ma good, Little Gloria! Stick to your ma! You be nice to your ma!'"

On one occasion during the trial, when the judge allowed her mother to visit her at her aunt's house in Old Westbury, she locked herself in her room and hid the key in the bottom of a powder box so as not to have to see her. She believed mistakenly that if she were put in the custody of her Aunt Gertrude, she would have Dodo with her forever, and Dodo was the only person in the world with whom she did not feel she was an impostor. The irony of the case is that in awarding the custody of Little Gloria to her aunt instead of her mother the judge imposed as a condition of the verdict that the nanny be discharged. Gloria was not allowed to maintain any contact with her. To further the isolation caused by the verdict, Vanderbilt writes, her favorite Whitney cousin, Gerta Henry, who also lived on the estate in Old Westbury, was told by her father that she could no longer play with or be friends with Gloria, because Gloria was a bad influence, who would grow up to be exactly like her mother.

"All those people took this child and made mashed potatoes out of her, and when it was all over, everyone was back on square one," observed Vanderbilt a half-century later about the proceedings. Her mother was allowed to see her on weekends for one month during the summer, but their meetings were strained, and most of their time together they spent going to movies. The rest of the time Vanderbilt lived in Old Westbury at her aunt's house, but once the trial was over, contact with Gertrude Whitney was minimal. "There was the time we looked at a magazine together," she remembered. "Oh, I think she loved me, but I think the tragedy of her was that she couldn't express her love."

Expressions of love were equally difficult between her and her mother in the years following the trial. In her book she writes about a

July visit to her mother in Los Angeles during her early teenage years. At one point they are in the backseat of a limousine, driving up the coast of California to spend a weekend at San Simeon, the castle of William Randolph Hearst and Marion Davies. "Long before we reached Santa Barbara," Vanderbilt writes, "my mother ran out of conversation, and when she ran out of conversation, I ran out of conversation too."

Looking out the windows to the East River, Vanderbilt explained that they went through their lives without ever once discussing the trial together, although it was the thing that had changed them all. Then she corrected herself. "Thelma did say one thing to me, actually, now that I come to think of it." Thelma, which she pronounces Telma, was her mother's twin. "She said, 'Probably Mrs. Whitney believed all those things Mama said about your mother.' Thank God my mother had Thelma, because they really were like a mirror image of each other, and not only that, but so supportive of each other. It was as if my mother and Thelma were married. When you think of it, imagine, from birth, being in a room with someone who looks exactly like you and is just there as an extension of yourself. I almost never saw my mother really alone. Thelma was always there, and I realized later that my mother was as frightened of me as I was of her. Did I tell you how Thelma died? She dropped dead on Seventy-third and Lexington on her way to see the doctor. In her bag was this miniature teddy bear that the Prince of Wales had given her, years and years before, when she came to be with my mother at the custody trial, and it was worn down to the nub."

She has, in adulthood, made her peace with her Vanderbilt and Whitney relations, from whom she felt so alienated while she was growing up. The word *impostor* keeps coming into her conversation; she felt as a child that she was in their midst under false pretenses and would be found out and banished. "I couldn't wait to grow up," she said. The past Thanksgiving, she and her sons spent the day with eighty Whitney relations in Westbury.

"The estate is all chopped up now," she said. "It's amazing what happened to it. My cousin Pam lives in Aunt Gertrude's studio now. The house where I lived, my aunt's house, is where Flora Miller lives, who is Pam's mother. And Sonny Whitney's house and the indoor pool and the stables are a country club now. Sonny sold the estate right from under them, and they don't speak now because of that. I mean, the golf club comes right up to my cousin Flora's front lawn. From her bedroom, which was my aunt's room, she looks out and there are people in Bermuda shorts walking around."

Vanderbilt shook her head and twisted one of the three signet rings she was wearing on her fingers. "You know," she said, remembering back to the old days in Westbury, "it seemed as if it would last forever. It seemed to just happen. Effortlessly. You never saw people with vacuums or anything, and flowers would be changed overnight by unseen hands. It was just . . . perfect."

About the Vanderbilt side of the family, she said, "I'm very friendly now with all of them. In fact, every summer we go to Newport and stay at the Breakers. I hadn't been back to the Breakers since I was a child, and of course now it's a museum, with hordes of people going through. My cousin Sylvie, Countess Szapary, the daughter of my Aunt Gladys, who was my father's other sister, lives on the top floor, and I always stay in what was my father's room. It's sort of fascinating. Everything is exactly the way it was, except the tubs, those incredible bathtubs. Nothing comes out of the tap for hot salt water piped in from the sea anymore."

Once Upon a Time ends when Vanderbilt is seventeen, racing down the beach away from a Fourth of July party in Malibu, six months before the first of her four marriages to such wildly different types as actors' agent Pat di Cicco, conductor Leopold Stokowski, film director Sidney Lumet, and writer Wyatt Cooper. She was reluctant to talk about her first three marriages or her unsuccessful reunion with her nanny, Dodo, whom she hired as a nurse for the two sons of her second marriage, to Stokowski, for these are things she will be dealing with in the remaining five, or possibly six, volumes of her memoirs. The second volume, almost finished, takes her from age seventeen to twenty-one, and the third from twenty-one to twenty-nine. "I intend to live a very long life. My Grandmother Vanderbilt lived to ninety-five, and my Grandmother Morgan to a hundred and five. Of course, she lied about her age, but we knew. People say to me that I have total recall, but everything is a relative thing. I'm also a natural-born writer. It's how you perceive it, how you invent it, how you choose to tell it."

On several occasions the late Truman Capote wrote about her. In *Breakfast at Tiffany's*, her stutter, "genuine but still a bit laid on," was supposedly the inspiration for the model Mag Wildwood, Holly Golightly's best friend. In "La Côte Basque, 1965," the most celebrated chapter of Capote's never completed novel, *Answered Prayers,* published in *Esquire* in 1975, Vanderbilt appeared as herself, together with her chum Carol Marcus Saroyan Saroyan Matthau. In the story, Vanderbilt fails to recognize her first husband, Pat di Cicco, when he stops by her table to chat.

Her close friendships with women, especially Carol Matthau and Oona Chaplin, tend to be lasting. At one time all three married much older men. Carol Matthau married writer William Saroyan twice. Oona Chaplin, daughter of playwright Eugene O'Neill, married Charlie Chaplin. And Vanderbilt wed Leopold Stokowski, who was forty years her senior. For the last few years the two women closest to her have been New York socialites Judy Peabody and Isabel Eberstadt. Like Vanderbilt, they are artistically inclined. Judy Peabody is chairman of the board of directors of the Dance Theatre of Harlem, and Isabel Eberstadt is a novelist. "I really trust women," said Vanderbilt. "And I believe they trust me."

She has been at various times in her life an actress, a painter, a collagist, a playwright, and a poet, each time baring herself to public criticism. In the late fifties she costarred with Ginger Rogers in an all-star television special of Noel Coward's *Tonight at 8:30*, acted opposite television star Gardner McKay in an episode of "Adventures in Paradise," and toured in Molnar's play *The Swan.* Her paintings have been exhibited, and a book of her collages has been published. She has written two plays, which are both under option but which have not been produced. In recent years Vanderbilt has achieved spectacular financial success, earning more money than she inherited, by signing a licensing agreement with Murjani International, which put her name on its line of jeans at the peak of the designer-jeans craze. The label reportedly took in $500 million a year, and Vanderbilt's face, in Murjani television commercials, became familiar to a whole new generation of Americans. She is also a designer of home furnishings, luggage, and handbags, all of which bear her name. Currently she is producing a perfume called Vanderbilt, which her business manager, Tom An-

drews, claims is "far and away the biggest seller in American per-
fume." She has recently made her entry into the food area with Gloria
Vanderbilt tofu glacé, a frozen dessert manufactured by the Dolly
Madison company, and the Danbury Mint has just introduced the
Gloria Vanderbilt bride doll, the first designer doll in its series. When
I asked her which was better, inherited or earned wealth, she did not
hesitate to reply, "Oh, darling, the money you make is better."

Copies of Wyatt Cooper's book, *Families: A Memoir and a Celebration,* are everywhere in her apartment. "Wyatt was the most extraordinary father," said Vanderbilt. "From the beginning, he treated our
children as persons. It was everything I never had growing up." Everything she did not have as a child, in the way of love and family and
emotional security, her sons by Cooper have had, and the affection
that exists between mother and sons is evident. Carter is a sophomore
at Princeton, and Anderson will graduate from the Dalton School in
June. Last summer Anderson worked as a waiter at Mortimer's. "Of
anything I have achieved in my life, really, to be the parent that I feel
I am is for me the greatest thing that I could ever possibly achieve,"
she said.

When I asked her if she would ever remarry, she answered, "I tell
you, it's seven years now since Wyatt has gone. It's only now that I'm
really not numb. My boys are getting older. They're going to be really
gone soon. And I would like to live with somebody. Now we don't
have those pressures of getting married. But I'm not going to settle for
anybody. I'm very, very fussy. Listen, in a strange way my book has become another person. I want to finish the other books, and all my direction is going toward that. But, of course, one wants to share things
with one person."

It was time to go to lunch and give Bill Blass the cigarette case Noel
Coward had once given Gertrude Lawrence. After that she had a
meeting at Knopf to go over the final placement of the photographs in
her book. The poor little rich girl of the thirties is very much in control
of her life in the eighties. As she stood looking down on Gracie
Square, a thought occurred to her, something Wannsie, her mother's
maid for forty years, once said to her about the trial: "It was all a terrible misunderstanding."

Since this article was written, Gloria Vanderbilt has undergone one of life's greatest tragedies in the death of her son, Carter Cooper. She has also suffered severe financial distress brought about by unscrupulous people who managed her affairs and took advantage of her. She has long moved from Gracie Square and lives in elegant simplicity in far smaller quarters. But in no way has life defeated her. Her spirits have never flagged. She is at present preparing an exhibition of her new artworks.

FATAL CHARM: THE SOCIAL WEB
OF CLAUS VON BÜLOW

"The problem with Claus," said one of Claus von Bülow's closest friends at a Park Avenue dinner party, "is that he does not dwell in the Palace of Truth. You see, he's a fake. He's always been a fake. His name is a fake. His life is a fake. He has created a character that he plays. Claus is trompe l'oeil."

"Come in, come in," said von Bülow expansively as he opened the front door to Helmut Newton, the photographer, who had just arrived from Monte Carlo for the session, and me. Von Bülow was standing in the marble-floored, green-walled, gilt-mirrored hallway of the Fifth Avenue apartment of his multimillionairess wife, whom he was accused of twice trying to kill. In the background a very old Chinese butler hovered, watching the master of the house usurp his duties. On that May Sunday of the seventh week of his second trial, the Danish society figure was dressed in tight blue jeans and a black leather jacket.

"This is the first time I've actually posed for a picture since my front and side shots," said von Bülow in his deep, resonant, English-school, international-set voice.

From the beginning, the von Bülow proceedings, legal and otherwise, had had an air of unreality about them. His once beautiful wife was one of the country's richest heiresses. His stepchildren were a prince and princess. His daughter was a disinherited teenager. His former mistress was a socialite actress. His current lady friend was a thrice-married Hungarian adventuress who was not the countess she was often described as being. The maid who testified against him had once worked for the Krupps. And lurking darkly in the background was a publicity-mad con man bent on destroying him.

The apartment of Sunny von Bülow, even by Fifth Avenue standards, is very grand. Located in one of the most exclusive buildings in New York, its current market value is estimated by one of the city's top Realtors at nearly $8 million. Although a sophisticated friend of von Bülow's complained that the forty-foot drawing room has "far, far too many legs," it should be pointed out that the legs are by Chippendale and of museum quality, as is nearly every object in the fourteen-room apartment looking down on Central Park.

According to the terms of Sunny von Bülow's will, the apartment will go to von Bülow when she dies. So will Clarendon Court, the fabulous mansion set on ten acres overlooking the sea in Newport, Rhode Island, where her two comas took place during successive Christmas holidays, in 1979 and 1980. So will $14 million of her $75 million fortune. In the meantime the maintenance on the apartment is paid for by Sunny's estate, so in effect von Bülow and his self-proclaimed mistress, Andrea Reynolds, have been largely supported by his comatose wife since his conviction in 1982 for her attempted murder. That verdict was overturned on appeal because certain materials had been withheld from the defense and others had been improperly admitted as evidence.

"How is my old friend Bobby Moltke?" von Bülow asked Newton as he was setting up his photographic equipment. Then he added, "Not well, I hear." Newton resides in Monte Carlo, where Count Moltke lives part of the year, and the inquiry was distinctly perverse. Count Moltke is the father of Alexandra Isles, von Bülow's former mistress, for whom, in the opinion of many, he sought to be rid of his wife. That day her name was prominent in the newspapers because another former lover of hers, the theater critic John Simon, had given an interview to the *New York Post* saying that he was in almost daily contact with the missing actress and that she had no intention of returning to testify at the second trial. Furthermore, Count Moltke, a Danish aristocrat, is known to loathe his fellow countryman for having involved the count's daughter in a scandal that has haunted her for years.

When I admired the carpet in the drawing room, von Bülow said, "I believe in building a room from the rug up. Did you ever know Billy Wallace in England? His father ordered this rug from Portugal before the war, and by the time it arrived the war had started, and it was put in storage and never used. I bought it from the family after the war." As usual, his attitude and conversation totally belied the fact that he was at that very moment a candidate for a long sojourn in one of Rhode Island's adult correctional institutions.

While von Bülow posed for Newton in front of a portrait of himself painted in Paris when he was twenty-one, Mrs. Reynolds, dressed in a white satin, lace-trimmed negligee, her eyes rimmed with black eyeliner, appeared and led me back to Sunny von Bülow's bedroom. On the bed Mrs. Reynolds had laid out evening dresses and a black leather outfit that matched von Bülow's for the shoot. One of the many stories about Andrea Reynolds that circulated at the trial in Providence and in the Upper East Side dining rooms of New York was that she wore Mrs. von Bülow's clothes and jewels, and that she had the clothes altered by a seamstress from the Yves Saint Laurent boutique on Madison Avenue.

"Not true!" Mrs. Reynolds had exclaimed when I mentioned these allegations a few days earlier. "I have far better jewels than Sunny von Bülow ever had. I've had fantastic jewels all my life. I wasn't even twenty when I had one of the biggest diamonds around. Be careful what you say about my jewels; I don't want to be robbed again."

She suffered a million-dollar jewel heist at her villa in Saint-Tropez in the late sixties, and was quoted then by the French columnist Jacques Chazot as saying, "They were only my *bijoux de plage*." Another robbery occurred in her New York hotel suite while she was at the movies seeing *Deep Throat*, and once a pair of $80,000 earrings disappeared from a dressing room at Dior in Paris after she removed them to try on fur turbans. She suspects that they were lifted by an American-born duchess of historical importance who used the dressing room after her. She opened several velvet boxes on the bed, revealing a treasure trove of emeralds, diamonds, and pearls. "Mummy sent me these," she said.

During the final days of the first trial, Andrea Reynolds and her third husband, television producer Sheldon Reynolds, wrote a letter to von Bülow telling him they believed he was innocent. Lonely and isolated, von Bülow responded. They met in New York the day after his return there from Newport following the guilty verdict, and a warm friendship quickly developed. He spent weekends at the couple's country house in Livingston Manor, New York, and they stayed frequently at the von Bülow apartment. They made plans to have Reynolds be the agent for von Bülow's proposed autobiography and the miniseries based on it. (Von Bülow believes Robert Duvall should play him if a film or miniseries *is* ever made.) These plans fell apart when Reynolds, on a business trip in London, read in a gossip column that his wife and von Bülow were having an affair. A divorce is in progress. Mrs. Reynolds claims she was a neglected wife: "We were both unhappy when we met, Claus and I."

"Look," said one of von Bülow's swellest friends, who doesn't see him anymore, "six years ago, before all this happened, Claus wouldn't have had time for Andrea Reynolds." Although she claims to have known von Bülow for years, they did not travel in the same echelons of high society. She has a history of taking up with men who are at their low ebb and reviving them. A man just convicted of twice attempting to murder his wife would not seem like much of a catch to most women, but to Andrea Reynolds, Claus von Bülow, sentenced to thirty years pending appeal, was the ticket to center stage that she had always craved.

They made one of their first public appearances together in New York at a party given by Lady Jeanne Campbell, a former wife of Norman Mailer and the daughter of the eleventh Duke of Argyll. It was a glittering gathering of social names, literary names, titles, and a few film stars, and when von Bülow and Mrs. Reynolds entered late, after the theater, all conversation stopped. The occasion established Claus von Bülow's tremendous social celebrity; after that the couple maintained a high profile in the upper register of New York. They attended the opera regularly, on the smart night, and were frequent guests at the parties of such well-chronicled hostesses as von Bülow's old friend Mercedes Kellogg, the wife of Ambassador Francis Kellogg, and his new friend and staunch supporter Alice Mason, the New York Realtor. They were also regulars at Mortimer's, the Upper East Side restaurant that caters to Manhattan's people-you-love-to-read-about.

Von Bülow inspires feelings that range from detestation to zealotry. At one of Alice Mason's parties, the editor of a magazine, appalled to be in the same room with a man found guilty of attempting to murder his wife, said she would leave if she were seated at the same table with him. Another woman at the party remarked, "He might look like the devil, but he's such a cozy old thing, and so amusing to sit next to at dinner. Have you seen him do his imitation of Queen Victoria?"

As a couple, they entertained frequently and elegantly at Sunny's Fifth Avenue apartment. "Very good food and lots of waiters," said man-about-town Johnny Galliher. One party was a *vernissage* for Andrea Reynolds's eyelift; the guest of honor was Dr. Daniel Baker, the plastic surgeon who had performed the operation. Their frantic pace continued right up to the second trial, and included an eighteenth-birthday party for Claus and Sunny's daughter, Cosima, at Mortimer's, attended by such *bon vivants* of New York as John Richardson, Kenny Lane, and Reinaldo and Carolina Herrera, but not by a single person of Cosima's age. "As long as they take Cosima with them when they go out, her trust pays the bill," said an informed source. They spent their last evening in New York before the second trial at a party given by Cornelia Guest, the city's most highly publicized post-debutante, whose mother, C. Z. Guest, the noted horsewoman, gardener, and socialite, was prepared to give testimony in von Bülow's behalf at the trial and corroborate the allegations of the late Truman Capote and others that Sunny von Bülow was a drug addict and a drunk.

For the first several weeks of the trial in Providence, my room at the Biltmore Plaza Hotel was on the same floor as the rooms von Bülow and Mrs. Reynolds shared. For several years I had seen the two of them around New York. Although we had never spoken, we had often been at the same parties or in the same restaurants. The first day in the courtroom, von Bülow recognized me but did not acknowledge me. The second day he nodded to me in the men's room. When we met in the corridor on the fourteenth floor of the hotel, he struck up a conversation about a portable word processor I was carrying. At that moment the door to their suite opened, and Andrea Reynolds came out into the hall.

She said to von Bülow, "I don't know Mr. Dunne's first name."

"Dominick," I said.

Von Bülow, leaning toward her, said slowly and deliberately, "And Mr. Dunne is not friendly toward us."

"I'm being friendly now," I said.

They invited me into their room, which had a sitting area at one end of it. An open closet was crammed with Mrs. Reynolds's clothes and at least twenty pairs of her shoes.

"We mustn't talk about the trial," said von Bülow.

For a while we talked about Cosima von Bülow, who had that day been accepted at Brown University and would soon graduate from Brooks School in Massachusetts. Von Bülow spoke proudly and affectionately of her.

"Cosima has the best qualities of both her parents," said Andrea Reynolds. "She has the beauty and serenity of Sunny, and the intelligence and strength of Claus." Von Bülow acknowledged to me later Mrs. Reynolds's importance in Cosima's life. "She had been the adult woman to whom Cosima would constantly turn with her little flirtations or whatever a young girl wants to talk about. . . . No new woman in my life could have survived a lack of affinity with Cosima."

"Senator Pell called this morning and wanted to have lunch with Claus in Providence," said Andrea Reynolds, "and you can print that." She was referring to Senator Claiborne Pell of Rhode Island. "He obviously doesn't think he's guilty." Von Bülow remarked with the self-deprecatory kind of humor that had become a trademark with him, that he had declined the invitation because he didn't want to spoil the senator's chances of winning a sixth term by being seen with him in public.

That night I happened to fly back to New York on the same plane that Senator and Mrs. Pell were on. I struck up a conversation with Mrs. Pell and revealed that I was covering the von Bülow trial.

"I was with Claus von Bülow this afternoon and heard that the senator had called to ask him for lunch," I said.

"Is that what you were told?" Mrs. Pell asked. Nuala Pell is the daughter of Jo Hartford Bryce, the Great Atlantic & Pacific Tea Company heiress, and a Newport neighbor of the von Bülows.

"Yes," I replied.

"Mr. von Bülow called my husband. My husband didn't call Mr. von Bülow," she said.

———

Every Friday afternoon during the trial the von Bülow station wagon was packed and ready to depart the instant court adjourned. The doorman of the Biltmore Plaza Hotel held open the rear door, and the golden retriever, Tiger Lily, bolted into her regular place, eager to be gone. As Mrs. Reynolds, behind the wheel, waved gaily to photographers, von Bülow, wearing one of his handsomely cut cuffed-sleeved, foulard-lined tweed jackets, slipped into the front seat beside her, and they took off to New York. After the third week of the trial, they gave a christening party for Mrs. Reynolds's granddaughter, Eliza McCarthy. Von Bülow was the godfather, and the infant wore the christening dress Cosima had worn. Mrs. Reynolds, in a hat of red poppies with a veil and a blue high-fashion dress, nipped into Mortimer's for a celebratory drink between the religious service at St. Jean Baptiste Church and the seated lunch for twenty at the apartment: cold poached salmon, cucumber salad, and champagne, served by three waiters in addition to Tai, the Chinese butler.

Mrs. Reynolds interrupted von Bülow's toast to say, "Claus, Ann-Mari Bismarck is calling from London."

"Excuse me," said the host, leaving the table to talk with Princess von Bismarck, one of his strongest supporters.

"He's innocent," said the woman next to me. "It's those awful drugged-out children who have brought all this on and framed him. I can't sleep nights worrying about Claus."

A few days before the christening, von Bülow had gone with the jury, the judge, and both teams of lawyers for a view of Clarendon Court, the Newport mansion he and Sunny and their children had shared during the marriage. Clarendon Court was the location of the two alleged murder attempts. The gates leading to the courtyard of the Georgian mansion were boarded up to discourage passersby from snooping. Entering the grounds of his former home through a service entrance in a side wall, von Bülow broke down and cried, wiping away his tears with a silk handkerchief. Skeptics were quick to note that he was directly in line with a television camera raised high on a cherry picker to film what went on behind the walls, where the media were denied access.

"Why did you cry?" I asked him.

"It was the dogs," he replied, meaning three yellow Labradors that had belonged to him and Sunny and had often slept on their bed. "I remembered the dogs as young and lean, and they had become old and fat. But they remembered me, and they jumped up on me and greeted me, and I felt like Ulysses returning. And I broke down."

The only outward indication that Claus von Bülow was ever under severe strain was a habit he developed of stretching his neck and jutting out his chin at the same time, like a horse trying to throw the bit out of its mouth, or a man resisting a noose. Whatever one felt personally about the guilt or innocence of the man, one could not deny his charm, which was enormous, in a European, upper-class, courtly sort of way. One of the first calls he made after his arrest was to John Aspinall, his English gambler friend, to say that, alas, he would not be able to attend the ball Aspinall and his wife were giving that weekend in Kent.

The slightest incident would trigger an inexhaustible supply of heavy-furniture anecdotes about the titled, the famous, and the wealthy—his standard points of reference. He would regale you with the fact that Christian VII of Denmark, whose portrait hangs in his drawing room, died of syphilis and drink. Or that the marble of his dining table, as blue as malachite is green, is called azurite. "I hate malachite, don't you?" he asked. "It reminds me of the fellow who was so proud of his malachite cuff links until a Russian grand duke said to him, 'Ah, yes, I used to have a staircase made of that.' " Once when a waiter poured him wine, he sniffed it, sipped it, savored it, nodded his approval of it, and then continued with the anecdote he was telling about the Dowager Marchioness of Dufferin and Ava, concerning Sunny von Bülow's maid, Maria Schrallhammer, who testified against him in both trials. " 'I know how difficult it is to get a good maid,' Maureen said, 'but this is ridiculous.' "

He would cite as his Newport supporters Alan Pryce-Jones, Oatsie Charles, Mr. and Mrs. John Winslow, and especially Anne Brown, the septuagenarian dowager Mrs. John Nicholas Brown, born a Kinsolving, who took the stand in von Bülow's behalf as a character witness at the first trial and became his most devoted champion in the deeply divided summer colony. At a dinner in Palm Beach last winter given by

Mr. and Mrs. Walter Gubelmann, also of Newport, Mrs. Brown announced that her faith in Claus von Bülow remained undiminished, and she asked the other guests to raise their glasses in a toast to him. No one rose to join her.

Von Bülow continued to wear the wedding ring from his marriage to Sunny, although he said any number of times that they would have divorced if what happened had not happened. The ring was in fact returned to him before the first trial by Alexandra Isles, his former mistress, whose appearance at that trial helped to convict him and whose melodramatic appearance at the second trial again turned sentiment against him. Mrs. Isles had had the wedding ring in her possession because it embarrassed her to have him wear it during the course of their affair.

Sometimes he spoke of Sunny as if she were a beloved late wife. "That was one of Sunny's favorite books," he said one day when he saw me reading *The Raj Quartet* during a break in the jury selection. Another time, at the apartment on Fifth Avenue, he saw me looking at a silver-framed photograph of her, taken by Horst. "God, she was beautiful," he said quietly.

"Were you ever in love with Sunny?" I asked.

"Oh, yes. Very much so," he replied in his dark baritone. "I'm really not letting out any secrets when I say that Sunny and I were geographically apart, but in every other sense together, for two years before we got married."

Who exactly is Claus von Bülow? For most of his life, dark rumors have circulated about him: that he was a page boy at Hermann Göring's wedding, that he is a necrophiliac, that he killed his mother and kept her body on ice, that he was involved in international espionage. Von Bülow either has a logical explanation for each rumor or shrugs it off as ludicrous. The necrophilia story, he says, was pinned on him in 1949, as a joke, on Capri, by Fiat owner Gianni Agnelli and Prince Dado Ruspoli. "Like dirt, it stuck," he says.

He was born Claus Cecil Borberg on August 11, 1926, in Copenhagen to Jonna and Svend Borberg, who divorced when he was four. His mother was a beauty who throughout her life developed strong friendships with men in high places. His father was a drama critic who

greatly admired the Germans, even after they occupied Denmark in
World War II. "He gave a good name to a bad cause," says von Bülow
about his father. "He dined with the wrong people." After the war he
was arrested as a collaborator and sentenced to four years in prison.
Von Bülow says that his father's conviction—like his own thirty-six
years later—was thrown out on appeal, and he was released after eighteen months. However, when von Bülow returned to Denmark, he did
not go to see his father, who died broken and ostracized a year after his
release.

His mother was residing in England at the time of the German invasion of Denmark. Claus was spirited there via Sweden in the early
years of the war through the efforts of both his parents. Claus took the
name of his maternal grandfather, Frits Bülow, a former minister of
justice, since the name Borberg had been besmirched. The *von* was
added later.

When he was sixteen, he was accepted at Cambridge University,
from which he graduated in 1946 with a law degree. Too young to take
the bar, he spent a year in Paris auditing courses at the École des Sciences Politiques and introducing himself to the world of international
high society. After working with Hambros bank in London, he joined
the law offices of Quintin Hogg, later Lord Hailsham. An interesting
fact that was not brought up in either trial is that during the 1950s his
law firm handled the first known case of murder by insulin injection.

Von Bülow and his mother, with whom he lived until her death,
bought one of the grandest apartments in London, in Belgrave Square,
which, von Bülow says, "dined two hundred with ease and slept three
with difficulty." Before gambling became legal, he rented it out to his
friend John Aspinall for private gambling parties. He also made
friends with Lord Lucan who later murdered his children's nanny in
the mistaken belief that she was his wife, and whose subsequent
whereabouts have never been ascertained. Tall and handsome, with an
eye for the right social contacts, von Bülow soon knew all the people
who mattered. In Saint Moritz he had an affair with socialite Ann
Woodward after she killed her husband.

In the early sixties, when he was thirty-three years old, von Bülow
was hired as an administrative assistant to the legendary oil tycoon

J. Paul Getty, who had recently moved his headquarters of the Los Angeles-based company to London. There has been much speculation as to exactly what von Bülow's importance was in the Getty empire, whether he was an errand boy or a figure of consequence. Getty hated to fly, so von Bülow frequently represented him at meetings and reported back to him. A woman friend of Getty's told me that von Bülow arranged parties in his apartment at which the old man could meet girls. What is certain is that his income from working for one of the richest men in the world was less than $20,000 a year. Von Bülow speaks of Mr. Getty with enormous affection and says that one of the major mistakes of his life was leaving England and that job.

Margaret, Duchess of Argyll, was a great friend of Paul Getty's and often served as hostess at his parties. She remembers one occasion when she returned to London from Getty's estate in Surrey with von Bülow, whom she did not know well at the time. She was then involved in one of the most scandalous divorces in English history. Von Bülow asked her if she knew that her husband had taken a room at the Ritz in London that connected with the room of a certain Mrs. So-and-so. She did not know. "But, you can imagine, it was very important information for me to have at that time," said the duchess, "and Mr. von Bülow didn't even know the duke."

In 1966 von Bülow married the American Princess Martha "Sunny" Crawford von Auersperg, thirteen months after her divorce from her first husband, Prince Alfie von Auersperg, on whom she had settled a million dollars and two houses. Tired of living in Austria, tired of her husband's philandering, tired of big-game hunting in Africa, Sunny wanted to bring up her two children from that marriage, Princess Annie-Laurie von Auersperg and Prince Alexander von Auersperg, aged seven and six, in the United States. Fifteen years later those same two children would charge their stepfather with attempting to murder her. The couple settled in New York in Sunny's apartment at 960 Fifth Avenue, the same apartment where von Bülow and Mrs. Reynolds reside.

A year later, their only child, Cosima, was born. Prince Otto von Bismarck, J. Paul Getty, the Marchioness of Londonderry, and Isabel Glover were her godparents.

"Did you see yourself on Dan Rather last night?" I asked Andrea Reynolds the morning after CBS had run a long sequence of the trial, showing her watching Alexandra Isles, von Bülow's mistress before her, testify against him.

"No, darling, I didn't know it was on. But so many people have been filming me—can you imagine if I spent my days seeing if I can see myself on TV? How did I look?"

Clearly the star of the second trial was Mrs. Reynolds, although she was, much to her chagrin, not allowed to sit in the courtroom. She was here, there, and everywhere else, though, known to every employee in the Biltmore Plaza Hotel, to all the cabdrivers of Providence, and to each member of the press. Forty-eight years old, she was born in Hungary and raised and educated in Switzerland. She speaks seven languages. Vivacious, curvaceous, and flirtatious, she seems a sort of latter-day Gabor, with a determination factor somewhere on the scale between Imelda Marcos and Leona Helmsley. She was openly loathed by Claus von Bülow's lawyers long before she told a reporter from *People* magazine that the jury didn't like Thomas Puccio: "They draw away from him when he approaches the jury box." Puccio, von Bülow's tough defense attorney, gained national recognition as the Abscam prosecutor. Friends claim Mrs. Reynolds knew more about the first trial than the lawyers did. One reporter counted twenty-nine pages of Sunny von Bülow's medical records spread out on tables and chairs in her suite.

She was Claus von Bülow's most passionate defender, fighting to vindicate her man and at the same time establishing a name for herself. It was she, according to Sheldon Reynolds, who got most of the affidavits from prominent people saying that Sunny von Bülow was an alcoholic. Von Bülow said about her, "I realize that that Hungarian hussar has, often to one's total exhaustion, whipped everybody, including me, into activity." Nowhere was this more evident than in von Bülow's dealings with the media.

During the first trial, in Newport, von Bülow sometimes spoke to members of the press in the corridors of the courthouse during recesses, but he never socialized with them. During the second trial, in Providence, with Mrs. Reynolds at the helm, he openly courted the media with masterly manipulation. They were on a first-name basis with most of the members, dined regularly with them in the various restaurants of Providence, and drove at least one reporter to New York in their station wagon for the weekend, dazzling them all, or so they thought, with their glamour, while always stipulating that anything they said was strictly off the record. Mrs. Reynolds often telephoned reporters if she didn't like the way they reported on the trial, and occasionally went over their heads to their editors. When Tony Burton wrote in the *New York Daily News* that while the jury was sequestered in the Holiday Inn, cut off from family and friends, the defendant and his lady friend were dining nightly in the best restaurants in Providence, Mrs. Reynolds called him a Commie pinko faggot. Eventually reporters grew sick of the off-the-record quotes fed to them by the pair. One journalist baited Mrs. Reynolds by asking her, "Come on, Andrea, what kind of fuck is Claus?" She replied, without a second's hesitation, "How can you expect me to answer that? If I tell you he's good, there will be even more women after him than there already are, and if I tell you he's no good, how does that make me look?"

Barred from the courtroom, Mrs. Reynolds watched the trial in the truck of Cable News Network, which carried the proceedings live, gavel to gavel. There she was able to see exactly what went on in the courtroom, without all the commercials and cutaways. To the dismay of the CNN personnel, she slowly began to take over the small booth. When Alexander von Auersperg's lawyer entered one day, he was met by Mrs. Reynolds. When Judge Corinne Grande called the booth, Mrs. Reynolds answered the telephone. Mrs. Reynolds was then asked not to return. She begged to be readmitted for just one more day in order to watch a hearing for one of several mistrials requested by the defense, but CNN declined. "Even a maid gets two weeks' notice," snapped Mrs. Reynolds.

Mrs. Reynolds's style was a curious mixture of femininity and rough language. Her stories about the von Auersperg children, whom she had never met, were scurrilous. "Everyone who ever went to Xenon knows all about them," she said. On a secret tape submitted to the producers of "60 Minutes," she referred to Alexander as an asshole.

One day I asked her, "Is it true that you shot your first husband?"

"Absolutely not."

"That's a pretty well circulated story about you, Andrea."

"It wasn't my first husband. It was my second husband," she said. "And I didn't shoot him. He shot himself. When I left him. I'm the one who saved him. Not the one who shot him."

Andrea Reynolds was born Andrea Milos. Her family was described to me by a Hungarian who knew them as noble without a title. She and her mother fled Hungary for Switzerland when the Russians arrived, but her father, a banker, was forced to stay behind. Eventually he escaped to Morocco with the family jewels, sewn, according to Mrs. Reynolds, into the seams of his lederhosen. In Casablanca, he opened a dry-cleaning establishment called Mille Fleurs, and his fortune started to flourish again after he secured the business of the United States Army base in Casablanca. After her parents divorced, her mother married Sir Oliver Duncan, an immensely rich Englishman with pro-German leanings who sat out the war in Switzerland. Older by far than his new wife and suffering from Parkinson's disease, he was an heir to the Pfizer pharmaceutical company. The facts of his death are murky, but nearly all sources agree that he was kidnapped from Switzerland and hidden in a convent in Rome. At some point during his incarceration, he was carried to Monte Carlo and forced to sign away his fortune to his abductors. Some Europeans familiar with the story told me his body had never been found, but Mrs. Reynolds said she knew exactly where her stepfather was buried and that his funeral was attended by hundreds of prominent people. Her mother, the widowed Lady Duncan, now lives in Brazil. "During all these topsy-turvy things, I always went to the best schools," said Mrs. Reynolds.

Her first husband was a French-Italian named Ellis Giorgini. They had, according to Mrs. Reynolds, "a beautiful wedding in Paris." But the marriage was short-lived: "He drank a bit too much." Her second husband, Pierre Frottier-Duche, a Frenchman, is the father of her only child, Caroline, who is a student of veterinary medicine at the University of Pennsylvania and the mother of Eliza McCarthy. They lived in a house in Paris that had once belonged to Anatole France, and had a villa in Saint-Tropez. At one time very rich, Frottier suffered severe financial reverses. When he later went bankrupt, Mrs. Reynolds gave him back all the jewels he had given her. "I'm a gentleman," she said. Asked to comment on the story that Frottier had been forced to become a taxi driver after he went broke, she replied, "No, no, no, a limousine driver, and he would pick up people like Henry Ford, whom he knew from before, and Henry would sit up in the front seat with him when he realized it was Pierre."

Her conversation is peppered with fashionable names. The late Florence Gould, daughter-in-law of robber baron Jay Gould, was the godmother of her daughter, Caroline. The late Babe Paley was the matron of honor at her third marriage, to film producer Sheldon Reynolds. When pressed, she admitted, "Well, actually, Babe was sick on the day of the wedding, with a toothache, and someone else had to stand in, but I think of her as my matron of honor."

She claims to be on excellent terms with all her husbands, but at least one did not share this opinion. "If Claus has to marry Andrea," said Sheldon Reynolds, "he will wish he'd been convicted."

One night the telephone rang in my hotel room in Providence. It was Mrs. Reynolds. She asked me not to mention something she had told me about her first husband, and I agreed not to.

"I talk too much when I'm with you," she said. "I'm going to have to arrange for you to have a little accident."

We both laughed and hung up.

A rich person on trial is very different from an ordinary person on trial. The powerful defense team assembled by von Bülow for the second trial so outshone the prosecution that the trial often seemed like a football game between the New York Jets and Providence High. Outsiders versed in legal costs estimated that the second trial alone cost von Bülow somewhere in the neighborhood of a million dollars. Besides Thomas Puccio and Alan Dershowitz, the Harvard law professor who won the appeal, four other lawyers, two of them from New York, attended the trial daily. Von Bülow even hired his own court stenographer, because the court-appointed one could not turn out transcripts fast enough to suit the defense. That cost alone, combined with printing, binding, and messenger fees, was probably close to $1,500 a day. Where the money for this extravagant operation came from was anyone's guess. Von Bülow's personal income is $120,000 a year, the interest on a $2 million trust Sunny von Bülow donated to the Metropolitan Opera with the stipulation that the income should go to von Bülow for life. Some said he sold art objects. Others said he had a loan of $900,000 from the Getty Oil Company. Still others said Mrs. Reynolds controlled the backers who provided the money.

"Are you in love with Andrea?" I asked von Bülow one Sunday morning late in the trial, when we were sitting on a bench in Central Park.

His eyes were closed. He was catching the warm May rays of the sun on his face. "I love Andrea," he replied slowly, measuring his words. "I find this very hard. Being *in* love is very different from loving somebody. There has to be the right timing and the right climate. . . . The climate and timing are wrong. I just don't have enough left for the enthusiasm and recklessness and carefreeness that are inherent in falling in love. I'm a man with a noose around my neck."

David Marriott was meticulously suited and vested in beige gabardine, with an *M* monogrammed on his French cuffs. Tall, slender, twenty-seven years old, he had arrived for our meeting, as he arrived for all of his public appearances, in a limousine. His chauffeur-bodyguard sat with us in the cocktail lounge of the Biltmore Plaza, munching peanuts.

"Would you describe the color of your glasses as grape?"

"No, rose. The press always calls them rose. Call them rose. Not grape," insisted David Marriott.

One of the most bizarre and unresolved aspects of the complicated von Bülow story was this mysterious young man from Wakefield, Massachusetts, where he lived with his mother. David Marriott had a voracious appetite for publicity and a deep hatred of Claus von Bülow and Andrea Reynolds. He surfaced after the first trial and was, for some time, embraced by von Bülow, Mrs. Reynolds, and Alan Dershowitz. Because of Marriott, von Bülow announced that he had discovered dramatic new evidence which he claimed would establish his innocence. At the urging of a later discredited Catholic priest, Father Philip Magaldi, Marriott swore that he had delivered packages containing hypodermic needles, bags of white powder, syringes, vials of Demerol, and pills to Alexander von Auersperg, who had told him that some of the material was for his mother, "to keep her off my back."

This evidence was a direct contradiction of the state's claim that the only person in the von Bülow household who had access to, or familiarity with, drugs and paraphernalia was Claus von Bülow. Affidavits signed by both Marriott and Father Magaldi were therefore important to von Bülow for his appeal.

Marriott paid visits to von Bülow's Fifth Avenue apartment and to the Reynoldses' country house in Livingston Manor, had lunches and dinners in fashionable restaurants, and took several trips to Puerto Rico, paid for by von Bülow. But then a falling-out occurred. By the start of the second trial, Marriott had recanted his original confession, and was claiming instead that his story had been concocted by von Bülow and that the drugs and needles he had delivered "didn't go to Sunny and Alex, they went to Claus." Marriott further revealed that he had secreted a tape recorder in his Jockey shorts and taped von Bülow, Mrs. Reynolds, Father Magaldi, and Alan Dershowitz in compromising conversations. He invited members of the press to his house in Wakefield to listen to them. Although the voices of von Bülow, Mrs. Reynolds, and Father Magaldi were distinguishable, the content of their talk, while suspicious in nature, was not incriminating. That left Marriott unwanted by either side.

Marriott was variously described by the media as an undertaker, a male prostitute, and a drug dealer. He claimed to me to be none of these, although he said that von Bülow had once offered to send him to mortician's school, and his remarks about von Bülow were filled with homosexual innuendo. Von Bülow said he had never heard of David Marriott before he came forward with his story of having sold drugs at Clarendon Court. Marriott, on the other hand, said he had known von Bülow for seven or eight years, having met him through a now deceased twenty-three-year-old drug dealer and hustler named Gilbert Jackson, who was, in Marriott's words, "bound up in elastic cord and strangled and stabbed many, many times on August 28, 1978." Two vagrants are serving time for that murder. When I asked

Andrea Reynolds whether von Bülow ever knew Gilbert Jackson, she said, "Darling, one doesn't know people like that."

In a move of desperation to achieve the notoriety that was eluding him, Marriott passed out defamatory leaflets about his onetime cohort, Father Magaldi, during mass at St. Anthony Church in North Providence, but the local television stations, alerted by Marriott of his intentions to make scandalous allegations about the priest, ignored the stunt.

When I called Marriott to double-check his version of how he had met von Bülow, he said, "I'm not telling you this unless I get paid for it. I'm saving that for my book."

"Listen, it doesn't matter, I'm running short of space anyway. I don't need to use you at all."

"It's all right. You can use it. I met him through Gilbert Jackson in 1978."

During the seventh week of the trial, David Marriott was severely beaten up. His nose was broken and his eyes were blackened. No explanation was given for the assault.

After the jury retired to deliberate, Father Magaldi was indicted for perjury and conspiring to obstruct justice by lying in behalf of Claus von Bülow.

Our mother, as you know, has been in an irreversible coma for four years: she cannot see, hear or speak. She is a victim in every sense. Our mother gave us unfailing love and devotion. She taught us the very big difference between right and wrong. We carry her sensitivities and her teachings as, perhaps, only children can. . . . She was not there to tell what had happened to her. She was not there to speak for herself when her character was assaulted. Lying in a deep coma, our mother became a non-person.

That is a portion of a letter written by Alexander von Auersperg and Annie-Laurie Kneissl that appeared in the newsletter of an organization known as Justice for Surviving Victims, Inc. Alexander and Annie-Laurie, who is known as Ala, remained remote figures throughout most of the second trial, but then they emerged in a blaze of worldwide publicity at a press conference in which they begged their stepfather's former mistress, Alexandra Isles, who had fled the country, to come forward and provide critical testimony. "We realize that coming forward the last time was an act of courage on your part. We ask that you summon the same courage again."

Sunny's children by her first marriage, backed by their maternal grandmother, Annie Laurie Aitken, who died last year, undertook the original investigation of their stepfather and hired former New York District Attorney Richard Kuh to confirm their suspicions. Jonathan Houston, executive director of Justice Assistance in Providence, brought me together with Ala Kneissl early in the trial. We met for the first time in the New York apartment of Pamela Combemale, a close friend of Sunny von Bülow's and the cousin of another ill-fated heiress, Barbara Hutton.

Married to an Austrian, the beautiful Ala Kneissl was pregnant with her second child when we met. Her brother, who is equally good-looking, graduated from Brown University in 1983 and works in the retirement division of E. F. Hutton. Deeply devoted to their mother, they acknowledged that she and von Bülow were happy for many years, and that they themselves had had affection for him. They had called him Uncle Claus or Ducky. Why Ducky? In those days, while his hair transplant was growing in, he wore a toupee, and when he swam he held his head far out of the water like a duck. Their mother, they said, preferred home life to social life, and they reminisced about family meals and going to films together and lying on their mother's bed watching television.

While the jury was out deliberating, Ala and Alexander invited me to Newport to spend the night at Clarendon Court. We dined across Bellevue Avenue at the home of the Countess Elizabeth de Ramel, an American friend of Ala's titled by a former marriage, whose Newport antecedents, the Prince and Wood-Prince families, date back for generations. There were a dozen guests. Despite attempts at joviality, the conversation throughout dinner never strayed far from the trial and the looming verdict. Ala and Alexander, who were dubbed "the kids" by the press during the trial, are remarkably unspoiled for young people who have grown up amid a kind of wealth and opulence that is almost incomprehensible.

Clarendon Court faces Bellevue Avenue on one side and the Atlantic

Ocean on the other. In 1956 it was used as the setting for Grace Kelly's home in the film *High Society*. Another page of its colorful history concerns a young man named Paul Molitor, who was hired by Claus von Bülow in 1979 from the China Trade Museum in Massachusetts to work for the Newport Preservation Society, of which von Bülow was then an officer. Molitor beat out 120 other applicants for the job. Shortly after his arrival in Newport, von Bülow invited him to move into the carriage house on the grounds of Clarendon Court. Extremely personable, he soon became a popular extra man at dinner parties. He was in residence at the time of Sunny von Bülow's second coma, and his Newport friends recall that he was extremely fearful of having to testify at the first trial. He was not called to the stand, but one night six months later, he jumped off the Newport Bridge. A persistent rumor in the resort colony is that he was pushed. He was wearing a dinner jacket. An early report in the *Providence Journal*, later denied, said that his feet were bound with chicken wire.

Clarendon Court is a house where you walk through huge rooms to get to other huge rooms. Outside, between the terrace and the sea, is the mammoth swimming pool built by Sunny when she acquired the house after her second marriage; two fountains in the pool shoot water twenty feet into the air. She gave her last great party here, a twenty-first-birthday celebration for Alexander, at which all the guests wore white and played croquet on the sweeping lawns as the mist rolled in from the ocean.

"That was Claus's," said Ala, with a shudder of distaste, pointing to a cast-iron jardiniere held up by three mythological figures with erect penises. Some of the furniture in the house belongs to von Bülow, from his Belgrave Square apartment. At the end of the first trial, when he put in a list of the pieces of furniture that were his, he claimed a partners' desk. Later it was discovered in an old photograph that the desk had been in Sunny's house in Kitzbühel during her marriage to Alfie von Auersperg. The furniture in von Bülow's study has a different feeling entirely from the rest of the house; exotic formula-laden pieces crowd the room, and opium pipes hang on the wall. It was here that he left the note containing the phrase "metal box," which led to the discovery of the infamous black bag that contained the syringe and insulin that were at the heart and soul of the case.

In a world of people who call their mother Mummy, Ala and Alexander call theirs Mom. As I walked through the house with them, they said things like "This was my mom's favorite color," pointing to the coral-painted walls of an upstairs sitting room, or "You should have seen my mom arrange flowers."

Their mother's bedroom remains exactly the way it was on the night of the second coma. Her elegantly canopied bed consists of two beds pushed together, made up separately with Porthault sheets and monogrammed blanket covers. On von Bülow's side of the bed is an old, silver-framed photograph of him in a striking, almost noble pose. I opened a handsome box on his bed table. It was filled with cartridge shells. Under the shells was a used syringe. In one of Sunny's closets, next to her evening dresses, are unopened gifts from that last Christmas of 1980—one from her lifelong friend Isabel Glover, another from her now deceased mother. Their festive wrappings are faded and limp.

On the day that Alexandra Isles returned to the United States to testify against von Bülow, Cosima graduated from Brooks School. She was the only member of the graduating class with no relatives present, but her classmates rallied behind her and cheered loudly when she received her diploma.

The estrangement from her half brother and half sister was over Clarendon Court. Although she was welcome to use the house at any time, Ala and Alexander would not vacate the place for her. When I told von Bülow that Ala and Alexander still cared for Cosima, he replied, "I just think they have to put their money where their mouth is. I am not impressed with constant repetitions of love and holding on to her money. I'd much rather hear them say they hate the brat and that's why they're holding on to her money."

Both von Bülow and Mrs. Reynolds were obsessed with the fact that Cosima had been cut out of the $110 million estate of her grandmother, Annie Laurie Aitken, for siding with her father. "She's out twenty-five million," Mrs. Reynolds said to me one day after Cosima and her boyfriend had left the table at Mortimer's.

One of the most poignant moments of the trial occurred on the last day, when all three of Sunny von Bülow's children appeared in the courthouse. It was the first time Ala and Cosima had seen each other since a chance encounter on the street three years earlier. As the divided family passed in the corridor, they looked straight ahead and did not speak. "She's gotten so beautiful," Ala said to me later of Cosima. "My mother would be very proud of her."

No one else in the trial came near to the sheer dramatic power of Alexandra Isles. Often described in the media as a soap-opera actress, the patrician Mrs. Isles attended the same schools as Sunny von Bülow: Chapin and St. Timothy's. Her mother, the Countess Mab Moltke, was born into the Wilson family of San Francisco, whose fortune, diminished now, traces its roots back to the Comstock Lode. Mrs. Isles is divorced from Philip Isles, a member of the wealthy Lehman banking family; his father changed his name from Ickelheimer in the 1950s. Following their divorce, Isles married the former wife of Dr. Richard Raskind, who changed his name to Renée Richards when he became a woman.

Deeply wounded by the hostile reaction she received at the end of the first trial, von Bülow's former mistress fled the country rather than testify again, believing, she said, that a videotape of her testimony in the first trial could be used in the second. At a New York party, Mrs. Isles's friend John Simon told me that under no condition would she return. He claimed, and later repeated to the press, that she did not want her son, Adam, fifteen, a student at Groton, to suffer the embarrassment of having his mother on the stand as the mistress and motive of the defendant in an attempted murder trial; that her mother was ill and had begged her not to take the stand; that she was terrified of being cross-examined by Thomas Puccio because she knew von Bülow's lawyer would expose her private life; and that she had received threatening letters from von Bülow warning her not to testify. Von Bülow vehemently and angrily denied this, claiming he had not been in touch with her since the first trial.

Mrs. Isles, who was reported to be hiding out at Forest Mere, an exclusive fat farm in England, flew from Frankfurt, Germany, the day after the von Auersperg children made their plea for her to return. After conferring with the prosecution team in Boston, she spent the night under an assumed name in the Ritz-Carlton Hotel, watching a Celtics game with her son. The next morning she testified that von

Bülow had called her at her mother's house in Ireland after the first coma to say that he had lain on the bed next to his wife for hours waiting for her to die, but that at the last minute he had not been able to go through with it and had called the doctor. Feisty and unwavering, she withstood the pummeling of Thomas Puccio. When he asked her to explain how she could have continued an affair with a man she suspected of trying to kill his wife, she shouted, "Have you ever been in love?" Then she added, "I doubt it."

Mrs. Reynolds was openly contemptuous of Mrs. Isles. Speaking of the jury, she said to me, "They have been told Claus was consumed by so much passion he was willing to kill his wife and get her money so that he could marry Alexandra Isles. In real life, two days after the end of the first trial, he and I fell in love with each other." Later the press said that she bared her claws and declared that Alexandra Isles had had two or three men at a time. Mrs. Isles had no comment to make about Mrs. Reynolds.

Meanwhile, the subject, or object, of all this conflict, Sunny von Bülow, lies in the sixth year of her coma on the tenth floor of the Harkness Pavilion in the Columbia-Presbyterian Medical Center in New York City. She is not, as many believe, on a life-support system, nor is she the total vegetable she is often described as being. I was told that the yearly cost of maintaining her is considerably in excess of half a million dollars. Her $725-a-day room is guarded around the clock by a special security force, and private nurses and a maid look after her at all times. A maze of curtained screens further protects her from the remote possibility that an outsider should gain entry to her room. A current photograph of the comatose woman would be worth a fortune.

Dr. Richard Stock, who has been her physician for twenty-nine years, as he was her mother's and grandmother's, visits her several times a week. She is fed through a tube in her nose. She receives physical therapy and dental care, and her hair is washed and set twice a week. Her own skin creams are used on her hands and face. She wears her own nightgowns and bed jackets and sleeps on Porthault sheets. Music plays in the room, and there are always highly scented flowers on her bedside table.

Ala and Alexander visit her regularly. Sometimes Ala brings her two-year-old daughter, also called Sunny, so that her mother can know she has a grandchild. They talk to her. They touch her. They tell her about things.

In a bizarre twist of fate, their father, Prince Alfie von Auersperg, is also in an irreversible coma, in Salzburg, the result of an automobile accident two years ago, when he was driving with Alexander. Their father's sister, Princess Hetty von Auersperg von Bohlen, the wife of Arndt von Bohlen and Halbach, the Krupp munitions heir, has found a healer in Europe who specializes in comas. She plans to bring the healer to New York to minister to her former sister-in-law. There are those who say that when Alfie von Auersperg and Sunny von Bülow stood side by side in the receiving line at their daughter's marriage to Franz Kneissl, he asked her to divorce Claus von Bülow and remarry him.

Maria Schrallhammer, the German maid so devoted to her mistress that she refused to divulge to two sets of defense attorneys the fact that Sunny von Bülow had had a face-lift because she had promised her she would never tell, also visits regularly, as does G. Morris Gurley, the Chemical Bank trust officer for Sunny's estate. Old friends are occasionally admitted, and one of them told me, "She has a personality just like you or I do. She reacts differently to different people. Some days you have a termagant on your hands. You try to brush her hair and you will have hell to pay. Other times, if the shades aren't open, she still looks beautiful in the half-light, although her hair has gone completely gray."

Cosima von Bülow has not been to the hospital since December 1981. Nor has Claus von Bülow.

In the three years that preceded Sunny von Bülow's second coma, most of her friends did not see her, or saw her only rarely. Some of them claim that von Bülow isolated her, answered the telephone for her, took messages that they felt she never received.

One of Sunny's last public appearances in New York was at the funeral of her childhood friend Peggy Bedford, a Standard Oil heiress with an inheritance comparable to Sunny's, although she was reputed to have gone through most of it by the time of her death in an automobile accident. Married first to Thomas Bancroft, she had later become the Princess d'Arenberg and then the Duchess d'Uzes. Friends say they spoke with Sunny on the steps of St. James Church following the service and found her warm and friendly and eager to make plans to see them. Then von Bülow appeared at her side, took hold of her elbow, and led her off to their waiting limousine. One old friend, Diego Del Vayo, remembers that she waved a gloved hand to him out of the car window.

For the eight weeks that the trial mesmerized the country, a related development of the strange case ran its parallel course. Nowhere was the scent of rot more pervasive than in the minimally publicized story of a Providence parish priest, Father Philip Magaldi, and his onetime companion David Marriott, an unemployed mystery man who drove around in limousines and who was happy to show anyone who cared to look Xeroxed copies of his hotel bills from Puerto Rican resorts, which he claimed were paid for by Claus von Bülow. Why, people wondered, if von Bülow was innocent, would he have involved himself in such an unsavory atmosphere?

Let us backtrack.

On July 21, 1983, Father Magaldi, on the stationery of Saint Anthony Church, 5 Gibbs Street, North Providence, Rhode Island, wrote and signed the following statement in the presence of a notary:

TO WHOM IT MAY CONCERN:

. . . I wish to state that I am ready to testify, if necessary, and under oath, that DAVID MARRIOTT did in fact discuss with me in professional consultation, his delivering to Mr. Claus von Bülow's stepson, Alexander [von Auersperg], packages which he thought contained drapery materials from his friend Gilbert [Jackson] in Boston, but on one occasion a package which he opened contained drugs which were delivered to the Newport mansion and accepted by Mrs. Sunny von Bülow who stated Alexander was not home but she had been expecting the package.

My reason for writing this affidavit is that in the event of accident or death, I wish to leave testimony as to the veracity of the statements made to me by DAVID MARRIOTT and also that as his counselor in spiritual matters, I advised him to inform Mr. Claus von Bülow and his lawyers as to what he knew concerning drug involvement by Alexander. I intend to speak to Mr. Roberts, the Attorney General of the State of Rhode Island, concerning these matters in August.

Five days later, on white watermarked stationery bearing the engraved address 960 Fifth Avenue, New York, New York, Claus von Bülow wrote Father Magaldi a letter that was quoted in the *New York Post* by gossip columnist Cindy Adams at the conclusion of the second trial. It reads in part:

Dear Father Magaldi:

I want to thank you for your kindness and courage in braving the storm and the airport delays, and then coming to meet me in New York. Had I been able to contact you in Boston I would gladly have faced those problems myself.

We were however rewarded with a very enjoyable evening, and I am grateful to you.

I want to repeat my wish to consult with you in finding an acceptable charity for donating the royalties of my book. The total profits, including film rights, could be anything between $500,000 and $1,000,000. . . . I will be happy to meet with you in Providence, Boston, or New York at your convenience.

On September 30, 1983, Father Magaldi, in a document notarized by his attorney, William A. Dimitri, Jr. (who later became the attorney for von Bülow's mistress, Andrea Reynolds), made the following statement:

In addition to my affidavit I wish to state something which I feel is too delicate a matter to come before the media and public at this time.

I refer to pictures shown me by David Marriott in which Alexander is engaged in homosexual activity with an unidentified male whom David told me was Gilbert Jackson.

Because these pictures in my estimation served no purpose and were patently pornographic, I destroyed them. However I can state that I recognized Alexander in the picture but cannot verify that the other was Gilbert Jackson since I have never seen him.

In actuality, Father Magaldi had never met Alexander von Auersperg, and Alexander von Auersperg had never met Gilbert Jackson, who was murdered in 1978, and therefore no such pornographic pictures ever existed for Father Magaldi to destroy. In other, more exotic areas of his life, Father Magaldi traveled in the netherland of Boston under the alias Paul Marino. It was in this role that he met David Marriott, in the Greyhound bus terminal in 1977, and not in the spiritual capacity he claimed in his affidavit. David Marriott told me that he did not know his benefactor was a Catholic priest until Magaldi was in a minor automobile accident several years after their friendship began and his true identity came out.

Marriott, who participated in preparing these and other affidavits besmirching the names of Claus von Bülow's wife, Sunny, and his step-son, Alexander von Auersperg, later claimed that they were all lies and that he had been paid by von Bülow for his part in the deception. Furthermore, Marriott had secretly tape-recorded conversations with Father Magaldi, von Bülow, and Andrea Reynolds to attempt to support his claim. On one tape that I listened to, Father Magaldi and Marriott discuss von Bülow's alleged offer to help the priest be elevated to bishop. On another there is talk about getting the late Raymond Patriarca, the Mafia chieftain of Providence, to get a drug dealer serving time in jail to say that Alexander von Auersperg had been one of his customers.

This murky matter played no part in Claus von Bülow's second trial in Providence. However, there were frequent rumors that Father Magaldi, who is a popular priest in the city, was about to be indicted for lying in a sworn statement he had given in 1983 to help von Bülow get a new trial, and that may have been the principal reason why Judge Corinne Grande insisted that the jury be sequestered for the eight weeks of the trial, especially since several of the members were acquainted with Father Magaldi. The priest was not indicted until after the jury had retired to deliberate, and the contents of the sealed indictment were not made known.

On the day before the jury returned its verdict, Claus von Bülow and Father Magaldi met—perhaps by accident, perhaps by design—in the lobby of the Biltmore Plaza Hotel. The encounter took place at seven o'clock on a Sunday morning and was witnessed by one of the bellmen, who used to serve as an altar boy for Father Magaldi. The priest, the bellman told me, had made the fifteen-minute drive from North Providence to buy the Sunday papers at the newsstand in the lobby of the hotel. Just as he arrived, the elevator doors opened and von Bülow emerged to walk Mrs. Reynolds's golden retriever, Tiger Lily. The encounter between the two men was brief, but the bellman was sure they had exchanged a few words.

That night, twelve members of the media who had covered the trial gathered for a farewell dinner in a Providence restaurant. Their conversation never strayed far from the subject that had held them together for nearly nine weeks—the trial. They discussed the fact that once again Claus von Bülow had not taken the stand, and they felt that it had been a foregone conclusion in the defense strategy from the start that he was never going to. The defense was aware that the prosecution was in possession of an exhaustive report by a European private-detective agency on the life of von Bülow before his marriage to Sunny, and a clever prosecutor, given the opportunity to examine the defendant directly, would have been able to ask many potentially embarrassing questions. Another topic of conversation was Judge Corinne Grande, whose frequent rulings favorable to the defense raised questions of her impartiality. In what was certainly the most controversial ruling of the trial, Judge Grande had agreed with von Bülow's lawyers that the testimony of G. Morris Gurley, Sunny's banker at the Chemical Bank in New York, should be barred. Gurley would certainly have testified that, according to a prenuptial agreement, von Bülow would receive nothing from his wife in a divorce. However, according to her will, he would inherit $14 million if she died.

I repeated a story I had heard that afternoon from someone who had been present at an exchange between Mr. Gurley and Alexandra Isles in the witness room. Mrs. Isles had just completed her testimony when Gurley was informed that he would not be called to the stand. Gurley was stunned. So was Mrs. Isles. "I can't believe they're not letting you testify," she told him. "I wasn't the motive, Morris. The money was the motive. He had me for free."

Late in the evening someone came up with the idea, since there were twelve of us, of pretending to be a jury and voting a verdict, not as we anticipated the jury would vote, but as we would vote if we were members of the jury and knew everything we knew rather than what Judge Grande had selected for us to know. The waitress brought a pad and pencils, and each person cast his vote. Our verdict, we all agreed, would remain our secret.

During the four days the jury was out deliberating, Claus von Bülow wandered up and down the crowded corridors of the courthouse, chain-smoking Vantage cigarettes and behaving like a genial host at a liquorless cocktail party, moving from one group of reporters to another with his endless supply of anecdotes. He even took time to call his most consistently loyal friend, the art historian John Richardson, to ask when he planned to leave for London. Monday week, he was told. He asked Richardson if he would take twelve large bags of potato chips to Paul Getty, Jr., who loved potato chips, but only the American kind.

On Monday morning, June 10, 1985, while waiting for the jury to reappear, von Bülow was tense and withdrawn. In the minutes before the jury entered, Barbara Nevins, a popular CBS reporter, leaned over from the press box and asked him if he had any final words before the verdict was delivered. In an uncharacteristic gesture, von Bülow raised the middle finger of his left hand to her.

"Is that for me, Mr. von Bülow, or for the press in general?" asked Miss Nevins. Thinking better of his gesture, he pretended that he had meant to scratch his forehead. At that moment the jury entered.

The proceedings were swift. The verdict was, predictably, "Not Guilty" on both charges. Von Bülow bowed his head for an instant and blinked back a tear. Then he and his lawyer Thomas Puccio nodded to each other without emotion. The courtroom was strangely mute despite a few cheers from elderly Clausettes in the back of the room. Very little of the ecstasy that accompanies a vindication was present, except in the histrionics of Mrs. Reynolds, whose moment had finally come, and she played it to the hilt. Flanked by two of her favorite reporters and directly in line with the television camera, she raised her diamond-ringed fingers to her diamond-earringed ears and wept.

In his moment of victory, von Bülow bypassed the embrace and kiss offered him by Mrs. Reynolds, who was wearing the same blue party dress she had worn at her granddaughter's christening, and gave her a peck on the cheek. Then he raced to a telephone to call Cosima.

During the triumphant press conference after the trial, von Bülow, surrounded by seven lawyers glowing with the flush of victory, returned to his old arrogance as he fielded questions from media representatives he no longer needed to court. Following a champagne visit with the jury that had acquitted him, he and Mrs. Reynolds returned to New York. Even in his moment of victory, dramatic rumors preceded his arrival. At Mortimer's restaurant, a French visitor said that if Claus had been found guilty, there was a plan to spirit him out of the country on the private jet of a vastly rich Texan.

"If I took you down to our beach and you started asking people, the two hundred of us who have dinner and swim and play golf together, you would find nearly everybody will say he did it," Mrs. John Slocum, a member of Newport society whose pedigree goes back twelve generations, told a reporter a week before von Bülow was acquitted. "And I'll tell you something else," she added, "people are afraid of Claus."

A few days after the trial, I went to Newport to check out the scene, and found that the battle lines between the pro- and anti-von Bülow factions remained drawn, and seemed possibly even fiercer than ever. On the front page of the *Newport Daily News*, Mrs. Slocum crossed swords with Mrs. John Nicholas Brown, who had been von Bülow's staunchest defender in Newport society from the beginning, in their respective damnation and praise of Judge Grande and the verdict. In the same article Mrs. Claiborne Pell, the wife of Senator Pell of Rhode Island, said she was "delighted" that von Bülow had walked from the courthouse a free man, while Hugh D. Auchincloss, the stepbrother of Jacqueline Kennedy Onassis, who had once written a letter in von Bülow's behalf to help him gain membership in the Knickerbocker Club, had harsh words for the verdict, the judge, and his former friend.

At the exclusive Clambake Club, Russell Aitken, the widower of Sunny von Bülow's mother, Annie-Laurie Aitken, stared ahead stone-faced as Mr. and Mrs. John Winslow, who had once said that the Aitkens would not be welcome at Bailey's Beach if Claus were acquitted, were seated nearby with their party. The Winslows were equally stone-faced.

Russell Aitken's dislike of his stepson-in-law is ferocious, and it predates the two charges of attempted murder by insulin injection. Standing on the terrace of Champs Soleil, the Bellevue Avenue estate he inherited from his late wife, which rivals, perhaps even surpasses, Clarendon Court in splendor, Mr. Aitken recalled for me the first time he and his wife ever met Claus von Bülow. It was in 1966 in London, in the lounge of Claridge's Hotel, when von Bülow was a suitor for Sunny, who had just divorced Prince Alfie von Auersperg. Von Bülow arrived for the meeting with Sunny's parents with his head covered in bandages, explaining that he had been in an automobile accident. Later Mr. and Mrs. Aitken heard from Sunny that the truth was rather different: his head was bandaged because he had just had his first hair-transplant operation.

Behind Russell Aitken, on the rolling lawns of the French manor house, a new croquet court was under construction, which promises to be the handsomest croquet court on the Eastern Seaboard. A respected sculptor, he had had one of his own artworks installed on a wall overlooking the new court. Mr. Aitken interrupted his tour to continue our conversation about his stepson-in-law. "He is an extremely dangerous man," he said, "because he's a Cambridge-educated con man with legal training. He is totally amoral, greedy as a wolverine, cold-blooded as a snake. And I apologize to the snake."

"May I quote you saying that, Mr. Aitken?" I asked.

"Oh, yes, indeed," he replied.

While von Bülow saved himself for an exclusive interview with Barbara Walters on "20/20," his mistress did a saturation booking on the television shows. Back in Providence, Judge Grande defended herself against a barrage of criticism that she had let a guilty man walk free. "I DIDN'T HELP CLAUS BEAT RAP," went one headline. Out in Seattle, Jennie Bülow, the elderly widow of Frits Bülow, Claus von Bülow's long-dead maternal grandfather, from whom he acquired his name when he changed it from Borberg, made no secret of her dissatisfaction with both the judge and the verdict.

In New York, von Bülow announced that he would visit Sunny at Columbia-Presbyterian Medical Center for the first time in four years as a gesture of his continuing love for her. Later, seated in the library of his wife's Fifth Avenue apartment, he met with Barbara Walters, as he had met with her at the conclusion of his first trial. He talked about his desire to go back to work. "I was never going to divorce Sunny because of any other woman," he told her. "I was going to divorce Sunny because she didn't tolerate my work." At the end of the interview, Miss Walters announced that von Bülow would soon be leaving for England to begin work for Paul Getty, Jr., the son of his former boss.

Getty, who was very possibly the donor of both von Bülow's bail money and his defense fund, is fifty-two years old and makes his home in England. He recently gave $63 million to the National Gallery in London. In 1984, according to *Fortune* magazine, he had an income from the Getty trust of $110 million. A virtual recluse, Getty is said to be a registered drug addict in England. His second wife, Talitha Pol, a popular member of the jet set, died in her husband's penthouse apartment in Rome of a massive overdose of heroin in 1971. To this day many of her friends insist that the fatal injection was not self-administered. The oldest of Getty's five children, John Paul III, lost an ear during his kidnapping in Italy in 1973. He later suffered a methadone-induced stroke that left him blind and crippled. Getty's youngest child, Tara Gabriel Galaxy Gramaphone Getty, seventeen, the son of Talitha, is at present engaged in legal proceedings against the $4 billion Getty trust.

In the ongoing controversy that constantly surrounds him, von Bülow for some reason denied to reporter Ellen Fleysher during a news conference an item in Liz Smith's syndicated column saying that he and Mrs. Reynolds had posed for *Vanity Fair* magazine and photographer Helmut Newton dressed in black leather. "No, I think you've got the wrong case," he told the reporter. Liz Smith, quick to respond, printed in her column two days later, "Once you see Claus inside the magazine in his black leather jacket, I want you to tell me how we can believe anything he says."

The same day that Liz Smith questioned von Bülow's veracity, the

New York Times reported that the indictment against Father Magaldi in Providence had been unsealed and that the priest was charged with perjury and conspiring to obstruct justice to affect the outcome of Claus von Bülow's appeal. Early that morning the telephone rang in my New York apartment. It was Mrs. Reynolds. Displeased with the latest developments in the media, she accused me of planting the story in Liz Smith's column to attract publicity for my article in *Vanity Fair*.

"Do you have any fear of being subpoenaed in the Father Magaldi case?" I asked her.

"They wouldn't subpoena me over their dead bodies," replied Mrs. Reynolds.

"Why?"

"I can totally demolish Mr. Marriott," she said. There was ice in her voice.

I asked her if it was true that she and von Bülow were only waiting for the return of his passport so that they could get out of the country before they were subpoenaed. She angrily denied to me that they had played any part in the false affidavits.

Von Bülow now got on the line, and his anger equaled that of Mrs. Reynolds. "I suggest you talk with Professor Dershowitz at Harvard," he told me sternly.

"Let me give you his telephone number," snapped Mrs. Reynolds, "to save you the seventy-five cents it will cost you to dial information."

The burning question was, would Claus von Bülow's acquittal give him automatic use of his comatose wife's $3.5 million annual income, minus, of course, the half-million dollars a year it costs to maintain her in Columbia-Presbyterian Medical Center? If so, his access to the money was not immediate, and civil litigation loomed that could tie up Sunny's fortune for years. In the meantime, unless Sunny dies and von Bülow inherits the $14 million that he is guaranteed in her will, he will have to make do with the interest on the $2 million trust his wife gave to the Metropolitan Opera, which amounts to $120,000 a year before taxes. There was talk in the first week of his freedom that money was tight.

Despite the wide coverage of von Bülow's acquittal across the country, the accolades of victory were spare in New York. The jewelry designer Kenneth Jay Lane entertained von Bülow and Mrs. Reynolds at a lunch in their honor—cold curried chicken, pasta salad, raspberries and blueberries with crème fraîche—and the guest list included John Richardson; Giorgio co-owner Gale Hayman; the English film star Rachel Ward; her husband, Australian actor Bryan Brown; and her mother, Claire Ward, longtime companion of von Bülow's great friend Lord Lambton, a former parliamentary undersecretary for the Royal Air Force who was forced to resign after his involvement in a government sex scandal. The lunch coincided with the announcement in the *New York Times* of Father Magaldi's indictment, and one guest reported that the atmosphere was subdued.

While von Bülow waited for his passport to be returned, he and Mrs. Reynolds became—for them, at least—almost socially invisible. They lunched quietly at Le Cirque, with their staunch ally Alice Mason, the New York Realtor and hostess. On another occasion Mrs. Reynolds entertained two members of the press at lunch at the Four Seasons. They attended a coming-out party given in honor of two daughters of the family with whom Cosima had lived during the first trial. For some reason they did not once venture into Mortimer's, the Upper East Side restaurant that had become their favorite haunt between trials.

Mrs. Reynolds told friends she was writing a miniseries based on the trial. Von Bülow made plans with his publisher for his autobiography and according to one friend, made arrangements for a face-lift. Together they visited the Livingston Manor house of Mrs. Reynolds's about-to-be-former husband, Sheldon Reynolds, to look at trees she had planted and pick up clothes she had left there. A witness to the scene reported that von Bülow's attitude to Mrs. Reynolds was chilly.

Alexandra Isles declined to be interviewed at the end of the trial. "We all have our own ways of surviving," she wrote me. "Mine is to try to put it out of my head and get on with other things. I know you will understand that an interview somehow keeps it all 'unfinished business,' but here is a bit of irony you are welcome to use: It was my father who, in the Danish underground, got little Claus Borberg (in his boy scout uniform!) out of Denmark."

The participants began to scatter. Maria Schrallhammer, after twenty-eight years of service with Sunny Crawford von Auersperg von Bülow and her children, retired and returned to Germany the day after the verdict. Cosima von Bülow, eighteen, threw herself into the hectic whirl of a summer of debutante parties. Alexander von Auersperg returned to his job in the retirement division of E. F. Hutton. Ala Kneissl, pregnant with her second child, began work on a documentary film about victims of homicide. Together Ala and Alexander, through the Chemical Bank, which handles the fortunes of their mother and grandmother, are in the process of establishing two major foundations. One will provide funds for the solace of the families of homicide victims and for changes in legislation to allow victims' rights to equate with the rights of criminals. A second foundation, commemorating both their parents, will be for medical research in the field of comas. G. Morris Gurley, the bank officer who was not allowed to testify at the trial, is in charge of overseeing the foundations.

Von Bülow did not visit his wife at Columbia-Presbyterian Medical Center. Two weeks after the acquittal, his passport was returned to him, and for the first time in five years he was free to travel abroad. The next day he and Mrs. Reynolds left New York. They did not fly first class. He stopped in London to visit friends. Mrs. Reynolds, after a one-day stopover in London, went on to Geneva to visit her father. A few days later they rendezvoused at the Grand Hotel & de la Pace in the Italian spa of Montecatini Terme.

The third act of the von Bülow affair is still to be played. Will Father Magaldi be tried for lying in a sworn statement he gave to help von Bülow get a new trial? Will David Marriott, who once said and later recanted that he had delivered drugs, needles, and a hypodermic syringe to Clarendon Court, testify against his former friend and benefactor? Will Claus von Bülow and Mrs. Reynolds be called to testify at Father Magaldi's trial? Will the relationship of von Bülow and Mrs. Reynolds sustain the serenity of his acquittal, with or without Sunny's income of $3.5 million a year? Will New York and London society receive the couple back into the charmed circle at the top?

The drama seems a long way from the final curtain, although

Claus von Bülow's dark and spacious place in social history has been assured.

The romance of Claus von Bülow and Andrea Reynolds did not endure long after his acquittal. A civil case that followed the criminal case was settled out of court. Cosima von Bülow was reestablished in her grandmother's will. Von Bülow and Cosima moved to London, where he still lives. Cosima has married. Claus has reestablished himself in society there. The von Auersperg children, Ala and Alexander, are both married. They are the founders of the National Victim Center, a national umbrella organization that helps victims of crime. I am a member of the Board of Directors of the organization. Andrea Reynolds married an English aristocrat, the Hon. Sean Plunkett, and runs a bed-and-breakfast in the Catskills. Sunny von Bülow is still alive as of this writing and still in the coma from which she has never awakened.

THE MANSIONS OF
LIMBO

INTRODUCTION

Years ago, reading a book whose title I no longer remember, I came across a sentence in which the words "the mansions of limbo" appeared. I was struck by those words. I loved the sound of them, and they have always stayed with me. In my Catholic youth, I learned that limbo was a blissful repository for the souls of infants who died before they were baptized, a community whose perfection was marred only by the fact that they were denied the sight of God. As I grew older, the meaning of limbo broadened to signify a state of privileged oblivion with a missing ingredient. When I began to put together the pieces from *Vanity Fair* that make up this collection, I tried to find a unifying factor in the kind of people and situations I write about, and the words that I read so long ago returned to me. However, I could never find the book in which I read them. Neither could scholarly friends or *Bartlett's Quotations* reveal their source. So I have simply usurped the words to make up the title of this book.

Not all, but most of the people I write about here soared in the decade of the eighties, a period in which the fortunes of the rich seemed limitless, and our information about them equally limitless. We knew, often with their cooperation, everything there was to know about them: how much money they were worth, how much they paid for their houses, their paintings, their curtains, their dresses, their centerpieces, and their parties. They acquired and acquired, and climbed and climbed. One man earned $550 million in a single year. The cost of another man's new house reached nearly $100 million. Perhaps it was bliss for them, but, certainly, it was bliss with a missing ingredient. Toward the end, some of the luminous figures went to jail for fiscal irregularities. The marriages of others began to disentangle. And a horrible new disease was killing the innocent in appalling numbers. Then the decade ended.

Has any other decade ever ended so promptly? On the twelfth stroke of midnight on December 31, 1989, it was over, finished, done with, history. The sixties, as they will always be remembered, were reluctant to go. The sixties continued to dance to the music of time until the fourth year of the seventies, before allowing that patient decade to define itself. But people were sick of the eighties, sick of the criminal improprieties of Wall Street, sick of the obeisance to money while the homeless occupied more and more sidewalk space in our cities. People wanted the eighties to be finished. And yet, for as long as it lasted, there was a hilariously horrifying fascination in watching the people who overindulged in extravagance, especially the ones who fell so resoundingly from grace and favor. Twice I went to prisons, one in Lucca, Italy, the other in Bern, Switzerland, to interview financial figures whose lifestyles and careers had only recently blazed on the social and financial pages. In Venice an Australian heiress almost married a prince in an international social event, but the heiress was not really an heiress and the prince turned out to be a steward on Qantas Airlines, who eloped with his best man the night before the wedding. In Geneva I watched rich people, mad for instant heritage, stand on chairs and wildly overbid and overpay for the late Duchess of Windsor's jewels at an auction staged by Sotheby's in a circus atmosphere worthy of P. T. Barnum. Once I was the lone American on a sailing ship of English aristocrats and minor royals on a cruise through several tropical islands in the Caribbean, a nobleman's odyssey culminating in a bizarre costume ball on the sands of an island mansion where grand ladies wore tiaras and men adorned themselves with plumes, pearls, and white satin. On Lake Lugano, the beauty queen fifth wife of the man with the second largest art collection in the world, after that of the Queen of England, brought about the transfer of her husband's famed artworks from Switzerland to her native Spain in hopes of obtaining the title of duchess from the Spanish king. In New York, a great photographer, who recorded with acute precision the dark side of the netherworld as it has never been recorded before, took my picture only a short time before he died. In a Beverly Hills mansion, a film mogul and his wife were brutally slain gangland style, and, seven months later, their two handsome and privileged sons were arrested for the crime, after a massive spending spree with their new inheritance.

All the pieces do not fit into the pattern of the late decade. There are the eternal figures like the singer Phyllis McGuire, once the mistress of the gangster Sam Giancana, in her Las Vegas mansion, and the actress Jane Wyman, the only divorced wife of a United States president, who have defied time and continue to fascinate. There is Lady Kenmare, the chatelaine of a great house in the South of France, who flourished in international society in the thirties, forties, and fifties as the rumored murderess of her four husbands. And, finally, there is the beautiful and highly intelligent Queen Noor of Jordan, the American fourth wife of King Hussein, who sits on a precarious throne between Israel and Iraq during the war that will define the new decade.

Dominick Dunne
New York, 1991

NIGHTMARE ON ELM DRIVE

O n a recent New York–to–Los Angeles trip on MGM Grand Air, that most luxurious of all coast-to-coast flights, I was chilled to the bone marrow during a brief encounter with a fellow passenger, a boy of perhaps fourteen, or fifteen, or maybe even sixteen, who lounged restlessly in a sprawled-out fashion, arms and legs akimbo, avidly reading racing-car magazines, chewing gum, and beating time to the music on his Walkman. Although I rarely engage in conversations with strangers on airplanes, I always have a certain curiosity to know who everyone is on MGM Grand Air, which I imagine is a bit like the Orient Express in its heyday. The young traveler in the swivel chair was returning to California after a sojourn in Europe. There were signals of affluence in his chat; the Concorde was mentioned. His carry-on luggage was expensive, filled with audiotapes, playing cards, and more magazines. During the meal, we talked. A week before, two rich and privileged young men named Lyle and Erik Menendez had been arrested for the brutal slaying of their parents in the family's $5 million mansion on Elm Drive, a sedate tree-lined street that is considered one of the most prestigious addresses in Beverly Hills. The tale in all its gory grimness was the cover story that week in *People* magazine, many copies of which were being read on the plane.

"Do you live in Beverly Hills?" I asked.

"Yes."

"Where?"

He told me the name of his street, which was every bit as prestigious as Elm Drive. I once lived in Beverly Hills and knew the terrain well. His home was in the same general area as the house where Kitty and Jose Menendez had been gunned down several months earlier in a fusillade of fourteen twelve-gauge shotgun blasts—five to the head and body of the father, nine to the face and body of the mother—that left them virtually unrecognizable as human beings, according to eyewitness reports. The slaying was so violent that it was assumed at first to have been of Mafia origins—a hit, or Mob rubout, as it was called, even in the *Wall Street Journal*. The arrest of the two handsome, athletic Menendez sons after so many months of investigation had shocked an unshockable community.

"Did you ever know the Menendez brothers?" I asked the teenager.

"No," he replied. They had gone to different schools. They were older. Lyle was twenty-two, Erik nineteen. In that age group, a few years makes an enormous difference.

"A terrible thing," I said.

"Yeah," he replied, "But I heard the father was pretty rough on those kids."

With that, our conversation was concluded.

Patricide is not an altogether new crime in the second echelon of Southland society. Nor is matricide. On March 24, 1983, twenty-year-old Michael Miller, the son of President Reagan's personal lawyer, Roy Miller, raped and clubbed to death his mother, Marguerite. In a minimally publicized trial, from which the media was barred, Miller was found guilty of first-degree murder but was acquitted of the rape charge, presumably on the technicality that the rape had occurred after his mother was dead. The judge then ruled that young Miller, who had been diagnosed as schizophrenic, was legally innocent of murder by reason of insanity. "Hallelujah," muttered Michael Miller after the verdict. He was sent to Patton State Hospital, a mental institution in California.

On July 22, 1983, in a Sunset Boulevard mansion in Bel Air, twenty-year-old Ricky Kyle shot his father, millionaire Henry Harrison Kyle, the president of Four Star International, a television-and-movie-production firm, in the back after awakening him in the middle of the night to tell him there was a prowler in the house. Several witnesses testified that Ricky had confided in them about a longstanding desire to kill his father, who was alleged to have been physically and mentally abusive to his son. The prosecution argued that Ricky was consumed with hatred for his father and greed for his fortune, and that, fearing that he was about to be disinherited, he plotted the ruse of the prowler. With the extraordinary leniency of the Southern California courts for first-time murderers, young Kyle was sentenced to five years for the slaying. Expressing dismay with the verdict, Ricky's mother told reporters she had hoped her son would be spared a prison term. "I think he has suffered enough," she said. Ricky agreed. "I feel like I don't deserve to go to prison," he said.

And then there were the Woodman brothers, Stewart and Neil, accused of hiring two assassins to gun down their rich parents in Brentwood. Tried separately, Stewart was convicted of first-degree murder. To escape the death penalty, he incriminated his brother. Neil's trial is about to start.

Further elaboration is not necessary: the point has been made. One other case, however, on a lesser social stratum but of equal importance, under the circumstances, should be mentioned: the Salvatierra murder, which received international attention. In 1986, Oscar Salvatierra, the Los Angeles–based executive of a newspaper called *Philippine News*, was shot while he was asleep in bed, after having received a death threat that was at first believed to be tied to the newspaper's opposition to former Philippine president Ferdinand Marcos. Later, Arnel Salvatierra, his seventeen-year-old son, admitted sending the letter and killing his father. In court, Arnel Salvatierra's lawyer convinced the jury that Arnel was the victim of a lifetime of physical and psychological abuse by his father. The lawyer, Leslie Abramson, who is considered to be the most brilliant Los Angeles defense lawyer for death-row cases, compared Arnel Salvatierra to the tragic Lisa Steinberg of New York, whose father, Joel Steinberg, had been convicted of murdering her after relentlessly abusing her. "What happens if the Lisa Steinbergs don't die?" Abramson asked the jury. "What happens if they get older, and if the cumulative effect of all these years of abuse finally drives them over the edge, and Lisa Steinberg pulls out a gun and kills Joel Steinberg?" Arnel Salvatierra, who had been charged with first-degree murder, was convicted of voluntary manslaughter and placed on probation.

This story is relevant to the Menendez case in that the same Leslie Abramson is one-half the team defending the affluent Menendez brothers. Her client is Erik Menendez, the younger brother. Gerald Chaleff, with whom she frequently teams, is representing Lyle. On an earlier burglary case involving the brother, Chaleff, who gained prominence in criminal law as the defender of the Hillside Strangler, represented Erik. It is rumored that Abramson and Chaleff are each being paid $700,000. Psychological abuse is a constant theme in articles written about the brothers, and will probably be the basis of the defense strategy when the case comes to trial. There are even whispers—shocker of shockers—of sexual abuse in the Menendez family.

Jose Enrique Menendez was an American success story. A Cuban émigré, he was sent to the United States by his parents in 1960 at age fifteen to escape from Castro's Cuba. His father, a onetime soccer star, and his mother, a former champion swimmer, stayed behind until their last properties were seized by Castro. Young Jose, who excelled in swimming, basketball, and soccer, won a swimming scholarship to Southern Illinois University, but he gave it up when he married Mary Louise Andersen, known as Kitty, at the age of nineteen and moved to New York. He earned a degree in accounting at Queens College in Flushing, New York, while working part-time as a dishwasher at the swank "21" Club in Manhattan, where, later, successful and prosperous, he would often dine. Then began a career of astonishing ascendancy which took him through Hertz, where he was in charge of car and commercial leasing, to the record division of RCA, where he signed such high-earning acts as Menudo, the Eurythmics, and Duran Duran. By this time he and Kitty had had two sons and settled down to a graceful life on a million-dollar estate in Princeton, New Jersey. The boys attended the exclusive Princeton Day School and, urged on by their father, began developing into first-rate tennis and soccer players. Their mother attended every match and game they played. When Jose clashed with a senior executive at RCA in 1986, after having been passed over for the executive vice presidency of RCA Records, he uprooted his family, much to the distress of Kitty, who loved her life and house in Princeton, and moved to Los Angeles. There he leapfrogged to I.V.E., International Video Entertainment, a video distributor which eventually became Live Entertainment, a division of the hugely successful Carolco Pictures, the company that produced the Rambo films of Sylvester Stallone as well as some of Arnold Schwarzenegger's action films. Jose Menendez's success at Live Entertainment was dazzling. In 1986 the company lost $20 million; a year later, under Menendez, Live earned $8 million and in 1988 doubled that. "He was the perfect corporate executive," I was told by one of his lieutenants. "He had an incredible dedication to business. He was focused, specific about what he wanted from the business, very much in control. He believed that whatever had to be done should be done—with no heart, if necessary."

The family lived at first in Calabasas, an upper-middle-class suburb of Los Angeles, inland beyond Malibu, where they occupied one house while building a more spectacular one on thirteen acres with mountaintop views. Then unexpectedly, almost overnight, the family abandoned Calabasas and moved to Beverly Hills, where Jose bought the house on Elm Drive, a six-bedroom Mediterranean-style house with a red tile roof, a courtyard, a swimming pool, a tennis court, and a guesthouse. Built in 1927, rebuilt in 1974, the house had good credentials. It had previously been rented to Elton John. And Prince. And Hal Prince. And a Saudi prince, for $35,000 a month. Erik Menendez, the younger son, transferred from Calabasas High to Beverly Hills High, probably the most snobbish public school in America. Lyle was a student at Princeton University, fulfilling one of the many American dreams of his immigrant father.

They were the ideal family; everyone said so. "They were extraordinarily close-knit," an executive of Live Entertainment told me. "It was one big happy family," said John E. Mason, a friend and Live Entertainment director. They did things together. They almost always had dinner together, which, in a community where most parents go to parties or screenings every night and leave their children to their own devices, is a rare thing. They talked about world events, as well as about what was happening in Jose's business. On the day before the catastrophic event, a Saturday, they chartered a boat called *Motion Picture Marine* in Marina del Rey and spent the day together shark-fishing, just the four of them.

On the evening of the following day, August 20, 1989, the seemingly idyllic world that Jose Menendez had created was shattered. With their kids at the movies in Century City, Jose and Kitty settled in for a comfortable evening of television and videos in the television room at the rear of their house. Jose was in shorts and a sweatshirt; Kitty was in a sweatshirt, jogging pants, and sneakers. They had dishes of strawberries and ice cream on the table in front of the sofa where they were sitting. Later, after everything happened, a neighbor would report hearing sounds like firecrackers coming from the house at about ten o'clock, but he took no notice. It wasn't until a hysterical 911 call came in to the Beverly Hills police station around midnight that there was any indication that the sounds had not been made by firecrackers. The sons of the house, Lyle and Erik, having returned from the movies, where they said they saw *Batman* again after they couldn't get into *License to Kill* because of the lines, drove in the gate at 722 North Elm Drive, parked their car in the courtyard, entered the house by the front door, and found their parents dead, sprawled on the floor and couch in the television room. In shock at the grisly sight, Lyle telephoned for help. "They shot and killed my parents!" he shrieked into the instrument. "I don't know ... I didn't hear anything ... I just came home. Erik! Shut up! Get away from them!"

Another neighbor said on television that she had seen one of the Menendez boys curled up in a ball on the lawn in front of their house and screaming in grief. "I have heard of very few murders that were more savage," said Beverly Hills police chief Marvin Iannone. Dan Stewart, a retired police detective hired by the family to investigate the murders, gave the most graphic description of the sight in the television room. "I've seen a lot of homicides, but nothing quite that brutal. Blood, flesh, skulls. It would be hard to describe, especially Jose, as resembling a human that you would recognize. That's how bad it was." According to the autopsy report, one blast caused "explosive decapitation with evisceration of the brain" and "deformity of the face" to Jose Menendez. The first round of shots apparently struck Kitty in her chest, right arm, left hip, and left leg. Her murderers then reloaded and fired into her face, causing "multiple lacerations of the brain." Her face was an unrecognizable pulp.

The prevalent theory in the days following the murders was that it had been a Mob hit. Erik Menendez went so far as to point the finger at Noel Bloom, a distributor of pornographic films and a former associate of the Bonanno organized-crime family, as a possible suspect. Erik told police and early reporters on the story that Bloom and his father had despised each other after a business deal turned sour. (When questioned, Bloom denied any involvement whatsoever.) Expressing fear that the Mob might be after them as well, the brothers moved from hotel to hotel in the aftermath of the murders. Marlene Mizzy, the front-desk supervisor at the Beverly Hills Hotel, said that Lyle arrived at the hotel without a reservation two days after the murders and asked for a two-bedroom suite. Not liking the suites that were available on such short notice, he went to another hotel.

Seven months later, after the boys were arrested, I visited the house on Elm Drive. It is deceptive in size, far larger than one would imagine from the outside. You enter a spacious hallway with a white marble floor and a skylight above. Ahead, to the right, is a stairway carpeted in pale green. Off the hallway on one side is an immense drawing room, forty feet in length. The lone piece of sheet music on the grand piano was "American Pie," by Don McLean. On the other side are a small paneled sitting room and a large dining room. At the far end of the hallway, in full view of the front door, is the television room, where Kitty and Jose spent their last evening together. On the back wall is a floor-to-ceiling bookcase, filled with books, many of them paperbacks, including all the American-history novels of Gore Vidal, Jose's favorite author. On the top shelf of the bookcase were sixty tennis trophies—all first place—that had been won over the years by Lyle and Erik.

Like a lot of houses of the movie nouveaux riches still in their social and business rise, the grand exterior is not matched by a grand interior. When the Menendez family bought the house, it was handsomely furnished, and they could have bought the furniture from the former owner for an extra $350,000, but they declined. With the exception of some reproduction Chippendale chairs in the dining room, the house is appallingly furnished with second-rate pieces; either the purchase price left nothing for interior decoration or there was just a lack of interest. In any case, your attention, once you are in the house, is not on the furniture. You are drawn, like a magnet, to the television room.

Trying to imagine what happened that night, I found it unlikely that the boys—if indeed it was the boys, and there is a very vocal contingent who believe it was not—would have come down the stairs with the guns, turned right, and entered the television room, facing their parents. Since Jose was hit point-blank in the back of the head, it seems far more likely that the killers entered the television room through the terrace doors behind the sofa on which Kitty and Jose were sitting, their backs to the doors, facing the television set. The killers would probably have unlocked the doors in advance. In every account of the murders, Kitty was said to have run toward the kitchen. This would suggest, assuming she was running away from her assailants, that they had entered from behind.

Every person who saw the death scene has described the blood, the guts, and the carnage in sick-making detail. The furniture I saw in that room was replacement furniture, rented after the murders from Antiquarian Traders in West Hollywood. The original blood-drenched furniture and Oriental carpet had been hauled away, never to be sat on or walked on again. It is not farfetched to imagine that splatterings of blood and guts found their way onto the clothes and shoes of the killers, which would have necessitated a change of clothing and possibly a shower. There is no way the killers could have gone up the stairs, however; the blood on their shoes would have left tracks on the pale green stair carpet. The lavatory beneath the stairs and adjacent to the television room does not have a shower. What probably happened is that the killers retreated out the same terrace doors they had entered, and went back to the guesthouse to shower and change into clothes they had left there. The guesthouse is a separate, two-story unit beyond the swimming pool and adjacent to the tennis court, with a sitting room, a bedroom, a full bath, and a two-car garage opening onto an alley.

There is also the possibility that the killers, knowing the carnage twelve-gauge-shotgun blasts would cause, wore boots, gloves, and overalls. In that event, they would have only had to discard the clothes and boots into a large garbage bag and make a dash for it. One of the most interesting aspects of the case is that the fourteen shell casings were picked up and removed. I have been told that such fastidiousness is out of character in a Mafia hit, where a speedy getaway is essential. There is a sense of leisurely time here, of people not in a hurry, not expecting anyone, when they delay their departure from a massacre to pick the shell casings out of the bloody remains of their victims' bodies. They almost certainly wore rubber gloves to do it.

Then they had to get rid of the guns. The guns, as of this writing, have still not been found. We will come back to the guns. The car the killers left in was probably parked in the guesthouse garage; from there they could make their exit unobserved down the alley behind the house. Had they left out the front gate on Elm Drive, they would have risked being observed by neighbors or passersby. Between the time the killers left the house and the time the boys made the call to the police, the bloody clothes were probably disposed of.

On the day before the fishing trip on the *Motion Picture Marine*, Erik Menendez allegedly drove south to San Diego and purchased two Mossberg twelve-gauge shotguns in a Big 5 sporting-goods store, using for identification the stolen driver's license of a young man named Donovan Goodreau. Under federal law, to purchase a weapon, an individual must fill out a 4473 form, which requires the buyer to provide his name, address, and signature, as well as an identification card with picture. Donovan Goodreau had subsequently said on television that he can prove he was in New York at the time of the gun purchase in San Diego. Goodreau had once roomed with Jamie Pisarcik, who was, and still is, Lyle Menendez's girlfriend and stalwart supporter, visiting him daily in jail and attending his every court session. When Goodreau stopped rooming with Jamie, he moved into Lyle's room at Princeton, which was against the rules, since he was not a student at the university. But then, Lyle had once kept a puppy in his room at Princeton, and having animals in the rooms was against the rules too.

What has emerged most significantly in the year since the murders is that all was not what it seemed in the seemingly perfect Menendez household. There are people who will tell you that Jose was well liked. There are more people by far who will tell you that he was greatly disliked. Even despised. He had made enemies all along the way in his rise to the high middle of the entertainment industry, but everyone agrees that had he lived he would have gone right to the top. He did not have many personal friends, and he and Kitty were not involved in the party circuit of Beverly Hills. His life was family and business. I was told that at the memorial service in Los Angeles, which preceded the funeral in Princeton, most of the two hundred people who attended had a business rather than a personal relationship with him. Stung by the allegations that Jose had Mob connections in his business dealings at Live Entertainment, allegations that surfaced immediately after the murders, the company hired Warren Cowan, the famed public-relations man, to arrange the memorial service. His idea was to present Menendez as Jose the family man. He suggested starting a Jose Menendez scholarship fund, a suggestion that never came to fruition. It was also his idea to hold the memorial service in an auditorium at the Directors Guild in Hollywood, in order to show that Jose was a member of the entertainment community, although it is doubtful that Jose had ever been there. Two people from Live Entertainment gave flowing eulogies. Brian Andersen, Kitty's brother, spoke lovingly about Kitty, and each son spoke reverently about his parents. One person leaving the service was heard to say, "The only word not used to describe Jose was 'prick.' "

Although Jose spoke with a very slight accent, a business cohort described him to me as "very non-Hispanic." He was once offended when he received a letter of congratulations for having achieved such a high place in the business world "for a Hispanic." "He hated anyone who knew anything about his heritage," the colleague said. On the other hand, there was a part of Jose Menendez that secretly wanted to run for the U.S. Senate from Florida in order to free Cuba from the tyranny of Fidel Castro and make it a U.S. territory.

Kitty Menendez was another matter. You never hear a bad word about Kitty. Back in Princeton, people remember her on the tennis courts with affection. Those who knew her in the later years of her life felt affection too, but they also felt sorry for her. She was a deeply unhappy woman, and was becoming a pathetic one. Her husband was flagrantly unfaithful to her, and she was devastated by his infidelity. There has been much talk since the killings of Jose's having had a mistress, but that mistress was by no means his first, although he was said to have had "fidelity in his infidelity" in that particular relationship. Kitty fought hard to hold her marriage together, but it is unlikely that Jose would ever have divorced her. An employee of Live Entertainment said, "Kitty called Jose at his office every thirty minutes, sometimes just to tell him what kind of pizza to bring home for supper. She was a dependent person. She wanted to go on his business trips with him. She had June Allyson looks. Very warm. She also had a history of drinking and pills." Another business associate of Jose's at Live said,

"I knew Kitty at company dinners and cocktail parties. They used to say about Kitty that she was Jose with a wig. She was always very much at his side, part of his vision, dedicated to the cause, whatever the cause was."

A more intimate picture of Kitty comes from Karen Lamm, one of the most highly publicized secondary characters in the Menendez saga. A beautiful former actress and model who was once wed to the late Dennis Wilson of the Beach Boys, Lamm is now a television producer, and she and her partner, Zev Braun, are developing a miniseries based on the Menendez case. Lamm is often presented as Kitty's closest friend and confidante. However, friends of Erik and Lyle decry her claims of friendship with Kitty, asserting that the boys did not know her, and asking how she could have been such a great friend of Kitty's if she was totally unknown to the sons.

Most newspaper accounts say that Karen Lamm and Kitty Menendez met in an aerobics class, but Lamm, who says she dislikes exercise classes, gave a different account of the beginning of their friendship. About a year before the murders, she was living with a film executive named Stuart Benjamin, who was a business acquaintance of Jose Menendez. Benjamin was a partner of the film director Taylor Hackford in a production company called New Visions Pictures, which Menendez was interested in acquiring as a subsidiary for Live Entertainment. During the negotiation period, Benjamin, with Lamm as his date, attended a dinner party at the Menendez house on Elm Drive. Lamm, who is an effusive and witty conversationalist, and Kitty spent much of the evening talking together. It was the beginning of a friendship that would blossom. Lamm described Kitty to me as being deeply unhappy over her husband's philandering. She claims that Kitty had tried suicide on three occasions, the kind of at-home suicide attempts that are more cries for help than a longing for death. Kitty had once won a beauty contest and could still be pretty on occasion, but she had let her looks go, grown fat (her autopsy report described her as "fairly well-nourished" and gave her weight as 165), and dyed her hair an unbecoming blond color that did not suit her. Lamm suggested that she get back into shape, and took her to aerobics classes, as well as offering her advice on a darker hair color. During the year that followed, the two women became intimate friends, and Kitty confided in Lamm, not only about Jose's infidelity but also about the many problems they were having with their sons.

Lamm said she met the boys three times, but never talked to them in the house on Elm Drive. She told me, "Those kids watched their mother become a doormat for their father. Jose lived through Lyle. Jose made Lyle white bread. He sent him to Princeton. He gave him all the things that were not available to him as an immigrant." Lamm finally talked with Kitty's sons at the memorial service at the Directors Guild. She was introduced to Lyle, who, in turn, introduced her to Erik as "Mom's friend." She said that Lyle had become Jose overnight. He radiated confidence and showed no emotion, "unless it was a convenient moment." Erik, on the other hand, fell apart.

Over the previous two years, the handsome, athletic, and gifted Menendez sons had been getting into trouble. Although a great friend of the boys dismissed their scrapes as merely "rich kids' sick jokes," two events occurred in Calabasas, where the family lived before the move to Beverly Hills, that were to have momentous consequences for all the members of the family. The brothers got involved in two very serious criminal offenses, a burglary at the home of Michael Warren Ginsberg in Calabasas and grand theft at the home of John Richard List in Hidden Hills. In total, more than $100,000 in money and jewels was taken from the two houses—not an insignificant sum.

Jose dealt with his sons' transgressions the way he would deal with any prickly business problem, said a business associate, by "minimizing the damage and going forward, fixing something that was broken without actually dealing with the problem." He simply took over and solved it. The money and jewels were returned, and $11,000 in damages was paid. Since Erik was underage, it was decided that he would take the fall for both brothers, thereby safeguarding Jose's dream of having Lyle study at Princeton. Jose hired the criminal lawyer Gerald Chaleff to represent Erik—the same Gerald Chaleff who is now representing Lyle on the charge of murdering the man who once hired him to represent Erik on the burglary charge. Everything was solved to perfection. Erik got probation, no more. And compulsory counseling. And for that, Kitty asked her psychologist, Les Summerfield, to recommend someone her son could go to for the required number of hours ordered by the judge. Les Summerfield recommended a Beverly

Hills psychologist named Jerome Oziel, who, like Gerald Chaleff, continues his role in the Menendez saga right up to the present.

Prior to the thefts, Erik had made a friend at Calabasas High School who would also play a continuing part in the story. Craig Cignarelli, the son of a prominent executive in the television industry, is a Tom Cruise look-alike currently studying at the University of California in Santa Barbara. Craig was the captain of the Calabasas High School tennis team, and Erik, who had recently transferred from Princeton Day, was the number-one singles player on the team. One day, while playing a match together, they were taunted by two students from El Camino High School, a rival school in a less affluent neighborhood. Menendez and Cignarelli went out to the street to face their adversaries, and a fight started. Suddenly, a whole group of El Camino boys jumped out of cars and joined the fray. Erik and Craig were both badly beaten up. Erik's jaw was broken, and Craig received severe damage to his ribs. The incident sparked a close friendship between the two, which would culminate in the cowriting of a movie script called *Friends*, in which a young man named Hamilton Cromwell murders his extremely rich parents for his inheritance. One of the most quoted passages from this screenplay comes from the mouth of Hamilton Cromwell, speaking about his father: "Sometimes he would tell me that I was not worthy to be his son. When he did that, it would make me strive harder . . . just so I could hear the words 'I love you, son.' . . . And I never heard those words." To add to the awful irony, Kitty, the loving mother who could not do enough for her sons, typed the screenplay in which her own demise seems to have been predicted. In the embarrassing aftermath of the burglaries, the family moved to the house on Elm Drive in Beverly Hills. Jose told people at Live Entertainment that he was upset by the drug activity in Calabasas and that the tires of his car had been slashed, but it is quite possible that these stories were a diversionary tactic, or smoke screen, created to cover the disgrace of his son's criminal record.

A further setback for the family, also partly covered up, had occurred the previous winter, when Lyle was suspended from Princeton after one semester for cheating in Psychology 101. Taken before a disciplinary committee, he was told he could leave the university voluntarily or be expelled. He chose to leave. This was a grave blow to Jose, who loved to tell people that he had a son at Princeton. Again taking over, he tried to talk the authorities at Princeton into reinstating his son, but this time the pressure he applied did not work. The suspension lasted a year. In a typical reaction, Jose became more angry at the school than he was at his son. He urged Lyle to stay on in Princeton rather than return to Beverly Hills, so that he would not have to admit to anyone that Lyle had been kicked out.

But Lyle did return, and worked briefly at Live Entertainment, where he showed all the worst qualities of the spoiled rich boy holding down a grace-and-favor job in his father's company. He was consistently late for work. His attention span was brief. He worked short hours, leaving in the afternoon to play tennis. He was unpopular with the career-oriented staff. "The kids had a sense of being young royalty," said an employee of the company. "They could be nasty, arrogant, and self-centered." But, the same person said, Jose had a blind spot about his sons. And tennis held the family together. Once, Jose took the Concorde to Europe just to watch Lyle play in a tennis tournament, and then came right back. However, for all the seeming closeness of the family, the sons were proving to be disappointments, even failures, in the eyes of their perfection-demanding father. Jose had apparently come to the end of financing his recalcitrant sons' rebellion, and there are indications that he planned to revise his will.

After the Calabasas debacle, Erik transferred to Beverly Hills High School for his senior year. His classmates remember him chiefly as a loner, walking around in tennis shorts, always carrying his tennis racket.

"A girl I was going out with lusted after him," a student told me. "She said he had good legs."

"Was he spoiled?"

"Everyone at Beverly High is spoiled."

Like his father, Lyle is said to have been a great ladies' man, which pleased Jose, but several of Lyle's girlfriends, mostly older than he, were not considered to be suitable by his parents, and clashes occurred. When Jose forbade Lyle to go to Europe with an older girlfriend, Lyle went anyway. A person extremely close to the family told me that another of Lyle's girlfriends—not Jamie Pisarcik, who has been so loyal to him during his incarceration—was "manipulating him," which I took to mean manipulating him into marriage. This girl became pregnant. Jose, in his usual method of dealing with his sons' problems, moved in and paid off the girl to abort the child. The manner of Jose's interference in so personal a matter—not allowing Lyle to deal with his own problem—is said to have infuriated Lyle and caused a deep rift between father and son. Lyle moved out of the main house into the guesthouse at the back of the property. He was still living there at the time of the murders, although Erik continued to live in the main house.

Karen Lamm told me that in her final conversation with Kitty, three days before the killing and one day before the purchase of the guns in San Diego, Kitty told her that Lyle had been verbally abusive to her in a long, late-night call from the guesthouse to the main house.

From the beginning, the police were disinclined to buy the highly publicized Mafia-hit story, on the grounds that Mafia hits are rarely done in the home, that the victim is usually executed with a single shot to the back of the head, and that the wife is not usually killed also. The hit, if hit it was, looked more like a Colombian drug-lord hit, like the bloody massacre carried out by Al Pacino in the film *Scarface*, which, incidentally, was one of Lyle's favorite movies.

Months later, after the arrests, the Beverly Hills police claimed to have been suspicious of the Menendez brothers from the beginning, even from the first night. One detective at the scene asked the boys if they had the ticket stubs from the film they said they had just seen in Century City. "When both parents are hit, our feeling is usually that the kids did it," said a Beverly Hills police officer. Another officer declared, two days after the event, "These kids fried their parents. They cooked them." But there was no proof, nothing to go on, merely gut reactions.

Inadvertently, the boys brought suspicion upon themselves. In the aftermath of the terrible event, close observers noted the extraordinary calm the boys exhibited, almost as if the murders had happened to another family. They were seen renting furniture at Antiquarian Traders to replace the furniture that had been removed from the television room. And, as new heirs, they embarked on a spending spree that even the merriest widow, who had married for money, would have refrained from going on—for propriety's sake, if nothing else—in the first flush of her mourning period. They bought and bought and bought. Estimates of their spending have gone as high as $700,000. Lyle bought a $60,000 Porsche 911 Carrera to replace the Alfa Romeo his father had given him. Erik turned in his Ford Mustang 5.0 hardtop and bought a tan Jeep Wrangler, which his girlfriend, Noelle Terelsky, is now driving. Lyle bought $40,000 worth of clothes and a $15,000 Rolex watch. Erik hired a $50,000-a-year tennis coach. Lyle decided to go into the restaurant business, and paid a reported $550,000 for a cafeteria-style eatery in Princeton, which he renamed Mr. Buffalo's, flying back and forth coast to coast on MGM Grand Air. "It was one of my mother's delights that I pursue a small restaurant chain and serve healthy food with friendly service," he said in an interview with *The Daily Princetonian*, the campus newspaper. Erik, less successful as an entrepreneur than Lyle, put up $40,000 for a rock concert at the Palladium, but got ripped off by a con-man partner and lost the entire amount. Erik decided not to attend U.C.L.A., which had been his father's plan for him, but to pursue a career in tennis instead. After moving from hotel to hotel to elude the Mafia, who they claimed were watching them, the brothers leased adjoining condos in the tony Marina City Club Towers. "They liked high-tech surrounds, and they wanted to get out of the house," one of their friends said to me. Then there was the ghoulish sense of humor another of their friends spoke about: Sitting with a gang of pals one night, deciding what videos to rent for the evening, Erik suggested *Dad* and *Parenthood*. Even as close a friend as Glenn Stevens, who was in the car with Lyle when he was arrested, later told the *Los Angeles Times* that two days after the murders, when he asked Lyle how he was holding up emotionally, his friend replied, "I've been waiting so long to be in this position that the transition came easy." The police were also aware that Lyle Menendez had hired a computer expert who eradicated from the hard disk of the family computer a revised will that Jose had been working on. Most remarkable of all was that, unlike the families of most homicide victims, the sons of Jose and Kitty Menendez did not have the obsessive interest in the police search for the killers of their parents that usually supersedes all else in the wake of such a tragedy.

As the C.E.O. of Live Entertainment, Jose Menendez earned a base pay of $500,000 a year, with a maximum bonus of $850,000 based on the company's yearly earnings. On top of that, there were life-insurance policies. An interesting sidebar to the story concerns two policies that were thought to have been taken out on Menendez by Live Entertainment. The bigger of the two was a $15 million keyman policy; $10 million of which was with Bankers Trust and $5 million with Crédit Lyonnais. Taking out a keyman life-insurance policy on a top executive is common practice in business, with the company being named as beneficiary. Live Entertainment was also required to maintain a second policy on Menendez in the amount of $5 million, with the beneficiary to be named by him. Given the family's much-talked-about closeness, it is not unlikely that Kitty and the boys were aware of this policy. Presumably, the beneficiary of the insurance policy would have been the same as the beneficiary of Jose's will. In the will, it was stated that if Kitty died first everything would go to Jose, and if Jose died first everything would go Kitty. In the event that both died, everything would go to the boys.

The murders happened on a Sunday night. On the afternoon of the following Tuesday, Lyle and Erik, accompanied by two uncles, Kitty's brother Brian Andersen and Jose's brother-in-law Carlos Baralt, who was the executor of Jose's will, met with officials of Live Entertainment at the company's headquarters to go over Jose's financial situation. At that meeting, it became the difficult duty of Jose's successor to inform the heirs that the $5 million policy with beneficiaries named by Jose had not gone into effect, because Jose had failed to take the required physical examination, believing that the one he had taken for the $15 million policy applied to both policies. It did not. A person present at that meeting told me of the resounding silence that followed the reception of that information. To expect $5 million, payable upon death, and to find that it was not forthcoming, would be a crushing disappointment. Finally, Erik Menendez spoke. His voice was cold. "And the $15 million policy in favor of the company? Was that in order?" he asked. It was. Jose had apparently been told that he would have to take another physical for the second policy, but he had postponed it. As an officer of the company said to me, "That anything could ever happen to Jose never occurred to Jose."

The news that the policy was invalid caused bad blood between the family and the company, especially since the immediate payment of the $15 million keyman policy gave Carolco one of its biggest quarters since the inception of the company. One of Jose's former employees in New York, who was close enough to the family to warrant having a limousine sent to take him from a suburb of New York to the funeral in Princeton, said to me, "The grandmother? Did you talk to her? Did she tell you her theory? Did she tell you the company had Jose taken care of for the $15 million insurance policy?" The grandmother had not told me this, but it is a theory that the dwindling group of people who believe in the innocence of the Menendez boys cling to with passion. The same former employee continued, "Jose must have made a lot of money in California. I don't know where all that money came from that I've been hearing about and reading about."

Further bad feelings between the family and Live Entertainment have arisen over the house on Elm Drive, which, like the house in Calabasas, is heavily mortgaged: Approximately $2 million is still owed on the Elm Drive house, with estimated payments of $225,000 a year, plus $40,000 a year in taxes and approximately $40,000 in maintenance. In addition, the house in Calabasas has been on the market for some time and remains unsold; $1.5 million is still owed on it. So, in effect, the expenses on the two houses are approximately $500,000 a year, a staggering amount for the two sons to have dealt with before their arrest. During the meeting on the Tuesday after the murders, when the boys were told that the $5 million life insurance policy had not gone into effect, it was suggested that Live Entertainment might buy the house on Elm Drive from the estate, thereby removing the financial burden from the boys while the house was waiting to be resold. Furthermore, Live Entertainment was prepared to take less for the house than Jose had paid for it, knowing that houses where murders have taken place are hard sells, even in as inflated a real estate market as Beverly Hills.

Ads have run in the real estate section of the *Los Angeles Times* for the Elm Drive house. The asking price is $5.95 million. Surprisingly, a buyer did come along. The unidentified person offered only $4.5 million, a bargain for a house on that street, and the offer was hastily accepted. Later, however, the deal fell through. The

purchaser was said to have been intimidated by the event that occurred there, and worried about the reaction neighborhood children
would have to his own children for living in the house.

The arrangement for Live Entertainment to purchase the property
from the estate failed to go into effect, once the police investigation
pointed more and more toward the boys, and so the estate has had to
assume the immense cost of maintaining the properties. Recently, the
Elm Drive house has been leased to a member of the Saudi royal
family—not the same prince who rented it before—for $50,000 a
month to allay expenses.

Carolco, wishing to stifle rumors that Live Entertainment had Mob
connections because of its acquisition of companies like Strawberries,
an audio-video retailing chain, from Morris Levy, who allegedly has
Genovese crime-family connections, and its bitter battle with Noel
Bloom, hired the prestigious New York firm of Kaye, Scholer, Fier-
man, Hays & Handler to investigate the company for underworld ties.
The 220-page report, which cynics in the industry mock as a white-
wash, exonerated the company of any such involvement. The report
was read at a board meeting on March 8, and the conclusion made
clear that the Beverly Hills police, in their investigation of the Menendez murders, were increasingly focusing on their sons, not the Mob.
An ironic bit of drama came at precisely that moment, when a vice
president of the company burst in on the meeting with the news that
Lyle Menendez had just been arrested.

Concurrently, in another, less fashionable area of the city known as
Carthay Circle, an attractive thirty-seven-year-old woman named Judalon Rose Smyth, pronounced Smith, was living out her own drama
in a complicated love affair. Judalon Smyth's lover was a Beverly Hills
psychologist named Jerome Oziel, whom she called Jerry. Dr. Oziel
was the same Dr. Oziel whom Kitty Menendez's psychologist, Les
Summerfield, had recommended to her a year earlier as the doctor for
her troubled son, after the judge in the burglary case in Calabasas had
ruled that Erik must have counseling while he was on probation. During that brief period of court-ordered therapy, Jerome Oziel had met
the entire Menendez family. Judalon Smyth, however, was as unknown
to Lyle and Erik as they were to her, and yet, seven months from the

time of the double murder, she would be responsible for their arrest on the charge of killing their parents.

On March 8, Lyle Menendez was flagged down by more than a dozen heavily armed Beverly Hills policemen as he was leaving the house on Elm Drive in his brother's Jeep Wrangler, accompanied by his former Princeton classmate Glenn Stevens. Lyle was made to lie on the street, in full view of his neighbors, while the police, with drawn guns, manacled his hands behind his back before taking him to the police station to book him for suspicion of murder. The arrest came as a complete surprise to Lyle, who had been playing chess, a game at which he excelled, until two the night before at the home of a friend in Beverly Hills.

Three days earlier, Judalon Smyth had contacted the police in Beverly Hills and told them of the existence of audiotapes in the Bedford Drive office of Dr. Oziel on which the Menendez brothers had allegedly confessed to the murders of their parents. She also told police that the brothers had threatened to kill Oziel if he reported them. Lastly, she told them that the two twelve-gauge shotguns had been purchased at a sporting-goods store in San Diego. All of this information was unknown to the Beverly Hills police, after seven months of investigation. They obtained a subpoena to search all of Oziel's locations. The tapes were found in a safe-deposit box in a bank on Ventura Boulevard.

Lyle's arrest was reported almost immediately on the local Los Angeles newscasts. Among those who heard the news was Noel Nedli, a tennis-team friend from Beverly Hills High who was Erik Menendez's roommate in a condominium that Erik was leasing for six months at the Marina City Club Towers, next to the condominium that his brother had leased with his girlfriend, Jamie Pisarcik. Erik was playing in a tennis tournament in Israel, where he had been for two weeks, accompanied by Mark Heffernan, his $50,000-a-year tennis coach. By a curious coincidence, Erik happened to telephone Nedli at almost the same moment Nedli was listening to the report of Lyle's arrest on the radio. It was merely a routine checking-up-on-everything call, and Nedli realized at once that Erik did not know about Lyle's arrest. He is reported to have said to Erik, "I hope you're sitting down." Then he said, "Lyle was just arrested."

"Erik became hysterical. He was crying, the whole nine yards," said a friend of Nedli's who had heard the story from him. This friend went on to say that the immediate problem for Erik was to get out of Israel before he was arrested there. Accompanied by Heffernan, who was not aware of the seriousness of the situation, the two got on a plane without incident, bound for London. There they split up. Heffernan returned to Los Angeles. Erik flew to Miami, where several members of the Menendez side of the family reside. An aunt advised him to return to Los Angeles and turn himself in. Erik notified police of his travel plans and gave himself up at Los Angeles International Airport, where he was taken into custody by four detectives. He was later booked at the Los Angeles County Men's Central Jail on suspicion of murder and held without bond.

According to Judalon Smyth, and the California Court of Appeals decision, she had stood outside the door of Dr. Oziel's office and, unbeknownst to the Menendez brothers, listened to their confession and threats. Dr. Oziel has denied this.

Approximately a year before any of the above happened, Judalon Smyth told me, she telephoned Jerome Oziel's clinic, the Phobia Institute of Beverly Hills, after having heard a series of tapes called *Through the Briar Patch*, which had impressed her. She was then thirty-six, had been married twice, and was desirous of having a relationship and a family, but she tended to choose the wrong kind of men, men who were controlling. The *Briar Patch* tapes told her she could break the pattern of picking the wrong kind of men in five minutes.

She says Oziel began telephoning her, and she found him very nice on the phone. She felt he seemed genuinely interested in her. After Oziel's third call, she sent him a tape of love poems she had written and called *Love Tears*. She also told him she was in the tape-duplicating business. She found his calls were like therapy, and she began to tell him intimate things about herself, like the fact that she had been going to a professional matchmaker she had seen on television. "I was falling in love over the phone," she said. "You don't think someone's married when he calls you from home at night."

Eventually, he came to her house with two enormous bouquets.

"The minute I opened the door I was relieved," she said. "I wasn't attracted to him. He was shorter than me, blond, balding, with a round face." She told me she was attracted to men who looked like the actor Ken Wahl or Tom Cruise. Oziel was forty-two at the time. "He kept trying to get physical right away. I said, 'Look, you're not my type. I'm not attracted to you.' He said he just wanted a hug. I said, 'Just because you know all this intimate stuff about me doesn't mean . . .'

"Finally I gave in. It was the worst sex I ever had in my life. To have good sex you either have to be in love or in lust. I wasn't either. It was also awful the second time. The third time was better. I broke off with him four or five times between September and October. Then Erik Menendez came."

Although Dr. Oziel had not seen any members of the Menendez family since Erik's counseling had ended, when news of the murders was announced in August 1989, according to Smyth, he became consumed with excitement at his proximity to the tragedy. "Right away, he called the boys and offered his help." At the time, the boys were hiding out in hotels, saying they thought the Mafia was after them. "Jerry would go to where the boys were. He was advising them about attorneys for the will, etc. He had an I'll-be-your-father attitude."

At the end of October, Smyth told me, Oziel got a call from Erik, who said he needed to talk with him. Erik came at four in the afternoon of Halloween, October 31, to the office at 435 North Bedford Drive. There is a small waiting room outside the office, with a table for magazines and several places to sit, but there is no receptionist. An arriving patient pushes a button with the name of the doctor he is there to see, and a light goes on in the inner office to let the doctor know that his next patient has arrived. Off the waiting room is a doorway that opens into a small inner hallway off which are three small offices. Oziel shares the space with several other doctors, one of them his wife, Dr. Laurel Oziel, the mother of his two daughters.

Once there, Erik did not want to talk in the office, so he and Oziel went for a walk. On the walk, according to Smyth, Erik confessed that he and his brother had killed their parents. Lyle, who was at the Elm Drive house at the time, did not know that Erik was seeing Oziel for that purpose. Lyle did not know either that Erik had apparently also confessed to his good friend Craig Cignarelli, with whom he had written the screenplay called *Friends*.

When Smyth arrived at the office, Erik and Oziel had returned from their walk and were in the inner office. According to Smyth, Oziel wanted Erik to tell Lyle that he had confessed to him. Erik did not want to do that. He said that he and Lyle were soon going to the Caribbean to get rid of the guns and that he would tell him then. The plan, according to Erik, Judalon Smyth told me, was to break down the guns, put them into suitcases, and dump the bags in the Caribbean. On the night of the murders, the boys had hidden the two shotguns in the trunk of one of their parents' cars in the garage. The police had searched only the cars in the courtyard in front of the house, not the cars in the garage. Subsequently, the boys had buried the guns on Mulholland Drive. Smyth says Dr. Oziel convinced Erik that the boys would certainly be caught if they were carrying guns in their luggage. He also persuaded him to call Lyle and ask him to come to the office immediately.

It took ten minutes for Lyle to get to the office from the house on Elm Drive. Smyth says he did not know before he got there that Erik had confessed. When he walked into the waiting room, he picked up a magazine and chatted briefly with Smyth, assuming that she was another patient. "Been waiting long?" he asked her. He also pushed the button to indicate to Oziel that he had arrived. Oziel came out and asked Lyle to come in.

According to the California Court of Appeals decision, Smyth says she listened through the door to the doctor's meeting with the boys and heard Lyle become furious with Erik for having confessed. She told me he made threats to Oziel that they were going to kill him. "I never thought I believed in evil, but when I heard those boys speak, I did," she said.

The particulars of the murders she is not allowed to discuss, because of an agreement with the Beverly Hills police, but occasionally, in our conversation, things would creep in. "They did go to the theater to buy the tickets," she said one time. Or, "The mother kept moving, which is why she was hit more." Or, "If they just killed the father, the mother would have inherited the money. So they had to kill her too."

Or, "Lyle said he thought he committed the perfect murder, that his father would have had to congratulate him—for once, he couldn't put him down."

Judalon went on to say, and it is in the opinion of the California Court of Appeals, that she was frightened that she might be caught listening if the boys came out of the office. She went back to the waiting room. Almost immediately, the door opened. "Erik came running out, crying. Then Lyle and Jerry came out. At the elevator, I heard Jerry ask if Lyle was threatening him. Erik had already gone down. Lyle and Jerry followed." From a window in the office, Smyth could see Lyle and Oziel talking to Erik, who was in his Jeep on Bedford Drive.

According to Smyth, Erik knew, from his period of therapy with Oziel after the burglaries, where the doctor lived in Sherman Oaks, a suburb of Los Angeles in the San Fernando Valley. Fearing the boys might come after him, Oziel called his wife and told her to get the children and move out of the house. "Laurel and the kids went to stay with friends," said Smyth. Oziel then moved into Smyth's apartment, the ground floor of a two-family house in the Carthay Circle area of Los Angeles.

In the days that followed, Smyth told several people what she had heard. She has her own business, an audio-video duplicating service called Judalon Sound and Light, in the Fairfax section of Los Angeles. Behind her shop, in which she also sells crystals, quartz, and greeting cards, there is a small office which she rents to two friends, Bruce and Grant, who also have a video-duplicating service. As self-protection, she told them that the Menendez boys had killed their parents. She also told her mother and father and her best friend, Donna.

Then Oziel set up another meeting with the boys. He told them on the second visit that everything they had told him was taped. According to Smyth, the original confession, on October 31, was not taped. What was taped was Oziel's documentation of everything that happened in that session and subsequent sessions with the boys, giving times and dates, telling about the confession and the threat on his life, "a log of what was happening during the time his life was in danger." Smyth further contends that, as time went on, the relationship between the doctor and the boys grew more stable, and the doctor no longer felt threatened.

She said that Oziel convinced the boys "he was their only ally—that if they were arrested he would be their only ally. He was the only one who knew they were abused children, who knew how horrible their home life was, who knew that Jose was a monster father, who knew that Kitty was an abused wife. He convinced them that if they had any hope of ever getting off, they needed him."

Meanwhile, the personal relationship between Smyth and Oziel deteriorated. In a lawsuit filed in the Superior Court of the State of California by Judalon Rose Smyth against L. Jerome Oziel, Ph.D., on May 31, three months after the arrest of the Menendez brothers, it is charged that while Smyth was receiving psychiatric and psychological counseling from defendant Oziel he "improperly maintained Smyth on large doses of drugs and, during said time periods, manipulated and took advantage of Smyth, controlled Smyth, and limited Smyth's ability to care for herself . . . creating a belief in Smyth that she could not handle her affairs without the guidance of Oziel, and convincing Smyth that no other therapist could provide the insight and benefit to her life that Oziel could." In the second cause of action in the suit, Smyth charges that on or about February 16, 1990, defendant Oziel "placed his hands around her throat attempting to choke her, and pulled her hair with great force. Subsequently, on the same day, Defendant Oziel forced Smyth to engage in an act of forcible and unconsented sexual intercourse." According to the California Court of Appeals decision, approximately three weeks after the alleged attack, Smyth contacted the police in Beverly Hills to inform them about the confession she said the Menendez brothers had made to Oziel.

Oziel's lawyer, Bradley Brunon, called Smyth's allegations "completely untrue," and characterized her behavior as "an unfortunate real-life enactment of the scenario in *Fatal Attraction*. . . . She has twisted reality to the point where it is unrecognizable."

"The boys are *adorable*. They're like two foundlings. You want to take them home with you," said the defense attorney Leslie Abramson, who has saved a dozen people from death row. She was talking about the Menendez brothers. Leslie Abramson is Erik's lawyer. Gerald Chaleff is Lyle's.

"Leslie will fight to the grave for her clients," I heard from reporters in Los Angeles who have followed her career. "When there is a murder rap, Leslie is the best in town."

Abramson and Chaleff have worked together before. "We're fifty-fifty, but she's in charge," Chaleff said in an interview. They like each other, and are friends in private life. Abramson met her present husband, Tim Rutten, an editorial writer for the *Los Angeles Times*, at a dinner party at Chaleff's home.

During the arraignment in the Beverly Hills courthouse, I was struck by the glamour of the young Menendez brothers, whom I was seeing face-to-face for the first time. They entered the courtroom, heads held high, like leading actors in a television series. They walked like colts. Their clothes, if not by Armani himself, were by a designer heavily influenced by Armani, probably purchased in the brief period of their independent affluence, between the murders and their arrest. Their demeanor seemed remarkably lighthearted for people in the kind of trouble they were in, as they smiled dimpled smiles and laughed at the steady stream of Abramson's jocular banter. Their two girlfriends, Jamie Pisarcik and Noelle Terelsky, were in the front row next to Erik's tennis coach, Mark Heffernan. Everyone waved. Maria Menendez, the loyal grandmother, was also in the front row, and aunts and uncles and a probate lawyer were in the same section of the courtroom. Several times the boys turned around and flashed smiles at their pretty girlfriends.

They were told to rise. The judge, Judith Stein, spoke in a lugubrious, knell-like voice. The brothers smiled, almost smirked, as she read the charges. "You have been charged with multiple murder for financial gain, while lying in wait, with a loaded firearm, for which, if convicted, you could receive the death penalty. How do you plead?"

"Not guilty, Your Honor," said Erik.

"Not guilty," said Lyle.

Later I asked a friend of theirs who believes in their innocence why they were smiling.

"At the judge's voice," she replied.

Leslie Abramson's curly blond hair bounces, Orphan Annie style, when she walks and talks. She is funny. She is fearless. And she is tough. Oh, is she tough. She walked down the entire corridor of the Beverly Hills courthouse giving the middle finger to an NBC cameraman. "This what you want? You want that?" she said with an angry sneer into the camera. thrusting the finger at the lens, a shot that appeared on the NBC special *Exposé*, narrated by Tom Brokaw. Her passion for the welfare of the accused murderers she defends is legendary. She is considered one of the most merciless cross-examiners in the legal business, with a remarkable ability to degrade and confuse prosecution witnesses. "She loves to intimidate people," I was told. "She thrives on it. She knows when she has you. She can twist and turn a witness's memory like no one else can." John Gregory Dunne, in his 1987 novel *The Red White and Blue*, based the character Leah Kaye, a left-leaning criminal-defense attorney, on Leslie Abramson.

"Why did you give the finger to the cameraman?" I asked her.

"I'll tell you why," she answered, bristling at the memory. "Because I was talking privately to a member of the Menendez family, and NBC turned the camera on, one inch from my face. I said, 'Take that fucker out of my face.' These people think they own the courthouse. They will go to any sleazoid end these days. So I said, 'Is this what you want?' That's when I gave them the finger. Imagine, Tom Brokaw on a show like that.

"I do not understand the publicity of the case," she continued, although of course she understood perfectly. "I mean, the president of the United States wasn't shot."

Before I could reply with such words as "patricide," "matricide," "wealth," "Beverly Hills," she had thought over what she had said. "Well, I rate murder cases different from the public." Most of her cases are from less swell circumstances. In the Bob's Big Boy case, the only death-penalty case she has ever lost, her clients herded nine employees and two customers into the restaurant's walk-in freezer and fired shotguns into their bodies at close range. Three died and four were maimed. One of those who lived had part of her brain removed. Another lost an eye.

"What's the mood of the boys?" I asked.

"I can't comment on my clients," she said. "All I can say is, they're among the very best clients I've ever had, as far as relating. Both of them. It's nonsense, all this talk that there's a good brother and a bad brother. Lyle is wonderful. They're both adorable."

———

NIGHTMARE ON ELM DRIVE

In the avalanche of media blitz that followed the arrest of the Menendez brothers, no one close to Lyle and Erik was the object of more intense fascination and scrutiny than Craig Cignarelli, Erik's tennis partner, with whom he had written the screenplay *Friends*. A family spokesperson told me that in one day alone Craig Cignarelli received thirty-two calls from the media, including "one from Dan Rather, 'A Current Affair,' 'Hard Copy,' etc., etc. I can't remember them all. We had to hire an attorney to field calls." The spokesperson said that "from the beginning it was presumed that Craig knew something."

Craig, clearly enjoying his moments of stardom following the arrests of his best friend and best friend's brother, talked freely to the press and was, by all accounts of other friends of the brothers, too talkative by far. In articles by Ron Soble and John Johnson in the *Los Angeles Times*, Craig said he was attracted to Erik by a shared sense that they were special. He recalled how they would drive out to Malibu late at night, park on a hilltop overlooking the ocean, and talk about their hopes for the future, about how much smarter they were than everyone else, and about how to commit the perfect crime. They had nicknames for each other: Craig was "King," and Erik was "Shepherd." "People really looked up to us. We have an aura of superiority," he said.

As the months passed, it was whispered that Erik had confessed the murders to Craig. This was borne out to me by Judalon Smyth. But he confessed them in an elliptical manner, according to Smyth, in a suppose-it-happened-like-this way, as if planning another screenplay. It was further said that Craig told the police about the confession, but there were not the hard facts on which to make an arrest, such as came later from Judalon Smyth.

Craig's loquaciousness gave rise to many rumors about the two boys, as well as about the possibility that a second screenplay by them exists, one that parallels the murders even more closely. Craig has since been requested by the police not to speak to the press.

At one point, Cignarelli was presumed to be in danger because of what he knew, and was sent away by his family to a place known only to them. An ongoing story is that a relation of the Menendez brothers threatened Craig after hearing that he had gone to the police. The spokesperson for Craig wanted me to make it clear that, contrary to rumors, Craig "never approached the police. The police approached Craig. At a point Craig decided to tell them what he knew." When I asked this same spokesperson about the possibility of a second screenplay written by Craig and Erik, he said he had never seen one. He also said that the deputy district attorney, Elliott Alhadeff, was satisfied that all the information on the confession tapes was known to Craig, so in the event that the tapes were ruled inadmissible by the court he would be able to supply the information on the stand.

Sometime last January, two months before the arrests, the friendship between the two boys cooled. That may have been because Erik suspected that Craig had talked to the police.

Earlier that month, during a New Year's skiing vacation at Lake Tahoe, Erik had met and fallen in love with Noelle Terelsky, a pretty blond student at the University of California in Santa Barbara from Cincinnati. The romance was instantaneous. "Erik's not a hard guy to fall for," said a friend of Noelle. "He's very sweet, very sexy, has a great body, and is an all-around great guy." Noelle, together with Jamie Pisarcik, Lyle's girlfriend, visits the brothers in jail every day, and has been present at every court appearance of the brothers since their arrest. Until recently, when the house on Elm Drive was rented to the member of the Saudi royal family, the two girls lived in the guesthouse, as the guests of Maria Menendez, the proud and passionate grandmother of Lyle and Erik, who believes completely in the innocence of her grandsons. Maria Menendez, Noelle, and Jamie are now living in the Menendezes' Calabasas house, which has still not been sold.

Five months had passed since the arrest. Five months of hearings and deliberations to see whether the audiotapes of Dr. Jerome Oziel were admissible in the murder trial of Lyle and Erik Menendez. Police seizure of therapy tapes is rare, because ordinarily conversations between patients and therapists are secret. But there are occasional exceptions to the secrecy rule, one being that the therapist believes the patient is a serious threat to himself or others. Only the defense attorneys, who did not want the tapes to be heard, had been allowed to participate in the hearings. The prosecution, which did want them to be heard, was barred. Oziel had been on the stand in private hearings from which the family, the media, and the public were barred. Judalon

Smyth had also been on the stand for two days in private sessions, being grilled by Leslie Abramson. The day of the decision had arrived.

There was great tension in the courtroom. Noelle and Jamie, the girlfriends, were there. And Maria, the grandmother. And an aunt from Miami. And a cousin. And the probate lawyer. And others.

Then the Menendez brothers walked in. The swagger, the smirks, the smiles were all gone. And the glamour. So were the Armani-type suits. Their ever-loyal grandmother had arrived with their clothes in suit bags, but the bags were returned to her by the bailiff. They appeared in V-necked, short-sleeved jailhouse blues with T-shirts underneath. Their tennis tans had long since faded. It was impossible not to notice the deterioration in the appearance of the boys, especially Erik. His eyes looked tormented, tortured, haunted. At his neck was a tiny gold cross. He nodded to Noelle Terelsky. He nodded to his grandmother. There were no smiles that day.

Leslie Abramson and Gerald Chaleff went to Judge James Albracht's chambers to hear his ruling on the admissibility of the tapes before it was read to the court. The brothers sat alone at the defense table, stripped of their support system. "Everybody's staring at us," said Erik to the bailiff in a pleading voice, as if the bailiff could do something about it, but there was nothing the bailiff could do. Everybody did stare at them. Lyle leaned forward and whispered something to his brother.

The fierce demeanor of Leslie Abramson when she returned to the courtroom left no doubt that the judge's ruling had not gone in favor of the defense. As the judge read his ruling to the crowded courtroom, Abramson, with her back to the judge, kept up a nonstop commentary in Erik Menendez's ear.

"I have ruled that none of the communications are privileged," said the judge. There was an audible sound of dismay from the Menendez family members. The tapes would be admissible. The judge found that psychologist Jerome Oziel had reasonable cause to believe that Lyle and Erik Menendez "constituted a threat, and it was necessary to disclose the communications to prevent a danger." There was no doubt that this was a serious setback to the defense.

Abramson and Chaleff immediately announced at a news conference that they would appeal the judge's ruling. Abramson called Oziel a gossip, a liar, and "less than credible." Neither Judalon Smyth's name nor her role in the proceedings was ever mentioned.

A mere eight days later, in a stunning reversal of Judge Albracht's ruling, the 2nd District Court of Appeals blocked the release of the tapes, to the undisguised delight of Abramson and Chaleff. Prosecutors were then given a date by which to file opposing arguments. Another complication occurred when Erik Menendez, from jail, refused to provide the prosecution with a handwriting sample to compare with the handwriting found on forms for the purchase of two shotguns in San Diego, despite a warning by the court that his refusal to do so could be used as evidence against him. In a further surprise, Deputy District Attorney Elliott Alhadeff, who won the original court ruling that the tapes would be admissible, was abruptly replaced on the notorious case by Deputy District Attorney Pamela Ferrero.

Since their arrest in March, Lyle and Erik Menendez have dwelt in the Los Angeles County Men's Central Jail, in the section reserved for prisoners awaiting trial in heavily publicized cases. The brothers' cells are not side by side. They order reading material from Book Soup, the trendy Sunset Strip bookshop. Erik has been sent *The Dead Zone*, by Stephen King, and a book on chess. They have frequent visits from family members, and talk with one friend almost daily by telephone. That friend told me that they have to pay for protection in jail. "Other prisoners, who are tough, hate them—who they are, what they've been accused of. They've been threatened." He also told me they feel they have lost every one of their friends. Late in August, when three razor blades were reportedly found in Erik's possession, he was put in solitary confinement, deprived of visitors, books except for the Bible, telephone calls, and exercise. That same week, Lyle suddenly shaved his head.

Los Angeles District Attorney Ira Reiner stated on television that one motive for the murders was greed. Certainly it is possible for a child to kill his parents for money, to wish to continue the easy life on easy street without the encumbrance of parental restrictions. But is it really possible for a child to kill, for merely financial gain, in the manner Kitty and Jose Menendez were killed? To blast holes into one's parents? To deface them? To obliterate them? In the fatal, *coup de grâce* shot, the barrel of one shotgun touched the cheek of Kitty Menendez. You wonder if her eyes met the eyes of her killer in the last second of her life. In this case, we have two children who allegedly participated in the killing of each parent, not in the heat of rage but in a carefully orchestrated scenario after a long gestation period. There is more than money involved here. There is a deep, deep hatred, a hatred that goes beyond hate.

The closest friend of the Menendez brothers, with whom I talked at length on the condition of anonymity, kept saying to me over and over, "It's only the tip of the iceberg." No amount of persuasion on my part could make him explain what the iceberg was. Months earlier, however, a person close to the situation mouthed but did not speak the word "incest" to me. Subsequently, a rich woman in Los Angeles told me that her bodyguard, a former cop, had heard from a friend of his on the Beverly Hills police force that Kitty Menendez had been shot in the vagina. At a Malibu barbecue, a film star said to me, "I heard the mother was shot up the wazoo." There is, however, no indication of such a penetration in the autopsy report, which carefully delineates each of the ten wounds from the nine shots fired into Kitty Menendez's body. But the subject continues to surface. Could it be possible that these boys were puppets of their father's dark side? "They had sexual hatred for their parents," one of the friends told me. This same person went on to say, "The tapes will show that Jose molested Lyle at a very young age."

Is this true? Only the boys know. If it is, it could be the defense argument that will return them to their tennis court, swimming pool, and chess set, as inheritors of a $14 million estate that they could not have inherited if they had been found guilty. Karen Lamm, however, does not believe such a story, although it is unlikely that Kitty would have revealed to her a secret of that dimension. Judalon Smyth was also skeptical of this information when I brought up the subject of sexual abuse. She said she had heard nothing of the kind on Halloween afternoon when, according to the California Court of Appeals decision, she listened outside Dr. Oziel's office door as Lyle and Erik talked about the murders. She said that last December, almost two months after the October 31 confession to Oziel, which was not taped, the boys, feeling that the police were beginning to suspect them, voluntarily made a tape in which they confessed to the crime. In it, they spoke of their remorse. In it, apparently, they told of psychological abuse. But sexual abuse? Judalon Smyth did not hear this tape, and by that time Dr. Oziel was no longer confiding in her.

October 1990

I became deeply and personally involved in this story. The trial went on for months. Erik and Lyle Menendez, the young killers, became romantic figures in the televised proceedings. In cases of high crime, I've never made any attempt to present a balanced picture. This was no exception. I was appalled by the lies I heard defense attorneys tell in the courtroom. I became despised by Leslie Abramson, the lead defense attorney. I couldn't have cared less. The trial ended in a hung jury, which was considered a victory for the defense. Their luck did not hold for the second trial. They are both doing life without the possibility of parole in separate prisons in California.

QUEENS OF THE ROAD

J ust when you thought you knew all there was to know about the highly publicized Collins sisters, Joan and Jackie, or Jackie and Joan, comes the news that big sister Joan, the soap-opera superstar, whose divorces and romantic exploits have been making tabloid headlines for thirty years, has turned literary in her fifty-fifth year and is moving in on the printed-page turf of her little sister Jackie, the superstar novelist, whose eleven-volume *oeuvre* has sold 65 million copies in thirty languages throughout the world over the last two decades. Yes, friends, Joan Collins, between takes as the beloved bitch Alexis Carrington Colby on "Dynasty," has written her *own* novel, called *Prime Time,* about a top-rated soap opera on American television, with eight or ten characters, all of them actors and actresses, and a leading lady who has overcome obstacles, both personal and financial, to regain her stardom.

And as if that weren't enough, Joan's literary agent, the legendary Irving "Swifty" Lazar, a superstar in his own right, has sold Joan's book for a million bucks to, you guessed it, Jackie's publisher, Simon and Schuster, where her editor is another superstar, Michael Korda, a novelist in his own right, who—hang on to your hat—also happens to be Jackie's editor. (Lazar sold it abroad for an additional $2 million—$1 million in England alone—without showing one written word.)

"I get along very well with both of them," said Korda. "I'm very fond of them."

There are those who will tell you that Jackie isn't happy with the proximity, and neither is her superstar agent, Morton Janklow, who long ago moved in on Swifty Lazar's turf as the agent who got the most bucks for his writer clients. As a reaffirmation of Simon and Schuster's warm feeling for its massive money-maker, Michael Korda signed Jackie up for two additional books after the completion of her current contract.

"I don't like to talk figures," said Jackie Collins in her Beverly Hills home about her new deal, "but I will say it's a record-breaking contract."

Michael Korda, from his New York office, added, "If this isn't the largest amount of money in American book publishing, it sure ought to be. It's about the same size as the Brazilian national debt." Then he added, almost as an afterthought, "But I also bought two more books from Joan."

"Is there a feud going on between them?" I asked.

"Probably so, at some level," he answered. "Jackie can't help but feel that Joan is crowding her territory."

Said Irving Lazar, "Certainly, there is sibling rivalry at times."

Said Joni Evans, formerly of Simon and Schuster, now publisher at Random House, "Of course, there has to be."

Said Morton Janklow, "Yes, Jackie and Joan have flareups, but since Simon and Schuster has both books, Irving and I can see to it that they don't come out head to head. So both sisters will have a couple of great months."

The Collins sisters themselves are quick to tell you that there is no trouble between them at all, although their publicist, Jeffrey Lane, who is actually Joan's publicist, best pal, and traveling companion, but who doubled as Jackie's publicist for this article, laid down some ground rules for me to abide by, namely that if Jackie's name was used first in one sentence, then Joan's must be used first in the next, and that there was to be equal copy on each sister. Like that.

The fact is, I know both of these ladies. The first time I ever saw Joan was in 1957. She walked up off the beach in Santa Monica, California, where I was renting a beach house, wearing a bikini before anyone I knew was wearing a bikini, and asked if she could use the bathroom. She was then in the first of her two stardoms, the one that didn't last. Of course she could use the bathroom. In my scrapbooks I have pictures of her from the sixties, at parties my wife and I had in

Beverly Hills: with Mia Farrow, before she married Frank Sinatra; with Ryan O'Neal, after he split from Joanna Moore; with Michael Caine, long before he married Shakira; and with Natalie Wood, after her first marriage to Robert Wagner. Joan was then in the second of her four marriages, to the English star Anthony Newley. In every picture she is having a good time.

Jackie I met much later. We sat next to each other at one of Irving Lazar's Academy Awards parties at Spago. It struck me then how alike the sisters are, and also how different. Last year at the Writers' Conference in Santa Barbara, Jackie and I were both speakers, along with Thomas McGuane, Irving Stone, William F. Buckley, Jr., and others. Jackie arrived only minutes before she was scheduled to speak, in a stretch limousine with a great deal of video equipment to record her speech. Only, she didn't make a speech the way the rest of us did. The conference provided her with an interviewer, and the interviewer asked her questions. There wasn't an empty seat in the hall. "Can you give the writers here some advice?" the interviewer asked. "Write only about what you know," she told them. Later, when the floor was thrown open to questions from the audience, the audience was told in advance by the interviewer, "Miss Collins will answer no questions about her sister." Her sister was, at the time, involved in the highly publicized extrication from her fourth marriage.

It's nonsense," said Jackie when I asked her about the rumors of a rift. "We're very amicable together."

"I don't have a rivalry with my sister," said Joan when I asked her. "People are always saying I have rivalries—particularly with Elizabeth Taylor and Linda Evans. I've never said a bad word about another actress, at least in print. And now they're saying I have this rivalry with Jackie. It's not true."

"Let me put it this way," said Jackie. "We're not in each other's pockets, but we're good friends. We're not the kind of sisters who call each other every day, but she knows I'm there for her."

"Jackie lives a totally different life from me," said Joan. "If I get five days off from work, I take off. I like Los Angeles, but I'm more European than she is in my outlook. I like staying up late. I like sleeping late. I like two-hour lunches, with wine. I do not like tennis, golf, lying by the pool. What I like doing here is to work very hard and then leave."

"We have a lot of the same friends," said Jackie. "Roger and Luisa Moore, Dudley Moore, Michael and Shakira Caine. Then Joan has *her* whole group of friends, and I have *my* whole group."

"I like getting on planes and going on trips," said Joan.

Hollywood Wives gave me a high profile," said Jackie. "Before that, in England, I was always Joan's little sister. I was lucky to have made it in America before Joan hit in 'Dynasty.' What I love about Joan is that she's one of the great survivors. She did things ahead of her time that have since become accepted. She always lived her life like a man. She was a free spirit. If she saw a guy she wanted to go to bed with, she went after him, and that was unacceptable behavior at the time."

"Oh, God, Jackie, that's great," said Joan, touching the emerald of a borrowed necklace her sister was wearing for the shoot. "Is it yours?"

Jackie laughed. "No, darling."

"You should buy it for yourself," said Joan. "You can afford it."

Joan Collins is the embodiment of the kind of characters that Jackie Collins writes about. She is beautiful, famous, rich, was once a movie star, has been what is known in Hollywood as on her ass, meaning washed up and nearly broke, and then resurrected herself as a greater television star than she ever was a movie star. Jackie flatly denies that her character Silver Anderson in *Hollywood Husbands* was based on her sister, although Silver Anderson is a washed-up, middle-aged star who makes it back, bigger than ever, in a soap opera, who "wasn't twenty-two and didn't give a damn," and who "had a compact, sinewy body, with firm breasts and hard nipples."

Joan has been married and divorced four times. "I've always left my husbands," she said, about Maxwell Reed, Anthony Newley, the late Ron Kass, and the recent and unlamented Peter Holm, who asked for, but didn't receive, a divorce settlement of $80,000 a month. Her host of romances over the years, which she delineated in detail in her auto-biography, *Past Imperfect,* have included Laurence Harvey, Warren Beatty, Sydney Chaplin, Ryan O'Neal, and Rafael Trujillo, the son of the dictator of the Dominican Republic, an affairette masterminded in the fifties by Zsa Zsa Gabor. She currently lives in a house that Joan Crawford might have lived in at the height of her fame. Built by Laurence Harvey but redone totally by Joan, it has a marble entrance hall and white carpets and white sofas and a peach bedroom with an Art Deco headboard and a spectacular view of the city of Los Angeles. She has posed for more than five hundred magazine covers, and many of them are framed on the walls of her office. She has diamonds for all occasions, and Bob Mackie and Nolan Miller design the glittering evening gowns she favors for her public appearances. Swifty Lazar says, "Joan is addicted to the precept that life is for fun and having a great time. She throws caution to the wind. It has brought her troubles at times. She has been broke when she didn't have to be. She is much less cautious than Jackie. She worries much less about what's going to happen in ten years. She lives totally in the present."

Known as a great hostess, she loves having parties as much as she loves going to them. She gives Sunday lunches, seated dinners for eighteen, and buffet suppers for forty, and recently she tented over her swimming pool and had several hundred of her nearest and dearest friends, mostly famous, in for a black-tie dinner dance, with, according to Swifty Lazar, "great music, great wines, and place cards," the kind of party that people in Hollywood always say they used to give out here but don't give anymore. She loves nightlife, and one of her complaints about Hollywood, where she has lived on and off since the 1950s, is that everyone goes to bed too early. As often as possible, every three weeks or so, she is on a plane to London for four or five days, because her three children are there. Tara and Sacha, twenty-five and twenty-three, by her marriage to Anthony Newley, are living on their own. Her other daughter, Katyana, called Katy, by Ron Kass, who died in 1986, is the child she literally willed back to life after she was struck by a car and hovered between life and death for weeks in an intensive-care unit when she was eight. Katy, now fifteen, attends school in London and lives in a rented flat with Joan's longtime English secretary and a nanny. Although Joan is said to party nonstop during her London weekends, it is to see her children that she travels there so often, and not to see her latest love, Bill Wiggins, known as Bungalow by the English tabloids because he has "nothing upstairs and everything down below." As of this writing he is no longer her latest love but just "a dear friend." "She loves it there," said Douglas Cramer, an executive producer on "Dynasty." "Next to the Queen, she's the queen."

"How do the producers feel about your traveling so much to England while the show is in production?" I asked Joan.

"They're quite accommodating, actually, because they want me back next season," said Joan.

"Are you coming back next season?"

"I would only do it on my terms. I would not want to be in every episode."

While Joan is known as a great hostess, Jackie is known as a great housekeeper. She cooks. She markets. She dusts. She has no live-in servants, only a cleaning woman three times a week, and her children have their household chores. At Christmastime, she presided over a family dinner for seventeen, including Joan, which she cooked and served herself, urging seconds and thirds on everyone, and then organized charades. She is a very concerned family person.

Like her sister, she has a tremendous drive to be on top. "Being number one in America means being number one in the world," she said. She has been married for over twenty years to Oscar Lerman, who co-owns discotheques in London and Los Angeles. Ad Lib, his famous London club of the sixties, was a favorite hangout of the Beatles and the Stones. It was there Jackie conceived the idea for her about-to-be-released novel, *Rock Star.* Tramp, the Los Angeles branch of his London disco, is a hangout for young stars like Sean Penn and Timothy Hutton. Jackie goes there one night a week to watch the action and store away information. She married for the first time at the age of nineteen, but the marriage ended tragically when her husband overdosed on drugs. Her oldest daughter, Tracy, is from that marriage, and she has two more daughters by Oscar, Tiffany, twenty, and Rory, eighteen, who are not, absolutely not, she will tell you, "Hollywood kids," which will be the subject of the book after *Lady Boss,* which will be the book after *Rock Star.* All three girls live at home, in a deceptively large white house in the flats of Beverly Hills which Carroll Baker once bought with her *Baby Doll* earnings. It is definitely not the kind of house where Joan Crawford would have lived, but rather a house that screams family and family life. There are so many cars in the driveway it looks like a parking lot: Jackie's '66 Mustang and her two Cadillacs, Oscar's Mercury, her daughters' cars, and sometimes their boyfriends' cars. Every room has bookcases brimming over with books, most of them best-sellers of the Harold Robbins and Sidney Sheldon school, and so many paintings that they are stacked against the walls. Pictures of movie stars at movie-star parties, all taken by the famous author herself, who never goes to a party without her camera, line the walls of her powder room.

On my first visit to Jackie's home, two large yellow Labradors were flaked out on the white sofas in the living room, and she did not tell them to move. "Poor old thing, he's fifteen," she said about one of the dogs, and we moved to another room rather than disturb them.

When the doorbell rang later, the dogs charged for the door. Joan Collins, in a fox coat, had stopped by to have tea with her sister.

"Am I going to be jumped on by these wild animals?" she screamed from the front hall. All Joan's entrances are entrances. The day before, she had walked down a stairway wearing a—for her—demure dress. "This is my *jeune fille* look," she said in greeting. "Still trying after all these years."

"Joan's not crazy about dogs," Jackie explained to me, rising to take the dogs elsewhere. It occurred to me that Silver Anderson in *Hollywood Husbands* is not crazy about dogs either.

The sisters greeted each other with a kiss on each cheek. One had tea. One had coffee. They talked about movies they had seen the night before. They always see movies in friends' projection rooms or at studio screenings. Jackie had seen *The Last Emperor* at Roger Moore's house. Joan had seen *Baby Boom* at someone else's house. "It's my favorite movie. Diane is so good," she said about Diane Keaton. "She had one of the best scenes I ever saw." She then reenacted it while Jackie watched. Whatever you hear about these two sisters having a feud, just remember this. They like each other. They laugh at each other's stories. They listen to each other, and they're proud of each other's success.

"We are the triumph of the immigrant," said Joan. "That's what America's all about. People dream that the streets are paved with gold, and my sister and I showed that they are. If only Mummy had lived to see the two of us now, she would have been so proud."

Their father, now in his eighties, they remember as aloof, strict, and austere when they were children. "English men are rather cool and into themselves," Joan said. He was a theatrical agent with Lew Grade, later Sir Lew Grade, now Lord Grade. But it was their mother, who died in 1962, whom both sisters spoke of in the most loving terms, as being affectionate and feminine and protective of them. There are pictures of her in both sisters' houses.

"We wish our mother was alive to see what's happened to us. She would have enjoyed this more than anyone," said Jackie.

Joan said it was not true, as I had heard, that she was so broke in 1981 that Aaron Spelling had to pay her grocery bills before she could return to California to do "Dynasty." "Where do these stories start?" she asked.

In a large album of color photographs on the tea table, there is a picture of Joan, taken by Jackie, at the party Joan gave to celebrate her recent divorce from Peter Holm, the toy-boy husband who almost made Joan look foolish, but didn't, because she laughed at herself first. In the photograph, she is wearing a T-shirt that says, "HOMEless," a gift from her friend David Niven, Jr. She is laughing, but behind her mascara'd eyes there is the unmistakable look, at once gallant and sad, of the Hollywood survivor.

When I asked her about Peter Holm, who is rumored to be writing a book called *Joan and Me*, she began to sing. It is a topic she is thoroughly sick of. "I wonder what's happened to him," she said finally.

"Do you care?" I asked.

She shrugged her shoulders.

"One of these days I just know I'm going to meet somebody with whom I would like to share my life," she said.

Later, as I was leaving, she called after me a variation on that line in *Tea and Sympathy*, "When you write about this, and you will, be kind!"

Jackie Collins is a high-school dropout and was a self-confessed juvenile delinquent at age fifteen. "I'm glad I got all of that out of my system at an early age," she said. She arrived in Hollywood at sixteen to visit her sister, then a contract player at Twentieth Century-Fox. Joan was just leaving to go on location for a film, and she tossed her sister the keys to her apartment. "Learn how to drive" was her only L.A. advice. Jackie said she started out her Hollywood life with Joan's famous friends and the friends she made herself—kids who pumped gas and waited on tables. She still draws on the latter group for inspiration. In all her books, there are characters who embody the underlying hostility of the have-nots for the haves. Chauffeurs and gardeners urinate in movie stars' swimming pools; hired waiters steal cases of liquor at A Group parties where they serve; butlers sell their employers' secrets to the trash press.

Jackie's style is different from Joan's, but it's style. Watch her walk into Le Dome for lunch, a superstar in action. Le Dome, on the Sunset Strip, is the hot hot hot spot for the in movie crowd to lunch these days. Outside the front door, fans with cameras wait for the stars. "Look this way, Miss Collins," they yell when we arrive, and she obliges, adjusting her head to the perfect angle, smiling the friendly but not too friendly smile that celebrities use for their fans. Inside, Michael Yhuelo, one of the owners, greets her with open arms and gives her an air kiss near each cheek. Waiters turn to look at her as if she were a film star rather than a novelist. She walks through the terrace room and makes a turn into the dining room to the table she has asked for in the far corner. "Hi, Michelle," she calls to Michelle Phillips on the way. "Hi, Jack," she calls to the columnist Jack Martin.

"I really love L.A.," she said. "In England, I grew up reading Harold Robbins, Mickey Spillane, and Raymond Chandler." L.A. to Jackie means strictly Hollywood, which she affectionately calls the kiss-ass capital of the world. She loves the picture business, the television business, the record business, and the people in them, the stars, celebrities, directors, and producers. She is also a great partygoer, but more in the role of observer than participant, someone doing research. Like all seasoned Hollywood people, she refers to Hollywood as "this town." "One of the reasons I've gotten along here is that I've never needed this town, or anything from anyone here." As she said at the writers' conference last summer, "Write about what you know." And what this lady knows about is Hollywood. Sue Mengers, the famed Hollywood actors' agent, now in semiretirement, called *Hollywood*

Husbands the definitive book about Hollywood in the eighties. "Jackie got the feeling of this town better than anyone ever caught it. She understands it."

"I love what I do," said Jackie. "I fall in love with my characters. They become me, and I become them. They're part of me forever, even when I'm finished with them."

Her writing schedule is rigid. She works seven days a week, writing in longhand in spiral notebooks in a room she calls her study. On a good day she can write twenty pages. On a bad day she knocks off ten. When she gets to about seven hundred pages, she starts to bring the novel to an ending. She does not type; a secretary transfers her long-hand to a word processor. Jackie is aware that her grammar is not always perfect, but that is the way she wants it. Once she asked her secretary to change anything she thought was wrong, and she then realized that her work lost in the translation to correct grammar.

"I never show *anything* to my publishers until after I finish writing the entire book," said Jackie. At the time I talked with her in December, she had not yet submitted *Rock Star* to Simon and Schuster, although it was coming out in April. Most books are not published until eight or ten months after submission. Confirming this, Michael Korda diplomatically said, "I would rather not have it this way." Only someone who has shown the same consistent success year after year could command that kind of leverage with a publisher.

Finally we get around to the subject of Joan Collins the novelist.

"Everybody wants to write a book once in their life," said Jackie about Joan's book, which she has not read. "If Joan can do it, good luck to her. She does everything well." She looked at her menu and continued: "I don't see Joan as becoming a novelist. I see it as a diversion for her. I've been a published novelist for twenty years. All eleven of my books have never been out of print." She thought over what she had said. "Of course, the fact that I've been offered the lead in a soap opera has nothing to do with her book!"

Joan Collins is the kind of woman you expect women to hate, but they don't. When her friends talk about her, they use the adjectives "indomitable" and "indefatigable." Her former agent, Sue Mengers, who handled the crème de la crème of Hollywood stars when she was still in the picture business, confirmed for me a story that Joan had told me. During Joan's down years, when the movie offers had stopped coming, Sue took Joan, whom she truly liked, out to lunch and told her she had to face up to the fact that after forty it was tough for actresses. "You have to realize that nothing more may happen in your career. Go home and concentrate on real life." Mengers went on to say that Joan cried a little that day, but she refused to give up. "Never," she said. "I'm so happy she proved me wrong," said Mengers. "Even Aaron Spelling, when he cast Joan in the part of Alexis, could not have imagined how strongly the public would take to her—especially women. The femme fatale number she plays is in good fun. In her own life, she has more women friends than any woman I know."

Joan Collins can carry on a conversation with you on the set of "Dynasty" at the same time she is being pinned up by one person, powdered by another, and having her hair sprayed by a third. She continues her conversation while she looks in a mirror that someone holds for her, checks her left side, checks her right, and makes a minute readjustment of a curl. She has been on movie sets since she was seventeen, and she retains the figure of a teenager and a bosom so superb that she recently had to threaten to sue the London *Sun* and *News of the World* after they reported that she had had a breast implant. She hadn't had a breast implant at all, and she got a retraction.

"Actually, I started writing novels when I was seven or eight," said Joan, about her new career as a novelist. " 'The Little Ballerinas,' 'The Gypsy and the Prince.' That kind of thing."

She is called to the set to shoot a scene with Linda Evans, a variation of half a hundred other confrontation scenes between Alexis and Krystle that have been shot in the six years that she has been on "Dynasty." Joan, as Alexis, paced back and forth in her office, reading a stock report, and Linda Evans, as Krystle Carrington, entered.

ALEXIS: What do you want, Krystle?

KRYSTLE: To go over a few things with you.

ALEXIS: Such as?

KRYSTLE: Your life.

ALEXIS: Is this some sort of joke?

KRYSTLE: I'm getting closer and closer to the truth of who and what you really are.

ALEXIS: I'm going to call security.

The director yelled, "Cut!" Joan returned to where we had been talking, and picked up the conversation as if a scene had not just been filmed. "I write in bed, on planes, under the hair dryer, on the set. Sometimes I write twelve to fifteen hours a day for a week, and then I don't touch it for a while. It's erratic, because it's a second career for me."

"Most of her manuscript comes in on the most extraordinary pieces of paper," says Michael Korda, who is working closely with her on her novel, as he did on her autobiography. "But every word is from her. Every revision. There is no ghostwriter, no helper, no hidden person. Her concentration is remarkable, given all the things going on in her life." Korda, the nephew of Sir Alexander Korda, the film producer, is an old acquaintance of Joan's from their teenage years in London. He remembers that when he was nineteen he took her to a party for Sonny Tufts at the house of Sir Carol Reed, but he adds that Joan did not remember this early date when he reminded her of it.

He thinks that when the two books come out the media will manufacture a rivalry between Joan and Jackie. "But if the time should ever come when the two of them are neck and neck on the *New York Times* best-seller list," he says, "I'm going to have a hot time of it."

March 1988

———————————

Things remain touch-and-go between the Collins sisters, and probably always will. They're never going to be buddies, but they're civilized when they meet. Jackie is totally content in her Beverly Hills life in the Joan Crawford–style mansion she built for herself. Joan lives a peripatetic life. She's likely to be seen racing through the lobby of the Ritz Hotel in Paris, or entertaining a group at lunch at Harry's Bar in London, or resting up from it all in Saint-Tropez.

TEARDOWN

Teardown is the new word on everyone's lips in what has become known as the Platinum Triangle, the prestigious residential area of Los Angeles that encompasses Beverly Hills, Holmby Hills, and Bel Air, and teardowns are rampant on almost every one of its fashionable streets. Sounds of hammering and drilling fill the air, and the once-quiet drives are jammed with cement mixers, cherry pickers, trucks, and lunch wagons as one of the greatest and most expensive building booms in real-estate history takes place. If *teardown* is a new word to you, it means buying a house, very often a beautiful house, for a great deal of money, and tearing it down in order to build a bigger house, for a great deal more money, on the same piece of land, a process that results, very often, in the construction of houses that are vastly overscaled for the size of the property on which they sit. The value of the land alone is so high that people are paying $3 million and up for an acre.

"We're in a renaissance out here. There's nothing like it in the world," said the enormously successful Realtor Bruce Nelson as he drove me around the various high-priced areas in his pale yellow Rolls Corniche, in which the telephone never stopped ringing. "Excuse me," he said at one point, stopping in the middle of a sentence to answer the phone and discuss a deal with a possible buyer for the house of a Saudi Arabian prince, which the prince had bought a few years earlier from the shipping and real-estate magnate D. K. Ludwig, reportedly the richest man in America until recent business reversals in the Amazon region of Brazil toppled him from that lofty perch to a current net worth of a mere $550 million.

"All the great homes here were built in the thirties," Nelson continued after he hung up. "At that time, two-acre lots went for $15,000 or $20,000. Now the same property goes for between $7 million and $10 million, but without the house." Nelson was not exaggerating. In fact, a few days later the *Los Angeles Times* reported in its real estate column that a two-acre vacant lot in Beverly Hills had been sold by the film and record producer David Geffen for $7.45 million. Geffen had bought the land only a year and a half earlier for $3.85 million, and after having plans for a house drawn up had decided against building it. Even more amazing was the story of a young couple who had purchased eight acres in the Pacific Palisades for $6.5 million. Only two of the eight acres were flat; the rest was downhill. Yet even before the couple started to build, they had an offer of $24 million in cash for the land. And they refused it!

Real-estate agent Thelma Orloff, who was a show girl in the great days of the MGM musicals, holds court in the coffee shop of the Beverly Hills Hotel at 8:30 every morning, before leaving for her office. Still statuesque, she arrives each day to a chorus of "Hello, Thelma" from the regular breakfasters at the counter. Thelma Orloff has been around a long time, first as a show girl, then as an actress, wife, and mother, and now—stardom at last—as a real-estate agent *extraordinaire*. She recently celebrated fifty years of friendship with her best pal, Lucille Ball. She used to swim in Fanny Brice's pool in Holmby Hills, and can tell you every person who's lived in that house since Fanny died and what he paid. It is said that Thelma Orloff made the former television gossip celebrity Rona Barrett rich by turning over Beverly Hills real estate for her. As she drove me through the streets in her sleek black Cadillac, her comments on the houses of the famous were like an oral history of the area. "That's Eva Gabor's house, which is now up for sale; she bought it from Henry Berger after Anita Louise died. That's Betsy Bloomingdale's house, and up there next to it there used to be a one-story house that burned down; this developer bought it and has built a $7.8 million spec house, using every square inch of the land. Over there's Bonita Granville Wrather's house, which is about to come on the market. I went to Ann Warner with an offer of $30 million for her house, but she said, 'Forget it.' " Ann Warner is the widow of Jack Warner, of Warner Brothers, and her magnificent house, set on nine prime Beverly Hills acres, is considered one of the great estates of the area. Mrs. Warner, who lives in virtual seclusion in a few upstairs rooms in the house, has turned down offer after offer for her mansion. One real-estate agent told me she would probably accept $25 million for it on the condition that she have the right to live there for the rest of her life, with everything as it is.

In my early days in Hollywood, the grandest house of all to get into, once you had arrived socially, was the white Georgian mansion belonging to the late William and Edith Mayer Goetz. A famed Hollywood wit as well as a distinguished film producer, Bill Goetz was one of the earliest major art collectors in the film colony. His wife, Edie, the daughter of Louis B. Mayer, the legendary head of MGM in its heyday, and the sister of Irene Mayer Selznick, who was once married to David O. Selznick, before he married Jennifer Jones, was a Hollywood princess in every sense of the word, and, as Mrs. Goetz, became the undisputed social queen of Hollywood for decades. Her chef knew no peer in the community, and her guest lists were as carefully honed as fine ivory. No outsiders in Edie Goetz's drawing room, ever. After dinner, there was always the latest movie, and as Mrs. Goetz's guests settled back into the sofas and chairs of her drawing room, designed by William Haines, a screen was lowered at one end of the room, obliterating for two hours Picasso's *Mother and Child*. It was heady stuff. Now the Goetzes are dead, their pictures have been sold in a recent auction that netted $85 million for their two daughters, and their lovely, graceful house is up for sale. Imagine my surprise, while having breakfast in the coffee shop of the Beverly Hills Hotel, to hear it casually referred to as a teardown—a $12 million teardown, but a teardown nonetheless. According to Bruce Nelson, the Goetz mansion, though swank in the extreme in its day, now needs "everything done. The Leonard Goldbergs offered $8 million cash, and were turned down." Another of the big Realtors told me, "Streisand looked at it, but decided against it. Too much work." In all probability, the purchaser, whoever he or she may be, will raze the house to build a bigger and grander one. It's the trend. It's in the air. The talk is so pervasive and persuasive that you find yourself agreeing with the logic of buying a $10 million mansion in order to tear it down and build a $20 million one.

———

Some people will tell you that Columbia Savings in Beverly Hills started the teardown trend; a few residents will go so far as to say that Columbia Savings has just about ruined Beverly Hills. But the people who will always be most associated with the trend are the vastly rich television mogul Aaron Spelling and his wife, Candy. Over five years ago, the Spellings bought the old Bing Crosby house on one of the best streets in Holmby Hills for $10 million. It turned out that the cost of bringing the house up to date and redesigning it to the eighties' needs of the Spelling family was prohibitive—it would be cheaper to tear it down and start over. The neighbors in the swank neighborhood were appalled, but the Spellings persevered. If all goes according to plan, they will finally be able to move into their French-style palace a year from now.

The Spelling house is the most discussed house in the city, and all other houses are compared with it. As of this moment, it is the largest by far of the many large houses being built. There was a time when houses were talked of in terms of how many rooms they had, but now all such discussions are in terms of square feet. The Spelling house is, give or take a thousand square feet or two, 56,000 square feet, approximately the size of a football field. An acre is 43,560 square feet, so the Spelling place is roughly an acre and a quarter of house. Probably not since Ludwig of Bavaria brought his country to the verge of bankruptcy with the extravagance of his palace-building has a residence been as publicly criticized as the Spelling house. Television newscasters have hovered over it in helicopters, pointing out to their viewers that it is being built for a family of only four. Comedians tell jokes about it. The fact remains that if the Spelling house had not been so prominently placed, so visible to the public eye, it would have been far less criticized. Budd Holden, a former set designer on "The Dinah Shore Show" who is now designing many of the most expensive L.A. homes, though not the Spelling mansion, has said of it, "It's mind-boggling, the space. Just beautiful." Four different real-estate agents told me that "some Japanese" had secretly gone through the Spelling house and offered $52 million for it.

"Do you mean the Spelling house is for sale?" I asked.

"No, no, of course it isn't for sale. But everything out here is for sale."

The mode of upscale spending is bewildering to longtime residents of Beverly Hills, who shake their heads in sadness at the evaporation of their once-charming community with its side-by-side potpourri of architectural styles. There is no remembrance of things past. "Beverly Hills has been destroyed. It's gone," one resident told me. New people moving in can't tear down fast enough. "New money wants new houses," said Stan Herman, a Beverly Hills Realtor with eighteen agents working under him in an elegant office that sports a bar. Herman, who has a press agent and a press kit that lists the names of 131 famous people "who have lived in Stan Herman's homes," used to be married to Linda Evans of "Dynasty," and he moves in the fast lanes of Beverly Hills and Malibu life. Over the years he has bought many houses, redone them, and then resold them at enormous profit. He bought, for instance, the house Frank Sinatra lived in during his brief marriage to Mia Farrow in the 1960s, redid it entirely, even adding one of his trademarks, a wall urinal in the marble master bathroom, and then resold it to the theatrical producer James Nederlander and his wife for over $4 million. Herman says that if he had just held on to it until the teardown period started, he wouldn't have had to bother to do it over; he could have sold it for the same price without doing one thing. "There's megabucks here today. The Australians, the Japanese, people from Hong Kong. The Taiwanese money isn't here yet, but it's coming, and, of course, the French and the Italians. These people build enormous kitchens, the size of commercial kitchens, but they never cook, because they go out every night, and only the maids cook their own dinners in them." The big question everyone wants answered is, Who *are* these people who are knocking down all the houses and building new ones, putting as many square feet of house on the property as they can? Stan Herman said, "You'd think you would know, or should know, who someone is who has $10 million to spend on a house, but these days you don't."

KEEP OUT signs are posted everywhere to prevent the curious multitudes from staring in. Any sign of unauthorized entry brings a foreman yelling "Uh-uh" in no uncertain terms, meaning *"Out!"* and the grander places under construction have uniformed security guards. However, by arriving on the sites in Bruce Nelson's yellow Corniche and using "attitude," as Nelson calls it, I was able to gain entry to a surprising number.

Four of the most extraordinary new houses that I visited are being built by men in their early forties, most of them self-made men who acquired their fortunes during the Reagan years and who have probably been influenced by the flamboyance of Donald Trump's highly publicized lifestyle. In one instance, two houses on adjoining lots were torn down to build one 24,000-square-foot home for the couple and their three children, three nannies, and four maids. In another, two houses on adjoining lots were gutted, rebuilt, and joined together as one, encircled by a miniature railroad for the owner's two young sons. "You're only this age once. You may as well do it," one architect quoted his client as saying.

"We're talking all cash in these houses. There are no loans on any of them," said Bruce Nelson. "Vast fortunes have been coming into the Los Angeles area for years now, but very quietly."

Standing in the curve of a sweeping staircase, looking out over the marble-columned hallway, I said, "My God, these people could give a dance in this hall."

The contractor who had let me in answered, "They don't have to. There's a discotheque downstairs."

"Who is the owner?" I asked.

"He is not anyone you ever heard of," said the contractor.

Whoever these people are, they have not only a grand style in mind for their houses but also a grand style for the lives they intend to live in their houses once they are complete. In one *petit palais* under construction that I entered, the architect told me that the owner, described only as being "in airplane parts," had been so impatient to show off his vast new structure that he had increased the already large work staff of masons and bricklayers and agreed to pay them double and triple time to face the front of the mansion with red brick before Christmas so that he could give an outdoor party in the courtyard and let his friends see his work in progress.

"This is the only place in the world where real-estate agents become stars. I'm writing a novel about it," said real-estate agent Elaine

Young. "What I'd really like to have is a three- or four-minute segment on the news dealing with real estate. When I first went into
the business thirty years ago, there were only men in real estate, and
older women. Real-estate people have been getting better- and better-
looking. We just hired three new people in our office, two gorgeous
girls and one handsome man. A man buying a $5 million house would
rather buy from a beautiful woman than a homely one. It's such a personal business—we're in people's houses, in their bedrooms and their
bathrooms. I love what I do. I could have gone into show business, but
I ended up making a lot more money than some of the producers I've
dated. We're sort of the periphery of show business."

A glamorous figure, Elaine Young lunches daily at the same table in
the Polo Lounge of the Beverly Hills Hotel. An hour before I talked
with her, she had been interviewed by another writer for another
magazine. She was once married to the late film star Gig Young, who,
years later, in the third week of a subsequent marriage, shot and killed
his bride and himself in an unexplained mystery. Her hair is very very
blond, her dress is very very pink, and her glasses have white frames.
People turn to look at Elaine Young. "It's awesome," she said about
the boom. "Every year I've said it can't go up any more, and then it
does. Nothing hurts California real estate. Nothing. The rest of the
country can get into a recession and California doesn't know. Even the
earthquakes don't stop it. Did you feel the earthquake last night? I
slept right through it."

Four or five times during the hour we spent together, the captain in
the Polo Lounge brought her a remote-control telephone. "I told
them not to put calls through," she said each time, and then took the
call and transacted some business. "The Burt Reynolds house is up for
sale for $6 million, and I've got some people interested," she said.
"Burt's moving back to Florida lock, stock, and barrel. It's the Japanese who are driving up the prices. They don't want anything over five
years old. Even an older house redone they're not interested in. That's
why there's so many teardowns. The Koreans are pretty much the
same. I don't believe the prices! I have rentals for $40,000 a month.
And there's no end in sight. Oh, God, here's another call. I told them
not to put calls through."

_____

In Europe, in the fifteenth century, laws called sumptuary laws were created to limit the excesses of the rich: the tower of a castle could be only so high, the length of a jeweled train only so long. "These people don't know when to stop," said Bruce Nelson about the new builders. "There are only two or three really great architects working in all this boom. What you're getting mostly is schlock. Look at this house. French balustrades and Corinthian columns. Everything is overbuilt. They don't know that the essence of elegance is simplicity. It's hard for them to stop. Now water is the new status symbol. I don't just mean Jacuzzis and very, very large swimming pools. Waterfalls are becoming very popular, and lakes."

At this point we drove into the courtyard of a $30 million spec house. I had been reminded by one real-estate agent to explain that a spec house did not mean a spectacular house, although it might very well be spectacular. A spec house is a house built on speculation, for sale to anyone with the necessary bucks. This $30 million spec house was being built right next door to an almost matching house. They were being built by two former business partners who reportedly no longer speak. Each house has a tennis court that is cantilevered out over Coldwater Canyon. The houses can be seen for miles around, and have caused outrage in the neighborhood. One Beverly Hills society figure, who lives directly below them, said, "I know it's terrible to talk about money, but my husband had to have $50,000 worth of shrubbery put in our lawn to block out those two monstrosities." The one I was allowed to enter has more gigantic marble columns than Hadrian's Villa. The master suite has his-and-her bathrooms of unparalleled luxury, with Jacuzzis, sunken tubs, and etched-glass doors. The floor of the dining room has clear glass panels that reveal an indoor swimming pool below. Leaving through the front door, which is eighteen feet high, the real-estate agent pointed to the house next door and said to me, "Imagine spending $30 million on this house and having that ugger right on top of you."

"Do you think this will sell?" I asked.

"Hell, yes," he said. "We're at the beginning of this boom. We're not at the end of it. No matter what happens to the economy, these people won't be affected."

The real big shots are taken by helicopter to look at property. That includes the very rich Japanese, members of the Saudi royal family, and agents representing the Sultan of Brunei's family. "I sold one house to a man from Hong Kong," said Bruce Nelson. "It always surprised me that he never wanted to see it when he was in town. Then I was told it was a subterfuge for the brother of the Sultan of Brunei. He paid $15 million for the house, but he's never moved in."

Brooks Barton, the patrician real-estate broker who is the first vice president of Coldwell Banker, spent hours in the air showing places to Sir James Goldsmith, the international financier, before Goldsmith abandoned the idea of living in Los Angeles and settled on Mexico instead. "The economy of Southern California is incredible, and growing all the time," Barton told me as he pointed out the Jerry Perenchio estate below. Although any spread with two acres is referred to as an estate by most brokers, there are only four major estates left that have not been broken up into smaller lots. One of them is the aforementioned Ann Warner estate. Another is the former Conrad Hilton estate in Bel Air, which, like the Warner place, has nine acres. Now owned by the tremendously rich widower David Murdock, who is listed by *Forbes* magazine as being worth "well over $900 million," the property was described by one broker as the "the perfect estate. You can't see it from the road. The driveway goes into a proper courtyard. The house opens onto the gardens." Another is the Knoll, considered by many to be the most beautiful house in Beverly Hills. The Knoll was built in the 1950s and lived in for many years by a Doheny heiress, Lucy Doheny Battson, whose family at one time owned four hundred acres in Beverly Hills. In 1975 Mrs. Battson sold the house for what was considered at the time the astronomical price of $2 million to the Italian film producer Dino De Laurentiis, who sold it six years later to the country-western star Kenny Rogers for $13 million. Rogers in turn sold it three years later to the Denver oil billionaire Marvin Davis for $20-plus million. Davis, who owned Twentieth Century-Fox Studios briefly and then sold it, and owned the Beverly Hills Hotel briefly and then sold it, and his popular wife, Barbara, are cutting a wide social swath in both the film community and the group that hovers around former president Reagan and Mrs. Reagan. The Davises' annual Christmas party in their new house is said to outdo for sheer splendor and movie star attendance any other party in the community in years and years. The last of the four great estates is the Bel Air showplace known as the former Kirkeby house, which became well known around the world as the house in the television series "The Beverly Hillbillies." Driven to despair by the constant tourist traffic past the place, the late Carlotta Kirkeby very much regretted ever having let the house be used. The French-château-style mansion is now owned by Jerry Perenchio, the former talent agent turned sports promoter who was later partners with television mogul Norman Lear until he sold his interests to Coca-Cola for $485 million. Perenchio paid $13.5 million for the estate, then bought the house on each side for an additional $7 million in order to protect his property. He is living in one of them until the big house is finished; he tore down the other to build a new driveway. Perenchio is doing what in real-estate circles is called a total gut job on the elegant mansion, keeping the shell of the house but realigning and opening up the inside—all under the supervision of Henri Samuel, the great Parisian decorator, who also guided to completion the magnificent apartment of the socially visible John and Susan Gutfreund in New York.

Move over, Aaron Spelling. Someone with even grander plans than yours is moving in on your turf, and the only way to get an idea of the extent of this envisioned Shangri-la is to see the property from the air: 157 acres of Beverly Hills land called Benedict Canyon Mountain, purchased about twelve years ago by Princess Shams for her brother the Shah of Iran as the site for a palace for his years in exile. Fate, however, had plans for the Shah other than retirement in Beverly Hills. Now the property is owned by Merv Griffin, the former big-band vocalist turned talk-show host and game-show entrepreneur, who sold his interest in "Wheel of Fortune" to Coca-Cola for $250 million plus. He then bought the Beverly Hilton Hotel for $100 million, and has subsequently built a greater fortune in radio stations and real estate, even vying with the formidable Donald Trump for supremacy in the Resorts International chain. At present Griffin lives in a handsome gray stone Georgian mansion in Beverly Hills, which is on the market for $20 million. The new pool pavilion for this temporary house was inaugurated with a lunch party for Mrs. Ronald Reagan, at which Griffin's great friend Eva Gabor acted as hostess. "It's a shame we had to back the gates with canvas," said Waldo Fernandez, who decorated the house and designed the pavilion, "but there were too many people looking in and taking pictures." Fernandez was also the architect for the very large weekend house Griffin built in Palm Springs, which burned to the ground the week it was completed and then had to be completely rebuilt. But nothing, absolutely nothing, can compare with the about-to-be-started house on the top of Benedict Canyon Mountain.

I was driven there in the black Bentley of Waldo Fernandez, who also decorated the Bel Air home of Elizabeth Taylor. Fernandez, forty-ish, mustached, stylishly dressed by Giorgio Armani, will design Griffin's mountaintop palace with views in all directions. Fernandez's aide followed the Bentley in a Land Rover, and when we got to what will be the entry gates of the estate, we got out of the Bentley and into the Land Rover in order to negotiate the terrain. Fernandez was in charge of grading the mountaintop to the present seventeen flat acres, at a cost of $4 million. Three lakes are being built on it. At one point, the driveway will pass between two of the lakes. There will be two sets of gates for security, with armed guards at each. All cars will be stopped for clearance at both. There will be a guest parking area for ninety cars. There will be a helicopter pad. Permission to build the helicopter pad was secured only with the understanding that Griffin's helicopter would service the hills in case of fire. And there will be all the other requisites of the good life: a theater, tennis courts, a gymnasium with a pool, not to be confused with the other pool by the pool pavilion. "We didn't want to see the courts or the pool from the house," said Fernandez. "There will be trails to those areas." He pointed to another area. "The vineyards will be there."

The house, which will take from two and a half to three years to build, will be 60,000 square feet, 4,000 square feet larger than the Spelling house. It will be Palladian in style, with an atrium fifty feet by fifty feet by fifty feet in the middle. The facing will be limestone; the roof, red tile. The estimated cost of the building: $50 million.

"I'll soon be going to Europe to tag furniture for the house," said Fernandez.

"It all sounds very Hearstian," I said, referring to San Simeon, the palace William Randolph Hearst completed in 1939.

"It is," said Fernandez. Looking over the beautiful acreage, he said, "It's a dream of a job."

Despite all the hoopla connected with the Griffin estate, several highly placed people among the real-estate cognoscenti believe the house will never be built. "He's got ten in it now," they say, meaning $10 million. "You can buy Merv's land and Waldo Fernandez's blueprints for the house for $25 million."

But not to worry. There's always Robert Manoukian, an international figure of Armenian descent, who is a trusted friend of the Sultan of Brunei, and who also acts as his emissary. He negotiated to buy the Beverly Hills Hotel from Marvin Davis for the Sultan. Manoukian's new house, which is in the planning stages, is being designed by Budd Holden. It is to be built on 3.75 acres, on three descending lots, one of which was the old James Coburn estate, and, depending on whose version you believe, is going to be 58,000 square feet, 60,000 square feet, or 70,000 square feet. Fit for a king.

"Which is the Reagans' house?" I asked Brooks Barton in the helicopter.

"There," he answered, pointing down.

"Where?"

"There, that one."

"*That* little thing?"

"Yes."

Spoiled now by mansions of all sizes, styles, and shapes, I peered down critically at the modest ranch-style structure that is the new home of the former president of the United States and Mrs. Reagan—modest, at least in comparison with the houses in the neighborhood. It is a one-story, three bedroom house of about 7,300 square feet (roughly the size of Candy Spelling's dressing room and closets), with pool, which friends of the Reagans bought for them for $2.5 million. Local rumor has it that Nancy Reagan does not enjoy having the house described as ranch-style. A block away on one side is the elaborate spec house designed by Budd Holden on 1.9 acres which recently sold for $15 million to the man from Hong Kong. On the other side is Jerry Perenchio's French château.

April 1989

The prices quoted in this piece, which seemed so outrageous in 1989 when I wrote it, now seem altogether normal and even bargain basement in some cases. Back then, billionaires were spoken of in hushed tones, so few were they. Now they're practically a dime a dozen.

HIGH ROLLER: THE PHYLLIS
McGUIRE STORY

One day several years ago I was lunching at Le Cirque, arguably New York's most fashionable noontime restaurant, when my attention was drawn from my companions to three vaguely familiar-looking ladies of a certain age whom I at first mistook for triplets, since they were dressed identically in beige Chanel suits with matching bags, bracelets, pins, and honey-colored hairdos and were all speaking at the same time in an animated fashion. Seated at one of the very best tables, they were not unaware of the stir they were creating as they received the kind of deferential treatment from the sometimes haughty Le Cirque staff that Mrs. Astor or Mrs. Rockefeller might receive. The limitless curiosity of the socially inquisitive traveled from table to table: "Who are they?" And the answer came back, "The McGuire Sisters." A snap of the fingers—of course! The McGuire Sisters, the beautiful trio from Middletown, Ohio, who had had thirty hit records and given command performances for five presidents and the Queen Mother of England. One of the most popular singing groups of the fifties, discovered and made famous by Arthur Godfrey, they had by then been long out of circulation.

"Which one is Phyllis?" I asked the captain.

"In the middle," he answered.

"Wasn't she the—?"

Before I could finish my sentence, he nodded, *Yes, she was.* If I *had* finished my sentence that day at Le Cirque, it would have been, "Wasn't she the girlfriend of Sam Giancana?" Giancana, for decades one of the Mafia's most notorious and highly publicized figures, was also renowned for his role in the CIA plot to assassinate Fidel Castro, for his friendship with Frank Sinatra, and for his carrying on a love affair with Judith Campbell Exner at the same time she was having an affair with John F. Kennedy, the president of the United States.

Phyllis McGuire met Sam Giancana, according to legend, in Las Vegas in 1960, when the McGuire Sisters were performing there four times a year and pulling down $30,000 a week. Sam was a widower of fifty-two, and Phyllis, barely thirty, had already divorced Neal Van Ells, a radio/television announcer from Dayton, Ohio. Like many another Vegas performer, Phyllis had taken a liking to the gaming tables and had run up a hefty marker. As the story goes, Sam, spotting her, and liking her, went to Moe Dalitz, who ran the Desert Inn, and asked him how much the McGuire girl owed. Moe told him $100,000, a large marker at any time but enormous then. Sam is alleged to have said to Moe, "Eat it," meaning, in gangland parlance, erase the debt, which is different, of course, from paying the debt, but nonetheless it was a gesture not without charm and romantic appeal, especially since Sam followed it up with a suiteful of flowers. They fell in love.

For a time, the romance remained a well-kept secret, but wherever the trio traveled, Sam was there. In 1962, when the sisters were appearing at a nightclub in London, they were photographed there with their hairdresser, Frederic Jones, and Sam Giancana was also in the picture, with his arm wrapped around Phyllis. The photograph was flashed around the world, with enormous repercussions. The press and the public expressed a sense of outrage that the popular singer would associate with a person like Sam Giancana. In a tearful interview with the late gossip columnist Dorothy Kilgallen, Phyllis McGuire denied the rumors that she and Sam had been secretly married in Sweden, and also swore that she was never going to see Sam again. In 1968, the McGuires performed for the last time as a trio on "The Ed Sullivan Show," broadcast from Caesars Palace in Las Vegas. Since then, Phyllis has occasionally appeared as a solo act, as well as in musicals around the country, most recently in *Applause!* in Atlantic City.

Sam Giancana's life was ended in 1975, while he was cooking Italian sausage in the basement kitchen of his Oak Park, Illinois, home by a shot from a High-Standard Duromatic .22 target pistol, with a silencer attached, fired into the back of his head. That shot was followed by a second, fired into his mouth after he fell to the floor, and then by a third, fourth, fifth, sixth, and seventh, which were fired upward into his chin, shattering his lower jaw, ripping through his tongue, and lodging in the back of his skull. The FBI believes to this day that the deliverer of the blasts was a friend of many years, who still lives in the Chicago area, and that Sam was murdered because he had refused to cut the Chicago Mob in on the gambling empire he had set up outside the United States, in Iran, Haiti, and Central and South America, as well as on five gambling ships he ran in the Caribbean. Furthermore, Sam had become old, he was in poor health, and it was time for a change.

Long before then, Phyllis and Sam had ceased being lovers, but they had remained friends and she had visited him on numerous occasions during his eight-year exile in Mexico. Both the Mob nobility and the show-business greats with whom Sam had hobnobbed snubbed his Chicago funeral. Only Phyllis McGuire and Keely Smith, who had once sung with Louis Prima, arrived to pay their respects to Giancana's three daughters and to say farewell to Sam in his $8,000 silver casket.

For several years the McGuire Sisters have been planning a nightclub comeback. In February they performed at Rainbow & Stars in New York, and shortly after that, I made arrangements to interview Phyllis McGuire. "Don't mention Sam Giancana to her," people warned me, but not mentioning Sam Giancana when writing about Phyllis McGuire would be like not mentioning Richard Burton when writing about Elizabeth Taylor, or, in a more parallel situation, like not mentioning Nicky Arnstein when writing about Fanny Brice. As it turned out, I didn't have to bring up Sam's name, because Phyllis McGuire brought it up first. Their story has all the stuff of which myths are made.

I arrived in Las Vegas with elaborate directions for how to get from the airport to Rancho Circle, the exclusive enclave behind a guarded gate where she has lived for years. "Past the Lit'l Scholar Schoolhouse," I read from my instruction sheet, but the driver said he didn't need any instructions. "Everybody in Vegas knows where Phyllis McGuire lives."

From outside, the place looked like a suburban ranch-style house built in the fifties, but all resemblance to ranch-style life ended at the front door, which was opened by a man wearing a gun in a holster under his open suit jacket. Paul Romines has been her bodyguard for fourteen years. I stood for a moment in the hallway. To the right was a dining room with a mirrored floor. Through a door was a men's lavatory with two wall urinals side by side. Ahead was a replica of the Arc de Triomphe, which separated the hall from the living room. The living room was one of the largest I have ever been in, so large that a forty-four-foot-high replica of the Eiffel Tower did not seem to cramp the space. Beyond that was a vast area which included the formal dining room and, to the right of it, a bar with twelve bar chairs. To the left was an area identified by the bodyguard as the Chinese area, and to the right an area he designated as the French area. The windows, he informed me, were all bulletproof and could take a magnum shot, and at the touch of a button steel doors would drop from the eaves over all the windows, securing the house completely, fortress-style.

The floor of the living room was black and white marble. The rugs in the French area were Aubusson and Tabriz, and the walls were covered in rose damask. The chandeliers and sconces were Bavarian, with amber light bulbs. The mirrors on the walls were Venetian, and the chairs and sofas were all French, in multiple groupings, so many chairs that I lost count at sixty. That was when Phyllis McGuire came in.

She was dressed in a nautical style, with white flannel trousers and a white cashmere sweater with naval insignia on it. Her earrings were anchors. She was not at all what I was expecting, and from the moment she spoke I liked her. She was friendly, funny, gracious, utterly enthusiastic, constantly up, with boundless energy. And pretty, very pretty.

"Did anyone offer you a cup of coffee?" she asked. "Or anything?" She flung up her hands in mock exasperation and called into the kitchen, "Enice, take care of Mr. Dunne. And I'll have some coffee too. And some Perriers." She asked me, "Did you meet Enice? Enice Jobe? She's been with me for thirty-three years."

We sat on French chairs in the French area. "Is the music too loud?" she asked. "I can turn it down. Turn it down, Enice, will you, and put the coffee right here on this table."

I asked about the sisters, Dorothy and Christine, and she said,

"We've been singing together since I was four years old. We sang in the car, using the windshield wiper for a metronome. My sisters are the most incredible harmony singers. I can start in any key, and they pick it up." The sisters got their start singing in the First Church of God in Middletown, Ohio, where their mother, an ordained minister, was an associate pastor.

"We were middle class," she said. "My father worked for forty-six years for Armco Steel. He made steel before there were jet furnaces, working at an open hearth, shoveling in the pig iron. He wore safety shoes and long thick underwear, safety shirts and gloves, and a hard hat. At night after work, his clothes were coated with salt from his sweat. When my sisters and I started making money, we asked our parents what they owed, and we paid off everything. We made my father retire, and ordered a custom-made Cadillac with a gold plaque on it that said, FOR ASA AND LILLIE MCGUIRE, FROM DOROTHY, CHRISTINE, AND PHYLLIS. We sent them all over the world."

Looking around the French area, she said, "Some of this furniture is very valuable, and some is just personal to me. That Aubusson should be hanging on the wall rather than be on the floor. A lot of furniture and the paneling came from the house of Helen Bonfils in Denver, Colorado. Her father was the editor and publisher of the *Denver Post*. She was one of the finest women I ever knew. That desk belonged to Helen's father."

One thing I'll say about Phyllis McGuire, she's not hard to converse with. Raise any topic—with few exceptions—and she will talk away. She told me that one of the newspapers had called her a motor-mouth.

"Do you want to see everything?" she asked.

"Sure."

She took me through the house and grounds. There are eight acres and two guesthouses. "That's where my sisters stay when they come here to rehearse. The rest of the time they live in Arizona. They came to Vegas during the week and went home on weekends while we were getting ready for the comeback. We worked six to eight hours a day. We worked out and did stretching exercises in the mornings and did three hours each afternoon with Jim Hendricks, our pianist. One night I had Altovese and Sammy Davis over to hear the act. Chris and Dorothy each have their own bedroom and television set, and they share the living room and kitchen."

Sister Dorothy is no stranger to romantic headlines herself, having engaged in 1958 in a steamy love affair with fellow Arthur Godfrey singing star Julius La Rosa, which resulted in a public scolding on-air by Godfrey. Although the choirgirl image was tarnished, that affair caused no lessening of the group's popularity.

Behind the main house, we came to a moatlike area where Phyllis's twenty-three swans swim. "Those are the black Australian swans there," she said. "That one is about ready to hatch." Pointing to her tennis court, she said, "That's where Johnny Carson learned how to play tennis. It needs to be swept," she added, shaking her head.

"Someone told me all the flowers in your garden are fake," I said. She laughed and said, "Honey, I keep five gardeners."

In the pool house, noticing a crack in one of the windows, she picked up the telephone and called the main house. "Enice, tell maintenance there's a crack in the window of the pool house. Have him replace it, will you?" A bit farther on, she said, "Over there's my putting green. My waterfalls aren't on today—sorry."

Back in the house, she took me downstairs. "This is my nightclub. It even has a neon sign. The carpet rolls up and it's a dance floor underneath. The dance floor is in the shape of a piano. There have been lots of parties in this room. Over here is a blackjack table. Moe Dalitz gave me this table as a gift. I've taught more people how to play blackjack here at this table."

There is a beauty salon in the house, with several chairs and dryers so that the sisters, or houseguests, can have their hair done at the same time. In the health club, next to the beauty salon, are three change-rooms and three massage tables next to one another, where three masseurs can work on three guests at the same time. "The steam room is always ready," she said, peering into a window of the steam room.

Her huge bathtub is part of her bedroom, and her closets are enormous. "This is all Chanel," she said, pointing to one area. "Over there, it's all Galanos, and there in that room is all Pauline Trigère." It was a tour she was used to giving. "This is for my furs. The lynx, ermine, and sable are here. The older furs are over there. I keep a record of everything I wear so that I don't ever repeat with the same people. All my clothes are on a computer. So are all the books in my library, and all the furniture. They're all on video as well."

She picked up a model airplane. "This was my G-II," she said. "It had a sign saying, WELCOME ABOARD THE PHYLLIS SPECIAL. I've decorated the interiors of three planes. Do you feel like lunch?"

"Sure."

The mail had arrived. "Enice, I don't want to see the tabloids. The Searles across the street said there was something in them about us. Don't show me." We sat in the small dining room, and Enice, having given the mail to a secretary, brought in the lunch. "I have the greatest kitchens in the world," Phyllis said. "I don't cook, but I always have great chefs. And some of my maids have been with me for fourteen or seventeen years."

"How many people work for you in this house?" I asked, having noticed several in the background.

She began to count, looking up, looking over at Enice for verification, placing the forefinger of her left hand against the pinkie finger of her right hand, then against the ring finger, then the center finger, then against the other forefinger, and then repeating the process, at the same time reeling off a seemingly endless list of names—maids, cooks, guards, gardeners, drivers, secretaries.

"Twenty-eight," she said finally.

She thinks a great deal about security. "My limo driver carries a gun," she said. "But if they want to get you, they're going to get you. For me, it's the most secure feeling in the world when those steel doors are down."

Phyllis McGuire has a more elaborate lifestyle than most television and nightclub performers of the fifties whose stars have dimmed with time and the fickle musical tastes of the public, and nowhere is her wealth more visible than in her wondrous jewelry. No one who knows about jewels has not heard about her fantastic collection, which ranks among the best in the world, right up there with the famous collections of Elizabeth Taylor, Imelda Marcos, Candy Spelling, Mrs. Marvin Davis, and the fifth Baroness Thyssen. Harry Winston, the great jeweler, once said to her, "If ever there was a lady meant to wear jewels, it's you." She told me, "There was a time when I was purchasing millions of dollars' worth of jewelry. I was one of Harry Winston's best customers." She paused for a moment and then added, "Maybe some Saudis were ahead of me. Jewels really turned me on then, and they still do. I wear the jewels, they don't wear me."

On the day I was in her house, most of her jewels had been put in the vault because she was leaving imminently for a singing engagement with her sisters at the Moulin Rouge in Chicago. But a few were still at hand. "Enice," she called out, "bring in the canaries." The canaries consisted of a forty-two-carat yellow diamond set in a ring, surrounded by smaller diamonds, and some loose yellow diamonds which she was planning to have made into earrings. She examined her stones like a jeweler. "I'm not sure I like the way they put the diamonds around the canary," she said, "but I'm trying it this way." From the same package she pulled a twenty-eight-carat marquise-shaped diamond ring, which she called "one of the babies" because of its small size—small, at least, in comparison with some of her other rings. The canaries brought to mind a fairly recent drama in her life.

In 1979, she said she took a D-flawless-diamond ring to Harry Winston's to have it cleaned and to have the prongs checked. When the ring was returned to her, it didn't seem to have the same sparkle it had had previously. Even now, a decade later, recounting the story, she held her hand up and examined her ring finger as if she were looking at the ring in question. She said that she had said at the time, "This can't be my ring. It doesn't sparkle the same." She said she had begun to question her own sanity. "I said to Enice, 'Is this my ring, Enice?' and she said, 'I think it is, Miss Phyllis.' But there is a process called cubic zirconia, where a fake diamond can be cut exactly to match a real diamond. I knew that my ring had been switched. I turned in one to be cleaned, and they gave me back another. I sued Winston for $60 million. They countersued me for $100 million." At the time, a spokesman for Winston denied the allegations "absolutely."

"I was only trying to recover my jewels," she continued. "I deposed for three days at Foley Square in New York. I discovered the diamond wasn't mine at Christmas of '79, and the case was settled in '82." She seemed to be finished with her story.

"But what happened?" I asked.

"I'm not allowed to discuss the outcome of the suit. That's part of the agreement," she said, giving a helpless shrug, but neither her smile nor her attitude indicated any discontent with the outcome.

A spokesman for Winston told me the company had no comment to make.

Her conversation is peppered with the names of the very rich and very famous, with whom she has spent most of her time over the last twenty-five years. "I met Imelda Marcos at a party at Adnan Khashoggi's," she told me, and she and her sisters were scheduled to sing at the ninety-fifth birthday party of Armand Hammer, the billionaire philanthropist. Ann-Margret's name came up, and she said, "Let's call her." Ann-Margret was playing at Caesars Palace. She dialed the number. "This is Phyllis McGuire," she said to the telephone operator. "I'd like to speak to Ann-Margret. She's still sleeping? At two o'clock in the afternoon? My God, she only had one show last night. OK, tell her I called."

"New York is like roots for me," she said. "It was the first big city we saw after Ohio." For years she kept a Park Avenue apartment. Then she bought a town house on one of the most exclusive streets on the Upper East Side of Manhattan. "Do you know where Givenchy is? Two houses behind that." She bought the house, she said, "lock, stock, and barrel, including antiques, china, crystal, and silverware, from a son of King Fahd of Saudi Arabia," who was afraid of being assassinated, following the assassination of Anwar Sadat in Egypt, and took up residence instead in the Waldorf Towers, where many heads of state, and families of heads of state, stay for purposes of security. Phyllis loved the house dearly but spent only twenty-one days in it in 1987, so when her great friend Meshulam Riklis, the vastly rich ($440 million) financier husband of Pia Zadora, asked if he could buy it, she sold it to him. In order not to be without a nest in New York, she borrowed the Pierre Hotel apartment of another great friend, the vastly rich ($950 million) financier Kirk Kerkorian, and liked it so much that she talked Kerkorian into selling it to her, completely furnished.

"I'm a good businesswoman," she said, a fact that is borne out by most of her acquaintances. "If I weren't performing, I would have to constantly be working at something. I love business."

I didn't have to mention Sam Giancana. She brought him up. "I've had four serious involvements in my life, and one was a marriage. That was only for about ten minutes. Two of the men are still my friends, Simon Srybnik and Dr. Stanley Behrman, the head of oral surgery at New York Hospital. Even after Simon married Judy, and Stanley married Nancy, we stayed friends." She paused before continuing. "And then there was Sam." When she said Sam, she whispered his name. There is no doubt she loved him.

Even William Roemer, the former FBI agent who dogged Sam's life for a decade, says, "Phyllis really loved Sam, and Sam loved her." Phyllis's great friend the Broadway producer Dasha Epstein says, "She disappeared out of our lives when she was going with Sam. She said, 'I know it's difficult for my friends, and I understand.' That was so like Phyllis."

"My life is so much more than that—with Sam," Phyllis said. "That was only a chapter. I'm not ashamed of my past. I was doing what I honestly felt." She sat back in her rose damask Bergère chair and continued. "Sam was the greatest teacher I ever could have had. He was so wise about so many things. Sam is always depicted as unattractive. He wasn't. He was a very nice-looking man. He wasn't flashy. He didn't drive a pink Cadillac, like they used to say. He was a beautiful dresser. Dorothy Kilgallen thought he was my attorney when she met him. The two great losses of my life were my father and Sam."

She is now working on her autobiography to set the record straight. "I've got to get this out. I've got to get on with my life. It's holding me up. I have things to say that haven't been said," she told me. "Like about the late Mayor Daley of Chicago, even if his son is the new mayor." "It's a heavy-duty story," she was quoted in Marilyn Beck's column as saying. "I've been in thirty-four books in the last twelve to fifteen years, and it's time my story was finally told correctly. I don't need a Kitty Kelley doing to me what she did to Sinatra and [what she's doing to] Nancy Reagan."

She denies, for example, the story about the $100,000 marker that Giancana told Moe Dalitz to eat. "I never lost more than $16,000 gambling at any one time," she said. She also discounts many of the stories about her in the book *Mafia Princess*, written by Sam Giancana's daughter Antoinette. "I tried to stop that book," she said. "It wasn't accurate. Toni got all her information through the Freedom of Information Act. She didn't know any firsthand. She and her father hadn't been close. She used to come and stay here, in the guesthouse."

In 1961, at the height of Phyllis's fame, her affair with Giancana was still not known to the public. The FBI, which tracked Giancana's every move, had chosen not to expose the relationship, understanding that such publicity would be detrimental to McGuire's career. But in the spring of that year, agents bugged their motel room in Phoenix and learned they would be traveling on American Airlines to New York with a stopover at O'Hare Airport in Chicago. The FBI decided to subpoena Phyllis with the proviso that if she cooperated with them by answering their questions in a room within the terminal, they would withdraw the subpoena and she would not have to appear the next day. She knew that if she were to appear, it would become publicly known that she was the mistress of the Mob chief. What the FBI agents asked her to do was cooperate with them in the future by letting them know where Sam was at all times. Phyllis agreed to do what they asked, and they took the subpoena back, but, according to several reliable sources, she didn't keep her promise.

William Roemer's job that day was to keep Giancana occupied while Phyllis was being questioned, and he and Giancana got into a screaming match at the airport, climaxing when Sam said he was going to have his friend Butch Blasi machine-gun him down. Roemer, probably the greatest authority on Sam Giancana, remembers him very differently from the way Phyllis does. His book, *Roemer: Man Against the Mob,* will be published in October by Donald I. Fine. He told me on the phone from his home in Tucson, "Sam was ugly, balding—wore a wig at the end of his life. Little, slight, dumpy, a deese-dem-dose guy, scum of the earth, killer, the dregs of society, the worst kind of person. We hated each other. I hated him, and he hated me."

Roemer said that the Mob was extremely upset with Giancana when he was going with Phyllis. They thought he wasn't minding the store. "He fell in love with her and traveled all over the world with her," Roemer said. He agrees that Phyllis, in the tradition of wives, daughters, and lovers of Mob members, knew little of Sam's life away from her. He told me that when Phyllis first thought about writing her book, she called him—Sam's nemesis—to say that she had met a lot of people during her years with Sam but that she didn't actually know who they were or what they had done. Some of them, she said, she knew only by their nicknames, like "Chuckie" (English), "Butch" (Blasi), and "Skinny" (D'Amato)—all figures in the racketeering life of Sam Giancana.

"Did Sam leave any money to Phyllis?"

"Nobody could ever prove that he left her money," answered Roemer. Although Giancana left an estate valued at only $132,583.16 when he died, that meant nothing. The kind of money that people like Sam Giancana have is not banked or left in the ordinary ways of money management. Roemer said it is possible that Giancana had a hundred million dollars.

"It very definitely hurt our careers for about a year," Phyllis McGuire said about her affair with Giancana. "We were blacklisted on TV, but that ended."

In your interview with Dorothy Kilgallen, you said you were going to give him up," I said.

"Yes, I know. I said in that interview that I'd never see him again. Well, I did." She shrugged, and then threw out one of the amazing bits of information that flow freely from her tongue. "Kilgallen was murdered," she said. "She didn't commit suicide." Dorothy Kilgallen, who supposedly died of a sleeping-pill overdose in 1964, had in that same year interviewed Jack Ruby, the assassin of Lee Harvey Oswald, the man who assassinated President Kennedy. "I saw her three days before, dancing at El Morocco with Johnnie Ray. She was murdered. I didn't believe the suicide story then. I don't believe it now. Dorothy was the most beautiful corpse I ever saw."

Although Phyllis McGuire did not mention him in her list of suitors, there has been another romantic involvement since Sam, a bigger-than-life character named Mike Davis, and they are still close friends. The owner of Tiger Oil, Davis is based in Houston, but he is always on the move. Phrases like "my jet" pop up in his conversation, as do such names as Bunker Hunt, of the Texas Hunts, and Adnan Khashoggi, the international arms dealer, currently in hot water, with whom Davis has been a sometime partner. "Tiger Mike," as some people call him, is of Lebanese extraction. He was once the chauffeur of Phyllis's great friend Helen Bonfils, and married Bonfils upon the death of her husband in 1956. Helen Bonfils was reportedly in her late sixties at the time, and Davis was in his late twenties. Bonfils, who took over the running of the *Denver Post* when her father died, was also involved in producing Broadway shows. She helped finance Davis's start-up in Tiger Oil. Davis's interest in Phyllis began while she was still involved with Giancana. McGuire told me she once pulled him behind a slot machine and warned him. "You better stay away from me. Do you want to end up on the bottom of Lake Mead?"

On several occasions, Frank Sinatra's name came up in our conversation, and I sensed a certain amount of animosity. "We are cautiously friends," she said slowly. "He is the most talented but most contradictory person. He has surrounded himself with an entourage who yes him to death. How can you expand yourself surrounded by yes-men? I've stayed in his house, and he has bored me to death. He tells the *sa-a-ame* stories he's been telling for years, and all I ever heard were his records, which he played *over and over* again." She covered her ears as she told this. "I thought to myself, I'll never do that in my house with my records. You *never* hear my own music played on my system."

She recounted to me a story that I had read in Kitty Kelley's unauthorized biography of Sinatra, *His Way*. Sinatra, who was making $100,000 a week in Las Vegas, agreed, along with Sammy Davis, Jr., Dean Martin, and Eddie Fisher, to appear for nothing in a club called Villa Venice, which was a front for Giancana. Afterward, Giancana wanted to send a gift to each of them, and Phyllis picked out Sinatra's gift. She suggested sending Steuben crystal, having seen stemware in Sinatra's house that he told her was Steuben. "I say Steuben. Frank said Steu*banne*. He thought what he had was Steuben, but it wasn't. Steuben always says Steuben on the bottom, but his didn't. I called Gloria, who was Frank's secretary, to see if they should be monogrammed, but she said no to the monogram, because people tended to walk off with anything that had Sinatra's monogram on it. I sent him a service for thirty—martini glasses, white-wine glasses, red-wine glasses, champagne glasses, and water tumblers. I spent over $7,000 on that gift, and the S.O.B. never sent a thank-you note."

"Did you get any flak from Sinatra from telling Kitty Kelley the story about the Steuben glasses?"

"None whatever," she said, shaking her head emphatically. "He knows better. Let me tell you about Frank. He doesn't know how to say, 'I'm sorry,' and he doesn't know how to say, 'Thank you.' He could never admit he made a mistake. I sent my Lear to Houston to pick up Dr. DeBakey when Frank's mother was killed, because they were friends, but he never said thank you for that either."

"Didn't you make a movie with Sinatra?"

"Hmmm," she answered, nodding her head. "*Come Blow Your Horn.* Everyone said Sam got that movie for me with Frank, which was *not* true. I played a buyer from Neiman-Marcus, a part that was not in the stage play. He was supposed to kiss me in one scene, and I was wearing my diamond drop earrings." She held up her fingers to indicate a good three inches of diamonds, from the lobes to the shoulders. "When he kissed me, he put his hands over my ears like this." She covered her ears with her hands. "That was the last important picture Frank did."

"Why did you ever stop singing?"

"Oh, we lost our confidence at different times—me less than Dorothy and Christine," said Phyllis. "Dorothy got married. Christine got married. They had guilt trips thinking they should be home with their children."

When she sings, she said, she feels tidal waves of love coming from the audience, "like a full moon when the ocean is active." On the night I flew to Chicago to watch the McGuire Sisters perform at the Moulin Rouge in the new Fairmont Hotel, the room was packed. The crowd was an older crowd, but then, the cover charge was twenty-five dollars per person, on top of drinks and dinner. "People feel they know us," said Phyllis. "They love us. They watched us grow up on TV." Sitting at a front-row table was Irv Kupcinet, the dean of Chicago columnists, and his wife, Essie. "Ladies and gentlemen," came the announcement over the loudspeaker, "*the McGuire Sisters!*"

And there they were, Dorothy, Christine, and Phyllis, with Phyllis, as always, in the middle. Fake eyelashes, glitter on their blue eyeshadow, honey-colored falls on their honey-colored hair, and peach dresses covered with crystals. When they sang their familiar hits, like "The Naughty Lady of Shady Lane," "Melody of Love," and "Sugartime," which put them on the cover of *Life* magazine in 1958, they got excited applause of recognition. Phyllis gave the audience their cover charge's worth. She did vocal impersonations of Judy Garland, Louis Armstrong, Ethel Merman, Pearl Bailey, and other stars of her era. And she was right: the audience loved them.

"Where do you sing next?"

"We might make a deal with Steve Wynn for the Mirage," said Phyllis. The Mirage, due to open before the end of the year, is the newest of the hotels on the Vegas Strip. We were sitting at a table in a corner of the bar of the Fairmont, late, after her second show. Her sisters had gone upstairs. She was in a long red dress and wore dark glasses because she was still wearing her stage makeup.

"I don't fear living, and I don't fear dying," she said. "You only live once, and I'm going to live it to the fullest, until away I go. And I'm going to continue singing as long as somebody wants me."

June 1989

I really adored Phyllis McGuire. I had such a good time with her when I was writing this story, and we've stayed friends since. I've seen her in Vegas and L.A. and New York, and, believe me, people react when you walk into a restaurant with her. She always looks like a million bucks, and the fact that the notorious Sam Giancana was the great love of her life gives her a sort of special dimension no one else has. Hers is not the sort of histoire *you usually hear about a lady in the circles in which I move.*

SOCIAL DEATH IN VENICE

At first it seemed like a reenactment of the sort of turn-of-the-century match Henry James or Edith Wharton might have written about, the marriage of a New World heiress and an Old World prince, a swap of money and title beneficial to both sides. Indeed, as we approach the turn of another century, the allure of grand titles for socially ambitious mothers with marriageable daughters seems not to have diminished, judging by the remarkable events in Venice during Easter weekend this year. No story by Henry James or Edith Wharton, however, would have ended with headlines such as this: HEIRESS JILTED AS BRIDEGROOM RUNS OFF WITH BEST MAN.

In this version of the tale, the heiress is an Australian named Primrose Dunlop, and the nobleman is the awesomely titled Prince Lorenzo Giustiniani Montesini, Count of the Phanaar, Knight of Saint Sophia, Baron Alexandroff. A poor prince who claims to be "a small link in a chain that goes back to Constantine," Prince Giustiniani, known to his friends as Laurie, is employed as a steward on Qantas Airlines. Lorenzo Montesini, as he was then called, appeared on the social scene of Sydney in 1983, at a charity party at Fairwater, the mansion of Lady Fairfax, the widow of the Australian press lord. Affable, charming, socially adept, Lorenzo soon was in demand as an extra man. "He charmed his way into everyone's house here," one Sydney social figure told me. "He was asked to all the parties, between flights."

When the Egyptian-born Montesini, who is forty-four, chubby, bouncy, elfin, and very short, arrived in Sydney from Melbourne, he came with his longtime companion, Robert Straub, with whom he had

271

served in Vietnam. In Woolloomooloo, a middle-class suburb of Sydney, the men converted two rose-pink cottages into their home, which they filled with gilded mirrors, Persian carpets, rococo furnishings, and tables covered with framed photographs of well-known people. Montesini described the princely possessions as "family things."

Primrose Dunlop, the woman in question, was not a blushing debutante in her first bloom. Nor was she really an heiress, but merely the stepdaughter of a rich man who has two daughters of his own, who do not care much for their stepsister. Primrose is thirty-six, had been married before, briefly and unhappily, and is called Pitty Pat to distinguish her from her mother, Lady Potter, who is also named Primrose. Pitty Pat has had a variety of jobs over the years: she sold pots and pans in a department store, wrote social columns for two Sydney tabloids, did public-relations work for the British mogul Lord McAlpine, and, most recently, clerked as an eight-dollar-an-hour assistant to a haberdasher named John Lane, a great friend of her mother's, who sometimes escorted Lady Potter on the endless round of parties and boutique openings that her much older husband did not wish to attend.

Lady Potter, who once raised French poodles and is most often described by her friends as vivacious, became the fourth wife of Sir Ian Potter in 1975. Sleek, stylish, and very well dressed, she speaks in the grand vocal tones of a society lady. Her previous marriage, to Dr. Roger Dunlop, a surgeon, who is the father of Primrose, ended in divorce. Lady Potter, a tireless fund-raiser for charity, with a hearty appetite for publicity and social recognition, had set her sights far beyond Sydney and Melbourne. Described by an English acquaintance who has sat next to her at dinner on several occasions as "an expert dropper of key names meant to establish her credentials," Lady Potter is referred to in the Australian social columns as "the Empress" and is said to revel in her nickname. She is considered by many to be the queen bee of the Sydney-Melbourne social axis, and her public-relations consultant, Barry Everingham, has gone so far as to describe Sir Ian and Lady Potter as the closest thing that Australia has to royalty.

Sir Ian, eighty-eight, is one of Australia's most respected businessmen, but age has caught up with the old man. A number of people I spoke with described him as slightly "gaga." Others said he was amazingly sharp for a man of his age. He played an integral, albeit passive, part in the Venetian nuptials, however, because his money was paying for everything. His fortune, which has been estimated at $48 million by some, less by others, was to finance the splendid wedding for the bride, and it was thought by many to be the lure for the groom. Sir Ian has a daughter named Robin from his first marriage, and a daughter named Carolyn Parker Bowles from his second marriage. Mrs. Parker Bowles, who lives in London, is the mother of Sir Ian's two grandsons. "Sir Ian is a self-made man of enormous ability who, until all this, has been very quiet. He is a great Australian," one Australian businessman told me. "The poor man has been dragged into a situation which will appear in his obituary."

Last year Lorenzo Montesini brought out a novel about Sydney society called *Cardboard Cantata*, which he dedicated to Lady Potter. Since no publisher picked up on it, the book was printed privately. It has been rumored that Lady Potter financed the publication for the four thousand copies, and she gave a launch party for the book, in an art gallery, which attracted three hundred of the city's smartest citizens. It was on the occasion of that party that Lorenzo first aired his previously unsuspected titles of prince, count, knight, and baron.

The sheer awfulness of Lorenzo Montesini's book was conveyed to me by the editor of an Australian magazine, who said, "I defy you to read it." In an earlier, snobbier time, it would have been called a shop-girl's book. The three leading characters, who vie with one another for leadership of Sydney society, are named Babylonia Grushman, Cooii Rundle, and Lady Millicent Bosenquet. Another character is described as coming from a "well-to-do but poor family." Despite its social send-off, the book was, predictably, a colossal flop. Stacks of unsold copies gathered dust until the recent publicity created a belated demand and elevated them to the status of collector's items. But the point was not the book, and the literary life was not the prince's ambition. It seemed that it was the book *party* that led to the plans for a wedding. That night Lady Potter told the press, "I've known Lorenzo for years. He's a dear sweet boy. Ian and I look upon him as family." The steward-author-prince smiled and said, "I have arrived."

From there, things moved quickly. The rose-pink cottages became the setting for a round of parties, at which Pitty Pat and Lady Potter were always present. "Unless you entertain, you're dead," said

Lorenzo in an early television interview, speaking in his chatty manner, seated on a thronelike chair. "Montesini brought a manservant down from Thailand and dressed him in a *King and I* costume with the Giustiniani coronet on it," said a friend who attended his parties. Surprisingly, it was Robert Straub, Lorenzo's great friend, who inadvertently brought about the engagement when he jokingly remarked one evening after dinner, "Think about it, Primrose. If you were to marry Lorenzo, you would become a princess." Although the remark was greeted with hoots of laughter, it set the idea in motion.

Soon after that, Lady Potter confirmed in a magazine interview that Lorenzo "telephoned and formally asked for my daughter's hand in marriage. . . . I said that as long as he makes her happy, the answer's yes." He gave her an engagement ring of aquamarine and diamonds, modernized from a piece handed down to him by his grandmother.

No one loves a party more than Lady Potter, and she saw fit to celebrate the joyous news of her daughter's engagement with two, one in Melbourne and a second in New York, at fashionable Mortimer's, to which she invited some of the most promotable of New York's social names, including Leonard Lauder and Nan Kempner.

The romantic city of Venice was decided on as the location of the wedding. Not only was Giustiniani one of the great titles of Venice, but Lady Potter had been renting palazzi there for several years and had come to know the small and exclusive English-speaking colony. In preparation, Pitty Pat became a Catholic; she received instruction from Father Vincent Kiss, and she was sponsored by John Lane, her boss and her mother's walker. The Sydney and Melbourne newspapers followed every detail of the arrangements. The date was set for April 16, the day after Easter. The wedding would take place in the Basilica di San Pietro, to which the bride would be oared in one of a flotilla of gondolas, followed by a grand reception and candlelit dinner in the marble hall of the Palazzetto Pisani on the Grand Canal, which the bride's mother had leased for the occasion. Seventy Australian guests were invited to the lavish event.

Despite encouragement from Lady Potter, the affianced couple appeared in public infrequently, giving rise to rumors that theirs was a nonromantic liaison reeking of ulterior motives on both sides. When

Montesini and Robert Straub, whose relationship was causing titters in Lady Potter's circle, showed up at a party to celebrate the opening of a Chanel boutique in Sydney, John Lane, acting for Lady Potter, said to Lorenzo, "Don't be seen in public with that man again." The bride's family was less than enthusiastic when Lorenzo announced that Straub would be his best man. Dissension arose. There were rumors, all unconfirmed, that lurid photographs existed.

Stories persisted in Sydney society that the prince was in it for the money. He himself reported to Pitty Pat that John Laws, one of the highest-paid radio announcers in the world, had told him, while he was pouring champagne for him in the first-class cabin on a Qantas flight, that his title should be worth at least $2 million to the Potters. Lorenzo was shocked. "People suggest that there is money in this for me. That's utter rubbish," he protested.

Before their departure for Venice, the prince and his princess-to-be posed for pictures and gave an interview for a long article in *Good Weekend* magazine in the *Sydney Morning Herald*, and it was that article, with the royal-looking photographs, that began the unraveling of their plans. Previously unknown relations of the prince came out of the woodwork and mocked his pretensions, disputing both the title and his right to use it. One cousin, Nelson Trapani, a forty-nine-year-old retired Queensland builder, told the press, "Really, all this speculation about a title is a load of bulldust. I'd sooner sit down with a pie and watch the telly."

Nonetheless, the group, which included Father Kiss, who was to perform the ceremony, took off amid whispers that all was not as it was supposed to be, with either the title or the romance, or anything else. Dr. Roger Dunlop, Pitty Pat's real father, was so opposed to his daughter's choice of husband that he boycotted the wedding ceremony.

If Lorenzo was having second thoughts, he nonetheless went along with the plans, flying to Venice with Robert Straub and John Lane, Lady Potter's great friend, who had been assigned the paternal function of giving the bride away, owing to the refusal of her real father and the inability of her stepfather because of his age. The groom-to-be was the only member of the wedding party without a confirmed seat on the plane. He traveled standby economy-class at his own expense.

A curious twist of alliances occurred during the trip. Lane, who had previously been unfriendly to Montesini and Straub and had warned them at the Chanel opening not to appear together in public, discovered, Lorenzo later said, that "we were really quite nice guys after all and not as bad as we had been painted."

On Good Friday, as Leo Schofield, an Australian journalist, and other guests were boarding their plane in Sydney for the long flight to Venice, they heard that the wedding had been called off.

What had up to then been merely a Sydney-Melbourne gossip-column story quickly turned into international headlines, and Pitty Pat and Lorenzo became, however briefly, household names, more famous in their disaster than they would ever have been in their marriage. "If it was publicity they all wanted," said one friend, "they have succeeded beyond their wildest dreams."

Although it was widely touted in the Australian press that the guest list had been made up of a glittering gaggle of international socialites, there wasn't a recognizable name in the group. "Not a single man, woman, or dog in Venice ever heard of any of these people," said one longtime resident of the city.

There was a problem with accommodations from the beginning. Lord and Lady Potter and Pitty Pat were housed on an upper floor of the Palazzetto Pisani, and the prince, his best man, and John Lane were housed in a small flat on the ground floor, or water floor, consisting of two tiny rooms. The space was crowded and uncomfortable, and the bathroom facilities were not to the trio's liking. At a cocktail party held at the Palazzetto, which is owned by the Countess Maria Pia Ferri, another Venetian countess is said to have exclaimed to the bridegroom when he was introduced to her as Prince Giustiniani, "Oh, you must be related to my friend Cecy Giustiniani." Cecy Giustiniani is the venerable Dowager Countess Giustiniani, and soon telephones were jingling up and down the Grand Canal. People ran to their *Libro d'Oro*, the Italian book of nobility, but no one could find a Prince Giustiniani. Every Venetian with whom I spoke drew attention, often huffily, to the fact that "Prince" is not a Venetian title. "Count" is the title that counts in Venice, as any countess will tell you.

The Dowager Countess Giustiniani vehemently refuted the claim of

Lorenzo Montesini that he was Prince Giustiniani, stating that her name had been violated. "The male line of the Venetian Giustinianis ended thirty years ago with the death of my dear husband, the Count Alvise Giustiniani," she said. "A Prince Giustiniani does not exist. To claim this is the most monstrous rubbish. This alleged title is false, false, false." So began the wedding week.

The Palazzetto Pisani soon became a battleground, with a butler carrying notes back and forth between floors. According to reports, the Potter family asked Lorenzo to substantiate his claim to the title before the wedding took place. The relationship with Robert Straub was also in dispute. The family was concerned about a projected news-paper story on Straub which would provide details of his life in Mel-bourne before he and Lorenzo moved to Sydney. Straub believed that someone considered more suitable was waiting in the wings to replace him as his best man. Lady Potter had reckoned that, once in Venice, Lorenzo would capitulate and Robert would go away, but this was not to be. Lorenzo and Straub and Lane left the Pisani and moved to a pension on the Giudecca Canal, which Lorenzo later described as "a hotel for middle-class English traveling el-cheapo." In the course of the move, Lorenzo claimed to have lost their passports, and he re-ported this to Pitty Pat.

The next morning, on the advice of John Lane, Lorenzo got on the telephone and told Lady Potter, not his wife-to-be, that the wedding was off. It then became the sad duty of Lady Potter to inform her daughter, the bride, that the groom was jilting her.

One of the Australian guests told me, "I thought they'd go through with it. After all, it seemed very much a marriage of convenience, all because of the title. It was really a larky thing to do, a combination of an ambitious mother wanting to feel well placed and a financially am-bitious groom." The same guest described running into Lorenzo in the bar of the Hotel Cipriani after the breakup but before he bolted from Venice with his best man. "He seemed totally devastated by the whole thing. He said, about himself and Pitty Pat, 'We'd been old friends. It was to have been a marriage of style.' "

Evelyn Lambert, the Texas chatelaine of the Villa Lambert in the Veneto outside of Venice, who rented her house to Lady Potter one year, told me, "I called her after the cancellation and she said she was not angry with Lorenzo. Venice thinks the whole thing was a publicity stunt, but I don't think so. The three men decided this was not going to work. I read in the *Sydney Morning Herald* that I was giving a bridal lunch on Good Friday. Honey, I'm a Catholic by conversion. I don't give lunch parties on Good Friday. I don't even *eat* on Good Friday."

One of Pitty Pat's cousins acted as family spokesman and made calls to all the guests to inform them that the wedding was off. "The families of both the bride and groom have searched high and low for an answer to an inexplicable riddle and a way to redeem the damage— spiritual, psychological, and material," he said. "To say the bride and her mother are distraught is understatement. They are utterly devastated. It is as though a bomb had exploded. The groom's decision and what made him take this step came out of the blue. His family had already handed over generations of jewels and heirlooms to Primrose.

"We had no inkling. No one fully understands the emotional bond between those two men who ran away together. We are trying to trace them. They might be in Timbuktu as far as we know.

"We would love a dialogue with Lorenzo to see exactly why it happened and to put things in perspective. Nothing is irredeemable. If only he had spoken openly with the bride, we would have understood. If at this late stage he were to come forward with regrets, we feel the bride would still accept him. Primrose is a tough girl, and she is fighting against distress, shame, and a feeling of ridicule. Fortunes have been spent by scores of people on this stylish wedding—return airfares from Melbourne, not to mention presents. But this matters least of all. It is the wounded bride we first have to deal with."

Many of the people who spoke with both mother and daughter were amazed by their composure. But, after all, in their world appearance is everything. A few days after the fiasco, the Potters and Pitty Pat left Venice and proceeded to Paris, where Lady Potter celebrated her birthday at Maxim's just as she had planned to right along.

A few days later in Melbourne, the premier of the state of Victoria, in a televised speech from the floor of Parliament House, accused the opposition party of being a mismatched marriage—worse than that of Pitty Pat Dunlop and the prince. The Melbourne newspapers carried the remark on their front pages.

In Sydney the called-off marriage was the most exciting event in years. "We fell about laughing here," said a friend of both parties. "It was all a publicity stunt to turn them into international figures, and it backfired on them."

People talked of nothing else. And when they finished talking to one another, they talked to the press, if asked. In an article by Daphne Guinness, Caroline Simpson, a member of the powerful Fairfax family, spoke her mind. "Hasn't this whole thing been a joke from the beginning?" she asked. "None of us thought it would get to the wedding stage and the church, did we? Dr. Dunlop came to see my mother [Betty Fairfax] this afternoon. They talked for hours. I think he had a lot to do with stopping it. It is really an extraordinary thing for a mother to push a child in that way." There was a certain amount of glee in social circles that Lady Potter "had egg all over her face." "The person I feel sorry for is Ian Potter," said Sheila Scotter, another social leader, "and his absolutely darling daughter Carolyn Parker Bowles, who *does* move in society circles in London with certain royals, including the monarch."

On her way back to Sydney via Paris and New York, Primrose Dunlop arranged to go public with her story on Australia's "60 Minutes" when she returned. The rumor was that she was paid $38,000 by the network, and that she would drop a bombshell on the show.

If the producers of "60 Minutes" really *did* pay Pitty Pat $38,000, they were rooked, for there was no bombshell. Or perhaps, as has been suggested, libel laws being what they are, the bomb was considered inadvisable, and was defused. The interview was benign, even boring. "Everyone here feels cheated by it," said a friend of Montesini's. "Such a pathetic amount was produced. Anyway, I heard they only paid her $23,000."

Pitty Pat was interviewed in the apartment of her mother and stepfather, and viewers had no sense of watching a sad and sympathetic jilted woman. She seemed arch and superior, holding her eyebrows high and looking down her nose at Jeff McMullen, the Morley Safer of Australia's "60 Minutes," as if she were granting an audience to a troublesome commoner.

"That's Mummy and H.M. the Queen," she said, showing a photograph of Lady Potter in a deep curtsy before Queen Elizabeth.

The only surprise in the program came when McMullen asked, "Were you sexually compatible with the prince?"

"Yes, we were. Wouldn't you be with someone you were going to marry?"

"Would you take him back?"

"Yeah. He's a decent guy."

She said she did not believe that Lorenzo was gay. If something had happened in his past, it was of no concern to either of them. She mentioned the possibility of lurid photographs—that was probably the predicted bombshell—but said she didn't believe they existed.

"Do you think Lorenzo's a prince?" asked Jeff McMullen, pointing out that Montesini's relatives had mocked the title.

"I don't know," replied Pitty Pat. "I would like to see his grandmother's will. She wanted him to take up the title. That's where it all started." She added that titles did not matter to her.

She said that she didn't think Lorenzo had been in it for the money. "Besides," she said, "my stepfather does not give away his money lightly." She said that the story had been started by John Laws, the radio announcer, who suggested to Lorenzo while airborne that his title was worth a fortune to the Potters. For that, she said, she felt a great deal of resentment for John Laws.

When asked how she felt about the premier's mentioning her name in Parliament, she became imperious in her dismissal of him. "How tacky. What a common remark," she snapped.

She then allowed herself to be talked into telephoning her almost-husband on national television in order to ask him why he had never consulted her about calling off the marriage. The prince-steward was out, on a flight presumably, and she got his answering machine.

"It's me," she said, and asked him to call her when he returned. In closing, she told McMullen that the heartache she felt was worse than the embarrassment.

Montesini, in an intimate moment with his friend the Australian journalist Daphne Guinness, gave his account of the fiasco. He claimed that Lady Potter had announced his engagement without his knowledge when he was in Tokyo for Qantas. "I felt trapped by it," he said, "pushed on by Pitty Pat's mother into something that got out of hand." However, he went along with it, "swept into the euphoria of such a grand occasion as a wedding in Venice."

"I could not see past April 16. I could not think beyond getting to Venice and going to the church. I could not begin to think of the night of the sixteenth, and where I would sleep after the wedding. I even rehearsed going up the aisle and standing in front of Father Vincent Kiss and when it came to the bit about 'Do you take Primrose to be your lawful wedded wife?' shouting 'NO!' and turning round and running out of the church."

However, he did not mention these inner torments, at least not to his fiancée and her family. According to him, the real reason for the breakup was the Potters' desire to terminate his friendship with Straub. When asked about the rumor that there had been a wedding settlement of some $2 million, Lorenzo said, "Take a naught off and you'd be nearer the mark, but I haven't been given a penny." In Venice, he said, John Lane told him that Lady Potter had changed her will so that he couldn't get his hands on the fortune that will eventually be Pitty Pat's. That, Lorenzo claimed, coupled with the information that Pitty Pat had said that after the sixteenth she would be a princess traveling first-class, made him feel used.

One week later, however, he also went public, in the Australian magazine *Women's Day*. Whether, like Pitty Pat, he was getting paid for his revelations is not known. But his statement, like hers, was a party-line exercise in face-saving. "I did not have the money to give her the lifestyle she would have expected," he said. "I loved her—and I always will—but as the rumors, all of which are untrue, began to circulate, I realized I was out of my depth and that it would be best to call off the marriage." He said that he had had a close and satisfying sexual relationship with Primrose, and he described her as sensual. "Every time I looked at her, I was reminded of a Byzantine empress." He denied that he was gay, and he downplayed the importance of his title. "It must be understood that Prince Giustiniani is a courtesy title only, and there is no way Primrose could use it on her passport, or use it in real life. She understood that completely. We often talked about it and laughed about it."

He was most grieved, he said, by her appearance on "60 Minutes."

"It was horrendous when, on the program, she tried to ring me and I heard my own voice on my telephone answering machine."

SPECIAL REPORTING FROM SYDNEY BY DAPHNE GUINNESS

August 1990

I had totally forgotten about these ridiculous people until I reread this piece recently. Primrose Dunlop, the jilted bride, her mother, Lady Potter, and her fiancé, Prince Giustiniani, blazed forth in gossip columns the world over for a few months in 1990 when the groom ran off romantically with his best man the night before the wedding. Now they have all faded from sight and sound, probably somewhere in Australia, from whence they came. I no longer had the interest in them to find out what happened to them.

KHASHOGGI'S FALL:
A CRASH IN THE LIMO LANE

A dnan Khashoggi was never the richest man in the world, ever, but he flaunted the myth that he was with such relentless perseverance and public-relations know-how that most of the world believed him. The power of great wealth is awesome. If you have enough money, you can bamboozle anyone. Even if you can create the *illusion* that you have enough money you can bamboozle anyone, as Adnan Khashoggi did over and over again. He understood high visibility better than the most shameless Hollywood press agent, and he made himself one of the most famous names of our time. Who doesn't know about his yachts, his planes, his dozen houses, his wives, his hookers, his gifts, his parties, his friendships with movie stars and jet-set members, and his companionship with kings and world leaders? His dazzling existence outshone even that of his prime benefactors in the royal family of Saudi Arabia—a bedazzlement that led to their eventual disaffection for him.

Now, reportedly broke, or broke by the standards of people with great wealth—his yacht gone, his planes gone, his dozen houses gone, or going, and his reputation in smithereens—he has recently spent three months pacing restlessly in a six-by-eight-foot prison cell in Bern, Switzerland, where the majority of his fellow prisoners were in on drug charges. True, he dined there on gourmet food from the Schweizerhof Hotel, but he also had to clean his own cell and toilet as a small army of international lawyers fought to prevent his extradition to the United States to face charges of racketeering and obstruction of justice. Finally, Khashoggi dropped his efforts to avoid extradition when the Swiss ruled that he would face prosecution only for obstruction of justice and mail fraud, not for the more serious charges of racketeering and conspiracy. On July 19, accompanied by Swiss law-enforcement agents, he arrived in New York from Geneva first-class on a Swissair flight, handcuffed like a common criminal but dressed in an olive-drab safari suit with gold buttons and epaulets. He was immediately whisked to the federal courthouse on Foley Square, a tiny figure surrounded by a cadre of lawyers and federal marshals, where Judge John F. Keenan refused to grant him bail. He spent his first night in three years in America not in his Olympic Tower aerie but in the Metropolitan Correctional Center. No member of his immediate family was present to witness his humiliation.

Allegedly, he helped his friends Ferdinand and Imelda Marcos plunder the Philippines of some $160 million by fronting for them in illegal real-estate deals. When United States authorities attempted to return some of the Marcos booty to the new Philippine government, they discovered that the ownership of four large commercial buildings in New York City—the Crown Building at 730 Fifth Avenue, the Herald Center at 1 Herald Square, 40 Wall Street, and 200 Madison Avenue—had passed to Adnan Khashoggi. On paper it seemed that the sale of the buildings had taken place in 1985, before the fall of the Marcos regime, but authorities later charged that the documents had been fraudulently backdated. In addition, more than thirty paintings, valued at $200 million, that Imelda Marcos had allegedly purloined from the Metropolitan Museum of Manila, including works by Rubens, El Greco, Picasso, and Degas, were being stored by Khashoggi for the Marcoses, but it turned out that the pictures had been sold to Khashoggi as part of a cover-up. The art treasures were first hidden on his yacht and then moved to his penthouse in Cannes. The penthouse was raided by the French police in search of the pictures in April 1987, but it is believed that Khashoggi had been tipped off. He turned over nine of the paintings to the police, claiming to have sold the others to a Panamanian company, but investigators believe that he sold the pictures back to himself. The rest of the loot is thought to be in Athens. If he is found guilty, such charges could get him up to ten years in an American slammer.

In a vain delay tactic meant to forestall the extradition process as long as possible, he had at first refused to accept the hundreds of pages of English-language legal documentation in any language but Arabic, although he has spoken English nearly all his life and was educated partially in the United States.

People wonder why he went to Switzerland in the first place, when he was aware that arrest on an American warrant was a certainty there and that Switzerland could and probably would extradite him if the United States requested it. The answer is now known, although there is the possibility that Khashoggi, like others in that rarefied existence of power and great wealth, thought he was above the law and nothing would happen to him. Alternatively, there is the possibility, which has been suggested by some of his friends, that he was tired of the waiting game and went to Bern to face the situation, because he was convinced that he had done nothing wrong and was innocent of the charges against him. There was neither furtiveness nor stealth, certainly no lessening of his usual mode of magnificence, in his arrival in Switzerland on April 17. He flew to Zurich by private plane. A private helicopter took him from the airport to Bern, where he had three Mercedeses at his disposal and registered in a very grand suite at the exclusive Schweizerhof Hotel. Ostensibly, his reason for visiting the city was to be treated by the eminent cellular therapist Dr. Augusto Gianoli with revitalization shots, whereby live cells taken from the embryo of an unborn lamb are injected into the patient to ward off the aging process. Dr. Gianoli's well-to-do patients often rest in the Schweizerhof after receiving the shots.

But apparently the revitalization of vital organs wasn't the only reason Adnan Khashoggi was in Bern on the day of his bust. He was killing two birds with one stone, and the other bit of business was an arms deal. Those closest to him are highly sensitive about the fact that he is always described in the media as a Middle Eastern arms dealer. True, he started out like that, they say, but they object to the fact that the arms-dealer label has stuck, and cite, instead, his other achievements. As one former partner told me, "Adnan brought billions and billions of dollars' worth of business to Lockheed and Boeing." Be that as it may, Khashoggi will always be best remembered in this country for his anything-for-a-buck participation in the Iran-contra affair, one of the most pathetic episodes in the history of American foreign policy, as well as a blight forever on the Reagan administration. True to form, the business he was conducting in his suite at the Schweizerhof that day was a sale of armored weapons.

When the Swiss police arrived at the suite, the other two arms dealers mistakenly thought they were after them, and a slight panic ensued. The arms dealers left immediately by another door in the suite and were out of the country by private plane within an hour of Khashoggi's arrest. Khashoggi, remaining totally calm, asked the police if they would place him under house arrest in his suite in the Schweizerhof Hotel instead of putting him in jail, but the request was denied. Then he asked them not to handcuff him, and the request was granted. The prison in Bern where he was taken, booked, fingerprinted, and photographed is barely a five-minute walk from the Schweizerhof, but the group traveled by police car. The friends of Adnan Khashoggi deeply resent that the Swiss government released his mug shots to the media as if he were an ordinary criminal. "I went immediately to Bern after the arrest," said Prince Alfonso Hohenlohe, one of Khashoggi's very close friends in international society and a neighbor in Marbella, Spain, "but they wouldn't let me in to see him. I sent him a bottle of very good French red wine and a message to the jail. I hear he is the best prisoner they have ever had. I would cut off my arm to get him out of this situation."

For years now, misfortune has plagued Khashoggi. In 1987, Triad America Corporation, his American company, which was involved in a $400 million, twenty-five-acre complex of offices, shops, and a hotel in Salt Lake City, filed for bankruptcy after its creditors, including architects, contractors, and banks, demanded payment. Khashoggi blamed the failure on "cash-flow problems." His most recent woe, reported by Reuters after his imprisonment in Bern, is that the privately owned National Commercial Bank of Saudi Arabia is suing him for $22 million, plus interest. The process of falling from a great height is subtle in the beginning, but there are those who have an instinctive ability to sniff out the first signs of failure and fading fortune. Long before the public disclosures of seized planes and impounded houses and bankruptcies, word went out among some of the fashionable jewelers of the world, from Rome to Beverly Hills, that no more credit was to be given to Adnan Khashoggi, because he had ceased to pay his bills. Then came the whispered stories of how he was draining money from his own projects to maintain his lifestyle; of unpaid servants in the houses and unpaid crew members on the yacht; of unpaid maintenance on his two-floor, 7,200-square-foot condominium with indoor swimming pool at the Olympic Tower on Fifth Avenue in New York; of unpaid helicopter lessons for his daughter, Nabila, even while the extravagant parties proclaiming denial of the truth continued. In fact, the more persistent the rumors of Khashoggi's financial collapse grew, the more extravagant his parties became. Nico Minardos, a former associate of Khashoggi's who was arrested during Iranscam for his involvement in a $2.5 billion deal with Iran for forty-six Skyhawk aircraft and later cleared, said, "Adnan is a lovely man. I like him. He is the greatest P.R. man in the world. When he gave his fiftieth-birthday party, our company was overdrawn at the bank in Madrid by $6 million. And that's about what his party cost. Last year he sold an apartment to pay for his birthday party."

Probably the most telling story in Khashoggi's downfall was repeated to me in London by a witness to the scene, who wished not to be identified. The King of Morocco was staying in the royal suite of Claridge's. The King of Jordan, also visiting London at the time, came to call on the King of Morocco. There is a marble stairway in the main hall of Claridge's which leads up to the royal suite. Shortly after the doors of the suite closed, Adnan Khashoggi, having heard of the meeting, arrived breathlessly at the hotel by taxi. Used to keeping company with kings, he sent a message up to the royal suite that he was downstairs. He was told that he would not be received.

Shortly after I was asked to write about Adnan Khashoggi, following his arrest, his executive assistant, Robert Shaheen, contacted this magazine, aware of my assignment. He said that I should call him, and I did.

"I understand," I said, "that you are the number-two man to Mr. Khashoggi."

"I am Mr. Khashoggi's number-one man," he corrected me. Then he said, "What is it you want? What will your angle be in your story?" I told him that at this point I didn't know. Shaheen's reverence for his boss was evident in every sentence, and his descriptions of him were sometimes florid. "He dared to dream dreams that no one else dared to dream," he said with a bit of a catch to his voice. He proceeded to list some of the accomplishments of his boss, whom he always referred to as the Chief. "The Chief was responsible for opening the West to Saudi Arabia. The Chief saved the Cairo telephone system. The chief saved Lockheed from going bankrupt." He then told me, "You must talk with Max Helzel. He is a representative of Lockheed. Get him before he dies. He is getting old. Mention my name to him."

An American of Syrian descent, Shaheen went to Saudi Arabia to teach English in the late fifties, and there he met Khashoggi. He has described his job with Khashoggi in their long association as being similar to that of the chief of staff at the White House. Anyone wishing to meet with Khashoggi for a business proposition had to go through him first. He carried the Chief's money. He scheduled the air fleet's flights. He traveled with him. He became his apologist when things started to go wrong. After the debacle in Salt Lake City, he said, "People in Salt Lake City can't hold Adnan responsible. He delegated all responsibility to American executives, and it was up to them to make a success. Adnan still believes in Salt Lake City." And he became, like his boss, a very rich man himself through the contacts he made. At the close of our conversation, Shaheen told me that it was very unlikely that I would get into the prison in Bern, although he would do what he could to help me.

The night before I left New York, I was at a dinner party in a beautiful Fifth Avenue apartment overlooking Central Park. There were sixteen people, among them the high-flying Donald and Ivana Trump, one of New York's richest and most discussed couples, and a major topic of conversation was Khashoggi's imprisonment. "I read every word about Adnan Khashoggi," Donald Trump said to me.

A story that Trump frequently tells is about his purchase of Khashoggi's yacht, the 282-foot, $70 million *Nabila*, thought to be the most opulent private vessel afloat. In addition to the inevitable discotheque, with laser beams that projected Khashoggi's face, the floating palace also had an operating room and a morgue, with coffins. Forced to sell it for a mere $30 million, Khashoggi did not want Trump to keep the name *Nabila*, because it was his daughter's name. Trump had no intention, ever, of keeping the name. He had already decided to rename it the *Trump Princess*. But for some reason

Khashoggi thought Trump meant to retain the name, and he knocked a million dollars off the asking price to ensure the name change. Trump accepted the deduction.

"Khashoggi was a great broker and a lousy businessman," Trump said to me that night. "He understood the art of bringing people together and putting together a better deal than almost anyone—all the bullshitting part, of talk and entertainment—but he never knew how to invest his money. If he had put his commissions into a bank in Switzerland, he'd be a rich man today, but he invested it, and he made lousy choices."

In London, on my way to Bern, I contacted Viviane Ventura, an English public-relations woman who is a great friend of Khashoggi's. She attended Richard Nixon's second inauguration in January 1973 with him. Ventura told me more or less the same thing Shaheen had told me. "The lawyers won't let anyone near him. They don't want any statements. There's a lot more to it than we know. This is a terrible thing that your government is doing. Adnan is one of the most generous, most caring men."

The five-foot-four-inch, two-hundred-pound, financially troubled megastar was born in Saudi Arabia in 1935, the oldest of six children. His father, who was an enormous influence in his life, was a highly respected doctor, remembered for bringing the first X-ray machine to Saudi Arabia. He became the personal physician to King Ibn Saud, a position that brought him and his family into close proximity with court circles. Adnan was sent to Victoria College in Alexandria, Egypt, an exclusive boys' academy where King Hussein was a classmate and where the students were caned if they did not speak English. Later he went to California State University in Chico, and was overwhelmed by the freedom of the lifestyle of American girls. There he began to entertain as a way of establishing himself, and to broker his first few deals. Early on he won favor with many of the Saudi royal princes, particularly Prince Sultan, the eighteenth son, and Prince Talal, the twenty-third son, who became his champions. In the 1970s, when the price of Arab oil soared to new heights, he began operating in high gear. Although Northrop was his best-known client, he also represented Lockheed, Teledyne National, Chrysler, and Raytheon in the Middle East.

By the mid-1970s, his commissions from Lockheed alone totaled more than $100 million. In addition, his firm, Triad, had holdings that included thirteen banks and a chain of steak houses on the West Coast of the United States, cattle ranches in North and South America, resort developments in Fiji and Egypt, a chain of hotels in Australia, and various real-estate, insurance, and shipping concerns. The first Arab to develop land in the United States, he organized and invested many millions in Triad America Corporation in Salt Lake City. He became an intimate of kings and heads of state, a great gift giver, a provider of women, a perfect host, and the creator of a lifestyle that would become world-renowned for its extravagance. Even now, in the overlapping murkiness of deposed dictators, the baby Doc Duvaliers, those other Third World escapees with their nation's pillage, are living in the South of France in a house found for them by Adnan Khashoggi, belonging to his son.

Perhaps not surprisingly, having presented myself as a journalist from the United States, I was not allowed to visit Khashoggi in the prison at 22 Genfergasse in Bern. It is a modern jail, six stories high, located in the center of the city. The windows are vertically barred, and the prisoners take their exercise on the roof. At night the exterior walls are floodlit. For a city prison there is an amazing silence about the place. No prisoners were screaming out the windows at passersby. There were no guards in sight on the elevated catwalk. Much has been made of the fact that Khashoggi got his meals from the dining room of the nearby Schweizerhof Hotel, but that and a rented television set and access to a fax machine were in fact his only privileges. In the beginning, waiters in uniform from the hotel would carry the trays over, but they were photographed too much and asked too many quesions by reporters. The waiters and the maître d' that I spoke with in the restaurant of the Schweizerhof were reluctant to talk about the meals being sent to the jail, as if they were under orders not to speak. The evening I waited to see Khashoggi's meal arrive, a young girl brought it on a tray. She was not in uniform. She got to the jail at precisely six, and the gourmet meal was wrapped in silver foil to keep it hot.

Everywhere, people speak admiringly of Nabila Khashoggi, the first child and only daughter of Adnan, by his first wife, Soraya, the mother also of his first four sons. Nabila is the only family member who remained in Bern throughout her father's ordeal, although one of the sons, Mohammed, is said to have visited once. A handsome woman in her late twenties, Nabila at one time had aspirations to movie stardom. In 1981, she became so distraught over the notoriety and sensationalism of her mother's divorce action against her father that she attempted suicide by taking an overdose of sleeping pills. Between father and daughter there is enormous affection and mutual respect. It was after her that Khashoggi named his spectacular yacht.

Nabila visited the prison on an almost daily basis, providing comfort and news and relaying messages to her father. The rest of the time she remained in total seclusion in her suite at the Schweizerhof. On occasion she dined at off hours in the dining room, but she did not loiter in the public rooms of the hotel, and reporters, however long they sat in the lobby hoping to get a look at her, waited in vain. I wrote her a note introducing myself and left it at the desk. I mentioned the names of several mutual friends, among them George Hamilton, the Hollywood actor, who had sold Nabila his house in Beverly Hills for $7 million three years ago, during the period when Nabila was trying to launch a career as a film actress. The house was allegedly a gift to Hamilton from Imelda Marcos when she was still the First Lady of the Philippines. I also mentioned in my note that I had been in touch with Robert Shaheen, Khashoggi's aide and friend, and that he was aware that I would contact her.

From there, I walked back to my hotel, the Bellevue Palace, and as I entered my room the telephone was ringing. It was Nabila Khashoggi. Polite, courteous, she also sounded weary and wept out; there was incredible sadness in her voice. She said that the lawyers had forbidden her or any member of her family to speak to anyone from the press, and that it would therefore not be possible for me to interview her. She thanked me, when I asked her how she was holding up, and said that she was well. In closing, she said in a very strong voice, "I think you should know that Robert Shaheen has not worked for my father for several years, and that we do not speak to him." This information shocked me, after Shaheen's passionate representation of himself to me as Khashoggi's closest associate, but it was only the first of many surprises and contradictions I would encounter in the people who have surrounded Adnan Khashoggi during his extraordinary life. Intimates of Khashoggi told me that he often had fallings-out with those close to him, and that sometimes they would be reinstated in his good graces, and sometimes not.

Later that day Nabila Khashoggi called again to ask if I spoke German. I said no. She said there was an article in that day's *Der Bund*, the Swiss-German newspaper, that I should get and have translated. The article was positive in tone, and said that perhaps the Americans did not have sufficient evidence to cause the Swiss to extradite Khashoggi. John Marshall, a British newspaperman based in Bern, said about the article, "The supposition is that the Americans have jumped the gun. The charges presented so far will not stand up in the Swiss court." Everywhere, I heard people say, "If Khashoggi tells what he knows, there will be enormous embarrassment in Washington." The reference was not to the charges pending against Khashoggi in the matter of Imelda and Ferdinand Marcos. It had to do with Iranscam. Roy Boston, a wealthy developer in Marbella and a great friend of Khashoggi's, said, "I can't imagine that the Americans really want him back in the United States. It would be a mistake. The president and the former president would be smeared. And the same with the King of Saudi Arabia. Adnan would never say one word against the king. But the Americans? Why should he keep quiet? If he really starts talking, good gracious me, there will be red faces around the world."

One of the unknown factors in the Khashoggi predicament is whether the King of Saudi Arabia will come to his aid, and on that point opinions differ. "I don't know how the king feels about Adnan now," said Roy Boston. "He did a lot of handling of Saudi affairs, with the king and without the king. There is always the possibility that he is still doing things for the king."

John Marshall said, "If the King of Saudi Arabia stands behind him, he will never let Khashoggi go to jail in the United States."

"Do you think the king will come to Khashoggi's rescue?" I asked Nico Minardos.

"No way!" he said. "The king doesn't like him. Only Prince Sultan likes him now."

The most mystifying family matter, during Khashoggi's imprisonment, was the nonappearance of Lamia Khashoggi, the beautiful second wife of Adnan, who never visited her husband in Bern. Several people close to the Khashoggis feel that their marriage has for some time been more ceremonial than conjugal. Lamia sat out her husband's jail time at their penthouse in Cannes with their son, Ali. I listened in on a telephone call placed by a mutual European friend who asked if she would talk with me. Like Nabila, she declined, under lawyers' orders. When the friend persisted, she acted as if she had been disconnected, saying, "I can't hear you. I can't hear you. Hello . . . hello?" and then hung up.

Until recently, Lamia, who was born Laura Biancolini in Italy, was a highly visible member of the jet set, palling around with such luminous figures as the flamboyant Princess Gloria von Thurn und Taxis, the young wife of the billionaire aristocrat Prince Johannes von Thurn und Taxis. At the Thurn und Taxises' eighteenth-century costume ball in their five-hundred-room palace in Regensburg, Germany, in 1986, Lamia Khashoggi made an entrance that people still talk about. Dressed as Mme. de Pompadour, she came down the palace stairway flanked by two Nubians—"real Nubians, from the Sudan"—carrying long-handled feathered fans. Her wig was twice as high as the wig of her hostess, who was dressed as Marie Antoinette, and her gold-and-white gown was so wide that she could not navigate a turn in the stairway and had to descend sideways, assisted by her Nubians. It was felt that she had attempted to upstage her hostess, a no-no in high society, and since then, though not necessarily related to the incident, their friendship has cooled. In the midst of the Thurn und Taxises' milliondollar revel, attendees at the ball tell me, there was much behind-the-fan talk that the Khashoggi fortune was in peril. Khashoggi had secured oil and mining rights in the Republic of the Sudan and had used those rights as collateral to borrow money. When his friend Gaafar Nimeiry, the president of the Sudan, was overthrown in 1985, the succeeding administration canceled the contracts he had negotiated, and one Sudanese broadcaster protested that Nimeiry had sold the Sudan to Adnan Khashoggi.

Laura Biancolini began traveling on Khashoggi's yacht, along with what is known in some circles as a bevy of lovelies, at the age of seventeen. She converted to Islam, changed her name to Lamia, and became

Khashoggi's second wife before giving birth to her only child and Adnan's fifth son, Ali, now nine, in West Palm Beach, Florida. Marriage
to a man like Adnan Khashoggi cannot have been easy for either of his
wives. Women for hire were part and parcel of his everyday life, and
he often sent girls as gifts to men with whom he was attempting to do
business. "They lend beauty and fragrance to the surroundings," he
has been quoted as saying.

His previous wife, who was born Sandra Patricia Jarvis-Daly, the
daughter of a London waitress, married him when she was nineteen,
long before he was internationally famous. She also converted to Islam
and took the name Soraya. They first lived in Beirut and later in London. A great beauty, she is the mother of Nabila and the first four
Khashoggi sons: Mohammed, twenty-five, Khalid, twenty-three, Hussein, twenty-one, and Omar, nineteen. Although their marriage was an
open one, the end came when he heard that she was having an affair
with his pal President Gaafar Nimeiry of the Sudan. He was already
involved with the seventeen-year-old Laura Biancolini. In Islamic tradition, a divorce may be executed by the male's reciting "I divorce
thee" three times. Subsequently, Soraya experienced financial discontent with her lot and complained that the usually generous Khashoggi,
whose lifestyle cost him a quarter of a million dollars a day to maintain, was being tight with his alimony payments to the mother of his
first five children. With the aid of the celebrated divorce lawyer Marvin Mitchelson, she sued her former husband for $2.5 billion, which
she figured to be half his fortune. She had, in the meantime, married
and divorced a young man who had been the beau of a daughter she
had had out of wedlock before marrying Khashoggi and bearing
Nabila. She had also engaged in a highly publicized love affair with
Winston Churchill, the grandson of the late British prime minister and
the son of the socially unimpeachable Mrs. Averell Harriman of Washington, D.C. Concurrently with that romance, she bore another child,
her seventh, generally thought to be Churchill's child but never publicly acknowledged as such. As choreographed by Marvin Mitchelson,
the alimony case received notorious worldwide coverage, which caused
great embarrassment to all members of the family, as well as an increased disenchantment with Khashoggi on the part of the Saudi royal
family. Ultimately, Soraya received a measly $2 million divorce settle-

ment, but, more important, she was also reinstated in the family. Right up to the bust and confinement in Bern, she attended all the major Khashoggi parties and even posed with Adnan and Lamia and their combined children for a 1988 Christmas family photograph.

Khashoggi's private life has always been a public mess. "I haven't spoken to my ex-uncle since 1983, after the Cap d'Ail scandal, when one of his aides went to jail for prostitution and drugs," said Dodi Fayed, executive producer of the film *Chariots of Fire* and the son of the controversial international businessman Mohammed Al Fayed, the owner of the Ritz Hotel in Paris and Harrods department store in London, over which there was one of the bitterest takeover battles of the decade. Dodi Fayed's mother, Samira, who died two years ago, was Adnan Khashoggi's sister. Khashoggi and Mohammed Al Fayed were once business partners. Since the business partnership and the marriage of Samira and Fayed both broke up bitterly, the relationship between the two families has been poisonous. Dodi Fayed's use of the term "ex-uncle" indicates that he no longer even considers Khashoggi a relation.

The Cap d'Ail affair had to do with a French woman named Mireille Griffon, who became known on the Côte d'Azur as Madame Mimi, a serious though brief rival to the famous Madame Claude, the Parisian madam who serviced the upper classes and business elite of Europe for three decades with some of the most beautiful women in the world, many of whom have gone on to marry into the upper strata. Partnered with Madame Mimi was Khashoggi's employee Abdo Khawagi, a onetime masseur. Madame Mimi's operation boasted a roster of three hundred girls between the ages of eighteen and twenty-five. A perfectionist in her trade, Madame Mimi groomed and dressed her girls so that they would be presentable escorts for the important men they were servicing. The girls, who were sent to Khashoggi in groups of twos and threes, called him *papa gâteau*, or sugar daddy, because he was extremely generous with them. In addition to their fee, 40 percent of which went to Madame Mimi, the girls received furs and jewels and tips that sometimes equaled or surpassed the fee. One of the greatest whoremongers in the world, Khashoggi was generous to a fault and provided the same girls to members of the Saudi royal family as well as to business associates and party friends. His role as a provider of women for business purposes was not unlike the role his uncle Yussuf Yassin had performed for King Ibn Saud. After the French police on the Riviera were alerted, a watch was put on the operations and the madam's telephone lines were tapped. In time an arrest was made, and the case went to trial in Nice in February 1984, amid nasty publicity. Madame Mimi, who is believed to have personally grossed $1.2 million in ten months, got a year and a half in jail. Khawagi, the procurer, got a year in prison. And Khashoggi sailed away on the *Nabila*.

Of more recent vintage is the story of the beautiful Indian prostitute Pamella Bordes, who was discovered working as a researcher in the House of Commons after having bedded some of the most distinguished men in England. In a three-part interview in the London *Daily Mail*, she made her sexual revelations about Khashoggi shortly after he was imprisoned in Bern, a bit of bad timing for the beleaguered arms dealer. Pamella was introduced into the great world by Sri Chandra Swamiji Maharaj, a Hindu teacher with worldly aspirations known simply as the Swami or Swamiji, although sometimes he is addressed by his worshipers with the papal-sounding title of Your Holiness. The Swami, who is said to possess miraculous powers, has served as a spiritual and financial adviser to, among others, Ferdinand Marcos, who credited him with once saving his life, Adnan Khashoggi, Mohammed Al Fayed, and both the Sultan of Brunei and the second of his two wives, Princess Mariam, a half-Japanese former airline stewardess. (Princess Mariam is less popular with the royal family of Brunei than the sultan's first wife, Queen Saleha, his cousin, who bore him six children, but Princess Mariam is clearly the sultan's favorite.) The Swami played a key role in the Mohammed Al Fayed–Tiny Rowland battle for the ownership of Harrods in London when he secretly taped a conversation with Fayed which vaguely indicated that the money Fayed had used to purchase Harrods was really the Sultan of Brunei's. The Swami sold the tape to Rowland for $2 million. Subsequently, he was arrested in India on charges of breaking India's foreign-exchange regulations.

The Swami introduced Pamella Bordes to Khashoggi after she failed to be entered as Miss India in the Miss Universe contest of 1982. Pamella, a young woman of immense ambition, was invited to

Khashoggi's Marbella estate, La Baraka, shortly after meeting him. In her *Daily Mail* account of her five-day stay, she said, "I had a room to myself. I used to get up very late. They have the most fabulous room service. You can order up the most sensational food and drink anytime you want." She despised the other girls who were sent along on the junket with her, referring to them as "cheapo" girls who "ordered chips with everything. They smothered their food with tomato ketchup and slopped it all over the bed. It was disgusting." The girls were taken shopping in the boutiques of Marbella and told to buy anything they wanted, all at Khashoggi's expense. In the evening, they dressed for dinner. She described Khashoggi as always having a male secretary by his side with a cordless telephone. "Non-stop calls were coming in. . . . It was business, business non-stop." She slept with him in what she described as the largest bed she had ever seen. "I was very happy to have sex with him, and he did not want me to do anything kinky or sleazy."

After their liaison, she became part of the Khashoggi bank of women ready and willing to be used in his business deals. In the article, she described in detail a flight she was sent on from Geneva to Riyadh to service a Prince Mohammed, a senior member of the royal family, "who would be a key man in buying arms and vital technology." The prince came in, looked her over, and said something to his secretary in Arabic. The secretary then took Pamella into a bathroom, where she was told to bathe and to wash her hair and blow-dry it straight. The prince, it seemed, wanted her with straight hair. Then she went to the prince's room and had sex with him. The next day she was shipped back to Geneva. "He was somebody very, very important to Khashoggi. Khashoggi was keeping him supplied with girls. Khashoggi has all these deals going, and he needs a lot of girls for sexual bribes. I was just part of an enormous group. I was used as sexual bait."

In an astonishing book called *By Hook or by Crook*, written by the Washington lawyer Steven Martindale, who traveled for several years with Khashoggi and the Swami, the author catalogs Khashoggi's use of women in business deals. The book, which was published in England, was then banned there by a court order sought not by Khashoggi but by Mohammed Al Fayed.

In Marbella, Adnan Khashoggi is a ranking social figure and a very
popular man. He has a magnificent villa on a huge estate that he
bought from the father of Thierry Roussel, the last husband of the
tragic heiress Christina Onassis. After Khashoggi bought his house in
Marbella in the late seventies, he said to Alain Cavro, an architect who
for twenty years has worked exclusively for him and who refers to him
as A. K., "I want to add ten bedrooms, salons and a big kitchen, and I
want it right away. I need to have it finished in time for my party."
Cavro told me that he had ninety-three days, after the plans were approved. Workers worked twenty-four hours a day, in shifts, and the
house was completed in time for the party. "A. K. has a way of convincing you of almost anything," Cavro told me. "He can persuade
you with his charm to change your mind after you have made it up. He
builds people up. He introduces people in such a flattering way as to
make them blush. He finds very quickly the point to touch them the
most. Afterwards, people say, 'You saw how nice he was to me?' People feel flattered, almost in love with him."

Khashoggi was responsible for bringing Prince Fahd, now King
Fahd, of Saudi Arabia to Marbella for the first time. That visit, which
resulted in Fahd's building a mosque and a palace-type residence in
Marbella, designed by Cavro, changed the economy of the fashionable
resort.

In the summer of 1988, a Texas multimillionairess named Nancy
Hamon chartered the ship *Sea Goddess* and invited eighty friends,
mostly other Texas millionaires, on a four-day cruise, starting in
Málaga, Spain. The high point of the trip was an elaborate and expensive lunch party at the Khashoggi villa in Marbella. Khashoggi, already
in severe financial distress, put on the dog in the hope of lining up
some of these rich Texas backers to shore up his failing empire.

"Oh, darling, it was an experience," said one of the guests. "There
were guardhouses with guards with machine guns, and closed-circuit
television everywhere. The whole house is gaudy Saudi, if you know
what I mean. They have Liberace's piano, with rhinestones in it, and
the chairs are all trimmed with gilt, and a disco, naturally, with a floor
that lights up. Do you get the picture? You can see Africa and Gibraltar from the terrace—that was nice. They had flamenco music pound-

ing away at lunch. Some of the guests got into the flamenco act after a few drinks. I'll say this for Mr. Khashoggi, he was a tremendously gracious host. And so was the wife, Lamia. She had on a pink dress trimmed with gold—Saint Laurent, I think—and rubies, lots of rubies, with a décolletage to set off the rubies, and ruby earrings, great big drop earrings. This is lunch, remember. He has built a gazebo that could hold hundreds of people, with silver and gold tinsel decorations, like on a Christmas tree. The food was wonderful. Tons of staff, as well as a lot of men in black suits—his assistants, I suppose. After lunch we were taken on a tour of the stables. The stables are in better taste than the house. Everything pristine. And Arabian horses. It was marvelous. It was amazing he could continue living on that scale. Everyone knew he was on his uppies."

These days, Khashoggi is constantly discussed in the bar of the exclusive Marbella Club. Very few people who know him do not speak highly of his charm, his generosity, and the beauty of his parties. The cunning streak that flaws his character is less apparent to his society and party friends than it is to his business associates. "When Adnan comes back here, I told Nabila that I'll give the first dinner for him," said Roy Boston. "He has been a considerable friend to some people here in Marbella. He is always faithful to his friends. He remembers birthdays. He does very personal things. That's why we like him. Now that he's in trouble, no one here is saying 'I don't like him' or 'I saw it coming.' "

"He is a fantastic host," said Prince Alfonso Hohenlohe. "He takes care of his guests the whole night—heads of state, noble princes, archdukes. He has a genius for seating people in the correct place. He always knows everyone's name, and he can seat 150 people *exactly* right without using place cards. All these problems he is in are because of his great heart and his goodness. I was at a private dinner party in New York when Marcos asked him to help save them. For A. K., there were no laws, no skies, no limits. With all the money he had, he should have bought the *New York Times*, or the *Los Angeles Times*, and NBC. He should have bought the media. The media can destroy a president, and it can destroy Khashoggi."

One grand lady in Marbella reminisced, "Which party was it? I don't remember. Khashoggi's birthday, I think. There were balloons everywhere that said I AM THE GREATEST on them, and he crowned himself king that night and walked through the party wearing an ermine robe. It was so amusing. But odd now, under the circumstances." Another said, "He's the only host I've ever seen who walks each guest to the front door at the end of the party. Even when we left at 8:30 in the morning, he walked us out to our cars. He's marvelous, really." Another, an English peeress, said, "Alfonso Hohenlohe's sister, Beatriz, the Duchess of Arion, invited us to dinner at Khashoggi's. I said I wouldn't *dream* of going to Mr. Khashoggi's on a secondhand invitation, and the next thing I knew, the wife, what's-her-name, Lamia, called and invited us, and then they sent around a car, and so, of course, we went. There were eighty, seated. It was for that Swami, what's-his-name, with a vegetarian dinner, because of the Swami— delicious, as a matter of fact. I said to my husband, or he said to me, I don't remember which, 'That Swami's a big phony.' But Mr. Khashoggi was very nice, and he entertains beautifully. Most of the people down here just feel sorry for him. For God's sake, don't use my name in your article."

An American writer who spends time in the resort said to me, "That gang you were with last night at the Marbella Club, they're all going to like him, but I know a lot of people here in Marbella who don't like him, the kind of people he owes money to. He gives big parties and owes money to the help. I'll give you the number of the guy who fixes his lawn mowers. He owes the lawn-mower fixer $2,000."

Whether Khashoggi is really broke or not is anybody's guess. Roy Boston said, "Is he broke? I can't answer that. Four weeks before he was arrested, he gave a party here that must have cost a fortune. It was a big show, so he can't be that broke, but he might be officially broke. If you were once worth $5 billion, you must have a little nest egg somewhere. He's not stupid, you know." A former American associate, wishing anonymity, said, "Adnan is not broke. I don't care what anyone says. He's still got $40 million coming in from Lockheed. That's a commission alone." Steven Martindale thinks he really is broke. "He owes every friend he ever borrowed money from." When Khashoggi's bail was set in New York at $10 million one week after his extradition, however, his brothers paid it immediately.

In his business dealings with the Sultan of Brunei, Khashoggi never rushed things. "Khashoggi had a personal approach. He was willing to show the Sultan a good time, willing and eager to take the Sultan around London or bring a party to the Sultan's palace in Brunei. He gave every appearance of not needing the Sultan, but rather of being another rich man like the Sultan himself who just wanted to enjoy the Sultan's company," writes James Bartholomew in his biography of the Sultan of Brunei, *The Richest Man in the World*. Business, of course followed.

Alain Cavro, who supervised all the buildings and reconstruction projects undertaken by any of the companies within the Khashoggi empire, was a close observer of the business life of Adnan Khashoggi. In 1975, Cavro became president of Triad Condas International, a contemporary design firm that built both palaces and military bases, mostly in the Middle East and Saudi Arabia. When Khashoggi met with kings and heads of state, he would usually take Cavro with him. Khashoggi would say to his hosts, "Give me the honor to demonstrate what we can do, either something personal for you or for the country." He meant a new wing for the palace, a pavilion for the swimming pool, a new country club, or, possibly, but not usually, even something for the public good. Whatever it was that was desired, Cavro would do the drawings overnight and then Khashoggi would present the architectural renderings and follow that up with the immediate building of whatever it was, as his personal gift to the king or head of state. In the inner circle this process was called Mission Impossible; it was designed to show what A. K. could do. "In Africa, heads of state are impressed with magic," said Cavro. Business followed. Cavro, totally loyal to A. K., said, "But these gifts must not be construed as bribes, but rather as a demonstration of how he could do things fast and well. A. K. felt that the heads of state were doing him a favor to allow him to demonstrate how he did things."

Cavro described to me Khashoggi's total concentration when he was involved in a business deal. When the pilot of one of his three planes would announce that they were landing in twenty minutes and that the chief of state was waiting on the tarmac, Khashoggi would go right on with what he was doing until the last possible second. Then he would change into either Western or Eastern garb, depending on where he was landing. In each of his private jets were two wardrobes: one contained his beautifully tailored three-piece bespoke suits from London's Savile Row, in all sizes to deal with his constantly fluctuating weight; in the other were white cotton *thobes*, headdresses, and black ribbed headbands, the traditional Saudi dress. As he deplaned, he would go immediately into the next deal and give that affair his full attention. He was also able to conduct several meetings at the same time, going from room to room, always zeroing in on the exact point under discussion. He constantly emphasized how important it is to understand what the other party to a deal needs and wants.

But long before Adnan Khashoggi's arrest in Bern and his extradition to the United States, his time had passed. His position as the star broker of the Arab world was no longer unique. He had set the example, but now the sons of other wealthy Saudi families were being educated in the United States and England, in far better colleges and universities than Chico State, and were being trained to perform the same role as Khashoggi, with less flash and flamboyance. Khashoggi had, in fact, become an embarrassment. A Jordanian princess described him in May of this year as a disgrace to the Arab world.

With sadness, Cavro told me, "Salt Lake City was the beginning of the end for him. And he lost so much money A. K. began to change. The parties were too extravagant. And his personal life." He shook his head. "Everything was too frantic. Even his brother wanted him to lower his lifestyle. That kind of publicity is a disease."

September 1989

Khashoggi was furious about this article. One night I ran into him at a party at the Fifth Avenue apartment of Warren Avis, of the Avis rent-a-car Avises. He beckoned me in a commanding gesture to follow him into a bedroom, which I did. He claimed that there were three incorrect statements in my article, and he was offended by something I wrote about his second wife. Then he turned and walked out of the room. Quite a few years later, during the trial of the Menendez brothers in Los Angeles, I attended a dinner party given by Paige Rense, the editor of Architectural

Digest, *in an alcove of the main dining room of the Bel Air Hotel. Looking up, I saw Adnan Khashoggi walking toward me with a determined stride. For an instant, I thought he was going to shoot me. Instead, he put out his hand to shake mine, as if to say that all was forgiven. Only last year, I ran into him in Paris at one of the couture shows that he attended with his third wife, Shapira, a strikingly beautiful woman. We greeted each other like old friends and met later at the Ritz Hotel for drinks. He talked about the whereabouts of the Ferdinand Marcos wealth. The man is fascinating; there is no doubt about that.*

MEMENTO MORI

I have never murdered any one, for I was carefully brought-up, and brought-up to be careful. I have, however, known some murderers—pleasant enough fellows—and I have sometimes wanted to commit a murder.
　　—From *Valentine's Days*, London, 1934,
　　　by Valentine, Viscount Castlerosse,
　　　later the Earl of Kenmare, fourth husband of
　　　Enid Lindeman Cameron Cavendish Furness Kenmare.

There are people in fashionable society who, throughout their lives, carry with them the burden of their scandals, as ineradicable from their personality as a tattoo on their forearm. Ann Woodward, the beautiful widow of the handsome and very rich William Woodward, never again after her husband's death walked into a drawing room, or anywhere else, without someone whispering, "She's the woman who shot and killed her husband." Perhaps it was by accident, as she claimed. Perhaps not. It didn't matter. It was what people said about her, and she knew they said it. The same is true of Claus von Bülow, the husband of the beautiful and very rich Sunny von Bülow. Even acquitted, as he was, he will never enter a room, or a restaurant, or a theater, without someone whispering, "He's the man who was accused of trying to kill his wife."

Another such person, forever notorious, was the beautiful Enid Kenmare, or Lady Kenmare, or, to be perfectly correct, the Countess of Kenmare, a mythic figure of the French Riviera and chatelaine of a

great house, the villa La Fiorentina, who lost four husbands, all by
death. W. Somerset Maugham, at a lunch party on the Côte d'Azur
shortly after he moved permanently to the Riviera, said, "Apparently
there is a lady who lives on Cap Ferrat who has killed all her husbands." Unknown to him, the lady about whom he was speaking, Enid
Kenmare, was at the lunch party and heard the remark. She took no
offense, and in time she and Maugham became the greatest of friends
and played bridge together constantly; she even hid his Impressionist-
art collection from the Nazis for him. But people came to say about
her, wherever she went, "She's the lady who killed all her husbands," a
legend that persisted for thirty years, into her old age, and that still is
repeated eighteen years after her death.

The beauty of the much-married and much-widowed Enid Kenmare was so renowned in the years before and after the Second World
War that it was said people stood on chairs in the lobby of the Hôtel
de Paris in Monte Carlo to catch a glimpse of her as she passed
through. She was reported to be fabulously rich, owing to the various
inheritances from her deceased husbands, who included an American
millionaire, Roderick Cameron, and three English aristocrats: Brigadier General Frederick Cavendish, Viscount Furness, and the Earl of
Kenmare. She was also a constant and successful gambler, who fre-
quented the casinos of Monte Carlo and Beaulieu nightly, playing
mostly *trente-et-quarante*. Her friends of that period claim that people
would drop their cards or chips to look at her when she swept past the
entrance without bothering to show the required passport, so well
known was she. There were always great stacks of chips in front of her,
and she never showed any emotion, whether she lost or won. According to one popular story, she purchased her magnificent estate at Cap
Ferrat with her winnings from a single big gambling night at the
casino, but, like every story about her, it may or may not be true. "Enid
became such a character that people began to invent stories about her,
and she told stories about herself that contributed to that sort of talk,"
Anthony Pawson, a septuagenarian bon vivant, told me in London
shortly before his death in December. "Enid was a mythomaniac," said
an old bridge partner of Lady Kenmare's on the Riviera. "She'd invent
stories, and that could be dangerous. You don't know why those people lie, but they do."

"She had fantastic posture, wore cabochon emeralds or rubies, and dressed for the evening in diaphanous and flowing gowns," remembered one of her friends. "It wasn't so much that she was superior as that she was in another sphere almost. She sort of floated, and she had the most amazing eyes."

Enid Kenmare's "other sphere" was, from all accounts, dope. "She kept her beauty because she didn't drink, but she was a heroin addict. Legally a heroin addict. She was on the drug list, you know, registered. Marvelous skin, never went in the sun," said a gentleman in New York. Another gentleman, in London, said, "She smoked opium certainly, and took heroin." A lady friend, more cautious, said, "I never noticed when people took dope." But another lady friend said, "She lived in a haze of drugs." Everyone commented on the fact that she drank Coca-Cola morning, noon, and night.

"If Enid were alive today, she would be, let me see, ninety-eight or ninety-nine, I suppose," said the Honorable David Herbert of Tangier, the son of, brother of, and uncle of various Earls of Pembroke, who knew Enid Kenmare for years and attended her fourth wedding, to Valentine Kenmare. "She walked down the aisle like a first-time bride," he told me, remembering the occasion. "She was very, very wicked. Once, she said to me, 'Do I look like a murderess? Tell me, do I?' "

The other great beauties of her era, to whom she was often compared—Diana Cooper, Daisy Fellowes, and Violet Trefusis—are all dead. So, too, are most of the men she knew. But there are a number still, deep in their eighties now, or nineties, who remember her. Some are in rest homes. Some have come on hard times and live in greatly reduced circumstances from the period in which they flourished. Some are on walkers or canes. One died a week after I spoke with him in his modest bed-sitting-room in London. Another had a stroke. Still another had become so deaf that it was impossible to communicate with her. Different people remembered Lady Kenmare differently. One old gentleman said, "We used to call Enid the cement Venus. Actually, I think Emerald Cunard made up that name." Another said impatiently, "No, no, not *cement* Venus. It was the *stucco* Venus. That's what we called her. Stucco. Not cement." Some remembered her quite erroneously. A grand old dowager marchioness, wearing a fox fur around her shoulders, walked slowly across the lobby of Claridge's in London, leaning on her stick. "I remember Enid," she said. "She pushed Lord Furness out the porthole." And there are also the friends of her children, who are now in their sixties and seventies, who were, in those days, the younger crowd. "I don't think Enid killed anybody, but she might have given them drugs and helped them along," said one friend of her son Rory, who died in 1985 at the age of seventy.

She was born Enid Lindeman in Australia, one of five children. Her father, Charles Lindeman, raised horses and introduced vines to New South Wales, thereby pioneering the wine industry in that country. In later years, when she bred racehorses in Kenya, she would talk about riding bareback as a child. Her rise to international social status began at the age of sixteen, when she allegedly became the mistress of Bernard Baruch, the American financier and presidential adviser, who was then in his forties. During their liaison, Enid, an accomplished artist, had a brief stint in Hollywood as a scenery painter. Their friendship lasted until the end of Baruch's life, when Enid returned to New York to say good-bye to him before he died. A skeptic remarked to me that the trip was to ensure that she would be "remembered financially by Mr. Baruch."

Baruch felt that his beautiful young mistress should be married properly, and it was he who introduced her to her first husband, the American Roderick Cameron, who, like Baruch, was much older than she. They were married in 1913, and he died the following year, leaving her with a son, also called Roderick Cameron, known as Rory, who would himself in time become a known figure in social, literary, and decorating circles.

In 1917 she married for the second time, in England, where she had moved, to Brigadier General Frederick Cavendish, known as Caviar Cavendish. "At that time, it was the thing to do, to marry soldiers," said Tony Pawson. Peter Quennell, the octogenarian writer, described Enid then as "a very autocratic beauty, greatly admired by her husband's junior officers." At White's Club in London, an elderly gentleman listening to this description guffawed and winked, to indicate that the admiration of the young officers was romantic in nature. Enid was presented at court to King George and Queen Mary when she became Mrs. Cavendish, and was said to be the most beautiful Australian ever presented. The marriage to General Cavendish, who, had he lived longer, would have become Lord Waterpark, produced two children, Caryll, a son, who is the present Lord Waterpark, and Patricia, a daughter, who is now Mrs. Frank O'Neill, and lives in Cape Town, South Africa, where she continues to manage a stud farm that her mother purchased before her death. That marriage also produced a considerable inheritance.

In 1933, Enid Cavendish married the very rich Lord Furness, known as Duke, short for Marmaduke, heir to the Furness shipping fortune. He had a private railroad car, two yachts, and an airplane. They were each other's third spouse. Lord Furness was himself no stranger to homicidal rumor and controversy. His first wife, Daisy, had died aboard his yacht the *Sapphire*, on a pleasure cruise from England to the South of France, and he had buried her at sea. "They say she was pushed off the yacht, but no one could ever prove it," said Tony Pawson. Thelma Furness, his second wife, in her memoir, *Double Exposure,* glides over the event of her predecessor's death. "They were forced to bury her at sea. There were no embalming facilities on the yacht, and they were too far out to turn back to England and not near enough to Cannes to make port." Had he been tried and convicted, it is said that, as an English lord, he would have been hanged with a silk rope, but there was never an arrest or a trial. Thelma, during her marriage to Furness, had become the mistress of the then Prince of Wales, and it was she who, inadvertently, brought her friend Wallis Warfield Simpson into the orbit of the prince, thereby losing her lover, her friend, and her husband. After Furness's subsequent marriage to Enid, he several times sought out his former wife, with whom he remained on friendly terms, for solace. His marriage to Enid was never happy. Thelma Furness was of the opinion that Enid got Furness on drugs. In her book, she tells of an occasion when Furness was nervously biting his knuckles. "We went up to Duke's suite. . . . Duke took off his coat and asked me to give him an injection—a *piqûre.* I couldn't do this because I did not know how; I had never handled a hypodermic needle. Finally, he asked me simply to pinch his arm, and he gave himself the injection." Of the last time she saw him on the Riviera, she wrote, "I've never seen a man look so frail, so mixed-up, so ill. I cried, 'Oh, Duke, if I could only put you in my pocket and take you away.' "

Elvira de la Fuente, a longtime Riviera resident who was a great friend of both Enid and her son Rory and a fourth at bridge with Somerset Maugham, sat on the quay at Beaulieu recently and talked about Furness's death in 1940. "Furness died at La Fiorentina," she said. "He used to get drunk every night. He was carried out of there when he died. There was a rumor that Enid killed him. I don't think she did, but she was quite capable of letting him die." The most persistent story of Furness's death was that it took place in the little pavilion at La Fiorentina, which Enid had constructed overlooking the sea, and where she and her friends played cards every day. On the night Furness became ill, she went back to the house to get his pills, locking the door behind her. The next morning he was found dead in the pavilion. Furness's death left Enid a very rich woman, and Thelma Furness tried to have her charged with murder, but Walter Monckton, the preeminent lawyer of the day, refused to take the case, and it never went to trial.

Enid's last marriage, to the sixth Earl of Kenmare, took place in 1943. He was an enormously fat man, 255 pounds, who once accidentally sat on a dog and killed it. Known as Valentine Castlerosse until he became an earl, he had a reputation for lechery and avid gambling that made him disliked in certain segments of society. He was the first English aristocrat to write a gossip column. Hopelessly in debt, he was rescued by Lord Beaverbrook, who paid him £3,000 a year plus expenses to write a column for the *Sunday Express*. Kenmare's family estates in Ireland were massive, 118,600 acres, but yielded only a modest annual income by the standards of the day, £34,000. He once said of his life, "I dissipated my patrimony; I committed many sins; I wasn't important." Elvira de la Fuente remembers that Enid sent her son Rory a telegram saying, "Do you mind if I marry Valentine Castlerosse?" "Valentine used to be married to Doris Castlerosse, who was a great friend of Vita Sackville-West and Virginia Woolf. She'd be about a hundred now," said de la Fuente. Doris Castlerosse died of an overdose of sleeping pills mixed with drink in 1943. Three weeks after the inquest into her death, Enid and Kenmare were married in a Catholic ceremony in the Brompton Oratory. One guest described the event as "taking place in a nightclub setting, for all the titled crooks and rogues in London were there." When Kenmare died less than a year after the marriage, Chips Channon, the English diarist, wrote of him, "An immense, kindly, jovial, witty creature, Falstaffian, funny and boisterous, and always grossly overdressed; yet with a kindly heart and was not quite the fraud he pretended to be." "Enid was supposed to have given him an injection, but I never believed that," said Tony Pawson. As Kenmare had no direct heir, the inheritance was to go to his bachelor brother, Gerald. Eventually it went to Beatrice Grosvenor, the daughter of his sister, but Enid, in one of her boldest ventures, claimed to be pregnant, although she was approaching fifty at the time. She was thus able to hold on to the income from the Irish lands for an additional thirteen months. Said Tony Pawson about the pregnancy, "I never heard that, but Enid was up to that sort of thing."

David Hicks, the English decorator married to the daughter of Earl Mountbatten, was a frequent visitor at La Fiorentina. "They used to say about Enid, she married first for love: Cameron. And then to Cavendish, for position—it was a very good name. Then Furness for the money. And Kenmare for the title," he said. But there were lovers too. "The Duke of Westminster was in love with her," said Tom Parr, the chairman of Colefax and Fowler, the London decorating firm. The Duke of Westminster, Britain's richest man, had been a friend of two of Enid's husbands, Furness and Kenmare, and the third of his four wives, Loelia, Duchess of Westminster, was sometimes a visitor at La Fiorentina. "There was one of the Selfridges too, of the store," said Elvira de la Fuente. "A rich man. He gave her money. He was very unattractive too. Some women can only go to bed with handsome men. With Enid, it didn't seem to matter."

"Before the war, the international upper classes were doping a great deal, but none of them showed it," said Tony Pawson. "They weren't like those drug addicts today."

"There was a terrible scandal in New York, but I wouldn't want to talk about that," said an ancient lady in London. In Paris, an ancient gentleman said, lowering his voice, "Have you heard what happened in New York? Such a scandal!"

The New York scandal they were referring to was what has become known in social lore as the Bloomingdale scandal. Donald Bloomingdale, a sometime diplomat, was forty-two, handsome, a rich man who

enjoyed an international social life, maintaining apartments in Paris
and New York. "Donald had very chic French friends," said Elvira de
la Fuente. "He spoke French well. He was quite a snob. He married
one of the Rothschild heiresses, the sister of one of them, but the marriage didn't last." Donald Bloomingdale was also a particular friend of
Enid's son Rory. "Rory was very much in love with Donald Bloomingdale, but at the time Donald was in love with an Egyptian, called Jean-
Louis Toriel, who was very drugged," Elvira de la Fuente told me.
Toriel was an unpopular figure among the fashionable friends of Donald Bloomingdale. Tony Pawson remembered that Toriel had a dachs-
hund that he turned into a drug addict. "A horrid little skeletal thing.
Too awful. He was really evil." On several occasions, Bloomingdale
went away for drug cures, but, because of Toriel, he always went right
back on drugs, once while driving to Paris immediately after his release from a clinic in Switzerland.

In the winter of 1954, Enid Kenmare and Donald Bloomingdale
were in New York at the same time. People remember things differently. Some told me it happened at the Pierre. Some said it happened
at the Sherry-Netherland. And some said it happened at the since-
razed Savoy-Plaza Hotel, which used to stand where the General Motors Building now stands on Fifth Avenue. At any rate, Donald
Bloomingdale wanted some heroin, and Lady Kenmare gave it to him.
One New York friend of Donald Bloomingdale's told me the heroin
was delivered in a lace handkerchief with a coronet and Lady Kenmare's initials on it. Another New York friend said the heroin was in
the back of a silver picture frame containing a photograph of Lady
Kenmare. However it was delivered, the dosage proved fatal. "It was
apparently a bad mixture," said Tony Pawson. The rich Mr. Bloomingdale, who would have been far richer if he had outlived his very rich
mother, Rosalie Bloomingdale, was found dead of an overdose the
next morning by a faithful servant. Good servant that he was, he knew
how to handle the situation. It was not his first experience in such
matters. He called the family lawyer immediately. The lace handkerchief with the coronet, or the picture frame with Enid's picture, or
whatever receptacle the heroin had come in, was removed, as were
the implements of injection. The family lawyer called the family doctor, and the police were notified. Meanwhile, Lady Kenmare was put

on an afternoon plane with the assistance of her good friends Norman and Rosita Winston, the international socialites, who for years had leased the Clos, a house on the grounds of La Fiorentina. "She was out of the country before any mention of Donald's death was ever made," said Bert Whitley of New York, who leased another house on the grounds. The servant, who had been through previous scrapes with his employer, was left money in Bloomingdale's will, as were Rory Cameron and Jean-Louis Toriel, the Egyptian, who later also died of a heroin overdose. The newspapers reported that Bloomingdale's death had been caused by an overdose of barbiturates. No connection between the countess and the death of Donald Bloomingdale was ever made publicly. "But everybody knew," I was told over and over. "Everybody knew."

Probably nobody knew better what happened that night than Walter Beardshall, who was Lady Kenmare's butler and valet at the time and who remains her fervent supporter to this day. Now crippled by post-polio syndrome, Mr. Beardshall lives in Brooklyn, New York, where he is mostly confined to a motorized wheelchair. "I traveled around the world with Her Ladyship," he told me. "Elsa Maxwell spread the rumor that I was her gigolo, and everyone gossiped about us, but I wasn't. I was twenty-four at the time, and Lady Kenmare was sixty-two." According to Beardshall, the incident happened at the Sherry-Netherland. "Mr. Bloomingdale had a permanent suite at the Sherry-Netherland, and we were his guests there. He filled Lady Kenmare's room with flowers and everything. The next morning the telephone rang very early, and Her Ladyship asked me to come to her room as quickly as possible. 'How fast can you pack?' she asked. 'We're leaving for London.' We had only just arrived in New York. She said, 'I had dinner last night with Mr. Bloomingdale. He told me I could borrow his typewriter so that I could write Rory a letter. When I called him this morning, his servant told me that he was dead. I was the last person to see him alive. We have to leave. You know how the American police are.' "

After the Bloomingdale incident, Somerset Maugham dubbed his great friend Lady Kenmare Lady Killmore, although some people attribute the name to Noel Coward. At any rate the name stuck.

"Did Enid ever talk about Donald Bloomingdale?" I asked Anthony Pawson.

"It was always a tricky subject," he said. "She didn't talk too much about it, because of all the rumors going round."

"Did Rory talk about it?" I asked a lady friend of his in London.

"Those stories about Enid were never discussed. I mean, you can't ask if someone's mother murdered someone. Rory told me, though, that once, when she arrived on the *Queen Mary*, the tabloids said, 'Society Murderess Arrives,' " she replied.

"When Donald died in New York that time, we all expected to know more about it, but nothing came out," said Elvira de la Fuente. "She ran from New York after that."

Daisy Fellowes, another of the stunning women of the period and a famed society wit, maintained a sort of chilly friendship with Enid. The daughter of a French duke and an heiress to the Singer sewing-machine fortune, she didn't think Enid was sufficiently wellborn, describing her as "an Australian with a vague pedigree." Once, in conversation, Enid began a sentence with the phrase "people of our class." Mrs. Fellowes raised her hand and stopped the conversation. "Just a moment, Enid," she said. "Your class or mine?" After the Bloomingdale affair, Daisy Fellowes announced she was going to give a dinner party for twelve people. "I'm going to have all murderers," she said. "Very convenient. There are six men and six women. And Enid Kenmare will have the place of honor, because she killed the most people of anyone coming."

Lady Kenmare was aware of the stories told about her, and she was sometimes hurt by them. Roderick Coupe, an American who lives in Paris, told me of an occasion when the social figure Jimmy Donahue, a Woolworth heir, cousin of Enid's friend Barbara Hutton, and often rumored to have been the lover of the Duchess of Windsor, asked Enid to his house on Long Island. After a pleasant dinner, he began to ask her why she was known as Lady Killmore. She explained to him that it was a name that caused her a great deal of heartache. Donahue, who had a cruel streak, persisted. "But why do people say it?" he asked several more times. Enid Kenmare finally announced she was leaving. Donahue told her he had sent her car

back to New York. Undeterred, she made her way to the highway
and hitchhiked to the city.

"She was one of the most accomplished women. She rode. She shot.
She fished. She painted very well. She sculpted. She did beautiful
needlework. She cooked marvelously. There was nothing she couldn't
do," said Tony Pawson. Looking through album after album of photographs of life at La Fiorentina, with its unending parties, one doesn't
see an angry or worried face among the people pictured. Any age, any
generation, eighteen to eighty, in and out of the house, and dogs everywhere. Although Lady Kenmare was thought of as a famous hostess, a
word she greatly disliked, her lunch parties at La Fiorentina were
often haphazard affairs, with unmatched guests. Celebrities such as
Greta Garbo, Barbara Hutton, Claudette Colbert, Elsa Maxwell, and
the Duke of Vedura came, but so did people no one had ever heard of.
Guests would be thrown together—friends of Rory's, friends of hers,
the well known and the unknown, the young and the old, the inexperi-
enced and the accomplished—with no care as to a balance of the sexes
at her table. Enid was diligently unpunctual, arriving, vaguely, long after her guests had been seated, once prompting Daisy Fellowes to remark on her hostess's absence, "Busy with her needle, no doubt."
Another guest remembered, "She had no sense of time whatsoever.
She'd arrive when the meals were over, or be dressed for the casino, in
evening dress and jewels, in the afternoon." Tom Parr said, "She was
an ethereal character, nice to us who were Rory's friends, adorable
even, but then she'd float off." On one occasion, she was struck by the
handsomeness of a young man sunning himself by her swimming pool.
"Do please stay on for dinner," she said. "But, Lady Kenmare, I've
been staying with you for a week," the young man replied.

"Enid was completely original. Very elegant. Very distinguished.
She always made an entrance, like an actress, carrying a flower," said
Jacqueline Delubac, a retired French actress who was once married to
Sacha Guitry. She was always surrounded by dogs, "a mangy pack,"
according to John Galliher of New York. Walter Beardshall remembers her entrances more vividly. "All her guests would already be
seated. First you would hear the dogs barking. And then you would
hear her voice saying, 'Be quiet. Be quiet.' Then you would hear her

high heels clicking on the marble floor. And then the dogs would enter, sometimes twenty of them, miniature poodles, gray and black. And then she would come in, with a parrot on one shoulder and her hyrax on the other." She fed her hyrax from her own fork; although at the cinema she would sometimes pull lettuce leaves from her bosom to feed it. Many people mistook the hyrax for a rat. It is a small ungulate mammal characterized by a thickset body with short legs and ears and rudimentary tail, feet with soft pads and broad nails, and teeth of which the molars resemble those of a rhinoceros and the incisors those of rodents. She taught the hyrax to pee in the toilet, standing straight up on the seat, and sometimes she let her guests peek at it through the bathroom window, keeping out of sight, since the hyrax was very shy. She trained her parrot to speak exactly like her. When the telephone rang, the parrot would call out, "Pat, the telephone," so that Enid's daughter, Pat, would answer it.

The fashion arbiter Eleanor Lambert often stayed with Rosita and Norman Winston in the Clos on Enid's property. She said that Lady Kenmare never seemed to sleep. She remembered looking out of her window during the night and seeing her walking through her garden dressed in flowing white garments, with the hyrax on her shoulder. "She looked like the woman in white from Wilkie Collins's book," Eleanor Lambert said.

"Enid was never social, really," said Elvira de la Fuente. "You could ask her to sit next to a prince or a waiter, and it never mattered to her." Indeed, the girl from Australia never went grand in the grand life she espoused and kept marrying into. She remained fiercely loyal to her Australian family back home, at one time investing money in the failing wine business even though her lawyers advised her not to. "They are my family," she said to them, according to Beardshall, who traveled to Australia with her. Along the way in her rise, she lost her Australian accent. Tony Pawson said she had "an accent you couldn't quite define, Americanized but not really American." James Douglas, who used to escort Barbara Hutton to La Fiorentina, said, "There was no trace of Australian at all, but sometimes her sister came from Australia to visit her, and then you could hear the way she once had talked." However, she did acquire irregularities of speech that were unique for a woman in her position at that time. According to Walter Beardshall, she used certain four-letter words before people started printing those words in books. He remembered a time when the Countess of Drogheda asked her, "What was Kenmare's first name, Enid?" Enid replied, "Fucked if I know. I was only married to him nine months before he died."

Some people say that Enid thought she would marry Somerset Maugham after Lord Kenmare's death, but more people scoff at this. "Nonsense!" said David Herbert. Tony Pawson agreed. "I don't believe she ever wanted to marry Willie Maugham. Unless it was for the money. Willie wasn't interested in ladies, you know." Jimmy Douglas said, "It's too ridiculous. What about Alan Searle [Maugham's long-time companion], for God's sake?" And Elvira de la Fuente said, "Enid had no friends, really, except Willie Maugham. She adored him. She and Maugham were a funny couple. They were intimate because of bridge. They played all the time. He was already old and grumpy at the time. It was companionship and affection, but there was no thought of romance."

At one time, friends say, Enid, who kept a residence in Monte Carlo and was a citizen of Monaco, harbored a desire for her daughter to marry Prince Rainier and become Her Serene Highness, the Princess of Monaco, but the prince showed no romantic inclinations toward Pat, nor did Pat toward the prince. Pat preferred dogs and horses, and was not cut out for princess life, or even society life on the Riviera, and soon decamped to Kenya and Cape Town to breed horses. Bearing no grudge toward the prince, Enid happily attended his wedding to Grace Kelly. As the tall, statuesque Lady Kenmare emerged from the cathedral at the end of the service, she was cheered by the crowds, who mistook her for a visiting monarch.

"Before anything else, Enid was a mother," said Yves Vidal of Paris and Tangier, who was a frequent visitor at the villa. "Most of the things she did, marrying all those men, were for the children more than herself." "She never, *never* did what family people do—criticize and mumble about her children," said Elvira de la Fuente. Walter Beardshall said she tried to keep her drug taking from her children. "Once, Pat found one of her syringes. 'What's this, Mummy?' she asked. 'Oh, it's Walter's,' Lady Kenmare replied. 'He leaves his stuff all over the place. Get it out of here, Walter. Take it to your own room.' "

But it was with Rory, her older son, that she was the closest. "I always thought Rory was in love with Enid," said a London lady. "At Emerald Cunard's parties, they used to come in together, covered in rings and not speaking." Certainly they had an extremely close mother-son relationship. "It was really Rory's life that Enid came to lead, after all the marriages," said Elvira de la Fuente. "He used to say to her as a joke, 'Now you'll never find a fifth husband after you've killed four of them.' They lived as a couple, but it wasn't incestuous. Rory told Enid he was a homosexual when he was forty. She had never suspected. It was a terrible shock to her, but a shock she overcame in a day or two." Yves Vidal said, "She didn't really like social life. She was actually miscast in the grand life of a chatelaine and hostess of the Riviera." Another guest said, "She was in a way a passenger at La Fiorentina. As she got older, people began to think of it as Rory's house. This famous lady was always in the background. Sometimes she'd go for days without coming out of her bedroom."

The magnificent house, located on the finest property on the Riviera, commands the entrance to Beaulieu Bay. It was considered a strategic position during the war, and the Germans, who occupied the house, built extensive fortifications on their property against an Allied invasion. Near the end of the war they blew up the fortifications, destroying half of the house and most of the gardens. When the house was returned to the family, Rory redesigned it in the Palladian style, and the interiors were decorated by him. As Enid Kenmare grew older, she developed curvature of the spine, and her once-perfect posture gave way to a bent-over condition. She began leasing the house. Elizabeth Taylor and Mike Todd occupied it for a time, and for years the American philanthropist Mary Lasker rented it during the peak months. The house is now owned by Harding and Mary Wells Lawrence, the former chairman of Braniff Airways and the founder of the advertising agency Wells, Rich, Greene. Mary Lawrence said, "When we bought La Fiorentina, there were no lights in the bathrooms. Lady Kenmare couldn't bear to look at herself in the mirror anymore."

She moved to Cape Town, South Africa, where she bought a stud farm and raised racehorses. Her daughter, Pat, had preceded her there. For a while Enid employed Beryl Markham, the author of *West with the Night*, to train her horses, but the two women, who had known each other since Enid's marriage to Lord Furness, were such strong personalities that their partnership did not work out. Pat had two lions she had brought up from the time they were cubs that had the run of the house. A New York friend of Pat's who used to visit La Fiorentina every summer also visited the two women in Cape Town. She remembers seeing one of the lions drag an unperturbed Enid through the living room and out the French doors. "She was not remotely frightened, and later Pat told me, 'It happens all the time.' "

"Enid was mysterious," said Yves Vidal. "I remember once watching her run down the steps of La Fiorentina followed by her dogs. She was so beautiful, and she knew she was very beautiful. Until the end, she kept a wonderful allure. What made her life and ruined her life at the same time was her beauty."

March 1991

Two of Lady Kenmare's closest friends came to me to suggest that I write this story. I hadn't been up on the much-married, frequently widowed Enid Kenmare until then and, of course, I was interested. A bevy of very grand people in several different countries were all too eager to gossip about her to me. When the piece came out, several of them had second thoughts about their quotes. One, David Herbert of Tangier, castigated me in a book he wrote before his death, although he had gossiped about her the most. Nowhere in the piece did I say that she killed her husbands. I said that people always claimed that she had killed her husbands, which they did. It wasn't I who nicknamed her Lady Killmore. Her friend Noel Coward did that years before I ever heard of the lady.

THE PASSION OF BARON THYSSEN

It was a late-fall twilight on Lake Lugano. We were standing in the open window of an art-filled sitting room in the Villa Favorita, one of the loveliest houses in the world, looking out over the lake, listening to waves lap against the private dock below. Across the water the lights of Lugano, a city of 30,000 people and fifty banks in the Italian-speaking corner of Switzerland, were coming on. My companion in reverie, the Baron Hans Heinrich Thyssen-Bornemisza, has been looking out at the same view for over fifty years, since his father, Baron Heinrich Thyssen-Bornemisza, bought the seventeenth-century villa from Prince Friedrich Leopold of Prussia in 1932. For those who need an introduction, Baron Hans Heinrich Thyssen-Bornemisza is generally conceded to be one of the richest men in the world ("in the billions," say some people, "in the high hundred millions," according to others), as well as the possessor of one of the world's largest private art collections, which is rivaled in size and magnificence only by that of the Queen of England. It was the art collection I was there to discuss, for the baron, now in his sixty-seventh year, has begun to have thoughts about mortality, and for the last five years the disposition of his collection has been uppermost in his mind.

He is called Heini by those close to him, and that evening he was dressed in a dinner jacket and black tie, awaiting the arrival of guests for dinner. The Thyssen fortune, he was telling me, had been made originally in iron and steel in Germany. "My mother irons and my father steals," he said, in the manner of a man who has told the same joke over and over. Early in life, his father had left Germany and moved to Hungary, where he had married into the nobility; thus the title baron and the addition of the hyphen and the name Bornemisza. The current baron's older brother and two sisters were born in Hungary, but the Thyssen-Bornemisza family fled to Holland when the Communist leader of Hungary, Béla Kun, sentenced the children's father to death for being a landowner. Heini Thyssen was born in Holland and spent the first nineteen years of his life there.

The baron's attention was distracted from his story by the arrival at the dock below of a flag-bedecked lake boat bringing his guests, thirty-one formally attired members of the Board of Trustees and the Trustees' Council of the National Gallery of Art in Washington, D.C., who were on a two-week tour of Swiss and Italian churches, museums, and private collections, headed by the gallery's director, J. Carter Brown. Among the members of this art-loving group were the Perry Basses of Fort Worth, the Alexander Mellon Laughlins and the Thomas Mellon Evanses of New York, and the Robert Erburus of Los Angeles.

"But it's too early," said the baron, looking down. "They've come too early. The baroness is not ready to receive them." And then he added, to no one in particular, "Send them away." He had his gun-toting American bodyguard tell the driver of the boat to spin the distinguished guests around the lake for half an hour and then come back. As we watched the drama from upstairs, we could hear Carter Brown call out, "Ladies and gentlemen," and then explain to his group that they were not to get off the boat yet but would instead take another short ride. This announcement apparently created some discord, because people began to get off anyway. The baron shrugged, sighed, smiled, and went down to greet them. Drinks were served on an outdoor loggia overlooking the lake. A night chill had set in, and the ladies hugged fur jackets and cashmere shawls over their short black dinner dresses and pearls. For some time the Baroness Thyssen-Bornemisza did not appear.

Tita Thyssen, a former Miss Barcelona and later Miss Spain, picked by a jury that included the American-born Countess of Romanoes and the great bullfighter Luis Dominguín, is the baron's fifth and presumably last baroness and, if all goes according to plan, his first and last duchess, for the *on-dit* in swell circles is that the King of Spain is prepared to confer on her the title of duchess when the Thyssen collection, or at least 700 of the A and B pictures in the 1,400-picture collection, goes to Spain permanently. That "permanently" is the catch.

"Where is she?" one wife asked, meaning their hostess.

"We heard she's not coming at all," said the lady to whom she spoke.

"I heard that too," said the first lady, and they exchanged "Miss Barcelona" looks.

But then the baroness did appear, the last arrival at her own party, although she was only coming from upstairs. She was stunning, blond, tanned from the sun, dressed in a long black strapless evening gown. "Balmain," I heard her say to someone. She has the persona of a film star and understands perfectly the technique of making an entrance. In an instant she was the center of attention, and earlier opinions of her were soon favorably revised. Like all the baron's wives, his fifth baroness is the possessor of some very serious jewelry. On her engagement-ring finger was a large marquise diamond that had once belonged to the baron's second wife, the ill-fated Nina Dyer, who married the baron at the age of seventeen and divorced him at the age of twenty-five to marry Prince Sadruddin Aga Khan, the half-brother of the late Aly Khan and the uncle of the current Aga Khan. Indifferent to gender when it came to love partners, Nina also dallied with a succession of ladies, who called her Oliver and vied with her husbands when it came to showering her with jewels. One of her most ardent admirers, an international film actress, gave her a panther bracelet designed by Cartier with an inscription in French which read, "To my panther, untamed by man." Before she was forty, Nina committed suicide. "She'd just had it," was the explanation someone who knew her gave me. Her jewelry, according to the baron, was stolen by her friends at the time of her death. Years later, he saw a picture of the marquise-diamond ring in an auction catalog. Although it had no listed provenance, he recognized it as the diamond he had given Nina years before, and bought it back for his fifth wife for $1.5 million.

The baroness was wearing diamond-and-ruby earrings, and around her neck, hanging on a diamond necklace designed to accommodate it, was the Star of Peace, which she had told me earlier in the day was the "biggest flawless diamond in the world." I explained to one of the guests who gasped at its size that it was 167 carats. The baroness heard me say it. "One hundred and sixty-*nine*," she corrected me, and then, hearing herself, she roared with laughter.

Tita Thyssen speaks in a husky, international voice, often changing languages from sentence to sentence. She is fun, funny, and flirtatious, with a nature that is best described as vivacious. She is refreshingly outspoken, and makes no bones, for example, about her dislike of her immediate predecessor, the former Denise Shorto of Brazil, whose divorce from the baron was extremely acrimonious, resulting in a settlement rumored to be in the neighborhood of $50 million, in addition to jewels worth $80 million. At one point in the proceedings Denise Thyssen was briefly jailed in Liechtenstein for leaving Switzerland with unpaid bills in excess of $1.5 million, and the baron accused her of failing to return certain jewelry and other items belonging to his family. Ultimately, Denise was allowed to keep all the jewels, on the ground that they were gifts made to her during her marriage, not Thyssen heirlooms. "A gift is a gift," she was quoted as saying. We are talking here about very, very, very rich people. Now in her late forties, Denise Thyssen lives in Rome with Prince Mariano Hugo zu Windisch-Graetz, who is in his mid-thirties, and their liaison is not smiled upon by the prince's family. She refused to be interviewed for this article with the pointed comment that "Heini's present wife is very publicity-minded. This article belongs to her. I don't see my place in it."

"I believe in destiny," Tita Thyssen said, discussing the Star of Peace. "This stone proves to me that destiny is always there. I first saw it in the rough, before it was cut, in the Geneva office of Harry Winston, before I met Heini. They left me alone with it and let me play with it. They told me they were thinking of doing an adventure with somebody and cutting it. The person involved turned out to be Heini, but I did not know him yet. I talked with the store from time to time, and three times it was almost sold. Then Heini gave it to me."

Among the guests that evening was her friend and jeweler, Fred Horowitz, who used to be with Harry Winston and is now an independent jeweler with offices in Geneva and Monte Carlo. It was through Horowitz that the baroness met Heini Thyssen. She was staying with him and his then wife, Donatella, who is now married to the Mercedes-Benz heir Mick Flick, on their boat in Sardinia. "It was time for me to go back to my house on the Costa Brava, but my friends begged me to stay one more day, and I did," said the baroness. The next day Horowitz took her to a party on Heini Thyssen's yacht. "The look he gave me when we met, now that I know him better, is the look he gets when he sees a painting that he knows he is going to buy. He knew he was going to get it." Then she added, "Only I'm more expensive than a painting, and you don't have to change the frame with me." Her husband listened to her story, amused.

According to one guest on the Thyssen yacht that day, Tita and Heini remained aloof from the party and played backgammon for hours. Also on board was Thyssen's fourth wife, Denise, though their marriage was already in its last stages. Seeing her husband and Tita together for so long, she made a slighting remark of the "upstart" variety about Tita, and with that the two women's mutual dislike began.

"We have never been apart more than a day since we met," Tita said, taking her husband's hand. "We have been married three and a half years now, but we have been together seven. We discuss everything."

Spotting Fred Horowitz, she turned her attention from the National Gallery group to him. "It doesn't hang right," she said about the enormous stone she was wearing. Horowitz had made her the two-row necklace of matched diamonds from which the Star of Peace hung as a pendant. The diamond was too heavy for the necklace and tipped upward. For several minutes she and Horowitz and his new wife, Jasmine, also jewel-laden, discussed in French what was wrong with the diamond necklace. Then realizing that she was neglecting her guests, she turned back to them and said, in a playful, self-deprecating manner, "These are very nice problems to have."

At dinner we sat at five place-carded tables of eight, and she held her table in thrall, all the while chain-smoking cigarettes. The fifth baroness is steeped in the lore of her husband's family and, like him, is an expert storyteller. She told one story about Heini's stepmother, the beautiful Baroness Maud von Thyssen, who during her marriage to Baron Heinrich Thyssen, fell madly in love with twenty-six-year-old Prince Alexis Mdivani, "one of the marrying Mdivani brothers," as they were called. Alexis had just negotiated a lucrative divorce from the American heiress Barbara Hutton. The lovers rendezvoused in a remote village in Spain. After the tryst, Maud had to return to Paris, and the prince drove her to her train at breakneck speed in the Rolls-Royce that Hutton had given him. "There was a terrible crash," the baroness said. "Mdivani was killed. Maud's beautiful face was half-destroyed. Heini's father divorced her." At that point a waiter accidentally dropped a dozen dinner plates on the stone floor, with a crash that brought the room to silence. The baroness looked over, shrugged, and returned to her conversation with the same aplomb that her husband demonstrated at his table across the room. Why let a few broken plates ruin a good party?

A stranger to art before her marriage, the baroness has become deeply involved in her husband's collection, and if she is not as conversant as he on the subject of old masters, she has made herself more conversant than you or I—knowledgeable enough to be the main force behind her husband's selection of Spain, over England, West Germany, the United States, Japan, and France, as the resting place for his treasure. Many people consider the choice odd, since the baron himself has no real connection with Spain and no long-standing friendships there. It is the baroness's dream, however, according to one Spanish Tita watcher, to live in Spain and to be accepted by people who once neglected and even snubbed her.

There are pictures everywhere in the villa. Up a secondary stairway, outside the men's lavatory, hangs an Edvard Munch, and in every corridor is a profusion of pictures, around any one of which the average millionaire might build an entire room. The bar in the family sitting room is a seven-part coromandel screen, broken up to conceal a refrigerator, an icemaker, glasses, and liquor bottles. Walking through a drawing room that the baron and baroness almost never go into, we passed a Bonnard portrait of Misia Sert, and in a formal dining room so infrequently entered that the light switch didn't work—a room too large for intimate groups but not large enough for big groups from museums—hung a pair of Canalettos.

"Would you like to see our bedroom?" the baroness asked her guests.

Is the pope Catholic? Of course we wanted to see the bedroom, which contains three Pissarros, a Renoir, a Toulouse-Lautrec, a Winslow Homer, a Manet, and more that I don't remember. The pictures in the villa are quite different from the pictures that hang in the galleries of the museum next door—the Titians, the Tintorettos, the Carpaccio, the Goyas, and the El Grecos, which the baron would show the group the next day.

"Do you move these pictures with you to your other houses?" someone asked her.

"No, we have others."

Their bedroom, in contrast to most of the Mongiardino-decorated rooms, is soft and feminine, done in pale colors. It opens into Heini's enormous bathroom, which has a tub the size of a small pool, and into Tita's sitting room, which has an early Gauguin over the daybed and a Corot. Although it was October, the perpetual calendar on a side table still indicated June. The Thyssen-Bornemisza family crest is embossed on the message pad next to every telephone in the villa; the motto reads, *"Vertu surpasse richesse"*—Virtue surpasses riches.

The baroness opened the door of closet after closet full of clothes. "Most of my clothes are still in Marbella," she said. She is dressed mostly by the Paris couturiers Balmain and Scherrer. When her schedule makes it impossible for her to attend the couture showings in Paris, the designers send her videotapes of their collections and she chooses from them.

"What's it like to live this way?" she was asked.

"It took me some time to get used to all this beauty," said the baroness quite modestly. "At first I was in shock."

"How long did it take before you got used to this kind of life?" I asked her.

"About two days," she answered, and burst out laughing at her joke.

Her native language is Spanish, which the baron does not speak well. His native languages are Dutch, Hungarian, and German, which the baroness does not speak well. When they are alone together, they speak sometimes in French and sometimes in English, heavily accented English, his Teutonic-sounding, hers with a very Latin inflection. "But," said the baroness, "if we have been with French friends, we continue in French for a day or so."

Their life is planned months in advance, mostly around art openings, for loans from their collection are constantly traveling from country to country and exhibition to exhibition. In their family sitting room, there are the inevitable silver-framed photographs of them, together or alone, with the Reagans, the Gorbachevs, the pope, and the president and matronly First Lady of Portugal, with whom Tita posed in a miniskirt six inches above the knees. They entertain at lunch. They entertain at dinner. They are forever on the move. The baroness knew as we talked in Lugano that seven weeks from that day she would be giving a party at L'Orangerie in Los Angeles ("Liza Minnelli can't come," she said to her husband. "Betsy Bloomingdale can"), and that the night before they would be dining in Palm Springs with Sir James Hanson, the British financier, and that they would be lunching the day after their party with Niki Bautzer, the widow of the Hollywood showbiz lawyer Greg Bautzer, at the Bistro Garden in Beverly Hills.

The baron is considered a prime kidnapping target. In all the houses there is closed-circuit surveillance with electrically operated doors. And bodyguards. And dogs. The bodyguards are American, part of a security force that handles only three international clients. The bodyguard I became acquainted with was a cross between Charles Bronson and Clint Eastwood. He packed two weapons beneath his suit, a pistol in a holster and what appeared to be a sawed-off machine gun tucked into the back of his trousers. He is with the baron all the time. "We never stay anywhere for longer than a week," he told me.

There are people who knew Tita before her marriage to Baron Thyssen who will tell you that she's changed, but, in all fairness, to enter the life she has entered and *not* change would be difficult for almost anyone. In addition to the Villa Favorita in Lugano, they have a new house on the outskirts of Madrid that rivals in movie-star luxe and size the Aaron Spelling mansion in California, as well as houses in Barcelona and Marbella and a house on the Costa Brava that was hers before they married; a town house on Chester Square in London; a house in St. Moritz and what she called a "small palace—tiny, really," in Paris, which they just purchased from the late Christina Onassis's last husband; a house in Jamaica; a suite at the Pierre Hotel in New York; and probably more that I did not hear about. Of course, there is a private plane for their constant peregrinations from house to house and art opening to art opening, and somewhere a yacht, which they occasionally use, and there are the servants who travel and the servants who stay put, plus the ever-present security guards.

The people who say that Tita Cervera has changed are the same people who say, with a roll of the eyes, "Have you met Mama yet?" By Mama, they mean Carmen Fernández de la Guerra, Tita's mother, whom I did not meet. She is, from all reports, not unlike the mother of Robin Givens, a strong and determined woman who plays a major part in her daughter's life. The Cerveras were originally a family of extremely modest means from Valladolid, a small city several hours from Madrid. Tita has always been, and continues to be, a devoted daughter. In the period before she met Thyssen, she was at an extremely low ebb in her life, with a child to support and no money. At her mother's insistence, she went to Sardinia in the hopes of meeting a rich man. That she connected with one of the richest men in the world, and then married him, must have surpassed even Carmen's wildest dreams. The baron, who was at first amused by his mother-in-law, is said now to want to spend less and less time with her. Although Carmen is headquartered mostly in Barcelona and Marbella, where she is frequently photographed for the Spanish magazines, her influence is such that recently she tried to keep her son-in-law from bringing Alexander, his fourteen-year-old son by Denise, into the Thyssens' house in London for fear that the boy, through his mother, would put an evil spell on the house. In fact, Tita and her mother are both worried about having evil spells put on them, and they have been known to ask Brazilian friends to bring them sandalwood twigs to ward off hexes.

Tita's own son, Borja, born out of wedlock by an unnamed father, was adopted by Baron Thyssen even before their marriage. The child was given the name Bornemisza and baptized with great style in the Lady Chapel of St. Patrick's Cathedral in New York, with the American billionairess Ann Getty for his godmother and the Duke de Badajoz, the King of Spain's brother-in-law, for his godfather. Since his mother's marriage to the baron, he has been given the full last name, Thyssen-Bornemisza. The eight-year-old Borja was nowhere in sight during my visit. The baroness said, "He used to live in Lugano. He is now going to live in Madrid."

The Duke de Badajoz has been the most influential figure in Spain in working with the Thyssens to bring their art collection to his country. Along with the Duchess of Marlborough and the late automobile tycoon Henry Ford, the duke was a witness when the Thyssens were married three and a half years ago at Daylesford, a magnificent English estate that the baron had purchased sixteen years earlier from the late press lord Viscount Rothermere. Although Daylesford was Thyssen's favorite house after the Villa Favorita, the estate has since been sold, for a reputed $16 million. The new baroness felt they spent too little time there to justify keeping such a large establishment, and preferred a house in Madrid, where they would be spending more and more of their time. According to one Spanish lady, Tita is also pushing her husband to sell the Villa Favorita.

The baroness was happily married for eight years to the late Lex Barker, who gained international fame as one of the successors to Johnny Weissmuller in the Tarzan films. She was Barker's fifth wife, too. "He dropped dead on Fifty-ninth and Lex on his way to lunch at Gino's," the baroness said. "Greg Bautzer phoned me in Geneva with the news." Barker had formerly been married to the fifties film star Lana Turner, and in the last year he has been accused by Turner's daughter, Cheryl Crane, in her memoir, *Detour,* of having repeatedly abused her sexually when she was ten years old. Crane gained her own measure of international fame several years after the alleged child abuse by stabbing to death her mother's lover, gangster Johnny Stompanato. Baroness Thyssen is fiercely loyal to the memory of her late husband, and she decried Crane's book. "I was so mad at that book," she said. "I was furious. I wanted to sue, but my lawyers told me you cannot sue over someone who's dead. If you're married to a man, you know very well if he likes little girls or not. Women fell down in front of Lex. He liked me. He liked women, not little girls, believe me. That woman is destroying the memory of Lex. I am trying to restore Lex's image."

The baroness is more reticent about discussing her second husband, Espartaco Santoni, a Spanish-Venezuelan movie producer and nightclub owner who now lives in Los Angeles. "We were only married a year," she said. During that marriage she acted in two films, one with Curt Jurgens and Peter Graves and the other with Lee Van Cleef. "In both those films I was killed for being unfaithful," she told me, laughing.

She said that the time she spent acting was the happiest period of her life, but she ended her acting career when that marriage ended. Now she paints, and she feels the same inner satisfaction doing it that she once felt acting. An acquaintance described her paintings to me as "colorful, light, and tropical, the kind you see on guest-room walls." But painting is only an occasional occupation, for her peripatetic life does not allow for a commitment to it. It is what she does in Jamaica. They spend two weeks a year at the house in Jamaica, called Alligator Head, which Baron Thyssen has owned since the fifties. There they relax completely, and the baroness paints. "I always say to my guests, 'If you have any problems, go talk to the butler or the maid, not me. I came here to relax and paint.'"

"That's a van Gogh behind you," said the baroness.

"An early one," said the baron.

There was also a van Gogh to the right of me and another one to the left. We were at lunch in the small family dining alcove of the Villa Favorita with the photographer Helmut Newton.

In the center of the table were pink and yellow flowers from the Thyssen-Bornemisza gardens and greenhouse. The flowers are changed for each meal, and arranged by the head gardener of the "six or eight, I can't remember" gardeners on the grounds. Lunch was served by the butler and a footman, both in dark coats and white gloves. The butler, Giorgio Pusiol, is one of the servants who travel. "Don't you think he's chic?" asked the baroness when he left the room. The footman went from place to place shaving white truffles onto the saffron rice that accompanied our osso buco.

The baron and baroness were both most agreeable to all of Helmut Newton's suggestions for photographing them, even when he asked them to change into evening clothes in the middle of the day and pretend lunch was dinner. The baroness began the meal wearing a strand of perfect pearls, the size of large grapes, later changed to her sapphires, both blue and yellow, the baron's latest gift to her, and then to her rubies, and with each set came a different dress from Balmain or Scherrer. "Change of colors, I see," said the baron as he leaned over to examine one necklace.

Suddenly, surprisingly, from out of nowhere, as coffee was being served, the baroness turned to me and said, "Have you ever heard of Franco Rappetti?"

"Yes," I replied. I had heard of Franco Rappetti, but having come to Lugano to discuss the transfer of a great art collection from Switzerland to Spain, I had hardly expected to get into the darkest shadow in the life of the baron, yet here it was, offered up with the demitasse by the baron's fifth wife. Anyone who has ever dipped into the Thyssen saga has heard of Franco Rappetti, a tall, blond, handsome Roman who was at one time the baron's European art dealer. He was also— and this is no secret, at least in the social and art worlds in which the Thyssens moved—the lover of Denise, the fourth baroness, during her marriage to the baron. A onetime playboy, compulsive gambler, and drug user, Rappetti has been described to me by a woman who knew him well as a man who shared women with many powerful men. On June 8, 1978, while on a visit to New York, Rappetti, thirty-eight, went out a window at the Meurice, a building on West Fifty-eighth Street favored by artistic Europeans who keep apartments in New York. His mysterious death has fascinated society and the art world ever since.

"Did you hear how he died?" she asked.

"I heard he either jumped or was thrown out the window," I answered.

"Thrown," said the baroness, and then named the person who she believed had had it done. Only days before, a friend of mine had attended a lunch party in London following a memorial service for the Marquess of Dufferin and Ava; there the conversation had also turned to Franco Rappetti, for some reason, and one of the guests had named a well-known figure in the New York art world as the one who threw him out the window. The person the baroness named as having had Rappetti thrown and the person named at the London lunch party as having actually thrown him were not the same.

"He was thrown out the window," the baroness repeated. The baron was sitting with us but read a letter during the exchange. "He was going to have his face changed so he could not be recognized. He wanted to get away from someone."

"His faced changed?"

"Surgery." She named the person Franco Rappetti had wanted to get away from. "He was going to move somewhere and start a new life." She said that Rappetti had been acting in a hyper manner before the defenestration, and had been injected with a tranquilizer to calm him down. It was in that state that he was thrown.

Residents of the building who knew Rappetti disagree violently with the theory that he was pushed or thrown. "He was not murdered," said one emphatically. "He jumped. It's as simple as that. He was depressed. He had money problems."

Franco Rossellini, the Italian film producer and nephew of the great director Roberto Rossellini, lives in apartment 10-J of the building. He said that police came rushing into his apartment before he knew what had happened and asked him if he knew who had jumped out the window and he saw the body, clad only in undershorts and an elaborate gold chain with charms and medals, lying ten floors below on the roof of a Volkswagen bus. "My God, for a moment I thought it was my butler," he told me. The body had come from the apartment above his, 11-J, where Rappetti had just arrived as a guest. One article written about the case stated that he had arrived "with a small suitcase and some very pure cocaine."

When the police left, Rossellini contacted Diane Von Furstenberg, the dress designer and perfume manufacturer, who was an acquaintance of Denise Thyssen's and who had, coincidentally, spoken with her on the telephone only a short time before. Although Denise Thyssen and Rappetti were in the city at the same time, supposedly neither knew the other was there. Von Furstenberg called the baroness at the Waldorf, realized she had not yet heard about Rappetti's death, put her mother on the telephone in order to keep Denise's line busy, and raced to the Waldorf Towers to break the news before she heard it from the police or news media. "Denise was hysterical," remembered Rossellini. Von Furstenberg then called Heini Thyssen in Europe to tell him what had happened, and contacted Rappetti's sister, who absolutely refused to believe that her brother had jumped. Later, Von

Furstenberg accompanied Denise to the city morgue. Since Denise could not bear to go in and see her dead lover, Von Furstenberg identified the body. Only then was she able to relinquish the grieving baroness into the care of closer friends—Princess Yasmin Aga Khan, the daughter of Rita Hayworth; Nona Gordon Summers, then the wife of a London art dealer; and Cleo Goldsmith, the niece of international financier James Goldsmith.

"Nobody pushed him out," Rossellini asserted. "That is a fact. He was running away all the time. He was paranoid. He thought someone was after him. He was not eating anything anymore. He was afraid someone was trying to poison him."

Just as authoritatively, a woman who knew Rappetti well insists that he was not a suicide. "Oh, no, I don't believe Franco jumped. He was so vain about his looks, he would never have gone out the window in undershorts."

"It would be almost impossible to throw a six-foot-three-inch, well-developed man out the window," said Mariarosa Sclauzero, the person most likely to know the exact circumstances of the death. Sclauzero, a writer, still lives in Apartment 11-J, along with her husband, Enrico Tucci. They were both close to Rappetti, and Mariarosa was in the apartment at the time of the death, though in a different room. According to Sclauzero and Tucci, Rappetti had arrived in New York two days before and had registered at the Summit Hotel, after stopping to see Tucci at his office, where he told him, "There is no way out. I have nobody in the world I can trust anymore, not even my butler." Alerted by Tucci that Rappetti was in a highly excitable state, Sclauzero went to the Summit and brought him back to the apartment. He was indeed carrying a suitcase, but, Sclauzero maintains, it contained no cocaine, just clothes and a picture of his small son.

Rappetti kept saying over and over, "They're after me. They want me dead. If anyone asks for me, say I am not here." In the next hour, he tried several times to telephone someone in Switzerland, but he could not get through. There were also several calls for him, supposedly from Paris, but Sclauzero sensed that they were local calls and said that he was not there. Rappetti had left his watch in Paris, and asked to borrow one of Tucci's watches and a T-shirt. He used the bathroom and went into one of the two bedrooms of the apartment to rest. Mariarosa remained in the living room, reading. When the police knocked on her door, after leaving Rossellini's apartment, and asked if she had a guest, she followed Rappetti's instructions and said no. Realizing, however, that something was wrong, she went into the bedroom and found the window wide open. Franco Rappetti was not there. On a table by the window were the watch he had borrowed and the T-shirt, folded. She admits it was a mistake to lie to the police. Later she was grilled for six hours.

"Franco Rappetti was pushed, but not physically," Sclauzero told me as we sat in Apartment 11-J of the Meurice. "Other people brought him to this despair. What he never said was who or why." She said that Rappetti was convinced that he was being poisoned by a servant in Rome, who was being paid by "other people," and that he was being pursued. She denied reports that he had money problems, arguing that he was worth about $5 million in art at the time of his death. She also said that after his death all the paintings in his apartment in Rome disappeared overnight.

The death was declared a suicide. Several well-heeled friends who were approached to lend their private planes to fly Rappetti's body back to Italy refused, on the ground that it would be unlucky to fly the body of a suicide. The day following the death, Heini Thyssen arrived at the Waldorf Towers. An oft-repeated story in these circles is that, on his arrival, Heini asked, "Does Denise blame me?" It is generally acknowledged that he arranged for the broken corpse to be shipped back to Genoa, Rappetti's birthplace, in a chartered plane. The body was accompanied by the grief-stricken Denise Thyssen and her sister Penny, who is married to Jamie Granger, the son of film star Stewart Granger. There are those who say the body was shipped before an autopsy could be performed. There are others who believe that Rappetti was already dead when he was thrown from the window. The man who made the arrangements to ship the body for Thyssen was another art dealer he did business with. His name was Andrew Crispo.

Many people who once moved in the orbit of this charismatic art dealer now seek to distance themselves as widely as possible from him. To the baron's great distress, his name has frequently been associated in recent times with that of Crispo, who figured prominently and salaciously in the 1985 sadomasochistic murder of a Norwegian fashion student named Eigil Vesti. Crispo was a prime suspect in the murder, but his young assistant Bernard LeGeros was tried and sentenced for the crime. This past October, Crispo, who is currently in prison for tax evasion, was tried on a forcible-sodomy charge and acquitted.

Thyssen and Crispo originally met at Crispo's gallery during an exhibition called "Pioneers of American Abstraction." Thyssen had lent one of his pictures, a watercolor by Charles Demuth, for the show. He complained that on the loan card beneath the picture the name Thyssen-Bornemisza had been misspelled. "How do you know?" asked Crispo. "Because I am Baron Thyssen," was the reply. Thereafter, Thyssen began buying pictures from Crispo.

Franco Rappetti, trying to hold on to his business relationship with Thyssen at the same time that he was conducting an affair with Thyssen's wife, had once told Crispo that he would have to pay him a commission on any pictures he sold to the baron. Crispo had refused. After Rappetti's death, Crispo became firmly entrenched as Baron Thyssen's New York art dealer. In one month Thyssen spent $3 million on paintings, and the two men developed a close bond that has been the subject of endless speculation. Some people believe that the immensely rich baron financed Andrew Crispo's Fifty-seventh Street gallery. Others believe that there was a deep friendship between Crispo and the baron's oldest son, Georg-Heinrich, now thirty-seven. Georg-Heinrich, also called Heini, is the baron's child by his first wife, a German Princess of Lippe, who is now the Princess Teresa von Fürstenberg. "Teresa and Heini should have stayed married," said a grand European lady recently while lunching at Le Cirque. "She wouldn't have cared about his peccadilloes. Ridiculous, all those divorces." Young Heini lives in Monte Carlo and runs the vast family empire so that his father can devote himself entirely to the art collection. The Thyssen fortune, no longer connected with the original iron-and-steel business in Germany, is now derived from shipbuilding in Holland, sheep farms in Australia, glass, plastics, and automobile parts in America, and assorted interests in Canada and Japan. Whatever relationship or relationships once existed among father, son, and Andrew Crispo no longer do.

Tita Thyssen told a curious story about an American magazine which sent a crew to photograph her and her husband at their house in Jamaica and then used only a small picture of them, "Like a snap-shot." "There was something funny about it," she said, shaking her head at the memory. "They stayed too long for a photography shoot—five days. I felt they were after something. Then we found out that the photographer was the boyfriend of Crispo's boyfriend."

The baron now joined the conversation. "Crispo sold pictures to other people and then declared on the books that I had bought them so his buyers could avoid paying the New York City tax. Two-thirds of the pictures he said that I bought he actually sold to other people."

The baroness nodded her head in agreement.

"What do you call those films where people are killed?" he asked.

"Snuff?" I said. A snuff film is one in which a person is murdered, usually ritualistically, on-camera.

"Snuff, yes. One of the newspapers in New York tried to say that I financed snuff films for Andrew Crispo." He shuddered in disgust.

"Why didn't you sue?" I asked.

He waved my question away with a dismissive gesture. "This is such bad coffee," he said, putting his cup on the table and standing. "These people do not know how to make coffee. You can get better coffee in an airplane." The conversation was over. Neither Rappetti nor Crispo was mentioned again. Back to art.

"The baron is a man in love with his collection. Everything for him is his collection. He loves it. He is *in* love with it," said the Duke de Badajoz, who is not only the great good friend of both the baron and baroness but also the man who has been, after Tita, the prime influence in guiding the baron's decision to allow the collection to go to Spain. "After all the effort of his father and him to collect and amass 1,400 pictures, half of which are quite unique, it was more than natural that he was worried for a long time as to what would happen to the collection when he dies. He did not want it dispersed and auctioned. He has been looking around for some years for what could be a solution for the principal part of his collection, the A pictures."

Clearly, the pictures are the focus of the baron's life. "I'm a lucky fellow. These pictures of my father's I have known for fifty years, and I've been collecting for thirty-five years so I know them all." Walking through the graceful galleries that his father built to house the early part of the collection and that he opened to the public after his father's death in 1947, Thyssen was drawing more interest from the browsing tourists and art lovers than the paintings themselves. He moved with the assurance of a celebrity, knowing he was being looked at and talked about. When people came up to ask him to autograph their Thyssen-Bornemisza catalogs, he was completely charming. As he signed the books, he would say a few words or make a joke. He was dressed, as he almost always is, in a blue blazer with double vents, which his London tailor makes for him a dozen at a time, gray flannels, and a striped tie. In his hand he carried a large, old-fashioned key ring, unlocking certain rooms as we entered them and then locking them again as we left.

"I bought this yesterday," the baron said, looking at a Brueghel painting of animals. "I bought it from my sister. It's not in the catalog. It belonged to my father, and my sister inherited it." He moved on. "Now, this picture I bought from my other sister." Although the baron inherited the major part of the collection when his father died, he has spent years buying back the pictures that his two sisters inherited. It is for this reason that he is determined that his collection be kept intact when he dies. Thyssen also had an older brother, whose story remains somewhat vague. "He lived in Cuba," said the baron. "Then he moved to New York and lived at the Plaza Hotel. He lived completely on vitamins. He OD'd on vitamins."

"OD'd?"

"Hmm, dead," he said. He walked into another room.

"This is my favorite picture," he said, peering as if for the first time at a Ghirlandaio portrait of Giovanna Tornabuoni, a Florentine noblewoman, painted in 1488. "She died very young, in childbirth. We have never known if the picture was painted before or after her death. It was in the Morgan Library in New York. They had to buy some books, so they sold it." He continued to make comments as he passed from one painting to the next: "A Titian, very late. He was almost ninety when he painted that . . . Who was that man who gave the big ball in Venice after the war? Beistegui, wasn't it? That pair of Tintorettos comes from him . . . Everything in this room was bought by me and not by my father. I call it the Rothschild room. All the pictures in this room I bought from different members of the Rothschild family . . . My father bought this Hans Holbein of Henry VIII from the grand-father of Princess Di, the Earl of Spencer. The Earl bought a Bugatti with the money. When the picture was shown in England, Princess Margaret said to me, 'Harry is one up on you.' She was talking about his six wives, and my five. I said, 'He didn't have to go through all these tedious legal proceedings I do.' "

Of course, only a fraction of the baron's pictures were on view. Sev-eral of his Degas were in New York at the Metropolitan Museum of Art. Some of his old masters had been lent to the U.S.S.R. and were at that moment in Siberia. Still others were on loan to exhibitions around the world. He shook his head at the complexity of owning such a large collection.

The baron unlocked a door, and we entered a part of his private museum called the Reserve, It is here that pictures for which there is no room in the galleries hang on both sides of movable floor-to-ceiling racks twenty to twenty-five feet high. In one room a restorer with a broken arm, on loan from the J. Paul Getty Museum in California, was cleaning a fifteenth-century Italian portrait. "We have no room for this Edward Hopper," the baron said of a picture of a naked woman sitting on a bed, "and there's no place for that Monet." He rolled the racks back. There was also no place for a Georgia O'Keeffe and an Andrew Wyeth and what seemed like several hundred others.

"That's a fake Mondrian there," he said, approaching it and squint-ing at it. "I bought it by mistake. An expert told me he saw Mondrian paint it, and I believed him."

"Why do you keep it?"

"I prefer to keep a small fake to a big fake," he said, smiling.

Behind a door, almost out of sight, hung a picture of the baron him-self. He made no comment about the portrait until I mentioned it. "That's me by Lucian Freud," he said. The picture, which I had seen at the Lucian Freud exhibition at the National Gallery in Washington, is chilling; it suggests that there is a dark side to this billionaire. "I was getting a divorce at the time," he said, as if explaining Freud's unflattering rendition. People who know the baron well say that it is an extraordinarily accurate portrait. "That is Heini totally," said an

American woman who had apparently known the baron extremely well for a short time between marriages and asked not to be identified. "He went into unbelievable mood swings."

Helmut Newton asked the baron to pose next to the Lucian Freud portrait. He did. "Your chin up a bit," said Newton. The baron raised his chin. "Maybe that's how I will look someday, but it's not how I look now." As we were leaving the room, he said, "There's another Greco."

Once the Spanish government agreed to put up the necessary capital to house the paintings, and figured out what compensation should be made to the heirs of Baron Thyssen for renouncing their claim to his pictures, the deal was more or less in order. The baron has five children, starting with Georg-Heinrich from his first marriage. He has two children by his third wife, the former Fiona Campbell-Walter: Francesca, known as Chessy, who is an actress, and Lorne, an aspiring actor. After their divorce, Fiona, a beautiful English model, fell madly in love with Alexander Onassis, Aristotle's son by his first wife, Tina Livanos. Although Fiona was acknowledged to be a positive influence on Alexander, who was younger than she, Aristotle Onassis despised her. In 1973, Alexander Onassis was killed in a plane crash. Thyssen also has a child, Alexander, by his fourth wife, Denise, as well as his adopted son, Borja, brought by Tita to the fifth marriage.

"All the paintings legally belong to a Bermuda foundation, a trust, made by Baron Thyssen," the Duke de Badajoz explained to me in his office in Madrid. "After all the proposals from all the countries were together, the Bermuda foundation met and decided the ideal solution would be to make a temporary arrangement and, if it worked out, to make the final solution."

The Spanish government will provide a palace known as the Villa-hermosa to house the Thyssen-Bornemisza collection. When the old Duchess of Villahermosa died almost sixteen years ago, the time of block-long palaces for private living was at an end, and her daughters, two duchesses and a *marquesa*, sought to sell it. The enormous pink brick palace was first offered to the Spanish government for a relatively modest amount of money. For whatever reasons, the government turned down the offer, and a bank purchased the palace. In order to make the building work as a commercial institution, the inside was stripped, so all architectural details of the once-elegant structure have been obliterated, including what many people told me was one of the most beautiful staircases in Madrid. Then the bank went bankrupt, and the palace was bought by the Ministry of Culture, for more than five times what the government would originally have had to pay.

The palace is huge. There are two floors below ground level which will be made over for restaurants, an auditorium for lectures, and parking space. There will be three complete floors of galleries, and the top floor will be used for offices. Several hundred of the A and B pictures from the Thyssen collection will hang in the Villahermosa Palace. A convent in Barcelona is being refitted to hang seventy-five of the religious paintings in the collection. The rest will continue to hang in the private galleries of the Villa Favorita in Lugano.

The estimated time for the reconstruction of the palace is between eighteen months and two years. The ten-year loan period for the collection will not begin until the pictures are actually hung in the Villahermosa. In bottom-line terms, the loan of the pictures is in reality a rental for a ten-year period. "There is an annual fee of $5 million paid as a rent to the Bermuda foundation," said the Duke de Badajoz. Spain also has to provide insurance and security.

Critics of what has come to be known as the baron's Spanish decision say that he coyly received proposals from a host of suitors, playing one off against the other, when all the time he knew he was going to defer to his wife's wishes and send the collection to Spain, at least for a decade. Prince Charles flew to Lugano to lunch at the Villa Favorita in an effort to get the collection for England, and Helmut Kohl, the chancellor of West Germany, made a similar foray, offering a Baroque palace or a brand-new museum to house the collection. It is not out of the question that one or the other of these countries will be so favored when the baron's permanent decision is made. A London newspaper stated at the time of his last divorce that he had a tendency to ask for his gifts back, although the journalist was referring to jewels and not paintings. An interesting observation made to me by a prominent woman in Madrid was that, whatever decision is made, the Spanish pictures in the collection—the Velázquezes, the Goyas, the El

Grecos—will never be allowed to leave the country. All the reports over the last year about the agreement have included the added attraction of Tita Thyssen getting the title of duchess. "It has never been part of the negotiation," said the Duke de Badajoz. "It is the king's privilege to grant such a thing." In fact, Baron Thyssen will be offered a dukedom, which would elevate the baroness to duchess. "Of course, you cannot make a duke for ten years," said the Duke de Badajoz, which means, in practical terms, that the baron and baroness would not be elevated to duke and duchess if at the end of the ten-year loan period they decided to remove the pictures to England, or France, or West Germany, or Japan, or the United States. In the meantime, the Spanish government has already decorated Baron Thyssen with the Grand Cross of Carlos III, one of Spain's highest honors, for outstanding service to the Spanish government, and has decorated the baroness with an Isabel la Católica medal, for outstanding civil merit.

For the present, Baron and Baroness Thyssen will be spending more and more time in Madrid to be near the Villahermosa during the reconstruction period and to take part in deciding how the collection will be hung. Their new house on the outskirts of Madrid, in an area that is reminiscent of the Bel Air section of Los Angeles, is the kind of house that Californians talk about in terms of square feet. It is immense, with an indoor swimming pool next to the gymnasium, and an outdoor pool which may be one of the largest private swimming pools in the world. The décor is pure movie star: beige marble, beige terrazzo, beige travertine, indoor waterfalls, plate glass in all directions, and a security system that defies unwanted entry. "I want to get rid of all this," said the baroness after her first night there, waving her hands with a sweeping gesture at the custom-made beige leather sofa and chairs. "And all that in there," she continued, waving at the furniture in another of the many rooms, shaking her head at its lack of beauty. They bought the almost new house furnished. She said that she would give all this "modern furniture" to a benefit for the poor that the aristocratic ladies of Madrid were putting on and that she would furnish the new house with the antique furniture from Daylesford, which has been in storage since that estate was sold.

The Thyssens were scheduled to leave the following morning in their private plane for Barcelona, where the baroness and the Spanish opera singer José Carreras were to receive awards from the city of Barcelona. "It will be nice to settle down and decorate this new house. We are having the gardens all done over too. We've also bought the lot next door so there will be privacy. And there's the new house in Paris that I have to do over. All this traveling. It gets so tiring."

As we walked through her new gardens, she said, "When I die, I am going to leave all my jewelry to a museum. I hate auctions, when it says that the jewelry belonged to the late Mrs. So-and-so."

January 1989

I think I will never forget the beauty of the Thyssen art collection as it hung in Baron Thyssen's magnificent Villa Favorita on Lake Lugano. The collection is still magnificent, and more accessible to the public, hanging in the Villahermosa Palace in Madrid, but the intimacy of a great collection hanging in a great house has been lost. As of now, Baroness Thyssen has not been made a Spanish duchess by the Spanish government for her part in getting the collection to Spain. From time to time over the years, I have run into the baron and baroness in various cities, and I am always intrigued by the fascinating Tita Thyssen, who remains beautiful and seems always to be enjoying life to the fullest.

JANE'S TURN

"**R**emember, I've been in this business fifty-four years. I made eighty-six pictures and 350 television shows. I have not been idle." As she spoke, she leaned forward and her forefinger tapped the table to emphasize her accomplishment. The speaker was Jane Wyman, a no-nonsense star in her mid-seventies, who is one of the highest-paid ladies in show business. Her immensely successful television series for Lorimar, "Falcon Crest," is in its ninth year, and it is she, everyone agrees, in the centerpiece role of Angela Channing, that the public tunes in to see. She got an Academy Award in 1948 for *Johnny Belinda*, in which she played a deaf-mute who gets raped. She was nominated for Oscars on four other occasions, and she has also been nominated twice for Emmys. She has behind her what can well be called a distinguished career.

We met in a perfectly nice but certainly not fashionable restaurant called Bob Burns, at Second Street and Wilshire Boulevard in Santa Monica, California, not far from where she lives. Bob Burns is her favorite restaurant, where she has her regular table, a tufted-leather booth. It is one of those fifties-style California restaurants that are so dark inside that when you stop in from the blazing sunlight you are momentarily blinded and pause in the entrance, not sure which way to go. When she arrived, I was already at the table. My eyes had become accustomed to the dark, and I was able to watch her getting her bearings in the doorway. It was twelve noon on the dot, and we were the first two customers in the restaurant. Even to an empty house, though, she played it like a star. She is taller than I had expected. Her posture is superb. Her back is ramrod-straight. She is rail-thin, too thin, giving credence to the speculation that she is not in good health. She walks slowly and carefully. Some people say she is seventy-two, some say seventy-five, others say older. What's the difference? She looks great. Her hairdo, bangs over her forehead, is the trademark style she has worn for years. "Is that you?" she asked, peering.

"Yes." I rose and walked toward her.

She held out her hand, strong and positive. The darkness of the restaurant was flattering to a handsome woman of a certain age, but that is not her reason for liking the place. "The three people who own it went to school with my kids," she said. The words "my kids" were said in the easy manner any parent uses when talking about his or her children. She happens not to be close to either of hers, but we didn't talk about that.

She is private in the extreme, almost mysterious in her privacy, a rich recluse who chooses to live alone, without servants even, in an apartment in Santa Monica overlooking the Pacific Ocean. She is a woman in control at all times. There is not a moment off guard. What you see is the persona she wants you to see, and she reveals nothing further. Any aspect of her career is available for discussion, but don't tread beyond. And for God's sake, I was told, don't mention you-know-who or she'll get up and walk out. Simply put, it pains her that a marriage that ended forty-one years ago seems to interest the press and public more than her career.

"The reason I enjoy TV more than pictures now is that I like the pace better. You've got so many hours to do so much, and you have to get it done. I was on *The Yearling* for eleven and a half months! Sometimes we only did two pages of dialogue in four days," she said. She shook her head in wonderment at the difference in the two media. She was ready to order lunch. "Are the sand dabs breaded?" she asked the waitress. "Why don't we have a Caesar salad first?" she suggested.

For several years before "Falcon Crest" went on the air, she was in a state of semiretirement, spending most of her time painting. Although I have not seen any of her pictures, I have heard from her friends that she is an extremely talented landscape artist. In 1979 her work was exhibited in a gallery in Carmel, California, and so many of the pictures were sold that she now has none of her own work in her apartment. During those years, she said, she was always being sent film and television scripts, "like *Baby Jane*, or playing a lesbian, and I didn't want to do that. But when I was sent the pilot script for 'Falcon Crest,' I could see so many facets to the character of Angela Channing. I said, 'I'll give it two years.' It's now nine."

"People say that you control 'Falcon Crest,' " I said.

"I am a creative consultant only. They run things by me, or I run things by them. I just want to keep up the quality of the show," she replied. "I usually have my chair at an odd place on the set where no one can bother me. And I do help the young actors on the show. I hold a riding crop out, saying 'Don't do that!' "

"Is it true that actors on the show are told not to speak to you?"

"I hope not," she answered.

An actor who had appeared in a part that ran for three episodes told me that he had been informed by his agent, who in turn had heard it from the assistant director, that he was not to approach Miss Wyman on the set, as she did not like to be disturbed. He was also told never to go to her dressing room. He was also told that President Reagan was not be discussed on the set, ever. The surprise to this particular actor was that Miss Wyman "could not have been more delightful, or friendly. She came right up and introduced herself. One time I did knock on the door of her dressing room. I told her that I didn't think that the scene that we were to do together worked, and she asked me in, and we went over it and made some changes."

Susan Sullivan, who played her daughter-in-law on the series for eight years, said, "Jane is the most professional person I have ever worked with. I have seen her battle through illnesses and fatigue and still keep working. She says, 'Let's get this done. We have a job to do,' and everyone gets behind her. She is always willing to help younger actors. She gives instructions nicely and with humor. She once told me, 'You can tell anybody anything if you do it with humor.' She ruled the set with a kind and intelligent hand."

Rod Taylor, who plays her current husband in the series, agreed. "Sure, she rules the set, but everybody expects that. I adore her."

David Selby, who plays her son and has developed the closest friendship of any of the cast members with her, said, "Never once has she asked to be excused from standing in while the other actors in the scene are having their close-ups. She would be upset if you did your close-up without her. She has never once been late. If we go out to dinner, we go to her favorite little spot. I've never been to her apartment."

Another cast member said, "I've spent years working with her, and I still don't know her. She does not let herself be known."

An insider on the show had told me that an attempt would be made on Angela Channing's life in the new season of the series. "Is it true that you are going to be smothered with a pillow in the third episode and that the audience won't know whether you're dead or alive?"

Her eyes became very large. She was surprised that I knew that. She thought for a moment how to answer. "I *am* going into a coma for a while," she said. She has a way of letting you know when she is finished with a topic, without actually telling you that she is.

"Do you have a social life?" I asked.

"Not really. When you're on a series, it, the series, becomes your life. I don't go out." She gets up at 4:30 each morning the series is in production. "I can't drive in the dark, so I'm picked up by a studio driver. I leave my apartment at exactly 5:50. It's a long drive to the studio. I do my own makeup when I get there.

"I'm a great reader. And I have some close friends. We do a lot of telephoning. My friends understand me when I say, 'Everything is on hold until the series is finished.'" Among her closest friends are the two great film and television stars Loretta Young and Barbara Stanwyck, both of whom have had careers and led lives similar to Jane Wyman's. "Jane is a good girl. She's also a very determined woman," Barbara Stanwyck told me. "She has worked very hard for her successful career. I do mean hard, and she deserves all her success because she earned it." She then added, "I know this is a story about Jane, so be very good and very kind. She would be to you."

In an interview with Jane Wyman from the forties, published in a movie magazine of the period and discovered in the Warner Brothers archives at the University of Southern California, the writer noted, "Talking to her, one gets the impression she's wound up like a tight spring." Approximately forty years later, the same line could still be written about her, except for when she is talking about her career. Then she relaxes. She is a virtual oral historian of the decades she spent at Warner Brothers. She was under contract to Warner's for years, beginning in 1936 at $166 a week. She had been at Fox and Paramount before that. Somewhere along the line, her name was changed from Sarah Jane Fulks to Jane Wyman. "I stayed at Warner's until I went into television," she said. She started out as a wisecracking comedienne and singer, with no interest whatever in dramatic roles. "Jane Wyman has no yen for drama" read one of her early press releases. "Leave that to other people," she was quoted as saying. Her studio biography described her as "pert, vivacious, with plenty of pep. Jane Wyman is a human tornado." Not all of her films were distinguished, but her memory is as astonishingly sharp for details of the making of middling and less-than-middling films as it is for those of such classics as Billy Wilder's *The Lost Weekend.* "We were in a three-shot," she said, remembering one B-picture incident. "I was in the middle. Jack Carson was on one side, and Dennis Morgan on the other."

The star names flew from her lips. She calls James Cagney Cagney and Bob Hope Hope. "Cagney was my dream man," she said. "Hope wanted me to do this picture with him. You know Hope." Ann Sheridan. Humphrey Bogart. Joan Blondell. Bette Davis. "Bette Davis's dressing room was right next to mine, but we were never friends." Olivia de Havilland. Errol Flynn. "Jack Warner would never put me into any of their costume epics. He said I had the wrong looks. I think Jack was probably right."

She had an early marriage to Myron Futterman, a New Orleans dress manufacturer, about whom almost nothing is known. In 1940 she married Ronald Reagan, a fellow contract player at Warner Brothers, with whom she made four films. Their wedding reception was held at the home of the most famous of all Hollywood gossip columnists, Louella Parsons, who was raised in Dixon, Illinois, where Reagan grew up. Every movie magazine of the period recorded the idyll of the young stars' marriage, in the approved, studio-orchestrated publicity jargon. When Jane became pregnant, the studio announced that she was expecting a bundle from heaven. The bundle from heaven was Maureen Reagan, now forty-eight, who was born in 1941. Four years later the young couple adopted a son, Michael. They were promoted by Warner's as the dream Hollywood couple, and every fan magazine monitored their lives. "Ronnie and I are perfect counterparts for each other. I blow up, and Ronnie just laughs at me. We've never had a quarrel, because he's just too good-natured," said Jane in one interview. Several years after that, the lovebirds became known in the press as "Those Fightin' Reagans," and rumors of a rift in the marriage were rampant. Louella Parsons, who thrived on such matters, told Jane in a column, "I want to write a story and settle all this talk once and for all." Jane was quoted by Louella as replying, "Believe me, I'm going to find out who has started all this talk. . . . Can't gossips let us keep our happiness?"

In 1947 the marriage did break up. "We're through," Jane said to a columnist during a trip to New York. "We're finished, and it's all my fault." Reagan found out about the termination of his marriage when he read it in the column. He gave long interviews to Louella and to her archrival, Hedda Hopper, both of whom took his side. "If this comes to a divorce, I'll name *Johnny Belinda* as co-respondent," Hedda Hopper quoted him as saying. Jane had become so immersed in her new career as a dramatic actress that she wore pellets wrapped in wax in her ears so that she would not be able to hear during the filming of the deaf-mute movie. Hedda Hopper had more to say on the subject: "I can't really believe it yet. I don't think Ronald Reagan does either. It caught him so flatfooted, so pathetically by surprise. I talked to Ronnie the day he read in the newspapers what Jane should have told her husband first."

They were divorced in 1948, the same year she won the Academy Award. Jane got custody of the two children, and Reagan got weekend visitation rights. Jane testified that her husband's overriding interest in filmland union and political activity had driven them apart. Friends speculated at the time that Jane's emergence as a bona fide star and Reagan's concurrent slide from box-office favor contributed to the breakup. Others felt that Jane was simply bored with him. Before the governorship and his truly remarkable rise as a recognized world leader, friends from that period remember, he did indeed engage in long, ponderous, yawn-producing discourses on a variety of subjects. An ongoing joke in Hollywood during his campaign for the governorship of California was a remark attributed to Jane Wyman about her former husband. When asked what he was like, she allegedly said, "If you asked Ronnie the time, he'd tell you how to make a watch."

In 1954 Reagan married the actress Nancy Davis, who had been a contract player at MGM. Not long afterward, Jane married the bandleader and musical arranger Freddie Karger, a popular and handsome man-about-town in Hollywood. She divorced him a year later. Karger is often mentioned in Marilyn Monroe biographies as one of her lovers. Years later Wyman married Karger again, and then divorced him again. She has not married since.

In 1954 Jane was converted to Catholicism through the intervention of her great friend Loretta Young. Her Catholicism is a mainstay in her life. In fact, when asked her age, according to friends, she very often replies, "I'm thirty-five." She is counting from the year of her conversion to Catholicism. "She goes to Mass all the time," said a member of the cast of "Falcon Crest." "Sometimes she even has Mass said in her room." One of the ongoing characters in the series is a Catholic priest. "We need a lot of advice, because some of the characters are Catholic in the show," said Jane. The priest character is played by a real priest, Father Bob Curtis, a Paulist.

After *Johnny Belinda*, her career totally dominated her life. "She told me she could never even cook a hamburger. She taught her kids early that she wasn't going to be there," said an actor friend of hers. She had made the long and difficult transition from contract player to leading lady to star, and she hung on to that position through the forties and into the mid-fifties, playing what she has called four-handkerchief roles in such classic films of the genre as *Magnificent Obsession* and *The Blue Veil*, which remains her favorite. "I was in the middle of the woman's cycle in picture making," she said. She talked about her contemporaries. "Greer, Irene, Olivia, Joan, Bette, Loretta, Barbara, and don't forget Ginger ... I never really knew Ava." She was talking about Greer Garson, Irene Dunne, Olivia de Havilland, Joan Fontaine, Bette Davis, Loretta Young, Barbara Stanwyck, Ginger Rogers, and Ava Gardner. "The thing was, we were all different," she said. The *New York Times* film critic Bosley Crowther wrote about her in 1953, "Her acting of drudges has become a virtual standard on the screen." But then the cycle of women's films ended. She decided to retire in 1962.

Several seasons ago Lana Turner, who was one of the queens of MGM when Jane was one of the queens of Warner Brothers, came on

"Falcon Crest" as a semiregular. From the beginning, there was a cool-
ness between the two stars. Lana, according to one source, took five or
six hours to get ready, and Jane, for whom promptness is a passion,
could never tolerate that. Someone closely connected with the show
told me that Jane watched Lana on a talk show one night and felt that
she was taking credit for "Falcon Crest" 's coming in number two in
the ratings. "Imagine her taking credit for the show's success," said
Jane at the time. Lana did not appear on the show again.

In the old days of the studios and contract players, the young actors
were taught how to conduct themselves in interviews. They never said
anything negative about anyone, and that training is still evident today.

"Was there a difficulty between you and Lana Turner?" I asked.

"Enough said, right there," answered Jane Wyman. She looked at
me in a way that said very clearly that Miss Turner was a topic she had
finished discussing. Her praise for her fellow actors on the series is un-
qualified, however. "I love to work with David Selby." "Lorenzo
Lamas can do almost anything. He's a wonderful dramatic actor." "I
said, 'I want Rod Taylor in the show.' He was occupied doing something else. I said, 'We'll wait.' "

"I never asked anything about her children. I have never approached
that relationship with her," said an actor on the series. "I think she was
hurt by Michael's book, but she has never said one harsh word about
them. The only time I ever heard her mention the name of the president, she said something kind."

Both of her children have written books in which they announced things to their parents that they had not told them before.
Maureen wrote that she had been a severely battered wife in her
first marriage, and Michael confessed that he had been sexually molested by a man when he was a child. Since Joan Crawford's daughter Christina wrote *Mommie Dearest*, it has become the vogue
among the adult children of the famous to cash in on their privileged unhappiness by spilling the beans on their celebrity dad or
mom. Maureen wrote that Jane had not come to her first wedding.
Michael wrote that Jane had sent him away to boarding school when
he was six. Even the siblings did not seem to get along. Michael, in
his book, recounts an incident that happened when he was four

years old. He told Maureen that he knew a secret. "What?" she asked. He told her that she was getting a new blue dress for Christmas. Infuriated that he had ruined her Christmas surprise, she snapped, "I know a secret too. You're adopted."

"Do you see your grandchildren?" I asked. Maureen has no children, but Michael has two, Cameron and Ashley.

"Once in a while," she replied slowly. The subject was approaching the danger area. "They're in school when I'm working. They're adorable kids, Cameron and Ashley. Cameron's always saying to me, 'Gramma, how old are you?' And I say, 'I'm as old as my little finger.' And he says, 'How old is that?' and I say, 'As old as I am.' "

"Have you always been so reluctant to be interviewed?" I asked.

"No," she said. "My life's an open book. Everyone knows everything about me. There are all those magazines with lies in them." She had ordered a Diet Coke, and she took a sip. "I used to be interviewed a lot. But the last time I was, I had what seemed to be a very nice interview with the reporter, and then the piece came out. The first line was something like 'This is the president's ex-wife.' That's when the guillotine fell. I don't have to be known as that. I've been in this business longer than he has. It's such bad taste. They wouldn't say it if I was Joe Blow's ex-wife. It wouldn't even be mentioned."

With that said—and it was the closest she got to the unmentionable subject, the former president of the United States—she shifted topics abruptly. "We're going to have fun this year on the series. We have such a good producer, and the writers are wonderful. I feel like I'm doing the first show. The enthusiasm is just wonderful. The 'Falcon Crest' that *I* want is going on this year."

However reluctant she may be to discuss it, how can her relationship with Ronald Reagan not be discussed? She is the only former wife of a United States president in the history of the country. It is certainly true that if she had been married to Joe Blow it would never be mentioned. Her marriages to Myron Futterman, who manufactured dresses, and to Freddie Karger, who led the dance band on the roof of the Beverly Hilton Hotel in Beverly Hills, are never mentioned. But between those two marriages was her longest marriage, to a movie star of the period, with whom she had two children and who later became the governor of the state of California and then the president of the

United States. It is part of her history. It will be the lead in her obituary when she dies.

It is a curious coincidence of fate that the eight years of her emergence as the First Lady of television should almost exactly parallel the eight years of her former husband's second wife's emergence as the First Lady of the land. The relationship between the two women is, has always been, and ever will be poisonous, although Jane Wyman has never uttered a single word in public about or against Nancy Reagan. Apparently Mrs. Reagan has not returned the courtesy. There are publishing rumors that her forthcoming book, *My Turn,* contains several obliquely critical allusions to Jane Wyman in reference to the bringing up of the two children Jane had during her marriage to Ronald Reagan. "Jane was a star. Nancy never was," a Los Angeles socialite acquainted with both said to explain the bad blood between the two women. "For seventeen years, Jane has kept her mouth shut. Nancy hates Jane with such a passion because it's the only part of Ronnie that she doesn't control. If you had mentioned Ronnie to Jane, she would have gotten up and walked out." A person friendly with Nancy Reagan told me that in the scrapbooks she keeps of newspaper clippings about her romance and marriage to Ronald Reagan, all mentions of Jane Wyman have been blacked out. In turn, a person friendly with Jane Wyman told me in private Jane sometimes refers to Nancy Reagan as Nancyvita.

Until recently, Jane was a regular and favored patron of the famed Hollywood restaurant Chasen's, as well as a close personal friend of Maude Chasen, the widow of David Chasen, who founded the restaurant fifty-three years ago. Although her friendship with Maude continues, she is, by unstated mutual agreement, almost never seen there these days. Chasen's has become the more or less official restaurant of the recent president and his wife, and Jane Wyman's absence from the premises averts the possibility of a chance encounter.

A journalist friend told me about interviewing the former president in the private quarters of the White House. He had been warned in advance that the name Jane Wyman was never mentioned in the presence of the First Lady. But since Miss Wyman had been married to the president for eight years, the journalist ventured very cautiously, when they were deep into the conversation, to bring up her name. To his surprise, the president began to tell a friendly anecdote about his first wife. Midway through the story, Nancy Reagan walked into the room. Without a second's hesitation, the president shifted to another topic right in the middle of a sentence, and the subject of Miss Wyman did not come up again.

Every star of Jane Wyman's caliber pays a price for fame, and she has endured for over fifty years. Although she is husbandless and vaguely estranged from her children, her splendid isolation must not be confused with loneliness. Where she is is where she has always wanted to be from her early contract days.

Like all success-oriented people, she is not without her detractors. Robert Raison was Jane Wyman's agent for nearly thirty years, as well as her friend and sometime escort to social functions in the television industry. He was also the agent of Dennis Hopper, Michelle Phillips, and all of the Bottoms brothers. He had a reputation for developing close friendships with his clients. He negotiated the seven-year deal for Jane when she decided to play the role of Angela Channing on "Falcon Crest." At the end of the seventh year of the series, Raison heard from Jane's lawyer that he was through. "When she fired me, she never told me herself. I heard it from her lawyer," said Raison. When he asked why, the lawyer told him to call Jane and discuss it with her. "I did," said Raison. "I told her I wanted to hear it from her mouth. You know what she said?"

"No."

"She said, 'You and me, Bobby, we've run out of gas.' I was going to sue her, but the lawyers settled it for a given amount of money. I can't discuss that amount."

Raison is now writing a book about his years with Jane Wyman. It is tentatively titled *Jane Wyman, Less than a Legend: A Memoir in Close-Up*. Although angry and hurt, Raison still expresses residual tenderness for his former client. "Two days after the assassination attempt on the president, Jane sent him flowers to the hospital in Washington. Several days later, the president personally called to say thank you for the flowers," Raison recalled recently. He answered the telephone when the president called. "He said to me, 'Thank you for taking care of her, Bobby,' " said Raison.

———

The check came. In an interview situation like this one, the interviewer always picks up the check. As I reached for it, Jane Wyman tapped my hand and shook her head. "This is on Lorimar," she said.

We walked outside into the brilliant sunlight. Her red Jaguar was parked in the number-one space of the Bob Burns parking lot. We shook hands. "Where else can you meet such fascinating people and go to such places as people in our business do?" she said. "It's a fabulous life."

In an era of tell-all, Jane Wyman has made the decision to tell nothing. No confessions. No revelations. It's her life, and it's private. There are those who say it is her duty to inform historians of the eight years she shared with a man who later became the president of the United States, years that encompassed the peak of his minor movie stardom, his presidency of the Screen Actors Guild, and his role in the ignoble House Un-American Activities Committee hearings. But she sees it differently, and that's the way it is.

"She's one tough lady," said one of the cast members of "Falcon Crest." Yeah, but a lady.

November 1989

———

I really liked Jane Wyman. She was a no-nonsense lady who set the rules and expected you to play by them. She called me after this article came out to say that she hadn't liked the piece when it came out, but that friends of hers had told her that it was a good and positive piece and she had come round to that way of thinking herself. In recent years, she has stayed totally out of the limelight.

IT'S A FAMILY AFFAIR

It was a family affair. The father, the mother, the three sons, the two daughters, the estranged wife of one of the sons, a grandchild, boyfriends and girlfriends of all the children. And there were the father's half-sister and the mother's sisters and almost all their husbands, and a good many of their children. And cousins, lots of cousins, city cousins and country cousins, including, in the host's own words, "masses of Guinnesses." And friends, but only close friends, hardly a jet-setter in the whole bunch. This was, remember, a family affair.

But what a family and what an affair. Lord Glenconner, of England, Scotland, and the islands of Mustique and Saint Lucia in the British West Indies, who used to be called Colin Tennant before he inherited his father's title, was celebrating his sixtieth birthday in very grand style. For openers, he had chartered a brand-new 440-foot four-masted sailing vessel called the *Wind Star*, possibly the prettiest ship afloat, with a crew of eighty-seven, and had installed 130 of his nearest and dearest in its seventy-five staterooms, complete with VCRs and mini-bars, for a week-long cruise from Saint Lucia to Martinique to Bequia to Mustique, with parties all along the way, every noon and every night, culminating in a costume ball called the Peacock Ball at the Glenconners' place, which some people call a palace, on the beach in Mustique. And should there have been any question of the financial burden imposed by such an adventure, Lord Glenconner had taken care of that too, by paying the fares of all his guests from London to Saint Lucia, where he owns a second estate, called the Jalousie Plantation, which he plans, in time, to turn into a hotel and health spa. And should there have been any problem about rounding up a suitable cos-

tume for the lavish India-theme ball, Lord Glenconner had even
anticipated that. In his travels to India over the past year, while he was
preparing for his birthday celebration, he had purchased a variety of
kurtas and Aligarh trousers and turbans and ghagra/cholis and harem
dresses in a whole range of sizes and styles and had had them transported to the *Wind Star* so that his guests could pick out what they
liked. There were even two seamstresses on board to make any necessary alterations. The only thing you had to provide was your own jewelry. He drew the line at that. But he did have a hairdresser for the
ladies, who doubled as a barber for the men, and a masseuse and a
masseur. And 360 movies to choose from for the VCRs, including 58
pornographic ones. And all taxi rides on the various islands were to be
paid for by Lord Glenconner. And there was to be absolutely no tipping. Lord Glenconner had taken care of all that. It was, all the way
around, a class act.

I arrived in Saint Lucia the day before the plane from London arrived, and was met at Hewanorra airport by Lord Glenconner and his
estate manager, Lyton Lamontagne, at whose house I spent the first
night. Lyton Lamontagne, a native of Saint Lucia in his late twenties,
and his wife, Eroline, went to school together in the town of Soufrière.
He is handsome and she is beautiful. A trusted confidant of Lord
Glenconner's, Lamontagne traveled to India with him last year and
was instrumental in carrying out the farsighted and sometimes seemingly impossible plans of the eccentric lord. Glenconner feels, as do
others I saw in Saint Lucia, that in time Lyton Lamontagne could become the prime minister of the island. The Lamontagnes refer to Lord
Glenconner as Papa, as do many of the natives on both Saint Lucia and
Mustique, and there is a sense in their relationship of the nineteenth-
century British Empire builder and his devoted overseer. In Soufrière,
Glenconner lives in an old wooden house on the town square, so prim-
itive that it has no electricity or running water, although it will have at
some point in the future. He has to go to the nearby Texaco station to
use the bathroom or wash, and this sort of inconvenience seems to appeal to him, although it is at variance with his elegance of manner,
which is sometimes almost effete. He wears large straw hats, and for
his birthday week he always dressed in white or black.

Lord Glenconner talked briefly about several last-minute drop-outs from the party. Mick Jagger could not take the time out to attend, although Jerry Hall would be joining the group when the boat docked in Mustique. David Bowie could not come. Lord Dufferin and Ava were ill. Carolina Herrera had to finalize a perfume deal in New York. Glenconner rolled his eyes in disappointment. He rolls his eyes a great deal, in exasperation, or wonder, or over lapses of taste. His own lapses, however, take on a sort of aristocratic whimsy, at least in his mind. He once allowed himself to be photographed defecating by the side of the road in India and sent the pictures to *Vanity Fair*.

We sailed in a small open boat to the Jalousie Plantation, where one of the main events of the week-long celebration was going to take place several days hence. His plantation lies between two peaks called the Pitons. The original house, on what was once a sugar plantation built by the French in the seventeenth or eighteenth century, is long gone, but stone walls from the original waterwheel are still standing. The principal house now is a small wooden bungalow, onto which had just been added a covered porch for the picnic party. The bungalow, which has gingerbread trimmings, was painted pink with yellow shutters, green floors, and blue interior walls, and looked like a set from the musical *House of Flowers*. Gamboling happily around the scene of preparations was a frisky young elephant called Bupa, which Glenconner had bought from the Dublin zoo and had sent out to his plantation. A native painter was finishing a mural on one side of the house, and Lord Glenconner examined the lavender leaves and red and orange flowers closely. "No, no, no, I don't like that color red at all," he said to the painter. "There's far too much brown in that red. I want a red red." They found a red red.

Then we went for the first of two trips to the airport, to meet Lady Glenconner, known as Lady Anne, who was arriving from Mustique with the eldest of her three sons, Charles, as well as her daughter-in-law, Tessa Tennant, the wife of her second son, Henry, and Viscount Linley, the son of Princess Margaret by the Earl of Snowdon. The contingent from London, which included the Glenconners' twin teenage daughters, Amy and May, was arriving on a second plane several hours later. Another son, Christopher, was arriving from Mexico. On the way to the airport Glenconner had the driver stop the car several times so that he could cut wild lilies growing by the side of the road to present to his wife. Lady Anne is a lady-in-waiting to Princess Margaret. Such close friends are the Glenconners of the princess that they have been living at Kensington Palace as her houseguests for nearly a year while their new London house has been undergoing extensive renovations and decoration. "I sleep in what was Tony Snowdon's dressing room, just this far from Princess Margaret," Lord Glenconner told me. He said when they were moving out of their old house, Princess Margaret came to help them pack; she donned a working smock borrowed from a maid and wrapped china in newspapers.

"I thought surely you'd have had a steel band on the tarmac when the plane arrived," Lady Anne said to her husband, patting her hair beneath a straw hat and supervising the transfer of all the luggage to the van that would take us to the boat. She is blond and calm and attractive.

"I hadn't thought of it," replied Glenconner, and I felt that in his mind he was trying to figure out if he could do just that before the plane from London arrived a few hours later. Although they are married and live together, or at least live under the same roof when the separate schedules of their lives overlap, they speak to each other with the friendly distance of a divorced couple meeting at their child's wedding.

Their oldest son, Charles, called Charlie, thirty, looked pale and disheveled. His father told him to wash his face and get a haircut as soon as we got on the ship. Although Lord Glenconner has publicly disinherited his eldest son, who is a registered heroin addict, with an announcement in the London *Daily Mail*, there seems to be no lessening of affection for him, nor is there any sort of middle-class covering up of a family embarrassment. "My son Charlie is a heroin addict and has been ever since he was fifteen," said Glenconner openly, not only to me but to several other people encountering the situation for the first time. Charlie remains a part of the family, disinherited but not cast out, and loved by all. In time he will become Lord Glenconner, for titles must go to the eldest son, but the estates, fortune, and castle in Scotland will pass to his brother Henry, who is estranged from Tessa, by whom he has a son, Euan, three.

When we got to the pier where the *Wind Star* was docked, the fence was padlocked, and two armed guards stared at us as if we were usurpers, making no attempt to open the gates for the van to enter. "I am the lessee of the boat," called out Lord Glenconner from the backseat of the van. The guards did not react. "Just say Lord Glenconner," said Charles from the front seat to his father. "I am Lord Glenconner," called out Lord Glenconner. The gates were opened.

Standing on deck, we watched the London crowd arrive, hot and tired and bedraggled, and trudge up the gangplank. A Mrs. Wills had lost her keys, and there was a great to-do. "Where's Mark Palmer?" someone called out. "I can't find my suitcases," someone else wailed. John Stefanidis, the famed London interior decorator, who helped the Glenconners with the Great House in Mustique and who is currently doing up their new London house, remarked to his deck companions, Lord and Lady Neidpath, with whom he had flown over from Mustique, "Rather elite, having arrived early."

In typical English fashion, no one was introduced. Those who already knew one another stayed together and looked at the others. There were no passenger lists in the staterooms, so it was impossible to put names to faces. Even during lifeboat drill, when we were separated into small groups, they did not introduce themselves. After a few days, people began to come into focus as one-line descriptions were repeated over and over: "He's Princess Margaret's son." "She's Rachel Ward's mother." "He was recently fired by Mrs. Thatcher." "She's the Duke of Rutland's sister-in-law."

One passenger of interest was Barbara Barnes, on holiday from Kensington Palace, where she is nanny to the royal princes, William and Henry. Nanny Barnes, a popular figure on the ship, used to be nanny to the children of Colin and Anne Glenconner, and the Princess of Wales had given her time off to attend the celebration and visit her former charges.

For a week we heard no news of the outside world. We were hermetically sealed in the elegant confines of the *Wind Star* when we were not ashore being picnicked. There was swimming off the ship and in the pool, and gambling in the casino, and a gym to work out in, and bars to drink at, and a disco to dance in, and all those videos, including the fifty-eight pornographic ones, with titles like *For Your Thighs Only* and *Lust on the Orient Express*, and even a library. John Nutting read the recent biography of Lord Esher. His wife read a biography of

Francis Bacon. The Honorable Mrs. Marten read the new biography of Anthony Eden. Prince Rupert Löwenstein read the biography of Frank Sinatra by Kitty Kelley. Conversation, which never lagged, from breakfast to bedtime, was all about themselves. They never tired of discussing one another. One Englishman described the degree of friendship with another man on board as being not quite on farting terms.

"Tell me, how is young Lord Ivar Mountbatten, over there with the pretty Channon girl, related to Dickie?"

"He's through the Milford Haven branch."

"Claire tells me Tony Lambton's writing a biography of Dickie Mountbatten that's going to tell everything."

"Oh dear."

"The Guinnesses all stick together, have you noticed?"

"Lord Neidpath is very proud of his feet."

It is said that on all private boat trips the most unifying factor for harmony is a mutual dislike of one particular person aboard, and this trip was no exception. By the third day, all had agreed that they loathed the same certain person, and from that moment on, tales of that person's every move and statement were circulated.

"Don't believe any rumors unless you start them yourself," cautioned Lord Glenconner, in regard to all the rumors that were circulating about the trip. From passing yachts we heard that Michael Jackson was on board the *Wind Star*, but the person the passengers in the passing yachts mistook for Michael Jackson was called Kelvin Omard, a London actor and great friend of Henry Tennant, Lord Glenconner's second son. "Did you see *Water* with Michael Caine?" asked Tessa Tennant, Henry's wife. "Kelvin played the waiter."

"How much do you suppose this is all costing?" I inquired tentatively one day at lunch on Martinique, fully expecting to be put in my place with imperious stares for daring to ask such a vulgar question. I meant the whole week of it: the plane fares, the *Wind Star*, the parties, parties, parties, and the ball that was to come.

"That's what we're all wondering" was the immediate and unexpected answer, from one of my lunch companions, not a Tennant, at a table of Tennants. "We figure about a half-million." I didn't know if she meant pounds or dollars, but since she was English, I assumed pounds. As the week progressed, revealing constant new considerations on the part of our host for his guests, the cost question was brought up again and again, not only by me, an almost lone American on a boatload of Brits, but by a number of Brits as well.

"Colin is not limitlessly rich," said another passenger a few days later at dinner on board the *Wind Star*, pursuant to the same question. When I wrote down the phrase "not limitlessly rich," his wife said, "My God, you're not going to quote my husband, are you?"

"All I know is he sold some items at Sotheby's in order to charter the *Wind Star*, and paid for the charter in installments," offered someone else.

"Where is Lord Glenconner's money from?" I asked over and over.

"Sugar in the West Indies, nineteenth century, I would think" was one reply.

"Imperial Chemical" was another.

Lord Glenconner's explanation seemed to answer the question. "My great-grandfather invented the Industrial Revolution."

Like a mysterious shadow, a second ship was known to be looming in the distance, the *Maxim's des Mers*, the floating sister of the famed Parisian restaurant, carrying "the American crowd." At some point we would be rendezvousing with them. In speculation preceding the ball week, it had been rumored that Mick Jagger, David Bowie, Michael Caine, and others too famous for words would be among its passengers, supplying the magic mix of show biz with swells that guarantees fascination on both sides. At the helm of the *Maxim's des Mers*, at least as organizer of the famous, was André Weinfeld, the husband of Raquel Welch, and an invitation every bit as grand as the one to the Peacock Ball sent by Lady Glenconner and the one to a beach picnic on the morning following the ball sent by H.R.H. the Princess Margaret, Countess of Snowdon, had been dispatched by Miss Welch and Mr. Weinfeld bidding us, the passengers on the *Wind Star*, and other guests who would be joining our party in Mustique, to a dinner on board the *Maxim's des Mers* on the evening preceding the ball. Already, even before our rendezvous, rumors of defections from their guest list had circulated. We knew that such stalwarts of the international social scene as Carolina and Reinaldo Herrera and Ahmet and

Mica Ertegun had dropped out, not to mention Mick and David, as they were referred to, meaning Jagger and Bowie, who had long since changed their plans.

The *Maxim's des Mers* came side by side with the *Wind Star* in the cove in front of Lord Glenconner's Jalousie Plantation on Saint Lucia. The other boat was squat and inelegant next to our trim, patrician four-master; the battle lines were instantly drawn. No amount of interior Art Nouveau tarting up of the *Maxim's des Mers* could belie its minesweeper origins. The A group–B group distinction between the two parties could not be denied by even the most generous-hearted. It carried right down to the crew of the *Wind Star*, who snubbed the crew of the *Maxim's des Mers*. "Rather like being on the wrong side of the room at '21,' " remarked a *Wind Star* passenger about the *Maxim's des Mers*, which others were already referring to as the *Mal de Mer*. The celebrity guests that Mr. Weinfeld was able to produce arrived on-shore for the barbecue at the plantation. Vastly fat native women were dressed up in Aunt Jemima gear, a fourteen-piece steel band played nonstop, the elephant frolicked with the guests, and at one point Lyton and Eroline Lamontagne, got up as Scarlett O'Hara and Rhett Butler, drove down a mountain in a horse and buggy to be introduced by Lord Glenconner as his distinguished neighbors from the next plantation. Rum punch and more rum punch, and still more rum punch was consumed. And the sun beat down.

Heading Mr. Weinfeld's star list was the amply bosomed Dianne Brill, the New York underground cult figure often referred to in the gossip columns as the Queen of the Night. Although Miss Brill is a good sport, a good mixer, and a genuinely funny lady, even she could not bring about any real mixing between the passengers of the two ships. "Who do you suppose *they* are?" someone in our party asked about a trio of ladies. "In trade, I would think," said Prince Rupert Löwenstein playfully, "above a boutique and below a department store." André Weinfeld explained that because it was Thanksgiving, most of the people he had invited had backed out, and he had brought along a substitute crowd. Indeed, his wife, Raquel Welch, had not yet joined the company, but he assured us she would be along in time for her party on board the *Maxim's des Mers*.

———

In Mustique the inner circle widened to admit some new arrivals. Adding more than a dash of American glamour to the British festivities were two tall and sleek American beauties, Jean Harvey Vanderbilt, of New York, and Minnie Cushing Coleman, of Newport and New Orleans. On Mustique the groups within the group of the *Wind Star* began to divide up into splinter groups. "We're going to Ingrid Channon's house for lunch," said Mrs. Vyner. "We've been asked for drinks at Princess Margaret's house," said Mrs. Nutting. "We're having a box lunch at Macaroni Beach," said the ones who weren't invited to any of the private houses.

"What happens if you don't call Princess Margaret ma'am?" asked one of the new American arrivals.

"You don't get asked back," came the reply.

On the morning of Raquel Welch's party aboard the *Maxim's des Mers*, a telex arrived for Lord Glenconner from the star, saying that a contract negotiation prevented her from attending her own party. Lord Glenconner rolled his eyes in disappointment, but any attentive observer could also detect an element of anger in the eye roll. His last star had fallen by the wayside. From that moment on, Raquel Welch, who had always been referred to as Raquel in anticipation of her arrival, was referred to by one and all as Miss Welch.

"I think this is the rudest thing I have ever heard," fumed one of Lord Glenconner's guests, and then proceeded to fume against all Americans for Miss Welch's rudeness, especially since a member of the royal family had consented to attend her party.

"But Miss Welch is not American, Julian. She's English," said his wife.

"Oh dear," said her husband, calmly accepting the correction, although he had been right to begin with.

"If she can't be bothered to attend her own party, I can't be bothered to attend it either," said another guest.

"Disgraceful!"

"Movie stars always back out at the last minute."

"They're insecure in social situations."

"You don't suppose they're getting a divorce, do you, Mr. Weinfeld and Miss Welch?"

On the night of the ball, after a whole week of partying, guests ran up and down the passageways of the *Wind Star* borrowing feathers, remarking on one another's costumes, pinning and sewing up each other—all with the excitement of boarding-school students preparing for the annual spring dance. John Stefanidis had gone to Paris to borrow jewelry to wear with his Indian costume from Loulou de la Falaise, who works for Yves Saint Laurent, and indeed his pounds of pearls, rhinestone necklaces, and long drop earrings were the most elaborate jewelry at the ball—after the host's, that is.

All during the evening Lord Glenconner's eyes shone with the excitement of an accomplished creation—a symphony composed, an epic written, a masterpiece painted. Wearing a gold crown and ropes of pearls, he was dressed in white magnificence, his high collar and robes heavily encrusted with gold embroidery. The Glenconner house, called simply the Great House, is a Taj Mahal–like palace designed by the ultimate stage and ballet designer-fantasist, the late Oliver Messel, uncle of Lord Snowdon, former husband of Princess Margaret. Magical even in broad daylight, by night, for the ball, it was bathed in pink and turquoise fluorescent light, which gave the illusion of a Broadway-musical version of India. Handsome, almost nude black males from Saint Lucia and Mustique, their private parts encased in coconut shells painted gold, with strips of gold tinsel hanging from their shoulders to the ground, lined the pink-carpeted walkway to the house. Inside the double doors, more natives, in pink and blue Lurex fantasies of Indian dress inspired more by *The King and I* than by *The Jewel in the Crown*, stood cooling the air with giant peacock feather fans on poles.

Standing under a pink marquee, with the palm tree–lined beach in the background and the *Wind Star*, fully lit, on the sea beyond, Lord and Lady Glenconner, with their son Charlie by their side, received their elaborately dressed guests while their son Henry called out the names as they arrived.

"Mrs. Michael Brand," called out Henry Tennant.

"I am the Honorable Mrs. Brand, not Mrs. Michael Brand," corrected Mrs. Brand.

The natives on the island of Mustique call Princess Margaret simply Princess, with neither an article preceding nor a name following. Well, Princess was late, and the procession that was to open the ball could not take place until Princess arrived, because Princess was the principal participant. The fact was, Princess had arrived at the Great House, but she was still sitting in Lady Anne's bedroom, which boasts a silver bed with silver peacocks on the head- and footboards. One story had it that Raquel Welch had also finally arrived on the island, and that Princess, not wishing to be outdone by her, as she had been the previous evening, when Miss Welch had not shown up at her own party, where Princess was an honored guest, was delaying the procession until after Miss Welch's arrival. If such was the case, Princess lost another round.

Finally, despairing of Miss Welch's ever arriving, the royal procession started. The sisters of Lady Anne, Lady Carey Basset, with one of her three sons, and Lady Sarah Walter, with her husband, Prince and Princess Rupert Löwenstein, and the Americans, Miss Jerry Hall and Mr. and Mrs. James Coleman, Jr., moved slowly from the house to the receiving tent. They were followed by Viscount Linley, in a white peacock headdress, which he never removed for the whole night, and his beautiful girlfriend, Susannah Constantine. Then came Princess Margaret, the great friend of the Glenconners. On her head, complementing her dress, which was a gift from Lord Glenconner, she wore a black velvet headband tiara-style, onto which her maid, that afternoon, had sewn massive diamond clips. Her resplendence had been worth the wait.

"Her Royal Highness, Princess Margaret, Countess of Snowdon," called out Henry Tennant. All the Indian-clad ladies dropped in curtsies as she passed, and all the men bowed their heads. Under the tent, Lady Anne kissed her on both cheeks before doing a deep curtsy. Then Lord Glenconner removed his crown, as did his son Charlie, and they bowed to Princess.

When Princess Margaret first saw the Indian sari that Lord Glenconner had had made for her in India, she exclaimed, "I've been dreaming of having a dress like this since I was six." During dinner a maid spilled a tray of potatoes on the dress, but Princess's dinner partners, Sir John Plumb, the eighteenth-century historian, and John Nutting, an English barrister of note, were able to right the wrong with a minimum of fuss and very little stain.

Miss Welch, the lone dissenter from Indian costume, finally arrived during dinner, dressed in a gray metallic shirred evening gown and shoulder-length metallic shirred evening gloves, which she kept on while she ate. She was seated between Prince Rupert Löwenstein, a noted wit and conversationalist, and Mr. Roddy Llewellyn, the extremely affable suitor, before his marriage, of Princess Margaret, at whose Mustique house he and his wife, Tania, were houseguests, but conversation with the film star was pretty much uphill.

"Have you read the Sinatra biography?" Prince Rupert asked her.

"No," she said, "but I made a picture with Frank. If Frank likes you, he's behind you all the way. He wrote me a letter when my father died." Then she massaged her neck with her hand and said, "My neck's out. I've been wearing a neck brace, but I couldn't wear a neck brace with this dress to Colin's party. It's stress. I've been under a lot of stress. Would you get my husband, please? I need my pills for my neck. André, would you get my pills for my neck. Two of the yellow ones."

"They're back on the boat," joked Prince Rupert. "In the Dufy suite."

"No, I'm not staying on the boat," she said. "I'm at the Cotton House."

At the far end of Lord Glenconner's enormous swimming pool stands a maharajah's pleasure palace, discovered in India, purchased in India, and then brought to Mustique, along with two Indian stonemasons to put it together again. Constructed entirely of white marble, it has lattice marble screens on all four sides, which gives the interior constant dappled light by day. By night, for the ball, its interior was illuminated by gold fluorescent light, and smoke from smoke pots drifted through the lattice screens. A plan to have Raquel Welch emerge from the pleasure palace as part of the entertainment portion of the evening had been scratched, and an alternative plan had been substituted: another princess.

Princess was not the only princess at Lord Glenconner's ball. Princess Josephine Löwenstein was there, as well as her daughter, Princess Dora Löwenstein. And then there was Princess Tina—just Tina, no last name. Princess Tina provided the cabaret entertainment, appearing late in the evening in front of the pleasure palace, doing gymnastic gyrations while she balanced full glasses of something on her head and pelvic area. The crowd surged out to watch her—blacks and swells vying for the good positions from which to view the tantalizing spectacle. One heavily wined English lady sat in the reflecting pool in front of the pleasure palace and pulled up her skirts to the refreshing waters. "My God, look at her—she's showing her bush!" another lady cried out.

Thrice Miss Welch upstaged Princess Margaret. She didn't show up at her own party on the *Maxim's des Mers*, at which Princess Margaret was a guest. She arrived later than Princess Margaret at the Peacock Ball. And on the day following the ball, at Princess Margaret's party, a picnic luncheon on Macaroni Beach, under the same pink marquee from the ball of the night before, transported after dawn from the Great House, Miss Welch, accompanied by Mr. Weinfeld, made another late entrance, as the princess and her guests were finishing dessert. Miss Welch was all smiles as she greeted her hostess. Princess inhaled deeply on her cigarette through a long holder protruding from the corner of her mouth, exhaled, pointedly looked at her watch, wordlessly established the time, and then returned the greeting with a stiff smile. One-upmanship was back in the royal corner.

That night, Lord Glenconner's party drew to a close with a farewell dinner aboard the *Wind Star*. New friends were exchanging addresses. Bags were being packed. Princess arrived on board and was seated at the right of Lord Glenconner. People said over and over again that they would never forget the week-long celebration. John Wells, who writes the "Dear Bill" column in *Private Eye*, rose and in mock-Shakespearean rhetoric recited a long poem to our host which ended with these lines addressed to Princess Margaret:

> *Your Royal Highness, may I crave*
> *Leave not only to ask God to Save*
> *The Queen, your Sister, but to bless*
> *The Author of our Happiness—*
> *This Prospero, Magician King*
> *Who makes Enchanted Islands sing;*
> *King Colin, at whose mildest Bate*
> *King Kong himself might emigrate!*
> *So charge your Glasses, Friends, to honour*
> *Our reckless Host, dear Lord Glenconner.*

Amid cheers and tears, Lord Glenconner rose. Dressed all in black, his energies spent now, his production over, he thanked the people who had helped him in his yearlong preparations: Lyton Lamontagne, Nicholas Courtney, and others. He thanked his son Charlie "for getting a little better," he thanked his son Henry and Henry's friend Kelvin for working out the treasure hunt on the island of Bequia. He thanked his daughter-in-law Tessa for her constant assistance. He did not thank Lady Anne, who seemed not to notice not being thanked. "You all say you'll never forget," he said wistfully. "But you do, you know. You do forget. I can't even remember my own wedding day."

March 1987

The Glenconner family has suffered several tragedies since their festive cruise aboard the Wind Star *in 1987. One of their sons died of AIDS. Another was badly injured in a motorcycle crash. They sold their beautiful house in Mustique to the Russian-born former husband of the late shipping heiress, Christina Onassis. Lady Anne continues to be lady-in-waiting to Princess Margaret.*

GRANDIOSITY:
THE FALL OF ROBERTO POLO

In retrospect it's always easy to say, "Oh, yes, I knew, I always knew," about this one or that one, when this one or that one comes to a bad end or winds up in disgrace. Any number of people who knew Roberto Polo have told me that when they first heard that disaster was about to befall him, they said to the person who informed them, "I'm not surprised, are you?" and the informant invariably replied that he or she was not surprised either.

Polo, a thirty-seven-year-old Cuban-born American citizen with residences in Paris, New York, Monte Carlo, and Santo Domingo, is currently in prison in Italy, where he was arrested in June. He is wanted for questioning in Switzerland, France, and the United States concerning the alleged misappropriation of $110 million of his investors' money. At the time of his arrest, he had been a fugitive from the law for five weeks, and had been rumored either to have sought and bought refuge in Latin America or to have been murdered by the very people he was said to have swindled, on the theory that, if caught, he might reveal their identities.

"Roberto had so many personas it was hard to know which was the *real* person," one of his former employees said to me in describing him. A middle-class Cuban with dreams of glory, Polo appeared to be many things to many people, from family man to philanderer, from elegant boulevardier to preposterous phony, from fantasizer to fuckup of the American Dream. A man with the capacity to endear himself to many with his likability and charm and to enrage others with his grandiosity and pomposity, he provided uniformity of opinion among those who knew him in one thing only: He had exquisite taste.

I first met Roberto and his extremely attractive wife, Rosa, a Dominican by birth, the daughter of a diplomat and the cousin of a former president of that country, in 1984, at a small dinner for eight or
ten people in New York, at the home of John Loring, senior vice president of Tiffany & Co. They were the youngest couple in the group,
known to all the guests but me.

It was not until we sat down to dinner that I noticed the extraordinary ring Rosa Polo was wearing, a diamond so huge it would have
been impossible not to comment on it. As one who has held up the
hands and stared at the ice-skating-rink-size diamonds of Elizabeth
Taylor, Candy Spelling, and Imelda Marcos, I realized that the young
woman across from me was wearing one bigger and perhaps better
than all of them. I asked her about it, and before she could reply
Roberto called down from his end of the table and gave me the whole
history of the jewel. It was the Ashoka diamond, a 41.37-carat
D-flawless stone named after Ashoka Maurya, the third-century B.C.
Buddhist warrior-emperor. Polo had bought it for his wife from the
Mexican movie star Maria Felix.

Clearly the Polos were a young couple of consequence, but it was
hard to get a line on them. Rosa was quiet, almost shy, a Latin wife
who lived in the shadow of her husband, and Roberto sent out mixed
signals. He was said to be a financial wizard, and he had his own company called PAMG, for Private Asset Management Group. He handled the monetary affairs of a select group of very rich foreign
investors with assets in the United States.

He reclined in languid positions that first evening, and his talk was
decidedly nonfinancial, about jewelry and fashion and Jacob Frères,
Ltd., an antiques shop that had recently opened on Madison Avenue at
Seventy-eighth Street, which was run by Rosa's brother, Federico
Suro. They sold ormolu-encrusted furniture fit for palaces, and massive porcelain urns, all at prices in the hundreds of thousands of dollars. Roberto was obviously a genuine aesthete, mad about beautiful
things, and his interest in fashion, which would become obsessive in
the years ahead, was already evident. As a graduate student at Columbia in the early seventies, he had worked at Rizzoli, the art bookstore,
and had come up with the idea of doing a show called "Fashion As
Fantasy," with fashion designers showing clothes as art objects.

They were a couple in a hurry, or rather Roberto was in a hurry, and Rosa was swept along in his vortex. He had reportedly created his wife, turning her from a sweet Latin girl into a sleek and glamorous international figure. He picked out her clothes, told her what jewels to wear, chose their dinner guests, did the seating, and ordered the flowers and menu. He went to the collections in Paris with her, and in one season spent half a million dollars on clothes for her. He had a passion for jewelry and a knowledge of gemology. His role model, according to the interior designer and socialite Suzie Frankfurt, was Cosimo de' Medici.

"I didn't want it said I was just a rich boy," he said in an early interview, before his woes, as if he were the heir to a great fortune instead of an alleged usurper of other people's money. Like a Cuban Gatsby, an outsider with his nose pressed to the window, Roberto Polo wanted it all and he wanted it quick, and he saw, in the money-mad New York of the eighties, the way to achieve his ambitions.

July 1988. The picture was improbable. A young blond girl of extraordinary loveliness, wearing a light summer dress, was leaning against the pay-telephone booth in the courtyard of the prison in Lucca, an Italian walled town between Pisa and Florence. She was reading an English novel and occasionally taking sips of Pellegrino water from a green bottle. On the roof above her, a guard with a submachine gun paced back and forth on a catwalk in the scorching Tuscan sun. There was about the girl a sense of a person waiting.

I was waiting too, reading a day-old English newspaper and leaning against the fender of a dented red Fiat. I had been waiting for a week for a permit that was never to come, from the Procura Generale in Florence, to visit the most famous detainee in the prison. Roberto Polo had been arrested by the Italian police the week before in the nearby seaside village of Viareggio, after an alleged attempt, by wrist slashing, to commit suicide. Bleeding, believing himself to be dying, Polo had made farewell telephone calls proclaiming his innocence to one of his investors in Mexico, to members of his family, and to a former associate, the man who had set the case against him in motion.

It occurred to me, watching the young girl, that we were there for the same reason. I offered her my *Daily Mail*, and she said that she hadn't seen an English paper for days. She knew a girl whose name was in Nigel Dempster's column. "She's always in the papers," she said. We exchanged names, and it turned out that I knew the mother of her stepsisters in New York.

"Why are you here?" I asked. We had stepped through rope curtains into the shade of the Caffè la Patria, a bar and tobacco shop adjacent to the prison.

"I'm with people who are seeing someone inside," she said cautiously.

"Roberto Polo?" I asked.

"Yes."

"That's why I'm here," I said.

"I supposed you were," she replied.

The previous week I had made my presence and purpose known to Gaetano Berni, the Florentine lawyer retained by Polo's family. Berni had explained to me that Polo was fighting extradition to Switzerland. "It is better for him to remain in Italy," he had said. "The Swiss will be harder on him. Besides, there is insufficient evidence to extradite him. He didn't kill. He didn't deal drugs. He's not Mafia. As the judge pointed out, he was not escaping when he was arrested."

My new friend, Chantal Carr by name, was the girlfriend of Roberto Polo's brother, Marco, a banker in Milan, where she also lived. Early that morning she had driven Marco and his father, Roberto Polo, Sr., to Lucca in her tiny Italian car. Even for the family of such an illustrious prisoner, visiting hours were restricted to one hour a week, on either Saturday or Sunday.

When Chantal Carr saw Marco Polo come out of the prison, she joined him, and I could see her telling him that I was in the bar, hoping to talk to him. Marco Polo is thirty-three, younger than his brother by four years, and handsome. His hair is black and curly, combed straight back. He has the look of the rich Italian and Latin American playboys who disco at Regine's. Standing in the hot sun, he was weeping almost uncontrollably while Chantal Carr patted him comfortingly on the back. Behind him stood his father, a smaller man with wounded eyes. Roberto Polo, Sr., seemed desolated by the disgrace that had befallen his family, as well as by the shock of having just seen his son in such awful circumstances.

"My brother is devastated. He is destroyed," said Marco when he came into the café. The prison was filthy, he told me, the food inedible. Prisoners with money could purchase food and sundries in the prison store, but they were not allowed to spend more than 450,000 lire, or $350, a month. Roberto Polo, one of the few prisoners to have that kind of money, had spent his whole month's allowance in the first few days of his imprisonment. During the time I was in Lucca, he could not even buy stamps.

"I am living in subhuman conditions . . . with murderers, thieves, drug traffickers, etc.," Polo wrote in a press release from his cell. For two hours each morning, they were allowed to pace back and forth in an enclosed patio for exercise. "He is totally incommunicado. He does not know that people have come to see him," said Marco. The only visitors he was allowed to have were his lawyers and members of his immediate family, but even they were not allowed to bring him a prescription he needed or a brand of toothpaste he requested—only food.

Marco expressed shock at the newspaper coverage of his brother's dilemma. "They have convicted him without a trial," he said.

The family was hoping to obtain Roberto's release on bail. That afternoon the lawyers were due, Gaetano Berni from Florence and Jacques Kam from Paris. It seemed in keeping with the glamorous aspects of Roberto Polo's recent life that Maître Kam, the principal lawyer he had picked to defend his interests at the time the warrant for his arrest was issued, was also the lawyer of Marlene Dietrich, the late Orson Welles, Dior, and Van Cleef & Arpels. "Speed is of the essence," said Marco. "Everything comes to a standstill in August. The judicial system closes down. Of course, even if bail is granted, all his money has been frozen."

All around us in the café, waiting for the afternoon visiting hours to start, were prisoners' relatives, many with small children. Looking at them, Marco said, "Roberto wants to see Marina, his daughter. But Rosa and he have decided that it is best she not come. She is five. She would remember."

I asked about Rosa, who was expected in Lucca the following day from Paris, and whom I had spoken with a few days earlier. "Rosa has not cried once," replied Marco, and there was an implied criticism in his voice. It is a known fact among all their friends that Rosa Polo and her husband's mother have never gotten along. Rosa, however, who had every reason to be outraged at the position she found herself in, had been staunchly loyal to her beleaguered husband when I spoke with her. She is, after all, the daughter of a diplomat. Shortly after her husband's disappearance five weeks before his arrest, the French police confiscated $26 million in paintings and furnishings from the couple's Paris apartment, leaving Rosa and her daughter only mattresses on the floor to sleep on. "This whole thing has been a double cross," she had told me. "We know who has been feeding everything to the press. When the press destroys you, it is hard for anyone to ever believe you." The person who she believed had double-crossed her husband was Alfredo Ortiz-Murias, the former associate of Roberto Polo who had received one of his farewell calls. "We are united," she had said to me about Roberto and her.

Marco and his father were also scornful about Alfredo Ortiz-Murias. "He was always jealous of my brother," Marco said. Ortiz-Murias was the principal witness in the suit brought against Polo by Rostuca Holdings, Ltd., an offshore company operating out of the Cayman Islands, whose money was managed by Polo's company, PAMG. It came out in the conversation that the man behind the company known as Rostuca was the governor of one of the poorest states in Mexico. I remembered Gaetano Berni saying to me a few days earlier, about this same man, "What kind of person has $20 million in U.S. dollars *in cash* outside his own country? Even Mr. Agnelli or Mr. Henry Ford, when he was alive, did not have $20 million in cash." He had grimaced and shaken his head. The implication was clear.

"Will you tell me the circumstances of Roberto's arrest?" I asked Marco.

"I have heard three stories. I do not know which one is the truth," he replied, dismissing the subject.

I had heard several stories too, the first from Alfredo Ortiz-Murias in New York, about his farewell call from Roberto. According to Ortiz-Murias, who had blown the whistle on Polo, Roberto had said to him, "Good-bye, Alfredo. It's 6:30 A.M. in Europe. I am sorry you felt that way about me. Good-bye." When I asked Ortiz-Murias what his reaction to the call was, he said, "He was trying to make me feel guilty."

I had also heard from Pablo Aramburuzabala, one of Polo's

investors, a well-to-do Mexican businessman whose wife is the god-mother of the Polos' daughter, that Roberto had called his house four times to say that he was going to commit suicide. "The first three times I was out, but my wife spoke to him. He was calling from a public tele-phone. When I talked with him, he said he had never done anything wrong. He gave me the address in Viareggio and said that I could call Interpol if I wanted. He said he was full of blood and didn't have too much time. Then he must have called his mother. She called me to say that Roberto was dead. She said she didn't know where to go to claim his body. I gave her the address in Viareggio. Then the brother, Marco, called from Tokyo. Marco said that Roberto had been picked up by an ambulance and was in the hospital in Viareggio."

Roberto Polo gave his own version of his arrest in a press release: "I ate some fish which apparently made me very sick, because early in the morning, I called my brother (who lives in Milan), who speaks Italian, in order to ask him to call the police station to have them send a doc-tor because I felt like I was dying. My brother, who has a friend in Viareggio, asked his friend to call the police in order that they send a doctor to see me. By the time the doctor arrived, I had already vom-ited and had some tea: I felt much better. However, the doctor took my blood pressure, stated that it was a bit high, then left. A few hours later (I was already dressed to go to the beach on my bicycle), the po-lice returned without the doctor and asked me to go with them to the station. . . . I was interrogated. . . . After that I was taken, handcuffed, to the prison where I am in Lucca."

It seems odd that a person wanted by the police in three countries would call his brother in Milan to call the police in Viareggio to get a doctor for an attack of food poisoning. According to Gaetano Berni, the Florentine lawyer, Roberto himself called for an ambulance. It seems odd also that nowhere in Polo's account of the events in Viareg-gio does he mention Fabrizio Bagaglini. Only Gaetano Berni would speak about Bagaglini when I brought up the name. He said, "Fab-rizio stayed until the arrest." We will come to Fabrizio Bagaglini.

"Were you separated by a screen when you saw your brother?" I asked Marco Polo.

"No, we were able to embrace him."

"Was he wearing the ribbon?" Chantal Carr asked Marco.

"Yes," he replied.

Three weeks before Polo vanished, the French government had made him a Commander of the Order of the Arts and Letters in gratitude for his having donated to the Louvre Museum Fragonard's painting *The Adoration of the Shepherds* and a crown of gold, emeralds, and diamonds that had belonged to the Empress Eugénie.

"Does he wear a prison uniform?" I asked.

"No, he wears his own clothes. His body is clean. His clothes are clean. The place is filthy and horrible, but my brother looks classy. My brother is the classiest person I know."

In 1982 the Polos moved from a one-bedroom apartment on Lexington Avenue to a large Park Avenue apartment, for which they spent $450,000. That move signaled the beginning of their rise. They had a Botero in the dining room and a picture by Mary Cassatt of a woman reading *Le Figaro*, which Roberto later sold at Christie's for $1 million. "He took to buying paintings and then selling them a year later," said Alfredo Ortiz-Murias. "He had no attachment to anything. Everything he bought was for sale." Their only child, Marina, was born in 1983, while they were living in the Park Avenue apartment. The child's godfather was the Count of Odiel, whose wife is a cousin of the King of Spain. Early in 1984, Roberto bought a five-story town house on East Sixty-fourth Street for $2.7 million. Four years later, Ramona Colón, Polo's administrative assistant and office manager at the time of this purchase, stated in an affidavit filed with a New York civil suit, "I first became suspicious that not all of the clients' money was being invested as required. At that time Roberto directly or indirectly purchased a town house . . . and directed [an assistant] to transfer money, in the approximate amount of the purchase price of the town house, from clients' time deposits maturing at that time to an account at European American Bank on 41st Street, New York, and then to an account in the name of ITKA, at Crédit Suisse in the Bahamas. I believe that the ITKA account was Roberto Polo's personal account."

The redecorating of the new house from top to bottom—a job that would have normally taken anywhere from a year to two years—was done in six weeks, and Roberto was his own decorator. His men worked seven days a week, at the same frantic pace that his near neighbor

Imelda Marcos had set when she did over her new town house on East Sixty-sixth Street in time to give a party for the international arms dealer Adnan Khashoggi. He brought special upholsterers from England to install the green damask on the library walls. People who watched Polo during this period said that he worked like a man possessed in creating the perfect setting, as if he knew that his good fortune couldn't last. The dark-paneled dining room on the first floor was large enough to seat thirty-six comfortably, and the living room on the floor above was the size of a small ballroom, with a white damask banquette along one wall and ample space to hang the young couple's astonishing and ever-growing art collection. He sold his Impressionist art to make room for his new and even more impressive collection of eighteenth-century French paintings, Fragonards and Bouchers and Vigée-Lebruns, mostly purchased through the Wildenstein gallery in New York. In order to get insurance for the paintings, he had to have steel shutters installed on all the windows; at the push of a button, these dropped and plunged the interior of the house into total darkness.

He also moved his offices. He had started PAMG in the bedroom of his apartment. Then he had shared a small office with several other people. Next he had taken space at 101 Park Avenue. Now he rented grand offices on the forty-third floor of the General Motors Building on Fifth Avenue.

More and more, Roberto Polo began to be talked about. His antiques buying at auctions and in shops in New York and Paris was nonstop, and he always paid the top prices. A former associate of his described Roberto on a spree in Paris, going from shop to shop, buying $3 million worth of antiques to stock Jacob Frères. On one occasion Rosa wore $6 million in emeralds. On another, she pushed her baby's stroller through Central Park wearing a T-shirt and jeans, the Ashoka diamond, and a million-dollar strand of pearls. Roberto, no slouch in the jewelry department himself, wore a ring with a 10.5-carat Burmese ruby worth over $1 million. He was so meticulous that when he bought a picture for his office he would have a picture hanger come from Wildenstein to install it. He was a terror at home; one out-of-place ashtray or a table not dusted properly could drive him into a rage. On the other hand, when he had people to lunch at the town house, in the midst of all that grandeur he might serve his guests grilled-cheese sandwiches on paper plates, which a servant would pick up from a nearby luncheonette. He could not stand to be alone; he even took people on the Concorde with him so that he would not have to fly alone. He ran his multimillion-dollar business mainly from his house, on one rotary telephone without even call waiting, and held meetings there in darkened rooms.

My second encounter with the glamorous Polos was at a charity ball for Casita Maria, the oldest Hispanic settlement house in New York. Apart from the ball for the Spanish Institute, the Casita Maria Fiesta is considered to be *the* Latin party of the year in New York. A new and interesting way for rich social aspirants to get their name known in smart circles is to underwrite charity parties, and in 1985 Polo underwrote the Casita Maria ball. It was the custom of Casita Maria to present three prominent people with gold medals, and in previous years honored guests had included Placido Domingo and Dame Margot Fonteyn. That year the honorees were the Colombian painter Fernando Botero, former secretary of the treasury William Simon, and the film star Maria Felix, who was enormously popular in Mexico but, unlike her sister star Dolores Del Rio, little known in the United States. People say that Polo had an obsession with this septuagenarian actress, whom he had met through his mother, and from whom he had purchased the Ashoka diamond as well as a diamond snake necklace of extraordinary workmanship made by Cartier, both of which adorned Rosa Polo that night.

At the last minute, Maria Felix canceled, informing the committee that she had broken her ankle. So Polo and his brother-in-law, Federico Suro, put together an eleven-minute montage of Felix's film clips as a substitute for the no-show star. He had promised the glittering crowd a celebrity, and he delivered instead badly edited clips, far too long and in Spanish. Soon the audience in the Grand Ballroom of the Plaza Hotel grew bored, and began to talk and laugh as if the film were not going on. Polo became petulant, then furious, and at the end of the film he went up to the microphone and berated the audience for their bad manners. He said he was glad Maria Felix was not there.

At this outburst, looks were exchanged across the tables, the kind of looks that clearly said, Who the hell is this little upstart to lecture us on manners? To make matters worse, Roberto's mother, whom he had told people had once been an opera singer at La Scala, rose and applauded her son's speech.

"That night Roberto was finished in New York," said a Venezuelan society woman who resides in the city. Actually, he wasn't finished in New York that night. People with vast sums of money are never finished in social life as long as they keep picking up the checks, and Roberto Polo continued to pick up the checks for large dinners at Le Cirque and other fashionable restaurants, where he would sometimes order wine that cost a thousand dollars a bottle and take only a sip or two of it.

Some people are mesmerized by money. It covers all defects. Even people who suspected that something was not quite right about Polo overlooked his flaws and listened to him with rapt attention. Like a peacock, as soon as he met someone he wanted to impress, he would spread his feathers and show off all his colors, telling of his paintings, his furniture, his wife's jewels, his financial acumen, his social achievements. Often he would close this self-congratulatory catalog with the words "and only thirty-six"—his age at the time.

These same people, however, were beginning to speculate about who Roberto Polo was and where all his money came from. "We manage money for wealthy individuals," he would say. But talk was rampant that some of the money he managed was dirty money, meaning that he was laundering money, or drug-trafficking, or running arms. One former associate, however, who subsequently broke with him, told me he firmly believes that the clients' money was clean. The company served as financial adviser to a group of Mexicans, Latin Americans, and Europeans who happened to have money—often a great deal of money—in the United States. In most cases, however, it was illegal for these clients to have money invested secretly outside of their own country. In Spain, for instance, the government can confiscate all the Spanish holdings of an individual who has undeclared investments in the United States. At Citibank, where Polo had worked before founding PAMG, he became an account executive, but several times he was passed over for assistant vice president even though he attracted business to the bank. In 1981 he left to found his own company, which would serve the same function as the bank but with more personalized attention given to clients than the bank gave. PAMG arranged financial transactions for investors, and most of the money was in time deposits.

Although some former clients—Pablo Aramburuzabala, for one— say that they did not authorize Polo, or PAMG, to invest their money in art, Polo did entice new business to PAMG with a glossy brochure picturing his specialty in investments: paintings, jewels, and real estate. "Otherwise, his clients could have gone to Morgan Guaranty," said his lawyer Jacques Kam.

One of the great titans of Wall Street, who later refused to comment on his statement, is reported to have said about Roberto Polo, after meeting him at a small dinner party and listening to him talk, "There's something wrong. If there's that much money, I would have heard about him." He was echoing the old saying, "If they have the right kind of money, they're known at the bank."

"All of us, we may not know each other, but we know who each other is," said a New York social figure from a prominent Latin-American family, "and no one, not a single soul, knew anything about Roberto Polo or his family. Ask any of the Cubans we know. Never *heard* of Roberto Polo."

A New York fashion designer who was thinking of bringing out a fragrance backed by Polo was warned, "Do not touch him with the end of a barge pole."

Shortly after completing the town house, Polo gave a dinner for Amalita Fortabat, who is said to be the richest woman in Argentina. Many New York social figures attended. "Where did you get that fabulous Fragonard, Roberto?" someone asked him. "My parents brought it with them out of Cuba," he replied. People knew that wasn't the truth, but no one called him on it. "He bought the Fragonard at Wildenstein's, but he liked the old-money, old-family sound of his version of the acquisition," said a person who was present. Often he would point out a piece of his furniture by saying, "The twin to that is in Versailles."

Upper-class Cubans in New York and Florida are amazed by the stories Roberto Polo would tell of his family's background. "There is no mention of the Polo family in the old Social Registers from the days before Castro," said a Cuban lady in New York. Another said, "We know our own. The Polos were not in the clubs, and the boys did not go to either of the two schools everyone we know went to." Still another said, "He learned everything so fast. Just seven years ago, he was wearing black shoes and white socks." She paused and added, "He was always polite, very well mannered. I think he is to be admired for the myth he has created about himself. He really does think his family built all the oil refineries in Cuba. His family was perfectly nice— an engineer, or something like that, his father was—but they were certainly not a family that went about in social circles."

Like Imelda Marcos, who has spent a lifetime upgrading the circumstances of her birth, Polo had a tendency to paint a more aristocratic picture of his family than the truth would bear out. Even in stir, facing a long incarceration and sharing a cell and a toilet that doesn't work with two other prisoners, he issued a press release emphasizing the grandeur of his background. He quotes from early magazine articles written about him in which he was described as "the darkly handsome, wealthy Cuban refugee, son of Countess Celis de Maceda." He describes his father as having been, "like his father before him," a "very rich playboy" in Cuba, as if—even if it were true, which it appears not to be—it were an admirable thing to be the son and grandson of wealthy playboys. He also says, "On my father's side of the family the wealth came from the construction business; they built various oil refineries and industrial plants for Standard Oil Company, the Bacardi plants in Nassau and Puerto Rico, and parts of the United Fruit Company in Costa Rica. . . . My mother's family was wealthy, but less than my father's. However, whatever wealth they missed (compared to my father's family) they made up in a more aristocratic, artistic, and generally more socially prominent background. . . . My mother's nobiliary title came to her as the oldest child in her family through her grandmother; I inherited this title, which I have never used nor pretend to (even though there are those who want to make me a social climber, hardly necessary given my higher education, refinement, and family upbringing relative to my American counterparts), because I am the oldest child in my family."

Roberto Polo was born in Havana on August 20, 1951, the older of two sons of Roberto Polo, an engineer, and his wife, Maria Teresa. The family fled Cuba in the wake of Castro and moved to Peru, where they suffered serious financial losses when the government nationalized their business. They then moved to Miami, where Roberto and Marco went to school. Their mother, a trained opera singer, became a hospital nutritionist after they left Cuba. An aspiring artist, Roberto attended the Corcoran School in Washington on a scholarship from age fourteen to eighteen, and then graduated from the American University in Washington, where he met his future wife's brother, Federico Suro. He studied philosophy and art. He moved to Montreal in order to avoid the draft for the Vietnam War, but he was later classified 4-F due to curvature of the spine and flat feet. He then got a master's degree in painting and sculpture at Columbia University, and while he was there he took his first job, at Rizzoli. After Columbia, he joined Citibank.

In an article in *Women's Wear Daily* this year, he said of his wife's family, "My in-laws are very wealthy. My wife's uncle was the president of the Dominican Republic. His name was Antonio Guzman. His brother died of cancer and left a huge fortune. I left Citibank to oversee that money." In fact, the Suro family is intellectually prominent and highly respected, but it is not a rich family. Dario Suro, Rosa Polo's father, is considered to be one of the greatest Dominican painters. He became the cultural attaché at the embassy in Washington in 1963, under Ambassador Enriquillo Del Rosario, who is now an ambassador to the United Nations. Rosa Polo's mother, Maruxa Suro, was the first cousin of the late president Antonio Guzman, but since the pay at the embassy was low, Mrs. Suro, in order to provide her children with a good education, worked for a time in the dress department of Lord & Taylor in Washington. Rosa, after moving to New York, studied first at the Harkness School of Ballet and then at the Joffrey Ballet school until she married Roberto in 1972.

Soon after Polo started in business for himself, old friends began to notice a change in him. A grand Spanish lady who had been one of his investors said, "Several times I saw Roberto Polo in Le Cirque. A kid like that showing off at Le Cirque, pretending he was rich. Uh-uh." She withdrew her money from his management. An old friend of his wife's family, who had thought of himself as a friend of Roberto's as well, found that Roberto stopped speaking to him. "I often saw him in the company of the flashy type of Latin, wealthy but not of the top social class."

People began to say that the bubble was going to burst. Roberto was traveling more and more, leaving Rosa and the baby behind. Beneath the bravado was a man very unsure of himself. His look changed constantly. He didn't seem to know who he was. His hair was short, then it was long. One week he wore English clothes, the next week he wore Italian. I ran into him in the lobby of the Plaza-Athénée Hotel in Paris in 1986 and didn't recognize him when he spoke to me. He was wearing his hair in a ponytail, and either he was in the process of growing a beard or he was affecting an exaggerated version of the Don Johnson–*Miami Vice* look. Even his eyes looked different, and later I learned that he had taken to wearing blue contact lenses. He appeared at one evening party in a sort of bolero jacket, and people told me he had hoped to start a trend for bolero jackets in the evening. Close friends of Rosa said that she never looked happy. She complained that Roberto was constantly entertaining people from Mexico. She was always on call.

In May 1986, Polo moved his firm to Geneva and his family to Paris, so abruptly that it seemed as if he were leaving New York in a hurry. A Cuban lady who had followed his activities for several years said, "Roberto was disappointed with New York. You see, he was never really accepted by either the Latins or the Anglos. No matter how hard you try, very few Latins are really accepted in New York. He thought that that would not be true in Europe."

Polo claimed that the United States had cooperated with the governments of Haiti and the Philippines in revealing what assets were held in this country by the recently deposed Baby Doc Duvalier and Ferdinand and Imelda Marcos. He stated publicly that he thought President Reagan was throwing Duvalier and the Marcoses to the lions, and that PAMG investors deserved more discreet treatment than the U.S. government was offering. He sent a letter to his clients saying that Swiss banks offered them greater secrecy than other banks.

Several former associates have different views of Polo's quick move to Europe: "If you have more than fifteen clients that you are giving advice to, you need a license with the SEC. If the SEC had come to investigate after he bought the house on East Sixty-fourth Street, they would have known." Or: "He may have thought that by moving to

Switzerland he could hide under the Swiss secrecy laws." Or: "He had placed some time deposits in savings and loans in Maryland that went bankrupt. Jumbo CDs. The SEC was investigating those S&Ls."

Before leaving New York, Polo presented a Marisol sculpture to the Metropolitan Museum. He also did what had been in the cards for him to do for years: He entered the world of fashion. The dress designer Polo had always admired most was the brilliant and ill-fated British-American Charles James, whose dresses he thought of as pieces of sculpture. In James's declining years, when he was living in near destitution in the Chelsea Hotel, Polo had sent him $200 a week.

In December 1985 he purchased the fashion house of a designer named Miguel Cruz, a fellow Cuban whom he had met through Maria Felix. A second-echelon but respected designer with a faithful following, Cruz had been established in Rome since the 1960s. When he approached Polo to borrow money from him for his business, Polo is supposed to have said, "I don't lend money. I'll buy you." Fashion had always been a business that fascinated him. Now it became the business that would destroy him.

In Paris, he bought a fourteen-room apartment at 27 Quai Anatole-France which surpassed in elegance and grandeur the house on East Sixty-fourth Street. A Marisol sculpture of Rosa and Marina stood in the hallway. A Toulouse-Lautrec, van Dongens, Fragonards, and Bouchers lined the walls. Following in the steps of such other Latin American collectors who had lived in Paris as Arturo Lopez-Willshaw, Antenor Patino, and Carlos de Beistegui, Polo filled his apartment with the rarest of rare furniture, including pieces that had once belonged to Marie Antoinette. He tried to charm his way into French society with gifts and flowers, and he took tables in restaurants for fifteen or twenty people. Rosa became best friends with the wife of the antiques dealer Jean-Marie Rossi, who is the granddaughter of the late General Franco of Spain.

Polo hired the fashion consultant Eleanor Lambert to advise him on the buyout of the Miguel Cruz company. Cruz was paid a salary of $120,000 a year and a royalty on gross sales, although Polo claimed in an interview with *Women's Wear Daily* that he paid Cruz a minimum annual salary of $500,000. His intention was to vault Cruz into the ranks of the elite international designers of expensive ready-to-wear and to rival the houses of Giorgio Armani and Gianni Versace.

To launch the venture, Polo made an agreement with a retailer named Scarpa to turn her shops in Venice and Milan into Miguel Cruz boutiques. Scarpa received merchandise on consignment. Polo made a similar deal with a boutique owner on the island of Capri, and he paid $300,000 for the renovation of the shop. By the time the business opened, Polo had three boutiques, an office in the General Motors Building in New York with a rent of approximately $12,000 a month, and a showroom and warehouse in Milan. In spite of this huge overhead, Polo decided to launch an enormous advertising campaign. In the first season he spent $700,000 for media (media means buying space) and $30,000 on production. For the spring 1986 collection, there was an $800,000 advertising budget. For the fall 1986 collection, Polo spent $900,000 on advertising.

Consider, now, PAMG's contract with its investors: PAMG received a fee of one-half of 1 percent for managing an account. So on a $1 million account the annual fee would be $5,000. On a $100 million account, the fee would be $500,000. Therefore, people who worked for PAMG naturally began to wonder where the money was coming from to run the Miguel Cruz dress business as well as to cover Polo's continued buying of art and jewelry.

From the beginning, Polo played an active part in advertising and promotion, hiring the models, flying them to New York to be photographed, even staging the fashion shows. Fashion experts say that the campaign didn't work commercially, even if the photography was sometimes great. Like so much about Roberto Polo, his advertising sent out mixed signals; there was confusion as to whether he was selling his wares or his models. He claimed that he would make the name of Miguel Cruz known through the shock value of the ads. "We're living in a society that wants to be shocked," he told one interviewer. A Robert Mapplethorpe photograph for the Miguel Cruz men's line showed the back of a seated naked man removing a sweater over his head. For the women's line, a two-page ad showed a dimly lit female model in a black jeweled evening dress with one fully lit naked man behind her and another sitting on the floor in front of her.

It enraged Polo that while no one questioned the propriety of Calvin Klein's massively nude advertising campaign, which was going on at the same time, his own campaign was labeled prurient and offensive. "They object to my ads but not to Calvin Klein's." The advertisement showing the bull's-eye picture with the male rump may have offended one segment of the public, but a more lurid segment bombarded the New York office for copies of it.

Polo always knew more about everything than the experts. Soon he started directing Mapplethorpe's photo sessions, and Mapplethorpe, a bit of a prima donna himself, resented the interference. Eventually there was a falling-out, and Mapplethorpe resigned the account. Not to be topped, Polo wrote the photographer a letter firing him, and sent copies to several prominent people in New York.

Despite all the fanfare and hype, the Miguel Cruz line was a disaster almost from the beginning. The clothes were often badly made, delivery dates were missed, and orders were canceled. "I don't care about your four pages in *Vogue*—the clothes are not in my store" became a common complaint. It got to the point where the company was doing $1 million in advertising and only $100,000 in sales. In the fall of 1987, when all the collections of all the designers in Paris, New York, and Milan were showing skirts above the knee, Miguel Cruz was showing skirts down to the ankle. At that point Polo stepped in to give Cruz artistic advice on how the clothes should look, and he began writing memos telling him what colors and fabrics to use.

Unlike Polo's art acquisitions, which could be sold at a profit, the Miguel Cruz fashion venture was a bottomless pit. It is estimated that Polo lost between $12 million and $15 million on it, but he remained adamant in his belief that the clothes were beautiful and that the company was going to be a big success. He didn't want anyone to tell him the truth. He had a blind spot about Miguel Cruz, and he could not accept criticism. He thought that if he spent an enormous amount of money on advertising he should be rewarded with good reviews. He wrote irate letters to Polly Mellen of *Vogue* and Carrie Donovan of the *New York Times* threatening to pull his ads when they criticized the collections, and he had to be restrained from mailing a mocking letter to Hebe Dorsey, the late beloved fashion editor, demanding a retraction because she had mistakenly said Miguel Cruz designed in

Rome in the fifties when she meant the sixties. He had the idea that American editors could be bought. One of the most powerful women in fashion, who asked that she not be identified, told me that on the morning after one of the collections was shown in Milan she received in her hotel room a box containing a full-length black coat lined in sable. She tried it on, modeled it in front of a mirror, wrapped it up again, and returned it to Roberto Polo at the Miguel Cruz office. A former employee told me that Hebe Dorsey had returned many such gifts.

Peter Dubow, the owner of a company called European Collections Inc., was hired by Polo as a consultant to use his retailing contacts to penetrate the American stores. Dubow, who, like a lot of Roberto Polo's employees, is still owed a great deal of money in salary and expenses, says, "The easy speculation is that Roberto didn't care if the collections weren't good, that he was simply getting dirty money back into circulation. But he did care. He cared passionately."

One day in Paris, in the magnificent apartment on Quai Anatole-France, Dubow said to Polo, "We need someone to stage the fashion shows. We need an art director for the advertising."

"That's what I do," replied Roberto quietly.

Trying another tack, Dubow said about the latest collection, "It's not good enough. It's totally lacking in commerciality." He even went a step further. "It is ugly, Roberto."

Polo said, "How many Fragonards do you own?"

"None," replied Dubow.

With a gesture, Polo indicated his possessions in the drawing room where they were seated. "Do you own furniture like this?"

"No," said Dubow.

"Well, I think Miguel's collection is beautiful," said Polo, in his superiority, settling the matter. "I cannot imagine how ready-to-wear can be any more beautiful than this."

It is a curious quirk of Roberto's business sense that he gave priority to the evening dresses he presented as free gifts to society women in New York to wear to publicized social functions at a time when stores he depended on for business were not getting their shipments on time and orders were being canceled. To set things right, Roberto hired his brother, Marco, to be chief of production for the fashion house. There had always been a rivalry between the two brothers, particularly for the affection of their mother, and it was she who asked Roberto to take Marco into the company. Marco had wanted to go into the investment side of Roberto's business, not the fashion side, because he thought he knew more about banking than Roberto did. "When I was a kid, I used to beat the shit out of my brother, and now he's this big man ordering me around," Marco complained to an American employee of the business. At Miguel Cruz, Marco did a good job of putting the business in order, but the quality of the workmanship remained poor and orders were rarely delivered on time.

Late in 1987, at a party in Milan for the opening of a collection, Polo met Fabrizio Bagaglini. A sometime actor, sometime model, the twenty-five-year-old Bagaglini became a dominant figure in the life of Roberto Polo over the next seven months, right up until Polo's actual arrest in Viareggio. Shortly after meeting Fabrizio, Polo hired him to do his public-relations work, although Bagaglini was not known to have any experience or skill in that field.

In an interview conducted before the warrant went out for Polo's arrest, but published after, Nadine Frey of WWD wrote, "As a last gesture, [Polo] gave a mini-tour of his apartment, as Barry White blared out of a speaker somewhere and a handsome Roman aide-de-camp hustled out to make a lunch reservation." Roberto showed off Fabrizio as if he were a painting. He told people that he wanted to make Fabrizio the vice president of the perfume company he was planning to start, to be called Le Parfum de Miguel Cruz. Bagaglini began wearing Roberto's wristwatch, an eighteen-karat-gold Breitling, and Polo gave him a Ferrari Testarossa, worth $134,000, at a time when the unpaid bills and salaries at the Miguel Cruz office in New York amounted to $600,000. On several occasions, Polo said to his friends, "I have had three passions in my life: my wife, Rosa, my daughter, Marina, and Fabrizio." However, he persistently claimed that the friendship with Fabrizio was no more than a friendship.

Glamorous pictures of the glamorous Polos began appearing in all the fashionable magazines in France, usually showing them elegantly posed amid their museum-quality possessions. Elsewhere in the world, meanwhile, Mexican, Latin American, and European investors in PAMG were demanding to know where all the Polo money was coming from. "Roberto took too high a profile. He was too much in the

papers, lived on far too grand a scale. His investors didn't like it, especially as he was living on a far grander scale than they," said Alfredo
Ortiz-Murias, Polo's associate. Ortiz-Murias had at one time been
Roberto's superior at Citibank. He had left the bank to form his own
money-management firm, but, according to Polo, it had not done well,
and he later joined PAMG, bringing his own clients with him. Ortiz-
Murias claims to have introduced Roberto Polo to everyone in New
York, but Polo says otherwise. The former associates are now bitter
enemies.

Polo's behavior became more and more extreme. According to an
employee of Miguel Cruz's men's wear in Milan, "The stories he told
about himself became more and more fantastic, brilliant strokes of
genius—how he had bought things at one price and sold them a short
time later at enormous profits, like a pearl he bought for half a million
dollars and resold for a million. He said, 'I always have $10 million in
cash on hand.' "

Once, he showed up in the lobby of the Hotel Palace in Milan and
requested twenty-five rooms for important people he was flying in to
see the Miguel Cruz collection. The hotel, part of the CIGA hotel
group, owned by the Aga Khan, was totally booked for the fashion
week of the Milan collections and therefore unable to provide these
accommodations. Polo made a loud scene. "Get the Aga Khan on the
telephone!" he screamed indignantly.

He met Grace Jones and signed her up as a runway model for three
shows. At a time when the company was in serious trouble, he offered
her $50,000 for each appearance. Jones wisely insisted on being paid
in advance before each show.

He became a confider of intimate secrets, assuring each confidant
that he or she was the only person he could trust. "I find that I wake
up in a different bed each morning," he told an associate, who later
discovered he had shared the same intimacy with his publicist and a
number of friends. In October 1987, during the collections, he called
several people, some he didn't even know very well, sobbing, saying he
was getting a divorce. Rosa was said to be jealous of the female models
in the shows, and at one point she packed and left Milan for Paris.
There she remembered she had left her jewelry behind in the hotel
safe, so she returned, and everything was all right between them again.

One observer told me that Polo got "weirder and weirder." He dieted down to 145 pounds and began to dye the hair on his chest.

Last February, amid persistent widespread rumors of imminent financial troubles, he appeared at a sale in Monte Carlo with Fabrizio Bagaglini and a whippet dog and paid $500,000 for a pair of chairs by the French furniture-maker Sené, chairs so rare that they could not be taken out of France.

That same month, Pablo Aramburuzabala, who had been Roberto Polo's first major client and who had a sort of father-son relationship with him, flew from Mexico to Paris to confront him about all the rumors. "The investors were nervous and not happy hearing all the publicity he was getting, being described as a Cuban-American millionaire," he told me. "He didn't have time to make that kind of money unless he was doing something wrong. People start to do little things and get away with it and then start to take more and more. I gave him his chance. My wife is the godmother of his daughter. I met Roberto at Citibank. Then he started being money manager with me. It was just a matter of calling several banks to see which bank gave the best interest. I would see him four times a year, and he would tell me how my portfolio was. In February I asked him, 'Do you have financial problems?' He said no. He said that Mr. Ortiz-Murias was making trouble. I said to him, 'I don't think you have that kind of money.' I never authorized him to deal with art. He said that he had a syndicate of people for buying art. He told me he was managing a billion dollars. When I commented on Rosa's jewels, I was told that some of her jewels were lent by jewelers as a way of advertising. I said to him, 'I need some money. You have to give me some money back.' After a while I received part of it, not even 30 percent of the amount. Later, another small part, even smaller than the previous payment. I realized that things were in terrible shape. He promised to come to Mexico to straighten things out, but he never came."

The New York office of Miguel Cruz was run on money that was sent each month from Geneva. It took approximately $200,000 a month to keep the New York end of the business going, and more often than not only half that amount was sent. Salaries and bills went unpaid. By the end of 1987 there were bills in excess of $1 million. "A lot of people have been hurt by the unpaid bills, including Miguel

Cruz himself," said Peter Dubow. "Miguel always paid his bills, and the matter was highly embarrassing for him."

In the fall of 1987, Roberto Polo made his biggest play for social recognition, as well as a last-ditch bid to promote the flailing fashion line, by underwriting two famous balls, the Save Venice ball in Venice to help restore the Church of Santa Maria dei Miracoli, followed seventeen days later by the Chantilly Ball in France to benefit the Institute of France. They attracted the crème de la crème of international society. With rumors everywhere that he was financially strapped, Polo spent over $600,000—some say closer to a million—on the two events. In addition, it was reported in society columns that he flew guests from all over the world by private jet to attend the parties. The talk of the Save Venice ball was Rosa Polo's jewels, in all the colors. She swam each day in the swimming pool of the Hotel Cipriani in a different bathing suit with a necklace of precious stones to match. Meanwhile, the people in the warehouse in Milan had to pass the hat to pay for the gasoline to get the collection to the Chantilly Ball. After that they sent the collection to New York for the fashion week there, but the New York office didn't have the money to get it out of customs.

Polo's hope, apparently, was that his new perfume company would rescue his collapsing empire. At a cost of nearly $1 million, he built a new office for Le Parfum de Miguel Cruz on Avenue Marceau in Paris. He hired as the president of the company Jacques Bergerac, the fifties movie star, who had been married to Ginger Rogers and Dorothy Malone, and who had more recently—before the takeover by Ronald Perelman—been a high-ranking executive at Revlon. He also hired the New York architectural and design firm of de Marsillac Plunkett to design the bottles and packaging. He himself played an important part in choosing the scents for the perfume. The perfume business, however, is considered a seven-to-one shot for success, and it usually takes two to three years before profits begin to show. To finance Le Parfum and perhaps to settle with his disgruntled investors, who were beginning to demand their money back, Polo is reported to have sold $22 million in jewels between February and May.

He drew more international press by announcing that he had donated to the Louvre the Empress Eugénie crown, valued at $2.5 million, and Fragonard's *The Adoration of the Shepherds*, valued at between $2.5 million and $5 million. At a well-publicized ceremony attended by sixty guests in evening clothes, the French government expressed its gratitude by making him a Commander of the Order of Arts and Letters.

Next Polo announced that he was putting his famous collection of eighteenth-century French paintings up for sale. In what is thought to have been an I'll-pat-your-back-if-you-pat-mine gesture, Pierre Rosenberg, the distinguished curator of paintings at the Louvre, wrote the preface to the catalog for the sale, even though it is frowned on in museum circles for museum people to become involved in such commercial enterprises. To counteract the speculation that he was selling his collection to meet the demands of his investors, or to save his failing dress business, or to finance his perfume business, Roberto Polo wrote the foreword to the beautiful catalog, in which he said, "Collectors can be divided into two groups: those who satisfy their appetite by the endless accumulation of things and those who are most excited by the 'hunt,' the search and research of things. The latter kind of collector satisfies his appetite and curiosity for the collectible once he has it and squeezes out of it, as from a ripe fruit, all the juice that it has to give, then moves on to a different collectible . . . I am one of those collectors." Polo said he expected the sale to bring in between $18 million and $20 million.

When Alfredo Ortiz-Murias returned home from the Venice and Chantilly balls, he observed to Ramona Colón that he had seen a change in Roberto's personality. Ramona Colón told him that she thought Roberto had been transferring clients' money to "third parties." Ortiz-Murias claims that that was his first knowledge of malfeasance on the part of Polo. Colón stated in her affidavit that Polo would direct her to transfer a client's deposit to the PAMG-NY account and then to the ITKA account. "I noticed that some client time deposit cards were marked 'PAMG' in Roberto's handwriting. Although these time deposit cards were regularly updated and statements sent to the clients continued to report these time deposits, I believe that the entries and statements were fraudulent and that the time deposits no longer existed. . . . Sometime in mid-1984, I calculated the total shown on all cards marked 'PAMG' and the total was about $37 million."

Colón also stated in her affidavit, "I saw Roberto take home shopping bags full of client transfer records and other client information. Since I worked with the files on a daily basis, I know he never brought the records or information back. On one occasion, when Alfredo Ortiz-Murias requested some information on one of his clients and the record could not be found, Roberto explained that he had probably burned it in his fireplace by mistake. Also, during that time, Roberto instructed me to erase all the time deposit computer records. He told me that if they could not be erased, he would throw the computers into the river. Following Roberto's instructions, I contacted a man at Commercial Software, Inc., and he instructed me on how to erase the computer records, which I did."

Alfredo Ortiz-Murias began to notify his own clients and others that there was trouble, and the clients began to place calls on their assets, meaning, in layman's terms, they wanted their money back, immediately. In one of his letters from prison, Polo has said, "Rostuca advised PAMG in December 1987 that it wished to terminate its relationship; the other clients did the same in April and May of 1988; this means that PAMG was in the obligation to repay its clients between December of 1988 and June of 1989, at the earliest. Now as before this scandal, PAMG is prepared to pre-pay, but Alfredo is not interested, because as he said, 'I hate Roberto. I only want his blood.' "

When too many of Polo's investors demanded their money at the same time, it was like a run on the bank. He could not meet their demands. But that, his defenders say, did not make him a crook.

A Swiss arrest warrant was issued on April 30. The Swiss were expecting Polo to appear at the opening of the exhibition of twenty-six paintings that were to be auctioned on May 30, but he didn't show up. In the meantime the Swiss judge got in touch with the French police, and an international arrest warrant was issued. At that time Polo made a call from Paris to Milan from a street telephone. "Don't call me at home," he said. "The telephones are tapped."

On May 8, Roberto Polo and Fabrizio Bagaglini were in Haiti. Polo intended to start a new collection of pictures to replace his collection of French masterpieces. An American friend, Kurt Thometz, and his wife were in Paris at the time. They visited the Polo apartment and said there were already between thirty-five and forty Haitian paintings in one room. Roberto was also buying Dominican art, including some new works by his father-in-law.

On May 11, Polo was seen at a jewel auction in Geneva, selling.

On May 12, he was seen in the South of France with Rosa, Fabrizio, the child, the nanny, and Julio Cordero, Rosa's cousin, who was the manager of the Geneva office, and his wife.

On May 15, the group was in Monte Carlo, and Polo's life seemed out of control. With an international warrant out for his arrest, he arrived that afternoon at the Hôtel de Paris apartment of Baby Monteiro de Carvalho, the richest man in Brazil, to watch the Grand Prix, which raced by in the square below. He was accompanied by Rosa, Marina, and Fabrizio, and other guests commented that he seemed harassed.

On May 16, police entered the office of the Miguel Cruz perfume company in Paris and told the staff that Roberto Polo was under arrest. The feeling, according to Ortiz-Murias, is that perhaps the employees alerted Polo. He and his family returned from the South of France that night. Rosa and the child went to the apartment, but Roberto did not. Instead he went to a hotel.

On May 17, Roberto disappeared.

On May 18, at nine o'clock in the morning, the police and detectives walked into the Polo apartment. Rosa was there. The police seized $26 million in furniture and paintings, leaving her with only two mattresses on the floor. Rosa asked the police if she could keep her engagement ring, and they let her.

The Ferrari Testarossa was seized in Monte Carlo.

In the days that followed, several people in New York had direct-dial overseas calls from Polo. Eleanor Lambert told me, "He didn't give his name. He simply said, 'You know who this is, don't you?' I said yes, and he went on to say that all the stories about him were lies spread by Alfredo Ortiz-Murias, and that in time his name would be cleared." People who knew him best said that he would not allow the police to catch him, that he would take sleeping pills.

"I wouldn't be surprised if he was dead," said an antiques dealer in New York.

"A suicide?" I asked.

"No, murdered."

"Murdered?"

"You must understand that there are a lot of people who don't want him to be found, because he could incriminate them."

In addition to the investors who did not want to be identified, several of the antiques dealers Polo did business with in Europe were said to have been paid partially in their own country and partially in Switzerland, a practice not only frowned upon but considered criminal in some countries.

The whereabouts of Roberto Polo and Fabrizio Bagaglini between May 16 and the end of June, when they turned up in Viareggio, remains a mystery, although the most persistent speculation at the time, later proved incorrect, was that they were in Peru, Chile, or Brazil. Alfredo Ortiz-Murias believes that Polo was hiding out in an apartment in Paris, because Rosa Polo, who was then under surveillance, left her apartment each afternoon and went to the Hôtel Ritz on the Place Vendôme to use the public telephone, presumably to call her husband. In one of the press releases Polo wrote from the prison in Lucca, he says about this period, "Prior to going to Viareggio, I had been in my apartment in Monte Carlo, at the Hôtel de Paris (also in Monte Carlo), at the Hôtel Hermitage (also in Monte Carlo), at Hôtel Le Richemond in Geneva (registered in my name), and before that in Port-au-Prince in Haiti with friends and Santo Domingo, Dominican Republic, with family." There is no doubt that he was in all those places, but earlier than May 16. There is further speculation that the French police did not want to make the arrest in France because a nephew of President Mitterand, Maxime Mitterand, was an employee in the Geneva office of PAMG, Ltd.

On May 30, the auction of Polo's French masterpieces went on in Paris as scheduled. Five days earlier, Ader Picard Tajan, the auctioneer, had called a press conference to explain that the sale would be a "forced one" and that he would be the "receiver" for the courts. Surprisingly, the highly publicized sale did not draw crowds. The $14 million realized from it was $3.4 million less than had been expected. There was talk in art circles that if the works donated to the Louvre by Polo had been purchased with money that was not his own the Louvre would have to return them.

After Polo's arrest in Viareggio, Fabrizio Bagaglini returned to

Rome, where he remained for two weeks. From there he went to Paris and then on to London with a rich Argentinean girlfriend.

As of this writing, Roberto Polo has been denied bail by the Italians. Here in America, in addition to the ongoing investigations reportedly being conducted by the IRS and the SEC, the FBI is now allegedly involved in collecting evidence to see if there has been mail fraud, if, as Ramona Colón claimed in her affidavit, Polo sent false statements to his investors each month. On East Sixty-fourth Street in Manhattan, the gray stucco Italianate front of the Polos' town house is cracked and peeling. Inside, the lights stay on day and night. All the furniture is gone except for a set of six upholstered chairs, a chaise longue, and a sofa, all covered in chintz, that were left behind in the sitting room of the master bedroom, and an Aubusson rug, folded in one corner. On the front door is a notice that says, "Warning: "U.S. Government seizure. This property has been seized for non-payment of internal revenue taxes, due from Roberto Polo, by virtue of levy issued by the District Director of the Internal Revenue Service."

From prison Roberto Polo wrote me saying he was reading *One Hundred Years of Solitude* while awaiting the determination of his fate. He also issues communiqués and ultimatums, as if he were in the best bargaining position. In response to the criticism that his lifestyle surpassed that of the people whose money he handled, he wrote, "It is quite stupid to state that my lifestyle is better than that of my clients: I have a better education and sense of the quality of life, as well as make more money than any of them singly! Does the President or Chairman of the Board of Citibank, for example, live better than most of the bank's clients? Of course he does! PAMG, Ltd. has clients who are worth U.S. $20,000,000, but who don't know any better than to buy their clothes at Alexander's when they visit New York or who dine at coffee shops!"

From Mexico City, Pablo Aramburuzabala said, "Yesterday Polo said that if we didn't accept his offer to accept the money that had already been frozen he was going to tell everyone who we were. I said that my money is not dirty money. He can go ahead and tell."

In New York, Alfredo Ortiz-Murias says he has received irate calls from Roberto Polo's mother in Miami. She says she will not rest until she sees Alfredo in jail. Chantal Carr has become engaged to Marco Polo. Rosa Polo continues to live with Marina in the stripped-down apartment in Paris. The Miguel Cruz fashion house is defunct, and the perfume company is at a standstill. Everyone is waiting.

Jacques Kam, Polo's French lawyer, told me when he was in New York on the case, "There are many things in the stories that are quite wrong, 100 percent wrong." He added, "It is not the round that counts. It is the match. This whole case could boomerang."

Like the people who danced the nights away in the various discotheques of Imelda Marcos and then, after her fall from grace, pretended not to have known her, or claimed to have only met her, many of the recipients of Roberto Polo's largess act now as if the Polos had been no more than passing acquaintances, although they attended their parties and accepted free evening dresses from the ill-fated Miguel Cruz collections. Such is life in the fast lane. There are those, however, who remember Roberto Polo differently, for example the Chilean painter Benjamin Lira and his artist wife, Francisca Sutil. "The Roberto Polo we know doesn't match with this man we have been reading and hearing about," Lira said. They remember their friend Roberto as a devout family man and a loving and generous friend, with whom they went to concerts and films and galleries, and with whom they spent long evenings in their loft or in the Polos' town house, discussing art.

"Roberto's understanding of art goes far beyond taste," said Francisca Sutil. Eleanor Lambert agreed: "He was not just showing off. He was someone with real destiny. He could have been one of the great authorities on art, another Bernard Berenson."

October 1988

Roberto Polo was livid about this article. He sent me what I thought was a threatening letter, but I never did anything about it. He did time. He got out. There are occasional sightings of him. His jet set days are over. Most recently, he is said to be living quietly in Miami.

DANSE MACABRE: THE
ROCKEFELLER AND THE BALLET BOYS

There is no one, not even his severest detractor, and let me tell you at the outset of this tale that he has a great many severe detractors, who will not concede that Raymundo de Larrain, who sometimes uses the questionable title of the Marquis de Larrain, is, or at least was, before he took the road to riches by marrying a Rockefeller heiress nearly forty years his senior, a man of considerable talent, who, if he had persevered in his artistic pursuits, might have made a name for himself on his own merit. Instead his name, long a fixture in the international social columns, is today at the center of the latest in a rash of contested-will controversies in which wildly rich American families go to court to slug it out publicly for millions of dollars left to upstart spouses the same age as or, in this case, younger than the disinherited adult children.

The most interesting person in this story is the late possessor of the now disputed millions, Margaret Strong de Cuevas de Larrain, who died in Madrid on December 2, 1985, at the age of eighty-eight, and the key name to keep in mind is the magical one of Rockefeller. Margaret de Larrain had two children, Elizabeth and John, from her first marriage, to the Marquis George de Cuevas. The children do not know the whereabouts of her remains, or even whether she was, as a member of the family put it, incinerated in Madrid. What they do know is that during the eight years of their octogenarian mother's marriage to Raymundo de Larrain, her enormous real-estate holdings, which included adjoining town houses in New York, an apartment in Paris, a country house in France, a villa in Tuscany, and a resort home in Palm Beach, were given away or sold, although she had been known

397

throughout her life to hate parting with any of her belongings, even the most insubstantial things. At the time of her second marriage, in 1977, she had assets of approximately $30 million (some estimates go as high as $60 million), including 350,000 shares of Exxon stock in a custodian account at the Chase Manhattan Bank. The location of the Exxon shares is currently unknown, and documents presented by her widower show that his late wife's assets amount to only $400,000. Although these sums may seem modest in terms of today's billion-dollar fortunes, Margaret, at the time of her inheritance, was considered one of the richest women in the world. There are two wills in question: a 1968 will leaving the fortune to the children and a 1980 will leaving it to the widower. In the upcoming court case, the children, who are fifty-eight and fifty-six years old, are charging that the will submitted by de Larrain, who is fifty-two, represents "a massive fraud on an aging, physically ill, trusting lady."

Although Margaret Strong de Cuevas de Larrain was a reluctant news figure for five decades, the facts of her birth, her fortune, and the kind of men she married denied her the privacy she craved. However, her children, Elizabeth, known as Bessie, and John, have so successfully guarded their privacy, as well as that of their children, that they are practically anonymous in the social world in which they were raised. John de Cuevas, who has been described as almost a hermit, has never used the title of marquis. He is now divorced from his second wife, Sylvia Iolas de Cuevas, the niece of the art dealer Alexander Iolas, who was a friend of his father. His only child is a daughter from that marriage, now in her twenties. He maintains homes in St. James, Long Island, and Cambridge, Massachusetts, where he teaches scientific writing at Harvard. Bessie de Cuevas, a sculptor whose work resembles that of Archipenko, lives in New York City and East Hampton, Long Island. She is also divorced, and has one daughter, twenty-two, by her second husband, Joel Carmichael, the editor of *Midstream*, a Zionist magazine so reactionary that it recently published an article accusing the pope of being soft on Marxism. Friends of Bessie de Cuevas told me that she was never bothered by the short financial reins her mother kept her on, because she did not fall prey to fortune hunters the way her sister heiresses, like Sunny von Bülow, did.

Margaret Strong de Cuevas de Larrain, the twice-titled American heiress, grew up very much like a character in a Henry James novel. In fact, Henry James, as well as William James, visited her father's villa outside Florence when she was young. Margaret was the only child of Bessie Rockefeller, the eldest of John D. Rockefeller's five children, and Charles Augustus Strong, a philosopher and psychologist, whose father, Augustus Hopkins Strong, a Baptist clergyman and theologian, had been a great friend of old Rockefeller. A mark of the brilliance of Margaret's father was that, while at Harvard, he competed with fellow student George Santayana for a scholarship at a German university and won. He then shared the scholarship with Santayana, who remained his lifelong friend. Margaret was born in New York, but the family moved shortly thereafter to Paris. When Margaret was nine her mother died, and Strong, who never remarried, built his villa in Fiesole, outside Florence. There, in a dour and austere atmosphere, surrounded by intellectuals and philosophers, he raised his daughter and wrote more scholarly books. His world provided very little amusement for a child, and no frivolity.

Each year Margaret returned to the United States to see her grandfather, with whom she maintained a good relationship, and to visit her Rockefeller cousins. Old John D. was amused by his serious and foreign granddaughter, who spoke several languages and went to school in England. Later, she was one of only three women attending Cambridge University, where she studied chemistry. Never, even as a young girl, could she have been considered attractive. She was big, bulky, and shy, and until the age of twenty-eight she always wore variations of the same modest sailor dress.

Her father was eager for her to marry, and toward that end Margaret went to Paris to live, although she had few prospects in sight. Following the Russian Revolution there was an influx of Russian émigrés into Paris, and Margaret Strong developed a fascination for them that remained with her all her life. She was most excited to meet the tall and elegant Prince Felix Yusupov, the assassin of Rasputin, who was said to have used his beautiful wife, Princess Irina, as a lure to attract the womanizing Rasputin to his palace on the night of the murder. In Paris, Prince Yusupov had taken to wearing pink rouge and green eyeshadow, and he supported himself by heading up a house of couture called Irfé, a combination of the first syllables of his and his wife's names. Into this hothouse of fashion, one day in 1927, walked the thirty-year-old, prim, studious, and unfashionable Rockefeller heiress. At that time Prince Yusupov had working for him an epicene and penniless young Chilean named George de Cuevas, who was, according to friends who remember him from that period, "extremely amusing and lively." He spoke with a strong Spanish accent and expressed himself in a wildly camp manner hitherto totally unknown to the sheltered lady. The story goes that at first Margaret mistook George de Cuevas for the prince. "What do you do at the couture?" she asked. "I'm the saleslady," he replied. The plain, timid heiress was enchanted with him, and promptly fell in love, thereby establishing what would be a lifelong predilection for flamboyant, effete men. The improbable pair were married in 1928.

From then on Margaret abandoned almost all intellectual activity. She stepped out of the pages of a Henry James novel into the pages of a Ronald Firbank novel. If her father had been the dominant figure of her maidenhood, George de Cuevas was the controlling force of her adult existence. Their life became more and more frivolous, capricious, and eccentric. Through her husband she discovered an exotic new world that centered on the arts, especially the ballet, for which George had a deep and abiding passion. Their beautiful apartment on the Quai Voltaire, filled with pets and bibelots and opulent furnishings, became a gathering place for the *haute bohème* of Paris, as did their country house in St.-Germain-en-Laye, where their daughter, Bessie, was born in 1929. Their son, John, was born two years later. Along the way the title of marquis was granted by, or purchased from, the King of Spain. The Chilean son of a Spanish father, George de Cuevas is listed in some dance manuals as the eighth Marquis de Piedrablanca de Guana de Cuevas, but the wife of a Spanish grandee, who wished not to be identified, told me that the title was laughed at in Spain. Nonetheless, the Marquis and Marquesa de Cuevas remained a highly visible couple on the international and artistic scenes for the next thirty years.

When World War II broke out, they moved to the United States. Margaret, already a collector of real estate, began to add to her holdings. She bought a town house on East Sixty-eighth Street in New

York, a mansion in Palm Beach, and a weekend place in Bernardsville, New Jersey. She also acquired a house in Riverdale, New York, which they never lived in but visited, and one in New Mexico to be used in the event the United States was invaded. In New York, Margaret always kept a rented limousine, and sometimes two, all day every day in front of her house in case she wanted to go out.

Although Margaret had inherited a vast fortune, she was to inherit a vaster one through the persistence of her husband. George de Cuevas's wooing of his wife's grandfather, old John D. Rockefeller, turned Margaret from a rich woman into a very rich woman. While John D. had bestowed liberal inheritances on his four daughters during their lifetimes, he believed in primogeniture, and in his late seventies he turned over the bulk of his $500 million fortune to his only son, John D. Rockefeller, Jr., the father of Abby, John D. III, Nelson, Laurence, Winthrop, and David. He retained the income for himself. Margaret at that time was indifferent to her inheritance, but George, for whom the prospect of Rockefeller millions had surely been a lure in his choice of a life mate, was not one to sit back and watch what he felt should be his wife's share pass on to her already very rich Rockefeller cousins. He set about to charm his grandfather-in-law, and charm him he did. He even became his golfing companion. Rockefeller had never come across such a person as this eccentric bird of paradise that his granddaughter had married. Surprisingly, he not only was amused by him but genuinely liked him. The family legend goes that one day George took Bessie and John by the hand to the old man and said, "Do you want to see your great-grandchildren starve because their mother has not been taken care of the way the rest of the Rockefellers have been?" The tycoon calmly assured him that Margaret would be provided for. Old John D. then began investing his enormous income in the stock market and in the last years of his life made a second fortune, the bulk of which he left to Margaret on his death, when she was forty years old.

In 1940, in Toms River, New Jersey, George de Cuevas became an American citizen and renounced his Spanish title, claiming he would henceforth be known as merely George de Cuevas. However, he continued to be referred to by his title, and once his role as a ballet impresario grew to international prominence, he changed the name of the company associated with him throughout his career from the Ballet de Monte Carlo to the Grand Ballet du Marquis de Cuevas. From 1947 to 1960 the marquis toured the company all over the world, with the financial support of his wife, who donated 15 percent of her income to his troupe. He introduced American dancers to France and French dancers to America, and soon became a beloved figure in the dance world. The impresario Sol Hurok in his biography described him as "a colorful gentleman of taste and culture . . . perhaps the outstanding example we have today of the sincere and talented amateur in and patron of the arts."

Actually, de Cuevas is better remembered for one episode of histrionics and temperament than for any of his productions. In 1958 the dancer and choreographer Serge Lifar, then fifty-two years old, became angry when the marquis's company changed the choreography of his ballet *Black and White*. After a heated exchange of words the marquis, who was seventy-two at the time, slapped Lifar in the face with a handkerchief in public and then refused to apologize. Lifar challenged de Cuevas to a duel, and the marquis accepted. Although neither of the combatants was known as a swordsman, épées were chosen as the weapons. The location of the duel was to be kept secret because dueling was outlawed in France, but more than fifty tipped-off reporters and photographers showed up at the scene. The encounter was scheduled to last until blood was drawn. For the first four minutes of the duel Serge Lifar leapt about while the marquis remained stationary. In the third round the marquis forced Lifar back by simply advancing with his sword held straight out in front of him, and pinked his opponent. It was not clear, according to newspaper accounts of the duel, whether skill or accident brought the marquis's blade into contact with Lifar's arm. "Blood has flowed! Honor is saved!" cried Lifar. Both men burst into tears and rushed to embrace each other. Reporting the event on its front page, the *New York Times* said that the affair "might well have been the most delicate encounter in the history of French dueling."

As a couple, the Marquis and Marquesa de Cuevas became increasingly eccentric. "It was unconventional, their marriage, but, curiously, it worked," said Viscountess Jacqueline de Ribes, who was a frequent guest in their Paris apartment. "There were always people waiting in the hall to have an audience—it was like a court," said one family member. Another longtime observer of the inner workings of the de Cuevas household, Jean Pierre Lacloche, said, "Margaret was always in her room during the parties. She hated coming out, but usually she finally did. She gave in to all of George's pranks. She didn't care. He made life interesting around her." George de Cuevas often received visitors lying in bed wearing a black velvet robe with a sable collar and surrounded by his nine or ten Pekingese dogs, while Margaret grew more and more reclusive and slovenly in her dress. She always wore black and kept an in-residence dressmaker to make the same dress for her over and over again. When she traveled to Europe, she would book passage on as many as six ships and then be unable to make up her mind as to which she wanted to sail. If she wanted to go from Palm Beach to New York, she would book seats on every train for a week, and then not be able to make the commitment to move. Once, unable to secure a last-minute booking on a Paris-Biarritz train and determined to leave, no matter what, she piled her daughter, her maid, ten Pekingese dogs, and her luggage into a Paris taxicab and had the driver drive her the five hundred miles to Biarritz. The trip took three days.

George de Cuevas liked to entertain, and he filled their homes with society figures, titles, celebrated artists and dancers, and a constant flow of Russian émigrés. "At the Cuevas parties were such as the Queen Mother of Egypt, Maria Callas, and, of course, Salvador Dalí, who was a regular in the house," said Mafalda Davis, an Egyptian-born public-relations woman who was a great friend of George de Cuevas. George was a giver of gifts. He bought old furs and jewels from the poor Russians in Paris and gave them away as presents. He gave the Viscountess de Ribes a sable coat, and he gave Mrs. Gurney Munn of Palm Beach a watch on which he had had engraved "May the ticking of this watch remind you of the beauty of a faithful heart."

Somehow, in the midst of this affluent chaos on two continents, Bessie and John de Cuevas were raised. A relative of the family told me that Margaret had a good and strong relationship with her children. "Not a peasant-type relationship," he said, "not conventional," meaning, as I understood him, not many hugs and kisses, but strong in its way. Another relative said, "After a short period with her children—and later with her grandchildren—she was ready to send them out to play or to turn them over to their nanny. Margaret, who throughout her life was notorious for never being on time, arrived so late for her daughter's coming-out party at the Plaza Hotel in New York, which was attended by all of her Rockefeller relations, that she almost missed it. When Bessie was seventeen she met Hubert Faure, who became her first husband. "She was an extraordinary-looking person," said Faure about his former wife, with whom he has retained a close friendship. "English-American in intellect with a Spanish vitality behind that." Hubert Faure, now the chairman of United Technology, was not at the time considered a catch by the Marquis de Cuevas, who wanted his daughter to marry a Spanish grandee and possess a great title. But Bessie exhibited an early independence: she went ahead and married Faure in Paris in 1948, when she was nineteen, with no family and only another couple in attendance. John, her brother, was also married for the first time at an early age. The children, as Bessie and John are regularly referred to in the upcoming court case with Raymundo de Larrain, have at times shown a bemused attitude about their life. Once, when questioned about her nationality, Bessie described herself as a third-generation expatriate. John, during a brief Wall Street career, was asked by a colleague if he could possibly be related to a mad marquesa of the same name. "Yes," he is said to have replied, "she is a very distant mother."

The apex of the social career of George de Cuevas was reached in 1953 with a masked ball he gave in Biarritz: it vied with the Venetian masked ball given by Carlos de Beistegui in 1951 as the most elaborate fete of the decade. France at the time was paralyzed by a general strike. No planes or trains were running. Undaunted, the international nomads, with their couturier-designed eighteenth-century costumes tucked into their steamer trunks, made their way across Europe like migrating birds to participate in the *tableaux vivants* at the Marquis de Cuevas's ball, an event so extravagant that it was criticized by both the Vatican and the left wing. "People talked about it for months before," remembered Josephine Hartford Bryce, the A&P heiress, who recently donated her costume from the ball to the Metropolitan Museum of Art. "Everyone was dying to go to it. The costumes were fantastic, and people spent most of the evening just staring at each other." As they say in those circles, "everyone" came. Elsa Maxwell dressed as a man. The Duchess of Argyll, on the arm of the duke, who would later divorce her in the messiest divorce in the history of British society, came dressed as an angel. Ann Woodward, of the New York Woodwards, slapped a woman she thought was dancing too often with her husband, William, whom she was to shoot and kill two years later. King Peter of Yugoslavia waltzed with a diamond-tiaraed Merle Oberon. And at the center of it all was the Marquis George de Cuevas, in gold lamé with a headdress of grapes and towering ostrich plumes, who presided as the King of Nature. He was surrounded by the Four Seasons, in the costumed persons of the Count Charles de Ganay; Princess Marella Caracciolo, who would soon become the wife of Fiat king Gianni Agnelli; Bessie, his daughter; and her then husband, Hubert Faure. As always, Margaret de Cuevas did the unexpected. For days beforehand, her costume, designed by the great couturier Pierre Balmain, who had paid her the honor of coming to her for fittings, hung, like a presence, on a dress dummy in the hallway of the de Cuevas residence in Biarritz. But Margaret did not appear at the ball, although, of course, she paid for it. She may have been an unlikely Rockefeller, but she was still a Rockefeller, and the opulence, extravagance, and sheer size (four thousand people were asked and two thousand accepted) of the event offended her. She simply disappeared that night, and the party went on without her. She did, however, watch the arrival of the guests from a hidden location, and a much repeated, but unconfirmed story is that she sent her maid to the ball dressed in her Balmain costume.

George de Cuevas increasingly made his life and many homes available to a series of young male worldlings who enjoyed the company of older men. In the early 1950s Margaret de Cuevas purchased the town house adjoining hers on East Sixty-eighth Street in New York. The confirmation-of-sale letter from the realty firm of Douglas L. Elliman & Co. contained a cautionary line: "The Marquesa detests publicity and would appreciate it if her name weren't divulged." An unkind novel by Theodora Keogh, called *The Double Door*, depicted the marriage of George and Margaret and their teenage daughter. The double door of the title referred to the point of access between the two adjoining houses, beyond which the wife of the main character, a flamboyant nobleman, was not permitted to go, although the houses were hers. The drama of the novel revolved around the teenage daughter's clandestine romance with one of the handsome young men beyond the double door. Inevitably, the marriage of George and Margaret de Cuevas began to founder, and for the most part they occupied their various residences at different times. They maintained close communication, however, and Margaret would often call George in Paris or Cannes from New York or Palm Beach to deal with a domestic problem. Once when the marquesa's temperamental chef in Palm Beach became enraged at one of her unreasonable demands and threw her breakfast tray at her, she called her husband in Paris and asked him to call the chef and beseech him not only to quit but also to bring her another breakfast, because she was hungry. George finally persuaded the chef to recook the breakfast, but the man refused to carry it to Margaret. A maid in the house had to do that.

At this point in the story, Raymundo de Larrain entered the picture. "Raymundo is not just a little Chilean," said a lady of fashion in Paris about him. "He is from one of the four greatest families in Chile. The Larrains are aristocratic people, a better family by far than the de Cuevas family." Whatever he was, Raymundo de Larrain wanted to be something more than just another bachelor from Chile seeking extraman status in Paris society. He was talented, brilliant, and wildly extravagant, and soon began making a name for himself designing costumes and sets for George de Cuevas's ballet company. A protégé of the marquis's to start with, he soon became known as his nephew. An acquaintance who knew de Larrain at that time recalled that the card on the door of his sublet apartment first read M. Larrain. Later it became M. de Larrain. Later still it became the Marquis de Larrain.

In Bessie de Cuevas's affidavit in the upcoming probate proceedings, she emphatically states that although various newspapers have described de Larrain as the nephew of her father and suggested that he was raised by her parents, there was no blood relation between the two men. In a letter to an American friend in Paris, she wrote, "He is not my father's nephew. I think he planted the word long ago in Suzy's column. If there is any relationship at all, it is so remote as to be meaningless." Yet as recently as November, when I spoke with de Larrain in Palm Beach, he referred to George de Cuevas as "my uncle." The fact of the matter is that Raymundo de Larrain has been described as a de Cuevas nephew and has been using the title of marquis for years, and he was on a familiar basis with all members of the de Cuevas family. Longtime acquaintances in Paris remember Raymundo calling Margaret de Cuevas Tante Margaret or, sometimes, perhaps in levity, Tante Rockefeller. In her book *The Case of Salvador Dalí*, Fleur Cowles described the Dalí set in Paris as follows: "On May 9, 1957, the young nephew of the Marquis de Cuevas gave a ball in honor of the Dalís. According to Maggi Nolan, the social editor of the *Paris Herald-Tribune*, the Marquis Raymundo de Larrain's ball was 'unforgettable' in the apartment which had been converted . . . into a vast party confection," with "the most fabulous gala-attired members of international society." Fleur Cowles then went on to list the guests, including in their number the Marquis de Cuevas himself, without his wife, and M. and Mme. Hubert Faure, his daughter and son-in-law. Although Cowles did not say so, George de Cuevas almost certainly paid for Raymundo's ball.

Along the way de Larrain met the Viscountess Jacqueline de Ribes, one of the grandest ladies in Paris society and a ballet enthusiast to boot. "Before Jacqueline, no one had ever heard of Raymundo de Larrain except as a nephew of de Cuevas. Jacqueline was his stepping-stone into society," said another lady of international social fame who did not wish to be identified. The viscountess became an earlier admirer of his talent, and they entered into a close relationship that was to continue for years, sharing an interest in clothes and fashion as well as the ballet. Raymundo de Larrain is said to have made Jacqueline de Ribes over and given her the look that has remained her trademark for several decades. A famous photograph taken by Richard Avedon in 1961 shows the two of them in exotic matching profiles. At a charity party in New York known as the Embassy Ball, chaired by the Viscountess de Ribes, Mrs. Winston Guest, and the American-born Princess d'Arenberg, Raymundo de Larrain's fantastical butterfly décor was so extravagant that there was no money left for the charity that was meant to benefit from the event. In time the viscountess became known as the godmother of the ballet, and she, more than any other person, pushed the career of Raymundo de Larrain.

After the publication of *The Double Door*, the de Cuevases were often the subject of gossip in the sophisticated society in which they moved, but somehow they had the ability to keep scandal within the family perimeter. The relationship of both husband and wife with the unsavory Jan de Vroom, however, almost caused their peculiar habits to be open to public scrutiny. A family member said to me that at this point in Margaret de Cuevas's life she fell into a nest of vipers. Born in Dutch Indonesia, Jan de Vroom was a tall, blond adventurer who dominated drawing rooms by sheer force of personality rather than good looks. A wit, storyteller, and linguist, he had an eye for the main chance, and like a great many young men before him looking for the easy ride, he attached himself to George de Cuevas. De Vroom was quick to realize on which side the bread was buttered in the de Cuevas household, and, to the distress of the marquis, who soon grew to distrust him, he shifted his attentions to Margaret, whom he followed to the United States. At first Margaret was not disposed to like him, but, undeterred by her initial snubs, he schooled himself in Mozart, whom he knew to be her favorite composer, and soon found favor with her as a fellow Mozart addict. He got a small apartment in a brownstone a few blocks from Margaret's houses on East Sixty-eighth Street and was always available when she needed a companion for dinner. She set him up in business, as an importer of Italian glass and lamps. From Europe, George de Cuevas tried to break up the deepening intimacy, but Margaret, egged on by her friend Florence Gould, ignored her husband's protests. As the friendship grew, so did de Vroom's store of acquisitions. He was a sportsman, and through Margaret de Cuevas's bounty he soon owned a sleek sailing boat, a fleet of Ferrari cars, a Rolls-Royce, and—briefly, until it crashed—an airplane. He also acquired an important collection of rare watches.

Raymundo de Larrain and Jan de Vroom detested each other, and Jan, in the years when he was in favor with Margaret, refused to have Raymundo around. De Vroom had no wish to join the ranks of men who made their fortune at the altar; he was content to play the role of son to Margaret, a sort of naughty-boy son whose peccadilloes she easily forgave. A mixer in the darker worlds of New York and Florida, he entertained her with stories of his subterranean adventures. Often, in her own homes, she would be the only woman present at a dining table full of men who were disinterested in women.

In 1960 the Marquis de Cuevas, in failing health, offered Raymundo de Larrain, with whom he was now on the closest terms, the chance to create a whole new production of *The Sleeping Beauty*, to be performed at the Théâtre des Champs Élysées. De Larrain's *Sleeping Beauty* is still remembered as one of the most beautiful ballet productions of all time, and it was the greatest box-office success the company had ever experienced. The marquis was permitted by his physicians to attend the premiere. "If I am going to die, I will die backstage," he said. After the performance he was pushed out onto the stage in a wheelchair and received a standing ovation. George de Cuevas attended every performance up until two weeks before his death. He died at his favorite of the many de Cuevas homes, Les Délices, in Cannes, on February 22, 1961. Margaret, who was in New York, did not visit her husband of thirty-three years in the months of his decline. In his will George left the house in Cannes to his Argentinean secretary, Horacio Guerrico, but Margaret was displeased with her husband's bequest and managed to get the house back from the secretary in exchange for money and several objects of value.

Although Margaret had never truly shared her husband's passion for the ballet, or for the ballet company bearing his name, which she had financed for so many years, she did not immediately disband it after his death. Instead she appointed Raymundo de Larrain the new head of the company. There was always a sense of dilettantism about George de Cuevas's role as a Maecenas of the dance—not dissimilar to the role Rebekah Harkness would later play with her ballet company. The taste and caprices of the marquis determined the policy of the company, which relied on the box-office appeal of big star names. This same sense of dilettantism carried over into de Larrain's contribution. The de Cuevas company has been described to me by one balletomane as ballet for people who normally despise ballet, ballet for society audiences, as opposed to dance audiences.

De Larrain's stewardship of the company was brief but not undramatic. In June 1961 he played a significant role in the political defection of Rudolf Nureyev at the Paris airport when the Kirov Ballet of Leningrad was leaving France. The story has become romanticized over the years, and everyone's version of it differs. According to de Larrain, Nureyev had confessed to Clara Saint, a half-Chilean, half-Argentinean friend of de Larrain's, that he would rather commit suicide than go back to Russia. In one account, Clara Saint, feigning undying love for the departing star, screamed out to Nureyev that she must have one more kiss from him before he boarded the plane and returned to his homeland. Nureyev went back to kiss her, jumped over the barriers, and escaped in a waiting car as the plane carrying the company took off. De Larrain says that Clara Saint had alerted the French authorities that there was going to be a defection, and she advised Nureyev during a farewell drink at the airport bar that he must ask the French police at the departure gate for political asylum. He says that Nureyev spat in the face of the Russian security official. For a while Nureyev lived in de Larrain's Paris apartment, and the first time he danced after his defection was for the de Cuevas company, in de Larrain's production of *The Sleeping Beauty*. "He danced like a god, but he also had a spectacular story," de Larrain told me. At one of his first performances the balcony was filled with communists, who pelted the stage with tomatoes and almost caused a riot. People who were present that night remember that Nureyev continued to dance through the barrage, as if he were unaware of the commotion, until the performance was finally halted.

In Raymundo de Larrain's affidavit for the probate, he assesses his role in Nureyev's career in an I'm-not-the-nobody tone: "With the help of Margaret de Cuevas we made him into one of the biggest stars in the history of ballet." The professional association between de Larrain and Nureyev, which might have saved the de Cuevas ballet, did not last, just as most of de Larrain's professional associations did not last. "Raymundo and Rudolf did not have the same point of view on beauty and the theater, and they fought," explained the Viscountess de Ribes in Paris recently.

"Raymundo had great talent and tremendous imagination. He had the talent to be a stage director, but neither the health nor the courage to fight. He was very unrealistic. He didn't know how to talk to people. He was too grand. What Raymundo is is a total aesthete, not an intellectual. He wanted to live around beautiful things. He was very generous and gave beautiful presents. Even the smallest gift he ever gave me was perfect, absolutely perfect," she said. Another friend of de Larrain's said, "Raymundo had more taste and knowledge of dancing than anyone. His problem was that he was unprofessional. He couldn't get along with people. He had no discipline over himself." When the Marquesa de Cuevas decided in 1962 not to underwrite the ballet company any longer, it was disbanded. Then, under the sponsorship of the Viscountess de Ribes, de Larrain formed his own ballet company. He began by producing and directing *Cinderella*, in which he featured Geraldine Chaplin in a modest but much publicized role. The viscountess, however, couldn't afford for long to underwrite a ballet company, and withdrew after two years. Raymundo de Larrain then took to photographing celebrities for *Vogue*, *Town & Country*, and *Life*. His friends say that he had one obsession: to "make it" in the eyes of his family back in Chile. He mailed every newspaper clipping about himself to his mother, for whom, de Ribes says, "he had a passion."

For years Margaret de Cuevas's physical appearance had been deteriorating. Never the slightest bit interested in fashion or style, she began to assume the look of what has been described to me by some as a millionairess bag lady and by others as the Madwoman of Chaillot. "Before Fellini she was Fellini," said Count Vega del Ren about her, but other assessments were less romantic. Her nails were uncared for. Her teeth were in a deplorable state. She had knee problems that gave her difficulty in walking. She covered her face with a white paste and white powder, and she blackened her eyes in an eccentric way that made people think she had put her thumb and fingers in a full ashtray and rubbed them around her eyes. Her hair was dyed black with reddish tinges, and around her head she always wore a black net scarf, which she tied beneath her chin. She wrapped handkerchiefs and ribbons around her wrists to hide her diamonds, and her black dresses were frequently stained with food and spilled white powder and held together with safety pins. For shoes she wore either sneakers or a pair of pink polyester bedroom slippers, which were often on the wrong feet. Her lateness had reached a point where dinner guests would sit for several hours waiting for her to make an appearance, while Marcel, her butler of forty-five years, would pass them five or six times, carrying a martini on a silver tray to the marquesa's room. "She drank much too much for an old lady," one of her frequent guests told me. Finally her arrival for dinner would be heralded by the barking of her Pekingese dogs, and she would enter the dining room preceded by her favorite of them, Happy, who had a twisted neck and a glass eye and walked with a limp as the result of a stroke.

Her behavior also was increasingly eccentric. In her bedroom she had ten radios sitting on tables and chests of drawers. Each radio was set to a different music station—country-and-western, rock 'n' roll, classical—and when she wanted to hear music she would ring for Marcel and point to the radio she wished him to turn on. For years she paid for rooms at the Westbury Hotel for a group of White Russians she had taken under her wing.

In the meantime Jan de Vroom had grown increasingly alcoholic and pill-dependent. "If someone's eyes are dilated, does that mean they're taking drugs?" Margaret asked a friend of de Vroom's. "I've been too kind to him. I've spoiled him." Young men—mostly hustlers and drug dealers—paraded in and out of his apartment at all hours of the day and night. In 1973 two hustlers, whom he knew, rang the bell of his New York apartment. On a previous visit they had asked him for a loan of $2,000, and he had refused. When de Vroom answered the bell, they sent up a thug to frighten him and demand money again. Jan de Vroom, in keeping with his character, aggravated the thug and incited him to rage. A French houseguest found de Vroom's body: his throat had been cut, and he had been stabbed over and over again. Although he was known to be the person closest to Margaret de Cuevas at that time in her life, her name was not brought into any of the lurid accounts of his murder in the tabloid papers. De Vroom's body, covered from the chin down to conceal his slit throat, lay in an open casket in the Westbury Room of the Frank E. Campbell Funeral Chapel at Madison Avenue and Eighty-first Street. Except for a few of the curious, there were no visitors. A little-known fact of the sordid situation was that, through the intercession of Margaret de Cuevas, the body was laid to rest in the Rockefeller cemetery in Pocantico Hills, the family estate, although subsequently it was shipped to Holland. The

killers were caught and tried. There was no public outcry over the unsavory killing, and they received brief sentences. It is said that one of
them still frequents the bars in New York.

Into this void in the life of the Marquesa Margaret de Cuevas moved
Raymundo de Larrain. People meeting Margaret de Cuevas for the
first time at this point were inclined to think that the cultivated lady
was not intelligent, because she was unable to converse in the way people in society converse, and they suspected that she might be combin-
ing sedatives and drink. The same people are uniform in their praise of
Raymundo de Larrain during this time. For parties at her house in
New York, Raymundo would invite the guests and order the food and
arrange the flowers, in much the same way that her late husband had
during their marriage, and no one would argue the point that Raymundo surrounded her with a better crowd of people than Jan de
Vroom ever had. He would choreograph a steady stream of hand-
picked guests to Margaret's side during the evening. "'Go and sit with
Tante Margaret and talk with her, and I will send someone over in ten
minutes to relieve you,'" a frequent guest told me he used to say. "He
was lovely to her." Another view of Raymundo at this time came from
a New York lady who also visited the house: "He was so talented, Raymundo. Such a sense of fantasy. But he got sidetracked into money-
grubbing." Whatever the interpretation, Margaret de Cuevas and
Raymundo became the Harold and Maude of the Upper East Side and
Palm Beach. Bessie de Cuevas, in her affidavit, acknowledges that
"Raymundo was always attentive and extremely helpful to my mother,
particularly in her social life, which consisted almost exclusively of
gatherings and entertainments at her various residences."

On April 25, 1977, at the oceanfront estate of Mr. and Mrs. Wilson
C. Lucom in Palm Beach, the Marquesa Margaret de Cuevas, then
eighty years old, married Raymundo de Larrain, then forty-two, in a
hastily arranged surprise ceremony. The wedding was such a closely
guarded secret that Margaret de Cuevas's children, Bessie and John,
did not know of it until they read about it in Suzy's column in the New
York *Daily News*. Bessie de Cuevas's friends say that she felt betrayed
by Raymundo because he had not told her of his plans to marry her
mother. Among the prominent guests present at the wedding were

Rose Kennedy, Mrs. Winston Guest, and Mary Sanford, known as the queen of Palm Beach, who that night gave the newlyweds a wedding reception at her estate. In her affidavit Bessie de Cuevas states, "I had visited with my mother at some length at her home in New York just about two months before. She was clearly aging but we talked along quite well about personal and family things. She said she would be leaving soon to spend some time at her home in Florida. She did not in any way suggest that she was considering getting married. After I read the article, I called her at once in Florida. She could only speak briefly and seemed vague. I assured her that of course my brother John and I wanted anything that would make her comfortable and happy, but why, I asked, did she do it this way. Her reply was simple, 'It just happened.' "

Wilson C. Lucom, the host of the wedding, was also married to an older woman, the since-deceased Willys-Overland automobile heiress Virginia Willys. Lucom, who had trained as a lawyer, never practiced law but had served on the staff of the late secretary of state Edward Stettinius. Shortly after the wedding, in response to an inquiry from the Rockefeller family, he sent a Mailgram to John D. Rockefeller III, the first cousin of Margaret Strong de Cuevas de Larrain, stating his position as the representative of the marquesa and now of de Larrain. "Do not worry about her or be concerned about any rumors you may have heard," the Mailgram read. "She was married at our house with my wife and myself as witnesses. It was a solemn ceremony, and she was highly competent and knew precisely that she was being married and did so of her own free will being of sound mind." Bessie de Cuevas says in her affidavit, "I had never met or heard my mother speak of Mr. Lucom."

For the wedding, Raymundo told friends, he gave his bride a wheelchair and new teeth. He also supervised a transformation of her appearance. "You must understand this: Raymundo cleaned Margaret up. Why, her nails were manicured for the first time in years." He got rid of the white makeup and blackened eyes, and he supervised her hair, nails, cosmetics, and dress. "Margaret was never better cared for" is a remark made over and over about her after her marriage. De Larrain would invite people to lunch or for drinks and wheel her out to greet her guests; he basked in the compliments paid to his wife on her new appearance. However, lawyers for the Chase Manhattan Bank, which represents Bessie and John de Cuevas's interests, told me that the two health-care professionals who cared for the marquesa at different times in 1980 and 1982 recalled that de Larrain did not spend much time with his wife, and that she would often ask about him. But when attention was paid by him, it would be lavish; he would send roses in great quantity or do her makeup. Since he had arranged it so that no one would become close to his wife, "she was particularly vulnerable to such displays of charm and affection." During her second marriage, she became known as Margaret Rockefeller de Larrain. Although this was illustrious-sounding, it was incorrect, for it implied that she was born Margaret Rockefeller rather than Margaret Strong. "The snobbishness and enhancement were de Larrain's" sniffed a friend of her daughter's.

Shortly after the marriage, Sylvia de Cuevas, the then wife of John de Cuevas, took the marquesa's two granddaughters to visit her in Palm Beach. She says she was stopped at the front door by an armed guard, who would not let them enter until permission was granted by Raymundo. Soon other changes began to take place. Old servants who had been with the marquesa for years, including her favorite, Marcel, were fired by de Larrain. Bessie de Cuevas claims in her affidavit that he accused them of stealing and other misdeeds. Long-term relationships with lawyers and accountants were severed. Copies of correspondence to the marquesa from Richard Weldon, her lawyer for many years, and Albert Remmert, her secretary and financial adviser for many years, reflect that her directives to them were so unlike her usual method of communication that they questioned the authority of the letters. Shortly thereafter both men were replaced. Another long-time secretary, Lillian Grappone, told Bessie de Cuevas that her mother had complained of the fact that there were constantly new faces around her. During this period the many houses of the marquesa were sold or given to charity, among them her two houses on East Sixty-eighth Street in New York, which had always been her favorite as well as her principal residence. Bessie de Cuevas claims in her affidavit that her mother sometimes could not recall signing anything to effect the transfer of these houses. At other times she would talk as if she could get them back. On one occasion she acknowledged having signed away the houses but said she had been talked into it at a time when she was not feeling well. Her father's villa in Fiesole, where she had grown up, was given to Georgetown University. The house in Cannes was given to Bessie and John de Cuevas. Her official residence was moved from New York to Florida, but she was moved out of her house of many years on El Bravo Way in Palm Beach to a condominium on South Ocean Boulevard. Several people who visited her at the condominium said that she seemed confused as to why she should be living there instead of in her own house. Other friends explain the move as a practical one. The house on El Bravo Way was an old Spanish-style one on several floors and many levels, badly in need of repair, and for an invalid in a wheelchair life was simpler in the one-floor apartment.

During this period the financial affairs of the marquesa were handled more and more by Wilson C. Lucom, the host at the wedding. Bessie de Cuevas states in her affidavit, "I think my mother's belief that Lucom would safeguard her interests against de Larrain only highlights her lack of appreciation for the reality of her circumstances." Bessie de Cuevas tells of an occasion when she visited her mother at the Palm Beach condominium and Lucom "taunted" her by boasting that he and de Larrain were drinking "Rockefeller champagne." "My mother's total dependence on de Larrain is reflected in an explanation she gave for why she did not accompany de Larrain to Paris on a trip he made concerning her holdings there. De Larrain told her no American carrier flew to Paris any longer, and since my mother did not care for Air France, it was best for her not to go. Plainly, my mother had lost any independent touch with the real world."

Access to her mother became more and more difficult for Bessie de Cuevas. When she called, she was told her mother could not come to the telephone. Some friends who visited the marquesa say that she would complain that she never heard from her daughter. Others say that messages left by Bessie were never given to her. In 1982 Raymundo de Larrain took his wife out of the country, and they began what lawyers representing the de Cuevases' interests call an "itinerant existence." She never returned. They went first to Switzerland, then to Chile, where he was from and where they had built a house, and finally to Madrid, where de Larrain was made the cultural attaché at the

Chilean embassy. There Margaret died in a hotel room in 1985. Bessie de Cuevas saw her mother for the last time a few weeks before she died. Neither Bessie nor her brother has any idea where she is buried.

Certainly there was trouble between the Rockefeller family and the newly wed de Larrains from the time of the marriage. After the change of residence from New York to Florida, David Rockefeller urged his cousin to donate her two town houses at 52 and 54 East Sixty-eighth Street to an institution supported by the Rockefeller family called the Center for Inter-American Relations. The appraisal of the two houses was arranged by David Rockefeller, and the appraiser had been in the employ of the Rockefellers for years. He evaluated the two houses at $725,000. Subsequently Margaret de Larrain was distressed to hear that these properties, which she had donated to the Center for Inter-American Relations, were later sold to another favorite Rockefeller forum, the Council on Foreign Relations, for more than twice the amount of money they had been appraised at.

Raymundo de Larrain, in his affidavit for the probate proceedings, says that his wife's male Rockefeller cousins discriminated against the females of the family. "Not only did her cousin-trustee [John D. Rockefeller III] want to dominate her life and tell her how to spend her trust income, but wanted also to dictate and approve how she spent her non-trust personal principal and income. My wife strongly resented their intrusion in her personal life. . . . Her position was that her money was hers outright, not part of her trust, and that she and she alone was to decide how she spent it or what gifts she—not they— would make." Later in the affidavit, de Larrain says that his wife's trustees "wanted her to give virtually all her personal wealth away to her children long before she even thought of dying. Then they would control her through their control of her trust income."

De Larrain said that his wife had been generous with her two children, but that they were not satisfied with her gifts of millions to them. "They wanted more and more." After giving her children more than $7 million, she refused to transfer her personal wealth to them. Even after her gift of $7 million, he claimed, the trustees cut her trust income. "My wife was shocked and distressed at the unjust and cruel and illegal actions of the cousin-trustees in pressuring her to give millions to her children and then breaking their agreement not to cut her trust income. This further alienated her from her family. She felt cheated and a victim of a plan by the family and the Chase Manhattan Bank."

On February 21, 1978, a year after her marriage, Margaret de Larrain, at age eighty-one, revoked all prior wills and codicils executed by her. "I have personally destroyed the original wills in my possession, namely, two original wills dated February 14, 1941, and an original will dated April 26, 1950, and an original will dated May 14, 1956, and an original will dated May 17, 1968, and an original will dated June 11, 1968." Thereafter, Margaret de Larrain added two codicils to a new will of November 20, 1980. In the first, she stated that she had already transferred her fortune to her husband, and she made him the sole beneficiary and sole personal representative of her estate. In the second, she expressed her specific wish that her only two children and two grandchildren receive nothing. De Larrain ended his affidavit with this statement: "There is abundant testimony that my wife was entirely competent when she later added the two codicils which expressed that she wanted to give the property to me, her husband. She did this because her children neglected her and she had provided abundantly for them in her lifetime by giving them approximately $7 million in gifts."

It might be added that Margaret's will did not set a precedent in the stodgy Rockefeller family. Her mother's sister, Edith Rockefeller McCormick, who divorced her husband, Henry Fowler McCormick, heir to the International Harvester fortune, and then engaged in a series of flamboyant affairs with male secretaries, which caused her father great embarrassment, in 1932 bequeathed half of her fortune to a Swiss secretary.

Pending the upcoming court case, Raymundo de Larrain has dropped out of public view. When he is in Paris, he lives at the Meurice Hotel, but even his closest friends there, including the Viscountess de Ribes, do not hear from him, and he has dropped completely out of the smart social life that he once pursued so vigorously. On encountering Hubert Faure, the first husband of Bessie de Cuevas, in the bar of the Meurice recently, he turned his back on him. In Madrid he stays sometimes at the Palace Hotel and sometimes at less well-known ones. He has been seen dining alone in restaurants there. Sometimes he nods to former acquaintances, but he makes no attempt to renew friendships. He has also been seen in Rabat and Lausanne. In the past year he has made two substantial gifts to charity. He gave a check for $1 million to the Spanish Institute in New York, and, as a member of the board of the Spanish Institute said at a New York party, "The check didn't bounce." He also recently gave a check for $500,000 to Georgetown University to supplement the gift of his late wife's father's villa in Fiesole to Georgetown. "You have to figure that if Raymundo gave a million dollars to the Spanish Institute *before* the trial, he must have already squirreled away at least $10 million," said a dubious Raymundo follower in Paris recently.

This is not a sad story. The deprived will not go hungry. If the courts are able to ascertain what happened to Margaret Strong de Cuevas de Larrain's fortune in the years of her marriage and to decide on an equitable distribution of her wealth, already rich people will get richer. As a woman friend of Raymundo de Larrain said to me recently, "Raymundo will be bad in court, nervous and insecure. If there's a jury, the jury won't like him." She thought a bit and then added, "It's only going to end up wrong. If you don't behave correctly, nothing turns out well. I mean, would you like to fight the Rockefellers, darling?"

February 1987

Raymundo de Larrain died of AIDS several years after this article appeared. The whereabouts of his late wife's Rockefeller fortune has never come to light.

THE WINDSOR EPILOGUE

On April 2, 1987, in Geneva, A. Alfred Taubman, the Michigan mall millionaire who has become the *grand seigneur* of the auction world, put on an auction which, for sheer showmanship, rivaled the finest hours of the late P. T. Barnum, the *grand seigneur* of the circus world, who immodestly called his circus the greatest show on earth. Mr. Taubman, no shrinking violet himself, pitched his tent, or rather his red-and-white-striped marquee, on the banks of Lake Geneva and papered the house with some of the grandest names in the *Almanach de Gotha*—nonbidders, to be sure, but the swellest dress extras in auction history. Sprinkled among the princesses, the countesses, the baronesses, and an infanta were the buyers who meant business: dealers from New York and London, Japanese businessmen, a Hollywood divorce lawyer, representatives of the Sultan of Brunei and Prince Bernhard of the Netherlands, not to mention a battery of bidders who, because they did not wish to travel or like to be looked at, were connected by phone to Sotheby's in New York and Geneva. Under the red-and-white-striped marquee, after six months of an unparalleled publicity blitz, the gavel was finally raised on the opening lot of the sale of the jewels and love tokens of the late Duchess of Windsor, the American woman from Baltimore for whom a king gave up his throne. What followed was a jewel auction against which all jewel auctions to come will be compared.

In the month preceding the sale, the jewels, which I heard an English woman in Geneva describe as "frighteningly chic," traveled from Paris, where they had been under the protectorship of Maître Suzanne Blum, the Duchess's lawyer and a key figure in the story, to Palm

Beach and New York—all with great fanfare and hype generated by Sotheby's, the 243-year-old London-based auction house which took over New York's Parke-Bernet Galleries in 1964, in order to woo the rich Americans who were expected to be the chief buyers in Geneva. In both cities, Alfred Taubman, the owner and chairman of Sotheby's since 1983, hosted smart parties so that all the right people, like Mrs. Astor and Malcolm Forbes and the other heavy hitters, might have a leisurely view of the treasure trove that a besotted monarch had showered on his twice-divorced ladylove. Mr. Taubman, a hale and hearty sixty-two, whose assets are estimated in the *Forbes* magazine list of the four hundred richest people in America at $800 million, and his beautiful younger wife, Judy, a former Miss Israel who once worked behind the counter at Christie's, the rival auction house, handing out catalogs, are high-profile figures on the New York and Palm Beach social circuits. "Selling art is a lot like selling root beer," he once said.

Duchess fever swept New York. "The romance of the twentieth century," we heard over and over. In actual fact, it was not a romance that can bear very close scrutiny: the love story of a masculine woman of middle age, who was probably never once called beautiful in her life, and a Peter Pan king, who resisted responsibility and composed embarrassing love letters. "A boy loves a girl more and more and is holding her so tight these trying days of waiting," he wrote to her when he was forty-two. Be that as it may, royal romance was in the air. By day the hoi polloi, willing to wait in line for three or four hours just to pass by the jewel-filled vitrines, turned out in such record numbers that the *New York Times* reported the event on its front page. Public interest was so great that Sotheby's desisted from running advertisements in the newspapers and cut back plans to show the jewels on local television shows because the security force at the auction house could not handle any more people than were already jamming its halls.

Although the British press reported even more avidly than ours every detail of the presale hype, the traveling jewel show bypassed England. From a public-relations point of view, Sotheby's felt it best not to open old wounds or to stir up adverse criticism when such big bucks were at stake. Fifty years after Edward VIII gave up his throne for the woman he loved, his duchess, even in death, remains a controversial figure in that country, still disliked and still unforgiven by a generation that blames her for taking away from them a beloved king. A close friend of Princess Margaret, brimming with insider information straight from the palace, informed me, "The royal family hated her. Simply hated her."

Her American admirers felt very differently, of course. As one of them said to me in Geneva, "The English didn't get her. The English still don't get her. They should erect a statue to Wallis Windsor in every town in the realm for taking away their king."

The Duchess's sale lasted two days. The Hôtel Beau-Rivage, where Sotheby's is, was where the action was, but the Hôtel Richemond, directly next door, was unmistakably smarter. That was where the Taubmans stayed. The sale of the Duchess's jewelry was also the occasion of a Sotheby's board-of-directors meeting, and the Sotheby's board of directors, as assembled by Alfred Taubman, is the swellest board of directors in big business today, boasting such illustrious names as Her Royal Highness the Infanta Pilar de Borbón, Duchess of Badajoz, who happens to be the sister of the King of Spain, for starters, as well as the Right Honourable the Earl of Gowrie, the Earl of Westmorland, and Baron Hans Heinrich Thyssen-Bornemisza de Kaszon, who has the largest private art collection in the world after the Queen of England's, and such Americans as Henry Ford II, Mrs. Gordon Getty, and Mrs. Milton Petrie.

Society girls in the employ of Sotheby's, wearing black dresses and single strands of pearls, bristled with self-importance as they manned the telephones, dispensed press badges, sold catalogs, and gave terse replies to queries. The bars in both hotels were never not full, and the gossip was terrific, although not always reliable. "Absolutely not!" one indignant upper-class voice, overbrandied, rang out. "I don't care what you've heard! The Duchess of Windsor was not a man!"

Always, following the death of a prominent person, individuals come forward claiming to have had a closer acquaintance with the deceased than the facts would bear out. One favorite preoccupation among the insiders was minimizing the degree of familiarity certain people claimed to have had with the late Duke and Duchess. "So-and-so," they said, talking about a highly profiled man in New York, "was not nearly so close to the Duchess as he says he was. The Duke would never have had him around." Or, "I visited the Duchess for years and I never once heard her mention So-and-so," naming an international lady.

A thousand smartly dressed people piled into the tent to find their ticketed seats, all carrying the glossiest and most gossipy auction catalog ever printed. At fifty dollars a copy, it promptly sold out, and is now a collector's item. Friends met. Men greeted men with kisses on both cheeks, and women did the same. On closed-circuit television sets around the tent a film was shown, but no one watched, because they were all looking at one another. "The world was fascinated by them," intoned a voice on the sound track, "and they were obsessed with each other. . . . The Prince of Wales's father, George V, had Mrs. Simpson's past investigated and decided she was not a suitable companion for his son. . . . Queen Mary called her an adventuress." Year after year of newsreels of their glittering and empty life flashed by: weekends at Fort Belvedere when the Duke was still king, their somber wedding at the Château de Candé, the two of them arriving here, arriving there, fashion plates both, stepping out of limousines, waving from the decks of ocean liners, sweeping into parties, relentlessly up to the moment, in all the very jewels that were about to be sold, the Duchess leading, the Duke following, she gleaming, he scowling, or smiling sadly. Behind it all, a voice sang, "The party's over. It's all over, my friend." But no one was listening either, because they were all talking to each other. The Princess of Naples, married to Victor Emmanuel, who would have been the king of Italy if history had gone another way, chatted up Prince Dimitri of Yugoslavia, who works for Sotheby's jewelry department, while his brother, Prince Serge of Yugoslavia, chatted up the Baroness Tita Thyssen-Bornemisza, ablaze in sapphires, who chatted up the Countess of Romanoes, who was wearing the diamond bracelet she had inherited from the Duchess of Windsor and who in turn chatted up the Infanta Beatriz of Spain, who chatted up Grace, Countess of Dudley, who chatted up Princess Firyal of Jordan, who chatted up Judy Taubman, while her husband, Alfred Taubman, the *grand seigneur*, radiating power and importance, carried a huge unlit cigar and smiled and waved and greeted.

Then the auction began.

From the first of the 306 lots, a gold-ruby-and-sapphire clip made by Cartier in Paris in 1946, the air in the tent was charged with excitement.

A few moments later, lot 13, a diamond clip lorgnette by Van Cleef & Arpels, circa 1935, which was estimated to bring in $5,000, went to a private bidder for $117,000. The excitement began to build. Two lots later, when a pair of pavé diamond cuff links and three buttons and a stud, estimated to go for $10,000, went for $440,000 to a mysterious, deeply tanned man who was said to be bidding for the Egyptian who has taken over the Windsors' house outside Paris, the first applause broke out in the tent. People realized they were present at an event, engaged in the heady adventure of watching rich people acting rich, participating in a rite available only to them, the spending of big money, without a moment's hesitation or consideration. The sable-swathed Ann Getty, who wanted it known that she was there because of the board-of-directors meeting and not to bid, changed her seat from the fifth row to the first in order to be closer to the arena. By lot 91, a pair of yellow-diamond clips by Harry Winston, 1948, that went to the London jeweler Laurence Graff, one of the royal family's jewelers, for over $2 million, financial abandon filled the air with an almost erotic intensity, and it never lessened during the remaining hours of the sale. Powdered bosoms heaved in fiscal excitement at big bucks being spent. Each time the bidding got into the million-dollar range, for one of the ten or so world-class stones in the collection, the tension resembled the frenzy at a cockfight. Sotheby's employees manning the telephones waved their hands frantically to attract the auctioneer. People rose in their seats to get a better look at the mysterious Mr. Fabri, who bid and bid—money no object—on all the pieces directly linked to the love affair between Edward and Wallis. "The Duke would have hated all this," said a friend of the Duke's, shaking his head. "I'm surprised they're not auctioning off his fly buttons."

The auctioneer, like the judge at a trial, has the power to enthrall his audience. At the podium in Geneva was the tall and debonair Nicholas Rayner. It was he who first approached Maître Suzanne Blum, the keeper of the Windsor flame, about the disposition of the Duchess's jewels. A notoriously difficult woman, the octogenarian Maître Blum is said to have been charmed by Rayner, and because of him she entrusted the jewels to Sotheby's. The charm that captivated Maître Blum captivated all the women in the tent as well. "Divine," said one woman about Rayner. "And separated," said another, as if that fact added to his glamour. Although he was criticized by a few purists for several times allowing the bidding to continue after he had dropped the gavel—he said that since the money was going to charity the ordinary rules did not apply—he won over far more people than he alienated. He had a sense of theater, realized that he was in a leading role, and understood exactly how to keep this audience in the palm of his hand. Graceful, witty, he was Cary Grant at forty, giving the kind of performance that turns a good actor into a major star. At the end of the second day, when the total sales had reached $50 million, the audience rose and gave Rayner a standing ovation which rivaled any that Lord Olivier ever received.

It was a sad disappointment to auction voyeurs that they could not turn around and stare at Miss Elizabeth Taylor raising her already jeweled hand to bid $623,000 for a diamond clip known as the Prince of Wales feathers brooch, which Richard Burton had once admired on the Duchess, for the simple reason that Miss Taylor had chosen to make her bid by telephone while sun-tanning next to her swimming pool in Bel Air, California. They could not watch the multimillionaire dress designer Calvin Klein either, as he bid by telephone from New York $733,000 for a single-row pearl necklace by Cartier, or $198,000 for another single-row pearl necklace by Van Cleef & Arpels, or a mere $102,600 for a pearl-and-diamond eternity ring by Darde & Fils of Paris, or $300,600 for a pearl-and-diamond pendant by Cartier, for which he outbid the Duchess's friend and frequent New York hostess Estée Lauder, the cosmetics tycoon, and all for his beauteous new wife, Kelly. Expensive, yes, but Van Cleef & Arpels had told Calvin Klein it would take ten years to match pearls for the necklace he had in mind and cost several million dollars. He told the press that he was not going to wait for a special day, to give them to Kelly. "The best presents just happen," he said.

Under the marquee, only Marvin Mitchelson, the Hollywood divorce lawyer, who built his fortune on the failed marriages of the famous, broke the rules of anonymity and had himself announced as the purchaser of the Duchess's amethyst-and-turquoise necklace for $605,000. He further wanted it announced that he dedicated the purchase to the memory of his mother, who had worked to put him through law school. Mitchelson also purchased a huge sapphire brooch for $374,000 for someone else, a client whom he would not name, although he tantalized the press by hinting that it was Joan Collins, whom he was representing in her latest divorce.

In seats every bit as good as the seats occupied by the Princess of Naples and Princess Firyal of Jordan sat two dark-haired beauties in Chanel suits—real Chanel suits, not knockoffs—who were there to bid, not gape. They scrutinized their catalogs, and they had mink coats folded over their knees. Their stockings had seams, a subtle signal to the cognoscenti of such things that they were wearing garter belts, not panty hose. Ms. X and Ms. Y, two international ladies of the evening, told me they were staying at the Richemond, where they felt as at home as they do at the Plaza Athénée or the Beverly Hills Hotel. Ms. X had her heart set on lot 26, a pavé diamond heart with a gold-and-ruby crown and the initials W. and E., for Wallis and Edward, intertwined in emeralds. It had been the twentieth-wedding-anniversary present of the Duke to the Duchess. Ms. Y had *her* heart set on lot 31, a single-row diamond bracelet with nine gem-set Latin crosses hanging from it. The Duchess had worn it on her wedding day in 1937 and had once remarked that the crosses represented the crosses she had to bear. Ms. X said about Ms. Y, jokingly, that she wanted the bracelet with the crosses to wear on her whipping hand. Used to the best, Ms. Y has a custom-made bag by Hermès to carry her whips in. She didn't get the bracelet with the crosses, which went for $381,000. Ms. X didn't get the pavé diamond heart either. It went for $300,000. "The prices just got out of hand. We were a couple of zeros short," Ms. X told me during the break. "That heart probably belongs to Candy Spelling by now. Come and have tea tomorrow. We're free until ten."

Of course there was the inevitable Japanese, with millions at his disposal, who said he would have gone even higher than the $3.15 million he paid for the Duchess's solitary diamond. Hours later, no one could remember his name or his face.

There will be other jewel sales, even better jewel sales, but that night in Geneva, the jewel capital of the world, people wanted, at any price, no holds barred, something about which they could say, "This belonged to the Duchess of Windsor," because they knew that they were buying romance and history. Nowhere was this so evident as in lot 68, a pearl-and-diamond choker, which Nicholas Rayner carefully pointed out was imitation. The choker then sold for $51,000. The sale of the Duchess's jewels, coming as it did only a few days after the $39.9 million sale of a van Gogh sunflowers painting, whose chrome yellow paint had turned brown, made one realize the enormous amount of money there is in the world waiting to be spent, even for the imperfect, if the credentials are OK.

In the back of the tent, unknown to most of the people there, sat Georges Sanègre and his wife, Ofélia, the longtime butler and maid to the Duke and Duchess, quietly watching the personal possessions of their former employers make auction history. Not physically present, but prominently there in spirit, was the old and elusive Maître Blum, called Mrs. Blum by her detractors, who are legion. Maître Blum, who had met the Windsors in Portugal during World War II and then been their French lawyer for forty years, followed every moment of the auction by telephone from Paris and knew minute by minute everything that was going on.

Maître Blum's relationship with the former king and his duchess was strictly a business one. Social contact was limited to two dinners or lunches a year, and those in the context of business courtesy rather than friendship. The Duke was thought to have more regard for her than the Duchess, who, friends say, wanted to fire her after the Duke's death, but whose increasing mental confusion made this impossible.

"She lost her mind, you know," people told me about the Duchess, "during the last decade of her life." Or, "She was gaga." Or, "A veg." The *on-dit*, as these people say, meaning the gossip, or inside story, is that the Duchess insisted on having a final face-lift even though she was advised not to because of her age. Plastic surgeons in England and France declined to perform the operation, and warned her about the effects of anesthesia on people over seventy. Determined, she persevered. A plastic surgeon from another country performed the operation, in the course of which there was a technical difficulty with the anesthesia and the air to the Duchess's brain was briefly cut off. This is widely said to be the cause of the derangement that came on her after her husband's death. During her stay at Buckingham Palace at the time of the Duke's funeral, she often thought she was in Paris, and she mistook the Queen Victoria fountain, which she could see from the palace windows, for the Place de la Concorde. The Duke, before he died, aware that the Duchess's mind had begun to wander, entrusted her care to Maître Blum.

Shortly after the Duke's death, when the Duchess was in a confused and vulnerable state, all his private papers were confiscated, possibly under the direction of his cousin Lord Mountbatten, acting on behalf of the royal family. These papers now reside in the archives of Windsor Castle, unavailable to the public. Georges, the butler, is said to have hidden the love letters of the Duke and Duchess to prevent their being carried off in the same swoop. The letters he rescued were later published under the title *Wallis and Edward, Letters 1931–1937: The Intimate Correspondence of the Duke and Duchess of Windsor.*

It was the Duke's wish, so stated in his will, that the Duchess's jewels be removed from their settings after her death so that the pieces could never be worn by any other woman, but such was not the Duchess's wish. People who have had access to the Duchess's private papers tell me that several Americans tried to persuade the Duchess, because she was American, to leave her jewels, in whole or in part, to the Smithsonian Institution in Washington. Another suggestion was that she leave her jewels to the White House, as a permanent collection for the First Lady of the United States to wear. Although Maître Blum is most often blamed for nixing these American plans for the disposition of the collection, it was the Duchess herself who decided that France, the country that had given her refuge for fifty years, should be the beneficiary. There are unkind people who will tell you that if the Duchess had had her way, all her money would have been left to a dog hospital. The truth is, Maître Blum prevailed upon the Duchess to leave the money to the Pasteur Institute, the leading medical-research institution in France.

People familiar with the Windsors noticed, looking at the jewelry, that a great many pieces were missing. "What happened to all the Fulco di Verdura pieces?" they asked, referring to the designs of the Sicilian Duke di Verdura, whose scrapbooks show a great number of pieces he made for the Duchess which were not in the auction. Or, one heard in Geneva and later in New York, "All those marvelous things on her tables—her bibelots—what has become of those, we wonder?" The implication, each time the rhetorical question is asked, is that malfeasance was afoot. Michael Bloch, who edited the book of the couple's love letters, is adamant in his defense of Maître Blum. He affirms that she has not profited at all in the disposal of the estate, and his strong feelings are borne out by several other people close to the couple.

The Duchess had, in effect, an almost ten-year death, with nurses around the clock. The family fortune, in terms of hard cold cash, at the time of the Duke's death was around $1 million—not a great deal of money for people with their standard of living. The high cost of a royal death was prohibitive, and, curiously, the Duchess did not have medical insurance. From time to time during the years of the long illness, Maître Blum sold off pieces of jewelry, sets of china, or the odd Bergère chair or ormolu table to pay off the medical costs. Several years ago, for instance, Mrs. São Schlumberger of Paris bought a ruby necklace. A Sotheby's official assured me that the price she paid was at the top of the market at the time. Nate Cummings, the late American millionaire, collector, and friend of the Duke and Duchess, bought, among other things, a set of vermeil plates. Maître Blum also sold some bead necklaces in emeralds, rubies, and sapphires to the London firm of Hennell, who traveled to Beverly Hills with their wares before the auction. Candy Spelling, the wife of the television mogul Aaron Spelling and the possessor of one of the most spectacular jewel collections in the country, bought one of the necklaces. Another was sold to Mrs. Muriel Slatkin, the former owner, with her sister, Seema Boesky, the wife of the Wall Street swindler Ivan Boesky, of the Beverly Hills Hotel. A third was sold to Mrs. Marvin Davis, the wife of one of the country's richest men, who is, incidentally, the new owner of the Beverly Hills Hotel. Also, the Duchess gave away several pieces of her jewelry before she died. Princess Alexandra, a favorite niece of the Duke, received a piece. Princess Michael of Kent, whose own popularity in the royal family is on a par with the Duchess's, won the heart of her husband's aunt by marriage by calling her in a letter "Dear Aunt Wallis," thereby likening her own marriage to that of the Windsors, and she too was rewarded.

The Duchess in her will mentioned certain people, like the American-born Countess of Romanoes, who received a diamond bracelet with an inscription from the Duke to the Duchess engraved on the back of it.

When the item to be inherited was not specified, it was left to the discretion of Maître Blum, and in this role the mighty *maître* exerted her authority to the fullest. One lady of haughty bearing irritated Maître Blum exceedingly at the time of the Duchess's funeral by assuming too important a position and attitude among the mourners. Months later, her bijou of inheritance still undelivered, the haughty lady is said to have wailed to her friends, "Why does Maître Blum hate me so?" Her inheritance was the last to be distributed and the least important of the lot in both beauty and value.

No one lingers in Geneva. At fifteen minutes before eight the morning after the sale, Alfred Taubman, a huge unlit cigar balanced between his teeth, paced back and forth in front of the Hôtel Richemond, impatience in his every step. The auction was over, history made, he wanted to be gone. The jacket of his double-breasted gray flannel suit was unbuttoned. A cashmere scarf was wrapped Dickensian-style around his neck against the brisk lake breezes. By the curb three dark blue Mercedeses were being loaded with first-rate luggage, and he was directing the operation. Nervous minions offered assistance.

"How much . . . ?" someone started to ask him, meaning how much had the auction grossed.

"Forty-nine million plus," he answered, interrupting the question before it was finished. It was not the first time he had been asked the question since the night before, and he was proud of the figure.

"Call upstairs to Mrs. Taubman," he told the hall porter, walking back into the lobby of the hotel. "I left my yellow handkerchief behind. Tell her to find it." He walked back out to the street again. "C'mon. Let's get this show on the road." He did not like to be kept waiting. "Between Judy and Princess Firyal . . ." he said, shaking his head in exasperation at the delays women cause. Finally all was ready. "We're going to General Aviation, where my plane is," he said to the driver of the lead car.

The party was over, my friend.

In the six weeks that followed, two other notable jewel auctions took place. At Sotheby's in New York, the jewels of Flora Whitney Miller, the daughter of Gertrude Vanderbilt Whitney, were auctioned along with the jewels of a Romanian princess and the singer-actress Pia Zadora, among others. Back in Geneva, at Christie's, certain jewels of the Hon. Mrs. Reginald Fellowes, known as Daisy Fellowes, were sold in combination with jewelry from what the catalog listed merely as "various sources."

Unlike the Duchess of Windsor, both Mrs. Miller and Mrs. Fellowes, her contemporaries, were born to great wealth and great families. Mrs. Fellowes was the daughter of a French duke and a Singer-sewing-machine heiress. It was said that every time Mrs. Fellowes passed an advertisement for Singer sewing machines she crossed herself. Historically Daisy Fellowes is little more than a footnote in the memoirs and diary entries of social historians, although in fact she was just as relentlessly chic as the Duchess, far richer, and equally witty. She owned one of the largest yachts in the Mediterranean, the *Sister Anne*, on which the Windsors once sailed. Stories about her are endless. Once, a former footman with exceptional good looks, who had advanced himself from his position behind a dining-room chair to a seat at some of the best tables in the South of France, Palm Beach, and Beverly Hills, asked Daisy Fellowes if she missed her yacht, which she had recently sold. She looked at the fellow and answered, "Yes. Yes, I do. I miss it very much. Do you miss your tray?"

The auction of her jewels and the auction of the jewels of Flora Whitney Miller were dispirited occasions in comparison with the Windsor sale. "This won't be anything like that," a Christie's executive told me shortly before the Fellowes' jewelry auction. "In all my years in the auction business," she said wistfully, in remembrance of things past, "I never saw anything like the Duchess's sale."

In the weeks following the sale, the Duchess's jewels began appearing on fashionable necks, wrists, and bosoms. Elizabeth Taylor arrived at Malcolm Forbes's party-of-the-year in Far Hills, New Jersey, wearing her Prince of Wales Plumes, and Mrs. Milton Petrie, who, when she was the Marquesa de Portago, was a great friend of the Duchess, walked into New York hostess Alice Mason's party for former president and Mrs. Jimmy Carter wearing the Duchess's articulated tourmaline-and-quartz necklace.

At another dinner party in New York, I heard Mr. Taubman

describing, not immodestly, how he had restructured Sotheby's and made it a profitable company. "I computerized it. I got rid of the advertising department entirely. They were doing institutional advertising. I said to them, 'This isn't an institution. This is a business.' I didn't do wholesale firing, as everyone said. I kept the best people, but I brought in experts to go over every department. Now we have a working operation. When I took over the company, they were doing 350, 375 million a year. Last year we did 900 million. By the end of this year, I expect we'll do something like a billion two, a billion five, around there."

As far as the auction world is concerned, Mr. Taubman hit a peak with the sale of the Duchess's jewels. He made it the greatest show on earth. He took an estate appraised by his own experts at $7 million tops and, by means of hype and romance and showmanship, made it bring in over $50 million.

No matter how you slice it, though, Maître Blum emerges as the heroine of this tale. The Duchess of Windsor, unlike other ladies of the royal family she married into, was not a patroness of the arts or sciences. No orphanage or hospital ever knew her as a benefactress. Instead, she was the woman who defined the meaning of a life in society for her time. "Chic" and "stylish" were her adjectives of description. Her servants' livery was made by the same uniform maker who made the uniforms of General de Gaulle. Her days were spent preparing for the evening, telephoning friends, being massaged, being manicured, being coiffed, having fittings for her vast and ever-changing wardrobe, seating her dinners, choosing her china, ordering her flowers, having steamer trunks packed for their endless peregrinations in pursuit of pleasure. But fate stepped in to give a final importance to her life when Maître Blum suggested that the Pasteur Institute be the beneficiary of her will. At the time, no one could know that the Pasteur Institute would become the leading French medical institution involved in finding a cure for AIDS. Today, however, when the whole world is gripped with the fear of AIDS, the $45 million that the Pasteur Institute will receive from the sale of the Duchess's jewelry gives a sort of poetic finality to her life. Even, perhaps, the nobility that always eluded her.

August 1987

The extraordinary sale in Geneva of the Duchess of Windsor's jewels, where people stood on chairs to bid, so frantic were they to own something that had once belonged to the American duchess, was a sight I will probably never forget. It also paved the way for the many celebrity auctions that have followed: the Andy Warhol auction, the Jacqueline Onassis auction, the Princess Diana dress auction, etc., proving the point that celebrity sells.

ROBERT MAPPLETHORPE'S
PROUD FINALE

"No one expected him to live for the opening, and there he was, on a high," said Tom Armstrong, the director of the Whitney Museum of American Art in New York. Whether the artist would or would not be present was the question that occupied the minds of all the people involved, in the days preceding the highly publicized and eagerly anticipated *vernissage* of the work of Robert Mapplethorpe, the photographer who took his art to the outer limits of his own experience, at the Whitney last July.

For nearly two years the rumors of Robert Mapplethorpe's illness had been whispered in the New York art and social circles in which he moved as a celebrated and somewhat notorious figure. The death in January 1987 of the New York aristocrat and collector Sam Wagstaff from AIDS had brought the matter of Mapplethorpe's illness with the same disease out into the open. Mapplethorpe, the principal inheritor of Sam Wagstaff's fortune, had once been Wagstaff's lover and later, for years, his great and good friend. The inheritance, believed to be in the neighborhood of $7 million—some say more, depending on the value of his art and silver collection—made the already much-talked-about Mapplethorpe, a famed figure of the night in the netherworld of New York, even more talked about, especially when the will was contested by the sister of Sam Wagstaff, Mrs. Thomas Jefferson IV of New York. Mapplethorpe has never avoided publicity; indeed, he has carefully nurtured his celebrity since his work first came to public notice in the mid-seventies.

That summer night at the Whitney Museum, there were sighs of relief when he did arrive for the opening, having been released from St.

Vincent's Hospital only days before. He was in a wheelchair, surrounded by members of his entourage, carrying a cane with a death's-head top and wearing a stylish dinner jacket and black velvet slippers with his initials embroidered in gold on them—a vastly different uniform from the black leather gear that had been his trademark. For those who had not seen the once-handsome figure in some time, the deterioration of his health and physical appearance was apparent and quite shocking. His hair looked wispy. His thin neck protruded from the wing collar of his dinner shirt like a tortoise's from his shell. But even ill, he was a man who commanded attention, and who expected it. A grouping of furniture had been placed in the center of the second of the four galleries where the exhibition was hung, and there he sat, with his inner circle in attendance, receiving the homage of his friends and admirers, a complex olio of swells and freaks, famous and unknown, that makes up the world of Robert Mapplethorpe. His eyes, darting about, missed nothing. He nodded his head and smiled, speaking in a voice barely above a whisper. "It's a wonderful night," person after person said to him, and he agreed. He was enjoying himself immensely. On the wall facing him hung *Jim and Tom, Sausalito*, his 1977–1978 triptych of two men in black leather, adorned with the accoutrements of sadomasochistic bondage and torture. In the photographs, Jim, the master, is urinating into the willing, even eager, mouth of Tom, the tied-up slave. "Marvelous," said one after another of the fashionable crowd as they surveyed the work. "Surreal" was the word that came to my mind.

However much you may have heard that this exhibition was not a shocker, believe me, it was a shocker. Robert Mapplethorpe was described by everyone I interviewed as the man who had taken the sexual experience to the limits in his work, a documentarian of the homoerotic life in the 1970s at its most excessive. Even his floral photographs are erotic; as critics have pointed out, he makes it quite clear that flowers are the sexual organs of plants. But the crowds that poured in that night, and kept pouring in for the following three months that the exhibition remained up, had not come just to see the still lifes of stark flowers, or the portraits of bejeweled and elegant ladies of society, like Carolina Herrera and Princess Gloria von Thurn und Taxis and Paloma Picasso, and of artist friends, like

David Hockney and Louise Nevelson and Willem de Kooning, which are also very much a part of Mapplethorpe's *oeuvre*. They had come to see the sexually loaded pictures, freed of all inhibitions, that were hanging side by side with the above in the galleries of the Whitney, like the startling *Man in Polyester Suit*, in which an elephantine-size black penis simply hangs out of the unzipped fly of a man whose head is cropped, or the even more startling *Marty and Veronica*, in which Marty makes oral love to a stockinged and girdled Veronica, whose upper body is cropped off at her bare breasts. Mapplethorpe was a participant in the dark world he photographed, not a voyeur, a point he made clear by allowing a self-portrait showing his rectum—rarely considered to be one of the body's beauty spots—to be hung on the wall of the museum, with a bullwhip up it. The Mapplethorpe sexual influence is so great that in the otherwise scholarly introduction to the catalog of the show, Richard Marshall, an associate curator of the Whitney, made reference to this same photograph as the "*Self Portrait* with a whip inserted in his ass." That night, and on two subsequent visits to the exhibition, I watched the reactions of the viewers to the more graphically sexual pictures. They went from I-can't-believe-what-I'm-seeing-on-the-walls-of-the-Whitney-Museum looks to nudges and titters, to nervous, furtive glances to the left and right to see if it was safe to really move in and peer, and, finally, to a subdued sadness, a wondering, perhaps, of how many of the men whose genitalia they were looking at were still alive.

"On the opening night this amazing strength came to Robert," said Flora Biddle, the granddaughter of Gertrude Vanderbilt Whitney, who is the chairman of the board of trustees of the Whitney Museum, which her grandmother started. "At the end of the evening he got up and walked out, after he had come in a wheelchair."

Later, Mapplethorpe told me his feelings about the opening. "It was pretty good. I kept thinking what it would have been like if I'd been feeling better."

"You've become really famous, Robert," I said. "How does that feel?"

"Great," he said quietly, but shook his head at the same time. "I'm quite frustrated I'm not going to be around to enjoy it. The money's coming in, though. I'm making more money now than I've ever made before."

Today Mapplethorpe charges $10,000 for a sitting. His one-of-a-kind pictures sell for an average of $20,000 each. A Mapplethorpe print from the Robert Miller Gallery, his dealer in New York, starts at $5,000.

"I seem to read something about you every day in the press," I said.

"I do love publicity," he replied. "Good publicity."

In a sense, Sam Wagstaff created Robert Mapplethorpe, but anyone who knows Robert Mapplethorpe will tell you that he was ready and waiting to be created. They met over the telephone when Mapplethorpe was twenty-five and Sam was fifty. "Are you the shy pornographer?" Wagstaff asked when he telephoned him. Robert had heard of Sam before the call. "Everyone said there was a person in the art world I should meet. So Sam came over to look at my etchings, so to speak."

At the time the totally unknown Mapplethorpe was sharing an apartment in Brooklyn with the then totally unknown poet and later rock 'n' roll star Patti Smith, who has remained one of his closest friends. Although he was, in his own words, "doing photographs of sexuality" with a Polaroid camera back then, he did not yet consider himself a photographer. The Polaroid camera had been purchased for him by John McKendry, the curator of prints and photographs at the Metropolitan Museum. Mapplethorpe had become a sort of adopted son to McKendry and his wife, Maxine de la Falaise, the daughter of the English portrait painter Sir Oswald Birley, and was taken about by them into the smart circles of people who later became his friends and patrons. Wagstaff and Mapplethorpe became positive influences on each other's lives. The handsome and patrician Wagstaff, who graduated from Yale and once worked in advertising, had long since moved away from the Upper East Side and New York society world of his birth into the bohemian world downtown. A former museum curator, he had become more and more of a reclusive figure, involved with a group devoted to self-fulfillment called Arica, and sometimes, according to Mapplethorpe, observing whole days of silence. Wagstaff encouraged Mapplethorpe in his photography, and Mapplethorpe persuaded Wagstaff to start collecting photographs. "He became obsessed with photography," said Mapplethorpe. "He bought with a vengeance. It went beyond anything I imagined. Through him, I started looking at photographs in a much more serious way. I got to know dealers. I went with him when he was buying things. It was a great education, although I had my own vision right from the beginning. If you look at my early Polaroids, the style was then what I have now."

Richard Marshall states in his introduction in the catalog that Mapplethorpe "did not feel a strong ideological commitment to photography; rather it simply became the medium that could best convey his statement." Explaining this, Marshall said, "He wasn't a photographer who found his subject. The camera became the best way for him to express himself. Before that he was into collage, drawings, et cetera. He took up the camera to play with, and found that it was what he was looking for."

Barbara Jakobson, who was one of Mapplethorpe's first avid supporters as well as an old friend of Wagstaff's, said, "When I become enthusiastic about an artist, I do not keep my mouth shut. Within five minutes the jungle drums are beating. I like to see people I admire succeed. That was when our friendship started. Robert really saved Sam Wagstaff's life. At the beginning of the seventies, anyone who knew Sam said that he was virtually a recluse. Robert is the one who got him interested in collecting photography. Sam revolutionized the way we look at photographs. When he sold his collection to the Getty Museum, his position in photography was forever assured."

Mapplethorpe does not stint in his acknowledgment of his late friend's patronage. "I was a real hippie. Sam was a real hippie too. Financially he certainly helped me. He was very generous. We never actually lived together. I had a loft on Bond Street, which he bought for me. He had a loft on Bond Street too. We were lovers as well. I think if you're going to do a story, you should get all the facts. It lasted a couple of years. Then we became best friends. I even introduced him to James Nelson, who became his boyfriend after me." He paused before he added, "He's sick at this point too."

"With AIDS?"

"Yes. He's going through all his money. He's spending like crazy. He rents an apartment at Number One Fifth Avenue, where he and Sam lived, but Sam's apartment in that building has been sold."

Shortly after we talked, Jim Nelson died. Nelson, a former hairstylist for the television soap opera "All My Children," inherited 25 percent of Wagstaff's residuary estate, and Mapplethorpe inherited 75 percent. Nelson, aware that he was dying, wanted his money immediately, so Mapplethorpe, through their lawyers, bought out Nelson's share. As Nelson's life neared its end, he fulfilled a long-held dream and rented two suites on the *Queen Elizabeth 2*, one for himself and one for a companion, and sailed to England, where he stayed in a suite at the Ritz Hotel, and then took the Concorde back to New York. He spent the last day of his life making up a list of people he wanted to be notified of his death and another list of people he did not want to be notified, one of these being the person who told me this story.

Barbara Jakobson said, "It was great to observe Robert and Sam together. Sam got such a kick out of Robert, and Robert allowed Sam to be indulgent. Sam was a Yankee with cement in his pocket, but he was very generous with Robert. Sam always meant for Robert to have his money. I was very unhappy over the publicity about the will after Sam died."

Another close woman friend of both men, who did not want to be named, said, "Robert was looking for a patron, and along came Sam. Sam made Robert's career. He showed Robert this other way of life. Robert was into learning more than anyone I ever knew. When Robert met Sam, all the doors opened for him. Sam was his sugar daddy in a way."

Most of Wagstaff's money came from his stepfather, Donald Newhall, who left him and his sister shares of the Newhall Land and Farming Company in California, which later went public. Over the years, Wagstaff sold off some of his shares to buy his art, photography, and silver collections. In his will he left bequests of $100,000 each to the Museum of Modern Art, the Metropolitan Museum, and the New York Public Library, as well as $10,000 and the family silver to his sister, Mrs. Jefferson, and $10,000 to each of her three children.

"She's enormously rich," said Mapplethorpe about Mrs. Jefferson. "She didn't need the money."

"Then why did she contest the will?"

Mapplethorpe shrugged. "She needed entertainment," he said. In the long run, the litigation never went to trial; Wagstaff's sister decided against proceeding with the suit on the day of jury selection. Several subsequent lawsuits over Wagstaff's million-dollar silver collection, in which Mapplethorpe charged the New York Historical Society with "fraudulent conduct" in obtaining a five-year loan of Wagstaff's silver as he lay dying, were settled out of court.

Mapplethorpe's lawyer, Michael Stout, who handles many prominent people in the creative arts, said about him, "Robert is the most astute businessman of any of my clients. If there is a decision to be made, he understands the issues and votes the right way."

Although I had known Sam Wagstaff for years, my contact with Robert Mapplethorpe was minimal, no more than an acquaintanceship, so I was surprised when he asked me to write this article, and more surprised when he asked to photograph me. Two years ago, right after Sam Wagstaff died, when the rumors of litigation between his family and his heir over his will were rampant, I had thought of writing an article on the subject for this magazine. Mapplethorpe, however, let it be known through his great friend Suzie Frankfurt, the socialite interior decorator, that he did not wish me to write such a piece, and I immediately desisted. Later I saw him at the memorial service for Sam that was held at the Metropolitan Museum. Already ill himself, he made a point of thanking me for not writing the article.

I had met Mapplethorpe for the first time several years earlier, at a dinner given by the Earl of Warwick at his New York apartment. Although Mapplethorpe was then famous as a photographer, the celebrity that was so much a part of his persona was due equally to his reputation as a leading figure in the sadomasochistic subculture of New York. Indeed, he was the subject of endless stories involving dark bars and black men and bizarre behavior of the bondage and domination variety. He arrived late for the dinner, dressed for the post-dinner-party part of his night in black leather, and became in no time the focus of attention and unquestionably the star of Lord Warwick's party. He was at ease in his surroundings and, surprising to me, up on the latest gossip of the English smart set, telling stories in which Guinness and Tennant names abounded. When coffee was served, he took some marijuana and a package of papers out of his pocket, rolled a joint, lit it, inhaled deeply, all the time continuing a story he was telling, and passed the joint to the person on his right. It was not a marijuana-smoking group, and the joint was declined and passed on by each person to the next, except for one guest who, gamely, took a few tokes and then passed out at the table, after saying, "Strong stuff." Unperturbed, Mapplethorpe continued talking until it was time for his exit. After he was gone, those who remained talked about him.

Like everything else about Robert Mapplethorpe, the studio where he now lives and works on a major crosstown street in the Chelsea section of New York, which was also purchased for him by Wagstaff, is enormously stylish and handsomely done. In 1988 it was photographed by *HG* magazine, and Martin Filler wrote in the accompanying text, "Mapplethorpe's rooms revel in the pleasures of art for art's sake and reconfirm his aesthetic genealogy in a direct line of descent from Oscar Wilde and Aubrey Beardsley through Christian Bérard and Jean Cocteau." There are things to look at in every direction, a mélange of objects and pictures, but everything has its place. Order and restraint prevail. "You create your own world," said Mapplethorpe. "The one that I want to live in is very precise, very controlled." It fits in with his personality that he pays his bills instantly on receiving them.

Each time we met, we sat in a different area. In the back sitting room of the floor-through loft space, the windows have elegant brown-black taffeta tieback curtains designed by Suzie Frankfurt, which seem both incongruous and not at all incongruous. Frankfurt, who maintains a complicated friendship with him, said "Robert lives in the middle of a contradiction—part altar boy and part leather bar." That day he was wearing a black dressing gown from Gianni Versace, the Italian designer, and his black velvet slippers.

At one point he went into a paroxysm of coughing, and from the look he gave me I realized he didn't want me to see him like that. "Would you excuse me for a minute," he said. I got up and went to another part of the apartment until he called me back.

"Oh, I'm so sick," he said. "I've been throwing up all night. The nights are awful."

"When did you first know you had AIDS?" I asked.

"It was diagnosed as AIDS two years ago in October."

"Did you suspect beforehand that you had it?"

"Every faggot suspects beforehand."

He said that he had two nurses on twelve-hour shifts that cost him a thousand dollars a day. "But I'm lucky. I have insurance." He has been on AZT almost from the beginning. He worries constantly about friends who are less fortunate, specifically his black friends. In a conversation with Marlies Black, who assembled the Rivendell Collection of modern art and photography, which contains the largest selection of Mapplethorpe's work in the world, he once said, "At some point I started photographing black men. It was an area that hadn't been explored extensively. If you went through the history of nude male photography, there were very few black subjects. I found that I could take pictures of black men that were so subtle, and the form was so photographical." Now, musing on that, he said, "Most of the blacks don't have insurance and therefore can't afford AZT. They all die quickly, the blacks. If I go through my *Black Book*, half of them are dead."

When I sat for him to be photographed, I was nervous, even though he had asked me to sit. It was on a day that he was not feeling well. He had not slept the night before. He coughed a great deal. His skin was very pale. We sat on the sofa and talked while Brian English, his assistant, set up the camera and chair where I would sit for the picture. Although ill, Mapplethorpe kept working most days. He showed me pictures he had taken a day or two before of the three-year-old daughter of the actress Susan Sarandon, and he had arranged to photograph Carolina Herrera, the dress designer, as soon as he was finished with me. I was talking about anything I could think of, mostly about people we both knew, to postpone the inevitable. Finally, I told him I was nervous. "Why?" he asked. "I just am," I said. "Don't be," he said quietly. I was struck as always by his grace and manners, which seemed such a contradiction to the image most people have of Robert Mapplethorpe. Finally Brian placed me in the chair, and Robert got up and walked very slowly over to where the Hasselblad camera was set up. He looked in the viewfinder. He asked Brian to move a light. He made an adjustment on a lens opening. "Look to the left," he said. "Keep your head there. Look back toward me with your eyes." He was in charge.

Another time, I remarked that he was looking better. He told me that he was finally able to eat something called TPN, a totally nutritious substance which gave him 2,400 calories a day. "I don't actually eat. I'm fed mostly by tube. If I hadn't found this, I'd be dead by now. I couldn't keep any food down." And then he said a line I heard him say over and over. "This disease is hideous."

"My biggest problem now is walking. I have neuropathy, like when your foot's asleep. It's constant. It's in my hands too. If it weren't for that, I'd go out." His eyes moved toward the window. "I'd like to go to Central Park to see the new zoo. And I'd like to go back to the Whitney to see the show. I hear there are lines of people to see it."

He was born in a middle-class suburban neighborhood called Floral Park, which is on the edge of Queens, New York, the third of six children in a Catholic family of English, German, and Irish extraction. His mother is a housewife. His father does electrical work. He went to a public school in Floral Park, but he would have preferred to go to the Catholic school, which his younger brothers went to. Although he now says that Floral Park was a perfect place for his parents to raise a family, early yearnings in nonconformist directions brought his family life to a halt. "I wanted to have the freedom to do what I wanted to do. The only way to do that was to break away. I didn't want to have to worry about what my parents thought. When I was sixteen, I went to college at the Pratt Institute. That was when I began to live elsewhere."

Except for his brother Edward, the youngest of the six, who was at the studio each time I was there, he has not been close to his family for years, although he said that they are "closer since I told them I was sick, which was not too long ago."

"Did your parents come to see your show at the Whitney?" I asked him.

He shook his head no. "They intend to," he said. Then he added, "But they have come to see me here."

While still in school, he began living with Patti Smith, whom he met in Brooklyn. Maxine de la Falaise McKendry remembered that when

Robert first met Smith he kicked a hole through from his apartment to hers so that they could communicate better. "Patti and I built on each other's confidence. We were never jealous of each other's work. We inspired each other. She became recognized first. Then she had a record contract. She pushed ahead. There was a parallel happening to each career." Patti Smith, who is now married with two children, lives in Detroit. "We talk to each other all the time," he said.

"S&M is a certain percentage of Robert's work, and necessary to show, to give a representation of his work," said Richard Marshall. He told me that when they put the exhibition together there had never been any idea of censorship, or any reservation about including offensive material, although, he added, "there are some stronger pictures which do exist, some more explicitly graphic pictures, the uh, penetration of the arm." What Marshall was referring to was what Mapplethorpe calls his fist-fucking file. "Call Suzanne," he said to me, speaking of his lovely young secretary, Suzanne Donaldson, "and ask her, if you want to see the fist-fucking file, or the video of me having my tit pierced." When certain of these photographs were shown at an art gallery in Madrid, the gallery owner, who has since died of AIDS, was sent to jail.

"There were some letters of protest about the show, but not in great numbers at all," said Marshall. "We put up signs in three or four locations, warning parents that the show might not be applicable for children."

Flora Biddle concurs. "I went on a tour of the show the night before it opened with the Whitney Circle, which is the highest category of membership. Richard Marshall talked about the pictures to the group, dealing with the pictures you could call the most sexual, and spoke beautifully about them. The people in the Circle were attentive and open to them. Afterward, people came up and said they thought it was so wonderful the Whitney was hanging this show."

Barbara Jakobson said, "Sometimes I'd drive downtown in my yellow Volkswagen to have dinner with Robert. Then, later, I'd drop him off at the Mineshaft, or one of those places. God forbid he be seen having a woman drop him off, so I'd leave him a block away. I had no desire to see inside, but I once asked Robert to describe what it was like, in an architectural way. He said there were places of ritual. He told me how the rooms were divided, without telling me what actually went on. Once he showed me a sadomasochistic photograph. I said to him, 'I can't believe that a human being would allow this to be done.' He replied, 'The person who had it done wanted it to be done. Besides, he heals quickly.' Robert would find these people who enjoyed this. The interesting part is that they posed for him."

When I discussed this conversation with Mapplethorpe, he said, "I went to the Eagles Nest and the Spike to find models. Or I'd meet people from referrals. They'd hear you were good at such and such a thing, and call. I was more into the experience than the photography. The ones I thought were extraordinary enough, or the ones I related to, I'd eventually photograph."

"Were drugs involved?"

"Oh, yes. I've certainly had my share of drug experiences, but I don't need drugs to take pictures. They get in the way. However, drugs certainly played a big factor in sex at that time. MDA was a big drug in all this. It's somewhere between cocaine and acid.

"Most of the people in S&M were proud of what they were doing. It was giving pleasure to one another. It was not about hurting. It was sort of an art. Certainly there were people who were into brutality, but that wasn't my take. For me, it was about two people having a simultaneous orgasm. It was pleasure, even though it looked painful.

"Doing things to people who don't want it done to them is not sexy to me. The people in my pictures were doing it because they wanted to. No one was forced into it.

"For me, S&M means sex and magic, not sadomasochism. It was all about trust."

"If his S&M work were heterosexual, it wouldn't be acceptable," I was told by a world-famous photographer, who, because of Mapplethorpe's illness, did not wish to be quoted by name making critical remarks about him. "The smart society that has accepted his work has done so because it is so far removed from their own lives."

Even before the AIDS crisis, though, Mapplethorpe had begun to move away from the S&M scene as subject matter for his photography. One of his closest associates said to me, "Robert had gotten more and

more away from being a downtown personality. He had been observing the uptown life for some time, and I think he wanted to become a
society photographer. Once, leaving someone's town house on the Upper East Side, he said, 'I wouldn't mind living like that.' "

Carolina Herrera, the subject of one of Mapplethorpe's earliest and
most celebrated society portraits, has known him for years, "long before he was famous." They met on the island of Mustique in the
Caribbean in the early 1970s, when Herrera and her husband were
guests of Princess Margaret, and Mapplethorpe, along with his English friend Catherine Tennant, was a guest of Tennant's brother
Colin, who is now Lord Glenconner. Tennant remembers Mapplethorpe at the time wearing more ivory bracelets up his arms than the
rebellious Nancy Cunard wore in the famous portrait Cecil Beaton
took of her in 1927. When Mapplethorpe took Herrera's picture in a
hotel room in New York, he had only a minimum of photographic
equipment and no assistant. Herrera's husband, Reinaldo, had to hold
the silver umbrella reflector for him. Mapplethorpe photographed
Herrera wearing a hat and pearls, against a blank ground, and since
then his style in social portraiture has remained as stark as in his nude
figures, mirroring the sculptural influence of Man Ray more than the
ethereal settings of Cecil Beaton.

On Friday evening, November 4, 1988, Robert Mapplethorpe gave a
large cocktail party at his studio to celebrate his forty-second birthday. Incidentally, November 4 was also the birthday of Sam Wagstaff.
Birthday celebrations have always been important to Mapplethorpe,
according to Barbara Jakobson. She remembered other birthday parties in the past that Sam had given for Robert. " 'Sam is going to give
me a party,' Robert would say in advance."

At the peak of the birthday party, nearly two hundred people milled
through the vast studio, among them the film stars Susan Sarandon,
Sigourney Weaver, and Gregory Hines, all of whom had been photographed by Mapplethorpe. In the crowd were Prince and Princess Michael of Greece, the Earl of Warwick, Tom Armstrong of the Whitney
Museum, gallery owner Mary Boone, Bruce Mailman, who was a
managerial partner in the St. Marks Baths until it was closed down in
the wake of the AIDS epidemic, and Dimitri Levas, the art director

and principal stylist on Mapplethorpe's fashion shoots, who is said to be one of his heirs, as well as well-known figures from the magazine, gallery, auction, and museum worlds. And collectors. And people who were just friends. Inevitably, there were men in black leather, some wearing master caps, standing on the sidelines, watching. Everyone mixed.

Everybody brought gifts, wonderfully wrapped, and soon there was a mountain of them on a bench by the front door. Bouquets of flowers kept arriving throughout the party, including one of three dozen white roses in a perfect crystal vase. Waiters in black jackets moved through the crowd, carrying trays of fluted glasses of champagne. On several tables were large tins of beluga caviar, and Robert kept leaning over and helping himself.

Although there was certainly a sense that this was Robert Mapplethorpe's farewell party for his friends, there were no feelings of sadness in the studio that night. Robert, continually indomitable, provided his guests with an upbeat and optimistic celebration. He looked better than he had looked in weeks. He sat in his favorite chair, missing nothing, receiving guest after guest who came and knelt by his side to chat with him. Toward the end of the evening, he stood up and walked.

"This is Robert. This is his life. Everybody beautiful. Everybody successful," said one of the guests whom I did not know.

"Robert has style," said Prince Michael of Greece, surveying the event. "Personal style is not something you learn. It's something you have."

One of the most frequently asked questions these days is where Robert Mapplethorpe will leave his money when he dies. His lawyer, Michael Stout, refused to answer the question. But it is known that the photographer has recently set up the Robert Mapplethorpe Foundation, with a board of directors. Besides specific bequests to friends, the foundation will probably give money to the arts as well as to the American Foundation for AIDS Research (AmFAR), an organization with which Mapplethorpe had been associated since Sam Wagstaff's death. In a letter he sent out asking friends and acquaintances to pay $100 each to attend a private viewing of Sam Wagstaff's silver collection prior to its

sale at Christie's in January, he wrote, "I have asked AmFAR to use the
funds raised from this benefit to support community-based trials of
promising AIDS drugs, a pilot program which will greatly increase
patient access to treatments that may help extend their lives."

February 1989

---

*A terrible timing accident happened when this article, with its obituary-
sounding title, appeared on the stands* before *Robert Mapplethorpe's
death. His lawyer and friends were outraged, although Mapplethorpe
took it in good grace. He died nobly and bravely shortly afterward. On
my last visit with him, he took a photograph of me, one of the last he
ever shot. It arrived at my New York apartment after his death. I will always treasure it.*

THE LIGHT OF HUSSEIN

People came because she was beautiful, and were then awed by her brilliance. She had dispelled the fairy-tale image. "This is no fairy tale. This is not a fairy tale at all," said Sarah Pillsbury, the Hollywood film producer, about her Concord Academy classmate Queen Noor al Hussein after the queen had spoken in the United States in October, defending the controversial role of her husband, King Hussein of Jordan, in the Middle East crisis. The Arab kingdom is precariously situated, bordered by Iraq, Israel, Syria, and Saudi Arabia. Should a war erupt, Jordan could become a battlefield. But in Amman, the capital, there was no overt sense of turbulence, or of a country close to war, during my visit two weeks later.

Foreign correspondents, on their way to and from Baghdad or Riyadh, talked in the bar of the Inter-Continental Hotel of atrocities and war, but taxi drivers and shopkeepers did not. Over dinner, the minister of information, speaking for the king, told a group of American journalists, "We don't want war. We are extremely nervous about military action in the area. We cannot afford to have a war. Jordan will be destroyed." But life seemed to go on as usual. In Petra, "the rose-red city half as old as time," I asked a Bedouin guide, "Don't you worry about the crisis?" "No," he replied, "we live our life in crisis. We have our faith. We're not afraid of death."

I had come hoping to see the American queen, whom I had heard speak several weeks earlier at the Brookings Institute in Washington, D.C., but my visit began inauspiciously. Checking into the Inter-Continental Hotel, I was confronted by a figure from the palace, Fouad Ayoub, who informed me that there were obstacles. The appointment for an interview with Her Majesty, he said, was unfixed, uncertain, and unpromised. There was a reluctance to let me meet with her until certain guidelines had been agreed upon, guidelines that were never going to be agreed upon. The best I was able to muster up was an evening visit with the only female member of the Jordanian senate, Laila Sharaf. An unpromising interview, of real interest to neither Mrs. Sharaf nor me.

The taxi driver who took me from the Inter-Continental to Mrs. Sharaf's house, high up on a hill on the outskirts of the city, spoke English but resisted all my attempts at conversation. There was, I was soon to discover, an underlying dislike of Americans in the country. In the taxi was a photograph of King Hussein next to one of Iraqi president Saddam Hussein, the man described by President Bush as worse than Hitler. King Hussein, who for many years positioned Jordan as a "moderate" Arab monarchy—who, indeed, has long been one of Washington's staunchest allies in the region—refused to join the anti-Saddam coalition. The surface reasons were apparent: Palestinians, who have sided with Iraq, account for more than half of Jordan's population, and the king could ill afford to ignore their interests. Even those Jordanians opposed to the brutal policies of Saddam Hussein are more opposed to the presence of American troops in the area. Although Jordan has abided by the U.N. sanctions against Iraq, the king's position severely strained his relations with the Bush administration and Saudi Arabia, which reacted by cutting off oil shipments to Jordan, leaving Iraq as its only supplier, and deepening the economic crisis.

At Mrs. Sharaf's large and handsome villa, the scent of night-blooming jasmine filled the air. The flower garden was in full bloom, and birds in great profusion sang on the roof. It was a setting of Middle Eastern luxe, marred only by the presence of an armed guard in a sentry box. I asked the taxi driver to wait for me in the courtyard. He was reluctant until I assured him that I would pay for his waiting time.

Laila Sharaf, the widow of a prime minister, is a distinguished woman in her own right, involved in cultural affairs. With the queen, she was active in starting the Jerash Festival of Culture and Arts, an annual program of dance, poetry, and music held in an ancient Roman amphitheater. The festival brought thousands of tourists to the country and was a boon to the economy, but with the beginning of the Gulf crisis, tourism became nonexistent overnight. Her butler brought a tray with glasses of lemonade, orange juice, cola, and water. We settled on comfortable sofas, and she began to describe to me the duties and accomplishments of the American queen.

A fiercely private woman until the recent events in the Middle East focused attention on her, Queen Noor has never captured the imagination of the American public in the way that Princess Grace of Monaco, her obvious counterpart, did. Comparisons to the late princess are said to disconcert, even annoy, her. In London recently, she attended the play *Love Letters* with her great friend Tessa Kennedy, the interior designer who decorated several residences of the Jordanian royal family. After the show, the queen went backstage to visit one of the stars, another old American friend, Stefanie Powers. A friend of mine who sat behind the queen said she was virtually unrecognized by the audience. She has never become a fashion darling of the international paparazzi in the manner of the Princess of Wales, the Duchess of York, and the two princesses of Monaco. However, since Iraq invaded Kuwait in August, the queen has had a much higher profile, becoming the most visible woman in the Middle East. She played a major role in helping to organize aid for the nearly three-quarters of a million refugees who fled from Kuwait and flooded into her adopted country. The presence of the refugees placed an enormous burden on Jordan's already stricken economy. Her main priority was to help get the refugees home, and to accomplish that she personally enlisted the aid of Richard Branson, the British music and entertainment entrepreneur, who owns Virgin Atlantic Airways. The queen had recently returned from the United States, where she had spoken publicly in New York and Washington and had been interviewed by Barbara Walters on "Nightline." On that program she evidenced her skill in evading ticklish questions. When Walters asked her to describe her impression of Saddam Hussein, she replied that she had met him only once, very briefly. When Walters continued, "When your husband comes home after he's had these meetings, how does he describe him?" the queen replied, "My husband and I discuss issues more than personalities."

She was criticized in Jordan by those who felt it was not the natural role of the wife of the king to give speeches about foreign policy. In addressing such criticism, Mrs. Sharaf said, "The queen not only understands the facts, but she has put herself on the same perspective as the Arabs. Her way of thinking is very Western, but she has absorbed the Arab side."

Outside the house, arrival sounds could be heard. The butler hurried into the room and spoke excitedly to Mrs. Sharaf in Arabic. "She is here," Mrs. Sharaf said, surprised.

"Who?" I asked.

She rose and rapidly made her way to the hall and opened the door. A BMW motorcycle was driving into the courtyard. On it was King Hussein, the longest-ruling leader in the Arab world. Sitting behind him on the seat, arms around his waist, was Queen Noor. A military vehicle filled with soldiers came up behind them.

Suddenly feeling like an intruder, I said, "Would you like me to leave?"

"No, no. Wait in that room," my hostess told me.

I retreated to the salon and listened as she greeted the king and queen. The royal couple said they had been out for an evening spin in the hills above Amman and had decided to call on Mrs. Sharaf. Then I heard the lowered voice of Mrs. Sharaf explaining my presence in the adjoining room.

Suddenly the door opened, and the queen walked into the salon where I was standing. She is thirty-nine years old, tall, slender, and exceptionally good-looking. She was wearing blue jeans and a loose-fitting light blue sweater, but her carriage was as regal as if she had been in coronation regalia. Her long honey-colored hair fell to her shoulders, kept in place by a headband. Despite the informality of her dress and the situation we found ourselves in, however, the formal distance of royalty prevailed. She had come to pay an impromptu call on a friend and had found an unexpected visitor. "Sir," she said in greeting. Later I discovered she addresses most men as "sir."

Her looks are American. Her handshake is American. Her eye contact is American. And yet, somehow, she is ceasing, or has even ceased, to be American. In Washington earlier in the month, when she spoke at the Brookings Institute, she had several times said, "Speaking as an Arab . . ." Lisa Halaby, Princeton '74, has truly become, during the twelve years of her marriage, the Queen of Jordan. Her voice is American, but her manner of speech is not. So deliberate is her prose style that at times I had the ridiculous feeling that she was translating in her mind from Arabic to English. She often interjects phrases such as "if you will" and "as it were." There is no chitchat. There are no short answers. Every sentence is carefully thought out and spoken in a modulated, complicated, sometimes convoluted manner.

Behind her, a moment later, the king appeared. He, too, was dressed for biking, in a black leather jacket and aviator glasses, but even though his attire was informal, his history enveloped him. The thirty-eighth-generation descendant of the Prophet, he has been on the throne of the Hashemite kingdom of Jordan for thirty-eight years. At the age of fifteen, he witnessed the assassination of his grandfather King Abdullah during a visit to the Al Aqsa Mosque in Jerusalem. The same assassin then fired at him, but the bullet was deflected by a medal on the tunic of his military-school uniform. Two years later, he succeeded his mentally unstable father, King Talal, to the throne. If he was distressed at finding a reporter present during a rare private moment in his overcast life, he gave no indication of it. We shook hands. In all the official photographs that hang in the shop windows and office buildings of Amman, the king stands considerably taller than the queen. In reality, the queen is taller than the king by almost a head. Mrs. Sharaf motioned us to sit, and the butler reappeared with his tray of juices and cola. In the awkward moments that followed, I said that although I had hoped to meet them I had never expected to encounter them on a motorcycle.

"We courted on a motorcycle," said the queen. I was struck by the old-fashioned word "courted." "It was the only way we could get off by ourselves." Then she added, with a slight nod of her head to the courtyard outside, where the king's guards were, "Of course, we were always followed."

They discussed the Nobel Peace Prize, which had been awarded that day to Mikhail Gorbachev. The king had sent him a telegram of congratulations. They discussed Vaclav Havel. The queen said she had never met Havel, but would like to. She added that their days of travel were limited, at least for the time being. Invariably, the conversation

returned to the Gulf crisis. It is a constant in everyone's mind. It is the
dark cloud over their country and monarchy. "The country has never
been more united," she said.

Although she is a beautiful woman, her intelligence rather than her
beauty is her dominant force. She has weathered gossip and criticism,
but even those salon ladies, as they are called, meaning the upper-class
ladies of Amman, who most disliked her in the beginning have a
grudging respect for the manner in which she recently presented the
view of her country in the United States. Her husband, who has been
on the throne since his wife was one year old, is at the peak of his
popularity in his country. Several times during the visit, he looked over
at her and smiled. There is an open affection between them. When she
returned from her recent trip abroad in the royal family's Gulfstream
jet, the king was at the airport to meet her.

In the course of the conversation, the queen mentioned that she
would visit the new site of the Jubilee School the next day. The Jubilee
School is one of her pet projects, a three-year coeducational boarding
school for the most gifted high-school students in the region, providing them with scholarships to develop their leadership potential.

After fifteen minutes I departed, leaving them to their visit. Outside, in the courtyard, the king's motorcycle had been parked by the
front door. Eight soldiers carrying assault rifles hovered by the guard-
house waiting for their monarch. My taxi driver, who had been hereto-
fore so disagreeable, was now wide-eyed with awe. He was convinced
that the king had arrived by motorcycle at the hilltop villa specifically
to meet with me in secret conference. I did nothing to dissuade him of
his misperception. The following morning a call came from the palace,
inviting me to go along with the queen on her visit to the Jubilee
School. In the days that followed, every time I encountered the taxi
driver at the taxi stand in front of the hotel, we shook hands and chatted amiably, but by that time I was being picked up by silver Mercedes
sedans with soldier-chauffeurs provided by the palace, and had no
more need of taxis.

Queen Noor al Hussein was born Lisa Najeeb Halaby on August
23, 1951, into a prominent Arab-American family. Her well-known father, Najeeb Halaby, known as Jeeb, was of Syrian descent. He headed
the Federal Aviation Administration during the Kennedy-Johnson

years and was at one time the president of Pan American World Airways. Lisa was fashionably educated at the National Cathedral School in Washington, D.C., and the Concord Academy in Massachusetts before entering Princeton University in its first coeducational freshman class. She wore a black armband to protest the Vietnam War and became one of the first women cheerleaders. "She wore white ducks. She was the most gorgeous thing you ever saw, with her long hair," recalled television producer Gillian Gordon, one of her classmates and still a close friend. After her sophomore year, she took a year off and moved to Aspen, Colorado, where she supported herself as a waitress. She also did work in the library of the Aspen Institute and indulged her passion for skiing. Returning to Princeton, she took her degree in architecture and urban planning. Her graduation yearbook picture shows a rather plain girl with long, stringy hair and a quizzical, faraway look in her eyes. Beside their pictures, most of her classmates have a paragraph about themselves, describing academic accomplishments and future dreams. But not Lisa Halaby. Beside her picture is a blank white space, startling in retrospect, as if her past had already been put behind her and her future as the queen of a Middle Eastern country was too unfathomable even to imagine.

After Princeton she traveled to Australia and Iran, where she was hired as an assistant by Marietta Tree, the director of the American branch of the British architectural and planning firm of Llewelyn-Davis, Weeks. The firm had been commissioned by the late Shah of Iran to replan the city of Teheran, and Lisa Halaby lived there for six months doing architectural drafting. From Teheran she went to Jordan, where her father was closely connected with the head of Alia, the Jordanian airline, to work on a plan for the creation of an Arab air university. She was introduced to King Hussein when he was attending a ceremony to mark the arrival of the first jumbo jet to join Alia, which later became Royal Jordanian Airlines.

The king's first marriage, to Dina Abdul Hamid, whom he had met in London when still a schoolboy, took place in 1955, shortly after his nineteenth birthday. Dina, seven years his senior, was an intellectual with a university education and a keen understanding of the politics of the Arab world. The marriage was encouraged by his mother, Queen Zein, who admired Dina's intelligence and Hashemite credentials and was eager for her son to settle down. A daughter, Princess Alia, was born but the marriage collapsed only eighteen months after the wedding. While Dina was on a holiday in Egypt, the king divorced her. For the next six years, Princess Dina was allowed to see her daughter only once. Many years later, Dina married a Palestinian commando who was also seven years younger than she.

In 1961, King Hussein married for the second time. His bride, Antoinette "Toni" Gardiner, was a nineteen-year-old English girl, the daughter of a lieutenant colonel serving in Jordan. They were introduced at a dance. Toni became a Muslim and adopted an Arab name, Muna al Hussein, meaning "Hussein's wish." Like Dina, Muna was made a princess, but not queen, and when Hussein announced the engagement on the radio, he described Muna as a Muslim, but not as an Arab. Her English background was left for a subsequent announcement. A year later a much-hoped-for son was born. Prince Abdullah was named after Hussein's slain grandfather. Another son followed, Prince Feisal, and twin daughters, Princess Zein and Princess Aisha. In addition, Alia, his daughter from his marriage to Princess Dina, was brought up by Princess Muna as one of her own family.

By the end of 1972, King Hussein had met and fallen in love with Alia Toukan, the daughter of a Jordanian diplomat. To the surprise of most people in Jordan, who were unaware of any problem in his marriage, the king divorced Princess Muna and married Alia, whom he made Queen of Jordan. In 1977, Queen Alia was killed in a helicopter crash while returning from visiting a hospital in the south of Jordan. The queen left behind two children, Princess Haya and Prince Ali, as well as an adopted daughter, Abir. Abir as an infant had survived an air crash in which her mother was killed. She was found alive, cradled in her dead mother's arms. Alia was moved by the baby's plight and adopted her from her father, a Jordanian truck driver. Abir was brought up in the palace on equal footing with her royal siblings. In the five years of her marriage, Alia had become a popular and beloved queen. The king was grief-stricken by her death, and the nation was plunged into mourning. For a while he withdrew into seclusion.

When the king met Lisa Halaby, the attraction between the two was immediate. Marietta Tree, who was visiting in Jordan at the time, remembers being told by Lisa that the king had asked her to lunch.

Later that day, returning from a trip to Petra, Mrs. Tree asked, "How was the lunch?" Lisa told her, "It lasted five hours. He showed me the palace, and we played with the children." One of her close friends told me that she detested the word "dated" when speaking of her romance with the king. They "courted" for six weeks, escaping from the ever-watchful eye of Amman society, sometimes on the king's motorcycle for jaunts in the country and sometimes by helicopter for private dinners at Aqaba, the beach resort on the Red Sea, where the king maintains a summer residence.

Lisa Halaby converted to Islam and took the name Noor al Hussein, which means "light of Hussein." They were married on June 15, 1978, and the new queen became stepmother to the king's eight children, adopting Abir, who was then seven, and the two small children of Queen Alia. Sarah Pillsbury said of her old friend, "She was always very bright and very mature. We were always very impressed with her. She got in touch with me about a year after the wedding, and we have kept in touch since then. I was struck by her dignity and her determination to be the best wife and queen. The king never said to her, 'Do this. Do that.' She figured it out herself. Has she changed? None of us are the same people we were back then, and she's not, either." Another friend, the journalist Carinthia West, who attended the National Cathedral School with her, said, "Sure, it was hard for her in the beginning. She had no family. No buddies." It is a fact that there was a great deal of resentment toward the new queen at the beginning of her marriage, especially on the part of the fashionable ladies of Amman. There are indications also that jealousies occurred in the king's family over the new, fourth wife of the king. "It wasn't just because she's tall, blond, and American," a Jordanian woman told me. "It was because she became the queen." In the years that have followed, Queen Noor has had four children of her own. Prince Hamzah was born in 1980, Prince Hashim in 1981, Princess Iman in 1983, and Princess Raiyah in 1986.

When the queen goes about her daily duties, she travels in a motorcade, but there are no Daimlers, no Rollses, no Bentleys, no sirens, and no flags. This queen drives herself, in a jeep—a Mercedes jeep, but a jeep nonetheless. She chooses who is going to ride with her, and her companions change during the day so that she can talk privately with her attendants or her guests. Her jeep is in the middle of the motorcade, preceded and followed by military vans with soldiers.

On several occasions I rode in the jeep with the queen. She drives the way she speaks, carefully. Unlike the English princesses, who are always being stopped for speeding, she does not drive fast. She is sometimes recognized by passengers in other cars, who lean out their windows to wave at her. She always smiled and waved back. At a busy five-way intersection in the middle of the city, one of the soldiers in the vehicle ahead of the jeep hopped out to halt traffic in all directions so that the queen and her party could go through. "I don't like when they do that," she said. She stopped the jeep, shook her head, and waved the other cars through, sitting out the red light like any other driver. When the light turned green, she passed through the intersection. The traffic cop on duty smiled at her, and she waved back at him. "He knows me," she said.

After looking over the new facilities for the Jubilee School, she visited a school for girls, going from classroom to classroom, listening to children recite or perform, talking to as many of them as possible, giving her full attention to each conversation. About 50 percent of Jordan's population is under the age of fifteen. There is no bobbing and curtsying to her as there is to English royals making their official rounds in flowered hats. Rather, the queen extends her hand in the American manner and almost immediately engages in conversation. Her style of dress is extremely simple: Usually she wore a below-the-calf-length khaki skirt with a blue denim shirt and a blazer. She told me that when she was first married she was taken aside by an adviser and told that her duties would consist, for example, of cutting ribbons to open schools and buildings. She knew that her role would exceed such functions, but there was no precedent in the country for an activist queen. "I had always worked," she said. "My role has been a pioneering role."

When she is performing her official duties, she speaks only in Arabic. "It's my working language," she said. "I use no English when I am working with the people in the country, but I use both English and Arabic with people in the scientific fields." She now speaks the language fluently but says, "I will never be a great poet in Arabic. It's such a challenging language." With the king, who was educated in England at Harrow and Sandhurst, she speaks both languages, but they converse primarily in English. "My children are completely bilingual, more than I could ever be. I spoke only Arabic with my first child. I hope and pray they won't have to study Arabic as a second language. I want them to think in Arabic. They all go to Arabic schools. Their courses are taught in Arabic, except for English courses. Arithmetic and science are taught in both languages."

"Do they have accents?"

"They don't sound like foreigners speaking English," she replied.

Once, talking about her children, she said, "I was so lucky I was raised the way I was, and that I traveled and worked before I was married. I want my children to do the same before they marry."

"Will you send your children to school abroad?"

"I once said to the headmaster of my husband's school, 'I will send my children to the best school for each one of them when the time comes.' They will study abroad. Each is entitled to have some time to compete equally with everyone else. Within Jordan, they will always be the sons of the king. There will be those who will surround them with too much attention, judge them too easily, even take advantage of them. To really learn how to stand on their own feet, they need to get away."

Despite growing anti-American sentiment, which in some circles extends to the queen, she is in daily touch with her subjects. "The people on the street like her. They get excited when they see her. They don't look *up* to her. They look *to* her for help. They see her as the female, the softer figure whom they can reach out to for help. She has been here twelve years now. She has grown in her job," said Dr. Sima Bahous, an assistant professor of journalism at Yarmouk University, north of Amman.

I went with Queen Noor to the village of Al Bassah, an hour's drive from the capital. It was the first visit ever paid to the village by a member of the royal family. Schoolchildren lined up on both sides of the road to greet her motorcade. Like a latter-day character out of Lesley Blanch's *The Wilder Shores of Love*, the queen walked through rows of clapping schoolboys and cadets to shake hands with the elders of the village. She entered a Bedouin tent and sat on a sofa that had been placed there for her. Opposite her on chairs sat the men of the village, who told her what they needed for the village. She replied in Arabic, promising them help, asking her aides to make notes, speaking in the same deliberate manner as when she speaks in English. Up the hill from the tent, women with covered heads watched from the porch of a house. When she finished with the men, she walked up the hill to the women. They crowded around her, several hundred of them, wanting to be near her. They held up babies. They kissed her hand. She addressed herself with special care to the problems of the women. "We are equal with the men and work together, plus raise our children," they told her. During the harvest, they said, they needed a kindergarten for their children while they worked in the fields. She promised to help them. She went into the olive groves and picked olives with the women, and then walked down into a green valley that looked biblical, where the villagers grew pomegranates and figs.

On the way back to the city, I drove in the jeep with the queen. High on a mountaintop in the distance was a beautiful sprawling estate looking down on the Dead Sea. It was the country house of Prince Muhammad, a brother of the king. "My husband and I were given land up there as a wedding present, but we never built," she said. "Maybe someday, something simple, a place to get away."

The king and queen maintain a large house in London as well as an estate in the English countryside, grand enough to have been lent to the Duke and Duchess of York to live in while their own country house was being built. But their main home is Al Nadwa, the cream-colored royal palace in Amman. As palaces go, Al Nadwa is more like a rich man's mansion than a monarch's royal residence. If all twelve of the king's children were home at the same time—an unlikely event—it would probably be a tight squeeze. A large estate set in the middle of the city, it is in a well-guarded compound with staff offices, guest residences, barracks, and several other palaces, one of which, the old palace of King Abdullah, the king's grandfather, is used by Queen Noor for her foundation and offices.

We sat in the English-looking garden under a white marquee, looking out over a lush green lawn. The marquee seemed to have permanent status in the garden, since the poles were covered with ivy. The

lunch table was set for two. A butler wearing English butler clothes—
dark jacket, striped trousers—carried the food on trays from the
palace down a poplar-lined walkway to where we were sitting.

"This is my favorite room in the house," said the queen. "The garden is a recent thing. I put all this in. Gardening is something new for
me. I wish I'd done it long before. It established an equilibrium with
nature, putting my hands in the dirt, planting."

She looks as though she might have played field hockey in boarding
school, but she complained about not getting enough exercise. "I do
aerobics with a friend who comes here, and play tennis. We don't have
a swimming pool." Plans were drawn up for one several years ago, but
for security reasons it was never built. She likes to dispel the image of
luxury living behind the palace walls. "I like being able to say, 'We
don't have a pool.' "

"Have there been difficulties between you and other women in the
royal family?" I had heard there was a chilly relationship with a sister-
in-law and a former sister-in-law.

She shrugged. "I suppose it is the same in every family," she answered.

"Do you see Queen Zein?" The king's mother, Queen Zein, lives in
a large, well-guarded house on Jubaiha, the road in Amman where
most of the embassies are located. For years Queen Zein was the central figure in the royal family. After King Abdullah's assassination, she
was a powerful influence on her son when he became king.

"If there is a family wedding, part of the celebration will always
take place at her house," replied the queen carefully. "She came to see
me in the hospital each time one of the children was born."

Ever since her marriage, the queen has been gossiped about. She
has been accused of extravagance in clothes and jewels. She has also
been accused of having had plastic surgery on her face, but her friends
insist that clothes and jewels are not where her interests lie. "She is
passionately interested in what's going on," says Marietta Tree. While I
was in Jordan, a report was printed in an American newspaper that
said she had recently purchased an estate in Palm Beach, Florida.
When I asked her about it, she just smiled and shook her head in exasperation. "I am becoming inured to criticism. When you're in my position, people are always going to talk about you." She told me of a
story that went around about her several years ago in which she was

accused of purchasing a ring of extraordinary value. "Everyone knew someone who had seen the bill of sale, but it could never be found. It happened to Raisa Gorbachev too. I work with a wide variety of people from all segments of life. I'll never be approved of by everybody."

In all the time that I spent with her, there was never once when I felt I could have crossed the boundaries into the verbal intimacies of Americans meeting abroad. Her guard is never relaxed. Her conversation is without levity. It is not that she is humorless; it is simply that her sky is so darkened with the winds of war and its consequences that there is no time for laughter in her life. She is always addressed as Your Majesty. As an American, I found it difficult to call another American Your Majesty, but there is no other form of address. There are those in the court who address the king as Sidi, an affectionate term meaning "sir" or "My Lord," and address the queen as Sitti, meaning "My Lady," but I never did.

"How many assassination attempts have there been on the king?" I asked. I had been told there had been twenty-seven during his thirty-eight-year reign.

She waved her hands in front of her face as if to dispel my question. "I don't know. I don't want to know. My husband has learned from experience to be wise and prescient. He gives each moment of his life a maximum energy for good use. If we sealed ourselves off in a protective bubble, we wouldn't be able to reach out and touch and feel what people need. I feel they should be able to touch us. I'm willing to take the risk of being stampeded upon if it gives them hope. It runs against any security advice he has been given over the years. They feel he is not just a figurehead, or head of state in his office. He is there as a father to the people."

"Would you discuss the succession?" I asked her.

"At the moment, Prince Hassan, the king's brother, is the crown prince, so he is the king's successor. In this country, the succession has always been modified to accommodate. The monarchy should always be able to serve as a constructive and unifying force. The most important thing is that it serves the people of the country. For me, it's entirely in harmony with all I was raised to believe the role of the leader should be. It should not seek to protect its existence for its own sake."

When Prince Abdullah, the older son of Princess Muna, was born, in 1962, King Hussein named him as the crown prince, but since the country was in a constantly turbulent state, Hussein realized that a small child was not a reasonable successor. The king has two brothers, Prince Muhammad and Prince Hassan. Muhammad, who was next in line after the child Abdullah, was married to, and later divorced from, the international social figure Princess Firyal, who subsequently had a highly publicized liaison with the Greek shipping magnate Stavros Niarchos. After much consideration, the king bypassed Muhammad in favor of his younger brother, Prince Hassan, who is twelve years younger than the king. Oxford-educated and a brilliant public speaker, Hassan is considered the intellectual of the family. His wife, Princess Sarvath, is the daughter of a distinguished Pakistani leader and ambassador. Since the ratification of Hassan, the king has bypassed his two sons by the English Princess Muna and has named Prince Ali, his son by the Jordanian Queen Alia, as next in line after Prince Hassan. Prince Ali, now fifteen, attends Deerfield Academy in Massachusetts.

"I have heard it said that, because you are an American, you are becoming a liability to the king. Is that correct?"

She seemed surprised. "I haven't felt that. I have never felt it. I was born into an Arab-American family. My name, Halaby, is Arabic. I have returned to the Arab world. I am not aware that my Americanism is a liability."

Although most people in Amman dress in Western fashion, there is a growing group of Muslim fundamentalist women who have eschewed modern dress as a form of protest. "It has come out of the frustrations of the people," Sima Bahous had told me the day before. "Everybody wants an identity. It is more than a religious movement. If they unite behind a front, their voice will be heard."

"Do you feel threatened by the fundamentalists?" I asked the queen.

"I personally don't feel threatened, but I know that my work and what I have achieved could be threatened by them. Extremism will only feed off the economic inequalities. Traditionally, women in this area, even my mother-in-law, Queen Zein, wore their hair covered. It is part of the cultural tradition. As religious extremism started to develop, there came a form of dress that was devoid of color, that covered the body from head to toe. Over it is worn a headdress that is restrictive, an uglifying fashion psychologically, to defeminize, to desex, to make women totally unappealing, to negate their femininity. It is a symbol of submission. There is pressure brought to women to dress like that. I don't dress for the conservatives in society. At the same time, I don't dress the way Western women do, which would be immodest in this country."

"If war comes, do you fear losing your throne?"

"In the first place, I don't consider myself as having a throne. The only thing I would ever fear is if the peace and stability that the monarchy has offered to this country were destroyed, if all my husband struggled for, and what I have struggled for by his side, were lost. That is what I fear for. My happiness, satisfaction, and security do not come from the throne or the monarchy or having been privileged to carry the title of Queen of Jordan."

Her older son, Prince Hamzah, arrived from school and crossed the lawn to greet his mother. Dressed in a black T-shirt and light trousers, he looked like any American boy of ten arriving home from school, ready for playtime. In a garage on the opposite side of the palace, there were miniature Volkswagens and jeeps for the royal children, the kind that run on gasoline. Hamzah was joined by the princes' young American tutor. After greeting his mother and talking about the events of his school day, Hamzah pointed to the far end of the garden and asked, "Can we make some noise down there?"

The queen smiled and nodded to her son, and then resumed the conversation. "People are beginning to realize that we in Jordan don't conform to the worst stereotypes of the oil rich, or the worst stereotypes of the terrorists. Each Arab society is different from the others. For many in the Arab world, Saddam is a patriot. He represents someone who has stood up to the overwhelming forces of the West for what he believes in. He is against Western interference in Arab affairs. For many Arabs, whose history has been marked by Western interference over many decades, his tough stand is deemed to be courageous. Whatever happens, we shall follow King Hussein. For thirty-eight years, his humanity, experience, and wisdom have been what the people identify with."

In the background Prince Hamzah appeared from behind a tree, carrying a very realistic toy assault rifle. The tutor could be seen hiding behind another tree. The queen watched for a minute, shrugged, and said, "I guess he plays war with the boys."

It had turned dark. "Will you turn on the garden lights?" she called out to Prince Hamzah. Then her youngest child, Princess Raiyah, age four, arrived back at the palace from a children's music class. Dressed in pink jeans and a pink T-shirt, she raced to her mother. For several minutes they discussed the music class.

There was the beginning of a chill in the air. "The weather's going to change," she said. "This will be the last time I have lunch in the garden. It will soon be too cold to sit out like this. Sometimes there's even snow." She stood up. "Would you like to see the children's zoo?" she asked.

"If war comes, what will happen to Jordan?" I asked Sima Bahous.

"Some people think Jordan will suffer the most," she replied. "If it comes, the people in the streets will not be quiet. The youth of the country will not accept war without having a say in what will come about."

"Will the king survive?"

"War means change," she said. "Everything will be in danger. Not the king, who is popular, but the institution of monarchy."

On the night before I left Amman, the king and queen asked a small group of American journalists to dinner at the palace. On arriving there, each guest was given a seating plan showing where his or her place would be at the table. Thirty-five minutes after we had assembled and been served nonalcoholic drinks, the king and queen arrived in the reception room and, as a couple, moved around the room, greeting each guest. That night the queen wore tight black trousers and a loose-fitting black evening sweater. The king was wearing a dark business suit.

They did not sit at the head and foot of the long, narrow, elaborately set table. Instead, they sat opposite each other at the center of the table, so that during general conversation they were able to converse together. While we were served food passed by a staff of waiters, the king's plate was brought to him with food already on it. He ate almost nothing. Speaking in quiet tones, he held the attention of the entire table as he explained his role in trying to keep peace in the Middle East since August 2, when he had been awakened by King Fahd of Saudi Arabia at six o'clock in the morning to be told that the invasion of Kuwait had taken place. In the first forty-eight hours, he had gone off to mediate at the request of President Bush, President Mubarak, and King Fahd. He had been given assurances that there would be no condemnation of President Hussein, nothing to put him on the defensive. His efforts at peacekeeping, however, had been misunderstood, mistrusted, or rebuffed by former allies and friends. He seemed mired in personal melancholy, smoking cigarette after cigarette during the meal. Taking a cue from the king, a journalist seated to the left of the queen also lit up a cigarette. The queen mildly chastised the journalist for smoking, a chastisement clearly meant for the king.

Rising at the end of the dinner, the male reporters made a beeline for the queen, surrounding her to ask questions. From the sidelines, the king watched his wife at the center of the group of reporters and smiled proudly and affectionately. Lisa Halaby, Queen Noor al Hussein, had clearly come into her moment in time.

January 1991

I have seen the king and queen of Jordan several times since writing this article shortly before the outbreak of the Gulf War. When one of my sons was lost for five days in a mountain climbing accident during the O. J. Simpson criminal trial, I received a fax from the royal couple saying they were praying for my son's safe return. As of this time, the king, who is being treated for cancer in the United States, played an important part in the Arab-Israeli peace talks with President Clinton in Maryland. The beautiful American-born Queen Noor has become a world presence, known and admired.

. . . AND MORE

PARIS WHEN IT SIZZLES

You happen to be here at the most spectacular week the
couture has had in years.   —Polly Mellen, creative director
of *Allure*, in the elevator at the
Ritz hotel in Paris.

I wanted to do something different from murder trials for a change, and along came haute couture, which may not seem like a very logical transition, although the word "cutthroat," which applied perfectly to the last trial I covered, applied as well, in a business sense, to the rarefied goings-on I witnessed in Paris in January during what is called couture week. Whether sitting on a gold chair watching models parade past in astronomically priced dresses, or lunching at the Bar Vendôme in the Ritz hotel between shows, or dining with devotees of fashion at this or that opulent *hôtel particulier*, as they call town houses over there, I almost never heard anything discussed other than couture, couture, couture. If couture is dying, or dead, as naysayers have been predicting for years, you wouldn't have been aware of it. "It's a fabulous season, the best in years," people who know about such things kept saying to me in tones of joy. "Couture has its energy back!"

Price is not *the issue. It's absurd to talk about price. For*
these women the couture is a necessity: It's having something
no one else has. It's the same thing as collecting art.
—André Leon Talley, *Vanity Fair*
   contributing editor and *Vogue*'s contributing editor-at-large.

What I discovered fast is that there is a lot more to these shows than very rich ladies "who have lost their waists but not their appetite for couture"—to quote Suzy Menkes in the *International Herald Tribune*—planning their wardrobes around their upcoming social schedules. And it's a very different thing from ready-to-wear; no client paying what these dresses cost wants her ball gown to be mistaken for ready-to-wear. To give you an idea of the couture price range, a plain silk T-shirt to be worn under a suit costs $6,000, while the suit itself will set you back another $28,000 or so. A simple black evening dress with no beading or embroidery can cost about $18,000; more elaborate evening dresses go for as much as $250,000. Recently, the divorcing Jocelyne Wildenstein—who was expected at the January shows but did not appear—was photographed at a party in New York wearing a Chanel couture evening dress that cost $350,000. "She kept adding things," I was told.

Couture is considered such a refined art that it takes an exquisite sensibility to "get it," much as opera aficionados can assess and compare the beauty and timbre of great singers' voices in a way others can't. It would be absurd for me to say that I got that sensibility at the shows—you can't "get it" in a week—but I did come away with an understanding of the passion that those who do get it possess. They become transfixed as they talk about it, and an expression approaching rapture comes over their faces. They say things like "There are thousands of hours of embroidery on that" and "Everything made by hand!" For them, the genius of design combined with the craft of sewing is elevated to the level of the sublime.

For a little historical perspective on the matter, the French couture began in the 1860s, during the reign of Napoleon III, when the designer Charles Frederick Worth moved to Paris from London and dressed Empress Eugénie. It reached its apex in the 1950s, when Christian Dior, Jacques Fath, Cristóbal Balenciaga, Coco Chanel, and, later, Hubert de Givenchy ruled supreme as heads of their own houses, and Paris was the center of the fashion universe, from which all dictates pertaining to style emanated. These couturiers, colorful figures all, mixed in the Paris society of the day and understood the lives and needs of the women for whom they were designing. Hubert de Givenchy, the last of them, retired in 1995 and has recently become president of Christie's auction house in Paris, as well as a severe critic of French fashion today, particularly at the house that bears his name. Fashion is no longer a uniquely French institution. Foreigners have moved in on French turf, even into French ateliers. The English lads, as John Galliano and Alexander McQueen are often called, have taken over the reins at Dior and Givenchy. Oscar de la Renta of New York, where he has his own house, designs for Balmain and spends part of the year in Paris. The German Karl Lagerfeld has designed for Chanel for fifteen years, while maintaining his own line as well, and the Italian, Valentino, who recently sold his business and his services for $300 million to an Italian conglomerate, has opened palatial offices on the Place Vendôme, catty-corner to the Ritz, where he gave a splendid dinner for 150 very swell people following his show, which everyone said was his best in years.

This is couture. Nothing is impossible.
> —Katell le Bourhis, fashion adviser
> to Bernard Arnault, president of
> Moët Hennessy Louis Vuitton.

The Ritz, with its sad memory of a dead princess, is where "everyone" stays, meaning the people who get seats in the front row at all the shows, on either the customer or the press side of the aisles. The Ritz is where the action takes place, and it couldn't be more posh. When I arrived at my room, there were bouquets of flowers, baskets of fruit, gifts of cosmetics for men from Thierry Mugler, and invitations to the shows and the parties. Engraved cards soon began arriving—from Florence Grinda, director of public relations for Ungaro, for lunch in honor of Emanuel Ungaro after his show; from Valentino Garavani for dinner after his show in his new digs; from São Schlumberger for dinner in honor of Mrs. William McCormick Blair at her apartment on the Avenue Charles Fouquet; from Giancarlo Giammetti, Valentino's business partner, for lunch at his new, Peter Marino–decorated apartment on the Quai d'Orsay.

In the Ritz lobby, everyone seemed to be racing by on missions of importance. Anna Wintour, the editor of American *Vogue*, waved as she sped past in dark glasses, wearing a chinchilla-trimmed black suede jacket. Amanda Harlech, the muse for Karl Lagerfeld, hurried by, her hair in curlers, her Chanel dress covered in muslin. "I'm being photographed," she called out in passing. Marin Hopper, the fashion director of *Elle*, ran through on her way to the Saint Laurent show. Grace, Countess of Dudley, of New York society, all in black except for a turquoise shahtoush around her neck and clutching her front-row ticket to the Balmain show, paused only to say, "Nice tie." Actually, no one says "the Balmain show." They all say "Oscar's show." Or "We're going to Oscar's." Later, everyone said this was Oscar's best show in years.

From my journal:
The Bar Vendôme at the Ritz was hopping. Joan Collins, here from London for the Valentino show and looking great, was holding court at one table. Anna Wintour and Oscar de la Renta were in deep conversation at another. Baron Alexis de Redé. Princess Firyal of Jordan. Marina Palma. On and on, the kind of people you read about, who say things like "Mongiardino died this morning" and "Valentino wants you to come out to his château." Joy Henderiks, director of haute couture for Chanel, nodded in the direction of two of Paris's most enduring social figures, on a nearby banquette, and said, "They're having a social fling, those two." A social fling turns out to be not quite an affair, embracing all the intimacies except sex.

Last night Valentino had a big party after his show in his new Paris headquarters. The collection was a smash, and he was riding high. It was his best show in years, everyone said. Joan Collins, Princess Firyal, and my old pal Joan Buck were at my table. Joan, who is now the editor of *Paris Vogue*, is peaking, in both the looks and the career departments.

"Who is buying?" I asked a fashion-house directrice.
"Lots of women you've never heard of, whose husbands have made $50 million or so in the last few years."

In the late '50s, Elsa Schiaparelli predicted that jet travel would be the beginning of the end of couture. She said that in the jet age women wouldn't stay in Paris long enough for the fittings that are required for a couture dress to be properly made. Pierre Bergé, the partner of Yves Saint Laurent, predicted a while back that couture would be dead after Saint Laurent. And so it briefly seemed. Then along came Bernard Arnault, who many believe brought back to Paris the spotlight that shines on the couture. Arnault, who started what has become the huge luxury conglomerate Moët Hennessy Louis Vuitton (L.V.M.H.) in 1987, understood that there was gold in the great, known-around-the-world names of Dior and Givenchy, and he believed in perpetuating their magic.

After the death of Christian Dior in 1957, Yves Saint Laurent, whom Dior had named as his successor, took over. In 1962 he left to form his own house. Marc Bohan became design director. After him came Gianfranco Ferrè. In 1997, on the 50th anniversary of Dior's New Look, Arnault was looking for someone to take over the venerable house who would cause the kind of uproar that Dior himself had caused right after World War II. Many people expected that French-born designer Jean-Paul Gaultier would be handed the plum. "The press likes Gaultier," a woman in the business told me. "He's a very bright man and a great designer."

But Arnault surprised everyone. John Galliano had been in Paris for five years when Arnault plucked him from relative obscurity, gave him a brief stint at Givenchy, and then handed him the keys to the kingdom of Dior, while replacing him at Givenchy with 29-year-old Alexander McQueen—both appointments to spectacular effect.

"Do they sell enough dresses to offset the costs of these shows?" I asked Elizabeth Saltzman.
"Of course not."

Being new at the game, I was placed under the expert guidance of Elizabeth Saltzman, the fashion director of *Vanity Fair*, who, though young, is an old hand at the Paris couture, as was her mother, Ellin Saltzman—who covered couture for both Saks Fifth Avenue and Bergdorf Goodman—before her. To give you an idea about Elizabeth, the photographers took as many pictures of her as they did of the movie stars at the Thierry Mugler show, on the day she and I arrived in Paris with Jonathan Becker, our photographer.

I learned all sorts of things from Elizabeth. "The applause for a dress is usually started by someone who works in the house," she told me. She called it "backrow applause." Occasionally, though, the cognoscenti spot a winner and break into spontaneous front-row applause.

In her limited free time, Elizabeth had very chic chores to do. She had to find a special kind of toothpaste for her mother that you can get only in Paris, and she had to take her father's watch to be fixed at his Paris watchmaker's.

Galliano has carte blanche. How many bastions of art are left where an artist is given carte blanche?

— Katell le Bourhis

Whose collection was the best? I don't know. I am a neophyte, and I liked practically everything I saw. But for sheer theatrical thrills, surpassing anything I've seen on Broadway, including the first 20 minutes of *The Lion King*, no one came within a mile of Dior, or, rather, no one came within a mile of John Galliano, who was probably the most talked-about person of the week for showmanship. These days most of the individuals people call geniuses just plain aren't, but I think this guy might be. He has a vivid sense of what he wants to project, and he has made the spectacle his territory. For him, no fantasy is impossible.

Born in Gibraltar and raised in London, the 37-year-old Galliano put on a show at the Opéra National de Paris that was so dazzlingly theatrical, so utterly opulent, so extravagantly decadent that only someone bankrolled by a great conglomerate like L.V.M.H. could afford it. Patrick McCarthy, the editorial director of *Women's Wear Daily* and *W*, told me that Dior's contribution to the Opéra National alone, just for the use of the hall, was $150,000. The show was said to be in the $2 million range. Whatever it cost, it was worth every franc.

Backstage, before the show, it was like an opening night. The place was pulsating with excitement. Actors and extras dressed as adagio dancers, bullfighters, sailors, and ladies of the evening were preparing to set the scene. Galliano does not believe in having a mannequin model more than one dress, and each of the 40 models had her own dresser. When they were made up, coiffed, accessorized, and dressed, Galliano talked to them individually, briefing them on the personality he wanted to accompany each of his creations. He would say, "You're wonderful in that dress. It's marvelous, fantastic on you. Come, look in the mirror at yourself." He showed them how to walk, how to turn, how to swing a train. "He makes everyone feel so magical, so special," one of the models said. I watched him show his house model, Suzanne von Aichinger, who would open the show, how to run up the great marble staircase in a black strapless gown with a 12-foot train. "The collection is made on Suzanne's body," Katell le Bourhis told me. "Every time, he outdoes himself."

Galliano's inspiration for his extravaganza was the famous Boldini portrait of the Marchesa Luisa Casati, a turn-of-the-century figure with many lovers, who once gave a ball and then sold her house to pay for it. She died broke.

The British film and theater set designer Michael Howells, who dressed the opera house for the show, told me he had run Ken Russell's *Valentino* and the ball scene from Franco Zeffirelli's *La Traviata* for inspiration. Dripping candles had been burned down until they were an inch high. The heady scent of garlands of lavender and pink roses slightly past their prime filled the air. Even the seating was inspired. Gold ballroom chairs were artfully askew in all directions, as they would be at the end of a ball, with the name of a guest on each seat. "John likes people to sit not more than two feet away from the clothes," I was told. "If you're ten rows back, you can't see the work."

Diana Ross, just off the Concorde and looking fabulous, walked in and sat in the chair next to me. The Miller sisters, daughters of the duty-free tycoon, were in a box. Madame Pompidou was there. The man behind her was Bernard Arnault's bodyguard. Mrs. Martin Gruss from New York took a seat. There was Dodie Rosekrans from San Francisco. Arnault himself, sitting rigidly stiff, did not look like a man enjoying the opulence he was underwriting, as a crazed Nijinsky figure costumed for *Afternoon of a Faun*, with dyed yellow hair pointed upward, danced past him through the crowd.

"It's a happening," said Paris socialite São Schlumberger, who had been a supporter of Galliano's when he had his own house. A chauffeur in gray livery was pulled along by three borzois. Boys danced the tango together. A dignified, dark-skinned maharaja in silver raiment and diamond necklaces walked haughtily through the rooms in the company of exotic women. It didn't matter that the show started an hour late.

"You've got to be an actress to do that," said Diana Ross about Suzanne von Aichinger, as the house model did a deep curtsy in our direction. I told Diana, "You'd look great in every dress in this collection."

At the end, when Galliano came out for his bow between two models, he was in costume and makeup, as if he were another of the bizarre creatures at the Marchesa Casati's ball. He was dressed not as a duke or a prince but as a Cuban dancer with marcelled hair and his pencil-thin mustache. Just then thousands of green and orange paper butterflies fell from the ceiling. He seemed to be telling his adoring audience, "I am not one of you." As if the moment needed explaining, which it didn't, a French lady nearby said in English, "John does not mix in society. Nothing really interests him other than what he creates."

At the opposite sartorial extreme are Valentino and Oscar de la Renta, who are important figures in the world of the ladies they dress. Their apartments, country houses, and getaway retreats appear regularly in magazines. Both—tanned from holidays in the sun, in bespoke suits, shirts, and shoes—exuded style and success as they walked the runways at the conclusion of their shows.

Galliano's show lasted only 40 minutes, and only about a thousand people saw it, which is all part of the snob value attached to the couture. When the dresses cost $40,000 and more, the show is not meant for the masses. "Look at it this way: the magic is to astound," I was told by Katell le Bourhis. "It's glamorously, willfully decadent. It's a Versailles sort of experience."

"Beautiful, simply beautiful, but not a thing to wear," said one of the New York ladies on the way out. It was the kind of remark that infuriates the people who believe strongly in the couture. To those who called the clothes costumes, one fashion editor responded, "They're not costumes. Hidden away in that madness there were some very good things."

From my journal:

Went to Florence Grinda's lunch at her new apartment on the Rue de l'Université yesterday after the Ungaro show and before the Givenchy show. Lunch was for Florence's boss, Emanuel Ungaro, who received applause as he entered her crowded living room, as well as a kiss of homage on each cheek from the Viscountess Jacqueline de Ribes, a Paris social and fashion figure for four decades. Ungaro was triumphant. Everyone was saying, "It's his best show in years." The room was full of Greek royals. Princess Alexandra of Greece had just ordered her wedding gown from Ungaro. Crown Prince Pavlos was there with Princess Marie-Chantal, one of the three Miller sisters, who have all married so well. Marie-Chantal, who is called M.C., her sister Alexandra Von Fürstenberg, and Alexandra's mother-in-law, Diane Von Furstenberg, are at all the shows, front and center. Elizabeth Saltzman and I had our lunch sitting on Florence's bed with Jacqueline de Ribes. Pierfilippo Pieri, director of international press at Ungaro, told me that Florence is leaving after this show. Alfred Taubman has hired her to be head of European client development for Sotheby's, France.

The way you are seated is almost as important as the show itself. It's a terrible tragedy if you aren't seated well.
—A socially well-connected lady who said not to use her name, forgodsakes, or she wouldn't tell me anything.

A great part of the overall experience is watching the action in the rooms before the fashion show starts. Each of the gold chairs is marked with the name of an invited guest, and banish any thought of changing place cards. The first row means everything. As the celebs take their seats, the photographers run in and surround them. *Get the princess. Get the movie star. Get the Miller sisters.* The New York ladies, who are used to being photographed by the fashion press, walk that special walk society women walk when they know they are going to be photographed. They put even movie stars to shame, they do it so well.

I'm told by a fashion director that a lot of the regular buyers are missing this year. "People like Jayne Wrightsman come in later, after it dies down, and *then* order. Of course, now they take the collections to the United States—imagine what *that* costs—and show them to their clients there. Others they send videos to. There are women whose husbands don't want them to be seen. Besides, they've been doing the couture for so long that they don't get the thrill out of it that the young Miller sisters do."

"Did you order anything?" I asked a Middle Eastern woman I had seen at several shows.
"A few things."
"From where?"
"Two at Dior. Givenchy. Two at Valentino, and I'm on my way to Chanel. Just a few things."

"Glamorous" was the word for the show at Chanel, held in the Rue Cambon atelier of Coco Chanel. Nan Kempner, the New York social figure who has been a fashion perennial for as long as I have known her, which is about thirty-eight years, rushed in wearing a sable-lined raincoat, stopping to kiss a dozen or so people on both cheeks on the way to her seat. Princess Ira Von Fürstenberg and Princess Laure de Beauvau-Craon, of the Old Guard, sat next to Corinne Ricard—the wife of Patrick Ricard, the aperitif manufacturer—of the new guard, who is an important couture buyer. The actress Kristin Scott Thomas, who is about to appear in *The Horse Whisperer* opposite Robert Redford, sat in front of me, as did socialite Susan Gutfreund and business tycoon Linda Wachner of New York.

The models, wildly chic, walked down the famous winding and mirrored stairway, without looking at the steps as they descended. Some of them smoked cigarettes and were covered in jewels. Some wore black veils over their faces, looking like glamorous young widows who had just inherited a ton of money.

"It's so great to be in this house and having models coming down that stairway," said André Leon Talley. "She used to sit at the top of the stairs and watch the models from there." The "she" he was referring to was Coco Chanel, long dead, but resurrected in brilliant fashion by Karl Lagerfeld. "This is serious couture."

For years Talley, who is six feet seven, has been an unmistakable and outspoken presence in the world of fashion. Extravagantly snobbish and extravagantly low-down, hilarious in both modes, he is an oracle and a historian of the couture. Trained by the late, great Diana Vreeland, to whom he used to read books after she could no longer read for herself, he wore a gold-lamé jacket to the Dior show and sat with Isabella Blow, the madly camp former muse of Alexander McQueen of Givenchy, on his lap. Blow was wearing a dress that looked like an open parachute. "It was designed by this divine guy from Kansas City," she said, and everybody shrieked. Later, Talley told me that the mother of the young designer, Jeremy Scott, had mortgaged her house to pay for his first show in Paris.

Blow is the granddaughter of Sir Delves Broughton, who was cleared of the murder of Lord Erroll in the Happy Valley case in Kenya in 1941, made famous by James Fox in his book *White Mischief*. Blow is adored by a sizable coterie, although she is not everyone's cup of tea. "That sort of eccentricity works in England, but it doesn't go in France," said a French lady high in the couture.

From my journal:
Went to dinner last night at São Schlumberger's spectacular apartment, designed by Gabhan O'Keeffe. The Eiffel Tower is just outside her windows. Actually, it's difficult at first glance to know how to deal with the apartment other than to gasp. "It's bravura. That's what I like about it," said Suzy Menkes, who was wearing the turquoise velvet evening cloak that Helena Bonham Carter wears in *The Wings of the Dove*. The dinner was for Deeda Blair of Washington, a longtime couture customer. Diana Ross was there with Patrice Calmette, a Paris public-relations figure. São's dining table is long and narrow and seats forty, but there were only twenty for dinner. Across the table from me, São told Bernard Arnault, who was next to her, that she had been buying from the couture since 1961. Katell le Bourhis told São that Alexander

McQueen wanted to come and look at her closets, to see how she hung her clothes. Baroness Hélène de Ludinghausen, who works for Yves Saint Laurent, invited me to join a group she is taking to Russia in late June, on a tour that includes a ball at the Stroganoff Palace in St. Petersburg, which once belonged to her mother's family.

There was no doubt that Bernard Arnault was the most important person at the party. For all his brilliance as an entrepreneur, Arnault is a bit *formidable*, not much given to social chitchat. I said, in what I thought was a good opener to a conversation, "I heard you play the piano at a party in New York a few years ago." He replied, "My wife and I *both* played the piano that night." That was the end of the conversation.

There's a new erogenous zone in fashion.
> —Audrey Gruss, New York socialite,
> after the Alexander McQueen
> show for Givenchy.

There were groans of tribulation and woeful economic predictions at all the shows and parties over the financial collapse of the Asian stock market. "They're the ones who really spend on couture—or, rather, spent," one executive told me. McQueen staged his show for Givenchy in an industrial building so inconveniently located that several chauffeurs got lost en route. However, any petty annoyances were soon forgotten as it became apparent that McQueen was in top form, after several seasons that had been considered less than successful. The Japanese theme of the show—with its raked white pebbles, lonesome pine, single rock, and goldfish pond—was meant to be McQueen's bow to the Asian market. His models, wearing vinyl wigs cut at sharp angles and resembling geisha girls, posed dramatically in silhouette behind white screens before stepping onto the runway. Soon one could hear murmurs of approval from the audience.

I had begun to know whether something was good or not by watching the faces of the fashion editors as they watched the parade passing in front of them. The most expressive face was Polly Mellen's as she took in the overall picture, training her practiced eye on the hat and then down to the shoes, getting it, forming an opinion then and there, writing notes without looking at her pad. A few seats away, Joan Buck whispered comments to the man next to her without taking her eyes off the dress she was whispering about. Anna Wintour, Marin Hopper, *Harper's Bazaar* editor Liz Tilberis, Grace Coddington of American *Vogue*, Bridget Foley of *Women's Wear Daily*, and Constance White of the *New York Times* all stared with an intensity usually reserved for paintings. A talkative lady next to me, who was interested in watching people more than dresses—as was I—whispered to me, "Do you see the bodyguard?" She gestured in the direction of a man standing near a woman who was holding a sable coat in her lap, and shook her head in disapproval. "Such a mistake," she said. "People watch people being watched by bodyguards."

"Who is she?" I asked.

"One of the new ones," she replied.

At the end, McQueen came out for a bow and stood between his cutter and his head seamstress. "He's not hogging the limelight anymore," my friend on my left said, adding, "He's 30 pounds lighter than last year. The hair's now yellow, and look, he's wearing mules with high heels. He's changed. Alexander is much less angry than before."

From my journal:

Talked with the beautiful Amanda Harlech last night at Karl Lagerfeld's dinner for Liz Tilberis at his *hôtel particulier*. Lagerfeld's show earlier in the day had been a triumph. Everyone was saying, "It was Karl's best show in years." Amanda, who is Lady Harlech and lives in Wales, is Lagerfeld's muse, after having been muse to John Galliano before his ascension at Dior. When Galliano did not move quickly enough to take Harlech with him, Lagerfeld snatched her away. He designs with Amanda in mind. We sat together on a high-backed green damask sofa in Lagerfeld's drawing room, and she talked about the couture in that slightly mystical manner common to those who understand it. She had the same look on her face that I had seen on Anna Wintour's face earlier in the day over coffee in the Bar Vendôme, when she described the beauty of the Lagerfeld collection for Chanel. I was mesmerized by Amanda Harlech, whose late father-in-law, David

Ormsby Gore, was the British ambassador to Washington during Jack Kennedy's presidency. "If you could have been in the atelier at two this morning, watching them work, for everything to be ready for the show this morning. The only sound you hear is the sound of sewing," she said, miming the sewing in a long, graceful gesture. "They take such pride in their work. During the show they stand back and watch at the top of the stairs, where they can't be seen. If you could see their faces when their dress goes down the stairs."

Lagerfeld was fascinating, albeit a bit intimidating. His dark glasses are of an impenetrable blackness, and he never takes them off. It's hard to connect with someone when there's only one-sided eye contact. His is the house of a cultured man with perfect taste and many interests. I have never been in a residence where there were so many books. They are in every room, stacks of them, piled as high as the furniture. He told me that in his Paris house alone there are 180,000 volumes, and he is able to locate any book at any time. He has a photography studio in his house and has perfected a method of developing film by computer. They say he sleeps only four hours a night.

I heard Mugler had his nose broken surgically to make him look tough.   —Jonathan Becker, *Vanity Fair* photographer.

Once, seven or eight years ago, I sat next to Thierry Mugler on a New York-to-Los Angeles flight. We laughed for five hours. I never saw him again, but when I got to Paris there was a welcoming note from him at the Ritz and an invitation to go backstage before his show.

He's a dynamic personality, in great shape. His hair was very short and dyed yellow, as was the hair of a lot of men at the couture. "I'm very busy—can't talk," he said, shaking hands warmly but not stopping. "Thierry does everything—the music, the lighting fixtures on the wall," Ted Guefen, his publicist, told me. "He stands there by the television set and watches everything. Tell your photographer not to take any pictures of him until after the show."

Backstage, I ran into Alexandre of Paris, the Duchess of Windsor's

hairdresser, whom I hadn't seen since he did Elizabeth Taylor's hair in
Ash Wednesday, a film I produced in 1973. He was putting the finishing touches on the coiffures of the models, who had a tough, chic,
slightly butch dominatrix look. Mugler's clothes were overtly sexy. I
could see Jerry Hall looking great in them. Or Kim Basinger. Mrs. Adnan Khashoggi is one of his clients. The most discussed dress in the
collection hung from nipple rings on one of the models.

*"I'm going to have lunch with Adnan Khashoggi after the Chanel
show," I said to Elizabeth Saltzman.*
"You can't. You have to be at the Lacroix show at three."

Had tea with Adnan Khashoggi in the Bar Vendôme. He had once
been angry with me over an article I wrote about him, but we had had a
rapprochement at the Hotel Bel Air during the O. J. Simpson Trial.
The Ritz, by the way, is owned by Mohammed Al Fayed, father of the
doomed Dodi, employer of the drunk driver Henri Paul, and master
spinmeister of the tragic events of last August, who happens to be a
sworn enemy of Khashoggi's. Mohammed Al Fayed was once married
to Khashoggi's sister, and their divorce caused a bitter falling-out
between the two men which continues to this day, although Khashoggi
remained on good terms with his nephew Dodi. The first thing
Khashoggi said was that people all over the Middle East think that
Princess Diana's death was a conspiracy. I replied that a lot of people in
Paris think the same thing. When I asked him what he thought, he said
that he didn't used to think it was a conspiracy but now he sometimes
wonders. Just then his wife, Shapira, arrived. They have two small children. His son and his daughter Nabila's son are the same age. Shapira
had ordered clothes from the Thierry Mugler collection. We talked
about the whereabouts of Ferdinand Marcos's wealth and the dress
that hung from nipple rings.

On my way to the Chanel show, I tried to leave the Ritz by the Rue
Cambon entrance, only to find that it was locked and bolted. A bellman showed me a way out through a door into a back-hall anteroom
which had a door to the street. It seemed eerily familiar. Jonathan
Becker, who was with me, said, "Isn't this the Princess Diana exit?"

"Oui," replied the bellman. We all looked at one another in a Princess Diana moment.

From my journal:
Turned on CNN and watched Mike McCurry's press conference on the breaking Monica Lewinsky story. I was speechless. I've known about that story for six months at least, every detail of it, including the rumored stain on the dress, but I never took it as anything more than gossip. Back in November, I saw Vernon Jordan at lunch at the Four Seasons in New York. I almost told him what I knew, but then I thought, Suppose it isn't true, and I didn't speak up.

"People tell me couture is not relevant to today's world," I said to a *fashion editor.*
"Why should it be? It's a ravishing experience for a very few people."

With the exception of a brief appearance of Claudia Schiffer at Valentino, none of the supermodels whom we read about all the time were present at the couture. Over the hill, I was told. The models in Paris were mostly about seventeen.

"Hi, Mom. Hi, Dad," said Katie Ford, the president of Ford Models, as her parents, Eileen and Jerry Ford, who founded the agency in 1946, passed our table during lunch in the Bar Vendôme. Katie, who is married to André Balazs, who owns the Chateau Marmont in Los Angeles, booked many of the young American models who moved from show to show. "I called one of the models. I said I could book her for Paris. She said, 'How much?' I said, 'This isn't about money. Models get down on their knees and *beg* to go to the couture.'"

"Elizabeth, I can't look at one more dress," I said.
"You can't miss Gaultier. He designed for Madonna."

From my journal:
Went to the Dior atelier on the Avenue Montaigne with Katell le Bourhis, who told me, "These people never see the customer." The dresses are covered with muslin when they are not being worked on or

fitted. "It's a tradition. We veil everything. Otherwise someone might steal an idea."

Saw Mouna Ayoub—who used to be Mouna Al-Rashid when she was last written about in *Vanity Fair*—last night at Florence Grinda's second party for Emanuel Ungaro. Mouna, who took back her maiden name after her divorce, has been out of circulation in New York since her notorious change of auctioneers, from Sotheby's to Christie's, at the time her fabulous jewelry collection was to go on the block in late 1996, a last-minute switch that caused major social eruptions in circles that had once embraced her. She introduced me to her fiancé, François Curiel, who is the head of Christie's international jewelry department in Geneva. It was he who had persuaded her to switch houses. "And now we're getting married," she said.

Oh, the things they were saying about Yves Saint Laurent before his show! *He's fat. He's old. He's sick. He's doped. They're going to have to wheel him out. Can't walk. Loulou de la Falaise does the whole collection. She goes through the archives and does what has to be done to update everything.*

But all the Cassandras were wrong. They didn't wheel him out. The old King was still kinging it up. Looking a bit waxed and dyed, like Dirk Bogarde in *Death in Venice*, he shyly walked the full runway with a fixed smile that never altered to the enthusiastic applause of the crowded room. There were tears and cheers. The French love him. Everyone came out saying, "It was Yves's best show in years."

I saw this beautiful white dress with big, big sleeves that I loved, but how do you pack it?

—Mica Ertegun, after visiting
the Dior atelier the day
after the show.

After Gaultier—where everyone stared at Catherine Deneuve while mint tea was served by white-wigged lackeys in velvet breeches and a turban-clad harpsichordist played "My Way"—it was over. Some people were leaving Paris immediately. Some were staying on for a few days. Elizabeth wanted to go to Morocco for the weekend, but didn't. I went to see the Georges de la Tour exhibition at the Grand Palais museum and then bought my granddaughter a dress at Baby Dior. I had dinner with the Erteguns and Caroline Whitman, the former wife of actor Stuart Whitman, and a few others. No one talked about fashion. We talked about Clinton and Monica and how casually everyone was discussing blow jobs. Later, back at the Ritz, I got in the elevator with Polly Mellen, with whom I had gone to dancing school when she was eleven and I was ten. "Hey, Poll," I said on the way up to the sixth floor, "did you ever think when we were kids in Hartford that we'd end up in an elevator together in the Ritz hotel in Paris?"

For me, Paris is always sizzling, and the temperamental couturiers who spend millions twice a year at the couture shows will keep it sizzling for as long as there is fashion, and that means forever.

THREE FACES OF EVIL

What I have suspected since I became involved with the Los Angeles murder trials of the Menendez brothers and O. J. Simpson is that winning is everything, no matter what you have to do to win. If lies have to be told, if defenses have to be created, if juries have to be tampered with in order to weed out those who appear to be unsympathetic to the defendant, then so be it. The name of the game is to beat the system and let the guilty walk free. If you can get away with it. The stench of O. J. Simpson's acquittal grows stronger by the week as allegations of jury tampering abound, and reports surface concerning a flunked polygraph test taken by Simpson two days after the murders, in the company of two of his attorneys. Although the results were thought to have been destroyed, I am told that a copy exists. And then, as if that weren't enough, came the extraordinary moment during the penalty phase of the second Menendez trial when Leslie Abramson, the zealous defense attorney for Erik Menendez, was brought down with a resounding crash which stunned the legal profession and could possibly end with her disbarment, when her own expert witness Dr. William Vicary testified on the stand to prosecutor David Conn that changes in his notes had been made at Abramson's request, because she believed his original notes were prejudicial to her client. We'll get to this in sequence.

If there's another hung jury, look for my name in the
obituaries. —Detective Les Zoeller, who has been
on the Menendez case since the
night of the murders seven years
ago and has sat through both trials.

Since O. J. Simpson was arrested for the murders of Nicole Brown Simpson and Ronald Goldman on June 17, 1994, his case has so eclipsed the Menendez saga that most people were unaware that a second Menendez trial—not covered on Court TV—had been going on for five months until the verdict came in on March 20. A jury of eight men and four women found the used-to-be-rich brothers guilty of murder of both parents in the first degree with special circumstances—lying in wait and multiple murders.

Lyle and Erik Menendez knew before they sat down that day that the jurors had arrived at a verdict, even though Leslie Abramson in her closing argument had virtually begged for a hung jury. "It is better to not render a verdict than it is to render an unjust one or a compromise," she had said. They also knew there was no possibility that the verdict was going to be an acquittal, so they were prepared for bad news. The moment after the verdict was read by court clerk Penny Tinnell was breathtaking in its silence. There was not so much as a gasp heard. Even Maria Menendez, the mother of the murdered Jose Menendez and the grandmother of his killers, who had been known to make the occasional fuss, simply sat there, bravely mute. There were no breakdowns on the defense side or any traces of jubilation on the prosecution side. Leslie Abramson looked over at Erik, but said nothing. Charles Gessler, who represented Lyle, placed his hand on Lyle's back but said nothing. David Conn did not exchange even a look with Carol Najera, the second prosecutor. Then Erik, ashen-faced, old beyond his twenty-five years, turned to his grandmother and mouthed the words "I love you." It was heartbreakingly sad. I wanted to get out of that courtroom. I didn't want to talk to anybody about what had just happened, not even to David Conn to congratulate him on the brilliant job he had done by pointing out to the jury over and over again in his closing argument the absurdities of the defense case.

David Conn is an impressive figure in the courtroom, a presence to match Abramson but altogether different. Tall and lean, forty-five, with a full head of black hair, he bears an uncanny resemblance to Clark Kent, Superman's alter ego, as has been frequently noted. I had watched Conn in a courtroom before, during the 1990–91 trial of the hired killers who murdered Roy Radin, a showbiz impresario who had briefly been a partner of producer Robert Evans in the ill-fated film *The Cotton Club*. I was struck then by his calm toughness and firm command of the case. The killers got life without parole. After the Menendez verdict, I received a telephone call from Kate Radin, Roy's sister, in Hawaii. She was ecstatic over Conn's victory. "I hope David gets all the credit," she said. "All that I'm reading about out here is [Los Angeles district attorney] Gil Garcetti."

In this age of dysfunctional families and mindless violence, a verdict of any lesser degree than the one the jury came to in the Menendez case would have given the worst sort of message to the youth of America. What a waste, that two young men who had everything the material world could provide should end up in this disgraceful state, at the age for a first fatherhood neither will ever have, carrying the two words by which they will always be described: "murderer" and "convict." Whatever it was in their family that brought about the moments of madness that led to the brutal acts that ruined their lives irrevocably could not have been as bad as fifty or sixty or whatever number of years are left to them stagnating in a 10-foot-long prison cell. Now that they are stripped of the falsehoods that peppered their defense—the sexual abuse, the fear that their parents were going to kill them, none of which the jury bought the second time around—and left with the facts of what *really* happened on the night of August 20, 1989, and the days leading up to it, which only the two of them know, I wonder if they have come to realize how many options they had to deal with the hate they felt for their parents other than the violent one they picked. Their father's older sister, Teresita "Terry" Baralt, whom I have always admired, told me one day in the courthouse during the closing arguments that her nephews, whom she loves, were "horrified by what they have done, horrified, but it's too late."

For Leslie Abramson, who became a much-quoted celebrity during the first trial, the final verdict was a bitter defeat. She had always appeared ready to sacrifice Lyle to save Erik, whom she referred to as "my most cherished client." Parts of her three-day closing argument were so over the top that she verged on camp. She spoke with such passion for her client that she made winning an acquittal for a confessed killer seem like an act of nobility. An overpowering presence, a creative storyteller, an actress capable of playing Medea, she fiercely dared anyone to disbelieve her version of the murders. She ridiculed David Conn's premise that the killings were premeditated, explaining to the jury that driving to San Diego two days before the murders to purchase two shotguns with a stolen driver's license as identification was all logical behavior which had nothing to do with premeditation. There were times when you had to admire her sheer verve. At one point she bellowed to the courtroom in her most strident tone that the prosecution team were liars, who cared only about *winning*, not *truth*. When David Conn walked out of the courtroom into the corridor during one break, he jokingly held his hand over his ear, as if he had an earache from Abramson's yelling. Detective Les Zoeller laughed at Conn's performance. The trial historian Judy Spreckels cracked, "Louder ain't necessarily better." On the other hand, Joan Selznick, a former daughter-in-law of the late film producer David O. Selznick, who sat in a section reserved for the Menendez family, had a different reaction altogether. "Brilliant, don't you think?" she said. "I think she'll get Erik an acquittal."

As if sensing that her case for Erik wasn't playing to the jury the way it had in the first trial, Abramson injected bits of autobiographical information into her arguments. She told the jurors about her immigrant grandmother, who had worked in a sweatshop and seen friends jump out of windows during the Triangle Shirtwaist Company fire in 1911, and then had gone on to be a labor organizer. She worked in that her grown daughter has an I.Q. of 165, that her two-year-old son talks baby talk, and that her husband plays the lottery but doesn't win. She even brought in her physical ailments, by telling the jurors, for instance, that she needed a break to take her medication. She also told them that this was probably her last trial, and that it would be the "ultimate tragedy" of her life if she lost this case. Surely the jury must have been thinking the same thing a lot of us were: So what? She closed by asking the jury to hang if they couldn't agree to acquit Erik Menendez.

That night and the following day, Erik and Lyle Menendez were back in the headlines that Simpson had taken away from them, only this time the headlines were very different: MENENDEZ BROTHERS GUILTY!

It was the most interesting moment I ever spent in a court-
room. —Judy Spreckels, discussing the moment
                                Dr. William Vicary linked
                                Leslie Abramson to his deception.

The flamboyant Leslie Abramson, who had become a television personality on ABC after the first trial, may have flamboyantly cata-pulted herself right out of a career in both television and law if she knowingly advised Dr. William Vicary, a psychiatrist appearing as an expert witness on April 4, to deceive the jury.

This came to light during the penalty phase of the second trial, when the jurors who had found both Menendez brothers guilty of murder in the first degree were hearing testimony to decide whether their fate should be death by lethal injection or life in prison with-out the possibility of parole. If you read the transcript of that day's proceedings, it seems apparent from Abramson's immediate objec-tion to a question posed to Vicary by prosecutor David Conn that she was cognizant that the jig was about to be up for her. When Conn asked Vicary if Erik had talked of a conversation about what life would be like without parents, Conn suddenly realized that his copy of Vicary's notes didn't jibe with what Vicary was reading. "I'm going to object to this," Abramson said, but Judge Stanley Weisberg ignored her. Then came the line out of Vicary's mouth that silenced the courtroom: "I left that section out at the request of defense counsel."

"When did defense counsel ask you to rewrite your notes, leaving out material?" asked Conn.

"In preparation for my testimony at the first trial," replied Vicary.

"And which defense counsel made that request of you?" asked Conn.

"Ms. Abramson," replied Vicary.

"Did she tell you why she wanted you to rewrite your notes?" Conn persisted.

"She said this was prejudicial, and it was out of bounds, and it was not necessary," answered Vicary.

This is how the universe responds.
— Judy Hilsinger, C.E.O. of Hilsinger Mendohlson Inc.,
    the public-relations firm, discussing
    Leslie Abramson.

Within an hour or so of that fateful moment in Abramson's life, eleven people in California, some of whom had witnessed her humiliation in the courtroom, called me to say that she was "ruined," that she could be "disbarred." Vicary did not attempt to justify her instructions to him. But why should he? His career was also presumably in tatters. Who would ever put him on the stand again as an expert witness after he had deceived the court?

I don't like Leslie Abramson, and I know she doesn't like me. We sniffed each other early on, some six years ago, and didn't take to each other's smell. Back then she said to me, "The trouble with you is you always root for the wrong side." I told her, "It's hard to root for the kind of people you represent." Among her past courtroom triumphs at the time was the case of a Pakistani doctor named Khalid Parwez, who had been arrested on charges of strangling his eleven-year-old son and surgically cutting him into more than 200 pieces. Abramson had tried to work out a plea bargain for second-degree murder. A plea bargain carries with it an implication of guilt. The then district attorney, Ira Reiner, had turned her down, saying that the state was going for a conviction on first-degree murder. When the case went to trial, Abramson won an acquittal for Parwez, who even received a round of applause from the jury. Subsequently she sued Parwez for payment for her legal services.

The only thing that surprises me about the latest development is that such a smart woman—and, believe me, she is smart—might have done such a stupid thing. Over the years a lot of people have wanted to bring Leslie Abramson down, but in the end she seems to have brought herself down. She had turned over to Dr. Park Dietz, an expert witness for the prosecution in the second trial, a box of documents pertaining to Erik. In that box were notes Vicary had made in preparation for the first trial—*before* they had been redacted by him—and those were the notes Conn had in front of him. Once he realized that discrepancies existed, he approached Vicary to see what he was reading from. He picked up the notes and studied them carefully for almost a minute while the courtroom sat in silence. Then he pounced. Subsequently, Vicary testified that he had made twenty-four changes.

It was just a fluke, some people say, a lucky accident, the hand of God, but the novelist part of me wants to interpret it as an intervention by Jose Menendez, bellowing his rage at Abramson for the monstrous, distorted picture she had presented of him and his wife. There was not an iota of proof to support the sexual-molestation defense, nothing but the word of the two defendants, both of whom are world-class liars. I never believed them or fell for their tears on the stand. Abramson's clear intention from the very beginning was to portray Jose Menendez as a pervert who sexually molested her client for twelve years, right up to a night or two before the murders, in order to make the jury believe that he *deserved* to be killed. Eight of the things the brothers claimed their father had done to them are chronicled in other people's case histories in a book called *When a Child Kills*, by Paul Mones, who was an adviser to the defense in the first trial. The brothers' own aunt Terry Barralt, who loved them but did not believe the allegations of sexual abuse, told me during the first trial that they had both read Mones's book in jail. Baralt, who took the stand reluctantly during the first trial, told me she had said to Abramson at the time, "Be careful what you ask me, because I will not lie." If what the brothers said about their father was true, they didn't need to embellish their defense with other people's experiences.

When Dr. Vicary claimed that the alterations in his notes were made at the request of Abramson, the jury was present to witness her disgrace. So were print and television reporters, members of the family of the killers, and members of the public. Her defense team immediately distanced themselves from her, as if she had been carrying a communicable disease. A shot on television showed her standing apart from her confrères outside the courthouse during a break, smoking furiously, while they talked among themselves. Barry Levin, her co-counsel, told Judge Weisberg that he would advise Erik Menendez to ask the court to remove Abramson from the case. "Her credibility in front of this jury has been so severely tainted and damaged," he said, "that it's very unlikely that any of her arguments are going to persuade this jury." Charles Gessler and Terri Towery, Lyle's lawyers, argued that their client had been harmed, through no fault of his own, by Abramson's wrong call in putting Vicary on the stand with his altered notes. In what some experts are saying is a courtroom first, Abramson twice invoked her privilege against self-incrimination by taking the Fifth Amendment at the same time she was trying to keep a client from receiving the death penalty. Her alleged deception not only plunged the trial into total chaos but also cast her future into a doubtful state.

Abramson, who is never at a loss for words, was unable to declare her reaction to Vicary's allegations until a gag order imposed by Judge Weisberg was lifted after the jury came in on April 17 with the sentence of life in prison without the possibility of parole for both brothers. The following day, she gave her first extended interview, to the *Los Angeles Times*, where her husband, Tim Rutten, is a staff writer, one of the team that covered the O. J. Simpson trial. She told the reporter Ann O'Neill with a laugh, "I don't know how commonplace it is to have your psychiatric expert turn on you and lie on you in the middle of a trial. He has a guilty conscience that he rewrote his notes? That's his problem." To which Vicary responded, "I know that's what she's saying, and I honestly believe that she remembers it that way, but that's not my memory. I would never, ever take anything out of my notes that I think is important."

I have learned that a criminal investigation of Abramson will take place. Prosecutors from her past trials who are still in the district attorney's office, some of whom were eager to comment on her situation, were prevented from doing so by the gag order. One law-enforcement official said to me in disgust, "The system countenances this sort of thing as long as you get away with it."

People in publishing circles are wondering how this will affect her forthcoming book, *My Life in Crime*, for which Simon & Schuster paid $500,000. The title should still work. It has been reported that the last chapter will be Abramson's defense of her current situation.

O.J. will never be accepted back into the world he so desperately wants to be a part of. Never. They will never take him back. —Tina Sinatra at dinner at Le Colonial.

Knock, knock. Who's there? Kato. Kato who? That's my biggest fear. —Joke told by Kato Kaelin on television.

Unlike the Menendez brothers, O. J. Simpson has never, from the day of his arrest, ceased to be a newsmaker or a main topic of conversation, no matter what table you happen to be sitting at. Although his call-ins to radio and television shows don't get reported much anymore, he still makes them from time to time. Shortly after I returned to Los Angeles for the closing arguments in the Menendez case, he had something to say about me when he talked to radio station KJLH-FM, speaking in the patronizing voice of a man recently acquitted of two murders:

Look at the people [Geraldo Rivera] brings on his show. Why would anyone bring Dominick Dunne on for any kind of perspective? Because Dominick Dunne from day one has had one perspective. He sat there with his mouth open when the verdict came in, when reasonable people, even [Associated Press reporter] Linda Deutsch, and these other people who followed the trial daily, none of them were surprised by the verdict. They may have been surprised by the speed of the verdict, but, based on the evidence, none of them stated they were surprised. This guy was in shock. That shows just how far out of the mix he was.

I have a different reaction. I think his call depicts just how far out of the mix *he* is. People tell me he still doesn't really get how he is perceived by most people. Although, according to Japanese-American sportswriter Russell Kishi, he told a new golfing buddy during a match at Canyon Lakes Country club, near Temecula, about fifty miles from Los Angeles—not the sort of course where he used to play—that he is worth $120 million, a source close to the defense says he is broke and still owes money to some of his lawyers from the murder trial. Nevertheless, appearances being everything to him, the house on Rockingham shows no signs of lack of maintainance. His pay-per-view, which was supposed to bring him $20 million, never took place. His highly-touted $29.95 video, *O. J. Simpson: The Interview,* which was supposed to make him $1 million up front and a percentage of the profits, has been a bust. "They haven't sold 30,000 copies," Charles Steiner of ESPN told me at the Tyson-Bruno fight at the MGM Grand in Las Vegas. The video's producer, Tony Hoffman, known to some as "the king of the infomercial," disputes these accounts without disclosing the actual figures. Almost everybody else connected with the case is writing or has written a book for big money, and that is said to infuriate Simpson. According to the *National Enquirer,* Simpson has a new girlfriend named Kimberly Ashby, who looks exactly like Nicole and thinks he's guilty, but who loves him anyway. Ashby has denied the report. Can this story get any tackier?

H.R.H. Princess Margaret, on a recent visit to Los Angeles to raise funds for the British Museum, told me at a party that she thought the whole Simpson case was "such a bore," but I don't find it at all boring. I see it as a morality tale that is still playing itself out, like a Russian novel set in Los Angeles, with 1,000 characters and 1,000 subplots. It's my dream that one day all the pieces of this story will come out. There are so many people in this town who know things—bits and pieces of the puzzle—who won't come forward. People tell me, "I don't want to get involved," or "I'm scared," or "I'll tell you after the civil case is over." A man I know and trust, a friend of Simpson's for twenty years, says he's dying to tell me, but can't, the name of the person who called him from the crime scene on the night of the murders, before the police arrived.

"You knew about the murders before the police?" I asked.

"Yeah," he replied.

Even Kato Kaelin, Simpson's houseguest and star witness, said on

Geraldo Rivera's show in March that he believes that Simpson is guilty of the murders.

New Simpson stories continue to proliferate. On a wet Sunday morning in February, I met with a man I know in West Los Angeles who told me an extraordinary story about a plastic surgeon he is acquainted with in Beverly Hills whose name I cannot reveal. On two occasions during Simpson's glory days as a University of Southern California football star, the plastic surgeon claims, he was hired to repair the faces of two young women Simpson had allegedly beaten up. Like so many background people in the O.J. story, the doctor has had second thoughts about talking. "It was a long time ago, and besides, my hands didn't make the incision," he told me, implying that he was not the only doctor involved.

"I was at Eclipse one night having dinner. There was a large table next to us. I knew someone at the table and stopped to say hello. My friend said, 'I'd like you to meet Robert Shapiro'—who I hadn't noticed was at the table. Shapiro rose and held out his hand. I said, 'I'm sorry, Mr. Shapiro, but I cannot shake the hand of anyone who was responsible for O. J. Simpson's acquittal.'"
"Can I use that?" I asked.
"Sure, but you can't use my name."
　　　　—Conversation at the Hotel Bel-Air with a beautiful
　　　　　actress/model/television hostess/wife of an
　　　　　important industry figure.

Five months after O.J.'s unpopular acquittal, one member of his Dream Team, F. Lee Bailey, was hauled off to jail in leg-irons and handcuffs to do time for contempt of court for failing to hand over more than $20 million in stocks and cash appropriated from a drug-dealer client, money the Florida judge in the case believed belonged to the government. Linda Deutsch, the doyenne of crime reporters, said to me one day about the Simpson case, "It was a story of damage. Everyone connected with the case was damaged by it."

In late February, I ran into Barry Scheck and his wife in front of the

Beverly Hills Hotel. He said he wasn't in L.A. on Simpson business but to receive an award at a dinner that night. The Los Angeles Criminal Courts Bar Association presented him with an award that read, "In acknowledgment and recognition of his role as a member of the 'Dream Team' in the successful defense of *The People of the State of California* v. *Orenthal J. Simpson*, in the 'Trial of the Century.' " Subsequently, a case in which Scheck and his partner, Peter Neufeld, had gained notoriety in 1992 came back to haunt them. A convicted rapist, Kerry Kotler, whom they had cleared through DNA evidence after he had served eleven years, was charged with another rape after his release.

At the Brookins Community A.M.E. Church in South Central Los Angeles, Johnnie Cochran and Carl Douglas received "lawyers of the year" awards. In his acceptance speech, Cochran said that the defense team had won because God was on their side, that God was a brother. The congregation cheered. A lot of churchgoers I know were distressed by his claim of divine support. It has since come to light that two days after the murders Simpson, accompanied by Robert Shapiro and Robert Kardashian, went to the Los Angeles office of Dr. Edward Gelb—who once did a TV show with F. Lee Bailey called *Lie Detector*—and took a polygraph test on which his score was minus-20, which is classed as deceptive. The long-suppressed story was broken by Harvey Levin of KCBS in Los Angeles. When Levin tried to get Shapiro to make an on-camera statement at the signing of his book, *The Search for Justice,* at Book Soup on Sunset Boulevard, Shapiro, Levin said, "became manic" and went on signing books, ignoring him. I was told by Fred Goldman that during Simpson's deposition for the civil suit, several weeks earlier, Daniel Petrocelli, Goldman's attorney, had asked Simpson if he had taken a lie-detector test. Simpson, under oath, said no.

At Robert Shapiro's New York book party at "21," a man who looked familiar came up and spoke to me. He was Richard J. Zukerwar, the president and C.E.O. of the Grandoe Corporation in Gloversville, New York, which manufactures gloves. An expert witness for the defense, he had been in the courtroom one day during the trial, but he declined to take the stand. He startled me now by saying, "I could have proven that the glove *did* fit. The prosecution went completely wrong. Why didn't they go to the tanner who tanned the leather? I can show you that the glove fit. It's cut on a die. When I heard a juror say she acquitted Simpson because the glove didn't fit, I couldn't believe it."

Simpson's friend A. C. Cowlings, the driver of the white Bronco in the freeway chase, maintained a hostile silence about the case until he had to give his deposition for the civil suit on April 17. His statements were surprising. He acknowledged that he was aware that Simpson had viciously beaten Nicole and had once thrown her out of the house, which contradicted what Simpson had said in his deposition. Cowlings testified that Nicole had had an affair with football star Marcus Allen, who had been married in Simpson's house, but he refused to elaborate. And he took the Fifth Amendment on questions dealing with his activities between the morning after the murders and the freeway chase.

I was a friend of Nicole's. I introduced her to one of her boyfriends.   —A young man named Lonny who was standing on the step behind me on the escalator at Neiman Marcus in Beverly Hills.

Trial fame fades fast for some. Judge Lance Ito, who was for almost a year the most famous judge in the United States, as well as the inspiration for the Dancing Itos on Jay Leno's *Tonight Show*, had practically faded from sight—without ever making any public comment on the Simpson case—when he was rudely thrust back into the news in most unfavorable circumstances. The anonymity he had sought was not to be his. He took a shellacking from prosecutor Christopher Darden both in his book, *In Contempt*, and in an interview with Barbara Walters on *20/20*. Darden said that Johnnie Cochran had run the courtroom, not Judge Ito. Then *60 Minutes* did a report on jury tampering in the Simpson trial, and Judge Ito got it again, for dismissing juror Francine Florio-Bunten—who believed Simpson to be guilty and who would have hung the jury—without any investigation whatsoever after he received what I believe to have been an obviously fraudulent anonymous letter which made accusations about Florio-Bunten and her husband. On the heels of that, a guilty verdict pronounced on former Lincoln Savings and Loan boss Charles Keating in a state court in 1991—Ito's biggest case before Simpson—was overturned on appeal because of an error Ito had made in his instructions to the jury. Keating remains in prison on federal convictions.

They call Judge Weisberg Stanley Scissorhands since he cut so much out of the defense case.
> —Radio reporter who covered the second Menendez trial.

Marti Shelton called from Virginia after the Menendez verdicts. She had had a telephone friendship with Lyle Menendez during the first trial and had taped many of his calls. I have listened to some of the scare tactics that were later used to keep her from coming forward with what she knew. "It's the right verdict, but it's sad," she said.

Faye Resnick called me from Paris today. She's so glad to be out of here. She was getting death threats.
> —Stacy Gantzos, maître d' at Drai's, talking over her shoulder as she led me to my table.

Faye Resnick's coming back from Paris. She missed [her daughter] Francesca.   —Stacy Gantzos, talking over her shoulder as she led me to my table three weeks later.

One of the most interesting people I met on this trip out to Los Angeles—in the back room of Hamburger Hamlet on the Strip—was Anthony Davis, the great football star, who followed Simpson at U.S.C. and was on the cover of *Sports Illustrated* three times. Surprisingly, he also looks like Simpson, although he is heavier, and he is often mistaken for him, especially when he is in Brentwood. Davis, who is called A.D., is definitely not a Simpson supporter. "Socially, he was not part of his people. I know him like the back of my hand. I always hated being compared to him, because I'm nothing like him," he said. Davis, who speaks in a low voice, is a charismatic figure who demands your attention. He said he first met Nicole in Buffalo at Simpson's house, when he and O.J. were both in the pros. " 'Who's that?' I asked. 'That's O.J.'s woman,' I was told. I thought she was too young for *me*, and I was twenty-four at the time.

"O.J. doesn't like black women. It's like he forgot his own mother was black. The man forgot his roots. He forgot he was a black man. He abandoned his people," said Davis. He has equal contempt for Johnnie Cochran, and is furious that Cochran is representing U.S.C. against Marvin Cobb, a black former U.S.C. athlete whom the university removed from his position as assistant athletic director. "I'm embarrassed to be a black man with guys like that out there. Guys like that make it tough for me. You're looking at a real nigger, a black nigger," he said, pointing to himself. "These guys stepped over the line. I try to be an upstanding guy. I'm clean. I help my community. O.J.'s a goddamned sellout. This trial set us back; the verdict set us back years. There's been a mist in the air ever since the verdict. The only thing that beat the system was his money. The race card wasn't the issue; murder was. But Johnnie's for Johnnie, and O.J.'s for O.J. I can take you down to South Central and line up ten brothers, and nine of them would tell you he's a sellout. When you sell out, you lose. We still live in a racist society. You can be the greatest star on the cover of every magazine, you're still going to be a nigger here. I'm not here to blast the man. I'm here to talk right and wrong. Once the trial was over, he went to the black community one time only and never went back. My people, the black people, know what O.J. Simpson was about. We knew exactly where he stood for years. I believe we have a responsibility to our people."

Davis, who drives a black Lincoln and has an office in Beverly Hills, deals in affordable housing. His theory of the murders is very different from most versions. He believes that Simpson was involved "with bad people" in shady business deals involving drugs and that Nicole knew about them and had started to talk. "Nobody's going to do thirty years because of some pussy you're jealous of, man. This is something bigger. There's things about that story that no one knows about yet."

The guy would have been better off if he'd gone to jail. In jail he wouldn't look so bad. Another prisoner would say, "Oh, that's nothing, O.J., I killed five people." Or another guy would say, "Listen, O.J., I'm a child-molester. In here, they think that's worse." —A television reporter who didn't want his name used, during dinner at Eclipse.

I ran into prosecution lawyer Brian Kelberg one Saturday morning on Rodeo Drive in Beverly Hills. It was Kelberg who had acted out the murders in front of the Simpson jury—with himself as the victims and the chief medical examiner, Dr. Lakshmanan Sathyavagiswaran, as the perpetrator—staging each assault, with a ruler for a knife, the way he believed Simpson cut the throats of his wife Nicole and Ron Goldman. Although Kelberg had never been very friendly during the trial, that day on Rodeo Drive we instantly connected, like war veterans at a reunion, in the bond that unites all of us who sat in Judge Ito's courtroom for the long haul, and we began talking of the experience we had shared.

"What do you make of how O.J.'s behaving since the acquittal?" I asked.

"He has deluded himself into believing he didn't do it," said Kelberg.

We're not the original Smothers Brothers. But we are real brothers. I'm Erik. This is Lyle. We don't care who Mom liked best. —The Smothers Brothers in their nightclub act.

I had lunch at Dr. Deli on Van Nuys Boulevard with Craig Cignarelli, who stopped by the courthouse one day during the closing arguments. Cignarelli has been a principal figure in the Menendez case since a few days after the second memorial service for the slain parents, in Princeton, when Erik Menendez, who had been his best friend for two years, confessed to Cignarelli that he and Lyle had killed their parents. During the first trial, Cignarelli quoted Erik as having told him, "Lyle said, 'Shoot Mom.' " Jose Menendez had not liked Cignarelli and had once kicked him off the property of the Beverly Hills house. Cignarelli was a prosecution witness twice. Despised by Leslie Abramson, he despises her right back. During lunch he told me that Abramson had walked by him in the corridor and said, "Scumbag." Last year he graduated from the University of California at Santa Barbara. He is currently working on the political campaign of Republican candidate Richard Sybert, who is running for Congress from the 24th Congressional District. After the campaign, Cignarelli will attend law school. It is his hope to be a United States senator one day, an ambition mocked by Abramson in her closing argument.

Al Cowlings comes in here. I told the manager I wouldn't serve him, but they said I had to if he was a customer. Last time he was here, I called Petrocelli's office, because they were looking for him to serve a subpoena for the depositions for the civil suit, but no one called me back. If I had to wait on him, I'd tell him I didn't like to wait on someone who tried to help a killer get away. If he did anything to me, I'd call the National Enquirer. *I've got the number taped to the wall by the telephone in the kitchen.*

—Waitress at Nate 'n Al's, a popular
Beverly Hills deli, where many
industry figures have breakfast.

I want to show you something. See this trash bin? In the trial, this is what they said in court O.J. put the package in. They didn't even have this kind of trash bin until later. Here's the kind over here he put it in. See?

—Baggage handler for American Airlines at LAX.

Simpson's friend Robert Kardashian will always be remembered as the person who walked off Simpson's property the day after the murders carrying a Louis Vuitton bag that many people believed held the bloody clothes worn by the killer. I have never felt that that was so. I don't believe that Simpson would have brought the bloody clothes back to Los Angeles from Chicago, where he had gone after the murders to play in a golf tournament, knowing that he would be met by the police. I do wonder, however, if Kardashian could have played a part in the removal of the murder weapon from the golf bag that arrived at LAX the day after Simpson's return from Chicago, when he and Simpson, in the midst of his mourning, went to the airport to pick up Simpson's golf clubs. A knife in a golf bag might have gone through security undetected.

One day as I was walking in the American Airlines terminal at LAX, a woman I didn't know yelled out to me that I had just missed Kardashian, who was going to Minneapolis on a frequent-flier ticket. Then I ran into him in the Admirals Club. "I hear you're going to Minneapolis," I said. I have had a complicated relationship with Kardashian throughout the Simpson case. Once, I warned a lady from Johnnie Cochran's office, whom Kardashian was rumored to be involved with, that one of the tabloid papers was going to write about the relationship. He thanked me at the time. Although I had not written warmly about Kardashian, when my son Alex was missing in the Arizona mountains during the trial, he wrote me one of the nicest letters I have ever received, a father-to-father letter, which touched me very much. I never did find out why he was going to Minneapolis that day, but we had this exchange:

I said, "I've seen you on *Hard Copy* a couple of times when you and [writer Larry] Schiller were with Simpson when he was making his video."

Kardashian looked me straight in the eye, touched my arm, and said, "Not anymore, Dominick. I've pulled away."

"Really?"

"Really."

Later I heard that Kardashian and Simpson were no longer speaking. What I had known prior to this accidental meeting was that Kardashian was the secret partner of Larry Schiller on his book about the case, which was actually being written by James Willwerth of *Time* magazine, who covered the trial. The deal under discussion is that Kardashian will get a substantial portion of Schiller's fee but receive no credit. Someone I know who works for one of the tabloid papers told me that many of the Simpson stories that appeared after the verdict had been sold to them by Schiller and Kardashian.

Kardashian was at the time of the murders engaged to a beautiful, rich, blond widow in her thirties named Denice Halicki, with whom he lived in the house from which Simpson and A. C. Cowlings took off on the famous white-Bronco freeway chase after Simpson had been examined and photographed by Dr. Henry Lee, America's foremost forensic scientist, who was an expert witness for the defense at the trial. The couple had moved into the house just three weeks earlier. During the trial, I became friendly with Denice Halicki, although we were ostensibly on opposite sides. "Glamorous" is the best word to describe her. She has very long legs and wears very short skirts and is a knockout. After Kardashian and Halicki broke up, she moved out. The story went at the time that she took all the furniture and the television sets with her.

Halicki has the kind of looks that could make you think at first that she is all beauty and no brains, but that is certainly not the case. Although she and her late husband, H. B. "Toby" Halicki, a maverick independent-filmmaker known as "the car-crash king," had been married only three months when he was killed in an accident on the set of *Gone in 60 Seconds II*—an accident she witnessed—they had, she told me, "been together" six years. He left an estate of "close to $15 million," including heavy investments in real estate as well as enormous antique-toy and vintage-automobile collections. She was the principal beneficiary. Then two of her husband's twelve siblings and a few other people wanted a share. She went to Kardashian for legal advice, which is how they met. During the Simpson trial, she won five lawsuits over her inheritance, and two more, against the court-appointed administrator, are pending. She started a Bible-study group in order to alleviate the dark feelings that many people in the courtroom felt. Simpson's sisters, Shirley and Carmelita, were among those who attended, as were Simpson's daughter Arnelle and Johnnie Cochran's wife Dale. Halicki is a close friend of Jo-Ellan Dimitrius, the jury consultant for the defense. During the trial they went to the Cannes Film Festival together. Dimitrius, also tall and blond, came to the *Vanity Fair* Oscar party at Mortons in Beverly Hills in a strapless red satin dress on the arm of Larry King.

A few days after I ran into Kardashian, Halicki called me at my house in Connecticut.

"You had a mistake about me in your next-to-last 'Letter from Los Angeles,' " she said.

"What?"

"You said I was shopping on the day of the freeway chase and wasn't there in the house at the time."

I had indeed written that she had left the house before the Bronco chase.

"Who told you that?" she asked.

"I can't tell you."

"Was it ——?" She gave the name of a person who appeared to be a defense ally but wasn't. She was right.

"Don't you see what they're trying to do? They're trying to minimize me in the case. They're trying to make me look like a bimbo, out shopping all the time. Do you really think, knowing me, that I'm the kind of person who would be shopping at Neiman Marcus in Beverly Hills when all that was going on in *my* house? Of course I was there."

I laughed. She is a lady who likes to be at the center of the action.

"Remember, that was half my house at the time. Robert and I had just moved in there a few weeks before the murders. Let me ask you something: Did you also hear that I took all the furniture when I moved out on Robert?"

"And the TV sets too," I replied.

"They spread those stories. The furniture and the TV sets were all mine from my previous house."

When I returned to Los Angeles for the Menendez verdict, I met with Halicki at the Hotel Bel-Air. She spoke very graciously about her former fiancé. "O.J. used Robert," she said. "Robert went over there to the house on Rockingham as soon as he heard about the murders, like any friend would, and O.J. used him from then on. It's been terrible for Robert. His friends have left him."

"Did Simpson stay at your house?" I asked.

"From the night after the murders to the freeway chase, he slept at our house."

"Did Paula Barbieri sleep there?"

"Yes, except for one night."

"Do you ever get scared?" I asked.

"No," she replied.

When we parted, I watched a Hotel Bel-Air parking valet hold the door of her beige Rolls-Royce as she got in and waved good-bye.

Every memory is self-serving, and the occasional admission
of error offers the author an opportunity to congratulate
himself for his honesty and courage in mentioning it.
—John Gregory Dunne in his book review
of Christopher Darden's *In Contempt*
in the April 15, 1996, issue of *The New Yorker*.

Over a year ago, in April 1995, I wrote in this magazine that Christopher Darden was the person to watch in the Simpson trial. I have always admired Darden, often for just those things that his detractors criticize him for. I have rarely met a person who is as ethical as Darden. In a justice system in which truth has become a joke, his sense of truth is a beacon of light. I admired that he had the courage to cry during the press conference after he and Marcia Clark lost the case. Johnnie Cochran gave Darden a racially cruel time during the trial, and he took his lickings for the disastrous glove experiment. He *has* come out of this trial as a person to watch. What he has shown us is that, in the long run, losing may be more victorious than a victory without honor. As of April 7 of this year, his book, *In Contempt*, became No. 1 on the *New York Times* best-seller list.

Sydney smells Nicole's presence sometimes. She said,
"Mommy was just here. I can smell her perfume."
—Robin Greer, a friend of Nicole Brown Simpson's
and one of the authors of *You'll Never Make*
Love in This Town Again, discussing the
Simpson children during dinner at Drai's.

A young woman named Moya Rimp, whom I met during the Simpson trial, called to tell me that she and her mother, Pauline Rimp, a prominent real-estate woman in Brentwood, had moved into Nicole Brown Simpson's condo, the scene of the murders, in order to help the Brown family sell it. The Browns are eager to get rid of the condo, although as yet there have been no takers.

"What's it like living there?" I asked.

"Very strange. Tourists are still coming by to look at it. When I walk the dog, I meet all these people in the neighborhood who tell me things. There's one who swears she saw O.J. talking to Ron and Nicole before the murders, but she wouldn't come forward."

Moya Rimp invited me for dinner. I went. Robert Altman, the film director, and his wife, Kathryn, were also there. Altman is a cousin of Pauline Rimp's. With the reverence of a docent at the Getty Museum, Moya Rimp showed us through the condo. "This is where Nicole's exercise equipment was," she said, stopping in an area outside the master bedroom. We stared at the empty space, then moved on. "Now we're entering Nicole's bedroom. That was her bed, and beyond, in the bathroom, you can see her tub, which was filled with water that night and had lit candles around the edge." We became caught up in her surreal thrall.

As many times as I had walked by the condo and looked at the pictures of the crime scene, I was still amazed at how large the place is—3,400 square feet—and how small the killing area is. I perched on the spot outside the picture widow looking into the living room where Simpson would have sat when he reportedly spied on Nicole prior to the killings. It was the perfect place for a voyeur who had once watched his wife perform fellatio on another man, unseen by her—as happened with Keith Zlomsowitch. "We think he was watching Nicole through the window on the night of the murders, before she came outside," said Moya Rimp. In the ill-lit, eerie space, I felt as if I could almost hear the scuffling of rubber-soled Bruno Magli shoes and sneakers in the dirt and on the walkway. "This is where Ron fell," said Moya. "That's where Nicole was." As I looked at the scene, remembering the horrifying photographs shown in court, I didn't want to be there anymore, and we went inside.

One day I hope to visit Lyle and Erik Menendez in their separate prisons, where they are serving life terms without the possibility of parole, to see if they will talk truthfully about what actually happened in their Beverly Hills mansion on the night they mowed down their parents in a fusillade of shots. An aunt of the brothers tells me that they are riddled with guilt about the way they talked about their parents at the trial in the trumped-up defense that the jury didn't fall for the second time around.

As for O. J. Simpson, whose acquittal for the murders of Nicole Brown Simpson and Ronald Goldman stunned a great percentage of the nation, his life has been no bed of roses since. He is shunned and unaccepted in the world that he used to be such a part of, which is, of course, a better fate than the life-in-prison verdict of the Menendez brothers, but he is said to be unhappy with his lot. In an astonishing television interview with Ruby Wax on BBC, he did a mock knifing of the interviewer, using a banana as the weapon. That he could find humor in such an act seems to me that he learned nothing from the experience that he went through. Recently, the judge's decision to return his children to him during the civil trial has been overturned.

© Gasper Tringale

ABOUT THE AUTHOR

Dominick Dunne is the author of *The Two Mrs. Grenvilles, People Like Us, An Inconvenient Woman, The Mansions of Limbo, A Season in Purgatory,* and *Another City, Not My Own.* His essays for *Vanity Fair,* where he is Special Correspondent, have been collected in the book *Fatal Charms.* He produced the films *The Panic in Needle Park, Ash Wednesday, Play It As It Lays,* and *The Boys in the Band.* Dominick Dunne lives in New York City and Connecticut.